Automata an

Springer
London
Berlin
Heidelberg
New York
Barcelona
Hong Kong
Milan
Paris
Singapore
Tokyo

Alexander Meduna

Automata and Languages

Theory and Applications

Springer

Alexander Meduna, PhD
Department of Computer Science and Engineering, Technical University of Brno,
Božetěchova 2, Brno 61266, Czech Republic

ISBN 1-85233-074-0 Springer-Verlag London Berlin Heidelberg

British Library Cataloguing in Publication Data
Meduna, Alexander
    Automata and languages : theory and applications
    1. Machine theory 2. Formal languages 3. Computational intelligence
    I. Title
    511.3
ISBN 1852330740

Library of Congress Cataloging-in-Publication Data
Meduna, Alexander, 1957-
    Automata and languages : theory and applications / Alexander
    Meduna.
    p. cm.
    Includes bibliographical references and index.
    ISBN 1-85233-074-0 (alk. paper)
    1. Automata. 2. Formal languages. I. Title.
    QA267.M43 1999   98-52375
    511.3—dc21   CIP

Apart from any fair dealing for the purposes of research or private study, or criticism or review, as permitted under the Copyright, Designs and Patents Act 1988, this publication may only be reproduced, stored or transmitted, in any form or by any means, with the prior permission in writing of the publishers, or in the case of reprographic reproduction in accordance with the terms of licences issued by the Copyright Licensing Agency. Enquiries concerning reproduction outside those terms should be sent to the publishers.

© Springer-Verlag London Limited 2000
Printed in Great Britain

The use of registered names, trademarks etc. in this publication does not imply, even in the absence of a specific statement, that such names are exempt from the relevant laws and regulations and therefore free for general use.

The publisher makes no representation, express or implied, with regard to the accuracy of the information contained in this book and cannot accept any legal responsibility or liability for any errors or omissions that may be made.

Typesetting: Gray Publishing, Tunbridge Wells
Printed and bound at the Athenæum Press Ltd., Gateshead, Tyne & Wear
34/3830-543210 Printed on acid-free paper SPIN 10690768

In memory of Professor Jiří Kopřiva

Acknowledgements

This book is based on lecture notes that I use for my computer science classes dealing with automata, languages, computability, and compilers at various American and European universities. I taught these classes at the University of Missouri – Columbia for almost a decade during which time I greatly benefited from conversations with my colleagues and students. Regarding the final version of the text, I also profited from the suggestions of my colleagues at the Department of Computer Science and Engineering at the Technical University of Brno. Several staff members of Springer provided help during the preparation of this book; my special thanks go to my editor, Rebecca Mowat, my production controller, Joanne Cooling, and my typesetter, Robert Gray. Finally, I thank my wife Ivana for her support and, most importantly, her love.

Alexander Meduna

Preface

Automata represent fundamental abstract models of computation. This book presents an introduction to them. It concentrates on their three basic types — finite automata, pushdown automata, and Turing machines. The present text demonstrates properties and power of these automata by examining languages that they define. Besides automata, this book also covers some other models that define languages; most importantly, these models include regular expressions and context-free grammars. In addition, it adapts language models for translations and explains how to construct compilers by using these translation models. In its conclusion, based on the results concerning models for languages and translations, this book discusses the most essential topics of computational theory, such as computability, decidability and computational complexity.

Organization

The text consists of five parts:

Part I reviews basic mathematical concepts, including sets, relation, graphs, and proof techniques. In addition, it gives a rudimentary introduction to the basic models for languages and computation.

Part II deals with regular languages. This part studies two basic models for these languages — regular expressions and finite automata. In particular, it establishes the equivalence of these models and examines their properties.

Part III explores the fundamental models for context-free languages, namely, context-free grammars and pushdown automata; moreover, it defines some variants of these models. The properties of these models are studied in detail.

Part IV goes beyond the class of context-free languages. It defines and investigates Turing machines, two-pushdown automata, and unrestricted grammars. This part also presents the fundamental classification of languages, the Chomsky hierarchy.

Part V adapts the language models for translations. First, it obtains finite transducers from finite automata. Then, it develops pushdown transducers from pushdown automata. By using finite and pushdown transducers, a programming language translator is built up. Finally, this part derives Turing transducers from the Turing machines. Based upon Turing transducers, the text treats such important topics of computational theory as computability, decidability, and computational complexity.

Each of these parts ends with bibliographic notes, including suggestions for further reading.

Approach

This book primarily represents a theoretically oriented treatment. As a result, it introduces all formalism concerning automata with enough rigor to make all results quite clear and valid. By presenting many algorithms, worked-out examples, and computer programs, the present text also maintains an emphasis on the practical use of models for languages and translations. Most importantly, it builds up a complete compiler by using them.

Exercises

At the end of every chapter, a set of exercises is given to reinforce and augment the material covered in the chapter. Exercises are numbered as *i.j*, meaning the *j*th exercise related to the material in Section *i* of the chapter. They are listed according to level of difficulty, ranging from quite straightforward to more difficult exercises, which are indicated by stars. More specifically, singly starred exercises contain problems that require one significant insight for their solution, and doubly starred exercises require more than one such insight. In addition, programming projects also appear at the end of most chapters.

Use

This book is useful to everybody interested in understanding the fundamental models and ideas underlying computation. It can also be used as a textbook for an introductory course in automata theory at junior and senior levels. Although it contains enough material for a full year course, it is also recommended as the basis for a one-semester course, covering some selected essential topics of automata theory. Indeed, the text provides the flexibility needed to design several courses of this kind, such as the following five sample one-semester schedules.

1. Introduction to automata:
   1.1—1.3, 2.1—2.3, 3.1, 3.2.1—3.2.3, 3.3.1.1, 3.3.2—3.3.3, 4.1—4.2, 5.1, 5.2.1, 5.2.3, 5.3.1.1, 5.3.2—5.3.3, 6.1—6.2, 7.1, 7.3, 8.1.1—8.1.6, 8.3.1—8.3.2, 8.4, 9.1—9.2, 10.1—10.4.
2. Finite automata and regular expressions:
   1.1, 2.1, 3.1—3.3, 4.1-4.3, 7.2, 9.1, 9.3.1.
3. Pushdown automata and context-free grammars:
   1.1—1.3, 2.1—2.2, 5.1—5.3, 6.1—6.3, 7.1, 7.3, 8.2, 9.2, 9.3.2.
4. Introduction to compilers:
   1.1—1.3, 2.1—2.2, 3.1, 3.2.1—3.2.3, 3.3, 5.1.1—5.1.2, 5.2—5.3, 9.1—9.3.
5. Introduction to computational theory:
   1.1—1.3, 2.1—2.3, 8.1—8.4, 10.1—10.4.

Notes

Algorithms, examples, lemmas, and theorems are numbered sequentially within sections. The text also contains logical units, such as definitions. These units are concluded by the following symbols:

Symbol	Type of unit
◆	definition
●	convention
□	part of a proof
■	complete proof
△	part of an example
▲	complete example

Contents

Part I Introduction   1

Mathematical Background   3

0.1   Sets   3
0.2   Relations   7
0.3   Graphs   11
0.4   Proofs   15
       Exercises   18

Chapter 1 Languages   25

1.1   Formalization of languages   25
1.2   Expressions and grammars   33
       1.2.1   Expressions   33
       1.2.2   Grammars   34
       1.2.3   Specification of a programming language   39
1.3   Translations   48
       Exercises   52
       Programming Projects   57

Chapter 2 Automata   59

2.1   Conceptualization of automata   59
2.2   Transducers   71
2.3   Computability   78
       Exercises   82
       Programming Projects   88
Bibliographic notes   90

Part II Regular Languages   91

Chapter 3 Models for Regular Languages   93

3.1   Regular expressions   93
3.2   Finite automata   99
       3.2.1   Basic definitions   99
       3.2.2   Elimination of ε-moves   122

	3.2.3	Determinism	145
	3.2.4	Simplification	156
	3.2.5	Minimization	171
3.3	Finite Automata and regular expressions		175
	3.3.1	From regular expressions to finite automata	175
		3.3.1.1 Conversion of regular expressions to finite automata	175
		3.3.1.2 Scanning	196
	3.3.2	From finite automata to regular expressions	209
	3.3.3	Equivalence of finite automata and regular expressions	219
		Exercises	220
		Programming projects	227

Chapter 4 Properties of Regular Languages   229

4.1	Pumping lemma	229
4.2	Closure properties	237
4.3	Decidable problems	250
	Exercises	259
Bibliographic notes		265

Part III Context-Free Languages   267

Chapter 5 Models for Context-Free Languages   269

5.1	Context-free grammars		269
	5.1.1	Basic definitions	269
	5.1.2	Ambiguity	299
	5.1.3	Simplification	305
		5.1.3.1 Elimination of useless symbols	305
		5.1.3.2 Elimination of ε-productions	321
		5.1.3.3 Elimination of unit productions	334
		5.1.3.4 Proper context-free grammars	346
	5.1.4	Normal forms	347
		5.1.4.1 Chomsky normal form	348
		5.1.4.2 Greibach normal form	357
5.2	Pushdown automata		381
	5.2.1	Basic definitions	381
	5.2.2	Extension	415
	5.2.3	Determinism	432
5.3	Pushdown automata and context-free grammars		441
	5.3.1	From context-free grammars to pushdown automata	442

		5.3.1.1	Conversion of context-free grammars to pushdown automata	442

| | 5.3.1.2 | Parsing | 477 |

	5.3.2	From pushdown automata to context-free grammars	486
	5.3.3	Equivalence of pushdown automata and context-free grammars	494
		Exercises	495
		Programming projects	508

Chapter 6 Properties of Context-Free Languages   511

6.1	Pumping lemma	511
6.2	Closure properties	528
6.3	Decidable problems	551
	Exercises	558

Chapter 7 Special Types of Context-Free Languages and Their Models   565

7.1	Deterministic context-free languages	565
7.2	Linear and regular grammars	574
	Exercises	599
Bibliographic notes		605

Part IV Beyond Context-Free Languages   607

Chapter 8 Generalized Models   609

8.1	Turing machines		609
	8.1.1	Basic definitions	609
	8.1.2	Determinism	631
	8.1.3	Simplification	643
	8.1.4	Extension	652
	8.1.5	Universality	674
	8.1.6	Turing machines that always halt	693
	8.1.7	Linear-bounded automata	695
8.2	Two-pushdown automata		696
	8.2.1	Basic definitions	696
	8.2.2	Determinism	704
	8.2.3	Equivalence of two-pushdown automata and Turing machine	705

8.3	Unrestricted grammars	707
	8.3.1 Basic definition	708
	8.3.2 Equivalence of unrestricted grammars and Turing machines	713
	8.3.3 Normal forms	722
	8.3.4 Context-sensitive grammars	729
	8.3.4.1 Basic definition	730
	8.3.4.2 Context-sensitive grammars and linear-bounded automata	732
	8.3.4.3 Context-sensitive languages and recursive languages	735
	8.3.4.4 Normal forms of context-sensitive grammars	740
8.4	Hierarchy of language families	742
	Exercises	743
	Programming projects	753
Bibliographic notes		755

Part V Translations   757

Chapter 9 Finite and Pushdown Transducers   758

9.1	Finite transducers	758
9.2	Translation grammars and pushdown transducers	770
	9.2.1 Translation grammars	770
	9.2.2 Pushdown transducers	776
9.3	Compilers	787
	9.3.1 Compiler structure	788
	9.3.2 Scanner	789
	9.3.3 Parser, semantic analyzer, and code generator	806
	9.3.4 Optimizer	818
	9.3.5 Execution	820
	Exercises	822
	Programming projects	832

Chapter 10 Turing Transducers   833

10.1	Basic definitions	833
10.2	Computability	845
	10.2.1 Computers	845
	10.2.2 Computable functions	851
	10.2.3 Uncomputable functions	853
10.3	Decidability	856

10.3.1 Decision makers … 856
10.3.2 Decidable problems … 860
10.3.3 Computational complexity … 861
    10.3.3.1 Time complexity … 862
    10.3.3.2 Space complexity … 866
10.3.4 Undecidable problems … 867
10.3.5 Undecidability: a general approach … 872
    Exercises … 874
    Programming projects … 884
Bibliographic notes … 886

Bibliography   889

Indices   901

Index to Special Symbols   903

Index to Decision Problems   905

Index to Algorithms   907

Subject Index   911

Part I Introduction

This introductory part conceptualizes basic models for languages and computation. Chapter 0 reviews basic mathematical concepts used in this book. Then, Chapter 1 introduces languages, grammars, and translations. Finally, Chapter 2 describes automata and transducers. This part also explains how computer science uses these models to demonstrate the fundamental ideas underlying computation. As a result, the study of these models represents a metaphysic of computer science, whose significance is thus indisputable.

0 Mathematical Background

This chapter, consisting of three sections, describes the fundamental mathematical notions, concepts and techniques used in this book. Specifically, it reviews sets, relations, functions, graphs and proof techniques.

0.1 Sets

This section reviews fundamental notions concerning sets and operations on sets.

A *set*, Σ, is a collection of elements, which are taken from some prespecified universe. If a set, Σ, contains an element a, then this is written as $a \in A$ and refers to a as a member of Σ. However, if a does not belong to Σ, this is expressed as $a \notin \Sigma$. The *cardinality* of Σ, card(Σ), is the number of members of Σ. The set that has no member is the *empty set*, denoted $\emptyset$; note that card($\emptyset$) = 0. If a set Σ has a finite number of members, then Σ is a *finite set*; otherwise, Σ is an *infinite set*.

A finite set Σ is customarily specified by listing its members; that is,

$$\Sigma = \{a_1, a_2, ..., a_n\}$$

where a_1 through a_n are all members of Σ. An infinite set Ω is usually specified by a property π so that Ω contains all elements satisfying π; this specification has the following general format:

$$\Omega = \{a: \pi(a)\}$$

Example 0.1.1 Sets of numbers

Observe that

$$\{0\}$$

is a finite set; in fact, it contains only one member, 0. Furthermore, consider all *natural numbers*,

$$1, 2, ...$$

The set of all these numbers is infinite. As an example of an infinite set specified by a property, define the set of all *nonnegative integers* as

$$\{\,i: i \text{ equals 0 or } i \text{ is a natural number}\};$$

more briefly,

$$\{i : i \geq 0\}$$

▲

Example 0.1.2 Part 1 Sets of words and sentences

Consider the finite set of English articles, which are taken from the universe of English words. This set can be specified by listing its three members as

$$\text{Articles} = \{a, an, the\}$$

Observe that

$$\text{card}(\text{Articles}) = 3$$

Obviously,

$$a \in \text{Articles}$$

Notice that

$$\text{any} \notin \text{Articles}$$

because 'any' does not belong to Articles.

For every natural number i consider the following infinite set, whose elements are taken from the universe of English sentences:

$$\text{And}_i = \{ x : x \text{ is an English sentence with } i \text{ occurrences of } and\}.$$

For instance, And_2 contains

English and Russian are natural languages, but C and Pascal are artificial languages.

Finally, consider

$$\text{And} = \{\text{And}_i : i \geq 1\}$$

Notice that And represents an infinite set, whose members are also infinite sets.

△

As the conclusion of the previous example illustrates, sets may contain other sets; sets of this kind are customarily called *families* of sets, rather than sets of sets.

Let Σ and Ω be two sets. Σ is a *subset* of Ω, symbolically written

$$\Sigma \subseteq \Omega$$

if each member of Σ belongs to Ω. Σ is a *proper subset* of Ω, written as

$$\Sigma \subset \Omega$$

if $\Sigma \subseteq \Omega$ and Ω contains an element a such that $a \notin \Sigma$. Σ *equals* Ω, written as

$$\Sigma = \Omega$$

if $\Sigma \subseteq \Omega$ and $\Omega \subseteq \Sigma$.

Let Σ be a set. The *power set* of Σ, 2^Σ, is the set of all subsets of Σ; that is,

$$2^\Sigma = \{\, \Sigma' : \Sigma' \subseteq \Sigma \,\}$$

Observe that

$$\operatorname{card}(2^\Sigma) = 2^{\operatorname{card}(\Sigma)}$$

Example 0.1.2 Part 2 Subsets and power sets

Part 1 of Example 0.1.2 introduced

$$\text{Articles} = \{a, an, the\}$$

Consider

$$\text{IndefiniteArticles} = \{a, an\}$$

Observe that

$$\text{IndefiniteArticles} \subseteq \text{Articles}$$

Because Articles also contains 'the', which does not belong to IndefiniteArticles, IndefiniteArticles represents a proper subset of Articles.

The power set of Articles contains the following sets

$$\varnothing, \{a\}, \{an\}, \{the\}, \{a, an\}, \{a, the\}, \{an, the\}, \{a, an, the\};$$

symbolically,

$$2^{\text{Articles}} = \{\, \varnothing, \{a\}, \{an\}, \{the\}, \{a, an\}, \{a, the\}, \{an, the\}, \{a, an, the\} \,\}$$

Notice that

$$\operatorname{card}(2^{\text{Articles}}) = 2^{\operatorname{card}(\text{Articles})} = 2^3 = 8$$

△

Set operations

Let Σ_1 and Σ_2 be two sets. The *union* of Σ_1 and Σ_2, symbolically written as

$$\Sigma_1 \cup \Sigma_2$$

is defined as

$$\Sigma_1 \cup \Sigma_2 = \{\, x : x \in \Sigma_1 \text{ or } x \in \Sigma_2 \,\}.$$

The *intersection* of Σ_1 and Σ_2, written as

$$\Sigma_1 \cap \Sigma_2$$

is defined as

$$\Sigma_1 \cap \Sigma_2 = \{\, x : x \in \Sigma_1 \text{ and } x \in \Sigma_2 \,\}.$$

The *difference* of Σ_1 and Σ_2, written as

$$\Sigma_1 - \Sigma_2,$$

is defined as

$$\Sigma_1 - \Sigma_2 = \{\, x : x \in \Sigma_1 \text{ and } x \notin \Sigma_2 \,\}.$$

Example 0.1.2 Part 3 Union, intersection and difference
The first part of this example uses

$$\text{Articles} = \{a, an, the\}$$

In addition, consider the set

$$\text{TwoLetters} = \{a, b\}$$

Observe that

$$\text{Articles} \cup \text{TwoLetters} = \{a, an, b, the\}$$

$$\text{Articles} \cap \text{TwoLetters} = \{a\}$$

$$\text{Articles} - \text{TwoLetters} = \{an, the\}$$

$\triangle$

Mathematical background

Finally, consider a set Σ whose members are taken from a *universe*, U. Then, the *complement* of Σ, $\overline{\Sigma}$, is defined as

$$\overline{\Sigma} = U - \Sigma$$

Example 0.1.2 Part 4 Complement

Reconsider

$$\text{Articles} = \{a, an, the\},$$

whose members are taken from the universe of all English words. The complement of Articles contains all English words except 'a', 'an' and 'the'.

▲

0.2 Relations

The present section discusses relations and functions.

Let a and b be two elements. Then, (a, b) denotes the *ordered pair* consisting of a and b in this order. Let (a, b) and (c, d) be two ordered pairs. Then,

$$(a, b) = (c, d) \text{ if and only if } a = c \text{ and } b = d$$

Let Σ and Ω be two sets. The *Cartesian product* of Σ and Ω, $\Sigma \times \Omega$, is defined as

$$\Sigma \times \Omega = \{ (a, b): a \in \Sigma \text{ and } b \in \Omega\}$$

A *relation* ρ from Σ to Ω is a subset of $\Sigma \times \Omega$; that is,

$$\rho \subseteq \Sigma \times \Omega$$

Σ is the *domain* of ρ, and Ω is the *range* of ρ. If ρ represents a finite subset of $\Sigma \times \Omega$, then ρ is a *finite relation* from Σ to Ω. If $\Sigma = \Omega$, then ρ is a *relation on* Σ. A relation ρ' is a *subrelation* of ρ if ρ' represents a subset of ρ; that is, each ordered pair of ρ' also belongs to ρ. The *inverse of* ρ, ρ^{-1}, is defined as

$$\rho^{-1} = \{ (b, a): (a, b) \in \rho\}$$

Conventions

More precisely, a relation ρ is called a *binary relation*; for brevity, however, this book

usually refers to ρ as a *relation*. Furthermore, instead of $(a, b) \in \rho$, write $a \in \rho(b)$ or $a\rho b$; in other words, $(a, b) \in \rho$, $a\rho b$, and $a \in \rho(b)$ are used interchangeably.
●

Example 0.2.1 Relations
Recall that Example 0.1.2 uses

$$\text{Articles} = \{a, an, the\}$$

In addition, define the set

$$\text{TwoWords} = \{\text{author, reader}\}$$

The Cartesian product of Articles and TwoWords is defined as

$$\text{Articles} \times \text{TwoWords} = \{ \text{(a, author), (an, author),} \\ \text{(the, author), (a, reader),} \\ \text{(an, reader), (the, reader)}\}.$$

Consider the relation ProperArticles, from Articles to TwoWords; intuitively, ProperArticles properly relates English articles to the two English words – 'author' and 'reader':

$$\text{ProperArticles} = \{ \text{(an, author), (the, author),} \\ \text{(a, reader), (the, reader)}\}.$$

The inverse of ProperArticles is

$$\text{ProperArticles}^{-1} = \{ \text{(author, an), (author, the),} \\ \text{(reader, a), (reader, the)}\}.$$

▲

Closures of relations

Let ρ be a relation on a set Σ and let k be a natural number. The *k-fold product* of a relation, ρ^k, is defined as follows:

1. $a\rho^1 b$ if and only if $a\rho b$;
2. for $k \geq 2$, $a\rho^k b$ if and only if there exists $c \in \Sigma$ such that $a\rho c$ and $c\rho^{k-1} b$.

The previous definition illustrates the use of the *recursive definitional method*. To demonstrate the recursive aspect of this definition, consider $a\rho^4 b$. From the second part of this definition, there exists $c_1 \in \Sigma$ such that $a\rho c_1$ and $c_1 \rho^3 b$. By applying the second part again, there exists c_2 such that $c_1 \rho c_2$ and $c_2 \rho^2 b$. By another application of the second part, there exists c_3 such that $c_2 \rho c_3$ and $c_3 \rho^1 b$. Finally, by the first part of this definition, $c_3 \rho b$. Thus, there is a sequence of elements $c_1, c_2, c_3 \in A$ such that $a \rho c_1$, $c_1 \rho c_2, c_2 \rho c_3$, and $c_3 \rho b$. The upcoming chapters of this book frequently introduce new notions in this way.

Let ρ be a relation on a set Σ. The *transitive closure* of ρ, ρ^+, is defined as follows:

$$a \rho^+ b \text{ if and only if } a \rho^i b$$

for some $i \geq 1$. Consequently, $a \rho^+ b$ if and only if for some $n \geq 0$,

$$a \rho c_1, c_1 \rho c_2, \ldots, c_{n-1} \rho c_n, c_n \rho b$$

where $c_1, c_2, \ldots, c_n \in \Sigma$ (the case when $n = 0$ actually means $a \rho b$). The *reflexive and transitive closure of* ρ, ρ^*, is defined as follows

$$a \rho^* b \text{ if and only if } a \rho^i b$$

for some $i \geq 0$, where $a \rho^0 b$ is defined by

$$a \rho^0 b \text{ if and only if } a = b$$

In other words,

$$a \rho^* b \text{ if and only if } a \rho^+ b \text{ or } a = b.$$

Functions

Let Σ and Ω be two sets, and let ϕ be a relation from Σ to Ω such that for every $a \in \Sigma$,

$$\mathrm{card}(\{b: b \in \Omega \text{ and } a \phi b\}) \leq 1$$

Then, ϕ is a *function* from Σ to Ω. If ϕ satisfies

$$\mathrm{card}(\{b: b \in \Omega \text{ and } a \phi b\}) = 1$$

for every $a \in \Sigma$, then ϕ is a *total function* from Σ to Ω.

Conventions

Consider a function ϕ. If this book needs to point out that ϕ may not be total, then it refers to ϕ as a *partial function*. Instead of $a \phi b$, the present book often writes $\phi(a) = b$.

●

Let Σ and Ω be two sets, and let ϕ be a function from Σ to Ω. If card($\{a: a \in \Sigma$ and $a\phi b\}) \leq 1$, for all $b \in \Omega$, then ϕ is an *injection* from Σ to Ω. If ϕ is total and, in addition, card($\{a: a \in \Sigma$ and $a\phi b\}) = 1$, for all $b \in \Omega$, then ϕ is a *bijection* from Σ onto Ω.

Conventions

One-to-one function and *one-to-one correspondence* are synonymous with *injection* and *bijection*, respectively. For brevity, this book uses *injection* and *bijection*. ●

Example 0.2.2 Functions

Consider the two sets

$$\text{Pronouns} = \{I, you, he, she, it, we, they\}$$

$$\text{Be} = \{am, are, is\}$$

Pronouns contains the six English pronouns in their subject forms, and Be contains three present-tense forms of 'be' - 'am', 'are', and 'is'. Consider the total function, ProperPronoun, from Pronouns to Be; intuitively, ProperPronoun relates English pronouns to the corresponding present-tense form of 'be':

$$\text{ProperPronoun} = \{\ (I, am), (you, are), (he, is), (she, is),$$
$$(it, is), (we, are), (they, are)\}.$$

Observe that ProperPronoun does not represent an injection.
Consider the function RestrictedProperPronoun, from Pronouns to Be:

$$\text{RestrictedProperPronoun} = \{\ (I, am), (we, are)\}.$$

Notice that RestrictedProperPronoun is an injection.
Finally, assume that RestrictedProperPronoun is defined from { I, we } to { am, are }. Under this assumption, RestrictedProperPronoun represents a bijection. ▲

Let Σ, Ω and Δ be three sets, ϕ be a function from Σ to Ω, and γ be a function from Ω to Δ. The *composition of ϕ and γ*, denoted by $\gamma\phi$, is the function from Σ to Δ, defined as

$$\gamma\phi(a) = \gamma(\phi(a))$$

for all $a \in \Sigma$.

Before its conclusion, this section uses the notion of a bijection to introduce two important notions concerning infinite sets. An infinite set Σ is *countable* if there exists a bijection, β, from Σ to the set of natural numbers; otherwise, Σ is *uncountable*.

Example 0.2.3 Countable and uncountable sets

Consider the set of all even natural numbers; formally,

$$E = \{ n: n \text{ is an even natural number}\}.$$

Define the bijection β from E to the set of natural numbers as

$$\beta(2n) = n$$

for all natural numbers, n. Therefore, E is countable.

As proved in Section 2.3, the set of all functions from the set of natural numbers onto $\{0, 1\}$ is an uncountable set.

▲

0.3 Graphs

This section introduces graphs and some of their special cases. Most importantly, it defines trees, which fulfil a crucial role in this book.

Let Σ be a set. A *graph* is a pair $G = (\Sigma, \rho)$, where ρ is a relation on Σ.

Conventions

More precisely, a *graph* is called a *directed graph*. For brevity, this book uses the former.

●

Consider a graph $G = (\Sigma, \rho)$. Members of Σ are called *nodes*, and ordered pairs in ρ are called *edges*. If $(a, b) \in \rho$, then (a, b) *leaves* a and *enters* b; at this point, a is a *predecessor* of b, and b is a *successor* of a. Let $a \in \Sigma$; then, the *in-degree* of a equals card($\{ b: (b, a) \in \rho\}$), and the *out-degree* of a equals card($\{ c: (a, c) \in \rho\}$). A sequence of nodes, $(a_0, a_1, ..., a_n)$, where $n \geq 1$, is a *path of length n* from a_0 to a_n if $(a_{i-1}, a_i) \in \rho$ for all $i = 1, ..., n$; if, in addition, $a_0 = a_n$, then $(a_0, a_1, ..., a_n)$ is a *cycle of length n*.

A graph, $G = (\Sigma, \rho)$, is usually described pictorially so that each node, $a \in \Sigma$, is represented by a circle (see Figure 0.3.1), and each edge, $(a, b) \in \rho$, is represented by an arrow from circle a to circle b (see Figure 0.3.2).

Figure 0.3.1 Node a.

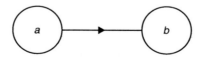

Figure 0.3.2 Edge (a, b).

Example 0.3.1 Graphs

Consider a Pascal program p and its *call graph*, $G = (\Sigma, \rho)$, defined so that Σ contains the set of subprograms in p, and

$$(a, b) \in \rho \text{ if and only if subprogram } a \text{ calls subprogram } b$$

For instance, let $\Sigma = \{A, B, C, D\}$, and $\rho = \{(A, B), (B, C), (C, A)\}$ (see Figure 0.3.3). According to this graph, A calls B, B calls C, and C calls A; D calls no subprogram.

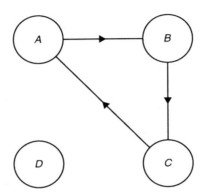

Figure 0.3.3 Call graph.

As $(A, B) \in \rho$, this edge leaves A and enters B, so A is a predecessor of B, and B is a successor of A. The in-degree of A is 1, and the out-degree of a is also 1. (A, B, C, A) is a path of length 3 from A to A; in fact, this path represents a cycle as it starts and ends in the same node, A.

▲

An *acyclic graph* is a graph $G = (\Sigma, \rho)$, that has no cycles. If $a \in \Sigma$ is a node having out-degree 0, then a is a *leaf*. If $(a_0, a_1, \ldots, a_n)$ is a path in G, then a_0 is an *ancestor* of a_n and a_n is a *descendent* of a_0; in addition, if $n = 1$, then a_0 is a *direct ancestor* of a_n and a_n is a *direct descendent* of a_0.

Trees

A *tree* is an acyclic graph, $G = (\Sigma, \rho)$, satisfying these three properties:

1. G has a specified node whose in-degree is 0; this node represents the *root* of G, denoted by root(G).
2. if $a \in \Sigma$ and $a \neq \text{root}(G)$, then a is a descendent of root(G) and the in-degree of a is 1.

Mathematical background

3. Each node $a \in \Sigma$, has its direct descendents, b_1 through b_n, ordered from the left to the right so that b_1 is the leftmost direct descendent of a and b_n is the rightmost direct descendent of a; at this point, a is the *parent* of b_1 through b_n and b_1 through b_n are a's *children*.

Let $G = (\Sigma, \rho)$ be a tree. The *frontier* of G, denoted by fr(G), is the sequence of G's leaves ordered from the left to the right. The *depth* of G, depth(G), is the length of the longest path in G; if depth(G) = 1, then G is an *elementary tree*. If $G' = (\Sigma', \rho')$ represents a tree satisfying these three conditions

1. $\Sigma' \neq \emptyset$, and $\Sigma' \subseteq \Sigma$
2. $\rho' = (\Sigma' \times \Sigma') \cap \rho$
3. in G, no node in $\Sigma - \Sigma'$ is a descendent of a node in Σ'

then G' is a *subtree* of G.

Conventions
Let G be any tree. This book draws G with its root on the top and with all edges directed down. For simplicity, it omits all arrowheads and all circles around G's nodes.

●

Example 0.3.2 Part 1 Trees
Consider a program p whose call graph $G = (\Sigma, \rho)$ is defined by $\Sigma = \{A, B, C, D, E\}$ and $\rho = \{ (A, B), (A, E), (B, C), (B, D)\}$. Notice that A calls B and E, and B calls C and D. Observe that G represents a tree (see Figure 0.3.4).

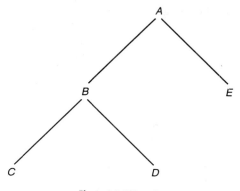

Figure 0.3.4 Tree G.

A represents the root of G because its in-degree is 0. B, C, D and E have their in-degrees equal to 1. B has two children, C and D; in other words, the parent of C and D is B. The frontier of G is CDE because these nodes appear as G's leaves ordered from the left to the right. As the length of the longest path in G is two, depth(G) = 2. Figure 0.3.5 presents a subtree of G.

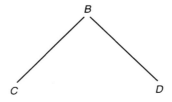

Figure 0.3.5 Subtree of G

Because the depth of the subtree in Figure 0.3.5 equals one, this subtree actually represents an elementary tree.

△

The edges of a graph are frequently labelled as illustrated next.

Example 0.3.2 Part 2 Labelled tree

Return to the call graph G depicted in Figure 0.3.4. Assume that the calls occur in this sequence:

1. A calls B
2. B calls C
3. B calls D
4. A calls E.

To specify this order, label G's edges as shown in Figure 0.3.6.

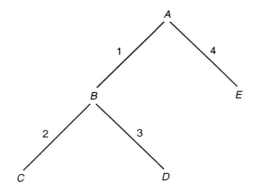

Figure 0.3.6 Labelled tree G.

▲

0.4 Proofs

This section explains the fundamental proof techniques used in this book.

Mathematical systems

A formal mathematical system S consists of these four fundamental parts:

1. basic symbols
2. formation rules
3. axioms
4. inference rules.

Basic symbols, such as constants and operators, form components of *statements*, which are composed according to formation rules. Axioms are primitive statements, whose validity is accepted without justification. By inference rules, some statements infer other statements. A *proof* of a statement s in S consists of a sequence of statements

$$s_1, \ldots, s_i, \ldots s_n$$

such that $s = s_n$ and each s_i is either an axiom of S or a statement inferred by some of the statements $s_1, \ldots, s_{i-1}$ according to inference rules. If s is proved in this way, then s is a *theorem* of S.

Logical connectives

Logical connectives join statements to create more complex statements. The most common logical connectives are

not, and, or, implies, if and only if

In this list, 'not' is unary while the other connectives are binary. That is, if s is a statement, then 'not s' is a statement as well. Similarly, if s_1 and s_2 are statements, then s_1 and s_2, s_1 or s_2, s_1 implies s_2, and s_1 if and only if s_2 are statements, too. The following two tables present the rules governing the truth, denoted by 1, or falsehood, denoted by 0, concerning statements containing these logical connectives.

s	not
0	1
1	0

s_1	s_2	and	or	implies	if and only if
0	0	0	0	1	1
0	1	0	1	1	0
1	0	0	1	0	0
1	1	1	1	1	1

Sometimes, this book symbolically denotes 'and' and 'or' by $\wedge$ and $\vee$, respectively. A statement of *equivalence*, which has the form

$$s_1 \text{ if and only if } s_2,$$

plays a crucial role in this book. A proof that s_1 if and only if s_2 is true requires a demonstration that the following two implications hold:

$$s_1 \text{ implies } s_2 \text{ and } s_2 \text{ implies } s_1$$

There are several methods of demonstrating that an implication is true – of these, proof by contraposition and proof by contradiction are given below.

Proof by contraposition

Proof by contraposition is based on the *contrapositive law*:

$$(s_1 \text{ implies } s_2) \text{ if and only if } ((\text{not } s_2) \text{ implies } (\text{not } s_1))$$

From this law, the implication s_1 implies s_2 can be verified by proving that (not s_2) implies (not s_1) is true.

Proof by contradiction

Proof by contradiction establishes that s_1 implies s_2 is true by demonstrating that the following implication holds true:

$$((\text{not } s_2) \text{ and } s_1) \text{ implies } 0$$

where 0 denotes falsehood. More precisely, assume that s_2 is false and s_1 is true. Then, demonstrate that under this assumption, a false statement arises. Consequently, s_1 implies s_2 is true.

Mathematical background

Example 0.4.1 Proof by contradiction

A natural number n is prime if its only positive divisors are 1 and n; for instance, 2 and 3 are primes. Consider

$$\text{Prime} = \{n: n \text{ is prime}\}$$

In other words, Prime contains all primes. By contradiction, prove that Prime is infinite. That is, assume that Prime is finite. Let

$$\text{card}(\text{Prime}) = k$$

for some natural number, k. In greater detail, express Prime as

$$\text{Prime} = \{p_1, p_2, \ldots, p_k\}$$

Set

$$n = p_1 \cdot p_2 \cdot \ldots \cdot p_k + 1$$

Observe that n is not divisible by p_i, for any $i = 1, \ldots, k$. As a result, either n is a new prime or n equals a product of new primes. In either case, there exists a prime greater than p_i, for $i = 1, \ldots, k$; therefore, Prime does not contain all primes. This contradiction implies that Prime is infinite.

▲

Proof by induction

A proof by induction demonstrates that a statement $s(n)$ is true for all integers, $n \geq b$, where b is a nonnegative integer. In general, a proof of this kind consists of these three parts:

Basis

> a proof that $s(b)$ is true

Inductive hypothesis

> an assumption that $s(i)$ is true for all $i = b, \ldots, j$, where j is an integer such that $j \geq b$

Inductive step:

> a proof that $s(j + 1)$ is true if the inductive hypothesis holds

Example 0.4.2 Proof by induction
Suppose that $s(n)$ is this statement

$$1 + 3 + 5 + \ldots + 2n - 1 = n^2$$

for $n = 1, 2, \ldots$. Less formally, $s(n)$ states that the sum of odd integers is a perfect square. An inductive proof of this statement follows next.

Basis
Because $1=1^2$, $s(1)$ is true.

Inductive hypothesis
Assume that $s(i)$ is true for all $i = 1, \ldots, j$, where j is a natural number.

Inductive step
This part of the proof verifies $s(j + 1)$, which means

$$1 + 3 + 5 + \ldots + (2j - 1) + (2(j + 1) - 1) = (j + 1)^2$$

By the inductive hypothesis, $s(i)$ is true for $i = 1, \ldots, j$. Specifically, for $i = j$,

$$1 + 3 + 5 + \ldots + (2j - 1) = j^2.$$

Hence,

$$1 + 3 + 5 + \ldots + (2j - 1) + (2(j + 1) - 1) = j^2 + 2j + 1 = (j + 1)^2.$$

Consequently, $s(j + 1)$ holds, and the inductive proof is completed. ▲

Exercises

1 Sets

1.1 Consider this set

$$\Sigma = \{0, 1, 2, 3, 4, 5, 6, 7, 8, 9\}.$$

Determine $\text{card}(\Sigma)$.
1.2 Give an example of an infinite set.
1.3 Let Ω denote the set of all English determiners. Describe 2^Ω.
1.4 Let $\Sigma_1 = \{a, b, c\}$ and $\Sigma_2 = \{c, d\}$. Determine $\Sigma_1 \cup \Sigma_2$, $\Sigma_1 \cap \Sigma_2$, and $\Sigma_1 - \Sigma_2$.

1.5 Let Σ be the following set, whose members are taken from the universe of natural numbers.

$$\Sigma = \{i\colon i \text{ is an even natural number}\}$$

Determine $\overline{\Sigma}$.

1.6 Russell's paradox is based on the predicate $\pi(X)$:

$$X \text{ is not a member of itself}$$

where X is a set. Reformulate $\pi(X)$ as

$$X \notin X$$

Consider

$$Y = \{\, X\colon X \notin X \}$$

Less formally, Y consists of the sets that are not members of themselves. Naturally, there exists the question of whether Y belongs to itself. If $Y \in Y$, then Y does not belong to Y, so $Y \notin Y$. However, if $Y \notin Y$, then by the definition of Y, Y contains Y, so $Y \in Y$. Consequently, $Y \in Y$ implies $Y \notin Y$, and $Y \notin Y$ implies $Y \in Y$ – an impossible situation. Therefore, Y does not exist. Is there a way of avoiding Russell's paradox?

2 Relations

2.1 Let Σ and Ω be two sets, and let ρ and ρ' be two relations from Σ to Ω. If ρ and ρ' represent two identical subsets of $\Sigma \times \Omega$, then ρ *equals* ρ', symbolically written as

$$\rho = \rho'$$

Illustrate this definition by an example.

2.2 Let Σ be a set, and let ρ be a relation on A. If for all $a \in \Sigma$,

$$a\rho a,$$

then ρ is *reflexive*. Give an example of a reflexive relation.

2.3 Let Σ be a set, and let ρ be a relation on A. If for all $a, b \in \Sigma$,

$$a\rho b \text{ implies } b\rho a,$$

then ρ is *symmetric*. Give an example of a symmetric relation.

2.4 Let Σ be a set, and let ρ be a relation on A. If for all $a, b, c \in \Sigma$,

($a\rho b$ and $b\rho c$) implies $a\rho c$,

then ρ is *transitive*. Give an example of a transitive relation.
2.5 Let Σ be a set, and let ρ be a relation on Σ. If ρ is reflexive, symmetric, and transitive, then ρ is an *equivalence relation*. Give an example of an equivalence relation.
2.6 Let Σ be a set, and let ρ be an equivalence relation on Σ. Then, ρ partitions Σ into disjoint subsets, called *equivalence classes*, so that for each $a \in \Sigma$, the equivalence class of a is denoted by $[a]$ and defined as

$$[a] = \{b: a\rho b\}.$$

Prove that for all a and b in A, either $[a] = [b]$ or $[a] \cap [b] = \emptyset$.
2.7 The *index* of an equivalence relation ρ on a set Σ is the number of equivalence classes into which A is partitioned by ρ. Give an example of an equivalence relation on a set Σ so that the index of this equivalence relation on Σ is 2.
2.8 Consider the following theorem and its proof.

Theorem A

Let Σ be a set, ρ be a relation on Σ, and ρ^+ be the transitive closure of ρ. Then, the following two properties hold:

(1) ρ^+ is a transitive relation.
(2) If ρ' is a transitive relation such that $\rho \subseteq \rho'$, then $\rho^+ \subseteq \rho'$.

Proof:
(1) To prove that ρ^+ is a transitive relation, demonstrate that

$$\text{if } a\rho^+ b \text{ and } b\rho^+ c, \text{ then } a\rho^+ c$$

As $a\rho^+ b$, there exist $x_1, ..., x_n$ in Σ so

$$x_1 \rho x_2, ..., x_{n-1} \rho x_n$$

where $x_1 = a$ and $x_n = b$. As $b\rho^+ c$, there also exist $y_1, ..., y_m$ in Σ so

$$y_1 \rho y_2, ..., y_{m-1} \rho y_m$$

where $y_1 = b$ and $y_m = c$. Consequently,

$$x_1 \rho x_2, ..., x_{n-1} \rho x_n, y_1 \rho y_2, ..., y_{m-1} \rho y_m$$

where $x_1 = a$, $x_n = b = y_1$, and $y_m = c$. As a result,

$$a\rho^+ c$$

Mathematical background

(2) In this part of the proof, demonstrate that if ρ' is a transitive relation such that $\rho \subseteq \rho'$, then $\rho^+ \subseteq \rho'$. Less formally, this implication means that ρ^+ is the smallest transitive relation that includes ρ.

Let ρ' be a transitive relation such that $\rho \subseteq \rho'$, and let $a\rho^+ b$. Then, there exist $x_1, ..., x_n$ in Σ so

$$x_1 \rho x_2, ..., x_{n-1} \rho x_n$$

where $x_1 = a$ and $x_n = b$. As $\rho \subseteq \rho'$,

$$x_1 \rho' x_2, ..., x_{n-1} \rho' x_n$$

where $x_1 = a$ and $x_n = b$. Because ρ' is transitive,

$$a\rho' b$$

Consequently,

$$a\rho^+ b \text{ implies } a\rho' b$$

Thus, Theorem A holds. ∎

By analogy with the proof of Theorem A, prove Theorem B, given next.

Theorem B
Let Σ be a set, ρ be a relation on Σ, and ρ^* be the transitive and reflexive closure of ρ. Then, the following two properties hold:

(1) ρ^* is a transitive and reflexive relation.
(2) If ρ' be a transitive and reflexive relation such that $\rho \subseteq \rho'$, then $\rho^* \subseteq \rho'$.

2.9 Consider the following definition.

Definition
Let Σ be a set, and let ρ be a transitive relation on Σ such that for every $a \in \Sigma$,

$$(a, a) \notin \rho$$

Then, ρ is a *partial order* on Σ.

Prove the next theorem.

Theorem

Let Σ be a set, and let ρ be a partial order on Σ. Then, for all $a, b \in \Sigma$, this implication holds

$$(a, b) \in \rho \text{ implies } (b, a) \notin \rho$$

2.10 Let Σ be a set having n elements. Set $\Omega = 2^\Sigma$. Let ρ be the relation on Ω defined by this equivalence

$$a\rho b \text{ if and only if } a \subset b$$

for all $a, b \in \Omega$. Prove that ρ is a partial order.

2.11 Generalize the notion of a binary relation to the notion of an nary relation, where n is a natural number.

2.12 Let Σ be a subset of the set of all nonnegative integers, and let ϕ be the total function from the set of all nonnegative integers to $\{0, 1\}$ defined by the equivalence

$$\phi(i) = 1 \text{ if and only if } i \in \Sigma$$

for all nonnegative integers, i. Then, ϕ is the *characteristic function* of Σ. Illustrate this notion by an example.

2.13 Introduce the notion of an nary function, where n is a natural number.

3 Graphs

3.1 Let Σ be a set. An *undirected graph* is a pair $G = (\Sigma, \rho)$, where $\rho \in \{\{a, b\}: a, b \in \Sigma\}$. Explain the fundamental difference between this definition and the definition of a graph given in Section 0.3.

3.2 Recall that Section 0.3 has defined a tree as an acyclic graph, $G = (\Sigma, \rho)$, satisfying these three properties:

(1) G has a specified node whose in-degree is 0; this node represents the *root* of G, denoted by root(G).
(2) If $a \in \Sigma$ and $a \neq \text{root}(G)$, then a is a descendent of root(G) and the in-degree of a is 1.
(3) Each node, $a \in \Sigma$, has its direct descendents, b_1 through b_n, ordered from the left to the right so that b_1 is the leftmost direct descendent of a and b_n is the rightmost direct descendent of a.

Reformulate (3) by using the notion of a partial order (see Exercise 2.9).

3.3 Design a one-dimensional representation for trees.

4 Proofs

4.1 A *tautology* is a statement that is true for all possible truth values of the statement variables. Explain why every theorem of a formal mathematical system represents a tautology.

4.2 Prove that the contrapositive law represents a tautology.

4.3 State a theorem and prove this theorem by using the contrapositive law.

4.4 A *Boolean algebra* is a formal mathematical system, which consists of a set, Σ, and operations 'and', 'or' and 'not'. The axioms of Boolean algebra follow next.

(1) *Associativity*

$$a \text{ or } (b \text{ or } c) = (a \text{ or } b) \text{ or } c$$

$$a \text{ and } (b \text{ and } c) = (a \text{ and } b) \text{ and } c$$

for all $a, b, c \in \Sigma$.

(2) *Commutativity*

$$a \text{ or } b = b \text{ or } a$$

$$a \text{ and } b = b \text{ and } a$$

for all $a, b, c \in \Sigma$.

(3) *Distributivity*

$$a \text{ and } (b \text{ or } c) = (a \text{ and } b) \text{ or } (a \text{ and } c)$$

$$a \text{ or } (b \text{ and } c) = (a \text{ or } b) \text{ and } (a \text{ or } c)$$

for all $a, b, c \in \Sigma$.

In addition, Σ contains two distinguished members, 0 and 1, which satisfy the following laws for all $a \in \Sigma$:

(4)

$$a \text{ or } 0 = a$$

$$a \text{ and } 1 = a$$

(5)

$$a \text{ or } (\text{not } a) = 1$$

$$a \text{ and } (\text{not } a) = 0$$

The rule of inference is substitution of equals for equals.

Give an example of a Boolean algebra.

1 Languages

This book expresses and studies computation by using various languages, ranging from binary languages through programming languages to natural languages. The present chapter, consisting of three sections, formalizes languages so as to encompass all this range.

Section 1.1 defines languages and some fundamental operations. Section 1.2 introduces basic language generators, including expressions and grammars, and illustrates their use by defining a new programming language. Finally, Section 1.3 discusses translations of languages.

1.1 Formalization of Languages

This section formalizes languages and then introduces several language operations.

Alphabets and words

To define languages, alphabets and words are first formalized.

Definition — alphabet and symbol
An *alphabet* is a finite, nonempty set of elements, which are called *symbols*.
◆

A sequence of symbols forms a word. The *empty word*, denoted by ε, is the word that contains no symbols. The next definition formally introduces words over an alphabet by using the recursive definitional method (see Section 0.2).

Definition — word
Let Σ be an alphabet.

1. ε is a word over Σ.
2. If x is a word over Σ and $a \in \Sigma$, then xa is a word over Σ.

◆

Convention
In the theory of languages, *word* is synonymous with *string*. This book uses the former throughout.
◆

The length of x is the number of all symbols in x.

Definition — length of word
Let x be a word over an alphabet, Σ. The *length* of x, $|x|$, is defined as follows:

1. if $x = \varepsilon$, then $|x| = 0$
2. if $x = a_1 \ldots a_n$, for some $n \geq 1$, where $a_i \in \Sigma$ for all $i = 1, \ldots, n$, then $|x| = n$.
◆

Let $a \in \Sigma$. Then, $\#_a x$ denotes the number of occurrences of a in x.

Operations on words

The following definitions introduce some basic operations over words.

Definition — concatenation of words
Let x and y be two words over an alphabet, Σ. Then, xy is the *concatenation* of x and y.
◆

For every word x,

$$x\varepsilon = \varepsilon x = x$$

Definition — power of word
Let x be a word over an alphabet, Σ. For $i \geq 0$, the *i*th *power* of x, x^i, is recursively defined as

1. $x^0 = \varepsilon$
2. $x^i = xx^{i-1}$, for $i \geq 1$.
◆

Observe that for any word x

$$x^i x^j = x^j x^i = x^{i+j}$$

where $i, j \geq 0$.
The reversal of a word is x written in the reverse order.

Definition — reversal of word

Let x be a word over an alphabet, Σ. The *reversal* of x, reversal(x), is defined as

1. if $x = \varepsilon$, then reversal(x) = ε
2. if $x = a_1 \ldots a_n$, for some $n \geq 1$, and $a_i \in \Sigma$, for $i = 1, \ldots, n$, then reversal($a_1 \ldots a_n$) = $a_n \ldots a_1$.

◆

Definition — prefix of word

Let x and y be two words over an alphabet, Σ. Then, x is a *prefix* of y if there exists a word, z, over Σ so $xz = y$; moreover, if $x \notin \{\varepsilon, y\}$, then x is a *proper prefix* of y.

◆

For a word y, prefix(y) denotes the set of all prefixes of y; that is,

$$\text{prefix}(y) = \{ x: x \text{ is a prefix of } y\}$$

Definition — suffix of word

Let x and y be two words over an alphabet, Σ. Then, x is a *suffix* of y if there exists a word, z, over Σ so $zx = y$; moreover, if $x \notin \{\varepsilon, y\}$, then x is a *proper suffix* of y.

◆

For a word y, suffix(y) denotes the set of all suffixes of y; that is,

$$\text{suffix}(y) = \{ x: x \text{ is a suffix of } y\}$$

Definition — subword

Let x and y be two words over an alphabet, Σ. Then, x is a *subword* of y if there exist two word, z and z', over Σ so $zxz' = y$; moreover, if $x \notin \{\varepsilon, y\}$, then x is a *proper subword* of y.

◆

For a word y, subword(y) denotes the set of all subwords of y; that is,

$$\text{subword}(y) = \{ x: x \text{ is a subword of } y\}$$

Observe that, for every word y, these three properties hold:

1. prefix(y) $\subseteq$ subword(y)
2. suffix(y) $\subseteq$ subword(y)
3. $\{\varepsilon, y\} \subseteq$ prefix(y) $\cap$ suffix(y) $\cap$ subword(y).

Example 1.1.1 Operations over words

This example illustrates some of the notions that the present section has introduced so far. Consider the *binary alphabet* – that is,

$$\{0, 1\}$$

Notice that

$$\varepsilon$$
$$1$$
$$010$$

are words over $\{0, 1\}$. Observe that

$$|\varepsilon| = 0$$
$$|1| = 1$$
$$|010| = 3$$

Furthermore, note that

$$\#_0 \varepsilon = 0$$
$$\#_0 1 = 0$$
$$\#_0 010 = 2$$

The concatenation of 1 and 010 equals

$$1010$$

The fourth power of 1010 equals

$$1010101010101010$$

Notice that

$$\text{reversal}(1010) = 0101$$

The words 10 and 1010 are prefixes of 1010. 10 is a proper prefix of 1010, whereas 1010 is not. Observe that

$$\text{prefix}(1010) = \{\varepsilon, 1, 10, 101, 1010\}$$

The words 010 and ε are suffixes of 1010. 010 is a proper prefix of 1010, whereas ε is not. Notice that

$$\text{suffix}(1010) = \{\varepsilon, 0, 10, 010, 1010\}$$

The words 01 and 1010 are subwords of 1010. 01 is a proper subword of 1010, but 1010 is not. Note that 01 is neither a prefix of 1010 nor a suffix of 1010. Finally, observe that

$$\text{subword}(1010) = \{\varepsilon, 0, 1, 01, 10, 010, 101, 1010\}$$

▲

Languages

Consider an alphabet, Σ. Let Σ^* denote the set of all words over Σ. Set

$$\Sigma^+ = \Sigma^* - \{\varepsilon\};$$

in other words, Σ^+ denotes the set of all nonempty words over Σ. The following definition formalizes a language over Σ as a set of words over Σ. Notice that this definition encompasses both artificial languages, such as Pascal, and natural languages, such as English.

Definition — language
Let Σ be an alphabet, and let $L \subseteq \Sigma^*$. Then, L is a *language* over Σ.

◆

By this definition, $\varnothing$ and $\{\varepsilon\}$ are languages over any alphabet. Notice, however, that

$$\varnothing \neq \{\varepsilon\}$$

because $\varnothing$ contains no element, while $\{\varepsilon\}$ has one element, namely ε. Observe that for every alphabet, Σ, Σ^* represents a language over Σ; as Σ^* consists of all words over Σ, this language is referred to as the *universal language* over Σ.

Because languages are defined as sets, the notions concerning sets apply to them (see Section 0.1). Consequently, a language, L, is finite if it has n members, for some $n \geq 0$.

Definition — finite and infinite language
Let L be a language. L is *finite* if $\text{card}(L) = n$, for some $n \geq 0$; otherwise, L is *infinite*.

◆

Operations on languages

Consider the set operations of union, intersection, and difference (see Section 0.1). Naturally, these operations apply to languages. That is, for two languages, L_1 and L_2,

$$L_1 \cup L_2 = \{\, x : x \in L_1 \text{ or } x \in L_2 \,\}$$

$$L_1 \cap L_2 = \{\, x : x \in L_1 \text{ and } x \in L_2 \,\}$$

$$L_1 - L_2 = \{\, x : x \in L_1 \text{ and } x \notin L_2 \,\}$$

Furthermore, consider a language L over an alphabet, Σ. The *complement of* L, $\overline{L}$, is defined as

$$\overline{L} = \Sigma^* - L$$

The present section has already introduced several operations on words. The following definitions extend these word operations to languages.

Definition — concatenation of languages
Let L_1 and L_2 be two languages. The *concatenation* of L_1 and L_2, $L_1 L_2$, is defined as

$$L_1 L_2 = \{\, xy : x \in L_1 \text{ and } y \in L_2 \,\}$$

♦

By this definition, every language L satisfies these two properties

1. $L\{\varepsilon\} = \{\varepsilon\}L = L$
2. $L\varnothing = \varnothing L = \varnothing$.

Definition — reversal of language
Let L be a language. The *reversal* of L, reversal(L), is defined as

$$\text{reversal}(L) = \{\, \text{reversal}(x) : x \in L \,\}$$

♦

Definition — power of language
Let L be a language. For $i \geq 0$, the *i*th *power* of L, L^i, is defined as

1. $L^0 = \varepsilon$
2. for all $i \geq 1$, $L^i = LL^{i-1}$.

♦

Definition — closure of language
Let L be a language. The *closure* of L, L^*, is defined as

$$L^* = \bigcup_{i=0}^{\infty} L^i$$

◆

Definition — positive closure of language
Let L be a language. The *positive closure* of L, L^+, is defined as

$$L^+ = \bigcup_{i=1}^{\infty} L^i$$

◆

By the previous two definitions, for every language L, these two properties hold:

1. $L^+ = LL^* = L^*L$
2. $L^* = L^+ \cup \{\varepsilon\}$.

The next example illustrates the set operations that this section has introduced so far. Besides the notations given in the previous definitions, this example also use these two notations

$$\text{prefix}(L) = \{\, y\colon y \in \text{prefix}(x) \text{ for some } x \in L\,\}$$

$$\text{suffix}(L) = \{\, y\colon y \in \text{suffix}(x) \text{ for some } x \in L\,\}$$

Example 1.1.2 Operations over languages
Let $\Sigma = \{0, 1\}$. Consider these two languages over Σ:

$$L_1 = \{\, 0, 01\} \text{ and } L_2 = \{1, 01\}$$

Observe that

$$L_1 \cup L_2 = \{\, 0, 1, 01\}$$
$$L_1 \cap L_2 = \{\, 01\}$$
$$L_1 - L_2 = \{\, 0\}$$
$$L_1 L_2 = \{\, 01, 001, 011, 0101\}$$

Furthermore, consider

$$L = \{10, 11\}$$

over Σ. Notice that

$$\overline{L} = \Sigma^* - \{10, 11\}$$
$$\text{reversal}(L) = \{01, 11\}$$
$$\text{prefix}(L) = \{\varepsilon, 1, 10, 11\}$$
$$\text{suffix}(L) = \{\varepsilon, 0, 1, 10, 11\}$$

For $i = 2$,

$$L^2 = \{1010, 1011, 1110, 1111\}$$

Observe that

$$L^* = \{\varepsilon, 10, 11, 1010, 1011, 1110, 1111, \ldots\}$$

and

$$L^+ = \{10, 11, 1010, 1011, 1110, 1111, \ldots\}$$

▲

Models for languages and their investigation

Various kinds of computation can be described and studied by using languages. This book concentrates on the examination of models for languages because these models actually represent models of computation described by these languages. Naturally, the same language can be described by many different models; models of this kind are known as *equivalent models*.

To examine language models systematically, these models are classified according to their expressive power; then, the resulting *classes of models* are investigated. Most importantly, this investigation determines the *families of languages* characterized by these classes. If several different classes characterize the same language family, then these classes of models *have the same power*. Frequently, there is a need to demonstrate that some equally powerful classes contain no model that can perform a given computational task, specified by a language L. In terms of languages, this demonstration consists in proving that the language family characterized by these classes does not contain L. As a rule, such a proof is based on *pumping lemmas*. *Closure properties* are also discussed in detail. To explain closure properties, consider a language family L and a language operation o. If L contains every language resulting from the application of o to any languages in L, then L is *closed* under o; otherwise, L is not closed under o.

Example 1.1.3 Closure properties

Let L be the family of languages over $\{a, b\}$ such that

$L \in \mathbf{L}$ if and only if each word in L begins with a

That is,

$$\mathbf{L} = \{ L: L \subseteq \{a\}\{a, b\}^* \}$$

Notice that **L** is closed under $\cup$ because for any $L, L' \in \mathbf{L}$, each word in $L \cup L'$ begins with a, so **L** contains $L \cup L'$.

On the other hand, **L** is not closed under reversal. Indeed, consider $\{ab\} \in \mathbf{L}$ and observe that reversal($\{ab\}$) = $\{ba\}$. As $\{ba\} \notin \mathbf{L}$, **L** is not closed under reversal.

▲

1.2 Expressions and Grammars

As pointed out in the conclusion of the previous section, the specification of languages represents an important topic. Finite languages can be specified by listing its components; for instance, the language consisting of all English articles is defined as

{a, an, the}

However, infinite languages cannot be described in this way. Therefore, special finite *metalanguages* – that is, languages that specify other languages – are used to generate infinite languages. This section introduces two language generators of this kind, expressions and grammars. First, Section 1.2.1 describes expressions, then Section 1.2.2 discusses grammar, finally Section 1.2.3 uses these language generators to design a new programming language, called COLA.

1.2.1 Expressions

A typical programming language contains logically cohesive lexical entities, such as identifiers or integers, over an alphabet, Σ. These entities, called *lexemes*, are customarily specified by *expressions*, recursively defined as follows:

1. $\emptyset$ is a regular expression denoting the empty set.
2. ε is a regular expression denoting $\{\varepsilon\}$.
3. a, where $a \in \Sigma$, is a regular expression denoting $\{a\}$.
4. If r and s are regular expressions denoting the languages R and S, respectively, then

    (a) $(r \cdot s)$ is a regular expression denoting RS
    (b) $(r + s)$ is a regular expression denoting $R \cup S$
    (c) (r^*) is a regular expression denoting R^*.

Whenever no ambiguity arises, parentheses are omitted in expressions. In this way, the next example describes Pascal identifiers.

Example 1.2.1.1 Identifiers

Consider Pascal identifiers, defined as arbitrarily long alphanumeric words that begin with a letter. Equivalently and concisely, Pascal identifiers can be specified by using the expression

$$\langle \text{letter} \rangle \langle \text{letter or digit} \rangle^*$$

where

$$\langle \text{letter} \rangle = A + \ldots + Z$$
$$\langle \text{letter or digit} \rangle = A + \ldots + Z + 0 + \ldots + 9$$

▲

Expressions, which are precisely called *regular expressions*, are studied in Section 3.1.

1.2.2 Grammars

The syntax of programming languages is usually described by specification tools based on grammars. This section presents the following three grammatically based specification tools for programming languages:

1. Backus-Naur form
2. extended Backus-Naur form
3. syntax graphs.

Backus-Naur form

The Backus-Naur form contains two kinds of symbols, terminals and nonterminals. Terminals denote lexemes, whereas nonterminals represent syntactic constructs, such as expressions. The heart of the Backus-Naur form is a finite set of productions. Each production has the form

$$A \rightarrow x_1 | \ldots | x_n$$

In $A \rightarrow x_1 | \ldots | x_n$, A is a nonterminal. This nonterminal, the left-hand side of $A \rightarrow x_1 | \ldots | x_n$, represents the syntactic construct that this production defines. The right-hand side is $x_1 | \ldots | x_n$, where x_i is a word consisting of terminals and nonterminals. The words x_1 through x_n represent n alternative definitions of A.

Example 1.2.2.1 Part 1 Backus-Naur form
Consider the Backus-Naur form defined by its three productions:

1. ⟨expression⟩ → ⟨term⟩|⟨term⟩+⟨expression⟩|⟨term⟩−⟨expression⟩
2. ⟨term⟩ → ⟨factor⟩|⟨ factor⟩*⟨ term⟩|⟨factor⟩/⟨term⟩
3. ⟨factor⟩ → i|(⟨expression⟩)

This form has terminals +, −, *, /, (,), and i, where i denotes an identifier or an integer. Furthermore, this form has three nonterminals, i.e. ⟨expression⟩, ⟨term⟩, and ⟨factor⟩.

△

The Backus-Naur form uses its productions to derive syntactically well-formed constructs. This derivation begins from a special nonterminal, called the start symbol, and consists of several derivation steps. The Backus-Naur form makes a derivation step, symbolically denoted by ⇒, according to a production, $A \to x_1|...|x_n$, so that in the derived word, an occurrence of A is replaced with x_i, for some $i = 1, ..., n$. The derivation ends when only terminals appear in the derived word.

Example 1.2.2.1 Part 2 Derivations
Return to the Backus-Naur form defined in part 1 of this example. The present part describes how this form derives

$$i+i*i$$

The derivation starts from ⟨expression⟩, which represents the start symbol. In the brackets, every step of this derivation specifies the applied definition, selected from all alternative definitions appearing on the right-hand side of the used production.

⟨expression⟩ ⇒ ⟨term⟩+⟨expression⟩   [⟨expression⟩ → ⟨term⟩+⟨expression⟩]
⇒⟨factor⟩+⟨expression⟩   [⟨term⟩ → ⟨factor⟩]
⇒ i+⟨expression⟩   [⟨factor⟩ → i]
⇒ i+⟨term⟩   [⟨expression⟩ → ⟨term⟩]
⇒ i+⟨factor⟩*⟨term⟩   [⟨term⟩ → ⟨factor⟩*⟨term⟩]
⇒ $i+i$*⟨term⟩   [⟨factor⟩ → i]
⇒ $i+i$*⟨factor⟩   [⟨term⟩ → ⟨factor⟩]
⇒ $i+i*i$ [⟨factor⟩ → i]

Observe that the Backus-Naur form discussed in here generates arithmetic expressions.

△

Extended Backus-Naur form

The extended Backus-Naur form extends the Backus-Naur form's productions by adding the following three options.

1. The right-hand side of a production may contain some optional parts, which are delimited by brackets, [and].
2. The right-hand side of a production may contain braces, { and }, to indicate a syntactic part that can be repeated any number times, including zero times.
3. The right-hand side of a production may contain ⌈ and ⌋ to indicate several options, which are separated by |.

Note that some versions of the extended Backus-Naur form use parentheses (and), instead of ⌈ and ⌋. However, because many programming languages contain parentheses as lexemes, the use of parentheses sometimes causes ambiguity; therefore, this book uses ⌈ and ⌋.

Example 1.2.2.1 Part 3 Extended Backus-Naur form

Recall that part 1 presented the following Backus-Naur form:

1. ⟨expression⟩ → ⟨term⟩|⟨term⟩+⟨expression⟩|⟨term⟩−⟨expression⟩
2. ⟨term⟩ → ⟨factor⟩|⟨ factor⟩*⟨ term⟩|⟨factor⟩/⟨term⟩
3. ⟨factor⟩ → i|(⟨expression⟩)

In terms of the extended Backus-Naur form, production 1 can equivalently be redefined as

1. ⟨expression⟩ → ⟨term⟩{⌈+|−⌋⟨term⟩}

Analogously, shorten the other productions. The resulting extended Backus-Naur form becomes

1. ⟨expression⟩ → ⟨term⟩{⌈+|−⌋⟨term⟩}
2. ⟨term⟩ → ⟨factor⟩{⌈*|/⌋⟨term⟩}
3. ⟨factor⟩ → i|(⟨expression⟩)

Notice that this form is more succinct than the original Backus-Naur form.

△

Syntax graph

As already pointed out, a production of the extended Backus-Naur form defines the structure of the syntactic unit denoted by the nonterminal that forms the left-hand side of the production. Such a production is represented by a *syntax graph*, which contains oval nodes and rectangular nodes. Oval nodes contain terminals, whereas rectangular nodes contain nonterminals. A syntax graph has an entering edge on the left and an exiting edge on the right. Each path that goes from the entering edge to the exiting edge gives rise to a valid structure of the syntactic unit defined by the graph.

Example 1.2.2.1 Part 4 Syntax graph
Part 3 gives the extended Backus-Naur form

1. ⟨expression⟩ → ⟨term⟩{⌈+|−⌋⟨term⟩}
2. ⟨term⟩ → ⟨factor⟩{⌈*|/⌋⟨term⟩}
3. ⟨factor⟩ → i|(⟨expression⟩)

Figures 1.2.2.1 to 1.2.2.3 depict the syntax graphs corresponding to these three productions.

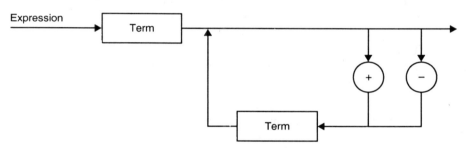

Figure 1.2.2.1 Syntax graph corresponding to ⟨expression⟩ → ⟨term⟩{⌈+|−⌋⟨term⟩}.

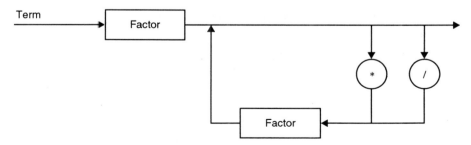

Figure 1.2.2.2 The syntax graph corresponding to ⟨term⟩ → ⟨factor⟩{⌈*|/⌋⟨term⟩}.

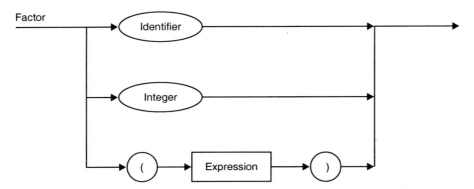

Figure 1.2.2.3 The syntax graph corresponding to ⟨factor⟩ → i|(⟨expression⟩).

△

Polish nation

Parenthesized infix expressions, such as (3+1)*2, are often represented by *Polish notation*, which uses no parenthesis and, therefore, simplifies the evaluation of these expressions. Next, two fundamental kinds of this notation, the prefix Polish expressions and the postfix Polish expressions are recursively defined.

Definition — prefix Polish expression
Let Σ be an alphabet, whose symbols denote operands. The *prefix Polish expressions* are defined recursively as follows:

1. If a is an infix expression, $a \in \Sigma$, then a is also the prefix Polish expression of a.
2. If U and V are infix expressions denoted by prefix Polish expressions X and Y, respectively, and o is an operator such that o $\in \{+, -, *, /\}$, then oXY is the prefix Polish expression denoting UoV.
3. If (U) is an infix expression, where U is denoted by the prefix Polish expression X, then X is the prefix Polish expression denoting (U).

♦

Definition — postfix Polish expression
Let Σ be an alphabet, whose symbols denote operands. The *postfix Polish expressions* are defined recursively as follows:

1. If a is an infix expression, $a \in \Sigma$, then a is also the postfix Polish expression of a.
2. If U and V are infix expressions denoted by prefix Polish expressions X and Y, respectively, and o is an operator such that o $\in \{+, -, *, /\}$, then XYo is the postfix Polish expression denoting UoV.
3. If (U) is an infix expression, where U is denoted by the postfix Polish expression X, then X is the postfix Polish expression denoting (U).

♦

Languages

The evaluation of the prefix Polish expressions is left to the Exercises.

Next, is described the method of evaluating postfix Polish expressions. This consists of the following two steps, which are iterated until no operator appears in the given postfix expression.

1. Let E be the current postfix Polish expression; find the leftmost operator, o, appearing in E and the two operands, a and b, preceding o.
2. Perform the operation aob and replace abo in E with the obtained result.

Example 1.2.2.1 Part 5 Postfix Polish notation

Consider the parenthesized infix expression

$$(3 + 1) * 2$$

Its postfix Polish equivalent is

$$31+2*$$

The evaluation of 31+2* follows next.

Iteration 1:
1. The leftmost operator appearing in 31+2* is + and the two operands preceding this operator are 3 and 1.
2. Perform 3 + 1 to obtain 4, and replace 31+ with 4 in 31+2*; the resulting expression has the form 42*.

Iteration 2:
1. The leftmost operator appearing in 42* is * and the two operands preceding this operator are 4 and 2.
2. Perform 4 * 2 to obtain 8, and replace 42* with 8.

Notice that this method correctly determines 8 as the resulting value of (3+1)*2.

▲

This section has introduced three pragmatically oriented specification tools for programming language syntax, the Backus-Naur form, the extended Backus-Naur form, and syntax graphs. To investigate these tools in a rigorous way, Chapter 5 formalizes them using *context-free grammars*, which are systematically investigated in Part III.

1.2.3 Specification of a programming language

This section demonstrates the use of the language generators introduced in Sections

1.2.1 and 1.2.2 by designing a new *co*mputer *la*nguage – COLA. This is a simple programming language, suitable for the evaluation of integer functions and sequences. To give an insight into COLA, consider the following COLA program:

begin
  read(n);
  write("resulting factorial", n, '! = ');
  factorial := 1;
  @iteration;
    if $n = 0$ **goto** @stop;
    factorial := factorial*n;
    $n := n - 1$;
  goto @iteration;
  @stop;
  write(factorial)
end

Although COLA has not been defined yet, it is intuitively clear that this program determines the factorial of n, where n is a nonnegative integer.

First, COLA lexemes are described by using expressions, discussed in Section 1.2.1. Then, COLA syntax is specified by using the extended Backus-Naur form and syntax graphs, introduced in Section 1.2.2.

COLA lexemes

Next are specified the following five COLA lexemes by using expressions. Notice that each of these lexemes has an unbounded length.

1. identifiers
2. integers
3. labels
4. text literals
5. new-line text literals.

Identifiers
COLA identifiers are nonempty alphanumeric words, which begin with a letter. Consequently, the COLA identifiers are specified by the expression

$$\langle\text{letter}\rangle\langle\text{letter or digit}\rangle^*$$

where <letter> and <letter or digit> are expressions defined as

$$\langle\text{letter}\rangle = a + \ldots + z$$
$$\langle\text{letter or digit}\rangle = a + \ldots + z + 0 + \ldots + 9$$

Integers
COLA integers are nonempty numeric words. They are defined as

$$\langle\text{digit}\rangle\langle\text{digit}\rangle^*$$

where

$$\langle\text{digit}\rangle = 0 + \ldots + 9$$

Labels
COLA labels have the form

$$@w$$

where w is a nonempty alphanumeric word; for instance, @stop is a well-formed COLA label. The COLA labels are defined by the expression

$$@\langle\text{letter or digit}\rangle\langle\text{letter or digit}\rangle^*$$

where

$$\langle\text{letter or digit}\rangle = a + \ldots + z + 0 + \ldots + 9$$

Text literals
COLA text literals have the form

$$'w'$$

where w is a word consisting of any symbols except ' or "; for instance, '! =' is a well-formed COLA text literal. The COLA text literals are defined by

$$'\langle\text{non-quotation symbol}\rangle^*'$$

where ⟨non-quotation symbol⟩ denotes the set of all symbols except ' or ".

New-line text literals
COLA new-line text literals have the form

$$"w"$$

where w is a word consisting of any symbols except ' or "; for instance, "resulting factorial" is a validly formed COLA new-line text literal. COLA new-line text literals are defined by

$$"\langle\text{non-quotation symbol}\rangle^*"$$

where ⟨non-quotation symbol⟩ denotes the set of all symbols except ' or ".

As identifiers, integers, labels, text literals, and new-line text literals have an unbounded length, they are specified here by using expressions. Observe that all remaining COLA lexemes have a bounded length:

arithmetic operators: +, −, *, /
relational operators: =, >, <
parentheses: (,)
separators: , and ;
assignment operator: :=
reserved words: **begin, end, goto, if, read, write**

COLA syntax

COLA syntax is specified here by the extended Backus-Naur form and by syntax graphs.

The COLA lexemes represent terminals in the extended Backus-Naur form for COLA. Furthermore, this form has these nine nonterminals:

⟨expression⟩
⟨factor⟩
⟨program⟩
⟨read list⟩
⟨statement list⟩
⟨statement⟩
⟨term⟩
⟨write list⟩
⟨write member⟩

where ⟨program⟩ is the start symbol. The extended Backus-Naur form for COLA possesses the following nine productions:

1. ⟨program⟩ → **begin**⟨statement list⟩**end**
2. ⟨statement list⟩ → ⟨statement⟩{;⟨statement⟩}
3. ⟨statement⟩ → identifier := ⟨expression⟩|
                   read(⟨read list⟩)|
                   write(⟨write list⟩)|
                   [[**if**⟨expression⟩⌈>|<|=⌋⟨expression⟩] **goto**]label
4. ⟨read list⟩ → identifier{, identifier}
5. ⟨write list⟩ → ⟨write member⟩{,⟨write member⟩}
6. ⟨write member⟩ → ⌈identifier|text literal|new-line text literal⌋
7. ⟨expression⟩ → ⟨term⟩{⌈+|−⌋<term⟩}
8. ⟨term⟩ → ⟨factor⟩{⌈*|/⌋⟨factor⟩}
9. ⟨factor⟩ → identifier |(⟨expression⟩)

Consider the first production

$$\langle \text{program} \rangle \rightarrow \textbf{begin}\langle \text{statement list} \rangle \textbf{end}$$

According to this production, a syntactically well-formed COLA program begins with **begin** and ends with **end**. Figure 1.2.3.1 presents the syntax graph visualizing this production.

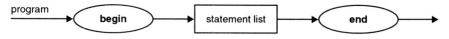

Figure 1.2.3.1 Syntax graph corresponding to production 1.

The nonterminal ⟨statement list⟩, appearing on the right-hand side of production 1, forms the left-hand side of the second production:

$$\langle \text{statement list} \rangle \rightarrow \langle \text{statement} \rangle \{;\langle \text{statement} \rangle\}$$

This production indicates that a COLA statement list consists of a sequence of statements, separated by semicolons. Figure 1.2.3.2 gives the syntax graph displaying this production.

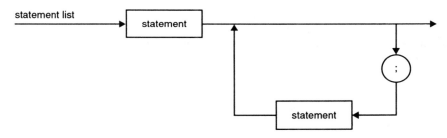

Figure 1.2.3.2 Syntax graph corresponding to production 2.

Consider the third production,

⟨statement⟩ → identifier := ⟨expression⟩|
        read(⟨read list⟩)|
        write(⟨write list⟩)|
        [[**if**⟨expression⟩⌈>|<|=⌋⟨expression⟩] **goto**]label

The four alternative definitions appearing on the right-hand side of this production specify the following COLA statements.

1. The definition

$$\text{identifier} := \langle \text{expression} \rangle$$

   specifies the COLA assignment statement; for instance,

$$\text{factorial} := \text{factorial}*n$$

is a valid COLA assignment statement. This instruction evaluates the expression appearing to the right of := and assigns the resulting value to the identifier appearing to the left of :=.

2. The definition

$$\textbf{read}(\langle \text{read list} \rangle)$$

specifies the COLA **read** statement; for instance,

$$\textbf{read}(n)$$

is a valid statement of this kind. This COLA **read** statement reads integers from the standard input and assigns these integer values to the members of the read list.

3. The definition

$$\textbf{write}(\langle \text{write list} \rangle)$$

describes the COLA **write** statement; for instance,

$$\textbf{write}(\text{factorial})$$

is a valid statement of this kind. This instruction writes the write list onto the standard output.

4. The definition

$$[[\textbf{if} \langle \text{expression} \rangle \lceil > | < | = \rfloor \langle \text{expression} \rangle] \,\textbf{goto}\,]\text{label}$$

contains three options:
(a) label
(b) **goto** label
(c) **if**⟨expression⟩⌈>|<|=⌋⟨expression⟩ **goto** label
which are discussed below.

(a) The definition

label

specifies the COLA label statement; for instance,

@stop

is a valid statement of this kind. This instruction acts as a label used by the following two branch instructions.

(b) The definition

goto label

specifies the COLA unconditional branch statement; for instance,

Languages

$$\textbf{goto}\ \text{@stop}$$

is a valid statement of this kind. This instruction causes the computation to continue at the label statement indicated by the label following **goto**.

(c) The definition

$$\textbf{if}\ \langle\text{expression}\rangle\ \lceil >|<|= \rfloor\ \langle\text{expression}\rangle\ \textbf{goto}\ \text{label}$$

specifies the COLA conditional branch statement; for instance,

$$\textbf{if}\ n = 0\ \textbf{goto}\ \text{@stop}$$

is a valid statement of this kind. This instruction compares the values of the two expressions by the relational operator appearing between these expressions. If this comparison holds true, the computation continues at the label statement indicated by the label following **goto**; otherwise, the instruction following this conditional branch statement is executed. Figure 1.2.3.3 presents the syntax graph displaying production 3.

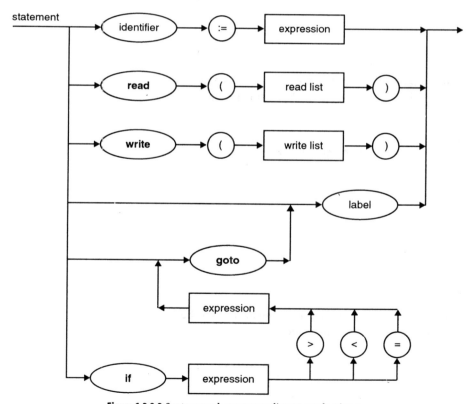

Figure 1.2.3.3 Syntax graph corresponding to production 3.

Consider production 4:

$$\langle \text{read list} \rangle \rightarrow \text{identifier}\{, \text{identifier}\}$$

This production indicates that a COLA read list consists of a sequence of identifiers, separated by colons. Figure 1.2.3.4 presents the syntax graph depicting this production.

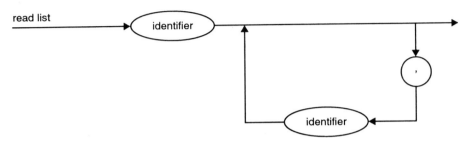

Figure 1.2.3.4 Syntax graph corresponding to production 4.

The fifth production,

$$\langle \text{write list} \rangle \rightarrow \langle \text{write member} \rangle \{, \langle \text{write member} \rangle \}$$

implies that a COLA write list consists of a sequence of write member, separated by colons. Figure 1.2.3.5 presents the syntax graph depicting this production.

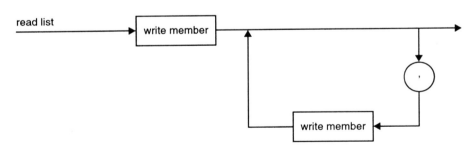

Figure 1.2.3.5 Syntax graph corresponding to production 5.

The nonterminal ⟨write member⟩, appearing on the right-hand side of production 5, forms the left-hand side of the sixth production:

$$\langle \text{write member} \rangle \rightarrow \lceil \text{identifier} | \text{text literal} | \text{new-line text literal} \rfloor$$

This production indicates that a write member is an identifier or a text literal or a new-line text literal. Figure 1.2.3.6 contains the corresponding syntax graph.

Languages

Finally, consider the remaining three productions 7–9:

$$\langle\text{expression}\rangle \to \langle\text{term}\rangle\{\lceil+|-\rfloor\langle\text{term}\rangle\}$$
$$\langle\text{term}\rangle \to \langle\text{factor}\rangle\{\lceil*|/\rfloor\langle\text{factor}\rangle\}$$
$$\langle\text{factor}\rangle \to \text{identifier}\,|(\langle\text{expression}\rangle)$$

Example 1.8, given in the previous section, has already discussed these productions and presented their syntax graphs (see Figures 1.2.2.1 to 1.2.2.3).

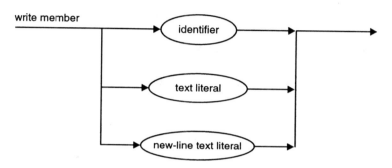

Figure 1.2.3.6 Syntax graph corresponding to production 6.

The specification of COLA is complete. Reconsider the COLA program given in the beginning of this section; that is,

```
begin
  read(n);
  write("resulting factorial", n, '! =');
  factorial := 1;
  @iteration;
    if n = 0 goto @stop;
    factorial := factorial*n;
    n := n - 1;
  goto @iteration;
  @stop;
  write(factorial)
end
```

By the specification of COLA, this represents a well-formed COLA program as verified in the exercises.

1.3 Translations

Sections 1.1 and 1.2 formalized and discussed languages. This section studies translations between languages.

Definition — translation
Let Σ be an *input alphabet*, and let Ω be an *output alphabet*. A *translation*, τ, from Σ^* to Ω^* is a relation from Σ^* to Ω^*. I_τ is called the *input language* of τ and denotes the domain of τ; that is,

$$I_\tau = \{ x : (x, y) \in \tau \text{ for some } y \in \Omega^* \}$$

O_τ is called the *output language* of τ and denotes the range of τ; that is,

$$O_\tau = \{ y : (x, y) \in \tau \text{ for some } x \in \Sigma^* \}$$

For each $x \in I_\tau$, $\tau(x)$ is defined as

$$\tau(x) = \{ y : (x, y) \in \tau \}$$

For each $L \subseteq I_\tau$, $\tau(L)$ is defined as

$$\tau(L) = \{ y : (x, y) \in \tau \text{ for some } x \in L \}$$

Notice that for every translation τ from Σ^* to Ω^*,

$$\tau(I_\tau) = O_\tau$$

Furthermore, for every language L such that $L \subseteq I_\tau$,

$$\tau(L) \subseteq O_\tau$$

Observe that translations are defined as relations, so all notations concerning relations (reviewed in Section 0.2) apply to translations as well. For instance, a translation τ is finite if τ represents a finite relation. ◆

Example 1.3.1 Finite translation
This example describes a finite translation τ that codes the decimal digits in binary. Formally, let $\Sigma = \{0, 1, 2, 3, 4, 5, 6, 7, 8, 9, 10\}$, $\Omega = \{0, 1\}$, and τ is the translation from Σ^* to Ω^*, defined as

$$\tau = \{(0, 0), (1, 1), (2, 10), (3, 11), (4, 100), (5, 101), (6, 110), (7, 111), (8, 1000), (9, 1001)\}.$$

Observe that

Languages

$$I_\tau = \{0, 1, 2, 3, 4, 5, 6, 7, 8, 9\}$$

$$O_\tau = \{0, 1, 10, 11, 100, 101, 110, 111, 1000, 1001\}$$

Notice that 8 is coded by τ as

$$\tau(8) = \{1000\}$$

Furthermore, consider $L = \{0, 2, 4, 6, 8\}$ and observe that

$$\tau(L) = \{0, 01, 100, 110, 1000\}$$

▲

Specification of translations

The specification of translations represents a similar problem to the specification of languages (see Section 1.2). As Example 1.3.1 illustrates, finite translations can be specified by listing their members. Naturally, this simple specification method is inapplicable to any infinite translations, τ. If, however, τ represents a special kind of infinite translation from Σ^* to Ω^*, where Σ and Ω are two alphabets, then the specification of τ can be reduced to the specification of $\tau(a)$, for each $a \in \Sigma$. Substitution represents a translation of this kind.

Definition — substitution
Let Σ and Ω be two alphabets, and let τ be a translation from Σ^* to Ω^* such that for all $x, y \in \Sigma^*$,

$$\tau(xy) = \tau(x)\tau(y).$$

Then, τ is a *substitution*, and τ^{-1} is an *inverse substitution*.

◆

Consider a substitution τ from Σ^* to Ω^*. By the previous definition, $\tau(\varepsilon) = \varepsilon$. This definition also implies that τ is completely specified by defining $\tau(a)$, for each $a \in \Sigma$. Indeed, for all $x, y \in \Sigma^*$, $\tau(xy) = \tau(x)\tau(y)$, so for all nonempty words w

$$\tau(w) = \tau(a_1) \ldots \tau(a_n)$$

where $|w| = n$, $w = a_1 \ldots a_n$, and $a_i \in \Sigma$ for $i = 1, \ldots, n$.

Example 1.3.2 Substitution
Consider the substitution τ from $\{0, 1\}^*$ to $\{0, 1, 2, 3, 4, 5, 6, 7, 8, 9\}^*$ defined by

$$\tau(0) = \{0, 2, 4, 6, 8\} \text{ and } \tau(1) = \{1, 3, 5, 7, 9\}$$

Less formally, τ transforms 0 and 1 to an even digit and an odd digit, respectively. As a result, τ can be seen as a denary cryptography of binary information. Indeed, all denary numbers contained in $\tau(w)$, where $w \in \{0, 1\}^*$, encode w. For example, as $\{5087, 1443\} \subseteq \tau(1001)$, 5087 and 1443 belong to the denary numbers cryptographing 1001. As $\tau^{-1}(\tau(w)) = w$, τ^{-1} actually acts as a decoder of τ. For example, τ^{-1} decodes both 5087 and 1443 to 1001 because $\tau^{-1}(5087) = 1001$ and $\tau^{-1}(1443) = 1001$.

▲

A special case of substitution is homomorphism.

Definition — homomorphism
Let Σ and Ω be two alphabets, and let τ be a substitution from Σ^* to Ω^*. If τ represents a function from Σ^* to Ω^*, then τ is a *homomorphism*, and τ^{-1} is an *inverse homomorphism*.

◆

Example 1.3.3 Homomorphism
Morse code, τ, represents an example of a homomorphism, mapping words consisting of Roman letters into $\{\cdot, -\}^*$:

$\tau(A) = \cdot -$
$\tau(B) = - \cdots$
$\tau(C) = - \cdot - \cdot$
$\tau(D) = - \cdot \cdot$
$\tau(E) = \cdot$
$\tau(F) = \cdot \cdot - \cdot$
$\tau(G) = - - \cdot$
$\tau(H) = \cdots \cdot$
$\tau(I) = \cdot \cdot$
$\tau(J) = \cdot - - -$
$\tau(K) = - \cdot -$
$\tau(L) = \cdot - \cdot \cdot$
$\tau(M) = - -$
$\tau(N) = - \cdot$
$\tau(O) = - - -$
$\tau(P) = \cdot - - \cdot$
$\tau(Q) = - - \cdot -$
$\tau(R) = \cdot - \cdot$
$\tau(S) = \cdot \cdot \cdot$
$\tau(T) = -$
$\tau(U) = \cdot \cdot -$
$\tau(V) = \cdot \cdot \cdot -$

$\tau(W) = \cdot--$
$\tau(X) = -\cdot\cdot-$
$\tau(Y) = -\cdot--$
$\tau(Z) = --\cdot\cdot$

▲

However, some infinite translations cannot be specified as simply as homomorphisms or substitutions; at this point, the language theory usually uses *translation grammars* to define them. Translation grammars resemble the Backus-Naur form (see Section 1.2.2). By analogy with the Backus-Naur form, translation grammars contain two kinds of symbols, terminals and nonterminals. Productions of translation grammars have the form

$$A \twoheadrightarrow x|y$$

Example 1.3.4 Part 1 Translation grammar

Consider the translation grammar having the following eight productions:

⟨expression⟩ ↠ ⟨expression⟩+⟨term⟩|⟨expression⟩⟨term⟩+

⟨expression⟩ ↠ ⟨expression⟩−⟨term⟩|⟨expression⟩⟨term⟩−

⟨expression⟩ ↠ ⟨term⟩|⟨term⟩

⟨term⟩ ↠ ⟨term⟩∗⟨factor⟩|⟨term⟩⟨factor⟩∗

⟨term⟩ ↠ ⟨term⟩/⟨factor⟩|⟨term⟩⟨factor⟩/

⟨term⟩ ↠ ⟨factor⟩|⟨factor⟩

⟨factor⟩ ↠ (⟨expression⟩)|⟨expression⟩

⟨factor⟩ ↠ i|i

where i denotes an identifier or an integer. This grammar contains terminals i, +, −, ∗, /, (, and). Furthermore, it has the nonterminals ⟨expression⟩, ⟨factor⟩, and ⟨term⟩, where ⟨expression⟩ is the start symbol.

▲

Starting from a pair consisting of two start symbols, a translation grammar uses its productions to derive pairs of words over terminals; each step in this derivation is symbolically denoted by ⇒⇒. The set of all pairs derived in this way represents the translation defined by the grammar.

Example 1.3.4 Part 2 Translation

The translation grammar given in the first part of this example translates infix arithmetic expressions to the equivalent postfix Polish expressions. Next, the present example describes the derivation steps that translate $i+i*i$ to $iii*+$.

⟨expression⟩|⟨expression⟩
$\Rightarrow$ ⟨expression⟩ + ⟨term⟩|⟨ expression ⟩⟨term⟩ +
$\Rightarrow$ ⟨term⟩ + ⟨term⟩|⟨term⟩⟨term⟩ +
$\Rightarrow$ ⟨factor⟩ + ⟨term⟩|⟨factor⟩⟨term⟩ +
$\Rightarrow$ i + ⟨term⟩|i⟨term⟩ +
$\Rightarrow$ i + ⟨term⟩*⟨factor⟩|i⟨term⟩⟨factor⟩* +
$\Rightarrow$ i + ⟨factor⟩*⟨factor⟩|i⟨factor⟩⟨factor⟩* +
$\Rightarrow$ i + i*⟨factor⟩|ii⟨factor⟩* +
$\Rightarrow$ i + $i*i$|$iii*$ +

▲

Section 9.2.1 discusses translation grammars in greater detail. In addition, Section 9.3 demonstrates their use in practice. Specifically, based on these grammars, Section 9.3 constructs a complete compiler for the programming language COLA, described in Section 1.2.3.

Exercises

Note: Making use of many formal notions introduced later on, Chapters 3 through 10 reconsider some of the following exercises in greater detail.

1 Formalization of Languages

1.1 Consider the definition
Let Σ be an alphabet:
(a) ε is a word over Σ
(b) if x is a word over Σ and $a \in \Sigma$, then ax is a word over Σ.
Section 1.1 has defined the words over Σ in a slightly different way. Are both definitions equivalent?

1.2 Prove that for all words x
$$x\varepsilon = \varepsilon x = x$$

1.3 Prove or disprove that for all $i \geq 0$,
$$\varepsilon^i = \varepsilon$$

1.4 Prove or disprove that there exists a nonnegative integer i such that for all words x
$$x^i = \varepsilon$$

1.5 Prove or disprove that for any two words, x and y,

$$xy = yx$$

1.6 Prove that concatenation is associative.

1.7 Give a nonempty word x such that

$$x = \text{reversal}(x)$$

1.8 Give a nonempty word x such that

$$x^i = \text{reversal}(x)^i$$

for all $i \geq 0$.

1.9 Give a word x such that

$$x^i = \text{reversal}(x)$$

for all $i \geq 0$.

1.10 Prove that for every word x

$$x^i x^j = x^j x^i = x^{i+j}$$

where $i, j \geq 0$.

1.11 Prove or disprove that for all words, x and y,

$$\text{reversal}(xy) = \text{reversal}(y)\text{reversal}(x)$$

1.12 Let $x = aaabababbb$. Determine prefix(x), suffix(y), and subword(x).

1.13 Prove that every word y satisfies these three properties
(a) prefix(y) $\subseteq$ subword(y)
(b) suffix(y) $\subseteq$ subword(y)
(c) $\{\varepsilon, y\} \subseteq$ prefix(y) $\cap$ suffix(y) $\cap$ subword(y)

1.14 Let $\Sigma = \{0, 1\}$. Consider the language

$$L = \{011, 111, 110\}$$

over Σ. Determine $\overline{L}$, reversal(L), prefix(L), suffix(L), L^2, L^*, and L^+.

1.15 Prove that the following four properties hold for every language, L:
(a) $L\{\varepsilon\} = \{\varepsilon\}L = L$
(b) $L\emptyset = \emptyset L = \emptyset$
(c) $L^+ = LL^* = L^*L$
(d) $L^* = L^+ \cup \{\varepsilon\}$.

1.16 Let L be a language. Characterize when $L^* = L$.

1.17 Define an enumerable language by analogy with the definition of an enumerable set.

1.18 Let Σ be an alphabet. Consider the family of all finite languages over Σ. Prove that this family is enumerable.

1.19* Let Σ be an alphabet. Prove that 2^{Σ^*} is not enumerable.

1.20 State the fundamental reason why some languages cannot be defined by any finite-size specification tools. (Section 8.1.5 discusses this crucial statement and its consequences in greater depth.)

1.21 Let $\Sigma = \{0, 1\}$. Consider the following two languages over Σ:

$$L_1 = \{00, 11\} \text{ and } L_2 = \{0, 00\}.$$

Determine $L_1 \cup L_2, L_1 \cap L_2, L_1 - L_2,$ and $L_1 L_2$.

1.22 Prove that the following two equations hold for any two languages, L_1 and L_2:
(a) $(L_1 \cup L_2)^* = (L_1^* L_2^*)^*$
(b) $(L_1 L_2 \cup L_2)^* = L_1 (L_2 L_1 \cup L_1)^*$.

1.23 Prove that the following three equations hold for any three languages $L_1, L_2,$ and L_3:
(a) $(L_1 L_2) L_3 = L_1 (L_2 L_3)$
(b) $(L_1 \cup L_2) L_3 = L_1 L_3 \cup L_2 L_1$
(c) $L_3 (L_1 \cup L_2) = L_3 L_1 \cup L_3 L_2$.

1.24 Prove or disprove that the following three equations hold for any three languages $L_1, L_2,$ and L_3:
(a) $(L_1 \cap L_2) L_3 = L_1 L_3 \cap L_2 L_1$
(b) $L_3 (L_1 \cap L_2) = L_3 L_1 \cap L_3 L_2$
(c) $L_3 (L_1 - L_2) = L_3 L_1 - L_3 L_2$

1.25 Determine all languages L_1 and L_2 satisfying

$$L_1 \cup L_2 = L_1 \cap L_2 = L_1 - L_2$$

1.26* By *DeMorgan's law*,

$$\overline{L_1 \cup L_2} = \overline{L_1} \cap \overline{L_2}$$

for any two languages, L_1 and L_2. Prove this law.

1.27 Example 1.1.3 discussed this family of languages

$$\mathbf{L} = \{L : L \subseteq \{a\}\{a, b\}^*\}$$

Consider each language operation defined in Section 1.1. Prove or disprove that **L** is closed under the operation.

1.28 Consider this family of languages

$$\mathbf{L} = \{L : L \subseteq \{a, b\}^* \{b\} \{a, b\}^*\}$$

Consider each language operation defined in Section 1.1. Prove or disprove that **L** is closed under the operation.

1.29 Consider the family of languages

$$L = \{ L: L \subseteq \{a, b\}^*, \text{ and } |x| \text{ is even for each } x \in L\}$$

Consider each language operation defined in Section 1.1. Prove or disprove that L is closed under the operation.

1.30 Consider the family of finite languages. In addition, consider each language operation defined in Section 1.1. Prove or disprove that this family is closed under the operation.

1.31* Consider the family of enumerable languages. In addition, consider each language operation defined in Section 1.1. Prove or disprove that this family is closed under the operation.

1.32* Consider the family of infinite languages, which properly contains the family of enumerable languages. In addition, consider each language operation defined in Section 1.1. Prove or disprove that this family is closed under the operation.

2. Expressions and Grammars

2.1 Consider the finite language consisting of all English determiners, such as *any* and *some*. Specify this language by listing all its members.

2.2 Consider the expression

$$\langle \text{letter}\rangle\langle \text{letter or digit}\rangle^*\langle \text{letter}\rangle$$

where $\langle \text{letter}\rangle = A + \ldots + Z$, and $\langle \text{letter or digit}\rangle = A + \ldots + Z + 0 + \ldots + 9$. Give an informal description of lexemes defined by this expression.

2.3 Construct expressions for all Pascal lexemes.

2.4 Let L be a language defined by an expression. Prove or disprove that any subset of L can be defined by an expression, too.

2.5 Select an infinite subset of English and define it by Backus-Naur form.

2.6 Construct the Backus-Naur form for the language consisting of the numbers in FORTRAN. By using this form, derive each of the following numbers:
(a) 16
(b) −61
(c) −6.12
(d) −32.61E+04
(e) −21.32E−02.

2.7 Construct the Backus-Naur form for the language consisting of all PL/I declaration statements. By using this form, derive each of the following statements:
(a) DECLARE A FIXED BINARY, B FLOAT
(b) DECLARE (A, B) FIXED
(c) DECLARE (A(10), B(-1:2), C) FLOAT.

2.8 Construct the Backus-Naur form for the language of parenthesized logical expressions consisting of the logical variable *p* and the logical operators **and**, **or**, and **not**. By using this form, derive each of the following statements:
(a) **not** *p* **or** *p*
(b) **not** (*p* **and** *p*) **or** *p*
(c) (*p* **or** *p*) **or** (*p* **and not** *p*).

2.9 Construct the extended Backus-Naur form that specifies the Pascal syntax.

2.10 Construct syntax graphs that specify the Pascal syntax.

2.11 Prove that the following three specification tools define the same family of language.
(a) the Backus-Naur form
(b) the extended Backus-Naur form
(c) syntax graphs

2.12 Modify the Backus-Naur form so
(a) the right-hand side of any production contains only one definition
(b) a nonterminal may form the left-hand side of several productions.
Formalize this modification and demonstrate its equivalence to the original Backus-Naur form.

2.13 Example 1.2.2.1 Part 1 discussed this three-production Backus-Naur form:

⟨expression⟩ → ⟨term⟩|⟨term⟩+⟨expression⟩|⟨term⟩−⟨expression⟩
⟨term⟩ → ⟨factor⟩|⟨factor⟩*⟨term⟩|⟨factor⟩/⟨term⟩
⟨factor⟩ → i|(⟨expression⟩)

Apply the modification discussed in Exercise 2.12 to this form.

2.14 Incorporate the Pascal relational and logical operators in the Backus-Naur form discussed in Part 1 of Example 1.2.2.1.

2.15 Make the extended Backus-Naur form more succinct by introducing some new notational options.

2.16 As noted in Section 1.2.2, some versions of the extended Backus-Naur form use (and) instead of ⌈ and ⌋, respectively. Demonstrate a practical disadvantage of the use of (and).

2.17 Section 1.2.2 has described syntax graphs informally. Define them rigorously.

2.18 Consider the infix expression (1+4)*((4+2)*3)+6. Determine and evaluate its postfix Polish equivalent.

2.19 Describe a method that evaluates the prefix Polish expressions.

2.20 Consider the infix expression 7*((3+1)*8)+2. Determine and evaluate its prefix Polish equivalent.

2.21 Consider the COLA program given in the beginning of Section 1.2.3. By the specification of COLA given in Section 1.2.3, demonstrate that this program represents a well-formed COLA program.

3. Translations

3.1 Specify the finite translation τ that translates the digits 0 through 9 to their octal representations.

3.2 Let Σ and Ω be two alphabets, and let τ be a substitution from Σ^* to Ω^*. Does there exist a word, $x \in \Omega^*$, such that $\tau^{-1}(x)$ is infinite? Does there exist a word, $x \in \Omega^*$, such that $\tau^{-1}(x) = \emptyset$? Does there exist a word, $x \in \Omega^*$, such that $\tau^{-1}(x) = \{\varepsilon\}$?

3.3* Let Σ and Ω be two alphabets, and let τ and τ' be two homomorphisms from Σ^* to Ω^*. If for all $x \in \Sigma^*$,

$$\tau(x) = \tau'(x)$$

then τ and τ' are equal. Design a method that decides whether two homomorphisms are equal.

3.4 Section 1.3 has stated that every homomorphism is a substitution? Explain this statement in detail.

3.5 Section 1.3 has stated that for every substitution τ, $\tau(\varepsilon) = \varepsilon$. Explain this statement in detail.

3.6 Section 1.3 has stated that for all $x, y \in \Sigma^*$,

$$\tau(xy) = \tau(x)\tau(y),$$

so, for all nonempty words w

$$\tau(w) = \tau(a_1 \ldots a_n) = \tau(a_1) \ldots \tau(a_n).$$

where $n \geq 1$, $w = a_1 \ldots a_n$, and $a_i \in \Sigma$ for $i = 1, \ldots, n$. Explain this statement in detail.

3.7 Design a translation grammar that translates infix expressions to the equivalent prefix Polish expressions.

3.8 Recall that syntax graphs graphically represent the Backus-Naur form. Design an analogical graphical representation for translation grammars – *translation graphs*.

Programming projects

1 Formalization of Languages

1.1 Consider each of the unary language operations introduced in Section 1.1. Write a program that reads a finite language L, applies this operation to L, and produces the languages resulting from this application.

1.2 Consider each of the binary language operations introduced in Section 1.1. Write a program that reads two finite language L and L', applies this operation to L and L', and produces the language resulting from this application.

1.3 Introduce a finite language L representing a dictionary. Write a program that provides insertion and deletion of words in L.

2 Expressions and Grammars

2.1 Design a data structure for representing expressions.
2.2 Design a data structure that represents the Backus-Naur form.
2.2 Consider the Backus-Naur form given in Part 1 of Example 1.2.2.1. Write a program that reads a natural number n and then generates all m-step derivations in this form, for $m = 1, \ldots, n$.
2.3 Consider the Backus-Naur form given in Part 1 of Example 1.2.2.1. Write a program that reads a word x and decides whether x is an arithmetic expression generated by this form.
2.4 Write a program that evaluates prefix Polish expressions.
2.5 Write a program that evaluates postfix Polish expressions.

3 Translations

3.1 Design a data structure for representing a substitution.
3.2 Design a data structure for representing a translation grammar.
3.3 Consider the translation grammar given in Part 1 of Example 1.3.3. Write a program that reads a natural number n and then generates all m-step derivations in this form, for $m = 1, \ldots, n$.
3.4 Write a program that reads a word x and decides whether x is a valid infix expression. If x is valid, the program translates x into its postfix equivalent by using the translation grammar given in Example 1.3.3.
3.5 Write a program that reads a word x and decides whether x is a valid infix expression. If x is valid, the program translates x into its prefix equivalent.

2 Automata

This chapter introduces three basic classes of computational models – finite automata, pushdown automata, and Turing machines. Section 2.1 conceptualizes the models and demonstrates that their investigation naturally leads to the study of languages that these models accept. Section 2.2 generalizes these models to transducers, which define translations; that is, it describes finite transducers, pushdown transducers, and Turing transducers. Finite and pushdown transducers underlie many software components, such as text editors and compilers. Section 2.3 discusses Turing transducers as a general model formalizing procedures; most importantly, it explains how Turing transducers allow computational theory to express and study crucial problems concerning computation rigorously.

2.1 Conceptualization of Automata

This section conceptualizes computational models, which are classified into three classes:

1. finite automata
2. pushdown automata
3. Turing machines.

This conceptualization is based on a pragmatically oriented approach to computation. Indeed, the three basic models result from the examination of quite common hardware and software components of computers. Most importantly, these models allow computer science to abstract these computer components and, thereby, investigate their behaviour in a formal way. The present section demonstrates that this investigation is inseparable from the study of the languages that these models define.

Finite automata

Example 2.1.1 Part 1 Finite automata as computational models
Consider a computer with a power button, by which the computer is turned on and off. Initially, the computer is off. A press of the power button turns the computer on, and a subsequent press of this button turns it off. During a time period, this button is pressed several times; however, the computer should be off after it is no longer used.

To formalize the use of this power button, observe that the computer can occur in two *states* – "on" or "off". The "off" state is the start state because the use of the computer begins when the computer is off. This state also represents the final state because the computer should be off after it is no longer used. In the "off" state, a press of the power button moves the computer to the "on" state, and a subsequent press of this button moves it back to the "off" state. To summarize, the computer works according to these two rules:

Rule 1: if the computer is in state "off" and a press occurs,
the computer moves from state "off" to state "on".

Rule 2: if the computer is in state "on" and a press occurs,
the computer moves from state "on" to state "off".

Figure 2.1.1 depicts the state diagram, that graphically formalizes the computer. In the diagram, the arrow indicates the start state; the final state is represented by double circled.

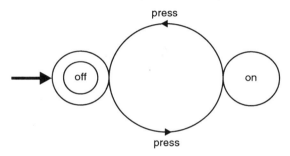

Figure 2.1.1 State diagram.

For simplicity, states "off" and "on" are denoted by 0 and 1, respectively, and instead of "press" symbol "a" is used (Figure 2.1.2.).

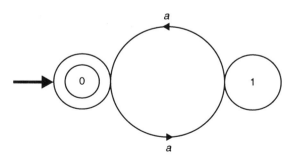

Figure 2.1.2 Simplified state diagram.

The state diagram in Figure 2.1.2 graphically represents a computational model called a finite automaton.

△

Automata

In general a *finite automaton*, denoted M, consists of five components:

1. a finite set of states
2. an alphabet of input symbols
3. a finite set of computational rules
4. the start state
5. a set of final states.

The automaton M works by making moves. Each move is made according to a computational rule, which describes how the current state is changed on a given input symbol. If a word of input symbols, $a_1 \ldots a_n$, causes M to make a sequence of moves that ends in a final state, then M *accepts* $a_1 \ldots a_n$. The collection of all words accepted in this way forms the *language accepted by* M; therefore, M can be seen as a language acceptor (see Figure 2.1.3).

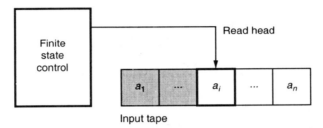

Figure 2.1.3 A finite automaton viewed as a language acceptor.

Viewed as a language acceptor, a finite automaton, M, consists of an input tape, a read head, and a finite state control. The input tape is divided into squares, each of which contains one symbol of an input word $a_1 \ldots a_n$. The finite control is represented by a finite set of states together with a finite set of computational rules. According to these rules, M changes states and moves the read head on the tape to the right. If M moves its head off the right end of the tape and, simultaneously, enters a final state, then it accepts $a_1 \ldots a_n$.

Example 2.1.1 Part 1 shows the state diagram of a finite automaton viewed as a computational model, which formalizes a computer (Figure 2.1.2). Part 2 of this example reconsiders this automaton as a language acceptor. Observe that both of these viewpoints are inseparable – indeed, this book approaches most computational models from both points of view.

Example 2.1.1 Part 2 Finite automata as language acceptors

Consider the finite automaton defined by the state diagram in Figure 2.1.2. This automaton moves according to these rules:

Rule 1: go from state 0 to state 1 on a

Rule 2: go from state 1 to state 0 on a

where 0 is both the start state and the final state. To illustrate the use of these rules, with *aaaa* on its input tape, the automaton makes the four-move computation depicted in Figure 2.1.4, where ⊢ denotes a move; in each of the four moves, this figure specifies the current state and the current head position.

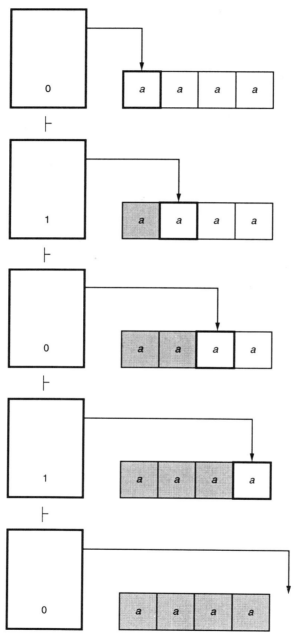

Figure 2.1.4 Acceptance of *aaaa*.

As shown in Figure 2.1.4, the automaton accepts *aaaa* because it enters the final state, 0, after having read *aaaa*. In general, this automaton accepts an input word, x, if and only if x consists of an even number of *a*s. In other words, the language accepted by this automaton is

$$\{a^{2n}: n \geq 0\}$$

Returning to Part 1 of this example, notice that $\{a^{2n}: n \geq 0\}$ contains precisely the words representing the sequences of presses that cause the computer to be turned off.

▲

The finite automaton discussed in the two parts of Example 2.1.1 works *deterministically* because, with *a*, it makes a unique move from either of its states. In general, however, a finite automaton works *nondeterministically* – that is, with the same symbol, it can make several different moves from the same state, as the following example illustrates.

Example 2.1.2 Part 1 Nondeterministic finite automata

Consider a computer's screen, which automatically dims when the computer is left idle for a minute. Initially, the computer has its screen dimmed. A press of a computer button brightens the screen. Then, the computer brightens the screen until it detects that it has been unused for a minute; at this point, the screen dims.

Denote a button press that brightens the screen by *a*, and use *b* to denote a one-minute run of the computer with its screen brightened. Also, denote states "off" and "on" by 0 and 1, respectively. By using this notation, Figure 2.1.5 depicts a finite automaton formalizing the screen dimming. Observe that this automaton works nondeterministically: with *b*, the automaton can move from 1 either to 1 or to 0.

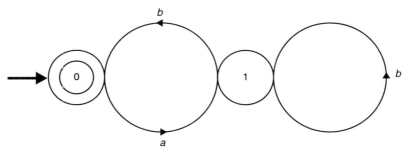

Figure 2.1.5 The nondeterministic finite automaton of Example 2.1.2.

△

Both deterministic finite automata and nondeterministic finite automata have their pros and cons. Deterministic finite automata are easy to implement, but they are too restricted to be a convenient formal tool for achieving mathematical results. However, nondeterministic finite automata represent an extremely convenient mathematical abstraction, but they are difficult to use in practice.

The determination of the language that a nondeterministic finite automaton M accepts may be a difficult task. Indeed, an input word x may cause a nondeterministic finite automaton M to make many different sequences of moves. If at least one of these sequences causes M to enter a final state, M accepts x; otherwise, it rejects x. The determination of the language accepted by M thus requires an examination of all possible move sequences that M can make on input words.

Example 2.1.2 Part 2 Nondeterministic acceptance

Return to the nondeterministic finite automaton in Figure 2.1.5. With ab as its input, this automaton can compute these two different move sequences:

1. With a it moves from 0 to 1, then with b it moves from 1 back to 1
2. With a it moves from 0 to 1, then with b it moves from 1 to 0.

Observe that the first move sequence ends in the nonfinal state 1, whereas the other sequence ends in the final state 0; therefore, this automaton accepts ab. As proved in the exercises, this automaton accepts the following language

$$\{ (ab^n)^m : m \geq 0 \text{ and } n \geq 1 \}$$

△

Any deterministic finite automaton is, in fact, a special case of a nondeterministic finite automaton. More surprisingly, for any nondeterministic finite automata M, there exists an equivalent deterministic finite automata M' – that is, M and M' accept the same languages. Consequently, the power of the deterministic finite automata coincides with the power of the nondeterministic finite automata.

Example 2.1.2 Part 3 Deterministic finite automata

Consider the deterministic finite automaton in Figure 2.1.6. This automaton has states A, B, C, where A is the start state, and A and C are final states. The input symbols are a and b. Observe that this deterministic finite automaton accepts

$$\{ (ab^n)^m : m \geq 0 \text{ and } n \geq 1 \}$$

Therefore, this automaton is equivalent to the nondeterministic finite automaton depicted in Figure 2.1.5, which accepts the same language.

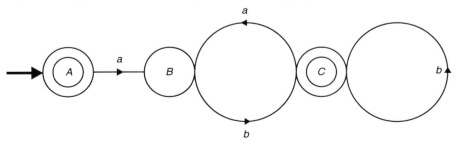

Figure 2.1.6 Deterministic finite automaton that accepts $\{ (ab^n)^m : m \geq 0 \text{ and } n \geq 1 \}$.

▲

Example 2.1.3 Part 1 Limit of the power of finite automata

The power of finite automata is rather limited. To illustrate this, notice that these automata cannot even verify that several occurrences of one symbol a are followed by the same number of occurrences of another symbol b. In other words, these automata are incapable of accepting

$$L = \{a^n b^n : n \geq 1\}$$

To appreciate this inability, observe that any computational model that accepts L needs to record the number of as to verify that this number coincides with the number of bs. As n in $\{a^n b^n : n \geq 1\}$ is unbounded, no finite automaton can accept L. Indeed, a finite automaton can record any information by using its set of states and, because this set is finite, it cannot record n, which runs to infinity.

To give a practical consequence of this example, assume that a and b represent (and), respectively. Under this assumption, the present example implies that finite automata fail to verify that n (s are followed by n)s, for $n = 1, \ldots$. Therefore, these automata are incapable of checking that arithmetic expressions are properly parenthesized.

▲

Pushdown automata

To increase the power of finite automata, it is possible to extend them by adding a potentially unbounded memory – a pushdown store. Automata extended in this way are called *pushdown automata*.

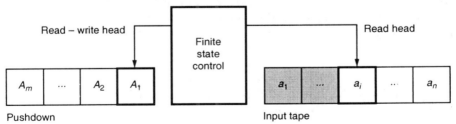

Figure 2.1.7 Pushdown automaton.

By analogy with a finite automaton, a pushdown automaton (Figure 2.1.7) works by making moves. However, in a pushdown automaton M, a move depends not only on the current state and the input symbol but also on the top symbol of the pushdown.

More precisely, in a move, M changes the state of the finite control, replaces the top symbol of the pushdown store with a word, and shifts the read head zero or one square to the right. M accepts a word, $a_1 \ldots a_n$, written on the input tape if M enters a final state after it has moved its read head off the right end of the tape and, thus, read all the input word, $a_1 \ldots a_n$.

Example 2.1.3 Part 2 Pushdown automata
Part 1 of this example noted that no finite automaton accepts language

$$L = \{a^n b^n : n \geq 1\}$$

However, this language is accepted by a pushdown automaton M, working as follows. First, M pushes down as. After having read all as, M pops up as and pairs them off with the input bs. If the bs exactly exhaust the as, the input is accepted; otherwise, it is rejected

More precisely, M has states 0 through 3, where 0 is the start state, and 3 is the final state. Furthermore, M has the input symbols a and b. Initially, M moves from 0 to 1 on a and pushes a onto the pushdown. Then, on each input a, M remains in 1 and pushes down a. When M reads the first b, it pops up a from the pushdown and, in addition, moves to state 2. In state 2, M reads b and pops up a from the pushdown. If M empties the pushdown and, simultaneously, reads all bs, then it has paired off all the as and bs and so it enters its final state, 3. With $aabb$ on its input tape, M makes the computation depicted in Figure 2.1.8 opposite.

▲

Chapters 5, 6, and 7 investigate pushdown automata and their properties in greater detail.

By presenting a language that no pushdown automaton can accept, the following example demonstrates a limit of pushdown automata's power.

Example 2.1.4 Part 1 Limit of the power of pushdown automata
Assume that a printer is to underline some text x consisting of n symbols. At this point, a typical word processor specifies this print by storing the word w in the form

$$w = xyz$$

where y consists of n backspaces, and z consists of n underlines. As a result, after printing x, the printer retraces n symbols back and then underlines x.

Consider the language L consisting of all words of the form w. To describe L symbolically, denote a letter in x, a backspace, and an underline by a, b, and c, respectively. By using this notation, L is defined as

$$L = \{a^n b^n c^n : n \geq 1\}$$

Automata

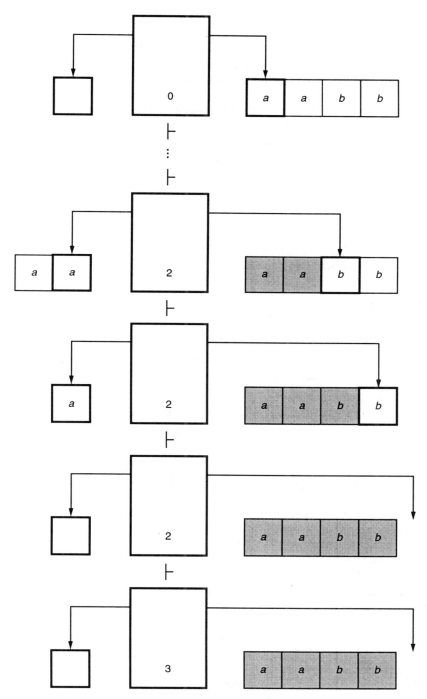

Figure 2.1.8 Acceptance of *aabb*.

Given an input word w, a computational model that defines L needs to record the number of as and verify that this number coincides with the number of both bs and cs. This verification cannot be accomplished by a single pushdown, as follows from the following observation. To verify the same number of as and bs, a pushdown automaton M needs to use a technique analogous to the method described in Example 2.1.3 Part 2. In other words, M first pushes down as, then it pops up these as and pairs them off with the input bs. At this point M loses the information about the number of as, so it cannot verify that the number of as coincides with the number of cs. Therefore, no pushdown automaton accepts L.

△

Turing machines

Figure 2.1.9 depicts another computational model, called a *Turing machine* after Alan Turing, who introduced this model in 1936.

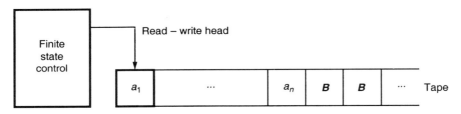

Figure 2.1.9 Turing machine.

In many respects, a Turing machine resembles a finite automaton. Indeed, like a finite automaton, a Turing machine consists of three components:

1. a tape, divided into squares
2. a tape read-write head
3. a finite state control.

However, there are two essential distinctions between a Turing machine and a finite automaton:

1. A finite automaton's tape is finite, whereas a Turing machine's tape is semi-infinite. That is, the tape has a leftmost square, but its squares may extend infinitely to the right.
2. Whereas the tape head of a finite automaton can only read, the tape head of a Turing machine can both read and write.

Automata

The finite state control of a Turing machine M is represented by a finite set of states together with a finite set of computational rules. According to these rules, M makes moves. During a move, M changes its current state, rewrites the scanned symbol with another tape symbol, and either keeps its head stationary or shifts its head one square to the right or left. To decide whether a given input word $a_1 \ldots a_n$ is accepted, M has one state defined as the start state and some states designated as final states. Initially, M's tape contains $a_1 \ldots a_n$ followed by Bs, where B denotes a blank symbol, and M's tape head is over a_1. If, starting from the start state, M can make a sequence of moves so it enters a final state, then M accepts $a_1 \ldots a_n$; otherwise, M rejects $a_1 \ldots a_n$. The collection of all words that M accepts in this way represents the language accepted by M.

Example 2.1.4 Part 2 Turing machines

As shown previously, no pushdown automaton accepts

$$L = \{a^n b^n c^n : n \geq 1\}$$

The present example constructs a Turing machine M that accepts this language. In addition to the input symbols a, b, and c, M uses the three additional symbols A, B, and C. M works by iterating the following five-step computational cycle:

1. If the input symbol is a, M replaces this a with A and moves the tape head one square right (and the computation continues at step 2); if the input symbol is B, M keeps moving right over Bs and Cs until it finds B, accepts, and halts (at this point, the computation ends).
2. Skipping over as and Bs, M keeps moving right until it finds b, which M replaces with B.
3. Skipping over bs and Cs, M keeps moving right until it finds c, which M replaces with C.
4. Skipping over Cs, bs, Bs, and as, M keeps moving left until it finds A.
5. M moves the tape head one square right (and the computation continues at step 1).

With $aabbcc$, M performs the move sequence depicted in Figure 2.1.10 on the next page.

▲

Chapter 8 investigates Turing machines and the family of *recursively enumerable languages*, which these machines characterize.

This section has introduced three fundamental computational models

1. finite automata
2. pushdown automata
3. Turing machines.

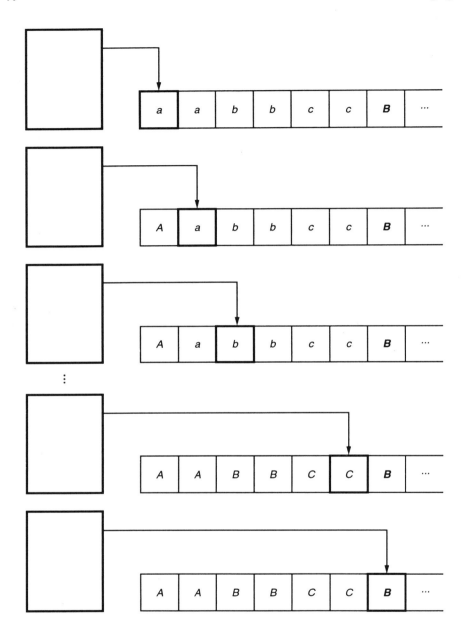

Figure 2.1.10 Acceptance of *aabbcc*.

By using these models, the chapters that follow investigate the fundamental ideas and principles behind computation from both its practical and theoretical standpoints. From a practical point of view, it is demonstrated that these models underlie common computer components, such as compilers. From a theoretical point of view, these models are used to formalize procedures and algorithms; based on this formalization, the power of computers is studied.

2.2 Transducers

The previous section has discussed computational models that accept languages. These models are now enhanced to transducers, which define translations. Transducers play a crucial role in the investigation of computation because they underlie most computer programs, which translate input data to output data according to some procedures.

Here the focus is on transducers acting as programs that execute unary functions over natural numbers. This is represented by the *unary* function, which maps all natural numbers i, into $\{1\}^+$ as follows

$$\text{unary}(i) = 1^i$$

In addition, this representation uses B to indicates the end of a word consisting of 1s. To illustrate the unary function, $1B$, $11B$, and $111111111111B$ represent 1, 2, and 12, respectively.

Example 2.2.1 Part 1 Successor function

The *successor function* is defined as

$$\phi(i) = i + 1$$

for $i = 1, \ldots$. By using unary, ϕ is specified as

$$\tau = \{\,(\text{unary}(i)B, \text{unary}(\phi(i)))B\colon i \geq 1\}$$

Equivalently,

$$\tau = \{\,(1^i B, 1^{i+1} B)\colon i \geq 1\}$$

▲

Every transducer discussed in the rest of this section computes a function over natural numbers so it defines the translation that specify the function. More precisely, a transducer computes a function ϕ so that, for every argument $i \geq 1$, it determines $\phi(i)$ by translating unary$(i)B$ to unary$(\phi(i))B$.

Finite transducers

A finite transducer represents a finite automaton modified for translation.

As Figure 2.2.1 shows, a finite transducer M consists of an input tape with a read head, a finite state control, and an output tape with a write head. The input tape is divided into squares, each of which contains one symbol of an input word x. The finite control is represented by a finite set of states together with a finite set of computational rules. According to these rules, M changes states, reads symbols on the input tape, and writes words on the output tape. If M moves its head off the right end of the input tape and, simultaneously, enters a final state, then it translates x to the word, y, written on the output tape (Figure 2.2.2). The set containing all pairs of words translated in this way forms the translation defined by M.

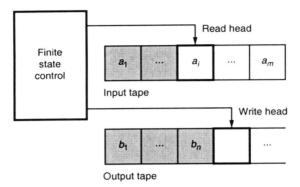

Figure 2.2.1 Finite transducer.

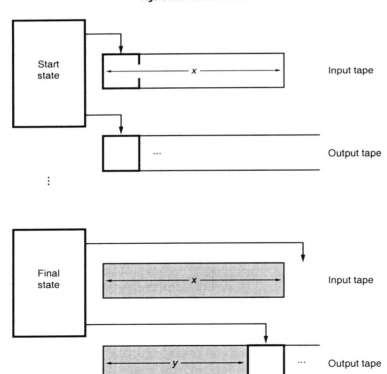

Figure 2.2.2 Translation of x to y made by a finite transducer.

Example 2.2.1 Part 2 Finite transducers

This example designs a finite transducer M that defines the translation $\tau = \{\,(1^i B, 1^{i+1}B) : i \geq 0\}$ and, thereby, computes the successor function ϕ defined in Part 1 of this example. M moves according to the following rules:

Rule 1: on 1, M remains in the start state s and writes 1
Rule 2: on B, M leaves s for the final state f and writes $1B$.

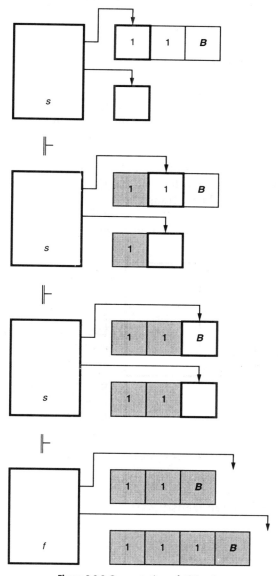

Figure 2.2.3 Computation of $\phi(2) = 3$.

With $11B$ on its input tape, M makes the three-move translation depicted in Figure 2.2.3 on the next page, where $\vdash$ denotes a translation move. Observe that this translation results in producing $111B$ on the output tape, so it correctly computes $\phi(2) = 3$.

▲

Sections 9.1 and 9.3 investigate finite transducers, their properties, and applications including a finite transducer acting as a scanner of a compiler for COLA (see Section 1.2.3).

Pushdown transducers

A pushdown transducer M consists of a pushdown, a finite state control, an input tape with a read head, and an output tape with a write head (Figure 2.2.4). The pushdown and the input tape have the same meaning as in a pushdown automaton. The finite control is represented by a finite set of states together with a finite set of computational rules. According to these rules, M replaces the pushdown top symbols with words, changes states, reads symbols on the input tape, and writes words on the output tape. If M moves its head off the right end of the tape and, simultaneously, enters a final state, then it translates the given input word x to the word y written on the output tape (Figure 2.2.5). The set that consists of all pairs of words translated in this way forms the translation defined by M.

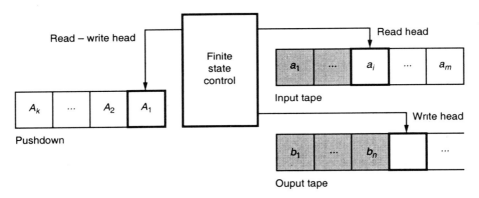

Figure 2.2.4 A pushdown transducer.

Example 2.2.2 Pushdown transducers

For all $i \geq 1$, define ϕ as

1. $\phi(i) = i$ if i is even
2. $\phi(i) = 1$ if i is odd.

Automata

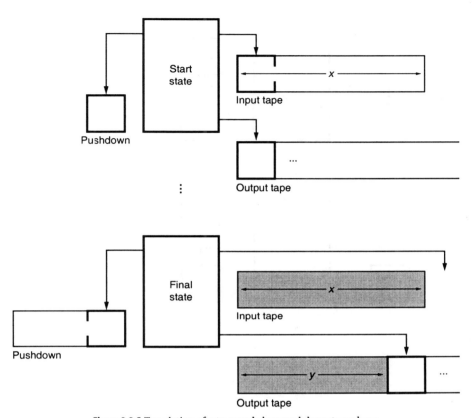

Figure 2.2.5 Translation of x to y made by a pushdown transducer.

For instance, $\phi(2) = 2$ because 2 is even; however, $\phi(3) = 1$ because 3 is odd. To construct a computational model that computes ϕ, the translation τ representing ϕ is specified as

$$\tau = \{ \text{unary}(i), \text{unary}(i): i \text{ is an even natural number}\}$$
$$\cup \{ \text{unary}(j), \text{unary}(1): j \text{ is an odd natural number}\}$$

Equivalently,

$$\tau = \{ (1^i B, 1^i B) : i \geq 1 \text{ and } i \text{ is even}\}$$
$$\cup \{ (1^i B, 1B) : i \geq 1 \text{ and } i \text{ is odd}\}$$

This example designs a pushdown transducer, M, which defines τ as follows. Initially, the input tape contains $1^i B$, for some $i \geq 1$. First, M pushes down input 1s until it reads B; in addition, during these pushes, M determines whether i is even or odd by analogy with the method described in Example 2.1.1 (see Figure 2.1.2). Based on this determination, M then performs these two kinds of computation.

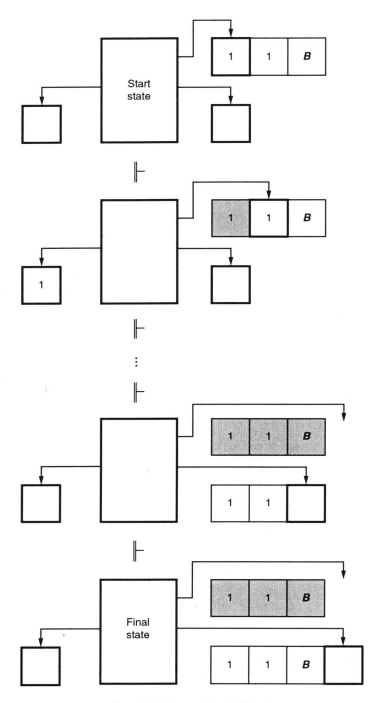

Figure 2.2.6 Computation of $\phi(2) = 2$.

1. Let i be even. At this point, M pops up 1 from the pushdown and, simultaneously, writes 1 on the output tape. When the pushdown is empty, M writes B on the output tape and enters a final state. In this way, M translates $1^i B$ to $1^i B$.
2. Let i be odd. Then, M writes $1B$ on the output tape and enters a final state so M translates $1^i B$ to $1B$.

Thus, M defines τ and, thereby, computes ϕ. To illustrate, with $11B$ on its input tape, the transducer makes the computation depicted in Figure 2.2.6; in other words, for $i = 2$, it properly computes $\phi(2) = 2$ as 2 is even.

▲

Sections 9.2 and 9.3 further investigate pushdown transducers.

Turing transducers

As Figure 2.2.7 shows, a Turing transducer M has an input tape and an output tape. M makes moves by analogy with a Turing machine. Initially, M's input tape contains a word x and its output tape is completely blank. If M can make a sequence of moves so that it erases x on the input tape, writes a word y on the output tape, and enters a final state with both heads over the leftmost squares, then M translates x into y (Figure 2.2.8). The set that contains all pairs of words translated in this way forms the translation defined by M.

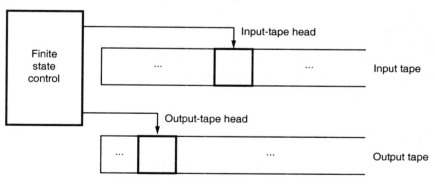

Figure 2.2.7 Turing transducer.

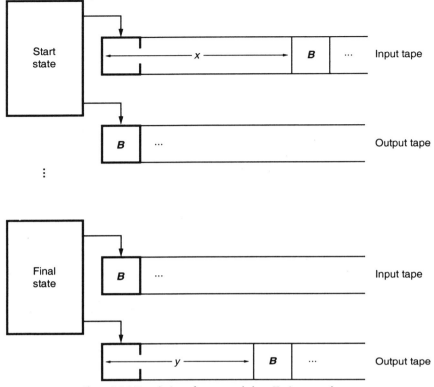

Figure 2.2.8 Translation of x to y made by a Turing transducer.

2.3 Computability

This section discusses crucial topics concerning computation and demonstrates that Turing transducers play a central role in the investigation of computation. First, it formalizes procedures and algorithms by using Turing transducers. Then, based on this formalization, the computing power of computers in general is discussed. Most importantly, a limit to this power is demonstrated by proving that some functions can never be computed by any computer. In addition, this section presents some problems that no computer can decide.

Procedures and their formalization

A *procedure* consists of a finite set of instructions, each of which can be executed in a fixed amount of time. When executed, a procedure reads input data, performs its instructions, and produces output data. An *algorithm* is a procedure that halts on all inputs. To illustrate these notions, a computer program represents a procedure. If a program halts on all input data, it is an algorithm. However, if a program enters an infinite loop on some input data, then it represents a procedure, which is not an algorithm.

As a rule, this book describes algorithms by using a Pascal-like notation. In general, this description has the following format:

Algorithm: Name.

Input: Input data.

Output: Output data.

Method:

begin
   Pascal-like description of the method that converts the input data to the output data
end.

Example 2.3.1 Part 1 Algorithm

Let n be a natural number. Recall that its factorial, $n!$, is defined as follows:

$$n! = i * (n-1) * (n-2) * \ldots * 2 * 1$$

The following algorithm reads a natural number n and determines $n!$ based on this equation:

Algorithm: Factorial.

Input: A nonnegative integer, n.

Output: The factorial of n, $n!$.

Method:

```
begin
  read(n);
  factorial := 1;
  while n > 1 do
  begin
    factorial := factorial*n;
    n := n - 1
  end{while};
  write(factorial)
end.
```

A verification of the algorithm Factorial leads to two proofs, referred to as Termination and Correctness. The former verifies that Factorial always terminates and, therefore, represents an algorithm. The latter demonstrates that Factorial correctly determines $n!$

1. Termination: Factorial first reads a natural number, n, by **read**(n). Then, it sets factorial to 1. After iterating the **while** loop n − 1 times, Factorial exits from this loop. Finally, it performs **write**(factorial) and halts. Consequently, Factorial always terminates.
2. Correctness: A verification that Factorial correctly determines $n!$ is left to the exercises.

▲

According to *Church's thesis* – a fundamental statement underlying all theoretically oriented computer science – the notion of a procedure is equivalent to the notion of a Turing transducer, introduced in the previous section. Consequently, in terms of computing power, the Turing transducer is equivalent to the digital computer.

Example 2.3.1 Part 2 Turing transducers as computers

This example constructs a Turing transducer M equivalent to Factorial, discussed above. In other words, for $n \geq 1$, M computes

$$\phi(n) = n!$$

where

$$n! = n * (n-1) * (n-2) * \ldots * 2 * 1$$

In terms of unary (see Section 2.2), this computation is expressed as

$$\tau = \{ (\text{unary}(n), \text{unary}(n!)) : i \geq 1 \}$$

Equivalently,

$$\tau = \{ (1^n B, 1^m B) : m, n \geq 1 \text{ and } m = n! \}$$

Initially, M's input tape contains $1^n B$, where $n \geq 1$, and its output tape is completely blank. M works by performing the following four-step computational cycle.

1. M writes the input tape containment, $1^n B$, on the output tape.
2. By replacing the rightmost 1 with B on the input tape, M decreases the number of input 1s by 1.
3. If the input tape contains $1^k B$ with $k \geq 1$, M continues at Step 4. If the input tape contains no 1, M completes the translation so it enters a final state with both heads over the leftmost squares.

4. If the output tape contains $1^m B$ (where $m \geq 1$), M replaces this containment with $1^{km} B$ (k has the same meaning as in the previous step), and continues at step 2.

A verification that M constructed in this way defines τ is left to the exercises.

▲

Uncomputable functions

By Church's thesis, a computer can compute a function if and only if a Turing transducer can compute the function. Therefore, if a Turing transducer cannot compute a function, then no computer can compute this function either; a function of this kind is called an *uncomputable function*. The existence of uncountable functions follows from the following counting argument, which demonstrates that there exist more functions than Turing transducers. Consider the set of all Turing transducers, T:

$$T = \{ M : M \text{ is a Turing transducer}\}$$

Because every Turing transducer has a finite description, T is countable. Let Φ be the set of all function from the set of natural numbers onto $\{0, 1\}$:

$$\Phi = \{ \phi : \phi \text{ is a function from the set of natural numbers onto } \{0, 1\}\}.$$

By contradiction, prove that Φ is uncountable as follows. Assume that Φ is countable. Let β be a bijection from Φ to the set of natural numbers. Let γ be the function from the set of natural numbers onto $\{0, 1\}$ defined for all natural numbers n as

$$\gamma(n) = 0 \text{ if and only if } \beta^{-1}(n) = \phi \text{ and } \phi(n) = 1, \text{ where } \phi \in \Phi; \text{ otherwise } \gamma(n) = 1.$$

As γ is a function from the set of natural numbers onto $\{0, 1\}$, $\gamma \in \Phi$. Let $\beta(\gamma) = m$. Then,

$$\gamma(m) = 0 \text{ if and only if } \gamma(m) = 1$$

This contradiction implies that that Φ is uncountable. Thus, there exist more functions than Turing transducers. Consequently, by Church's thesis, there exist functions that no computer can ever compute.

Decidability

Of interest are Turing transducers for formalizing algorithms that decide problems, and in particular problems to which there exist two answers – yes or no. A Turing transducer decides such a yes–no problem p so that it reads the specification of p on the input tape, determines the correct answer to p, and writes this answer on the output tape. The specification of p consists of two components, a *question* and an *instance*. The question formulates the problem. The set of problem instances forms the collection of all allowable values for the problem unknowns.

Some problems, however, cannot be decided by any Turing transducer. Therefore, by Church's thesis, these problems cannot be decided by any computer; problems of this kind are *undecidable*. To illustrate these problems, an undecidable problem, called the *halting problem*, is presented. Consider a deterministic Turing machine M with one final state f and a word w. The halting problem consists in asking whether, with w on its input tape, M halts in f. Formally, this problem is stated as:

Instance: A deterministic Turing machine, M, with one final state, f, and a word, w.
Question: Does M halt in f with w on its input?

In Section 10.3.4 it is demonstrated that this problem is undecidable. This undecidability implies several crucial results, including the following two consequences.

1. No algorithm can determine whether a given procedure is an algorithm; in other words, computer science can never algorithmically determine whether a given procedure terminates when applied to a given set of instances.

2. No algorithm can determine whether a given program enters an infinite loop with a given set of data.

Chapter 10 treats topics of the present section in detail.

Exercises

Note: Making use of the formalism introduced later on, Chapters 3 through 10 reconsider some of the following exercises in greater detail.

1. Conceptualization of Automata

1.1 Give a nondeterministic finite automaton M and an input word w, so that M accepts w by making two different sequences of moves.
1.2 Explain why no nondeterministic finite automaton accepts $\{a^n b^n : n \geq 1\}$.
1.3 Explain why no nondeterministic finite automaton accepts $\{w \text{reversal}(w): w \in \{a,b\}^+\}$.
1.4 Design a deterministic finite automaton that accepts $\{a^n b^m : m, n \geq 0\}$.
1.5 Consider each of the following languages. Does there exist a deterministic finite automaton that accepts the language?
  (a) $\{a^n b^m : 100 \geq m \geq n \geq 0\}$
  (b) $\{a^m b^n : 100 \geq m \geq n \geq 0\}$
  (c) $\{a^n b^m : m \geq n \geq 0\}$

1.6 Consider the COLA lexemes defined in Section 1.2.3. Design a deterministic finite automata that accept these lexemes.

1.7 Section 2.1 has stated that deterministic finite automata are easy to implement, but they are too restricted to be a convenient formal tool for achieving mathematical results. However, nondeterministic finite automata represent an extremely convenient mathematical abstraction, but they are difficult to use in practice. Explain these statements in greater detail, and illustrate them by examples.

1.8 Generalize deterministic finite automata so that they can make moves without reading input symbols. Formalize this generalization. Does this generalization change the power of finite automata?

1.9 By the general description given in Section 2.1, deterministic finite automata can enter a state from which they can make no move on some symbols. Restrict deterministic finite automata by ruling out this possibility; consequently, deterministic finite automata restricted in this way are capable of making a move from any state and on any input symbol. Formalize this restriction. Does this restriction change the power of deterministic finite automata?

1.10 Sketch a proof that the power of deterministic finite automata coincides with the power of nondeterministic finite automata. As a part of this proof, design an algorithm that coverts any deterministic finite automaton to an equivalent nondeterministic finite automaton.

1.11 Generalize finite automata so that they have a set of start states. Formalize this generalization. Does this generalization change the power of finite automata?

1.12 Generalize finite automata so that they can read a word in a move. Formalize this generalization. Does this generalization change the power of finite automata?

1.13* Generalize finite automata so that they can move either way on the tape. Formalize this generalization. Does this generalization change the power of finite automata?

1.14 Restrict finite automata so that they possess a single final state. Formalize this restriction. Does this restriction change the power of finite automata?

1.15 Sketch a proof to show that finite automata and regular expressions characterize the same family languages, i.e. the family of regular languages.

1.16 Sketch a proof to show that the power of finite automata is less than the power of pushdown automata.

1.17 Give an example of a pushdown automaton M and a word w so that M accepts w by making two different sequences of moves.

1.18 Design a pushdown automaton that accepts $\{w\text{reversal}(w): w \in \{a,b\}^+\}$.

1.19 Consider the programming language COLA, defined in Section 1.2.1. Design a pushdown automaton that accepts this language.

1.20 Explain why no pushdown automaton accepts $\{a^n b^n c^n: n \geq 1\}$.

1.21 Generalize pushdown automata so that they can read a word in a move. Formalize this generalization. Does this generalization increase the power of pushdown automata?

1.22 Generalize pushdown automata so that they have a set of start states. Formalize this generalization. Does this generalization increase the power of pushdown automata?
1.23 Generalize pushdown automata so that they can replace a word occurring on the pushdown top in a move. Formalize this generalization. Does this generalization increase the power of finite automata?
1.24* By analogy with deterministic finite automata, introduce deterministic pushdown automata. Prove that the power of deterministic pushdown automata is less than the power of nondeterministic pushdown automata.
1.25 Modify pushdown automata so that they possess two pushdowns. Formalize this modification. Prove that this modification changes the power of pushdown automata.
1.26 Consider pushdown automata. Replace pushdowns with queues in these automata. Formalize the models resulting from this modification. Compare the power of the resulting models with the power of pushdown automata.
1.27 Sketch a proof to show that pushdown automata and the Backus-Naur form define the same family of languages, i.e. the family of context-free languages.
1.28 Introduce a graphic representation of pushdown automata.
1.29 Sketch a proof to show that the power of pushdown automata is less than the power of Turing machines.
1.30 Give a Turing machine M and a word w so that M accepts w by making one sequence of moves.
1.31 Give a Turing machine M and a word w so that M accepts w by making two different sequences of moves.
1.32 Give a Turing machine M and a word w so that M accepts w by making infinitely many different sequences of moves.
1.33 Design Turing machines that accept the following languages:
(a) $\{a^i b^j c^k : i, j, k \geq 0 \text{ and } i < j > k\}$
(b) $\{a^i b^j : i, j \geq 0 \text{ and } j = 2i\}$
(c) $\{w : w \in \{a, b, c\}^*, \#_a w > \#_b w \text{ and } \#_a w < \#_c w\}$
(d) $\{a^i b^i c^j : i, j \geq 0 \text{ and } j \leq 2^i\}$
(e) $\{a^i b^i c^j : i, j \geq 0 \text{ and } i \leq j\}$
Sketch proofs that show the machines are correctly designed.
1.34* By analogy with deterministic finite automata, introduce deterministic Turing machines. Does the power of deterministic Turing machines coincide with the power of nondeterministic Turing machines?
1.35 From the description given in Section 2.1, Turing machines may keep the tape head stationary in a move. Rule out this possibility; in other words, restrict Turing machines so that they shift their tape heads to the left or to the right in every move. Formalize this restriction. Does this restriction change the power of Turing machines?
1.36 From the description given in Section 2.1, Turing machines can simultaneously change the state, rewrite the input tape, and shift the head. Restrict Turing machines so that they can either change the state and rewrite the input tape or change the state and shift the head. Formalize this restriction. Does this restriction change the power of Turing machines?

1.37 Introduce Turing machines with k tape heads, where $k \geq 1$. Does the power of these k-head Turing machines coincide with the power of one-head Turing machines?

1.38 Introduce Turing machines with k tapes, where $k \geq 1$. Does the power of these k-tape Turing machines coincide with the power of one-tape Turing machines?

1.39 Introduce Turing machines that can extend the tape to the left and to the right. Does the power of these machines coincide with the power of Turing machines?

1.40 Generalize Turing machines so that they have a set of start states. Formalize this generalization. Does this generalization increase the power of Turing machines?

1.41 Restrict Turing machines so that they cannot extend the tape, containing the input word. Formalize this restriction. Does this restriction decrease the power of Turing machines?

1.42* Give a language that no Turing machine accepts.

1.43 Design a graphic representation of Turing machines.

1.44 Consider common household machines, such as a microwave or a remote control. By analogy with Example 2.1.1. Part 1, simulate various kinds of behaviour of these machine by finite automata, pushdown automata, and Turing machines.

2 Transducers

2.1 Give a finite transducer M and two words v and w, so that M translates v to w by making two different sequences of moves.

2.2 Design finite transducers that define the following translations:
(a) $\{(axb, bxa): x \in \{c\}^*\}$
(b) $\{(x, xx): x \in \{c\}^*\}$
(c) $\{(a^i, a^i b^j): i, j \geq 0\}$

2.3 Design a finite transducer M that defines the translation

$$\tau = \{ (1^i B, 1^{3i} B): i \geq 1\}$$

By defining this translation, M actually computes a function over natural numbers. Determine this function.

2.4 Generalize finite transducers so that they have a set of start states. Formalize this generalization. Does this generalization increase the power of finite transducers?

2.5 Generalize finite transducers so that they can read a word in a move. Formalize this generalization. Does this generalization increase the power of finite transducers?

2.6* Generalize finite transducers so that they can move either way on the input tape. Formalize this generalization. Does this generalization increase the power of finite transducers?

2.7 Modify finite transducers so that they have a single input–output head, which both reads the input tape and writes on the output tape. Formalize this modification. Does this modification change the power of finite transducers?

2.8 Restrict finite transducers so that they cannot simultaneously read and write in a move. Formalize this restriction. Does this restriction change the power of finite transducers?
2.9 Introduce a graphic representation of finite transducers.
2.10 Return to the pushdown transducer M sketched in Example 2.2.2. Describe M in detail.
2.11 Prove that finite transducers define a proper subfamily of the family of translations defined by pushdown transducers.
2.12 Give a pushdown transducer M and two words v and w, so that M translates v to w by making five different sequences of moves.
2.13 Consider the translation

$$\tau = \{ (1^j B1^i B, 1^i B1^j B): i, j \geq 1 \}$$

Design a pushdown transducer M that defines τ.
2.14 Modify pushdown transducers so that they possess two pushdowns. Formalize this modification. Does this modification change the power of pushdown transducers?
2.15 Restrict pushdown transducers so that in a move, they can write no more than one symbol on the output tape. Formalize this restriction. Does this restriction change the power of pushdown transducers?
2.16 Restrict pushdown transducers so that in a move, they cannot simultaneously read and write. Formalize this restriction. Does this restriction change the power of pushdown transducers?
2.17* Prove that pushdown transducers and translation grammars define the same family of translations.
2.18 Generalize pushdown transducers so that they can read a word in a move. Formalize this generalization. Does this generalization add to the power of pushdown transducers?
2.19 Generalize pushdown transducers so that they have a set of start states. Formalize this generalization. Does this generalization add to the power of pushdown transducers?
2.20 Introduce a graphic representation of pushdown transducers.
2.21 Prove that pushdown transducers define a proper subfamily of the family of the translations defined by Turing transducers.
2.22 Give a Turing transducer M and two words x and y, so that M translates x to y by making infinitely many different sequences of moves.
2.23 Give a Turing transducer M and two words x and y, so that M translates x to y by making two different sequences of moves.
2.24 Give a Turing transducer M and two words x and y, so that M translates x to y by making one sequence of moves.
2.25 Design Turing transducers that define the following translations:
(A) $\{ (a^i b^j c^k, a^{i+j} b^{j+k} c^{k+i}): i, j, k \geq 1$ and $i < j$ and $k < i \}$
(B) $\{ (a^j, a^{2j}): j$ is a prime$\}$
(C) $\{ (ww, w): w \in \{a, b\}^* \}$

2.26* Introduce deterministic Turing transducers. Sketch a proof that the power of deterministic Turing transducers equals the power of nondeterministic Turing transducers.

2.27 Restrict Turing transducers so that they cannot simultaneously read and write. Formalize this restriction. Does this restriction change the power of Turing transducers?

2.28 Generalize Turing transducers so that they have a set of start states. Formalize this generalization. Does this generalization change the power of Turing transducers?

2.29 Generalize Turing transducers so that they can read a word in a move. Formalize this generalization. Does this generalization change the power of Turing transducers?

2.30 Introduce a graphic representation of Turing transducers.

3 Computability

3.1 Design Turing transducers that compute the following natural-number functions:
(a) $\gamma(n) = n^{n!}$
(b) $\gamma(n) = 2^n$
(c) $\gamma(n) = 2^{2^n}$

3.2 Section 2.3 has discussed Turing transducers that compute one-variable functions. Introduce Turing transducers that compute n-variable functions, where $n \geq 1$. Then, design Turing transducers that compute the following two-variable functions over natural numbers:
(a) $\gamma(n, m) = n + m$
(b) $\gamma(n, m) = nm$
(c) $\gamma(n, m) = n^m$

3.3* Consider the following problem, known as Post's correspondence:

Instance: A finite, binary relation, $R \subseteq T^+ \times T^+$, where T is an alphabet.
Question: Does there exist a sequence

$$(x_1, y_1), \ldots, (x_n, y_n)$$

for some $n \geq 1$ such that the following two conditions hold:

1. $(x_i, y_i) \in R$ for $i = 1, \ldots, n$;
2. $x_1 \ldots x_n = y_1 \ldots y_n$?

Sketch a proof showing that this problem is undecidable.

3.4* Consider the following special case of Post's correspondence, known as one-symbol Post's correspondence.

Instance: A finite, binary relationship, $R \subseteq T^+ \times T^+$, where T is an alphabet that contains one symbol.
Question: Does there exist a sequence

$$(x_1, y_1), \ldots, (x_n, y_n)$$

for some $n \geq 1$ such that the following two conditions hold:

1. $(x_i, y_i) \in R$ for $i = 1, \ldots, n$;
2. $x_1 \ldots x_n = y_1 \ldots y_n$?

Sketch a proof showing that one-symbol Post's correspondence is decidable.

3.5* Consider the problem of whether a program written in a programming language can loop forever. Formalize this problem. Sketch a proof showing that this problem is undecidable.

3.6* Consider the problem of whether a program written in a programming language can ever produce an output. Formalize this problem. Sketch a proof showing that this problem is undecidable.

3.7* Consider the problem of whether two programs written in a programming language produce the same output on all inputs. Formalize this problem. Sketch a proof showing that this problem is undecidable.

Programming projects

1. Basic concepts

1.1 Design a data structure that represents a nondeterministic finite automaton.
1.2 Write a program that decides whether a finite automaton is deterministic.
1.3 Write a program that simulates a deterministic finite automaton.
1.4 Write a program that simulates a nondeterministic finite automaton.
1.5 Write a program that can simulate every finite automaton.
1.6 Design a data structure that represents a pushdown automaton.
1.7 Write a program that simulates a pushdown automaton.
1.8 Design a data structure that represents a Turing machine.
1.9 Write a program that simulates a Turing machine.
1.10 Write a program that can simulate every Turing machine.

2. Transducers

2.1 Design a data structure that represents a finite transducer.
2.2 Write a program that simulates a finite transducer.
2.3 Design a data structure that represents a pushdown transducer.
2.4 Write a program that simulates a pushdown transducer.
2.5 Design a data structure that represents a Turing transducer.
2.6 Write a program that simulates a Turing transducer.

3 Computability

3.1 Example 2.3.1 Part 2 has constructed a Turing transducer M that computes the factorial of a natural number n. Write a program that simulates M.

3.2 Construct a Turing transducer M that computes a natural-number function, such as the Fibonacci function. Write a program that simulates M.

3.3 Write a program that simulates a Turing transducer that acts as a decision maker.

Bibliographical notes

Thue (1906, 1914) represent pioneer papers about formal languages. Chomsky (1956, 1957) introduced the notion of a grammar. Bar-Hillel (1964) and Chomsky and Schutzenberger (1963) are crucial early studies of context-free languages. Turing machines were introduced by Turing (1936). Rabin and Scott (1959) and Scott (1967) are also important early papers in the theory of automata.

It comes as no surprise that there exists a huge literature about formal languages and automata. Beigel and Floyd (1994), Brookshear (1989), Carroll and Long (1989), Cohen (1986), Harrison (1978), Hopcroft and Ullman (1979), Kelley (1995), Lewis and Papadimitriou (1981), Martin (1991), Minsky (1967), Salomaa (1969, 1973, 1985), Sudkamp (1988) and Wood (1987) belong to the most prominent books of this kind.

Part II Regular Languages

This part discusses regular languages and their basic models — regular expressions and finite automata. Chapter 3 formalizes both models, establishes their equivalence, and demonstrates their use in practice. Chapter 4 studies fundamental properties of regular languages. These properties cover a pumping lemma, closure properties, and basic results concerning decision problems.

3 Models for Regular Languages

This chapter characterizes regular languages by two basic models, regular expressions and finite automata. Regular expressions, outlined in Section 1.2.1, represent language-denoting formulas, based upon the operations concatenation, union, and *. Finite automata, conceptualized in Section 2.1, are simple language acceptors, that possess no auxiliary memory.

In practice, models for regular languages underlie many common software components. This is now illustrated by demonstrating that compilers' scanners actually act as finite automata. Scanners read programs written in high-level programming languages and group individual characters appearing in these programs into lexemes, such as identifiers. Most lexemes can be concisely specified as regular languages. For instance, Pascal identifiers, defined as arbitrarily long alphanumerical words beginning with a letter, are specified by the simple regular language

$$\{A, ..., Z\}(\{A, ..., Z\} \cup \{0, ..., 9\})^*$$

Consequently, lexical analyzers operate as finite automata, recognizing regular languages, that specify programming language lexemes.

Section 3.1 defines and studies regular expressions. Section 3.2 formalizes and discusses finite automata and their variants. Finally, Section 3.3 establishes the equivalence between finite automata and regular expressions, and demonstrates applications of both models.

3.1 Regular Expressions

This section formalizes and discusses regular expressions and the corresponding regular languages.

Definition — regular expression
Let Σ be an alphabet. The *regular expressions* over Σ and the languages that these expressions denote are defined recursively as follows:

1. $\emptyset$ is a regular expression denoting the empty set.
2. ε is a regular expression denoting $\{\varepsilon\}$.
3. a, where $a \in \Sigma$, is a regular expression denoting $\{a\}$.

4. If r and s are regular expressions denoting the languages R and S, respectively, then
   (a) $(r \cdot s)$ is a regular expression denoting RS
   (b) $(r + s)$ is a regular expression denoting $R \cup S$
   (c) (r^*) is a regular expression denoting R^*.

◆

We frequently simplify the *fully parenthesized regular expressions* made by this definition. To reduce the number of parentheses in these expressions, assume that * has a higher precedence than $\cdot$, and that $\cdot$ has higher precedence than $+$. Furthermore, abbreviate these expressions by omitting the symbol $\cdot$ in them. In addition, the expression rr^* is usually written as r^+ for brevity. These simplifications make regular expressions more succinct; for instance, $((a)^*(b \cdot (b)^*))$ can be written as a^*b^+.

For a regular expression r, $L(r)$ means the language denoted by r.

Definition — regular language
Let L be a language over an alphabet, Σ. L is a *regular language* over Σ if $L = L(r)$ for a regular expression r over Σ.

◆

Example 3.1.1 Symbol as a regular expression
Let Σ be an alphabet, and let a be a symbol in Σ; consider $\{a\}$. Observe that a is a regular expression over Σ. Because $\{a\} = L(a)$, $\{a\}$ is a regular language over Σ.

▲

The following example shows that any alphabet can be seen as a regular language.

Example 3.1.2 Alphabet as a regular language
Let Σ be an alphabet, $\Sigma = \{a_1, ..., a_n\}$ for some $n \geq 1$. We can write Σ as $\Sigma = \{a_1\} \cup ... \cup \{a_n\}$. From Example 3.1.1, $\{a_i\}$ is a regular language, denoted by the regular expression a_i. That is, $\{a_i\} = L(a_i)$, for all $i = 1, ..., n$. Consequently, $a_1 + ... + a_n$ is a regular expression denoting $\{a_1\} \cup ... \cup \{a_n\}$, so $\Sigma = L(a_1 + ... + a_n)$. Hence, Σ represents a regular language.

▲

The next example demonstrates that the universal language over any alphabet is a regular language.

Example 3.1.3 Universal language as a regular language
Let Σ be an alphabet. From Example 3.1.2, Σ is a regular language. Let r be a regular expression denoting Σ. Then, $L(r^*) = \Sigma^*$, so Σ^* is a regular language.

▲

Theorem 3.1.1, given next, states the relation between the family of finite languages and the family of regular languages.

Theorem 3.1.1
The family of finite languages is properly contained in the family of regular languages.

Proof
To demonstrate that the family of finite languages is contained in the family of regular languages, prove that every finite language is also a regular language. Let L be a finite language over an alphabet Σ:

$$L = \{x_1, ..., x_n\}$$

where $x_i \in \Sigma^*$, $i = 1, ..., n$, for some $n \geq 1$. Observe that

$$\{x_1, ..., x_n\} = \{x_1\} \cup ... \cup \{x_n\}$$

Clearly, x_i is a regular expression that denotes $\{x_i\}$, for $i = 1, ..., n$; formally,

$$\{x_i\} = L(x_i)$$

Hence,

$$x_1 + ... + x_n$$

is a regular expression that denotes $\{x_1, ..., x_n\}$, so L is a regular language. Thus, every finite language is a regular language.

To complete this proof, consider the universal language over Σ, Σ^*. From the definition of the universal language over an alphabet (see Section 1.1), Σ^* is infinite. From Example 3.1.3, Σ^* represents a regular language. Thus, Σ^* is an infinite regular language, and the theorem holds.
∎

The following two examples present and discuss binary infinite regular languages and the regular expressions denoting these languages.

Example 3.1.4 Binary infinite regular language
Consider the infinite regular language L consisting of all binary words that begin with 01 and end with 10; for instance, 011010 belongs to L, but 011011 does not belong to L. Formally,

$$L = 01\{0, 1\}^*10$$

A regular expression denoting L is

$$01(0+1)^*10$$

▲

Example 3.1.5 Another binary infinite regular language
Consider the infinite regular language L consisting of all binary words x satisfying these two properties:

1. x ends with 1
2. x does not contain 00.

For instance, 0101 belongs to L, but 01001 does not belong to L. Formally,

$$L = \{ x: x \in \{0,1\}^*\{1\} \text{ and } 00 \notin \text{subword}(x)\}$$

As the property $00 \notin \text{subword}(x)$ actually means that 1 follows each 0 appearing in x, L is equivalently defined as

$$L = \{1, 01\}\{1, 01\}^*$$

A regular expression denoting L is

$$(1+01)(1+01)^*$$

For brevity, simplify this expression to

$$(1+01)^+$$

▲

The next example describes regular expressions denoting real numbers in Pascal.

Example 3.1.6 Real numbers
As noted in Section 1.2.1, regular expressions concisely describe programming language lexemes. Indeed, Example 1.2.1.1 constructed a regular expression denoting the language consisting of all Pascal identifiers. In addition, the present example considers the regular language consisting of Pascal real numbers, namely

$$\{0,\ldots,9\}^+(\{\varepsilon\} \cup \{.\}\{0,\ldots,9\}^+)(\{\varepsilon\} \cup \{E\}\{\varepsilon, +, -\}\{0,\ldots,9\}^+)$$

A regular language denoting this language is

$$(0+\ldots+9)^+(\varepsilon + .(0+\ldots+9)^+)(\varepsilon + E(\varepsilon + + + -)(0+\ldots+9)^+)$$

▲

Models for regular languages

As Example 3.1.6 illustrates, regular expressions have important applications in practically oriented computer science applications, such as text editors and compiler scanners. In fact, Section 1.2.3 has already used regular expressions to describe all lexemes of the programming language COLA. Sections 3.3.1.2 and 9.3 also demonstrate some practical applications of regular expressions. The rest of the present section concentrates on theoretical properties of these expressions.

Taking a closer look at the definition of regular expressions, it can be seen that any regular language can be defined by infinitely many regular expressions. The regular expressions that denote the same language are considered to be equivalent.

Definition — equivalence of regular expressions
Two regular expressions r and s are *equivalent* if and only if $L(r) = L(s)$.   ◆

Several equations that hold for any regular expressions now follow.

Theorem 3.1.2
Let r, s, and t be regular expressions. Then, the following identities hold:

1. $L(\emptyset^*) = L(\varepsilon)$
2. $L(r\varepsilon) = L(r)$
3. $L(\varepsilon r) = L(r)$
4. $L(r\emptyset) = L(\emptyset)$
5. $L(\emptyset r) = L(\emptyset)$
6. $L(r + \emptyset) = L(r)$
7. $L(\emptyset + r) = L(r)$
8. $L(r + r) = L(r)$
9. $L(r^* + r) = L(r^*)$
10. $L((r^*)^*) = L(r^*)$
11. $L(r + s) = L(s + r)$
12. $L(r + (s + t)) = L(r + (s + t))$
13. $L(r(st)) = L((rs)t)$
14. $L((s + t)r) = L(sr + tr)$
15. $L(r(s + t)) = L(rs + rt)$

Proof
Leaving proofs of identities 2 through 14 to the exercises, verify the first identity and the last identity.

Proof of the first identity

$$L(\emptyset^*) = L(\varepsilon)$$

Observe that $\emptyset^*$ denotes the closure of the empty set. This closure equals $\{\varepsilon\}$:

$$L(\emptyset^*) = \{\varepsilon\}$$

By the definition of regular expressions,

$$\{\varepsilon\} = L(\varepsilon)$$

Therefore,

$$L(\emptyset^*) = L(\varepsilon)$$

Proof of the fifteenth identity

$$L(r(s+t)) = L(rs+rt)$$

Let r, s, and t be regular expressions defining the regular languages R, S, and T, respectively. Then,

$$L(r(s+t)) = R(S \cup T)$$

Observe that

1. $R(S \cup T) = \{xy : x \in R, y \in (S \cup T)\}$
2. $\{xy : x \in R, y \in (S \cup T)\} = \{xy_1 : x \in R, y_1 \in S\} \cup \{xy_2 : x \in R, y_2 \in T\}$
3. $\{xy_1 : x \in R, y_1 \in S\} \cup \{xy_2 : x \in R, y_2 \in T\} = RS \cup RT$

Hence,

$$R(S \cup T) = RS \cup RT$$

As $R(S \cup T) = L(r(s+t))$ and $RS \cup RT = L(rs+rt)$,

$$L(r(s+t)) = L(rs+rt)$$

■

At a glance, some statements seem to represent identities that hold for all regular expressions; in fact, however, there exist expressions that do not satisfy these statements. The following theorem presents six statements of this kind.

Theorem 3.1.3
There exist regular expressions r, s, and t so that

1. $L(rr) \neq L(r)$
2. $L(r + \varepsilon) \neq L(r)$

3. $L(sr) \neq L(rs)$
4. $L(r + (st)) \neq L((r + s)(r + t))$
5. $L((rs)^*) \neq L((r^*s^*)^*)$
6. $L((rs)^*) \neq L((r^* + s^*)^*)$

Proof
The establishment of statements 3 and 5 now follow; proofs of the other statements are left to the exercises.

Proof of the third statement
Set $r = 1$ and $s = 0$. At this point, $L(sr) \neq L(rs)$ because $01 \neq 10$.

Proof of the fifth statement
By analogy with the proof of the third statement, set $r = 1$ and $s = 0$. Observe that $1 \in L((r^*s^*)^*)$; however, $1 \notin L((rs)^*)$. Thus, $L((rs)^*) \neq L((r^*s^*)^*)$.
∎

3.2 Finite Automata

This section formalizes and investigates finite automata, conceptualized in Section 2.1. It covers both general and restricted variants of these automata. The general variants represent mathematically convenient models that are, however, difficult to apply in practice. On the other hand, the restricted variants are easy to use in practice, but their restrictions make them inconvenient from a theoretical point of view.

First, are introduced finite automata that can change states without reading input symbols. By ruling out changes of this kind, finite automata that read a symbol on every move are examined. In general, these automata work nondeterministically – with the same symbol, they can make several different moves from the same state. Therefore, special attention is paid to deterministic finite automata that disallow different moves from the same state on the same symbol. Also explained is how to minimize the number of states in deterministic finite automata. Most importantly, it is proved that all these models have the same power. Algorithms that convert the general versions of finite automata to their equivalent restricted versions are given.

3.2.1 Basic definitions

As described in Section 2.1, a finite automaton M consists of an input tape, a read head, and a finite state control (see Figure 3.2.1.1).

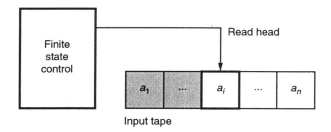

Figure 3.2.1.1 Finite automaton.

The input tape is divided into squares. Each square contains one symbol of an input word, $a_1 \ldots a_n$. The symbol under the read head, a_i, is the current input symbol. The finite control is represented by a finite set of states together with a relation, which is usually specified as a set of computational rules. M computes by making a sequence of moves. Each move is made according to a computational rule that describes how the current state is changed and whether the current input symbol is read. If the symbol is read, the read head is shifted one square to the right; otherwise, the read head is kept stationary. M's main task is to decide whether $a_1 \ldots a_n$ is accepted. For this purpose, M has one state defined as the start state and some states designated as final states. If M can read $a_1 \ldots a_n$ by making a sequence of moves from the start state to a final state, M accepts $a_1 \ldots a_n$; otherwise, M rejects $a_1 \ldots a_n$.

Example 3.2.1.1 Part 1 Intuitive design of a finite automaton

Before defining finite automata formally, let us try to describe a finite automaton intuitively. We want to design a finite automaton M that accepts every word w that can be decomposed into a concatenation of three subwords so that

$$w = w_1 w_2 w_3$$

where $w_1 \in \{a\}^*$, $w_2 \in \{b\}^+ \cup \{c\}^+$, and $w_3 \in \{a\}^*$. In other words, either $w = a^i b^j a^k$ or $w = a^i c^j a^k$, for some $i, k \geq 0$ and $j \geq 1$. The set of all these words form the language, L; that is,

$$L = \{a\}^*(\{b\}^+ \cup \{c\}^+)\{a\}^*$$

For example, $abba \in L$, but $baab \notin L$.

Construct M that works on $w = w_1 w_2 w_3$ of the above form as follows. M begins in its start state s. In this state, M reads the prefix w_1. From s, M can enter either state p or q without reading an input symbol. In p, M reads w_2 consisting of bs, whereas in q, M reads w_2 consisting of cs. From p, M can go to its final state f, on b. From q, M enters f on c. In f, M reads w_3 and, thereby, completes the acceptance of w.

To summarize the construction of M, we see that M's states are s, p, q, and f, where s is the start state and f is the final state. Its input symbols are a, b, and c. M makes its moves according to eight computational rules:

1. go from s to s on a
2. go from s to p without reading a symbol
3. go from p to p on b
4. go from p to f on b
5. go from s to q without reading a symbol
6. go from q to q on c
7. go from q to f on c
8. go from f to f on a

△

The basic definition of a finite automaton follows next.

Definition — finite automaton
A *finite automaton* is a quintuple:

$$M = (Q, \Sigma, R, s, F)$$

where

Q is a finite set of states
Σ is an input alphabet such that $\Sigma \cap Q = \varnothing$
$R \subseteq Q(\Sigma \cup \{\varepsilon\}) \times Q$ is a relation
$s \in Q$ is the start state
$F \subseteq Q$ is a set of final states.

◆

Members of R are called *computational rules* or, simply, *rules*; as a result, R is referred to as a *finite set of rules*. A rule, $(pa, q) \in R$ with $p, q \in Q$ and $a \in \Sigma \cup \{\varepsilon\}$, is usually written as

$$pa \vdash q$$

Example 3.2.1.1 Part 2 Formal specification of a finite automaton
Consider the finite automaton M, intuitively described in part 1 of this example. This example formalizes M as

$$M = (\{s, p, q, f\}, \{a, b, c\}, R, s, \{f\})$$

In M, $\{s, p, q, f\}$ is the set of M's states, where s is the start state and $\{f\}$ is the set of final states. Furthermore, $\{a, b, c\}$ represents the input alphabet of M. Consider Rule 1:

go from s to s on a

This rule is formally specified as

$$sa \vdash s$$

The other seven rules can be similarly formalized to obtain R, defined as

$$R = \{sa \vdash s, s \vdash p, pb \vdash p, pb \vdash f, s \vdash q, qc \vdash q, qc \vdash f, fa \vdash f\}$$

△

For brevity, the rules of a finite automaton are labelled and these labels are used to refer to the rules. If the rule $pa \vdash q$ is labelled r, then write

$$r: pa \vdash q$$

Here, pa is the left-hand side of rule r, which is denoted by lhs(r); analogously, the right-hand side of rule r, i.e. q, is denoted by rhs(r).

Conventions

Given a finite automaton, $M = (Q, \Sigma, R, s, F)$, this book describes M by using the following conventions:

1. The lowercase letters, f, p, q, and s, represent states in Q, where s is the start state, and f is a final state.
2. The lowercase letters $a, \ldots, d$ represent symbols in Σ.
3. The lowercase letters $u, \ldots, z$ represent words in Σ^*.
4. Rules in R are labeled by $1, \ldots, 9$ or by $r_1, r_2, \ldots$.
5. ρ represents a sequence of rules from R.

●

Subscripts and superscripts do not change these conventions, which are used hereafter unless explicitly stated otherwise.

Example 3.2.1.1 Part 3 Simplified specification of a finite automaton

By using the previous conventions, specify M as defined in part 2 of this example, by listing its rules. Label the eight rules of M by 1 through 8:

1: $sa \vdash s$
2: $s \vdash p$
3: $pb \vdash p$
4: $pb \vdash f$
5: $s \vdash q$
6: $qc \vdash q$
7: $qc \vdash f$
8: $fa \vdash f$

△

Models for regular languages

A finite automaton works by making moves according to its computational rules. In a move, it changes the current state and reads zero or one input symbol on the input tape.

Definition — configuration
Let $M = (Q, \Sigma, R, s, F)$ be a finite automaton. A *configuration* of M is a word χ satisfying

$$\chi \in Q\Sigma^*$$

♦

Definition — move
Let $M = (Q, \Sigma, R, s, F)$ be a finite automaton. If $\text{lhs}(r)y$ is a configuration of M, where $y \in \Sigma^*$ and $r \in R$, then M makes a move from $\text{lhs}(r)y$ to $\text{rhs}(r)y$ according to r, written as

$$\text{lhs}(r)y \vdash \text{rhs}(r)y \; [r]$$

♦

Convention
When the specification of the rule r used in $\text{lhs}(r)y \vdash \text{rhs}(r)y \; [r]$ is immaterial, simply write

$$\text{lhs}(r)y \vdash \text{rhs}(r)y$$

●

By specifying the current state and the unused portion of the input word, a configuration represents an instantaneous description of a given finite automaton, $M = (Q, \Sigma, R, s, F)$. To illustrate this, consider a configuration, $\text{lhs}(r)y$, and $r: pa \vdash q \in R$, so $\text{lhs}(r)y = pay$. This configuration indicates that p is the current state of M and ay is the unread part of the input word with the leftmost symbol of ay under the input head.

Observe that $\vdash$ represents a relationship over the configurations of M. This relationship formally specifies moves made by M. In a move, M either shifts its read head one square to the right or keeps the head stationary. More precisely, according to a rule of the form $r: pa \vdash q \in R$ with $a \in \Sigma$, M shifts the read head one square right; however, according to a rule of the form $r: p \vdash q \in R$, M does not shifts the read head. These two moves are now described in greater detail.

1. Consider $r: pa \vdash q \in R$ with $a \in \Sigma$. According to this rule, M changes state q to p, reads a, and shifts the read head one square to the right (Figure 3.2.1.2).

2. Consider the rule, $r: p \vdash q \in R$, called an ε-rule. According to this ε-rule, M makes an ε-move, which consists of changing p to q without reading any input symbol (Figure 3.2.1.3). As M does not shift the read head during an ε-move, in the next move M reads the same input symbol.

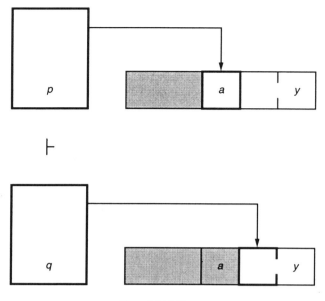

Figure 3.2.1.2 Move.

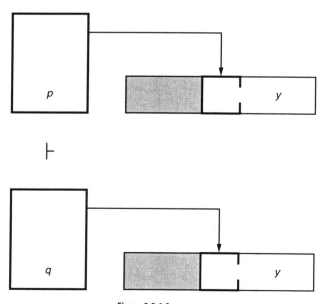

Figure 3.2.1.3 ε-move.

Example 3.2.1.1 Part 4 Moves

Return to the finite automaton M specified in part 3 of this example. Consider the configuration lhs(1)y with $y = bba$ and 1: $sa \vdash s$, so lhs(1)$y = sabba$. By rule 1, M makes this move:

$$sabba \vdash sbba \; [1]$$

From $sabba$, M can also make these two ε-moves:

$$sabba \vdash pabba \; [2] \text{ and } sabba \vdash qabba \; [5]$$

where 2: $s \vdash p$ and 5: $s \vdash q$.

△

Convention

Given a finite automaton M, χ_M denotes a configuration of M. When no confusion exists, use χ instead of χ_M.

●

The following definition extends a single move to a sequence of moves.

Definition — sequence of moves (part 1)

Let $M = (Q, \Sigma, R, s, F)$ be a finite automaton.

1. Let χ be any configuration of M. M makes *zero moves from χ to χ according to ε*, written as

$$\chi \vdash^0 \chi \; [\varepsilon]$$

2. Let there exist a sequence of configurations $\chi_0, ..., \chi_n$ for some $n \geq 1$ such that $\chi_{i-1} \vdash \chi_i \; [r_i]$ where $r_i \in R$, $i = 1, ..., n$; that is,

$$\chi_0 \vdash \chi_1 \; [r_1]$$
$$\vdash \chi_2 \; [r_2]$$
$$\vdots$$
$$\vdash \chi_n \; [r_n]$$

Then, M makes n moves from χ_0 to χ_n according to $r_1...r_n$, written as

$$\chi_0 \vdash^n \chi_n \; [r_1...r_n]$$

◆

Consider a finite automaton, $M = (Q, \Sigma, R, s, F)$. Assume that for some $n \geq 0$, $\chi \vdash^n \chi'$ $[\rho]$ in M, where $\rho = r_1 \ldots r_n$ with $r_i \in R$ for $i = 1, \ldots, n$ ($\rho = \varepsilon$ if $n = 0$). Notice that ρ, called the *rule word* corresponding to $\chi \vdash^n \chi'$ in M, specifies the sequence of n rules according to which M makes $\chi \vdash^n \chi'$. Recall that rules are customarily represented by their labels; at this point, rule words can be seen as ordinary words, consisting of rule labels. Thus, the operations on words, introduced in Section 1.1, apply to rule words, too. In this way, use is frequently made of rule words to describe move sequences rigorously and concisely. By way of illustration, suppose that a finite automaton makes n moves from χ_0 to χ_n by n applications of a rule, $r: qa \vdash q$. In terms of rule words, these n moves are succinctly expressed as $\chi_0 \vdash^n \chi_n$ $[\rho]$ with $\rho = \{r\}^n$. By contrast, if ρ represents an superfluous piece of information, $\chi \vdash^n \chi'$ $[\rho]$ is simplified to $\chi \vdash^n \chi'$.

Mathematically, $\vdash^n$ represents the n-fold product of $\vdash$. Based on $\vdash^n$, define two further notions, $\vdash^+$ and $\vdash^*$. The former denotes the transitive closure of $\vdash$, and the latter denotes the transitive and reflexive closure of $\vdash$.

Definition — sequence of moves (part 2)
Let $M = (Q, \Sigma, R, s, F)$ be a finite automaton, and let χ and χ' be two configurations of M.

1. If there exists $n \geq 1$ so $\chi \vdash^n \chi'$ $[\rho]$ in M, then $\chi \vdash^+ \chi'$ $[\rho]$.
2. If there exists $n \geq 0$ so $\chi \vdash^n \chi'$ $[\rho]$ in M, then $\chi \vdash^* \chi'$ $[\rho]$.

♦

By analogy with $\vdash^n$, it is possible to simplify $\vdash^+$ and $\vdash^*$ by writing $\chi \vdash^+ \chi'$ instead of $\chi \vdash^+ \chi'$ $[\rho]$ and $\chi \vdash^* \chi'$ instead of $\chi \vdash^* \chi'$ $[\rho]$.

Example 3.2.1.1 Part 5 Sequences of moves
Consider the configuration *sabba* of the finite automaton M discussed in previous examples. By using rules 1, 2, and 3 (Part 3 of this example contains all rules of M), M makes these three moves:

$$sabba \vdash sbba \quad [1]$$
$$\vdash pbba \quad [2]$$
$$\vdash pba \quad [3]$$

Therefore,

$$sabba \vdash^3 pba \quad [123]$$

or, briefly,

$$sabba \vdash^3 pba$$

As $sabba \vdash^3 pba$, this gives

$$sabba \vdash^+ pba$$

and

$$sabba \vdash^* pba$$

▲

A finite automaton, $M = (Q, \Sigma, R, s, F)$, accepts words over Σ in the following way. Initially, the input tape contains a word, $x \in \Sigma^*$. If M can make a sequence of moves so that it starts from s, reads x, and, then, enters a final state, M accepts x; otherwise, M rejects x. The collection of all words that M accepts is the language accepted by M, $L(M)$.

Definition — accepted language
Let $M = (Q, \Sigma, R, s, F)$ be a finite automaton and $w \in \Sigma^*$. If there exists an *accepting computation* of the form $sw \vdash^* f$, where $f \in F$, then M accepts w. The *language accepted by M*, denoted by $L(M)$, is defined as

$$L(M) = \{w: w \in \Sigma^*, \text{ and } M \text{ accepts } w\}$$

That is,

$$L(M) = \{w: w \in \Sigma^* \text{ and } sw \vdash^* f \text{ in } M \text{ for some } f \in F\}$$

◆

Example 3.2.1.1 Part 6 Accepted and rejected words
With $abba$, M makes this sequence of moves

$$\begin{aligned} sabba &\vdash sbba \\ &\vdash pbba \\ &\vdash pba \\ &\vdash fa \\ &\vdash f \end{aligned}$$

Therefore,

$$sabba \vdash^* f$$

Because f is final, M accepts $abba$ (Figure 3.2.1.4).

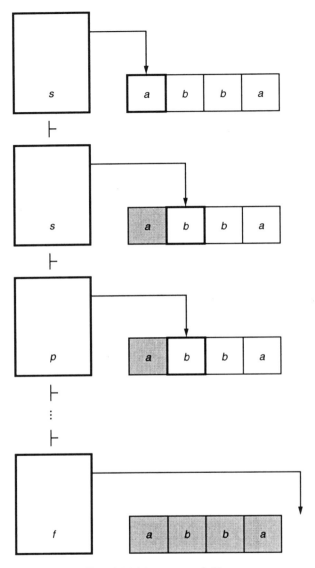

Figure 3.2.1.4 Acceptance of *abba*.

With *baab*, *M* makes no accepting computation, so *M* rejects *baab*.

△

Models for regular languages

Next, some tabular and graphical representations of finite automata are introduced.

A finite automaton, $M = (Q, \Sigma, R, s, F)$, can be represented by its *state table*, t (Figure 3.2.1.5). The columns of t are denoted by the members of $\Sigma \cup \{\varepsilon\}$, and the rows of t are denoted by the states of Q. The start state s denotes the first row, and the final states are underscored. For each $p \in Q$ and each $a \in \Sigma \cup \{\varepsilon\}$, the corresponding entry, $t(p, a)$, is defined as

$$t(p, a) = \{ q : pa \vdash q \in R \}$$

Less formally, $t(p, a)$ is the set of states that M can enter from p with a in a single move.

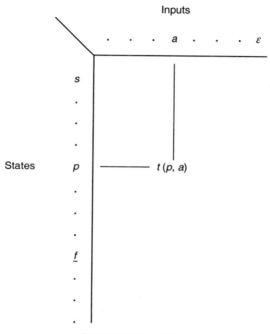

Figure 3.2.1.5 State table.

Example 3.2.1.1 Part 7 State table

Recall that this example deals with the finite automaton, M, defined by these rules

1: $sa \vdash s$
2: $s \ \vdash p$
3: $pb \vdash p$
4: $pb \vdash f$
5: $s \ \vdash q$

6: $qc \vdash q$
7: $qc \vdash f$
8: $fa \vdash f$

where s is the start state and f is the final state. Figure 3.2.1.6 depicts the state table corresponding to M.

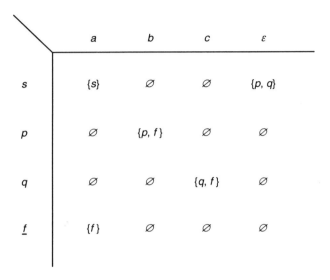

Figure 3.2.1.6 The state stable of M.

△

Graphically, a finite automaton $M = (Q, \Sigma, R, s, F)$, is represented by its *finite state diagram*. The nodes of this diagram are labelled with states of Q, where the start state is indicated by an arrow, and the final states are doubly circled. The edges are labelled with members of $\Sigma \cup \{\varepsilon\}$. A rule, $pa \vdash q$, is specified as displayed in Figure 3.2.1.7.

Figure 3.2.1.7 The representation of $pa \vdash q$ in a finite state diagram.

Example 3.2.1.1 Part 8 Finite state diagram

Figure 3.2.1.8 depicts the finite state diagram corresponding to M, examined in the previous parts of Example 3.2.1.1.

Models for regular languages

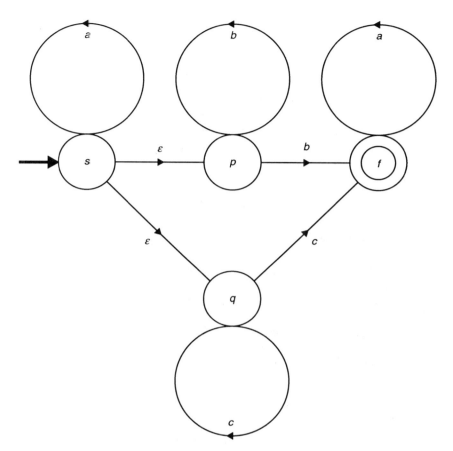

Figure 3.2.1.8 The finite state diagram of M.

△

The following example makes frequent use of finite state diagrams.

Example 3.2.1.1 Part 9 Accepted language
The first part of Example 3.2.1.1 informally designed the finite automaton M to accept $\{a\}^*(\{b\}^+ \cup \{c\}^+)\{a\}^*$. Next, by using several notions, such as rule words, introduced throughout this section, this example formally verifies the design. In other words, it rigorously establishes that

$$L(M) = \{a\}^* (\{b\}^+ \cup \{c\}^+)\{a\}^*$$

Recall that M is defined by the eight rules

1: $sa \vdash s$
2: $s \ \vdash p$

3: $pb \vdash p$
4: $pb \vdash f$
5: $s \vdash q$
6: $qc \vdash q$
7: $qc \vdash f$
8: $fa \vdash f$

where s is the start state and f is the final state. By using rule 1, M begins its computation in s, where it reads as. Then, M uses either rule 2 or rule 5; the following two cases — A and B — describe the computation resulting from the use of these rules.

Case A. By using rule 2, M enters state p without reading any symbol. In p, M reads bs by applying rules 3 or 4. Rule 3 causes M to remain in p and, thus, read another b in the next move. Rule 4 causes M to exit from p and enter f.
Case B. By using rule 5, M goes from s to q without reading any symbol. In q, M reads cs by using rules 6 or 7. By rule 6, M remains in q, so it reads another c in the next move. By rule 7, M goes from q to f.

In its final state f, M reads as according to rule 8. After reading all remaining a's of the input word, M stops and accepts.

From the previous description of the way M accepts input words, it is seen that M accepts an input word, $x \in \Sigma^*$, if and only if either $x = a^i b^j a^k$ or $x = a^i c^j a^k$, for some $j \geq 1$ and $i, k \geq 0$. In greater detail, M accepts $a^i b^j a^k$ according to a rule word of the form $1^i 2 3^{j-1} 4 8^k$, and M accepts $a^i c^j a^k$ according to $1^i 5 6^{j-1} 7 8^k$. These observations underlie the following formal determination of $L(M)$.

This determination begins with six claims, Claims A through F. Notice that Claim A, given next, implies

$$\{a\}^*(\{b\}^+ \cup \{c\}^+)\{a\}^* \subseteq L(M)$$

Claim A
Let $w \in \{a\}^*\{d\}^+\{a\}^*$, where $d \in \{b,c\}$. Then,

$$sw \vdash^* f \; [\rho_1 r_1 \rho_2 r_2 \rho_3]$$

where $\rho_1 \in \{1\}^*, \rho_3 \in \{8\}^*$, and the following two implications hold:

1. $d = b$ implies $r_1 = 2, \rho_2 \in \{3\}^*$, and $r_2 = 4$
2. $d = c$ implies $r_1 = 5, \rho_2 \in \{6\}^*$, and $r_2 = 7$

Proof
This claim is established by induction on $|w|$, for $|w| = 1, \ldots$.

Basis
Let $|w| = 1$. Then, $w = d$ with $d \in \{b,c\}$. Consider $d = b$. With b, M makes these two moves

$$sb \vdash pb \quad [2]$$
$$\vdash f \quad [4]$$

according to the rule word 24. Because $sb \vdash^* f$ [24] is a computation of the required form, this proves the basis of this inductive proof for the case when $w = b$. Analogously, this basis can be established for the case when $w = b$; this is left to the exercises.

Induction hypothesis
Assume that the claim holds for all words, $w \in \{a\}^*(\{b\}^+ \cup \{c\}^+)\{a\}^*$, satisfying $|w| \leq n$, for some $n \geq 1$.

Induction step
Consider $w \in \{a\}^*\{d\}^+\{a\}^*$, $d \in \{b,c\}$, such that $|w| = n + 1$. Suppose that $d = b$ and $w = a^i b^j a^k$, where $j \geq 1$ and $i, k \geq 0$. Consequently, $i + j + k = n + 1$. As $n + 1 \geq 2$, then $i + j + k \geq 2$, so $i \geq 1$ or $j \geq 2$ or $k \geq 1$. Assume $i \geq 1$ and express w as $w = a^{i-1}ab^j a^k$. Clearly, $|a^{i-1}b^j a^k| = n$ By the induction hypothesis,

$$sa^{i-1}b^j a^k \vdash^* f \quad [\rho_1 r_1 \rho_2 r_2 \rho_3]$$

with $\rho_1 \in \{1\}^*, r_1 = 2, \rho_2 \in \{3\}^*, r_2 = 4$, and $\rho_3 \in \{8\}^*$. This computation can be decomposed as follows:

$$sa^{i-1}b^j a^k \vdash^* sb^j a^k \quad [\rho_1]$$
$$\vdash^* f \quad [r_1 \rho_2 r_2 \rho_3]$$

Therefore, according to $\rho_1 1 r_1 \rho_2 r_2 \rho_3$,

$$a^{i-1}ab^j a^k \vdash^* sab^j a^k \quad [\rho_1]$$
$$\vdash sb^j a^k \quad [1]$$
$$\vdash^* f \quad [r_1 \rho_2 r_2 \rho_3]$$

That is,

$$sw \vdash^* f \quad [\rho_1 1 r_1 \rho_2 r_2 \rho_3]$$

where $\rho_1 1 \in \{1\}^*, r_1 = 2, \rho_2 \in \{3\}^*, r_2 = 4$, and $\rho_3 \in \{8\}^*$. At this point, we have proved the induction step for $w = a^i b^j a^k$, where $i, j \geq 1, k \geq 0$, and $i + j + k = n + 1$.

In addition to $w = a^i b^j a^k$ with $i, j \geq 1$, $k \geq 0$, and $i + j + k = n + 1$, there exist the following five possible forms of w with $|w| = n + 1$:

1. $w = b^j a^k$ with $k, j \geq 1$, and $j + k = n + 1$
2. $w = b^j$ with $j \geq 2$ and $j = n + 1$
3. $w = a^i c^j a^k$ with $i, j \geq 1$, $k \geq 0$, and $i + j + k = n + 1$
4. $w = c^j a^k$ with $j, k \geq 1$, and $j + k = n + 1$
5. $w = c^j$ with $j \geq 2$ and $j = n + 1$.

By analogy with the previous proof of the induction step for $w = a^i b^j a^k$ with $i, j \geq 1$, $k \geq 0$, and $i + j + k = n + 1$, it is possible to prove the inductive step for each of these five cases and, thereby, complete the proof of claim A. This is left to the exercises. □

Claim A implies that

$$\{a\}^*(\{b\}^+ \cup \{c\}^+)\{a\}^* \subseteq L(M)$$

To establish

$$L(M) = \{a\}^*(\{b\}^+ \cup \{c\}^+)\{a\}^*$$

requires a proof that

$$L(M) - \{a\}^*(\{b\}^+ \cup \{c\}^+)\{a\}^* = \varnothing$$

This proof is based on the following five claims, B through F.

Claim B studies M's computation that remains in state s (Figure 3.2.1.9). Specifically, this claim demonstrates that in s, M reads n as by n applications of rule 1: $sa \vdash s$, where $n \geq 0$.

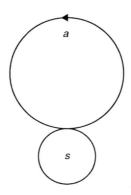

Figure 3.2.1.9 The computation of M in s.

Models for regular languages

Claim B
Let $sx \vdash^* s\,[\rho]$ in M. Then, $x = a^{|\rho|}$ and $\rho = 1^{|\rho|}$.

Proof
This claim is proved by induction on $|\rho|$.

Basis
Let $|\rho| = 0$. At this point, $x = \varepsilon$ and $\rho = \varepsilon$ in $sx \vdash^* s\,[\rho]$, so this computation is actually the 0-move computation $s \vdash^0 s\,[\varepsilon]$. Because $s \vdash^0 s\,[\varepsilon]$ represents a computation of the required form, the basis of this claim holds.

Induction hypothesis
Assume that Claim B holds for all rule words ρ satisfying $|\rho| \leq m$, for some $m \geq 0$.

Induction step
Consider a computation

$$sx \vdash^* s\,[\rho]$$

where $|\rho| = m + 1$. As $|\rho| \geq 1$, there exists a configuration χ such that

$$sx \vdash^* \chi\,[\rho']$$
$$\vdash s\,[r]$$

where $\rho = \rho'r$. Because the only rule with s on its right-hand side is rule 1, this gives $r = 1$. As a result, $\chi = sa$ and, therefore,

$$sx'a \vdash^* sa\,\,[\rho']$$
$$\vdash s\,\,\,\,\,[1]$$

where $x = x'a$ and $\rho = \rho'1$. Observe that $|\rho'| = |\rho| - 1$, so $|\rho'| = m$. Thus, by the induction hypothesis,

$$sx' \vdash^* s\,[\rho'] \text{ implies } x' = a^{|\rho'|} \text{ and } \rho' = 1^{|\rho'|}$$

Therefore,

$$x = x'a = a^{|\rho'|}a = a^{|\rho|}$$

and

$$\rho = \rho'1 = 1^{|\rho'|}1 = 1^{|\rho|}$$

In other words the inductive step is complete and Claim B is established by the principle of induction.

□

The following claim states that in p, M reads n bs by n applications of

$$3: pb \vdash p,$$

where $n \geq 0$ (Figure 3.2.1.10).

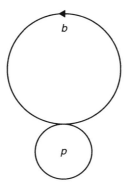

Figure 3.2.1.10 The computation of M in p.

Claim C
Let $px \vdash^* p\ [\rho]$ in M. Then, $x = b^{|\rho|}$ and $\rho = 3^{|\rho|}$.

Proof
This claim can be established by analogy with the proof of Claim B, so a detailed proof of Claim C is left to the exercises.

□

Claim D, given next, states that in q, M reads n cs by n applications of the rule 3: $qb \vdash q$, where $n \geq 0$ (Figure 3.2.1.11).

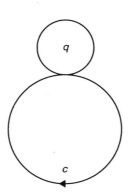

Figure 3.2.1.11 The computation of M in q.

Claim D
Let $qx \vdash^* q\,[\rho]$ in M. Then, $x = c^{|\rho|}$ and $\rho = 5^{|\rho|}$.

Proof
This proof is left to the exercises.

□

Remaining in its final state f, M reads n as by n applications of the rule 8: $fa \vdash f$ where $n \geq 0$ (Figure 3.2.1.12). Claim E formalizes this observation.

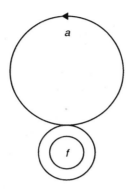

Figure 3.2.1.12 The computation of M in f.

Claim E
Let $fx \vdash^* f\,[\rho]$ in M. Then, $x = a^{|\rho|}$ and $\rho = 8^{|\rho|}$.

Proof
This proof is left to the exercises.

□

Making use of the previous four claims, the following claim determines the form for accepting computations made by M.

Claim F
Every accepting computation in M has the form

$$\begin{aligned}
sa^{|\rho_1|}d^{|\rho_2|}da^{|\rho_3|} &\vdash^* sd^{|\rho_2|}da^{|\rho_3|} && [\rho_1] \\
&\vdash od^{|\rho_3|}da^{|\rho_3|} && [r_1] \\
&\vdash^* oda^{|\rho_3|} && [\rho_2]
\end{aligned}$$

$$\vdash fa^{|\rho_3|} \quad\quad [r_2]$$
$$\vdash f \quad\quad [\rho_3]$$

where $\rho_1 \in \{1\}^*, \rho_3 \in \{8\}^*, d \in \{b, c\}$, and the following two implication hold:

1. $d = b$ implies $o = p, r_1 = 2, \rho_2 \in \{3\}^*$, and $r_2 = 4$
2. $d = c$ implies $o = q, r_1 = 5, \rho_2 \in \{6\}^*$, and $r_2 = 7$

Proof
Let

$$sz \vdash^* f[\rho]$$

be an accepting computation in M. This computation has the form of Computation 1 (Figure 3.2.1.13) or Computation 2 (Figure 3.2.1.14).

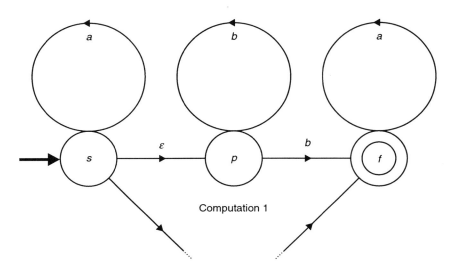

Figure 3.2.1.13 Accepting computation via p.

Computation 1
Here M enters p from s by making an ε-move according to 2: $s \vdash p$ (Figure 3.2.1.15).
Therefore, $sz \vdash^* f$ can be written as

$$sz \vdash^* sv$$
$$\vdash \chi_{\text{first-}p} \quad [2]$$
$$\vdash^* f$$

Models for regular languages

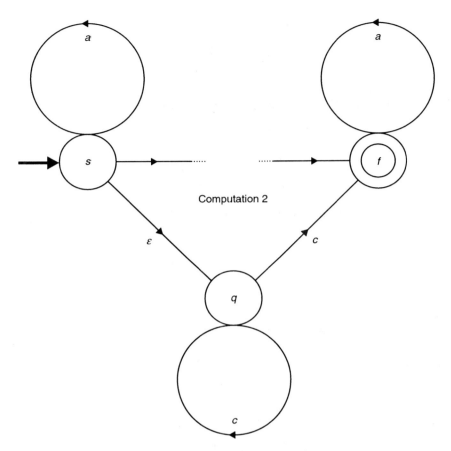

Figure 3.2.1.14 Accepting computation via q.

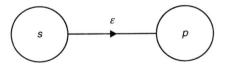

Figure 3.2.1.15 An ε-move that M makes from s to p.

where $\chi_{\text{first-}p}$ denotes the first configuration in state p. Let

$$sxv \vdash^* sv \ [\rho_1]$$

where $z = xv$. From Claim B, $sx \vdash^* s \ [\rho_1]$ implies $x = a^{|\rho_1|}$ and $\rho_1 = 1^{|\rho_1|}$, so

$$sa^{|\rho_1|}v \vdash^* sv \quad [\rho_1]$$
$$\vdash \chi_{\text{first-}p} \quad [2]$$
$$\vdash^* f$$

Because $sv \vdash \chi_{\text{first-}p}$ [2] is an ε-move, this can be written as

$$sa^{|\rho_1|}v \vdash^* sv \quad [\rho_1]$$
$$\vdash pv \quad [2]$$
$$\vdash^* f$$

From p to f, M makes a move according to the rule 4: $pb \vdash f$ (Figure 3.2.1.16).

Figure 3.2.1.16 A move that M makes from p to f.

Therefore, Computation 1 may be expressed as

$$sa^{|\rho_1|}v \vdash^* sv \quad [\rho_1]$$
$$\vdash pv \quad [2]$$
$$\vdash^* \chi_{\text{last-}p} \quad [\rho_2]$$
$$\vdash \chi_{\text{first-}f} \quad [4]$$
$$\vdash^* f$$

where $\chi_{\text{last-}p}$ denotes the last configuration in state p, and $\chi_{\text{first-}f}$ denotes the first configuration in state f. Let $v = wx$ and $\chi_{\text{last-}p} = px$. Because by Claim C, $pw \vdash^* p$ [ρ_2] implies $w = b^{|\rho_2|}$ and $\rho_2 = 3^{|\rho_2|}$,

$$sa^{|\rho_1|}b^{|\rho_2|}x \vdash^* sb^{|\rho_2|}x \quad [\rho_1]$$
$$\vdash pb^{|\rho_2|}x \quad [2]$$
$$\vdash^* \chi_{\text{last-}p} \quad [\rho_2]$$
$$\vdash \chi_{\text{first-}f} \quad [4]$$
$$\vdash^* f$$

According to 4: $pb \vdash f$, M goes from p to f with b. Consequently, $x = by$ and

Models for regular languages

$\chi_{\text{first-}f} = fy$, so

$$sa^{|\rho_1|}b^{|\rho_2|}by \vdash^* sb^{|\rho_2|}by \quad [\rho_1]$$
$$\vdash pb^{|\rho_2|}by \quad [2]$$
$$\vdash^* pby \quad [\rho_2]$$
$$\vdash fy \quad [4]$$
$$\vdash^* f \quad [\rho_3]$$

As no rule can cause M to leave f, $fy \vdash^* f \, [\rho_3]$ remains in f. From Claim E, $fy \vdash^* f [\rho_3]$ implies $y = a^{|\rho_3|}$ and $\rho_3 = 8^{|\rho_3|}$. Therefore, it is concluded that Computation 1 takes the form

$$sa^{|\rho_1|}b^{|\rho_2|}ba^{|\rho_3|} \vdash^* sb^{|\rho_2|}ba^{|\rho_3|} \quad [\rho_1]$$
$$\vdash pb^{|\rho_2|}ba^{|\rho_3|} \quad [2]$$
$$\vdash^* pba^{|\rho_3|} \quad [\rho_2]$$
$$\vdash fa^{|\rho_3|} \quad [4]$$
$$\vdash^* f \quad [\rho_3]$$

with $\rho_1 \in \{1\}^*$, $\rho_2 \in \{3\}^*$, and $\rho_3 \in \{8\}^*$.

Computation 2

By analogy with the demonstration of the form of Computation 1, prove that Computation 2 has the form

$$sa^{|\rho_1|}c^{|\rho_2|}ca^{|\rho_3|} \vdash^* sc^{|\rho_2|}ca^{|\rho_3|} \quad [\rho_1]$$
$$\vdash qc^{|\rho_2|}ca^{|\rho_3|} \quad [5]$$
$$\vdash^* qca^{|\rho_3|} \quad [\rho_2]$$
$$\vdash fa^{|\rho_3|} \quad [7]$$
$$\vdash^* f \quad [\rho_3]$$

with $\rho_1 \in \{1\}^*$, $\rho_2 \in \{6\}^*$, and $\rho_3 \in \{8\}^*$; a detailed version of this poof is left to the exercises.

We conclude that every accepting computation in M has the form

$$sa^{|\rho_1|}d^{|\rho_2|}da^{|\rho_3|} \vdash^* sd^{|\rho_2|}da^{|\rho_3|} \quad [\rho_1]$$
$$\vdash od^{|\rho_2|}da^{|\rho_3|} \quad [r_1]$$
$$\vdash^* oda^{|\rho_3|} \quad [\rho_2]$$

$$\vdash fa^{|\rho_3|} \quad [r_2]$$
$$\vdash f \quad [\rho_3]$$

where $\rho_1 \in \{1\}^*, \rho_3 \in \{8\}^*, d \in \{b, c\}$, and the following two implications hold:

1. $d = b$ implies $o = p, r_1 = 2, \rho_2 \in \{3\}^*$, and $r_2 = 4$
2. $d = c$ implies $o = q, r_1 = 5, \rho_2 \in \{6\}^*$, and $r_2 = 7$

Thus, Claim F holds.

□

From Claim A, for all $w \in \{a\}^*\{d\}^+\{a\}^*$, where $d \in \{b,c\}$,

$$sw \vdash^* f \; [\rho_1 r_1 \rho_2 r_2 \rho_3]$$

in M, where $\rho_1 \in \{1\}^*, \rho_3 \in \{8\}^*$, and the following two implications hold:

1. $d = b$ implies $r_1 = 2, \rho_2 \in \{3\}^*$, and $r_2 = 4$
2. $d = c$ implies $r_1 = 5, \rho2 \in \{6\}^*$, and $r_2 = 7$

Hence,

$$\{a\}^*(\{b\}^+ \cup \{c\}^+)\{a\}^* \subseteq L(M)$$

From Claim F, every accepting computation in M has the form described in Claim A. Thus,

$$L(M) - \{a\}^*(\{b\}^+ \cup \{c\}^+)\{a\}^* = \emptyset$$

Therefore,

$$L(M) = \{a\}^*(\{b\}^+ \cup \{c\}^+)\{a\}^*$$

▲

3.2.2 Elimination of ϵ-Moves

Finite automata, as defined in the previous section, can make ε-moves and, thereby, change states without reading an input symbol. This section demonstrates how to determine the computation that finite automata make by ε-moves. These automata are then restricted by disallowing ε-moves; consequently, finite automata restricted in this way read an input symbol on every move. It is demonstrated that this restriction does not change the power of finite automata. Finally, an implementation of finite automata that make no ϵ-moves is described.

Determination of computation without reading

Before explaining how to determine the set of states that a finite automaton can reach from another set of states without reading any input symbols, this section extends configurations to super-configurations, defined over sets of states.

Definition — superconfiguration
Let $M = (Q, \Sigma, R, s, F)$ be a finite automaton, $Q' \subseteq Q, x \in \Sigma^*$, and $X = Q'\{x\}$. Then, X is a *superconfiguration* of M.

♦

Consider a superconfiguration $Q'\{x\}$ of a finite automaton, $M = (Q, \Sigma, R, s, F)$. Observe that $Q' = \emptyset$ implies $Q'\{x\} = \emptyset$. Furthermore, if $x = \varepsilon$, then $Q'\{x\} = Q'\{e\} = Q'$; consequently, any subset of Q is a superconfiguration.

Convention
Given a finite automaton, M, X_M denotes a superconfiguration of M. Instead of X_M, simply write X when no confusion exists.

●

Definition — supermove
Let $M = (Q, \Sigma, R, s, F)$ be a finite automaton, and let $X_1 = Q_1\{ax\}$ and $X_2 = Q_2\{x\}$ be two superconfigurations of M, where $Q_1, Q_2 \subseteq Q, x \in \Sigma^*$, and $a \in (\Sigma \cup \{\varepsilon\})$. If

$$Q_2 = \{ p: qa \vdash p \in R \text{ for some } q \in Q_1 \},$$

then M makes a *supermove* from X_1 to X_2, written as

$$X_1 \vDash X_2$$

♦

Informally, Q_2 is the set of all states that M can enter from a state in Q_1 on a.

Example 3.2.2.1 Part 1 Supermoves
Reconsider the finite automaton M studied in Example 3.2.1.1. Recall that M has these rules:

1. $sa \vdash s$
2. $s \vdash p$
3. $pb \vdash p$
4. $pb \vdash f$
5. $s \vdash q$
6. $qc \vdash q$

7: $qc \vdash f$
8: $fa \vdash f$

Consider the superconfiguration $\{s\}\{abba\}$. As 1: $sa \vdash s$ is the only rule with sa on the left-hand side, $\{s\}$ is the set of states that M can enter from s. Therefore, M makes this supermove on a:

$$\{s\}\{abba\} \vDash \{s\}\{bba\}$$

However, from the same superconfiguration $\{s\}\{abba\}$, M can also make the following supermove without reading any input symbol

$$\{s\}\{abba\} \vDash \{p, q\}\{abba\}$$

Indeed, M contains two ε-rules with s on the left-hand side (2: $s \vdash p$ and 5: $s \vdash q$), so $\{p, q\}$ equals the set of states to which M can make an ε-move from s.

Consider $\{p, q\}\{bba\}$. Observe that $\{p, f\}$ is the set of all states that M can enter from states in $\{p, f\}$ on b because 3: $pb \vdash p$ and 4: $pb \vdash f$ are M's rules with pb on the left-hand side, and M has no rule with qb on the left-hand side. Therefore, M makes the supermove

$$\{p, q\}\{bba\} \vDash \{p, f\}\{ba\}$$

△

The previous section extended $\vdash$ to $\vdash^n$, $\vdash^*$, and $\vdash^+$ over configurations. Analogously, the following two definitions extend $\vDash$ to $\vDash^n$, $\vDash^*$, and $\vDash^+$ over superconfigurations.

Definition — sequence of supermoves (part 1)
Let $M = (Q, \Sigma, R, s, F)$ be a finite automaton.

1. Let X be any superconfiguration of M. Then, $X \vDash^0 X$ in M.

2. Let there exist a sequence of superconfigurations

$$X_0, ..., X_n$$

for some $n \geq 1$ such that

$$X_{i-1} \vDash X_i$$

for all $i = 1, ..., n$. Then, $X_0 \vDash^n X_n$ in M.

♦

Definition — sequence of supermoves (part 2)
Let $M = (Q, \Sigma, R, s, F)$ be a finite automaton, and let X and X' be two superconfigurations of M.

1. If there exists $n \geq 1$ so $X \vDash^n X'$ in M, then $X \vDash^+ X'$.
2. If there exists $n \geq 0$ so $X \vDash^n X'$ in M, then $X \vDash^* X'$.

◆

Example 3.2.2.1 Part 2 Sequences of supermoves

The previous part of this example demonstrated that the finite automaton M makes three super-moves:

$$\{s\}\{abba\} \vDash \{s\}\{bba\}$$
$$\vDash \{p, q\}\{bba\}$$
$$\vDash \{p, f\}\{ba\}$$

Therefore,

$$\{s\}\{abba\} \vDash^3 \{p, f\}\{ba\}$$

As $\{s\}\{abba\} \vDash^3 \{p, f\}\{ba\}$,

$$\{s\}\{abba\} \vDash^+ \{p, f\}\{ba\}$$

and

$$\{s\}\{abba\} \vDash^* \{p, f\}\{ba\}$$

△

Consider a finite automaton, $M = (Q, \Sigma, R, s, F)$. Based upon $\vdash^*$, the previous section has defined the language accepted by M, $L(M)$, as

$$L(M) = \{w: w \in \Sigma^* \text{ and } sw \vdash^* f \text{ for some } f \in F\}$$

Equivalently, $L(M)$ can be defined by using $\vDash^*$. Indeed, let $f \in F$, and $Q_f \subseteq Q$ such that $f \in Q_f$. From the definition of $\vDash^*$, for every $w \in \Sigma^*$,

$$sw \vdash^* f \text{ if and only if } \{s\}\{w\} \vDash^* Q_f$$

Therefore, $L(M)$ can be defined as

$$L(M) = \{w: w \in \Sigma^* \text{ and } \{s\}\{w\} \vDash^* F', \text{ where } F' \cap F \neq \varnothing\}$$

Example 3.2.2.1 Part 3 Accepted and rejected words

Consider the finite automaton M whose rules are listed in Part 1 of this example. With $abba$, M computes

$$\{s\}\{abba\} \vDash^* \{f\}$$

where f is the final state of M. Therefore, M accepts $abba$; that is, $abba \in L(M)$. With aa, M computes

$$\{s\}\{aa\} \vDash^* \{s\}$$

As $\{s\} \cap \{f\} = \emptyset$, M rejects aa, which is written as $aa \notin L(M)$.
Based on $\vDash^*$, Example 3.2.1.1 Part 7 proved that

$$L(M) = \{a\}^*(\{b\}^+ \cup \{c\}^+)\{a\}^*$$

The exercises establishe this equation by using the definition of $L(M)$ based on $\vDash^*$.

△

Given a finite automaton $M = (Q, \Sigma, R, s, F)$ and a set of states $Q_1 \subseteq Q$, the following algorithm determines the set of states Q_2 satisfying $Q_1 \vDash^* Q_2$ in M; in other words, Q_2 is the set of states that M can reach from states in Q_1 without reading any input symbols.

Algorithm 3.2.2.1: Determination of computation without reading

Input: A finite automaton, $M = (Q, \Sigma, R, s, F)$, and $Q_1 \subseteq Q$.

Output: Q_2 such that $Q_1 \vDash^* Q_2$.

Method
   begin
      $Q_2 := Q_1$;
      $Q_{old} := \emptyset$;
      repeat
         $Q_{new} := Q_2 - Q_{old}$;
         $Q_{old} := Q_2$;
         $Q_2 := Q_2 \cup \{p: q \vdash p \in R \text{ and } q \in Q_{new}\}$;
      until $Q_{old} = Q_2$;
end.

Lemma 3.2.2.2

Let $M = (Q, \Sigma, R, s, F)$ be a finite automaton, and let $Q_1 \subseteq Q$. Then, Algorithm 3.2.2.1 terminates and correctly determines Q_2 satisfying $Q_1 \vDash^* Q_2$.

Proof
Let Q_{2_i} denote the set of states included in Q_2 after iteration i of the **repeat** loop, for $i = 0, 1, \ldots$.

Termination
Observe that $Q_{2_i} \subseteq Q$, so

Models for regular languages

$$0 \le \text{card}(Q_{2_i}) \le \text{card}(Q)$$

for all $i \ge 0$. Notice that at each iteration the repeat loop can add some states to Q_2; however, it does not remove any states from this set. Therefore,

$$0 \le \text{card}(Q_{2_i}) \le \text{card}(Q_{2_{i+1}}) \le \text{card}(Q)$$

for all $i \ge 0$. The **repeat** loop is iterated provided that

$$\text{card}(Q_{2_i}) < \text{card}(Q_{2_{i+1}})$$

In other words, it exits when

$$\text{card}(Q_{2_j}) = \text{card}(Q_{2_{j+1}})$$

for some $j = 0, \ldots, \text{card}(Q)$. Thus, this algorithm terminates after it repeats the **repeat** loop no more than $\text{card}(Q) + 1$ times.

Correctness
To establish the correctness of this algorithm, claims A and B (below) must be proved. The former demonstrates that if Algorithm 3.2.2.1 adds a state p to Q_2 during an iteration of the **repeat** loop, then there exists a state $q \in Q_1$, such that $q \vdash^* p$.

Claim A
For all $i \ge 0$ and any $p \in Q$,

$$\text{if } p \in Q_{2_i}, \text{ then } q \vdash^* p \text{ for some } q \in Q_1.$$

Proof
This claim is proved by induction on i:

Basis
Let $i = 0$ and observe that $p \in Q_{2_0}$ if and only if $p \in Q_1$. Because $p \vdash^0 p$, the basis of this claim holds.

Induction hypothesis
Assume that the claim holds for all $Q_{2_0}, \ldots, Q_{2_i}$, for some $i \ge 0$.

Induction step
Let $p \in Q_{2_{i+1}}$ and consider two cases, $p \in Q_{2_j}$ for some $j \le i$, and $p \in Q_{2_{i+1}} - Q_{2_i}$.

1. Let $p \in Q_{2_j}$ for some $j \le i$. By the induction hypothesis, $q \vdash^* p$ for some $q \in Q_1$, so the inductive step holds in this case.

2. Let $p \in Q_{2_{i+1}} - Q_{2_i}$. By the description of the **repeat** loop, there exists a rule

$$r: q' \vdash p \in R$$

with $q' \in Q_{\text{new}}$. As $q' \in Q_{\text{new}}$, $q' \in Q_{2_i}$. By the induction hypothesis, $q \vdash^* q'$ in M for some $q \in Q_1$, so

$$q \vdash^* q'$$
$$\vdash p\,[r]$$

That is,

$$q \vdash^* p$$

where $q \in Q_1$. This establishes the inductive step in case 2, so Claim A holds. □

Claim B converts the implication given in Claim A.

Claim B
For all $i \geq 0$, if $q \vdash^i p$ with $q \in Q_1$, then $p \in Q_{2_i}$.

Proof
This claim is proved by induction on i.

Basis
Let $i = 0$. Then, $q \vdash^0 p$, so $q = p$. Then, p is included in Q_2 before the first iteration of the **repeat** loop; formally, $p \in Q_{2_0}$. Thus, the basis holds.

Induction hypothesis
Assume that the claim is true for all n-move computations, where $n = 0, \ldots, i$, for some $i \geq 1$.

Induction step
Let

$$q \vdash^{i+1} p$$

where $q \in Q_1$. Consider the two cases $p \in Q_{2j}$ for some $j = 0, \ldots, i$, and $p \notin Q_{2j}$ for any $j = 0, \ldots, i$.

1. Let $p \in Q_{2j}$, for some $j = 0, \ldots, i$. Recall that each iteration of the **repeat** loop can add some states to Q_2; however, no iteration of this loop removes any states from Q_2. Therefore,

$$Q_{2_n} \subseteq Q_{2_{n+1}}$$

for all $n \geq 0$. Thus, $p \in Q_{2_{i+1}}$.

2. Let $p \notin Q_{2_j}$, for any $j = 0, \ldots, i$. As $i + 1 \geq 1$, $q \vdash^{i+1} p$ can be written as

$$q \vdash^{i} q' \\ \vdash p \, [r]$$

where r is a rule of the form

$$r: q' \vdash p \in R$$

with $q' \in Q_{new}$. By the induction hypothesis, $q' \in Q_{2_i}$ because $q \vdash^{i} q'$. However, $q' \notin Q_{2_{i-1}}$ because $p \notin Q_{2_i}$ and $r: q' \vdash p \in R$. Thus,

$$q' \in Q_{2_i} - Q_{2_{i-1}}$$

Hence, by the **repeat** loop, $p \in Q_{2_{i-1}}$ because $q' \vdash p \in R$.

At this point, the induction step is completed, so Claim B holds. □

From Claims A and B,

$$p \in Q_2 \text{ if and only if } q \vdash^* p \text{ in } M \text{ for some } q \in Q_1$$

Hence, Q_2 is the set of states satisfying $Q_1 \vDash^* Q_2$. Therefore, the algorithm is correct, and the lemma holds. ■

Example 3.2.2.1 Part 4 Application of Algorithm 3.2.2.1

Return to the finite automaton M studied in the previous parts of this example, and consider $Q_1 = \{s\}$. Initially, Algorithm 3.2.2.1 sets

$$Q_2 = \{s\}$$

The first iteration of the **repeat** loop adds q and p to Q_2 because $s \vdash q$ and $s \vdash p$ are the ε-rules with s on the left-hand sides, so

$$Q_2 = \{s, q, p\}$$

As q and p represent new states in Q_2, the algorithm performs the second iteration of the **repeat** loop. However, this iteration adds no new state to Q_2, so the **repeat** loop exits. The following table summarizes the execution of Algorithm 3.2.2.1 with $\{s\}$ on its input.

Iteration	Q_2	New states
0	$\{s\}$	$\{s\}$
1	$\{s, p, q\}$	$\{p, q\}$
2	$\{s, p, q\}$	$\varnothing$

△

Finite automata without ε-rules

This discussion now demonstrates how to convert any finite automaton to an equivalent finite automaton without ε-rules.

Definition — ε-free finite automaton

Let $M = (Q, \Sigma, R, s, F)$ be a finite automaton. M is an *ε-free finite automaton* if for all $r \in R$,

$$\text{lhs}(r) \in Q\Sigma$$

♦

Algorithm 3.2.2.3: Conversion of a finite automaton to an equivalent ε-free finite automaton

Input: A finite automaton $M = (Q, \Sigma, R, s, F)$.

Output: An ε-free finite automaton, $M_{\varepsilon\text{-free}} = (Q, \Sigma, R_{\varepsilon\text{-free}}, s, F_{\varepsilon\text{-free}})$, such that $L(M_{\varepsilon\text{-free}}) = L(M)$.

Method
begin
  $F_{\varepsilon\text{-free}} := F$;
  $R_{\varepsilon\text{-free}} := \varnothing$;
  if $\{s\} \vdash^* F'$ in M and $F \cap F' \neq \varnothing$ **then** $F_{\varepsilon\text{-free}} := F_{\varepsilon\text{-free}} \cup \{s\}$;
  for each $q \in Q$ and $a \in \Sigma$ **do**
    $R_{\varepsilon\text{-free}} := R_{\varepsilon\text{-free}} \cup \{qa \mapsto p: \{q\}\{a\} \vdash^* Q_1\{a\} \vDash Q_2$ in M, for some $Q_1, Q_2 \subseteq Q$, and $p \in Q_2\}$;
end.

Intuitively, $M_{\varepsilon\text{-free}}$ simulates M in the following way. Concerning moves that read input symbols, $M_{\varepsilon\text{-free}}$ works as M. If M accepts ε by making several ε-moves and, then, entering a final state, then $F_{\varepsilon\text{-free}}$ contains s, so $M_{\varepsilon\text{-free}}$ accepts ε, too. If M makes a computation of the form $qa \vdash^* q'a \vdash p$, then $R_{\varepsilon\text{-free}}$ possesses $qa \mapsto p$, which simulates this computation in $M_{\varepsilon\text{-free}}$. Thus, $L(M) = L(M_{\varepsilon\text{-free}})$.

Before Lemma 3.2.2.4 formally verifies Algorithm 3.2.2.3, notice the relationship between this algorithm and Algorithm 3.2.2.1. Recall that for a finite automaton M

Models for regular languages

$= (Q, \Sigma, R, s, F)$ and a set of states $Q' \subseteq Q$, Algorithm 3.2.2.1 determines the set of states that M can reach from states in Q' without reading any input symbols. Observe that Algorithm 3.2.2.3 makes two determinations of this kind: first, it determines F' so $\{s\} \vDash^* F'$; second, Q_1 so $\{q\}\{a\} \vDash^* Q_1\{a\}$. Algorithm 3.2.2.1 thus provides a means for enabling Algorithm 3.2.2.3 to accomplish these determinations.

Lemma 3.2.2.4
Given a finite automaton $M = (Q, \Sigma, R, s, F)$, Algorithm 3.2.2.3 terminates and correctly constructs an ε-free finite automaton, $M_{\varepsilon\text{-free}} = (Q, \Sigma, R_{\varepsilon\text{-free}}, s, F_{\varepsilon\text{-free}})$, such that $L(M_{\varepsilon\text{-free}}) = L(M)$.

Proof
Termination
Because Q and Σ are finite sets, the **for** loop in the algorithm is repeated only a finite number of times, so this algorithm must terminate.

Correctness
$M_{\varepsilon\text{-free}}$ represents an ε-free finite automaton because $R_{\varepsilon\text{-free}}$ has no ε-rule. The identity

$$L(M_{\varepsilon\text{-free}}) = L(M)$$

is established by demonstrating that $M_{\varepsilon\text{-free}}$ accepts a word $w \in \Sigma^*$ if and only if M accepts w. First, the following claim for all non-empty words w is proved.

Claim
For all $w \in \Sigma^+$, $q \in Q$, and $Q' \subseteq Q$, the following equivalence holds:

$$\{q\}w \vDash^* Q' \text{ in } M_{\varepsilon\text{-free}} \text{ if and only if } \{q\}w \vDash^* Q' \text{ in } M.$$

Proof
Only if
By induction on $|w|$, prove that for all $w \in \Sigma^+$, $q \in Q$, and $Q' \subseteq Q$,

$$\{q\}w \vDash^* Q' \text{ in } M_{\varepsilon\text{-free}} \text{ implies } \{q\}w \vDash^* Q' \text{ in } M.$$

(The exercises proves this implication by induction on the length of computation in $M_{\varepsilon\text{-free}}$.)

Basis
Let $|w| = 1$, so $w = a$ and $\{q\}a \vDash^* Q'$ in $M_{\varepsilon\text{-free}}$. As $M_{\varepsilon\text{-free}}$ is an ε-free finite automaton, $\{q\}a \vDash^* Q'$ is actually a one-move computation; that is,

$$\{q\}a \vDash Q'$$

By the definition of $\vDash$, $Q' = \{p: qa \vdash p \in R_{\varepsilon\text{-free}}\}$. By the construction of $R_{\varepsilon\text{-free}}$, $qa \vdash p \in R_{\varepsilon\text{-free}}$ if and only if $\{q\}\{a\} \vDash^* Q_1\{a\} \vDash Q_2$ in M, where $Q_1, Q_2 \subseteq Q$ and $p \in Q_2$. Consequently, $Q' = Q_2$ and

$$\{q\}a \vDash^* Q'$$

in M. This concludes that the basis of the only-if part holds.

Induction hypothesis
Assume the only-if part of the claim holds for all $w \in \Sigma^+$ with $|w| \le n$, for some $n \ge 1$.

Induction step
Consider

$$\{q\}w \vDash^* Q'$$

in $M_{\varepsilon\text{-free}}$, where $|w| = n + 1$. Because $|w| \ge 1$, w can be expressed as $w = va$, where $a \in \Sigma$, and $\{q\}w \vDash^* Q'$ as

$$\{q\}va \vDash^* Q''\{a\} \vDash Q'$$

where $Q'' \subseteq Q$. As $|w| = n + 1$ and $a \in \Sigma$, then $|v| = n$. Because $\{q\}v \vDash^* Q''$ in $M_{\varepsilon\text{-free}}$,

$$\{q\}v \vDash^* Q''$$

in M by the inductive hypothesis. By the construction of $R_{\varepsilon\text{-free}}$, $q''a \vdash q' \in R_{\varepsilon\text{-free}}$ if and only if $\{q''\}\{a\} \vDash^* Q_1\{a\} \vDash Q_2$ in M where $Q_1, Q_2 \subseteq Q$ and $q' \in Q_2$. Consequently, $Q''\{a\} \vDash Q'$ in $M_{\varepsilon\text{-free}}$ implies

$$Q''\{a\} \vDash^* Q'$$

in M. Putting $\{q\}v \vDash^* Q''$ and $Q''\{a\} \vDash^* Q'$ together in M yields

$$\{q\}\{va\} \vDash^* Q''\{a\} \vDash Q'$$

in M. Because $va = w$,

$$\{q\}\{w\} \vDash^* Q'$$

in M. This concludes that the only-if part of the proof holds.

If
The 'if' part of the claim is left to the exercises.
It is therefore concluded that the claim holds.

□

Next, it is proved that

$$w \in L(M_{\varepsilon\text{-free}}) \text{ if and only if } w \in L(M)$$

by considering the two cases $w \in \Sigma^+$ and $w = \varepsilon$.

Case 1
Let $w = \Sigma^+$ and consider the claim for $q = s$. This gives

$$\{s\}w \vDash^* Q' \text{ in } M_{\varepsilon\text{-free}} \text{ if and only if } \{s\}w \vDash^* Q' \text{ in } M$$

where $Q' \subseteq Q$. In terms of $\vdash^*$,

$$sw \vdash^* q \text{ in } M_{\varepsilon\text{-free}} \text{ if and only if } sw \vdash^* q \text{ in } M$$

for all $q \in Q$. First assume (1.1 below) that $q \notin F_{\varepsilon\text{-free}} - F$; then assume (1.2) that $q \in F_{\varepsilon\text{-free}} - F$.

1.1 Let $q \notin F_{\varepsilon\text{-free}} - F$; then, $q \in F$ if and only if $q \in F_{\varepsilon\text{-free}}$, so that

$$w \in L(M_{\varepsilon\text{-free}}) \text{ if and only if } w \in L(M)$$

1.2 Let $q \in F_{\varepsilon\text{-free}} - F$, so $q = s$. From the claim,

$$sw \vdash^* s$$

in M. By the definition of $F_{\varepsilon\text{-free}}$,

$$s \in F_{\varepsilon\text{-free}} \text{ if and only if } s \vdash^* f \text{ in } M \text{ for some } f \in F$$

Thus,

$$sw \vdash^* s \text{ in } M_{\varepsilon\text{-free}} \text{ with } s \in F_{\varepsilon\text{-free}} \text{ if and only if } sw \vdash^* s \vdash^* f \text{ in } M$$

for some $f \in F$. Therefore,

$$w \in L(M_{\varepsilon\text{-free}}) \text{ if and only if } w \in L(M)$$

Case 2
Let $w = \varepsilon$; then, by the definition of $F_{\varepsilon\text{-free}}$,

$$s \in F_{\varepsilon\text{-free}} \text{ if and only if } \{s\} \vDash^* F' \text{ in } M \text{ and } F \cap F' \neq \varnothing$$

In terms of $\vdash^*$, this can be reformulated as

$$s \in F_{\varepsilon\text{-free}} \text{ if and only if } s \vdash^* f \text{ in } M \text{ for some } f \in F$$

Hence,

$$\varepsilon \in L(M_{\varepsilon\text{-free}}) \text{ if and only if } \varepsilon \in L(M)$$

Therefore, for all $w \in \Sigma^*$,

$$w \in L(M_{\varepsilon\text{-free}}) \text{ if and only if } w \in L(M)$$

Thus

$$L(M_{\varepsilon\text{-free}}) = L(M)$$

Therefore, the lemma holds. ∎

Corollary 3.2.2.5
Let L be a language. Then, $L = L(M)$ for a finite automaton M if and only if $L = L(M_{\varepsilon\text{-free}})$ for an ε-free finite automaton $M_{\varepsilon\text{-free}}$.

Proof
Only-if
This part follows from Algorithm 3.2.2.3 and Lemma 3.2.2.4.

If
Because every ε-free finite automaton is a special case of a finite automaton, the 'if' part of the corollary holds.

It is thus concluded that Corollary 3.2.2.5 is true. ∎

Example 3.2.2.1 Part 5 Application of Algorithm 3.2.2.3
Recall that the previous parts of this example investigated the finite automaton M

1: $sa \vdash s$
2: $s \vdash p$
3: $pb \vdash p$
4: $pb \vdash f$
5: $s \vdash q$
6: $qc \vdash q$
7: $qc \vdash f$
8: $fa \vdash f$

By Algorithm 3.2.2.3, this example converts M to an equivalent ε-free finite automaton,

Models for regular languages

$$M_{\varepsilon\text{-free}} = (Q, \Sigma, R_{\varepsilon\text{-free}}, s, F_{\varepsilon\text{-free}})$$

To determine $F_{\varepsilon\text{-free}}$, set $F_{\varepsilon\text{-free}}$ to $\{f\}$ and compute the **if** statement

if $\{s\} \vDash^* F'$ in M and $F \cap F' \neq \varnothing$ **then** $F_{\varepsilon\text{-free}} := F_{\varepsilon\text{-free}} \cup \{s\}$

Because $\{s\} \vDash^* \{p, q\}$ and $\{f\} \cap \{p, q\} = \varnothing$, the **if** statement does not change $F_{\varepsilon\text{-free}}$, so

$$F_{\varepsilon\text{-free}} = \{f\}$$

To determine $R_{\varepsilon\text{-free}}$, set $R_{\varepsilon\text{-free}}$ to $\varnothing$ and compute the **for** loop

for each $q \in Q$ and $a \in \Sigma$ **do**
$R_{\varepsilon\text{-free}} := R_{\varepsilon\text{-free}} \cup \{qa \vdash p: \{q\}\{a\} \vDash^* Q_1\{a\} \vDash Q_2$ in M
for some $Q_1, Q_2 \subseteq Q$ and $p \in Q_2\}$

Specifically, consider s and a in M. For this state and this input symbol add

$$sa \vdash s$$

to $R_{\varepsilon\text{-free}}$ because

$$\{s\}\{a\} \vDash^* \{s\}\{a\} \vDash \{s\} \text{ in } M$$

For s and b add

$$sb \vdash p$$

$$sb \vdash f$$

to $R_{\varepsilon\text{-free}}$ because

$$\{s\}\{b\} \vDash^* \{p\}\{b\} \vDash \{p, f\}$$

For s and c add

$$sc \vdash q$$

$$sc \vdash f$$

to $R_{\varepsilon\text{-free}}$. For state p and input b add

$$pb \vdash p$$

$$pb \vdash f$$

to $R_{\varepsilon\text{-free}}$. For state q and input c add

$$qc \vdash q$$
$$qc \vdash f$$

to $R_{\varepsilon\text{-free}}$. For f and a add

$$fa \vdash f$$

to $R_{\varepsilon\text{-free}}$. Observe that no other pair of a state and an input symbol results in including a new rule into $R_{\varepsilon\text{-free}}$. Labelling the new rules as r_1 through r_{10} yields $M_{\varepsilon\text{-free}}$ defined as

r_1: $sa \vdash s$
r_2: $sb \vdash p$
r_3: $sb \vdash f$
r_4: $pb \vdash p$
r_5: $pb \vdash f$
r_6: $sc \vdash q$
r_7: $sc \vdash f$
r_8: $qc \vdash q$
r_9: $qc \vdash f$
r_{10}: $fa \vdash f$

where s is the start state, and f is the final state (see Figure 3.2.2.1).

Notice that $M_{\varepsilon\text{-free}}$ can make a move from s to f either with b, according to r_3: $sb \vdash f$, or with c, according to r_7: $sc \vdash f$. For simplicity, instead of two separate edges, Figure 3.2.2.1 describes these two rules by a single edge (s, f), so it labels this edge with two inputs, b and c. Hereinafter, this simplified way is used to label the edge with all inputs on which the corresponding move can be made.

△

Implementation of ε-free finite automata

The remainder of this section describes an implementation of ε-free finite automata. Before this description, however, the behaviour of ε-free finite automata are compared with finite automata that allow ε-rules. Some additional notation is also introduced.

In general, a finite automaton M with ε-rules can make two different supermoves from the same superconfiguration X_1. Indeed, M can make one supermove with ε and another supermove with an input symbol. More formally, M computes

$$X_1 \vDash X_2 \text{ and } X_1 \vDash X_3 \text{ with } X_2 \neq X_3$$

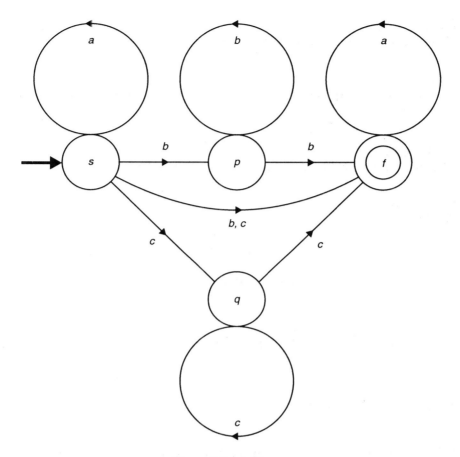

Figure 3.2.2.1 $M_{\varepsilon\text{-free}}$.

(For instance, the finite automaton discussed in Part 1 of Example 3.2.2.1 computes $\{s\}\{abba\} \vdash \{p, q\}\{abba\}$ and $\{s\}\{abba\} \vdash \{s\}\{bba\}$.) With a word having n symbols, M thus makes i different sequences of supermoves, for some $i \leq 2^n$. In contrast to a finite automata with ε-rules, an ε-free finite automaton makes a unique sequence of supermoves with any input word, as demonstrated below.

Lemma 3.2.2.6
Let $M = (Q, \Sigma, R, s, F)$ be an ε-free finite automaton, and let X_1 be a superconfiguration of M. Then, for all $i \geq 0$,

$$X_1 \vDash^i X_2 \text{ and } X_1 \vDash^i X_3 \text{ implies } X_2 = X_3$$

Proof
This lemma is proved by induction on $i \geq 0$.

Basis
Let $i = 0$. As $X_1 \models^0 X_2$ and $X_1 \models^0 X_3$, $X_1 = X_2 = X_3$. Thus, the basis of the lemma holds.

Induction hypothesis
Assume the lemma holds for all $i = 0, \ldots, n$, for some $n \geq 0$.

Induction step
Consider

$$X_1 \models^{n+1} X_2 \text{ and } X_1 \models^{n+1} X_3$$

As $n + 1 \geq 1$, we can express $X_1 \models^{n+1} X_2$ as

$$X_1 \models^n X'_2 \models X_2$$

Analogously, $X_1 \models^{n+1} X_3$ can be expressed as

$$X_1 \models^n X'_3 \models X_3$$

By the inductive hypothesis,

$$X'_2 = X'_3$$

Because M is ε-free, M reads a symbol, $a \in \Sigma$, during $X'_2 \models X_2$ and $X'_3 \models X_3$. Let $X'_2 = X'_3 = Q'\{ax\}$ with $x \in \Sigma^*$ and $Q' \subseteq Q$. By the definition of $\models$,

$$Q'\{ax\} \models Q''\{x\}$$

with $Q'' = \{ q'' : q' \in Q' \text{ and } q'a \vdash q'' \in R\}$, so $X_2 = X_3 = Q''\{x\}$. Therefore, the inductive step holds, and the lemma holds.
∎

Lemma 3.2.2.6 underlies the implementation of ε-free finite automata, given later in this section. This implementation also makes use of the following extended versions of logical connectives $\wedge$ and $\vee$, which denote *and* and *or*, respectively (see Section 0.4).

Consider the logical connective $\wedge$. Associating with each pair $\{0, 1\} \times \{0, 1\}$ a unique element $\{0, 1\}$, $\wedge$ can be seen as a bijection from $\{0, 1\} \times \{0, 1\}$ to $\{0, 1\}$. The following definition extends $\wedge$ by defining it from $\{0, 1\}^n \times \{0, 1\}^n$ to $\{0, 1\}^n$ for $n = 1, \ldots$.

Definition — extended *and*
Let $x = a_1...a_n$ and $y = b_1...b_n$ with $a_i, b_i \in \{0, 1\}$ for $i = 1, ..., n$, where $n \geq 1$. Then, $x \wedge y = (a_1 \wedge b_1)...(a_n \wedge b_n)$.

◆

For instance, if $x = 0011$ and $y = 0101$, then $0011 \wedge 0101 = (0 \wedge 0)(0 \wedge 1)(1 \wedge 0)(1 \wedge 1) = 0001$. By analogy with $\wedge$, the following definition extends $\vee$ by defining it from $\{0, 1\}^n \times \{0, 1\}^n$ to $\{0, 1\}^n$, for $n = 1, ...$.

Definition — extended *or*
Let $x = a_1...a_n$ and $y = b_1...b_n$ with $a_i, b_i \in \{0, 1\}$ for $i = 1, ..., n$, where $n \geq 1$. Then, $x \vee y = (a_1 \vee b_1)...(a_n \vee b_n)$.

◆

For $x = 0011$ and $y = 0101$, $0011 \vee 0101 = (0 \vee 0)(0 \vee 1)(1 \vee 0)(1 \vee 1) = 0111$.

The following implementation represents an ε-free finite automaton, $M = (Q, \Sigma, R, q_1, F)$, by its *binary state table t*. Let $\Sigma = \{a_1, ..., a_m\}$ and $Q = \{q_1, ..., q_n\}$, for some $m, n \geq 1$; at this point, t has m columns and n rows. The columns are denoted by a_1 through a_m so that the jth column corresponds to a_j. The rows are denoted by q_1 through q_n so that the ith row corresponds to q_i. The start state, q_1, denotes the first row, and the final states are indicated by underlining. Entries for t are specified by using the binary set representation 'BiRep', defined next.

Let $\Omega = \{a_1, ..., a_h\}$ be an h-member set, card$(\Omega) = h$, where $h \geq 1$. Then BiRep$_h$ is the bijection from Ω^h to $\{0, 1\}^h$ defined as

$$\text{BiRep}_h(Q') = b_h...b_1$$

where $Q' \subseteq Q^h$ and each $b_k \in \{0, 1\}$, for $k = h, ..., 1$, satisfies the equivalence

$$b_k = 1 \text{ if and only if } q_k \in Q'$$

Convention
Whenever h in BiRep$_h$ is understood, write BiRep instead of BiRep$_h$

●

By using BiRep$_n$, now define the entry $t(i, j)$, corresponding to q_i and a_j, for $i = 1, ..., n$ and $j = 1, ..., m$, as

$$t(i, j) = \text{BiRep}_n(Q')$$

where $Q' \subseteq Q$ so $\{q_i\}\{a\} \vDash Q'$; less formally, Q' contains the states that M can enter from q_i on a_j. From the definition of BiRep

$$t(i, j) = b_n...b_1$$

where $b_k \in \{0, 1\}, k = n, \ldots, 1$, so

$$b_k = 1 \text{ if and only if } q_i a_j \vdash q_k \in R$$

Figure 3.2.2.2 describes t pictorially.

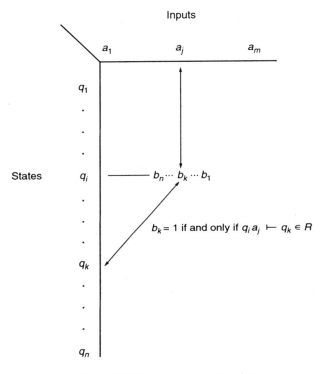

Figure 3.2.2.2 The binary state table of M.

Example 3.2.2.1 Part 6 Binary state table

Consider the ε-free finite automaton $M_{\varepsilon\text{-free}}$ obtained in Part 5 of this example. $M_{\varepsilon\text{-free}}$ has states s, p, q and f, where s and f are the start state and the final state, respectively. This automaton's input symbols are a, b and c. It contains ten rules:

r_1: $sa \vdash s$
r_2: $sb \vdash p$
r_3: $sb \vdash f$
r_4: $pb \vdash p$
r_5: $pb \vdash f$
r_6: $sc \vdash q$
r_7: $sc \vdash f$
r_8: $qc \vdash q$

r_9: $qc \vdash f$
r_{10}: $fa \vdash f$

Figure 3.2.2.3 presents the binary state table, t, representing $M_{\varepsilon\text{-free}}$.

		Inputs	
States	a	b	c
s	0001	1010	1100
p	0000	1010	0000
q	0000	0000	1100
f	1000	0000	0000

Figure 3.2.2.3 The binary state table t, representing $M_{\varepsilon\text{-free}}$.

Consider $t(1, 2) = 1010$, which represents $\{p, q\}$ as $\text{BiRep}(\{p, f\}) = 1010$; intuitively, $\{p, f\}$ is the set of states that $M_{\varepsilon\text{-free}}$ can enter from s, denoting row 1, on b, denoting column 2.

△

This section is now ready to describe the ε-free finite automaton implementation, which is theoretically based on Lemma 3.2.2.6. From this lemma, with an input word $w \in \Sigma^*$, an ε-free finite automaton $M = (Q, \Sigma, R, s, F)$, uniquely computes $\{s\}\{w\} \vdash^*$ Q' for some $Q' \subseteq Q$. If $Q' \cap F \neq \emptyset$, then $w \in L(M)$; otherwise, $w \notin L(G)$. The following implementation simulates $\{s\}\{w\} \vdash^* Q'$ and, then, tests whether $Q' \cap F \neq \emptyset$ to decide if $w \in L(M)$.

This implementation assumes that the end-of-input symbol # terminates a given input word, $w \in \Sigma^*$; in other words, the input has the form w#.

Algorithm 3.2.2.7: ε-Free finite automaton implementation

Input: An ε-free finite automaton, $M = (Q, \Sigma, R, q_1, F)$, where $Q = \{q_1, ...,q_n\}$, for some $n \geq 1$, and $\Sigma = \{a_1, ..., a_m\}$, for some $m \geq 1$, and w#, where w is an input word, $w \in \Sigma^*$.

Output: YES if $w \in L(M)$; NO if $w \notin L(M)$.

Method
type
  States = **array**[1..n] **of** 0..1;
  InputSymbols = 'a_1'...'a_n';
  BinaryStateTable = **array**[1..n, InputSymbols] **of** States;

var
  FinalStates, NewStates, CurrentStates: States;
  InputSymbol: InputSymbols;
  t: BinaryStateTable ;

begin
  Initialize t so it represents the binary state table of M;
  NewStates := $0^{n-1}1$ {NewStates Initialization};
  for k := n **downto** 1 **do**
    if q_k in F
    then FinalStates[n − k + 1] := 1
    else FinalStates[n − k + 1] := 0
    {FinalStates Initialization};

  read (InputSymbol);

  while InputSymbol ≠ '#' **do**
  begin
    CurrentStates := NewStates;
    NewStates := 0^n;
    for k := n **downto** 1 **do**
      if CurrentStates[n − k + 1] = 1
      then NewStates := NewStates ∨ t [n − k + 1, InputSymbol];
      read(InputSymbol)
  end;

  if FinalStates ∧ NewStates ≠ 0^n {determination of acceptance}
  then write('YES')
  else write('NO')
end.

Observe that for all $n \geq 0$, $\{q_1\}w \vdash^n Q'$ in M if and only if Algorithm 3.2.2.7 has NewStates = BiRep(Q') after the nth iteration of the **while** loop. When this algorithm reads the end-of-input symbol #, it exits from the **while** loop to test whether FinalStates ∧ NewStates ≠ 0^n. If FinalStates ∧ NewStates ≠ 0^n, Algorithm 3.2.2.6 writes YES because M can reach a final state after reading w and, thus, $w \in L(M)$. However, if FinalStates ∧ NewStates = 0, Algorithm 3.2.2.7 writes NO because there exists no final state that M can enter after reading w, so $w \notin L(M)$. The exercises formally verify that this algorithm works correctly by induction on the length of computation and the number of the **while** loop iterations.

Example 3.2.2.1 Part 7 Application of Algorithm 3.2.2.7

Apply Algorithm 3.2.2.7 to the automaton M and its binary state table (see Part 7 of this example). As M has four states ($s, p, q,$ and f), Algorithm 3.2.2.7 declares

$$\text{States} = \textbf{array}[1..4] \textbf{ of } 0..1$$

As M has three input symbols, $a, b,$ and c,

$$\text{InputSymbols} = \text{'}a\text{'}...\text{'}c\text{'}$$

Algorithm 3.2.2.7 initializes NewStates = 0001 and FinalStates = 1000. Consider *abba#* as the input of the algorithm. This input gives rise to the following four iterations of the while loop.

1. The first iteration begins with InputSymbol = a and computes

if CurrentStates[$n - k + 1$] = 1 **then** NewStates := NewStates $\vee$ $t[n - k + 1,$ InputSymbol]

for $k = 1$ because NewStates = 0001; that is, it sets

$$\text{NewStates} := 0000 \vee t[s, a]$$

where $t[s, a]$ = 0001. As a result, NewStates remains unchanged.

2. With InputSymbol = b, the second iteration sets NewStates = 1010 because $t[s, b]$ = 1010.

3. The third iteration begins with InputSymbol = b, the third symbol appearing in *abba*. As NewStates = 1010, this iteration performs the **if** statement for $k = 2$ and, then for $k = 4$. For $k = 2$, it computes NewStates := 0000 $\vee$ $t[p, b]$, where $t[p, b]$ = 1010 because p denotes row 2; as a result, NewStates = 1010. Then, for $k = 4$, it computes NewStates := 1010 $\vee$ $t[f, b]$, where $t[f, b]$ = 0000 because f denotes row 4; thus, NewStates = 1010.

4. The fourth iteration starts with InputSymbol = a. As NewStates = 1010, this iteration performs the **if** statement for $k = 2$, then 4. For $k = 2$, it sets NewStates := 0000 $\vee$ $t[p, a]$, where $t[p, a]$ = 0000, so NewStates = 0000. For $k = 4$, it sets NewStates := 0000 $\vee$ $t[f, a]$, where $t[f, a]$ = 1000, so NewStates = 1000. After these four iterations, # causes this algorithm to leave the **while** loop and test whether FinalStates $\wedge$ NewStates $\neq$ 0000. As FinalStates = 1000 and NewStates = 1000, this gives FinalStates $\wedge$ NewStates = 1000. Because 1000 $\neq$ 0000, Algorithm 3.2.2.6 writes **YES** to indicate that $abba \in L(M)$.

▲

From a practical point of view, Algorithm 3.2.2.7 performs operations over binary digits, so a programming language such as C, that elegantly handles bits represents an appropriate implementation language for this algorithm. However, Algorithm 3.2.2.7 can be adapted for a programming language such as Pascal, that supports set operations rather than bit operations. An algorithm adapted in this way represents ε-free finite automata by state tables, as introduced in the previous section, and performs set operations $\cup$ and $\cap$. Algorithm 3.2.2.8, which closes this section, represents an adaptation of this kind.

Algorithm 3.2.2.8: ϵ-Free finite automaton implementation based on set operations

Input: An ε-free finite automaton $M = (Q, \Sigma, R, q_1, F)$, where $Q = \{q_1, ..., q_n\}$, for some $n \geq 1$, $\Sigma = \{a_1, ..., a_m\}$, for some $m \geq 1$, and $w\#$, where w is an input word, $w \in \Sigma^*$.

Output: YES if $w \in L(M)$; NO if $w \notin L(M)$.

Method

type
    States = 'q_1'...'q_n';
    StateSet = **set of** States;
    StateTable = **array**[1..n, 1..m] **of** StateSet;
    InputSymbols = 'a_1'...'a_m';

var
    FinalStates, NewStates, CurrentStates: StateSet;
    InputSymbol: InputSymbols;
    t: StateTable;

begin
    Initialize t so it represents the state table of M;
    Initialize FinalStates to the states contained in F;
    NewStates := [q_1];

    read(InputSymbol);

    while InputSymbol $\neq$ '#' **do**
    begin
        CurrentStates := NewStates;
        NewStates := [];
        for $i := 1$ **to** n **do**
            if q_i **in** CurrentStates

```
        then NewStates := NewStates ∪ t['q_i', InputSymbol];
        read(InputSymbol)
    end;
    if (FinalStates * NewStates) ≠ []
    then write('YES')
    else write('NO')
end.
```

3.2.3 Determinism

In general, an ε-free finite automaton works nondeterministically: it can make several different moves from the same configuration. As a result, with the same input word, an ε-free finite automaton can make many different sequences of moves.

Example 3.2.3.1 Part 1 Nondeterminism
Reconsider the ε-free finite automaton $M_{\varepsilon\text{-free}}$, obtained in Part 6 of Example 3.2.2.1, and recall that $M_{\varepsilon\text{-free}}$ has these ten rules:

r_1: $sa \vdash s$
r_2: $sb \vdash p$
r_3: $sb \vdash f$
r_4: $pb \vdash p$
r_5: $pb \vdash f$
r_6: $sc \vdash q$
r_7: $sc \vdash f$
r_8: $qc \vdash q$
r_9: $qc \vdash f$
r_{10}: $fa \vdash f$

Observe that from the configuration $pbba$, $M_{\varepsilon\text{-free}}$ can make two different moves: $pbba \vdash pba$ [r_4] and $pbba \vdash fba$ [r_5]. Consequently, $M_{\varepsilon\text{-free}}$ works nondeterministically.
△

This section converts ε-free finite automata to equivalent deterministic finite automata, which make a unique move sequence with any input word.

Definition — deterministic finite automaton
Let $M = (Q, \Sigma, R, s, F)$ be an ε-free finite automaton such that for all $r, r' \in R$, $r \neq r'$ implies $\text{lhs}(r) \neq \text{lhs}(r')$. Then, M is a *deterministic finite automaton*.
◆

By the definition of a deterministic finite automaton $M = (Q, \Sigma, R, s, F)$, for each $q \in Q$ and each $a \in \Sigma$, qa forms the left-hand side of no more than one rule in R. Therefore, from the same configuration, M cannot make two different moves.

The following algorithm converts any ε-free finite automaton to an equivalent deterministic finite automaton.

Algorithm 3.2.3.1: Conversion of an ϵ-free finite automaton to an equivalent deterministic finite automaton — the subset method

Input: An ε-free finite automaton $M = (Q, \Sigma, R, s, F)$.

Output: A deterministic finite automaton $M_d = (Q_d, \Sigma, R_d, s_d, F_d)$, such that $L(M_d) = L(M)$.

Method

begin
  $Q_d := \{ \langle Q' \rangle : Q' \subseteq Q \}$;
  $s_d := \langle s \rangle$;
  $F_d := \{ \langle F' \rangle : \langle F' \rangle \in Q_d \text{ and } F' \cap F \neq \varnothing \}$;
  $R_d := \varnothing$;
  for each $\langle Q' \rangle \in Q_d$ and each $a \in \Sigma$ **do**
    begin
      determine Q'' such that $Q'\{a\} \vDash Q''$ in M;
      $R_d := R_d \cup \{\langle Q' \rangle a \vdash \langle Q'' \rangle\}$
    end
end.

In essence a supermove, $Q'\{a\} \vDash Q''$, in M is simulated by a rule of the form $\langle Q' \rangle a \vdash \langle Q'' \rangle$ in M_d. Therefore, with a word, $w \in \Sigma^*$, $Q_1\{w\} \vDash^* Q_2$ in M if and only if $\langle Q_1 \rangle w \vdash^* \langle Q_2 \rangle$ in M_d. As $\langle Q_2 \rangle \in F_d$ if and only if $Q_2 \cap F \neq \varnothing$, $L(M) = L(M_d)$. The following lemma demonstrates these observations in detail.

Lemma 3.2.3.2
Given a finite automaton $M = (Q, \Sigma, R, s, F)$, Algorithm 3.2.3.1 halts and correctly constructs a deterministic finite automaton, $M_d = (Q_d, \Sigma, R_d, s_d, F_d)$, such that $L(M_d) = L(M)$.

Proof

Termination
Because Q_d and Σ are finite, the **for** loop of Algorithm 3.2.3.1 iterates a finite number of times, so this algorithm surely terminates.

Correctness
First, this proof demonstrates that $M_d = (Q_d, \Sigma, R_d, s_d, F_d)$ is deterministic. Then, it proves that $L(M_d) = L(M)$.

Determinism

The input finite automaton $M = (Q, \Sigma, R, s, F)$ is ε-free. By Lemma 3.2.2.6, for any super-configuration, X_1, of M, $X_1 \vdash^i X_2$ and $X_1 \vdash^i X_3$ implies $X_2 = X_3$, for all $i \geq 0$. Hence, for any $Q' \subseteq Q$ and $a \in \Sigma$, $Q'\{a\} \vdash Q''$ in M for a unique Q'', where $Q'' \subseteq Q$; therefore, by the definition of R_d, $\langle Q' \rangle a \vdash \langle Q'' \rangle$ is the only rule of R_d that has $\langle Q' \rangle a$ on its left-hand side. That is, for all $r, r' \in R_d$, $r \neq r'$ implies $\text{lhs}(r) \neq \text{lhs}(r')$, so M_d is deterministic.

Equivalence

Leaving a detailed proof that $L(M_d) = L(M)$ to the exercises, this proof is only sketched here.

Let $x \in \Sigma^*$. By the definition of R_d, for all $i \geq 0$, this equivalence holds

$$\langle s \rangle x \vdash^i \langle Q' \rangle \text{ in } M_d \text{ if and only if } \{s\}\{x\} \vdash^i Q' \text{ in } M$$

where $Q' \subseteq Q$. By the definition of F_d, $Q' \cap F \neq \varnothing$ if and only if $\langle Q' \rangle \in F_d$. Therefore, for $i \geq 0$,

$$\langle s \rangle x \vdash^i \langle Q' \rangle \text{ in } M_d \text{ with } \langle Q' \rangle \in F_d$$

if and only if

$$sx \vdash^i Q' \text{ in } M \text{ with } Q' \cap F \neq \varnothing$$

In other words, M_d accepts x if and only if M accepts x. Hence,

$$L(M) = L(M_d)$$

Thus the lemma holds. ∎

Corollary 3.2.3.3

Let L be a language. Then, $L = L(M)$ for an ε-free finite automaton, M, if and only if $L(M_d)$ for a deterministic finite automaton M_d

Proof

Only-if
This part follows from Algorithm 3.2.3.1 and Lemma 3.2.3.2.

If
Because every deterministic finite automaton is a special case of an ε-free finite automaton, the 'if' part of this corollary holds.

Hence Corollary 3.2.3.3 is true. ∎

Convention

Returning to Algorithm 3.2.3.1, its output deterministic finite automaton, $M_d = $

$(Q_d, \Sigma, R_d, s_d, F_d)$, contains states of the form $\langle Q' \rangle$, where $Q' \subseteq Q$; therefore, if $Q' = \{q_1, ..., q_k\}$, $\langle Q' \rangle = \langle \{q_1, ..., q_k\} \rangle$. For brevity, the braces are dropped, so that $\langle q_1, ..., q_n \rangle$ is written instead of $\langle \{q_1, ..., q_k\} \rangle$.

●

Example 3.2.3.1 Part 2 Application of Algorithm 3.2.3.1

Consider the ε-free finite automaton $M_{\varepsilon\text{-free}}$ discussed in Part 1 of Example 3.2.3.1. By using Algorithm 3.2.3.1, the present part of this example converts $M_{\varepsilon\text{-free}}$ to a deterministic finite automaton $M_d = (Q_d, \Sigma, R_d, s_d, F_d)$ so that $L(M_{\varepsilon\text{-free}}) = L(M_d)$. By Algorithm 3.2.3.1

$$Q_d := \{\langle Q' \rangle : Q' \subseteq Q\}$$

where Q is the set of states in the input ε-free finite automaton. In this example, the input automaton $M_{\varepsilon\text{-free}}$ has the four states s, p, q and f, so that Q_d contains 16 states:

$\langle \rangle$
$\langle s \rangle$
$\langle p \rangle$
$\langle q \rangle$
$\langle f \rangle$
$\langle s, p \rangle$
$\langle s, q \rangle$
$\langle s, f \rangle$
$\langle p, q \rangle$
$\langle p, f \rangle$
$\langle q, f \rangle$
$\langle s, p, q \rangle$
$\langle s, p, f \rangle$
$\langle s, q, f \rangle$
$\langle p, q, f \rangle$
$\langle s, p, q, f \rangle$

The start state of M_d is defined by

$$s_d := \langle s \rangle$$

Algorithm 3.2.3.1 defines the set of final states in M_d as

$$F_d := \{\langle F' \rangle : \langle F' \rangle \in Q_d \text{ and } F' \cap F \neq \varnothing\}$$

where F is the set of final states in the input automaton. $M_{\varepsilon\text{-free}}$ contains a single final state f, so M_d has the final states

$\langle f \rangle$

$\langle s, f \rangle$

$\langle p, f \rangle$

$\langle q, f \rangle$

$\langle s, p, f \rangle$

$\langle s, q, f \rangle$

$\langle p, q, f \rangle$

$\langle s, p, q, f \rangle$

Algorithm 3.2.3.1 determines R_d by the **for** loop

for each $\langle Q' \rangle \in Q_d$ and each $a \in \Sigma$ **do**
   begin
      determine Q'' such that $Q'\{a\} \vDash Q''$ in M;
      $R_d := R_d \cup \{\langle Q' \rangle a \vdash \langle Q'' \rangle\}$
   end

Consider, for instance $\langle s, p, q, f \rangle$ and b; at this point, we add

$$\langle s, p, q, f \rangle b \vdash \langle p, f \rangle$$

to R_d because $\{s, p, q, f\}\{b\} \vDash \{p, f\}$ in $M_{\varepsilon\text{-free}}$. R_d contains these 48 rules:

$\langle \rangle a$	$\vdash \langle \rangle$	$\langle \rangle b$	$\vdash \langle \rangle$	$\langle \rangle c$	$\vdash \langle \rangle$		
$\langle s \rangle a$	$\vdash \langle s \rangle$	$\langle s \rangle b$	$\vdash \langle f \rangle$	$\langle s \rangle c$	$\vdash \langle f \rangle$		
$\langle p \rangle a$	$\vdash \langle \rangle$	$\langle p \rangle b$	$\vdash \langle p, f \rangle$	$\langle p \rangle c$	$\vdash \langle \rangle$		
$\langle q \rangle a$	$\vdash \langle \rangle$	$\langle q \rangle b$	$\vdash \langle \rangle$	$\langle q \rangle c$	$\vdash \langle q, f \rangle$		
$\langle f \rangle a$	$\vdash \langle f \rangle$	$\langle f \rangle b$	$\vdash \langle \rangle$	$\langle f \rangle c$	$\vdash \langle \rangle$		
$\langle s, p \rangle a$	$\vdash \langle s \rangle$	$\langle s, p \rangle b$	$\vdash \langle p, f \rangle$	$\langle s, p \rangle c$	$\vdash \langle f \rangle$		
$\langle s, q \rangle a$	$\vdash \langle s \rangle$	$\langle s, q \rangle b$	$\vdash \langle f \rangle$	$\langle s, q \rangle c$	$\vdash \langle q, f \rangle$		
$\langle s, f \rangle a$	$\vdash \langle s, f \rangle$	$\langle s, f \rangle b$	$\vdash \langle f \rangle$	$\langle s, f \rangle c$	$\vdash \langle f \rangle$		
$\langle s, f \rangle a$	$\vdash \langle s, f \rangle$	$\langle s, f \rangle b$	$\vdash \langle f \rangle$	$\langle s, f \rangle c$	$\vdash \langle f \rangle$		
$\langle p, q \rangle a$	$\vdash \langle \rangle$	$\langle p, q \rangle b$	$\vdash \langle p, f \rangle$	$\langle p, q \rangle c$	$\vdash \langle q, f \rangle$		
$\langle p, f \rangle a$	$\vdash \langle f \rangle$	$\langle p, f \rangle b$	$\vdash \langle p, f \rangle$	$\langle p, f \rangle c$	$\vdash \langle \rangle$		
$\langle q, f \rangle a$	$\vdash \langle f \rangle$	$\langle q, f \rangle b$	$\vdash \langle \rangle$	$\langle q, f \rangle c$	$\vdash \langle q, f \rangle$		
$\langle s, p, q \rangle a$	$\vdash \langle s, f \rangle$	$\langle s, p, q \rangle b$	$\vdash \langle p, f \rangle$	$\langle s, p, q \rangle c$	$\vdash \langle q, f \rangle$		
$\langle s, p, f \rangle a$	$\vdash \langle s, f \rangle$	$\langle s, p, f \rangle b$	$\vdash \langle p, f \rangle$	$\langle s, p, f \rangle c$	$\vdash \langle q, f \rangle$		
$\langle p, q, f \rangle a$	$\vdash \langle f \rangle$	$\langle p, q, f \rangle b$	$\vdash \langle p, f \rangle$	$\langle p, q, f \rangle c$	$\vdash \langle q, f \rangle$		
$\langle s, p, q, f \rangle a$	$\vdash \langle s, f \rangle$	$\langle s, p, q, f \rangle b$	$\vdash \langle p, f \rangle$	$\langle s, p, q, f \rangle c$	$\vdash \langle q, f \rangle$		

At this point, Algorithm 3.2.3.1 completes the construction of the deterministic finite automaton, M_d, from $M_{\varepsilon\text{-free}}$.

Consider, for instance, *abba*. With this word, M_d makes the following unique sequence of moves:

$$\langle s\rangle abba \quad \vdash \langle s\rangle bba \quad\quad [\langle s\rangle a \vdash \langle s\rangle]$$
$$\vdash \langle p,f\rangle ba \quad\quad [\langle s\rangle b \vdash \langle p,f\rangle]$$
$$\vdash \langle p,f\rangle a \quad\quad [\langle p,f\rangle b \vdash \langle p,f\rangle]$$
$$\vdash \langle f\rangle \quad\quad\quad [\langle p,f\rangle a \vdash \langle f\rangle]$$

▲

Consider Algorithm 3.2.3.1, which converts any ε-free finite automaton, $M = (Q, \Sigma, R, s, F)$, to an equivalent deterministic finite automaton $M_d = (Q_d, \Sigma, R_d, s_d, F_d)$. To obtain R_d, this algorithm iterates its **for** loop for each state in Q_d and each input symbol in Σ. Consequently, if M_d is represented by its state table, Algorithm 3.2.3.1 needs card(Q_d)card(Σ) iterations of this loop to complete this state table. Algorithm 3.2.3.4 speeds up this conversion, which constructs the state table of M_d from the binary state table of M (Section 3.2.2 gives the definition of the binary state table representing an ε-free finite automaton). This algorithm constructs each row of the state table for all input symbols in a single iteration step, so it needs card(Q_d) iterations to construct the whole table.

Algorithm 3.2.3.4 uses BiRep and the extended versions of $\wedge$ and $\vee$, introduced in the previous section. In addition, this algorithm also uses two new bijections, Binary and Decimal, defined next.

Let n be an integer. Then Binary_n is the bijection from $\{0, 1, \ldots, 2^n - 1\}$ to $\{x: x \in \{0, 1\}^*, |x| = n\}$ defined by the following equivalence:

$$\text{Binary}_n(i) = b_n\ldots b_1 \text{ if and only if } 2^{n-1}b_n + 2^{n-2}b_{n-1} + \ldots + 1b_1 = i$$

for all $i = 0, \ldots, 2^n - 1$. Decimal_n denotes the inverse of Binary_n. For instance, if $n = 2$, then, $\text{Binary}_2(0) = 00$, $\text{Binary}_2(1) = 01$, $\text{Binary}_2(2) = 10$, $\text{Binary}_2(3) = 11$, and $\text{Decimal}_2(00) = 0$, $\text{Decimal}_2(01) = 1$, $\text{Decimal}_2(10) = 2$, $\text{Decimal}_2(3) = 11$.

Convention

Drop the n in Binary_n and Decimal_n whenever no confusion exists; for instance, write $\text{Binary}(3) = 11$ and $\text{Decimal}(11) = 3$ instead of $\text{Binary}_2(3) = 11$ and $\text{Decimal}_2(11) = 3$, respectively.

●

Algorithm 3.2.3.4: Conversion of an ε-free finite automaton to an equivalent deterministic finite automaton — the binary method

Input: The binary state table, t_b, representing an ε-free finite automaton $M = (Q, \Sigma, R, q_1, F)$, where $Q = \{q_1, \ldots, q_n\}$, for some $n \geq 1$, and $\Sigma = \{a_1, \ldots, a_m\}$, for some $m \geq 1$.

Output: The $2^n \times m$ state table t representing a deterministic finite automaton, $M_d = (Q_d, \Sigma, R_d, s_d, F_d)$, such that $L(M) = L(M_d)$. $Q_d = \{$ Binary$(i): 0 \le i \le 2^n - 1\}$, and t's components are denoted in the following way:

1. for $i = 1, \ldots, 2^n - 1$, row i is denoted by Binary(i);
2. row 2^n is denoted by 0^n;
3. for $j = 1, \ldots, m$, column j is denoted by a_j;
4. for $i = 1, \ldots, 2^n - 1$, $t[i] = t[i, 1]t[i, 2]\ldots t[i, m]$; less formally, $t[i]$ denotes the binary word appearing at row i from column 1 to column m.

Method

begin
  $s_d := 0^{n-1}1$;
  $F_d := \{$Binary$(i) :$ Binary$(i) \in Q_d$ and Binary$(i) \wedge$ BiRep$(F) \ne 0^n\}$;
  for $i := 1$ **to** n **do**
    $t[2^{i-1}] := t_b[i]$ {the determination of all rows $t[j]$ where j is a power of two and $j < 2^n$};
  for $i := 1$ **to** $2^n - 1$ **do**
    if Binary$(i) = x1y$ with $x \in \{0\}^*$ and $y \in \{0,1\}^*\{1\}\{0,1\}^*$
    then $t[i] := t[$Decimal$(x10^{|y|})] \; \vee \; t[$Decimal $(x0y)]$ {the determination of all rows $t[k]$ where k is not a power of two};
  $t[2^n] := 0^{nm}$ {the determination of row $t[2^n]$}
end.

Observe that $t[i, j] =$ Binary(k) if and only if $Q'\{a_j\} \vDash^* Q''$ in M, where Binary$(i) =$ BiRep(Q') and Binary$(k) =$ BiRep(Q''). As a result, Binary$(i)a_j \vdash$ Binary(k) — the rule corresponding to $t[i, j]$ — simulates $Q'\{a_j\} \vDash Q''$ in M. Therefore, for $w \in \Sigma^*$, $Q_1\{w\} \vDash^* Q_2$ in M if and only if BiRep$(Q_1)w \vdash^*$ BiRep(Q_2) in M_d. As BiRep$(Q_2) \in F_d$ if and only if $Q_2 \cap F \ne \varnothing$ in M, $L(M) = L(M_d)$. The following lemma verifies these intuitive observations formally.

Lemma 3.2.3.5

Given a binary state table t_b representing an ε-free finite automaton M, Algorithm 3.2.3.4 halts and correctly constructs the state table representing a deterministic finite automaton $M_d = (Q_d, \Sigma, R_d, s_d, F_d)$, such that $L(M) = L(M_d)$.

Proof

Termination
Algorithm 3.2.3.4 halts because it repeats both **for** loops a finite number of times.

Correctness

Determinism
For every state BiRep(i) and every input a_j, R_d contains one rule — Binary$(i)a_j \vdash t[i, j]$. Therefore, M_d is deterministic.

Equivalence
Next, a proof that $L(M_d) = L(M)$ is sketched; a detailed proof of this equation is left to the exercises.

For all $i \geq 0$ and all $Q_1, Q_2 \subseteq Q$,

$$Q_1\{w\} \vDash^i Q_2 \text{ in } M \text{ if and only if } \text{BiRep}(Q_1)w \vdash^i \text{BiRep}(Q_2) \text{ in } M_d$$

Algorithm 3.2.3.4 sets $s_d = 0^{n-1}1$. Because $\text{BiRep}(\{q_1\}) = 0^{n-1}1$ and thus $\text{BiRep}(\{q_1\}) = s_d$, the previous equivalence implies

$$\{q_1\}\{w\} \vDash^* Q_2 \text{ in } M \text{ if and only if } s_d w \vdash^* \text{BiRep}(Q_2) \text{ in } M_d$$

Observe that $F \cap Q_2 \neq \varnothing$ if and only if $\text{BiRep}(Q_2) \wedge \text{BiRep}(F) \neq 0$. From the definition of F_d,

$$\{q_1\}\{w\} \vDash^* Q_2 \text{ in } M \text{ with } F \cap Q_2 \neq \varnothing$$

if and only if

$$s_d w \vdash^* \text{BiRep}(Q_2) \text{ in } M_d \text{ with } \text{BiRep}(Q_2) \text{ in } F_d$$

Consequently, M accepts x if and only if M_d accepts x, so

$$L(M) = L(M_d)$$

and the lemma holds.

∎

Example 3.2.3.1 Part 3 Application of Algorithm 3.2.3.4

Now return to Figure 3.2.2.3 which presents the binary state table t_b representing the ε-free finite automaton $M_{\varepsilon\text{-free}}$, discussed in the previous two parts of this example. Using Algorithm 3.2.3.4, this part of Example 3.2.3.1 demonstrates how to convert $M_{\varepsilon\text{-free}}$ to the state table t representing a deterministic finite automaton M_d satisfying $L(M_{\varepsilon\text{-free}}) = L(M_d)$. Because $M_{\varepsilon\text{-free}}$ has four states (s, p, q and f) and three inputs (a, b and c), t has 2^4 rows and three columns. M_d has 16 states — 0000, 0001, ..., 1111; states 0001 through 1111 denote t's rows 1 through 15, respectively, and state 0000 denotes row 16. Algorithm 3.2.3.4 defines 0001 as the start state of M_d. In general, this algorithm defines the set of final states F_d as

$$F_d := \{ \text{Binary}(i) : \text{Binary}(i) \in Q_d \text{ and } \text{Binary}(i) \wedge \text{BiRep}(F) \neq 0^n\}$$

The set of final states in $M_{\varepsilon\text{-free}}$ equals $\{f\}$, which denotes row 4 in t_b. As $\text{BiRep}(\{f\}) = 1000$, M_d has eight final states:

$$1000, 1001, 1010, 1011, 1100, 1101, 1110, 1111$$

Models for regular languages

Algorithm 3.2.3.4 computes

$$\text{for } i := 1 \text{ to } 4 \text{ do } t[2^{i-1}] := t_b[i]$$

so it defines these rows of t:

row $2^0 = 1$ (denoted by state 0001): 0001 1010 1100
row $2^1 = 2$ (denoted by state 0010): 0000 1010 0000
row $2^2 = 4$ (denoted by state 0100): 0000 0000 1100
row $2^3 = 8$ (denoted by state 1000): 1000 0000 0000

Then, Algorithm 3.2.3.3 computes

for $i := 1$ **to** $16 - 1$ **do**
  if Binary$(i) = x1y$ with $x \in \{0\}^*$ and $y \in \{0,1\}^*\{1\}\{0,1\}^*$
  then $t[i] = t[\text{Decimal}(x10^{|y|})] \vee t[\text{Decimal}(x0y)]$

In this loop, Algorithm 3.2.3.3 determines $t[i]$ for all $i \in (\{1, \ldots, 15\} - \{1, 2, 4, 8\})$. Consider, for instance, $i = 3$. Because Binary$(3) = 0011$,

$$t[3] = t[\text{Decimal }(0010)] \vee t[\text{Decimal}(0001)] = t[2] \vee t[1] =$$
$$0000\ 1010\ 0000 \vee 0001\ 1010\ 1100 = 0001\ 1010\ 1100$$

For $i = 5$, Binary$(5) = 0101$, so

$$t[5] = t[\text{Decimal}(0100)] \vee t[\text{Decimal}(0001)] = t[4] \vee t[1] =$$
$$0000\ 0000\ 1100 \vee 0000\ 1010\ 0000 = 0000\ 1010\ 1100$$

Figure 3.2.3.1 presents the complete state table t of the deterministic finite automaton M_d, satisfying $L(M_{\varepsilon\text{-free}}) = L(M_d)$.

By using Decimal, Figure 3.2.3.2 renames all the states of M_d so that the resulting equivalent deterministic finite automaton has states denoted by 0 through 15.

Consider the word *abba*. With this word, the deterministic finite automaton defined by the state table in Figure 3.2.3.2 makes the following unique sequence of four moves:

$$1abba \vdash 1bba \qquad [a \mapsto 1]$$
$$\vdash 10ba \qquad [1b \mapsto 10]$$
$$\vdash 10a \qquad [10b \mapsto 10]$$
$$\vdash 8 \qquad [10a \mapsto 8]$$

where 8 is a final state.

	a	b	c
0001	0001	1010	1100
0010	0000	1010	0000
0011	0001	1010	1100
0100	0000	1010	1100
0101	0001	1010	1100
0110	0000	1010	1100
0111	0001	1010	1100
<u>1000</u>	1000	0000	0000
<u>1001</u>	1001	1010	1100
<u>1010</u>	1000	1010	0000
<u>1011</u>	1001	1010	1100
<u>1100</u>	1000	0000	1100
<u>1101</u>	1001	1010	1100
<u>1110</u>	1000	1010	1100
<u>1111</u>	1001	1010	1100
0000	0000	0000	0000

Figure 3.2.3.1 The state table of M_d.

Models for regular languages

	a	b	c
1	1	10	12
2	0	10	0
3	1	10	12
4	0	0	12
5	1	10	12
6	0	10	12
7	1	10	12
<u>8</u>	8	0	0
<u>9</u>	9	10	12
<u>10</u>	8	10	0
<u>11</u>	9	10	12
<u>12</u>	8	0	12
<u>13</u>	9	10	12
<u>14</u>	8	10	12
<u>15</u>	9	10	12
0	0	0	0

Figure 3.2.3.2 The state table of M_d with states renamed 0 through 15.

3.2.4 Simplification

This section simplifies deterministic finite automata and makes them suitable for use in practice. It demonstrates that the resulting automata, called well-specified automata, are extremely easy to implement.

Accessibility

A deterministic finite automata M may have some inaccessible states, which M can never enter when making moves.

Definition — accessible state
Let $M = (Q, \Sigma, R, s, F)$ be a finite automaton. A state $q \in Q$ is *accessible* if there exists a word w in Σ^* such that $sw \vdash^* q$; otherwise, q is *inaccessible*.
◆

Example 3.2.4.1 Part 1 Inaccessible states
Consider the deterministic finite automaton defined by the state table in Figure 3.2.3.2. Its states 2, 3, 4, 5, 6, 7, 11, 13, 14, and 15 do not appear in this table, so no input word can take this automaton to any of these states. In other words, all these states are inaccessible.
△

Section 3.2.3 has presented Algorithm 3.2.3.4, which converts any ε-free finite automaton to an equivalent deterministic finite automaton in a very simple way. As illustrated by the previous example, however, the resulting deterministic finite automaton produced by Algorithm 3.2.3.4 may possess inaccessible states, which unnecessarily increase the size of this automaton. Therefore, this section modifies Algorithm 3.2.3.4 to the following algorithm, which converts any ε-free finite automaton to an equivalent deterministic finite automata without any inaccessible states.

Algorithm 3.2.4.1: Conversion of an ε-free finite automaton to an equivalent deterministic finite automaton without inaccessible states — the binary method

Input: The binary state table t_b representing an ε-free finite automaton $M = (Q, \Sigma, R, q_1, F)$, where $Q = \{q_1, ..., q_n\}$, for some $n \geq 1$, and $\Sigma = \{a_1, ..., a_m\}$, for some $m \geq 1$.

Output: The $i \times m$ state table t representing a deterministic finite automaton, $M_d = (Q_d, \Sigma, R_d, s_d, F_d)$, where t and M_d satisfy these three properties:

1. i is a natural number such that $i \leq 2^n$

2. $L(M) = L(M_d)$
3. $Q_d = \{1, ..., i\}$, where each state $j \in Q_d$ is accessible.

Method

begin
   Rows := $\varnothing$ {initially, t has no row};
   Entries := { $0^{n-1}1$ };

   $i := 0$;

   repeat
      if $b_n...b_1 \in$ Entries $-$ Rows
      then
      begin
         $i := i + 1$;
         Rows := Rows $\cup$ $\{b_n...b_1\}$;
         extend t by row $t[i]$ denoted with $b_n...b_1$;
         $t[i] := 0^{nm}$;
         for $k := n$ **downto** 1 **do**
            if $b_i = 1$ **then** $t[i] := t[i] \vee t_b[i]$;
         Entries := Entries $\cup$ { $t[i,j]: 1 \leq j \leq n$}
         {Entries contains all binary words appearing in t}
      end
   until Entries $-$ Rows = $\varnothing$;

   $Q_d := \{1, ..., i\}$ {states 1 through i correspond to the rows of the $i \times m$ state
           table, t};

   for $j := 1$ **to** i **do**
      if $b_n...b_1$ denotes $t[j]$
      then
      begin
         replace all appearances of $b_n...b_1$ with j in t;
         if $b_n...b_1 \wedge \text{BiRep}(F) \neq 0^n$ **then** $F_d := F_d + \{j\}$
      end {the replacement of t's binary entries with the corresponding states, and the
           determination of F_d}
end.

Algorithm 3.2.4.1 works by analogy with Algorithm 3.2.3.4 apart from the following two differences.

1. Algorithm 3.2.3.4 denotes t's entries in binary. Instead, Algorithm 3.2.4.1 denotes these entries with natural numbers. More precisely, Algorithm 3.2.4.1 uses binary words in t only during the execution of its **repeat** loop. Then, Algorithm 3.2.4.1

introduces i states, 1 through i, where i is the number of t's rows, and in its **for** loop, this algorithm substitutes these states for the corresponding binary words in t.
2. The first statement of Algorithm 3.2.3.4 introduces the 2^n states of M_d. Instead, Algorithm 3.2.4.1 introduces a new state only if M_d can enter this state; in this way, Algorithm 3.2.4.1 guarantees that each state in Q_d is accessible.

Lemma 3.2.4.2

Given the binary state table t_b representing an ε-free finite automaton M, Algorithm 3.2.4.1 halts and correctly constructs the state table t representing a deterministic finite automaton, $M_d = (Q_d, \Sigma, R_d, s_d, F_d)$, so that t and M_d satisfy the three properties described in the output of Algorithm 3.2.4.1.

Proof
This proof is left to the exercises. ∎

Example 3.2.4.1 Part 2 Application of Algorithm 3.2.4.1

Figure 3.2.2.3 describes the binary state table t_b representing the ε-free finite automaton $M_{\varepsilon\text{-free}}$ discussed in Example 3.2.3.1. This part of Example 3.2.4.1 uses Algorithm 3.2.4.1 to convert t_b to the state table t, representing a deterministic finite automaton M_d, so that $L(M_{\varepsilon\text{-free}}) = L(M_d)$ and, in addition, M_d has no inaccessible states.

Algorithm 3.2.4.1 sets Entries := $\{0^{n-1}1\}$ and then enters its **repeat** loop. Because Entries − Rows contains $0^{n-1}1$, this algorithm introduces $t[1]$, the first row of t, denotes $t[1]$ by 0001, and defines this row as

$$t[1] = 0001\ 1010\ 1100$$

As $t[1]$ has two new entries, 1010 and 1100, Algorithm 3.2.4.1 makes another two iterations of the **repeat** loop to introduce $t[2]$ and $t[3]$. It denotes $t[2]$ and $t[3]$ by 1010 and 1100, respectively, and determines their items as

$$t[2] = 1000\ 1010\ 0000$$

$$t[3] = 1000\ 0000\ 1100$$

To explain this determination, $t[2]$ equals 1000 1010 0000 because $t_b[4] \vee t_b[2] = 1000\ 0000\ 0000 \vee 0000\ 1010\ 0000 = 1000\ 1010\ 0000$, and $t[3] = 1000\ 0000\ 1100$ because $t_b[4] \vee t_b[3] = 1000\ 0000\ 0000 \vee 0000\ 0000\ 1100 = 1000\ 0000\ 1100$.

Because $t[2]$ and $t[3]$ contain two new items, 1000 and 0000, by another two iterations of the **repeat** loop, Algorithm 3.2.4.1 introduces $t[4]$ and $t[5]$ so it denotes $t[4]$ and $t[5]$ with 1000 and 0000, respectively, and defines them as

$$t[4] = 1000\ 0000\ 0000$$

$$t[5] = 0000\ 0000\ 0000$$

At this point, Entries − Rows = ∅, so the **repeat** loop exits with $i = 5$ and t as depicted in Figure 3.2.4.1.

	a	b	c
0001	0001	1010	1100
1010	1000	1010	0000
1100	1000	0000	1100
1000	1000	0000	0000
0000	0000	0000	0000

Figure 3.2.4.1 The binary-item state table resulting from the repeat loop.

As $i = 5$, Q_d has the five states 1, 2, 3, 4 and 5. In its **for** loop, Algorithm 3.2.4.1 renames 0001, 1010, 1100, 1000 and 0000 with 1, 2, 3, 4 and 5, respectively. Observe that f is the only final state of $M_{\varepsilon\text{-free}}$, and BiRep($\{f\}$) = 1000. Therefore, Algorithm 3.2.4.1 determines $F_d = \{2, 3, 4\}$ because states 2, 3 and 4 correspond to t's rows denoted by 1010, 1100 and 1000, respectively, and 1010 ∧ 1000 ≠ 1000, 1100 ∧ 1000 ≠ 1000, and 1000 ∧ 1000 ≠ 1000; however, states 1 and 5 are nonfinal because 1 and 5 correspond to t's rows denoted by 0001 and 0000, respectively, and 0001 ∧ 1000 = 0000 and 0000 ∧ 1000 ≠ 0000. Figure 3.2.4.2 depicts the resulting state table of M_d, and Figure 3.2.4.3 displays the state diagram of M_d.

	a	b	c
1	1	2	3
2	4	2	5
3	4	5	3
4	4	5	5
5	5	5	5

Figure 3.2.4.2 The state table of M_d.

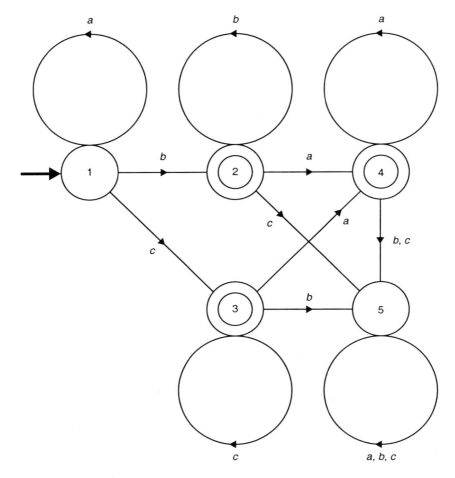

Figure 3.2.4.3 The state diagram of M_d.

With *abba*, M_d makes the following sequence of four moves:

$$\begin{array}{ll} 1abba \vdash 1bba & [\,1a \vdash 1\,] \\ \vdash 2ba & [\,1b \vdash 2\,] \\ \vdash 2a & [\,2b \vdash 2\,] \\ \vdash 4 & [\,2a \vdash 4\,] \end{array}$$

where 4 is final.

▲

Termination

A deterministic finite automaton M may have some states from which M cannot reach any final state, so M cannot accept any input word via these states.

Definition — terminating state
Let $M = (Q, \Sigma, R, s, F)$ be a deterministic finite automaton. A state $q \in Q$ is *terminating* if there exists a word $w \in \Sigma^*$ such that $qw \vdash^* f$ for some $f \in F$; otherwise, q is *nonterminating*.

◆

The following algorithm demonstrates how to remove nonterminating states from M.

Algorithm 3.2.4.3: Removal of nonterminating states from a deterministic finite automaton.

Input A deterministic finite automaton $M = (Q, \Sigma, R, s, F)$.

Output A deterministic finite automaton $M_t = (Q_t, \Sigma, R_t, s, F_t)$ such that $L(M_t) = L(M)$, and each state in Q_t is terminating.

Method

begin
    $Q_t := F$;
    repeat
        Old $:= Q_t$;
        $Q_t := Q_t \cup \{ q: qa \vdash p \in R \text{ where } a \in \Sigma \text{ and } p \in Q_t \}$
    until $Q_t - \text{Old} = \varnothing$;
    $R_t := R - \{ qa \vdash p : qa \vdash p \in R \text{ and } \{q,p\} \cap (Q - Q_t) \neq \varnothing \}$;
    $F_t := F$
end.

Algorithm 3.2.4.3 determines terminating states of M and places them into Q_t. As final states are always terminating, Algorithm 3.2.4.3 initializes Q_t to F. If Q_t contains a state p and if there exists a state q such that $qa \vdash p \in R$ for some $a \in \Sigma$, q is terminating, so the repeat loop adds q to Q_t. After the repeat loop moves all terminating states from Q to Q_t, this loop exits. Then, Algorithm 3.2.4.3 moves all rules containing terminating states from R to R_t. In addition, this algorithm sets F_t to F. At this point the algorithm obtains a deterministic finite automaton $M_t = (Q_t, \Sigma, R_t, s, F_t)$, so $L(M_t) = L(M)$, and each state in Q_t is terminating.

Lemma 3.2.4.4
Given a deterministic finite automaton $M = (Q, \Sigma, R, s, F)$, Algorithm 3.2.4.3 halts and correctly constructs a deterministic finite automaton $M_t = (Q_t, \Sigma, R_t, s, F_t)$ so $L(M_t) = L(M)$ and each state in Q_t is terminating.

Proof
This proof is left to the exercises.

■

Example 3.2.4.1 Part 3 Application of Algorithm 3.2.4.3
The previous part of this example has constructed the deterministic finite automaton M_d depicted in Figure 3.2.4.3. The present part of Example 3.2.4.1 uses Algorithm 3.2.4.3 to convert M_d to an equivalent deterministic finite automaton $M_t = (Q_t, \Sigma, R_t, s, F_t)$ without any nonterminating states.

Because M_d has three final states, 2, 3 and 4, the Algorithm initially sets

$$Q_t := \{2, 3, 4\}$$

Then, the **repeat** loop is entered, whose first iteration includes 1 into Q_t; as a result,

$$Q_t = \{1, 2, 3, 4\}$$

Because the second iteration adds no new state into Q_t, the repeat loop exits without 5 in Q_t, so 5 is a nonterminating state. Therefore, Algorithm 3.2.4.3 completes the construction of M_t by removing all rules containing 5 (Figure 3.2.4.4).

△

Completeness

A deterministic finite automaton M may lack rules for some states or input symbols; at this point M cannot complete reading some input words.

Definition — complete deterministic finite automaton
A deterministic finite automaton $M = (Q, \Sigma, R, s, F)$ is *complete* if $\{\text{lhs}(r): r \in R\} = Q\Sigma$; otherwise, M is *incomplete*.

◆

Example 3.2.4.1 Part 4 Incomplete deterministic finite automaton
Return to the deterministic finite automaton in Figure 3.2.4.4 and observe that this automaton can make no move from state 2 on c because none of this automaton's rules has $2c$ on the left-hand side. Besides, this automaton cannot move from 3 on b

Models for regular languages

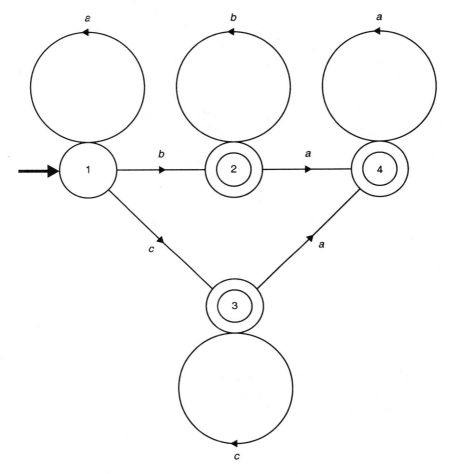

Figure 3.2.4.4 The state diagram of M_t.

or from 4 on b or c. Consequently, this automaton is incomplete. Consider bca as this automaton's input word. Having no rule with $2c$ on its left-hand side, this automaton cannot completely read this word. Indeed, after reading b, it enters state 2, from which this automaton cannot move on c.

△

Observe that if $M = (Q, \Sigma, R, s, F)$ is a complete deterministic finite automaton, then

$$\Sigma^* = \{w: w \in \Sigma^* \text{ and } sw \vdash^* q \text{ for some } q \in Q\}$$

Less formally, complete deterministic finite automata can read all symbols of every input word. Because of this advantage, most practical applications of finite automata use complete deterministic finite automata rather than their incomplete versions. The following algorithm provides practically oriented computer science with a simple method that converts any incomplete deterministic finite automaton into an equivalent complete deterministic finite automaton.

Algorithm 3.2.4.5: Conversion of an incomplete finite automaton to an equivalent complete deterministic finite automaton

Input: An incomplete deterministic finite automaton $M = (Q, \Sigma, R, s, F)$.

Output: A complete deterministic finite automaton $M_c = (Q_c, \Sigma, R_c, s, F)$ such that $L(M_c) = L(M)$.

Method

begin
$\quad Q_c := Q_c \cup \{q_{new}\}$ $\{q_{new}$ is a new state$\}$;
$\quad R_c := R_c \cup \{qa \vdash q_{new}: qa \in Q\Sigma - \{\text{lhs}(r): r \in R\}\}$
$\quad\quad \cup \{q_{new}a \vdash q_{new}: a \in \Sigma\}$
end.

Consider an incomplete deterministic pushdown automaton, M. Then, Algorithm 3.2.4.5 introduces a new state q_{new}. In addition, for each state q and each input a such that qa does not form the left-hand side of any rule in M, this algorithm defines a new rule of the form $qa \vdash q_{new}$. Moreover, for each input symbol a, it introduces a rule of the form $q_{new}a \vdash q_{new}$. The resulting automaton M_c represents a complete deterministic finite automaton satisfying $L(M_c) = L(M)$.

Lemma 3.2.4.6
Algorithm 3.2.4.5 halts and correctly converts an incomplete deterministic finite automaton M to a complete deterministic finite automaton M_c so $L(M_c) = L(M)$.

Proof
This proof is left to the exercises.

∎

Example 3.2.4.1 Part 5 Application of Algorithm 3.2.4.5
Reconsider the incomplete deterministic finite automaton discussed in the previous part of this example. Algorithm 3.2.4.5 converts this automaton to an equivalent complete deterministic finite automaton M_c. In fact, M_c produced by this algorithm coincides with the automaton in Figure 3.2.4.3, where 5 fulfills the role of q_{new}.

△

Well-specified finite automata

Consider a complete deterministic finite automaton. Observe that removing all its nonterminating states may make this automaton incomplete. To illustrate this, return to the complete deterministic finite automaton in Figure 3.2.4.3, remove its nonterminating state, 5, and notice that the resulting automaton is incomplete (Figure 3.2.4.4). However, this section next demonstrates how to convert any ε-free finite automaton to an equivalent complete deterministic finite automaton that has no inaccessible state and at most one nonterminating state.

Definition — well-specified finite automaton
Let $M = (Q, \Sigma, R, s, F)$ be a deterministic finite automaton satisfying these two properties:

1. Q has no inaccessible state;
2. Q has no more than one nonterminating state.

Then, M is a *well-specified* finite automaton.

◆

Algorithm 3.2.4.7: Conversion of a deterministic finite automaton to an equivalent well-specified finite automaton

Input: A deterministic finite automaton M.

Output: A well-specified finite automaton M_{ws}, such that $L(M_{ws}) = L(M)$.

Method

begin
    use Algorithm 3.2.4.1 to convert M to an equivalent deterministic finite automaton M_d without any inaccessible states;

    use Algorithm 3.2.4.3 to convert M_d to an equivalent deterministic finite automaton M_t without any nonterminating or inaccessible states;

    if M_t is complete
    then $M_t := M_{ws}$
    else Algorithm 3.2.4.5 converts M_t to an equivalent well-specified finite automaton M_{ws}
end.

Lemma 3.2.4.8
Algorithm 3.2.4.7 halts and correctly converts any ε-free finite automaton M to an equivalent well-specified finite automaton M_{ws}.

Proof
Termination
By Lemmas 3.2.4.2, 3.2.4.4 and 3.2.4.6, Algorithms 3.2.4.1, 3.2.4.3 and 3.2.4.5 halt, so Algorithm 3.2.4.7 halts, too.

Correctness
A proof that Algorithm 3.2.4.7 is correct is only sketched here; the complete proof is left to the exercises.

By Lemma 3.2.4.2, Algorithm 3.2.4.1 correctly converts M to an equivalent deterministic finite automaton M_d without any inaccessible states. By Lemma 3.2.4.4, Algorithm 3.2.4.3 correctly converts M_d to an equivalent deterministic finite automaton M_t without any nonterminating states. Because Algorithm 3.2.4.3 does not introduce any new states and because M_d is without any inaccessible states, M_t has only terminating and accessible states.

1. Assume M_t is complete; at this point M_t coincides with M. Because M_{ws} is a complete deterministic finite automaton that has only accessible and terminating states, M_{ws} is a well-specified finite automaton.

2. Assume M_t is incomplete; at this point Algorithm 3.2.4.5 converts M_t to an equivalent complete deterministic finite automaton M_{ws} and, by Lemma 3.2.4.6, this conversion is correct. Algorithm 3.2.4.5 introduces a new state q_{new}. Because this state is nonterminating, M_{ws} is a complete deterministic finite automaton that has no inaccessible state and one nonterminating state, q_{new}. Therefore, M_{ws} is a well-specified finite automaton.

In either case, M_{ws} represents a well-specified finite automaton. As M, M_d, M_t and M_{ws} are equivalent, $L(M) = L(M_{ws})$. Therefore, Lemma 3.2.4.8 holds. ∎

Corollary 3.2.4.9
Let L be a language. Then, $L = L(M)$ for a deterministic finite automaton M if and only if $L = L(M_{ws})$ for a well-specified finite automaton M_{ws}.

Proof
If
As every well-specified finite automaton is deterministic, the 'if' part of Corollary 3.2.4.9 holds.

Only-if
This part of the proof follows from Algorithm 3.2.4.7 and Lemma 3.2.4.8.

Therefore, Corollary 3.2.4.9 holds. ∎

Implementation

The remainder of this section demonstrates that well-specified finite automata are easy to use in practice. Specifically, it presents two algorithms that describe how to implement these automata. Both algorithms assume that a given input word w is followed by a special end-of-input symbol #.

Algorithm 3.2.4.10: Well-specified finite automaton implementation — the tabular method

Input: A well-specified finite automaton $M = (Q, \Sigma, R, q_1, F)$, where $Q = \{q_1, ..., q_n\}$ for some $n \geq 1$, $\Sigma = \{a_1, ..., a_m\}$ for some $m \geq 1$, and $w\#$, where w is an input word, $w \in \Sigma^*$.

Output: YES if $w \in L(M)$; NO if $w \notin L(M)$.

Method

type
   States = 1...n;
   InputSymbols = 'a_1' ...'a_m';
   Rules = **array**[States, InputSymbols] **of** States;
   StateSet = **set of** States;

var
   State:States;
   InputSymbol: InputSymbols;
   Rule: Rules;
   FinalStates: StateSet;

begin
   for $i := 1$ **to** n **do**
     for $j := 1$ **to** m **do**
       if $q_i a_j \vdash q_k$ **in** R **then** Rule[i, 'a_j'] := k {initializeRule according to R};

   for $i := 1$ **to** n **do**
     if q_i **in** F **then** FinalStates := FinalStates + [i]
     {Initialize FinalStates according to F};

```
State := 1;
read(InputSymbol);
while InputSymbol ≠ '#' do {the simulation of moves}
  begin
    State := Rule[State, InputSymbol];
    read(InputSymbol)
  end;

if State in FinalStates {Is the last state final?}
  then write('YES')
  else write('NO')
end.
```

In essence, a rule $q_i a_j \vdash q_k \in Q$ is represented by Rules$[i, 'a_j'] = k$. If State $= i$, InputSymbol $= a_j$, and Rules$[i, 'a_j'] = k$, the **while** loop of this algorithm sets State to k to simulate the application of $q_i a_j \vdash q_k$. When this loop reads #, it exits and the **if-then-else** statement tests whether State represents a final state. If so, this statement writes YES to indicate $w \in L(M)$; otherwise, it writes NO to indicate $w \notin L(M)$.

Example 3.2.4.1 Part 6 Application of Algorithm 3.2.4.10

Return to M_d in Figure 3.2.4.3. Observe that M_d represents a well-specified finite automaton. Based on Algorithm 3.2.4.10, the present part of this example builds a Pascal program simulating M_d. Instead of #, this program uses 'EOF' as its end-of-input symbol.

program FiniteAutomaton(*input, output*);

{This program simulates the well-specified finite automaton depicted in Figure 3.2.4.3. It reads an input word from file *input*. The input word is terminated with EOF. Input symbols out of range 'a' ... 'c' cause an error.}

```
type
  States = 1...5;
  InputSymbols = 'a' ...'c';
  Rules = array[States, InputSymbols] of States;
  StateSet = set of States;

var
  State: States;
  InputSymbol: InputSymbols;
  Rule: Rules;
  FinalStates: StateSet;
```

Models for regular languages

```
begin
    Rule[1, 'a'] := 1; Rule[1, 'b'] := 2; Rule[1, 'c'] := 3;
    Rule[2, 'a'] := 4; Rule[2, 'b'] := 2; Rule[2, 'c'] := 5;
    Rule[3, 'a'] := 4; Rule[3, 'b'] := 5; Rule[3, 'c'] := 3;
    Rule[4, 'a'] := 4; Rule[4, 'b'] := 5; Rule[4, 'c'] := 5;
    Rule[5, 'a'] := 5; Rule[5, 'b'] := 5; Rule[5, 'c'] := 5
    {Initialization of Rule};

    FinalStates := [2, 3, 4] {Initialization of FinalStates};

    State := 1;

    while not EOF do
        begin
            while not EOLN do {move simulation}
                begin
                    read(InputSymbol);
                    State := Rule[State, InputSymbol]
                end{while not EOLN};
            read(InputSymbol)
        end;


    if State in FinalStates {determination of acceptance}
        then writeln('YES')
        else writeln('NO')

end.
```

Suppose that this program simulates M_d working on $abba$EOF. At this point, the **while** loop iterates four times:

1. The first iteration begins with State = 1 and InputSymbol = a. Thus, it sets State := 1 because Rule[1, 'a'] = 1.
2. The second iteration has State = 1 and InputSymbol = b. At this point, State = 2 because Rule[1, 'b'] = 2.
3. The third iteration starts with State = 2 and InputSymbol = b, so it sets State := 2 because Rule[2, 'b'] = 2.
4. The fourth iteration begins with State = 2 and InputSymbol = a. Consequently, this iteration determines State = 4 by Rule[2, 'a'] = 4.

The next symbol is 'EOF', so the **while** loop exits and the **if-then-else** statement determines that State belongs to FinalStates because State = 4 and FinalStates = [2, 3, 4]. Therefore, this statement writes **YES** to specify that $abba \in L(M_d)$.

▲

Algorithm 3.2.4.10 represents the input well-specified finite automaton's rules by

$$\text{Rules} = \textbf{array}[\text{States, InputSymbols}] \textbf{ of States}$$

Observe that the following algorithm, which bases its implementation of a well-specified finite automaton upon a nested **case** statement, does not use any **array** declaration.

Algorithm 3.2.4.11: Well-specified finite automaton implementation — the case method

Input: A well-specified finite automaton $M = (Q, \Sigma, R, q_1, F)$, where $Q = \{q_1, ..., q_n\}$ for some $n \geq 1$, $\Sigma = \{a_1, ..., a_m\}$ for some $m \geq 1$, and $w\#$, where w is an input word, $w \in \Sigma^*$.

Output: YES if $w \in L(M)$; NO if $w \notin L(M)$.

Method

type
   States = 1...*n*;
   InputSymbols = 'a_1' ...'a_m';
   StateSet = **set of** States;

var
   State: States;
   InputSymbol: InputSymbols;
   FinalStates: StateSet;

begin

   for *i* := 1 **to** *n* **do**
     if q_i **in** *F* **then** FinalStates := FinalStates + [*i*]
       {Initialize FinalStates according to *F*};
   State := 1;
   read(InputSymbol);

   while InputSymbol <> '#' **do** {simulation of moves}
   begin
     case State **of**
       q_1: ...
         ⋮

```
    q_i: case InputSymbol of
        'a_1':...
        ⋮
        'a_j': State := q_k {if and only if q_i a_j ⊢ q_k ∈ R};
        ⋮
        'a_m':...
    end {case corresponding to q_i};
    ⋮
    q_n: ...
  end;
  read(InputSymbol)
end;

if State in FinalStates {determination of acceptance}
then write('YES')
else write('NO')

end.
```

To demonstrate a practical use of the implementation described by Algorithm 3.2.4.11, Section 3.3.1.2 designs a scanner based on this implementation.

3.2.5 Minimization

A well-specified finite automaton M may contain some redundant states, which can be merged together without any change of $L(M)$. By merging all these states in M, this section demonstrates how to minimize the size of M with respect to the number of M's states.

Definition — distinguishable states
Let $M = (Q, \Sigma, R, s, F)$ be a well-specified finite automaton, and let $p, q \in Q$ so $p \neq q$. If there exists a word $w \in \Sigma^*$, so that

$$pw \vdash^* p' \text{ and } qw \vdash^* q'$$

where $p', q' \in Q$ and $\text{card}(\{p', q'\} \cap F) = 1$, then w *distinguishes* p from q; at this point, p and q are *distinguishable*. If there exists no word that distinguishes p from q, p and q are *indistinguishable*. ◆

In other words, p is distinguishable from q if there exists a word $w \in \Sigma^*$, so $pw \vdash^* p'$, $qw \vdash^* q'$ and precisely one state in $\{p', q'\}$ is a final state. Observe that any final state, $p \in F$, and any nonfinal state, $q \in Q - F$, are distinguishable; indeed, ε distinguishes p from q.

Definition — minimum-state finite automaton

Let M be a well-specified finite automaton. Let M_{min} be a well-specified finite automaton satisfying these two properties:

1. M_{min} contains only distinguishable states;
2. $L(M) = L(M_{min})$.

Then, M_{min} is a *minimum-state finite automaton* equivalent to M.

♦

In terms of this definition, the following algorithm demonstrates how to construct M_{min} from M.·

Algorithm 3.2.5.1: Well-specified finite automaton minimization

Input: A well-specified finite automaton $M = (Q, \Sigma, R, s, F)$.

Output: A minimum-state finite automaton, $M_{min} = (Q_{min}, \Sigma, R_{min}, s_{min}, F_{min})$, that is equivalent to M.

Method

begin
    $Q_{min} := \{<Q - F>, <F>\}$;

    {splitting states in Q_{min}}
    while there exists a state, $<Q'> \in Q_{min}$, such that Q' contains a non-empty proper subset, $Q_1 \subset Q'$, so that for an input symbol, $a \in \Sigma$, $Q_1\{a\} \vDash Q_2$ in M, where $Q_2 \subseteq Q''$ and $<Q''> \in Q_{min}$, and $(Q' - Q_1)\{a\} \vDash Q_3$ in M, where $Q'' \cap Q_3 = \emptyset$ **do**
        $Q_{min} := (Q_{min} - \{<Q'>\}) \cup (\{<Q_1>, <Q' - Q_1>\}$;

    $R_{min} := \{ <Q_1>a \vdash <Q_2> : Q_1\{a\} \vDash Q_2$ in M and $<Q_1>, <Q_2> \in Q_{min}\}$;

    if $s \in Q'$ and $<Q'> \in Q_{min}$ **then** $s_{min} = <Q'>$;

    $F_{min} := \{ <Q'> : Q' \cap F \neq \emptyset$ and $<Q'> \in Q_{min}\}$;
end.

Because any final state and any nonfinal state are distinguishable, this algorithm initializes Q_{min} with two distinguishable states, $<F>$ and $<Q - F>$. Then, the **while** loop splits each state, $<Q'> \in Q_{min}$, satisfying the **while** loop conditions so it replaces $<Q'>$ with two new states, $<Q_1>$ and $<Q' - Q_1>$. When Q_{min} contains no state that can be split, the **repeat** loop exits; at this point, if $<Q'> \in Q_{min}$ and $p, q \in Q'$, then p and q are indistinguishable in M. Algorithm 3.2.5.1 then constructs R_{min} so that it contains $<Q_1>a \vdash <Q_2>$ if and only if $Q_1\{a\} \vDash Q_2$ in M and $<Q_1>, <Q_2>$ are in Q_{min}. Furthermore, this algorithm defines $s_{min} = <Q'>$, where $s \in Q'$ and $<Q'> \in Q_{min}$. Finally, it sets F_{min} to $\{ <Q'> : Q' \cap F \neq \emptyset$ and $<Q'> \in Q_{min}\}$. Observe that $L(M) = L(M_{min})$ and that Q_{min} contains only distinguishable states. In other words, M_{min} represents a minimum-state finite automaton equivalent to M.

Lemma 3.2.5.2

Algorithm 3.2.5.1 halts and correctly converts a well-specified finite automaton M to a minimum-state finite automaton, M_{min}, equivalent to M.

Proof
This proof is left to the exercises.

∎

Example 3.2.5.1 Part 1 Application of Algorithm 3.2.5.1

Figure 3.2.5.1 depicts a well-specified automaton M such that $L(M) = \{a\}^*\{b, c\}\{b\}^*\{a\}^*$.

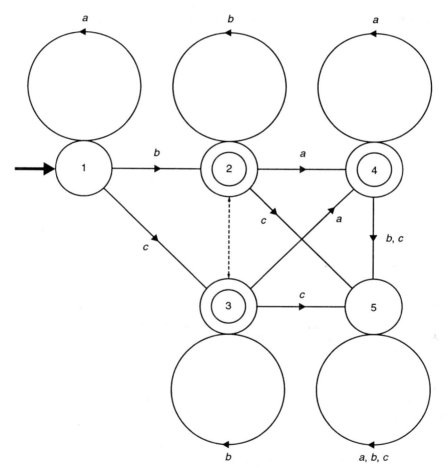

Figure 3.2.5.1 Well-specified finite automaton.

Algorithm 3.2.5.1 detects states 2 and 3 as indistinguishable, so it merges them together. As a result, this algorithm produces the minimum state finite automaton $M_{\min}$ displayed in Figure 3.2.5.2.

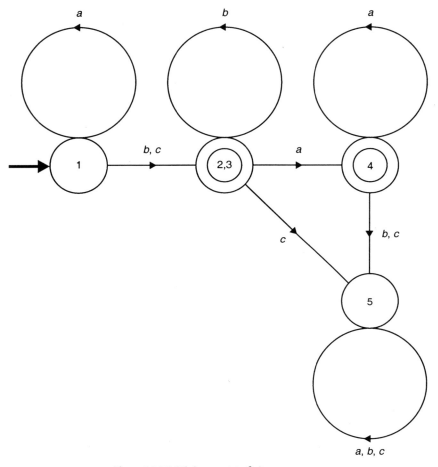

Figure 3.2.5.2 Minimum-state finite automaton.

Corollary 3.2.5.3
For any well-specified finite automaton, there exists a minimum-state finite automaton $M_{\min}$ equivalent to M.

Proof
This corollary follows from Algorithm 3.2.5.1 and Lemma 3.2.5.2. ∎

Algorithm 3.2.5.1 converts a well-specified finite automaton M to a minimum-state finite automaton, $M_{min} = (Q_{min}, \Sigma, R_{min}, s_{min}, F_{min})$, equivalent to M. As demonstrated in the exercises, M_{min} also satisfies a crucial property concerning the accepted language, $L(M)$: if $L(M') = L(M)$, where M' is a well-specified finite automaton, then M' contains at least card(Q_{min}) states. In other words, $L(M)$ cannot be accepted by any well-specified finite automaton with fewer than card(Q_{min}) states.

The exercises discusses some other algorithms that also minimize well-specified finite automata. Compared to Algorithm 3.2.5.1, these algorithm are more complex; however, they work more efficiently.

3.3 Finite automata and regular expressions

The following discussion demonstrates that the family of languages accepted by finite automata coincides with the family of regular languages. Section 3.3.1 converts regular expressions to equivalent finite automata; Section 3.3.2 transforms finite automata to equivalent regular expressions; finally, Section 3.3.3 states the equivalence of finite automata and regular expressions.

3.3.1 From regular expressions to finite automata

This section converts regular expressions to equivalent finite automata. More precisely, subsection 3.3.3.1 presents algorithms that accomplish this conversion. Then, subsection 3.3.3.2 demonstrates that these algorithms actually represent the fundamental methodology behind the construction of scanners used by compilers.

3.3.1.1 Conversion of regular expressions to finite automata

This section transforms regular expressions to equivalent finite automata. Recall that the regular expressions over an alphabet Σ and the languages that these expressions denote are defined as follows:

1. $\emptyset$ is a regular expression denoting the empty set;
2. ε is a regular expression denoting $\{\varepsilon\}$;
3. a, where $a \in \Sigma$, is a regular expression denoting $\{a\}$;
4. if r and s are regular expressions denoting the languages R and S, respectively, then
    A. $(r + s)$ is a regular expression denoting $R \cup S$;
    B. (rs) is a regular expression denoting RS;
    C. (r^*) is a regular expression denoting R^*.

For a regular expression r, the language that r denotes is symbolically referred to as $L(r)$. In terms of this notation, for any regular expression r the present section constructs a finite automaton M so $L(M) = L(r)$.

Empty set

Recall that $\emptyset$ is a regular expression denoting the empty set. The empty set is accepted by any finite automaton that has no final state. Figure 3.3.1.1 presents such a finite automaton, which has only one non-final state, s.

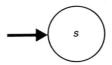

Figure 3.3.1.1 Finite automaton that accepts $L(\emptyset)$.

Lemma 3.3.1.1
There exists a finite automaton M such that $L(M) = L(\emptyset)$.

Proof
Let $M = (\{s\}, \Sigma, \emptyset, s, \emptyset)$ be a finite automaton (see Figure 3.3.1.1). Then, $L(M) = L(\emptyset)$.
∎

Empty word

Consider a finite automaton such that it has no rule and its start state is final. At this point, the language accepted by this automaton is $\{\varepsilon\}$. Figure 3.3.1.2 depicts a one-state finite automaton that accepts $\{\varepsilon\}$.

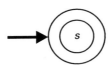

Figure 3.3.1.2 Finite automaton that accepts $L(\varepsilon)$.

Lemma 3.3.1.2
There exists a finite automaton M such that $L(M) = L(\varepsilon)$.

Proof
Let $M = (\{s\}, \Sigma, \emptyset, s, \{s\})$ be a finite automaton (see Figure 3.3.1.2). Then, $L(M) = L(\varepsilon)$.
∎

Symbol

Let Σ be an alphabet, and let a be a symbol, $a \in \Sigma$. Consider a finite automaton M with two states, s and f, where s is the start nonfinal state and f is the final state. M has only one rule, $sa \vdash f$ (see Figure 3.3.1.3). At this point, $L(M) = L(a)$.

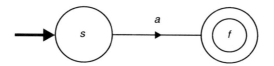

Figure 3.3.1.3 Finite automaton that accepts $L(a)$.

Lemma 3.3.1.3

Let Σ be an alphabet, and let a $\in \Sigma$. Then, there exists a finite automaton M such that $L(M) = L(a)$.

Proof

Let Σ be an alphabet, and let $a \in \Sigma$. Then, $M = (\{s, f\}, \Sigma, \{sa \vdash f\}, s, \{f\})$ is a finite automaton such that $L(M) = L(a)$.

∎

Union

Given two finite automata M_0 and M_1, the following algorithm constructs a finite automaton M satisfying $L(M) = L(M_1) \cup L(M_0)$.

Notice that this algorithm requires that M_0 and M_1 have disjoint sets of states. If M_0 and M_1 contain some states in common, we rename states in either of these automata to obtain two disjoint sets of states. In other words, this requirement is without any loss of generality.

Algorithm 3.3.1.4: Construction of a finite automaton for the union of two languages accepted by finite automata

Input: Two finite automata, $M_0 = (Q_0, \Sigma_0, R_0, s_0, F_0)$ and $M_1 = (Q_1, \Sigma_1, R_1, s_1, F_1)$, such that $Q_0 \cap Q_1 = \emptyset$.

Output: A finite automaton, $M = (Q, \Sigma, R, s, \{f\})$, where $\{s, f\} \cap (Q_1 \cup Q_0) \neq \emptyset$, such that $L(M) = L(M_0) \cup L(M_1)$.

Method

begin
    $Q := Q_0 \cup Q_1 \cup \{s, f\}$;
    $\Sigma := \Sigma_0 \cup \Sigma_1$;
    $R := R_0 \cup R_1 \cup \{s \vdash s_i : i = 0, 1\} \cup \{f_i \vdash f : f_i \in F_i, i = 0, 1\}$
end.

As Figure 3.3.1.4 indicates, Algorithm 3.3.1.4 constructs M consisting of M_0, M_1 and two new states, s and f, where s is M's start state, and f is its final state. From s,

M can make an ε-move to either of the two start states of M_0 and M_1. From any final state of M_0 or M_1, M can make an ε-move to f. Given a word, w,

$$sw \vdash s_iw \vdash^* f_i \vdash f \text{ in } M \text{ if and only if } s_iw \vdash^* f_i \text{ in } M_i$$

for some $i \in \{0, 1\}$ and $f_i \in F_i$, so

$$L(M) = L(M_0) \cup L(M_1)$$

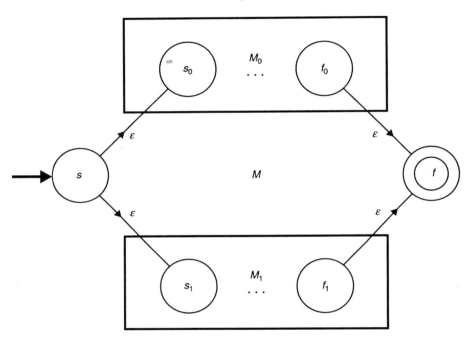

Figure 3.3.1.4 $L(M) = L(M_0) \cup L(M_1)$.

Lemma 3.3.1.5
Given two finite automata, $M_0 = (Q_0, \Sigma_0, R_0, s_0, F_0)$ and $M_1 = (Q_1, \Sigma_1, R_1, s_1, F_1)$, Algorithm 3.3.1.4 halts and correctly constructs a finite automaton, $M = (Q, \Sigma, R, s, \{f\})$, such that $L(M) = L(M_0) \cup L(M_1)$.

Proof
Termination
Clearly, this algorithm always terminates because the construction of Q, Σ and R involves only finite sets.

Correctness
To prove that $L(M) = L(M_0) \cup L(M_1)$, demonstrate that M accepts a word, $w \in \Sigma^*$, if

Models for regular languages

and only if M_i accepts w, for some $i \in \{0, 1\}$. First, the following claim needs to be established.

Claim
For every $w \in \Sigma^*$,

$$qw \vdash^* f_i \vdash f \text{ in } M \text{ if and only if } qw \vdash^* f_i \text{ in } M_i$$

where $q \in Q_i$ and $f_i \in F_i$, for some $i \in \{0, 1\}$.

Proof
Only if
By induction on j, this part of the proof demonstrates that for every $w \in \Sigma^*$,

$$qw \vdash^j f_i \vdash f \text{ in } M \text{ implies } qw \vdash^* f_i \text{ in } M_i$$

where $q \in Q_i$ and $f_i \in F_i$, for some $i \in \{0, 1\}$.

Basis
Let $j = 0$. That is, $qw \vdash^0 f_i \vdash f$ in M, where $i \in \{0, 1\}$ and $f_i \in F_i$. At this point, $q = f_i$ and $w = \varepsilon$. As $f_i \in F_i$ and $q = f_i$, $q \vdash^0 f_i$ in M_i with $q \in Q_i$, so the basis of the 'only if' part holds.

Induction hypothesis
Assume that the 'only if' part of the claim holds for all $j \leq n$, for some $n \geq 0$.

Induction step
Consider the computation

$$qw \vdash^{n+1} f_i$$
$$\vdash f$$

in M. Express this computation as

$$qw \vdash pv \;[qa \vdash p]$$
$$\vdash^n f_i$$
$$\vdash f$$

where $qa \vdash p \in R$ and $w = av$, for some $a \in \Sigma \cup \{\varepsilon\}$. Observe that $pv \vdash^n f_i \vdash f$ in M. By the inductive hypothesis,

$$pv \vdash^* f_i \text{ in } M_i$$

where $p \in Q_i$ and $f_i \in F_i$, for some $i \in \{0, 1\}$. As $Q_1 \cap Q_0 = \emptyset$, $q \in Q_i$, $qa \vdash p \in R_i - R_{1-i}$, and

$$qw \vdash pv \ [qa \vdash p]$$
$$\vdash^n f_i$$

in M_i. That is,

$$qw \vdash^* f_i$$

in M_i, where $q \in Q_i$ and $f_i \in F_i$. Therefore, the 'only if' part of the proof holds.

If
This part of the proof is left to the exercises.

Therefore the claim holds. □

Let $i \in \{0, 1\}$. Consider $w \in \Sigma_i^*$. Clearly,

$$w \in L(M_i) \text{ if and only if } s_i w \vdash^* f_i \text{ in } M_i$$

where $f_i \in F_i$. By the preceding claim for $q = s_i$,

$$s_i w \vdash^* f_i \text{ in } M_i \text{ if and only if } s_i w \vdash^* f_i \vdash f \text{ in } M$$

Obviously,

$$s_i w \vdash^* f_i \vdash f \text{ in } M \text{ if and only if } sw \vdash s_i w \vdash^* f_i \vdash f \text{ in } M$$

Every accepting computation in M has the form $sw \vdash s_i w \vdash^* f_i \vdash f$, so

$$sw \vdash s_i w \vdash^* f_i \vdash f \text{ in } M \text{ if and only if } w \in L(M)$$

These equivalences imply

$$w \in L(M_i) \text{ if and only if } w \in L(M)$$

where $i \in \{0, 1\}$. Consequently,

$$L(M) = L(M_0) \cup L(M_1)$$

Therefore the lemma holds.

∎

Models for regular languages

Corollary 3.3.1.6
Let $M_0 = (Q_0, \Sigma_0, R_0, s_0, F_0)$ be a finite automaton. Then, there exists a finite automaton, $M = (Q, \Sigma, R, s, \{f\})$, such that $L(M_0) = L(M)$ and M has only one final state, f.

Proof
Let $M_0 = (Q_0, \Sigma_0, R_0, s_0, F_0)$ be a finite automaton, and let $M_1 = (Q_1, \Sigma_1, R_1, s_1, F_1)$ be any finite automaton such that $L(M_1) = L(\emptyset)$ (see Lemma 3.3.1.1). Using Algorithm 3.3.1.4, convert M_0 and M_1 to a finite automaton, $M = (Q, \Sigma, R, s, \{f\})$, so $L(M) = L(M_1) \cup L(M_0)$ and M has only one final state, f. Because $L(M_1) \cup L(M_0) = L(\emptyset) \cup L(M_0) = L(M_0)$, $L(M) = L(M_0)$. Corollary 3.3.1.6 therefore holds.
∎

From this corollary, without any loss of generality, it is henceforth assumed that a finite automaton has only one final state. The next two algorithms make use of this assumption.

Concatenation

Given two finite automata M_0 and M_1 the following algorithm constructs a finite automaton M satisfying $L(M) = L(M_0)L(M_1)$.

Algorithm 3.3.1.7: Construction of a finite automaton for the concatenation of two languages accepted by finite automata

Input: Two finite automata, $M_0 = (Q_0, \Sigma_0, R_0, s_0, \{f_0\})$ and $M_1 = (Q_1, \Sigma_1, R_1, s_1, \{f_1\})$, such that $Q_1 \cap Q_0 = \emptyset$.

Output: A finite automaton, $M = (Q, \Sigma, R, s_0, \{f_1\})$, satisfying $L(M) = L(M_0)L(M_1)$.

Method

begin
$\quad Q := Q_0 \cup Q_1;$
$\quad \Sigma := \Sigma_0 \cup \Sigma_1;$
$\quad R := R_0 \cup R_1 \cup \{f_0 \vdash s_1\}$
end.

From Algorithm 3.3.1.7, M consists of M_0, M_1, and a new rule, $f_0 \vdash s_1$ (see Figure 3.3.1.5). M's start state equals s_0, and its final state is f_1. M accepts every word, $w \in \Sigma^*$, in the three following phases:

1. M simulates moves made by M_0 so this simulation ends up in f_0;
2. M makes an ε-move according to $f_0 \vdash s_1$;
3. M simulates moves made by M_1 so this simulation ends up in f_1.

This observation implies the following equivalence

$$w \in L(M)$$

if and only if

$$s_0 uv \vdash^* f_0 v$$
$$\vdash s_1 v \; [f_0 \vdash s_1]$$
$$\vdash^* f_1$$

in M, where $w = uv$, $u \in \Sigma_0^*$, and $v \in \Sigma_1^*$. Notice that

$$s_0 uv \vdash^* f_0 v$$
$$\vdash s_1 v \; [f_0 \vdash s_1]$$
$$\vdash^* f_1 \text{ in } M$$

if and only if

$$s_0 uv \vdash^* f_0 v \text{ in } M_0 \text{ and } s_1 v \vdash^* f_1 \text{ in } M_1$$

Furthermore,

$$s_0 uv \vdash^* f_0 v \text{ in } M_0 \text{ and } s_1 v \vdash^* f_1 \text{ in } M_1$$

if and only if

$$u \in L(M_0) \text{ and } v \in L(M_1)$$

These three equivalences imply

$$L(M) = \{ uv : u \in L(M_0) \text{ and } v \in L(M_1)\} = L(M_0)L(M_1)\}$$

Thus, this algorithm works correctly.

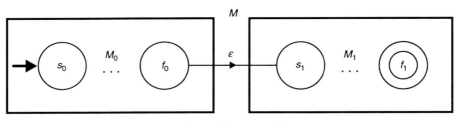

Figure 3.3.1.5 $L(M) = L(M_0)L(M_1)$.

Lemma 3.3.1.8

Given two finite automata, $M_0 = (Q_0, \Sigma_0, R_0, s_0, \{f_0\})$ and $M_1 = (Q_1, \Sigma_1, R_1, s_1, \{f_1\})$, Algorithm 3.3.1.7 halts and correctly constructs a finite automaton, $M = (Q, \Sigma, R, s, \{f\})$, such that $L(M) = L(M_0)L(M_1)$.

Proof
This proof is left to the exercises.

∎

Closure

Given a finite automaton M_0, the following algorithm constructs a finite automaton M satisfying $L(M) = L(M_0)^*$.

Algorithm 3.3.1.9: Construction of a finite automaton for the closure of the language accepted by a finite automaton

Input: A finite automaton, $M_0 = (Q_0, \Sigma_0, R_0, s_0, \{f_0\})$.

Output: A finite automaton, $M = (Q, \Sigma_0, R, s, \{f\})$, satisfying $L(M) = L(M_0)^*$.

Method

begin
  $Q := Q_0 \cup \{s, f\}$ $\{s, f \notin Q_0\}$;
  $R := R_0 \cup \{s \vdash s_0, s \vdash f, f_0 \vdash s_0, f_0 \vdash f\}$
end.

As Figure 3.3.1.6 depicts, Algorithm 3.3.1.9 constructs M consisting of M_0 and two new states, s and f, where s is the start state of M, and f is the final state of M. Besides R_0, M possesses four new rules: $s \vdash s_0, s \vdash f, f_0 \vdash s_0$ and $f_0 \vdash f$. Starting from s, M either enters f according to $s \vdash f$ and accepts ε, or M enters s_0 by using $s \vdash s_0$ to simulate a computation in M_0. Using $f_0 \vdash s_0$, M makes an ε-move from f_0 to s_0 to simulate another computation of M_0 from s_0 to f_0. By $f_0 \vdash f$, M enters f and halts. As a result, for any word $w \in \Sigma^*$

$$sw \vdash s_0w \vdash^* f_0 \vdash f \text{ in } M$$

if and only if

$$s_0 w_i \vdash^* f_0 \text{ in } M_0$$

where $i = 1, \ldots, n$, for some $n \geq 0$, and $w = w_1 \ldots w_n$. Consequently, $L(M) = L(M_0)^*$.

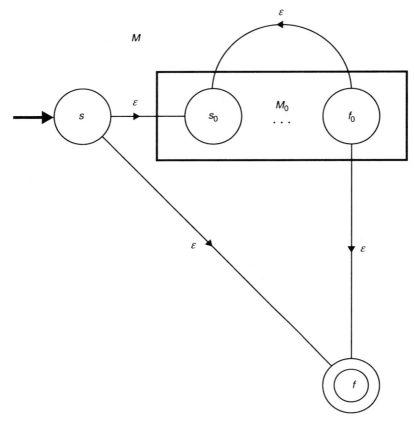

Figure 3.3.1.6 $L(M) = L(M_0)^*$.

Lemma 3.3.1.10
Let $M_0 = (Q_0, \Sigma_0, R_0, s_0, F_0)$ be a finite automaton on the input of Algorithm 3.3.1.9. Then, this algorithm halts and correctly constructs a finite automaton, $M = (Q, \Sigma_0, R, s_0, \{f\})$, satisfying $L(M) = L(M_0)^*$.

Proof
Termination

Because Q_0 and R_0 are finite, this algorithm surely terminates. *Correctness* To demonstrate that $L(M) = L(M_0)^*$, this proof first establishes the following claim.

Claim
For every $w \in \Sigma_0^*$,

$$s_0 w \vdash^* f_0$$
$$\vdash f \; [f_0 \vdash f] \text{ in } M$$

if and only if

there exist $n \geq 1$ and $w_1, \ldots, w_n \in \Sigma_0^*$ so

$w = w_1 \ldots w_n$ and $s_0 w_i \vdash^* f_0$ in M_0 for all $i = 1, \ldots, n$.

Proof
If
The 'if' part of this claim states that for all $n \geq 1$,

if $s_0 w_i \vdash^* f_0$ in M_0, $1 \leq i \leq n$, and $w = w_1 \ldots w_n$

then $s_0 w \vdash^* f_0 \vdash f [f_0 \vdash f]$ in M

This implication is proved by induction on n.

Basis
The basis of this inductive proof is left to the exercises.

Induction hypothesis
Assume that the 'if' part of the claim holds for all $n = 1, \ldots, m$, for some $m \geq 1$.

Induction step
Let

$s_0 w_i \vdash^* f_0$ in M_0, for $i = 1, \ldots, m+1$, and $w = w_1 \ldots w_m w_{m+1}$

Consider

$s_0 w_i \vdash^* f_0$ in M_0, $1 \leq i \leq m$, and $w' = w_1 \ldots w_m$

By the inductive hypothesis,

$s_0 w' \vdash^* f_0$
$\vdash f [f_0 \vdash f]$ in M

As $s_0 w_{m+1} \vdash^* f_0$ in M_0, $R_0 \subseteq R$, and $f_0 \vdash f \in R$, M also computes

$s_0 w_{m+1} \vdash^* f_0$
$\vdash f [f_0 \vdash f]$

Hence,

$$s_0w'w_{m+1} \vdash^* f_0 w_{m+1}$$
$$\vdash s_0 w_{m+1} \quad [f_0 \vdash s_0]$$
$$\vdash^* f_0$$
$$\vdash f \quad [f_0 \vdash f]$$

in M. As $w' = w_1...w_m$ and, thus, $w = w'w_{m+1}$,

$$s_0 w \vdash^* s_0$$
$$\vdash f \quad [s_0 \vdash f]$$

in M, so the if part of this proof holds.

Only if
This part of the proof is left to the exercises.

This concludes that the claim holds.

□

Let $w \in \Sigma_0^*$. Observe that M accepts w via a computation of the form

$$s_0 w \vdash^* f_0$$
$$\vdash f \quad [f_0 \vdash f]$$

More formally,

$$w \in L(M) \text{ if and only if } s_0 w \vdash^* f_0 \vdash f \ [f_0 \vdash f] \text{ in } M$$

By the previous claim,

$$s_0 w \vdash^* f_0 \vdash f \ [f_0 \vdash f] \text{ in } M$$

if and only if

$$s_0 w_i \vdash^* f_0 \text{ in } M_0 \text{ and } w = w_1 ... w_n$$

where $i = 1, ..., n$, for some $n \geq 1$. Obviously,

$$s_0 w_i \vdash^* f_0 \text{ in } M_0 \text{ if and only if } w_i \in L(M_0).$$

Consequently,

$$w \in L(M) \text{ if and only if } w = w_1 ... w_n \text{ with } w_i \in L(M_0)$$

where $i = 1, ..., n$, for some $n \geq 1$. Therefore,

$$L(M) - \{\varepsilon\} = L(M_0)^+$$

By using $s \vdash f$, M accepts ε, so $\varepsilon \in L(M)$. It is concluded that

$$L(M) = L(M_0)^*$$

Therefore, this lemma holds.

■

Conversion of regular expressions to equivalent finite automata

Algorithm 3.3.1.11, given next, transforms any regular expression to an equivalent finite automaton. More precisely, by using the previous five algorithms, this algorithm constructs partial finite automata, $M_1, M_2, \ldots$, which are equivalent to subexpressions of the input expression. By putting these partial automata together, it eventually obtains the resulting automaton equivalent to all the input expression.

Without any loss of generality, Algorithm 3.3.1.11 assumes that the input expression is fully parenthesized (see Section 3.1). This algorithm uses a special symbol, m_i, to denote the partial automaton M_i, for $i = 1, 2, \ldots$.

Algorithm 3.3.1.11: Conversion of any regular expression to an equivalent finite automaton

Input: A fully parenthesized regular expression E over an alphabet Σ.

Output: A finite automaton, $M = (Q, \Sigma, R, s, \{f\})$, satisfying $L(M) = L(E)$.

Method

begin
  $i := 0$;

  while the current expression contains a such that $a = \emptyset$ or $a = \varepsilon$ or $a \in \Sigma$ do
  begin
    $i := i + 1$;
    case a **of**
      $\emptyset$:   construct the finite automaton M_i such that
                $L(M_i) = L(\emptyset)$ by the proof of Lemma 3.3.1.1;
      ε: construct the finite automaton M_i such that
                $L(M_i) = L(\varepsilon)$ by the proof of Lemma 3.3.1.2;
      $a \in \Sigma$: construct the finite automaton M_i such that
                $L(M_i) = L(a)$ by the proof of Lemma 3.3.1.3;
    end;

    in the expression, replace a with m_i, where m_i denotes M_i
    {if this expression has the form $E_1 a E_2$, then this replacement produces the expression that has the form $E_1 m_i E_2$}
  end;

while the current expression has the form

$$E_1(E_2)E_3$$

where E_2 has one of these three forms

1. $E_2 = m_j + m_k$, for some $j, k = 1, \ldots, i$
2. $E_2 = m_j m_k$, for some $j, k = 1, \ldots, i$
3. $E_2 = m_j^*$, for some $j = 1, \ldots, i$

do
begin
  $i := i + 1$;
  case E_2 **of**
  $m_j + m_k$:   construct the finite automaton M_i such that
               $L(M_i) = L(M_j) \cup L(M_k)$ by Algorithm 3.3.1.4, where
               M_j and M_k are finite automata satisfying
               $L(M_j) = L(m_j)$ and $L(M_k) = L(m_k)$, respectively;
  $m_j m_k$:   construct the finite automaton M_i such that
               $L(M_i) = L(M_j)L(M_k)$ by Algorithm 3.3.1.7, where
               M_j and M_k are finite automata satisfying
               $L(M_j) = L(m_j)$ and $L(M_k) = L(m_k)$, respectively;
  m_j^*:   construct the finite automaton M_i such that
               $L(M_i) = L(M_j)^*$ by Algorithm 3.3.1.9, where
               M_j is a finite automaton satisfying $L(M_j) = L(m_j)$;
  end;
  in $E_1(E_2)E_3$, replace (E_2) with m_i, where m_i denotes M_i {this replacement produces the expression that has the form $E_1 m_i E_2$}
end;

the resulting automaton M_i is the output finite automaton M satisfying $L(M) = L(E)$
end.

The input to Algorithm 3.3.1.11 forms a fully parenthesized regular expression over an alphabet, Σ. Algorithm 3.3.1.11 uses an integer variable i to index the partial finite automata produced by the two **while** loops, which this algorithm contains.

*The first **while** loop*
Assume that the current expression has the form

$$E_1 a E_2$$

where $a = \emptyset$ or $a = \varepsilon$ or $a \in \Sigma$. At this point, an iteration of this loop produces a finite automaton M_i such that $L(M_i) = L(a)$ and, in addition, substitute m_i for a in $E_1 a E_2$, so the resulting expression has the form $E_1 m_i E_2$, where m_i denotes M_i. When, by iterating this loop, Algorithm 3.3.1.11 obtains an expression containing no $\varnothing$, ε, or a $\in \Sigma$, it leaves this loop for the second **while** loop.

The second **while** *loop*
Assume that the current expression has the form

$$E_1(E_2)E_3$$

where E_2 has one of these three forms

$$(m_j + m_k), (m_j m_k), \text{ or } (m_j^*)$$

Then, an iteration of the second **while** loop produces a finite automaton M_i equivalent to E_2 and, moreover, substitutes m_i for (E_2) in $E_1(E_2)E_3$. Each iteration of this loop thus removes a pair of parentheses from the expression. When this loop removes all parentheses and, therefore, exits, the algorithm has obtained the finite automaton, resulting from the last iteration of the second **while** loop, equivalent to all input expressions.

Notice that the second **while** loop takes advantage of the property that the input expression is fully parenthesized. Indeed, each iteration of this loop uses the parentheses appearing in the current expression to determine a subexpression that should be converted to an equivalent partial finite automaton. Consequently, the parentheses actually determine the order of these partial conversions.

Lemma 3.3.1.12
Let Σ be an alphabet, and let E be a fully parenthesized regular expression E such that $L(E) \subseteq \Sigma^*$. With E as its input, Algorithm 3.3.1.11 halts and correctly constructs a finite automaton, $M = (Q, \Sigma, R, s, \{f\})$, satisfying $L(M) = L(E)$.

Proof
Termination
This part of the proof is left to the exercises.

Correctness
The proof that $L(M) = L(E)$ is by induction on the number of operators ($+$, $\cdot$, and *) that appear in E.

Basis
Let E have zero operators. Then, $E = \varnothing$, $E = \varepsilon$, or E is a symbol of Σ. At this point, the algorithm enters only the first **while** loop, which constructs M_1 such that $L(M_1) = L(E)$. If $E = \varnothing$, this construction is made by the proof of Lemma 3.3.1.1. If $E = \varepsilon$, M_1 is constructed by the proof of Lemma 3.3.1.2. Finally, if E is a symbol of Σ, the construction of M_1 is made by the proof of Lemma 3.3.1.3. Before this algorithm halts, it sets $M = M_1$. Thus,

$$L(M) = L(M_1) = L(E)$$

It is concluded that the basis of this proof holds.

Induction hypothesis
Assume that the claim holds for all regular expressions containing no more than n operators, for some $n \geq 0$.

Induction step
Consider E having $n + 1$ operators. Because E is fully parenthesized, it can be expressed in one of the three forms

1. $E = (E_1 + E_2)$
2. $E = (E_1 E_2)$
3. $E = (E_1^*)$

where E_i has no more than n operators, $i = 1, 2$. 1.

Consider $E = (E_1 + E_2)$. By the inductive hypothesis, with E_1 on its input, Algorithm 3.3.1.11 constructs a finite automaton M' such that $L(M') = L(E_1)$ and, with E_2 on its input, this algorithm constructs a finite automaton M'' such that $L(M'') = L(E_2)$. Let E be on the input of Algorithm 3.3.1.11. Then, after n iterations of the second **while** loop, the expression has the form

$$(m_j + m_k)$$

where m_j denotes a finite automaton M_j such that $L(M') = L(M_j)$, and m_k denotes a finite automaton, M_k, satisfying $L(M'') = L(M_k)$, for some $j, k \geq 1$ such that $j \neq k$. Then, by using Algorithm 3.3.1.4, the next iteration produces a finite automaton M_i so

$$L(M_i) = L(M_j) \cup L(M_k)) = L(M') \cup L(M'') = L(E_1) \cup L(E_2) = L(E_1 + E_2) = L(E)$$

where $i = j + 1$ if $j > k$, and $i = k + 1$ if $k > j$. In addition, this iteration replaces $(m_j + m_k)$ with m_i; that is, an expression containing no operator. Thus, the second **while** loop exits, and Algorithm 3.3.1.11 sets $M = M_i$. Because $L(M) = L(M_i) = L(E)$, the resulting automaton M is equivalent to E.

2. Consider $E = (E_1 E_2)$. At this point, it can be verified that $L(M) = L(E)$ by analogy with the case when $E = (E_1 + E_2)$. This verification is left to the exercises.

3. Consider $E = (E_1^*)$. Then, it can be demonstrated that $L(M) = L(E)$ by a slight modification of the proof for $E = (E_1 + E_2)$. This demonstration is left to the exercises.

It is concluded that Lemma 3.3.1.12 holds. ■

Example 3.3.1.1 Application of Algorithm 3.3.1.11
Consider the fully parenthesized regular expression

$$(c((c + d)^*))$$

Models for regular languages

Assuming that c and d mean a letter and a digit, respectively, this expression denotes the language consisting of all Pascal identifiers, defined as arbitrarily long alphanumeric words that begin with a letter.

Algorithm 3.3.1.11 will convert $(c((c + d)^*))$ to an equivalent finite automaton.

The first while loop
In general, each iteration of the first **while** loop selects a in the current expression so $a = \emptyset$ or $a = \varepsilon$ or $a \in \Sigma$. In this example selection is indicated by underlining. Let the first iteration of the first **while** loop select the second appearance of c in $(c((c + d)^*))$; that is,

$$(c((\underline{c} + d)^*))$$

Then, from the proof of Lemma 3.3.1.3, this loop produces a finite automaton M_1, so $L(M_1) = \{c\}$ (Figure 3.3.1.7).

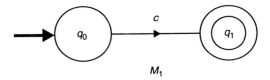

Figure 3.3.1.7 $L(M_1) = \{c\}$.

In addition, this loop changes $(c((\underline{c} + d)^*))$ to $(c((m_1 + d)^*))$ by substituting m_1 for the underlined c. The second iteration of this loop makes the selection

$$(c((m_1 + \underline{d})^*))$$

From the proof of Lemma 3.3.1.3, this loop constructs M_2 that accepts $\{d\}$ (Figure 3.3.1.8).

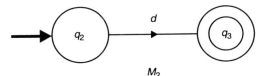

Figure 3.3.1.8 $L(M_2) = \{d\}$.

By replacing d with m_2, this loop changes $(c((m_1 + \underline{d})^*))$ to $(c((m_1 + m_2)^*))$. The third iteration selects the remaining c; that is,

$$(\underline{c}((m_1 + m_2)^*))$$

At this point, this iteration produces a new finite automaton M_3 so $L(M_3) = \{c\}$ (Figure 3.3.1.9).

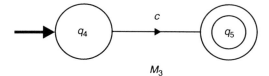

Figure 3.3.1.9 $L(M_3) = \{c\}$.

By rewriting c with m_2, this iteration yields $(m_3((m_1 + m_2)^*))$ as the current expression. As $(m_3((m_1 + m_2)^*))$ contains no $\emptyset, \varepsilon, c$ or d, the first **while** loop exits.

The second **while** *loop*
Each iteration of the second while loop selects a subexpresion of the form $(m_1 + m_2)$, $(m_1 \cdot m_2)$ or (m_1^*); as for the first **while** loop, selection is indicated by underlining. The first iteration of this loop makes the following selection

$$(m_3(\underline{(m_1 + m_2)^*}))$$

From Algorithm 3.3.1.4, this iteration produces a finite automaton M_4 that accepts $L(M_1) \cup L(M_2)$ (Figure 3.3.1.10).

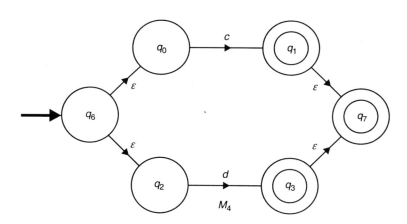

Figure 3.3.1.10 $L(M_4) = L(M_1) \cup L(M_2)$.

The first iteration of the second **while** loop also changes $(m_3((\underline{m_1 + m_2})^*))$ to $(m_3(m_4^*))$ by substituting m_4 for $(m_1 + m_2)$. The second iteration of this loop makes the selection

$$(m_3(\underline{m_4^*}))$$

Models for regular languages

and, by using Algorithm 3.3.1.7, constructs a finite automaton M_5 that accepts $L(M_4)^*$ (Figure 3.3.1.11).

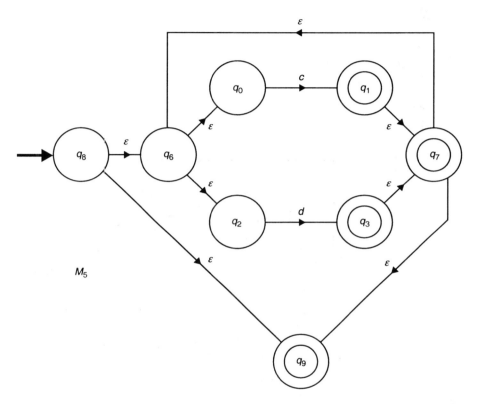

Figure 3.3.1.11 $L(M_5) = L(M_4)^*$.

This iteration also changes $(m_3(m_4^*))$ to $(m_3 m_5)$ by substituting m_5 for $(\underline{m_4^*})$. The third iteration selects

$$(\underline{m_3 m_5})$$

From Algorithm 3.3.1.9, this iteration produces a finite automaton M_6 that accepts $L(M_3)L(M_5)$ (Figure 3.3.1.12).

After the third iteration of the second **while** loop changes $(\underline{m_3 m_5})$ to m_6 this loop exits, so M_6 is the resulting automaton equivalent to the input expression $(c((c+d)^*))$.

To simplify M_6, the algorithms given in Section 3.2 are used to obtain the minimum-state finite automaton equivalent to M_6 (Figure 3.3.1.13).

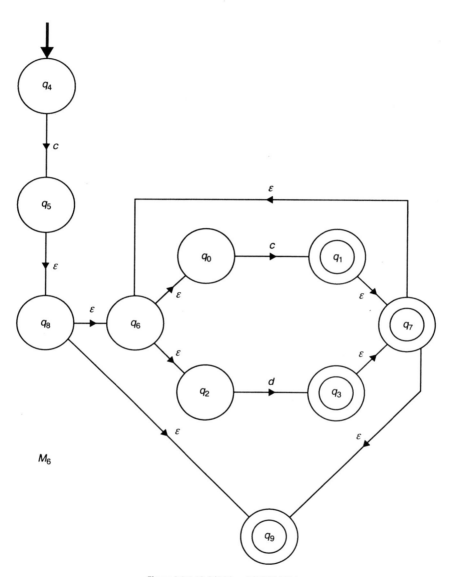

Figure 3.3.1.12 $L(M_6) = L(M_3)L(M_5)$.

Models for regular languages

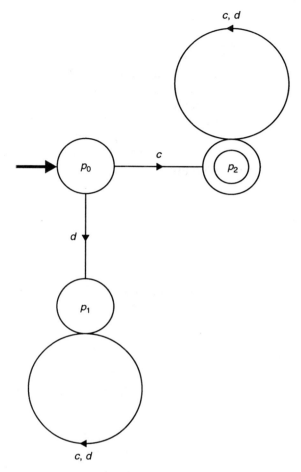

Figure 3.3.1.13 The minimum-state finite automaton equivalent to M_6.

When demonstrating the equivalence of finite automata and regular expressions, Section 3.3.3 makes use of the following crucial result of this section.

Corollary 3.3.1.13
Let L be a language. If $L = L(E)$, where E is a regular expression, then $L = L(M)$, where M is a finite automaton.

Proof
This statement follows from Algorithm 3.3.1.11 and Lemma 3.3.1.12.

3.3.1.2 Scanning

The previous section explains how to construct a finite automaton for any regular language, defined by a regular expression. In addition to its significant theoretical consequences (see Corollary 3.3.1.13, Theorem 3.3.3.1 and Theorem 3.3.3.2), this construction has important practical applications, including the design of scanners for compilers, the topic of the present section.

Given a program written in a high-level programming language, the main task of a scanner is to partition this program into the programming language lexemes — that is, logically cohesive lexical entities, such as identifiers or integers. To illustrate this, consider the following Pascal program:

program example(output);

begin
   writeln('SCANNING')
end.

A Pascal scanner divides this program into lexemes, listed together with the corresponding lexeme types in the following table.

Lexeme	Lexeme type
program	reserved word
example	identifier
(	left parenthesis
output	reserved word
)	right parenthesis
;	semicolon
begin	reserved word
writeln	reserved word
(	left parenthesis
'SCANNING'	text literal
)	right parenthesis
end	reserved word
.	period

Regular languages specify lexemes in an elegant and succinct way. Finite automata, in turn, define all regular languages. As a result, these automata, which are easy to implement, underlie most programming language scanners in reality. To demonstrate how to build up a real scanner, the rest of this section constructs a scanner for COLA, the programming language designed in Section 1.2.3.

COLA lexemes defined by regular languages

First, COLA lexemes are recalled, as represented by regular languages (Section 1.2.3 defined these lexemes by regular expressions).

Identifiers

$$XY^*$$

where X is the set of all letters, and Y is the set of all letters and digits.

Integers

$$X^+$$

where X is the set of all digits.

Labels

$$\{@\}X^+$$

where X is the set of all letters and digits.

Text literals

$$\{'\}X^*\{'\}$$

where X is the set of all symbols except ' or ".

New-line text literals

$$\{"\}X^*\{"\}$$

where X is the set of all symbols except ' or ".

Arithmetic operators

$$\{+, -, *, /\}$$

Relational operators

$$\{=, >, <\}$$

Parentheses

$$\{(,)\}$$

Separators

$$\{,\} \cup \{;\}$$

Assignment operator

$$\{:=\}$$

Reserved words

$$\{\text{begin, end, goto, if, read, write}\}$$

The following table classifies these COLA lexemes into 24 lexeme types and denotes each of these types by an integer:

	Lexeme type
1	Identifier
2	Integer
3	Label
4	Text literal
5	New-line text literal
6	+
7	−
8	*
9	/
10	=
11	>
12	<
13	(
14	)
15	,
16	;
17	:=
18	begin
19	end
20	goto
21	if
22	read
23	write
24	error

Type 24 indicates that the scanned word represents no validly formed COLA lexeme; in other words, the type-24 lexeme acts as a lexical error indicator.

Models for regular languages

Consider the following COLA program, whose purpose is to determine the factorial of a natural number, n:

```
begin
  read(n);
  write(" resulting factorial ", n, '! = ');
  factorial := 1;
  @iteration;
    if n = 0 goto @stop;
    factorial := factorial*n;
    n := n - 1;
  goto @iteration;
  @stop;
  write(factorial)
end
```

The following table presents the lexemes appearing in this program, together with their corresponding lexeme types:

Lexeme	Lexeme type
begin	18
read	22
(	13
n	1
)	14
;	16
write	23
(	13
"resulting factorial"	5
,	15
n	1
,	15
'! = '	4
)	14
;	16
factorial	1
:=	17
1	2
;	16
@iteration	3
;	16
if	21
n	1
=	10

0	2
goto	20
@stop	3
;	16
factorial	1
:=	17
factorial	1
*	8
n	1
;	16
n	1
:=	17
n	1
−	7
1	2
;	16
goto	20
@iteration	3
;	16
@stop	3
;	16
write	23
(	13
factorial	1
)	14
end	19

COLA scanner scheme

A COLA scanner is now constructed that recognizes the next lexeme occurring in the input COLA program and, moreover, indicates the type of this lexeme. Consequently, by repeatedly calling this scanner, the program can be partitioned into its lexemes and their types.

The COLA scanner contains 18 finite automata, being $M_1, ..., M_{17}$, and M_{24} (Figure 3.3.1.2.1). M_1 accepts lexemes of type 1 and, in addition, lexemes of types 18 through 23. Concerning M_2 through M_{17}, M_j accepts lexemes of type j (where $j = 2, ..., 17$). Finally, M_{24}, which corresponds to type-24 lexemes, indicates that the scanned word represents no COLA lexeme. Because each lexeme type begins with a symbol different from the first symbol of any other lexeme type, the scanner uses the first nonblank symbol appearing in the input COLA program to determine which of the 18 automata the scanner should call to read the next lexeme. For instance, if the next non-blank symbol is a digit, the scanner calls M_2, which accepts integers, because only integers begin with a digit.

Models for regular languages

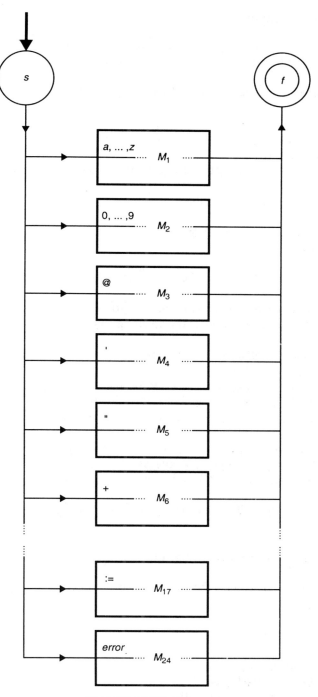

Figure 3.3.1.2.1 COLA scanner.

COLA scanner components

Before we present the Pascal-like procedure, GetLexeme, which implements the COLA scanner depicted by Figure 3.3.1.2.1, some components used by this procedure are described.

GetLexeme contains the following three global variables:

1. *Symbol* represents a variable of type **char**.
2. *Lexeme* is a linked list that stores a word whose symbols are of type **char**; this variable records a lexeme.
3. *LexemeType* is a variable of type **integer**; this variable stores a lexeme type.

GetLexeme also use two set variables:

1. Letters represents the set of all letters.
2. Digits denotes the set of all digits.

Finally, GetLexeme makes use of these four procedures:

1. A call of *Concatenate* produces the concatenation of the word in Lexeme and the character in Symbol, then places the resulting concatenation as the new contents of Lexeme.
2. A call of *Empty* empties Lexeme; in other words, this call corresponds to setting Lexeme to the empty word.
3. *GetSymbol* reads the next input character. More precisely, a call of GetSymbol places the next input character into Symbol. GetSymbol thus contains all necessary routines, such as skipping the end-of-line symbol, that reading from the standard input involves.
4. A call of UnGetSymbol pushes back the current character in Symbol onto the standard input. Most programming languages possess elegant tools for carrying out this procedure; for instance, C has the routine 'ungetc' for this purpose.

The exercises return to all these components of GetLexemes in greater detail.

Pascal-like implementation of the COLA scanner

GetLexeme, which implements the COLA scanner conceptualized in Figure 3.3.1.2.1, is as follows.

procedure GetLexeme;
begin
   Empty {Lexeme is empty};
   repeat GetSymbol **until** Symbol <> ' '
   {read the next non-blank symbol};

```
case Symbol of
    'a'..'z': P1;
    '0'..'9': P2;
    '@': P3;
    '''': P4;
    '''''': P5;
    '+': P6;
    ⋮
    ':': P17;
    otherwise: P24
end
end
```

In the above, P1, ..., P17 and P24 are procedures such that Pj implements M_j and, in addition, sets LexemeType to the type corresponding to the scanned lexeme. When GetLexeme exits, Lexeme contains the recognized lexeme, and LexemeType indicates the type of the recognized lexeme.

Procedures P1, ..., P17, and P24 follow next.

P1

Figure 3.3.1.2.2 depicts the finite automaton M_1 that accepts identifiers. In this figure, X and Y are the set of letters and the set of letters and digits, respectively, and $\bar{Y}$ denotes the complement of Y.

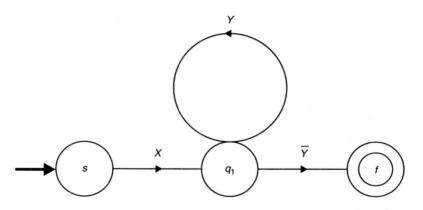

Figure 3.3.1.2.2 M_1.

Before presenting the Pascal-like procedure P1 that implements M_1, a procedure called ReservedWord is informally described. ReservedWord finds out whether the scanned lexeme, contained in Lexeme, represents a reserved word. To decide this question, this procedure determines whether Lexeme equals one of the following reserved words: **begin, end, goto, if, read** and **write**. If Lexeme equals a reserved word of type j, for some $j = 18, \ldots, 23$, then this procedure sets LexemeType to j; otherwise, ReservedWord sets LexemeType to 1 to indicate that Lexeme is an identifier, not a reserved word.

Recall that, when P1 begins, Symbol contains a member of Letters.

procedure P1;
begin
  repeat
    Concatenate{concatenation of Lexeme and Symbol};
    GetSymbol
  until not (Symbol **in** (Letters **or** Digits)) {this loop exits
        when it reads a nonalphanumeric symbol};
  UnGetSymbol   {the nonalphanumeric symbol in Symbol is
                    pushed back onto the standard input};
  ReservedWord   {LexemeType is set}
end

P2
The finite automaton accepting integers, M_2, is displayed in Figure 3.3.1.2.3, where X equals the set of digits, and $\overline{X}$ denotes the complement of X.

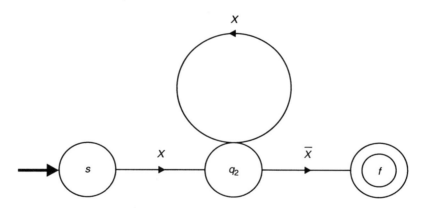

Figure 3.3.1.2.3 M_2.

Automaton M_2 is implemented by the procedure P2, which GetLexeme calls with Symbol containing a digit.

procedure P2;
begin
  repeat
    Concatenate;
    GetSymbol
  until not (Symbol **in** Digits) {this loop exits when it reads a nonnumeric
                  symbol};

UnGetSymbol {the nonnumeric symbol in Symbol is pushed back onto the
            standard input};
    LexemeType := 2
end

P3
Figure 3.3.1.2.4 shows the finite automaton M_3, which accepts labels. In this figure X denotes the set of letters and digits, and $\overline{X}$ is the complement of X.

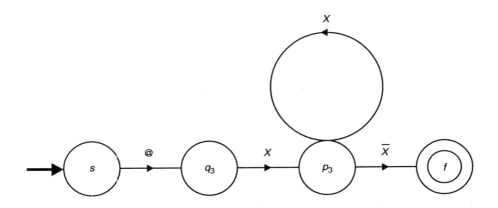

Figure 3.3.1.2.4 M_3.

The following procedure, P3, implements M_3. When GetLexeme calls P3, Symbol contains @. If M_3 recognizes a well formed label @x, where x is a non-empty alphanumeric word, P3 sets LexemeType = 3. If, however, no letter or digit follows @, P3 sets LexemeType = 24 to indicate a lexical error occurrence.

procedure P3;
begin
  repeat
    Concatenate;
    GetSymbol
  until not (Symbol **in** (Letters **or** Digits)) {this loop exits when it reads a
            nonalphanumeric symbol};
  UnGetSymbol {the nonalphanumeric symbol in Symbol is pushed back onto the
            standard input};
  if Lexeme contains only @
  then LexemeType := 24 {invalid label — no letter or digit follows @}
  else LexemeType := 3
end

P4
Figure 3.3.1.2.5 pictures M_4, the automaton that accepts text literals.

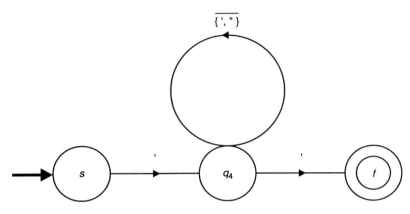

Figure 3.3.1.2.5 M_4.

Automaton M_4 is implemented by procedure P4. When GetLexeme calls P4, Symbol contains '. If P4 recognizes a well-formed text literal, which ends with ', P4 sets LexemeType = 4. If, however, P4 recognizes an invalid text literal that ends with ", P4 sets LexemeType = 24 to indicate a lexical error occurrence.

```
procedure P4;
begin
   repeat
      Concatenate;
      GetSymbol
   until Symbol in [', "] {this loop exits when it reads ' or "};
   if Symbol = '"'
   then LexemeType := 24 {invalid text literal — the
                          literal begins with ' but ends with "}
   else
   begin
      Concatenate;
      LexemeType := 4
   end
end
```

P5
Figure 3.3.1.2.6 depicts M_5, which accepts newline text literals.

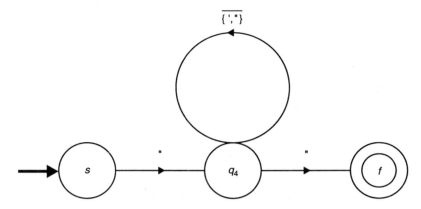

Figure 3.3.1.2.6 M_5.

When GetLexeme calls P5, the procedure that implements M_5, Symbol contains ". If P5 recognizes a well-formed newline text literal, it sets LexemeType = 5. However, if P5 recognizes an invalid new-line text literal that ends with ' instead of ", P5 sets LexemeType = 24.

procedure P5;
begin
   repeat
      Concatenate;
      GetSymbol
   until Symbol **in** [', "] {this loop exits when it reads ' or "};
   if Symbol = "'
   then LexemeType := 24 {invalid text literal — the literal begins with " but ends with '}
   else
   begin
      Concatenate;
      LexemeType := 5
   end
end

M6
Figure 3.3.1.2.7 depicts the finite automaton M_6, which accepts +.

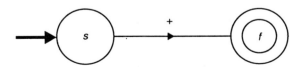

Figure 3.3.1.2.7 M_6.

When GetToken calls the following procedure, P6, which implements M_6, Symbol contains +.

> **procedure** P6;
> **begin**
>   Concatenate;
>   LexemeType := 6
> **end**

Procedures P7 through P16 are analogous to P6, so they are left to the exercises.

P17
The finite automaton M_{17}, which accepts :=, is shown in Figure 3.3.1.2.8.

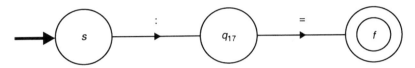

Figure 3.3.1.2.8 M_{17}.

The procedure P17, implements M_{17}. When GetLexeme calls P17, Symbol contains : . If P17 reads = as the next input symbol, P17 recognizes a well-formed assignment and sets LexemeType = 17; otherwise, P17 indicates an invalid assignment by setting LexemeType = 24.

procedure P17;
begin
  Concatenate;
  GetSymbol;
  if Symbol = '='
  then
  begin
    Concatenate
    LexemeType := 17
  end
  else LexemeType := 24 {invalid assignment operator — the second symbol differs
                from =}
end

Lexemes of types 18 through 23 are recognized within P1.

P24
If GetLexeme reads an illegal symbol, which does not form the beginning of any COLA lexeme, GetLexeme calls P24, defined as follows.

Models for regular languages

```
procedure M24;
begin
    LexemeType := 24
end
```

Note that four other procedures — P3, P4, P5 and P17 — can also set LexemeType to 24.

The discussion of GetLexeme continues later in this book; most importantly, Sections 5.3.1.2 and 9.3.1 frequently refer to this procedure.

3.3.2 From finite automata to regular expressions

The following discussion explains how to convert any deterministic finite automaton M to an equivalent regular expression E. This conversion uses two special languages, $L(M(i, j))$ and $L(M(i, j, k))$, introduced by the following definition.

Definition — special languages
Let $M = (Q, \Sigma, R, q_1, F)$ be a deterministic finite automaton, where

$$Q = \{q_1, \ldots, q_n\}$$

for some $n \geq 1$ (q_1 is the start state). Let $i, j \in \{1, \ldots, n\}$. Define $L(M(i,j))$ as

$$L(M(i,j)) = \{w : w \in \Sigma^* \text{ and } q_i w \vdash^* q_j\}$$

Let $i, j, k \in \{1, \ldots, n\}$ and define $L(M(i, j, k))$ as

$$L(M(i, j, k)) = \{w : w \in \Sigma^*, \text{ and } q_i w \vdash^* q_j \ [\rho]$$
$$\text{so that if } \rho \text{ contains } q_g a \vdash q_h \in R, \text{ then } g, h \in \{1, \ldots, k\} \}$$

♦

Informally, $L(M(i, j, k)$ denotes the language consisting of all words that cause M to make a sequence of moves from q_i to q_j so this sequence never enters q_m with $m > k$. Setting $k = n$ in $L(M(i, j, k)$ gives $L(M(i, j))$; that is,

$$L(M(i,j)) = L(M(i,j,n))$$

Notice that

$$L(M) = \bigcup_{q_i \in F} L(M(1, i))$$

where $i \in \{1, \ldots, n\}$.

Making use of $L(M(i,j))$ and $L(M(i,j,k))$, the following algorithm transforms any deterministic finite automaton, $M = (Q, \Sigma, R, q_1, F)$, to an equivalent regular expression, E. This algorithm first determines all languages $L(M(i,j,k))$. By using these languages, it determines all languages $L(M(i,j))$. Finally, by using the languages of the form $L(M(1,j))$ with q_j in F, this algorithm produces a regular expression, E, so

$$L(E) = L(M) = \bigcup_{q_i \in F} L(M(1, i))$$

In this algorithm, $E(i, j, k)$ and $E(i, j)$ are expressions denoting $L(M(i, j, k))$ and $L(M(i,j))$, respectively.

Algorithm 3.3.2.1: Conversion of a deterministic finite automaton to an equivalent regular expression

Input: A deterministic finite automaton $M = (Q, \Sigma, R, q_1, F)$, where $Q = \{q_1, \ldots, q_n\}$, for some $n \geq 1$.

Output: A regular expression E such that $L(E) = L(M)$.

Method

begin

    for $i = 1$ **to** n **do**
      for $j = 1$ **to** n **do**
        $E(i, j, 0) := \emptyset$
        {initialization of all $E(i, j, 0)$ to $\emptyset$};

    for $i = 1$ **to** n **do**
      for $j = 1$ **to** n **do**
        if $q_i a \vdash q_j \in R$
        then $E(i, j, 0) := E(i, j, 0) + a$
          {move from q_i to q_j on a};

    for $i = 1$ **to** n **do**
      $E(i, i, 0) := E(i, i, 0) + \varepsilon$
      {the zero-move computation from q_i to q_i};

    for $k = 0$ **to** $n - 1$ **do**
      for $i = 1$ **to** n **do**

Models for regular languages

```
        for j = 1 to n do
          E(i, j, k + 1) := E(i, j, k) + E(i, k + 1, k) E(k + 1, k + 1, k)*E(k + 1, j, k)
          {the determination of E(i, j, k + 1)};

      for i = 1 to n do
        for j = 1 to n do
          E(i, j) := E(i, j, n)
          {the determination of E(i, j)};

E := ∅;
for i = 1 to n do
  if qᵢ ∈ F then E := E + E(1, i)
                  {the construction of E}
end.
```

This algorithm first determines all $E(i, j, 0)$, denoting $L(M(i, j, 0))$, as follows. $L(M(i, j, 0))$ contains all symbols, $a \in \Sigma$, that takes M from q_i to q_j; therefore, Algorithm 3.3.2.1 constructs $E(i, j, 0)$ by the **for** loop:

for $i = 1$ **to** n **do**
  for $j = 1$ **to** n **do**
    if $q_i a \vdash q_j \in R$
    then $E(i, j, 0) := E(i, j, 0) + a$

In addition, if $i = j$, M also make the zero-move computation from q_i to q_j in zero moves so, at this point, $L(M(i, j, 0))$ contains ε. Thus, this algorithm has

for $i = 1$ **to** n **do**
  $E(i, i, 0) := E(i, i, 0) + \varepsilon$

After this **for** loop exits, Algorithm 3.3.2.1 has completed the determination of all languages that have the form $L(M(i, j, 0))$.

For all $k = 0, \ldots, n$, $L(M(i, j, k + 1))$ contains all words causing M to make a sequence of moves from q_i to q_j so that each state, q_h, occurring in this sequence satisfies $h \leq k + 1$. Language $L(M(i, j, k + 1))$ includes all words in $L(M(i, j, k))$ because these words cause M to make a sequence of moves from q_i to q_j so that each state, q_l, in this sequence satisfies $l \leq k$. Also, the words in $L(M(i, j, k))$ and $L(M(i, j, k + 1))$ also contain every word x that causes M to go from q_i to q_{k+1}, loop in q_{k+1} several times and, eventually, go from q_{k+1} to q_j provided that, during this computation, M always visits states, q_h, such that $h \leq k + 1$. In other words, x can be decomposed as $x = u v_1 \ldots v_m w$, where u takes M from q_i to q_{k+1}, v_t causes M to go from q_{k+1} back to q_{k+1}, for $t = 1, \ldots, m$, and w takes M from q_{k+1} to q_j. As $L(M(i, k + 1, k))$ $L(M(k + 1, k + 1, k))^* L(M(k + 1, j, k))$ contains the words that can be decomposed in this way, Algorithm 3.3.2.1 determines all $E(i, j, k + 1)$ by the following nested **for** loop:

for $k = 0$ to $n - 1$ do
  for $i = 1$ to n do
    for $j = 1$ to n do
      $E(i, j, k + 1) := E(i, j, k) + E(i, k + 1, k)E(k + 1, k + 1, k)^* E(k + 1, j, k)$

As $L(M(i, j)) = L(M(i, j, n))$, this algorithm then includes

for $i = 1$ to n do
  for $j = 1$ to n do
    $E(i, j) := E(i, j, n)$

Finally, because

$$L(M) = \bigcup_{q_i \in F} L(M(1, i))$$

this algorithm constructs the resulting expression E equivalent to M, by the **for** loop

for $i = 1$ to n do if $q_i \in F$ then $E := E + E(1, i)$

Lemma 3.3.2.2

Let $M = (Q, \Sigma, R, q_1, F)$ be a deterministic finite automaton, where $Q = \{q_1, ..., q_n\}$, for some $n \geq 1$. With M on its input, Algorithm 3.3.2.1 halts and correctly constructs a regular expression E such that $L(E) = L(M)$.

Proof

Termination

As $\{1, ..., n\}$ is finite, all **for** loops of the algorithm exit after making a finite number of iterations. Thus, this algorithm surely terminates.

Correctness

Well-Formed Regular Expression

Observe that Algorithm 3.3.2.1 constructs E so that its components consists of $\emptyset, \varepsilon$ and the symbols in Σ. These components are connected by the regular expression operators $+, ^*$ and concatenation. As a result, E represents a well-formed regular expression.

Equivalence

To demonstrate that E is equivalent to M, this proof first establishes the following claim.

Claim

Let $i, j \in \{1, ..., n\}$. $E(i, j, k)$ represents a regular expression denoting $L(M(i, j, k))$, for all $k = 0, ..., n$.

Proof
This claim is proved by induction on k.

Basis
Let $k = 0$. First, determine

$$L(M(i,j,0)) - \{\varepsilon\}$$

As $k = 0$, $L(M(i,j,0)) - \{\varepsilon\}$ contains all symbols, $a \in \Sigma$, such that with a, M makes a move from q_i to q_j; formally, such a move has the form

$$q_i a \vdash q_j \; [q_i a \vdash q_j]$$

where $q_i a \vdash q_j \in R$. Thus,

$$L(M(i,j,0)) - \{\varepsilon\} = \{\, a: a \in \Sigma \text{ and } q_i a \vdash q_j \in R\,\}$$

Furthermore, observe that

$$\varepsilon \in L(M(i,j,0)) \text{ if and only if } i = j$$

Therefore,

$$\varepsilon \notin L(M(i,j,0)) \text{ if and only if } i \neq j$$

1. Suppose that $i \neq j$ and, thus, $\varepsilon \notin L(M(i,j,0))$. Let

$$L(M(i,j,0)) = \{\, a: q_i a \vdash q_j \in R\,\} = \{a_1, \ldots, a_m\}$$

Because $i \neq j$, Algorithm 3.3.2.1 constructs $E(i,j,0)$ as

$$E(i,j,0) = \emptyset + a_1 + \ldots + a_m$$

As $\emptyset + a_1 + \ldots + a_m$ is a regular expression denoting $\{a_1, \ldots, a_m\}$, $E(i,j,0)$ denotes $L(M(i,j,0))$.

2. Suppose that $i = j$ and, thus, $\varepsilon \in L(M(i,j,0))$. Let

$$L(M(i,j,0)) - \{\varepsilon\} = \{\, a: q_i a \vdash q_j \in R\,\} = \{a_1, \ldots, a_m\}$$

Then,

$$L(M(i,j,0)) = \{a_1, \ldots, a_m\} \cup \{\varepsilon\}$$

As $i = j$, Algorithm 3.3.2.1 constructs $E(i,j,0)$ as

$$E(i,j,0) = \emptyset + a_1 + \ldots + a_m + \varepsilon$$

As $\emptyset + a_1 + \ldots + a_m + \varepsilon$ is a regular expression denoting $\{a_1, \ldots, a_m\} \cup \{\varepsilon\}$, $E(i,j,0)$ denotes $L(M(i,j,0))$.

We conclude that the basis of this claim holds.

Induction hypothesis
Assume that the claim holds for 0 through k, for some $k \in \{0, \ldots, n-1\}$.

Induction step
This part of the proof establishes the claim for $k+1$. Observe that

$$w \in L(M(i,j,k+1)) \text{ if and only if } q_i w \vdash^* q_j [\rho] \text{ in } M$$

where each rule, $q_g a \vdash q_h$, appearing in ρ satisfies $g, h \in \{0, \ldots, k+1\}$.

1. Assume that during the computation $q_i w \vdash^* q_j [\rho]$, M never visits q_{k+1}. Then, $w \in L(M(i,j,k))$.

2. Assume that during the computation $q_i w \vdash^* q_j [\rho]$, M visits q_{k+1} m times, for some $m \geq 1$. At this point, $q_i w \vdash^* q_j [\rho]$ can be decomposed as

$$\begin{aligned}
q_i u w_1 w_2 \ldots w_m v &\vdash^* q_{k+1} w_1 \ldots w_m v & [\rho_u] \\
&\vdash^* q_{k+1} w_2 \ldots w_m v & [\rho_1] \\
&\vdash^* q_{k+1} w_3 \ldots w_m v & [\rho_2] \\
&\vdots \\
&\vdash^* q_{k+1} w_m v & [\rho_{m-1}] \\
&\vdash^* q_{k+1} v & [\rho_m] \\
&\vdash^* q_j & [\rho_v]
\end{aligned}$$

where $w = u w_1 \ldots w_m v$, $\rho = \rho_u \rho_1 \rho_2 \ldots \rho_m \rho_v$, $u \in L(M(i, k+1, k))$, $w_i \in L(M(k+1, k+1, k))$ for $i = 1, \ldots, m$, and $v \in L(M(k+1, j, k))$. Hence,

$$w \in L(M(i, k+1, k)) L(M(k+1, k+1, k))^* L(M(k+1, j, k))$$

The above two cases imply that

$$L(M(i,j,k+1)) = L(M(i,j,k)) \\ \cup L(M(i, k+1, k)) L(M(k+1, k+1, k))^* L(M(k+1, j, k))$$

By the present algorithm,

$$E(i,j,k+1) = E(i,j,k) + E(i, k+1, k) E(k+1, k+1, k)^* E(k+1, j, k)$$

As $E(i,j,k) + E(i,k+1,k)E(k+1,k+1,k)^*E(k+1,j,k)$ is a regular expression denoting $L(M(i,j,k)) \cup L(M(i,k+1,k))L(M(k+1,k+1,k))^*L(M(k+1,j,k))$, then $E(i,j,k+1)$ denotes $L(M(i,j,k+1))$.

At this point, we have completed the induction step, so the claim holds.

$\square$

By this claim, $E(i,j,n)$ denotes $L(M(i,j,n))$, where $i,j = 1, \ldots, n$. Observe that Algorithm 3.3.2.1 sets $E(i,j) := E(i,j,n)$ for all $i,j = 1, \ldots, n$, so $E(i,j)$ represents a regular expression denoting $L(M(i,j))$ because $L(M(i,j)) = L(M(i,j,n))$. This algorithm then constructs the resulting regular expression, E, by

for $i = 1$ to n do
  if $q_i \in F$ then $E := E + E(1,i)$

E constructed in this way denotes $L(M)$ because

$$L(M) = \bigcup_{q_i \in F} L(M(1,i))$$

It is concluded that E and M are equivalent, so the lemma holds.

∎

Example 3.3.2.1 Application of Algorithm 3.3.2.1

Recall that Example 3.3.1.1 transforms the regular expression

$$c(c+d)^*$$

to the equivalent deterministic finite automaton M, depicted in Figure 3.3.2.1.

From Algorithm 3.3.2.1, the present example describes the converse transformation, changing M to $c(c+d)^*$.

M has these six rules:

$r_1: q_0 c \vdash q_2$
$r_2: q_0 d \vdash q_1$
$r_3: q_1 c \vdash q_1$
$r_4: q_1 d \vdash q_1$
$r_5: q_2 c \vdash q_2$
$r_6: q_2 d \vdash q_2$

where q_0 is the start state and q_2 is the final state.

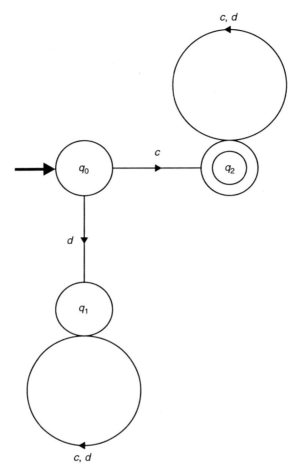

Figure 3.3.2.1 Deterministic finite automaton equivalent to $c(c+d)^*$.

The first **for** loop of Algorithm 3.3.2.1 sets

$$E(i, j, 0) = \emptyset$$

for all $i, j = 1, 2, 3$. Then, this algorithm performs

for $i = 1$ to 3 **do**
  for $j = 1$ to 3 **do**
    if $q_i a \vdash q_j \in R$
    then $E(i, j, 0) := E(i, j, 0) + a$

For $i = 1$ and $j = 1$,

$$E(1, 1, 0) = \emptyset$$

because no rule has q_1 on the left-hand side and on the right-hand side. For $i = 1$ and $j = 2$,

$$E(1, 2, 0) := \emptyset + d$$

because M has $r_2\colon q_0 d \vdash q_1$. For $i = 2$ and $j = 2$,

$$E(2, 2, 0) := \emptyset + c + d$$

as M contains $r_3\colon q_1 c \vdash q_1$ and $r_4\colon q_1 d \vdash q_1$. When this loop exits, Algorithm 3.3.2.1 has these expressions:

$E(1, 1, 0) = \emptyset$ $E(1, 2, 0) = \emptyset + d$ $E(1, 3, 0) = c$
$E(2, 1, 0) = \emptyset$ $E(2, 2, 0) = \emptyset + c + d$ $E(2, 3, 0) = \emptyset$
$E(3, 1, 0) = \emptyset$ $E(3, 2, 0) = \emptyset$ $E(3, 3, 0) = \emptyset + c + d$

Then, this algorithm performs

for $i = 1$ **to** 3 **do**
　　$E(i, i, 0) := E(i, i, 0) + \varepsilon$

This loop changes the previous nine expressions to

$E(1, 1, 0) = \emptyset - \varepsilon$ $E(1, 2, 0) = \emptyset + d$ $E(1, 3, 0) = c$
$E(2, 1, 0) = \emptyset$ $E(2, 2, 0) = \emptyset + c + d + \varepsilon$ $E(2, 3, 0) = \emptyset$
$E(3, 1, 0) = \emptyset$ $E(3, 2, 0) = \emptyset$ $E(3, 3, 0) = \emptyset + c + d + \varepsilon$

Algorithm 3.3.2.1 then executes

for $k = 0$ **to** 2 **do**
　for $i = 1$ **to** 3 **do**
　　for $j = 1$ **to** 3 **do**
　　　$E(i, j, k+1) := E(i, j, k) + E(i, k+1, k)E(k+1, k+1, k)^* E(k+1, j, k)$

For $i = j = 1$ and $k = 0$, it sets

$$E(1, 1, 1) := E(1, 1, 0) + E(1, 1, 0)E(1, 1, 0)^* E(1, 1, 0)$$

Hence,

$$E(1, 1, 1) := \emptyset + \varepsilon + (\emptyset + \varepsilon)(\emptyset + \varepsilon)^* (\emptyset + \varepsilon)$$

As $\emptyset + \varepsilon + (\emptyset + \varepsilon)(\emptyset + \varepsilon)^*(\emptyset + \varepsilon)$ is equivalent to ε,

$$E(1, 1, 1) := \varepsilon$$

For $i = 1, j = 2$, and $k = 0$,

$$E(1, 2, 1) := E(1, 2, 0) + E(1, 1, 0)E(1, 1, 0)^*E(1, 2, 0)$$

That is,

$$E(1, 2, 1) := \emptyset + d + (\emptyset + \varepsilon)(\emptyset + \varepsilon)^*(\emptyset + d)$$

As $\emptyset + d + (\emptyset + \varepsilon)(\emptyset + \varepsilon)^*(\emptyset + d)$ is equivalent to d,

$$E(1, 2, 1) := d$$

This nested **for** loop produces

$E(1, 1, 1) = \varepsilon$	$E(1, 2, 1) = d$	$E(1, 3, 1) = c$
$E(2, 1, 1) = \emptyset$	$E(2, 2, 1) = c + d + \varepsilon$	$E(2, 3, 1) = \emptyset$
$E(3, 1, 1) = \emptyset$	$E(3, 2, 1) = \emptyset$	$E(3, 3, 1) = c + d + \varepsilon$
$E(1, 1, 2) = \varepsilon$	$E(1, 2, 2) = d$	$E(1, 3, 2) = c$
$E(2, 1, 2) = \emptyset$	$E(2, 2, 2) = c + d + \varepsilon$	$E(2, 3, 2) = \emptyset$
$E(3, 1, 2) = \emptyset$	$E(3, 2, 2) = \emptyset$	$E(3, 3, 2) = c + d + \varepsilon$
$E(1, 1, 3) = \varepsilon$	$E(1, 2, 3) = d(c + d)^*$	$E(1, 3, 3) = c(c + d)^*$
$E(2, 1, 3) = \emptyset$	$E(2, 2, 3) = (c + d)^*$	$E(2, 3, 3) = \emptyset$
$E(3, 1, 3) = \emptyset$	$E(3, 2, 3) = \emptyset$	$E(3, 3, 3) = (c + d)^*$

By performing

for $i = 1$ to 3 **do**
  for $j = 1$ to 3 **do**
    $E(i, j) := E(i, j, 3)$

this algorithm constructs

$E(1, 1) = \varepsilon$	$E(1, 2) = d(c + d)^*$	$E(1, 3) = c(c + d)^*$
$E(2, 1) = \emptyset$	$E(2, 2) = (c + d)^*$	$E(2, 3) = \emptyset$
$E(3, 1) = \emptyset$	$E(3, 2) = \emptyset$	$E(3, 3) = (c + d)^*$

Finally, Algorithm 3.3.2.1 executes

$E := \emptyset$;
for $i = 1$ to 3 **do**
  if $q_i \in F$ **then** $E := E + E(1, i)$

As q_3 is the final state of M,

$$E = \emptyset + E(1, 3)$$

Because $E(1, 3) = c(c + d)^*$, Algorithm 3.3.2.1 yields

$$E = \emptyset + c(c + d)^*$$

This expression can be simplified to the resulting regular expression

$$E = c(c + d)^*$$

▲

When establishing the equivalence between finite automata and regular expressions, the following corollary is of value.

Corollary 3.3.2.3
Let L be a language. If $L = L(M)$ for a deterministic finite automaton M, then $L = L(E)$ for a regular expression E.

Proof
This corollary follows from Algorithm 3.3.2.1 and Lemma 3.3.2.2.

■

3.3.3 Equivalence of finite automata and regular expressions

This section establishes the equivalence of finite automata and regular expressions.

Theorem 3.3.3.1
Let L be a language. $L = L(M)$ for a finite automaton M if and only if $L = L(E)$ for a regular expressions E.

Proof
If
This part of the proof follows from Corollary 3.3.1.13.

Only if
Let L be a language. By Corollaries 3.2.2.5 and 3.2.3.3, $L = L(M)$ for a finite automaton M if and only if $L = L(M_d)$ for a deterministic finite automaton M_d. Thus, by Corollary 3.3.2.3, the 'only if' part of this proof holds.

This concludes that Theorem 3.3.3.1 holds.

■

The following theorem summarizes the main results of all Chapter 3.

Theorem 3.3.3.2

The following classes of expressions and automata characterize the family of regular languages:

1. regular expressions;
2. fully parenthesized regular expressions;
3. finite automata;
4. ε-free finite automata;
5. deterministic finite automata;
6. well-specified finite automata;
7. minimum-state finite automata.

Proof
This crucial theorem follows from Theorem 3.1.2, Corollary 3.2.2.7, Corollary 3.2.3.3, Corollary 3.2.4.9, Corollary 3.2.5.3 and Theorem 3.3.3.2.

∎

Exercises

1 Regular expressions

1.1 Prove or disprove that if L is a regular language, then any subset of L represents a regular language, too.

1.2 Consider these regular expressions over $\{a, b\}$:
  (a) $ab(bb)^*ba$
  (b) $a(aba)^*b(aba)^*a$
  (c) $((ab)^*ba(ab)^*)^*$
  (d) $((abba)^* + (baab)^*)^*$
  (e) $((ab + ba)^* + (aabb)^*)^*$
  (f) $a(a + b)^*b$
  (g) $((ab)^*b + ab^*)^*$
  (h) $aa(ba)* + b^*aba^*$
  (i) $(ab + (aab)^*)(aa + a)$
  For each of these expressions, solve the following five tasks:
  (A) give five words that belong to the language denoted by the expression;
  (B) give five words over $\{a, b\}$ that are not in the language denoted by the expression;
  (C) describe the language denoted by the expression informally;
  (D) describe the language denoted by the expression formally (use the set theory notation introduced in Section 1.1);
  (E) simplify the expression as much as possible.

1.3 Consider the following languages:
  (a) $\{a^i b^j c^k : i, k \geq 0 \text{ and } j \geq 1\}$

(b) $\{a^i b^j c^k : i, k \geq 1 \text{ and } j \geq 0\}$
(c) $\{a\}\{a,b\}^*\{b\} \cup \{\varepsilon\}$
(d) $\{x : x \subseteq \{a, b\}^* \text{ and } x \text{ has an equal number of } as \text{ and } bs \text{ such that no prefix of } x \text{ has two more } as \text{ than } bs \text{ or two more } bs \text{ than } as\}$
(e) $\{x : x \subseteq \{a, b\}^* \text{ and } x \text{ has an even number of } as \text{ and an odd number of } bs\}$
(f) $\{x : x \subseteq \{a, b\}^* \text{ and } x \text{ has an even number of } as \text{ and an even number of } bs\}$
(g) $\{x : x \subseteq \{a, b\}^* \text{ and } |x| \text{ is divisible by } 3\}$
(h) $\{x : x \subseteq \{a, b\}^* \text{ and } aaa \text{ does not appear in } x\}$
(i) $\{x : x \subseteq \{a, b\}^* \text{ and } aaa \text{ appears in } x\}$
(j) $\{x : x \subseteq \{a, b\}^* \text{ and } aaa \text{ appears in } x \text{ exactly once}\}$
(k) $\{x : x \subseteq \{a, b, c\}^* \text{ and } \#_a x = \#_b x = 3\}$
(l) $\{x : x \subseteq \{a, b, c\}^* \text{ and each appearance of } a \text{ is followed by } b\}$
(m) $\{x : x \subseteq \{a, b, c\}^* \text{ and each appearance of } a \text{ is preceded or followed by } b\}$
(n) $\{x : x \subseteq \{a, b, c\}^* \text{ and each appearance of } a \text{ is preceded and followed by } b\}$
(o) the intersection of (c) and (g) and (h).

For each of these languages, construct a regular expression denoting the language. Prove that the expression is correctly constructed.

1.4 Consider each lexeme of your favourite programming language. Write a regular expression that denotes the lexeme.

1.5 Consider these regular expressions
(a) $ab(cc)^* + a(bcc)^*$
(b) $a(bcc)^* + (abcc)^*$
(c) $\varnothing^*$
(d) ε^*
(e) $\varnothing + (\varepsilon + \varnothing)^*$
(f) $(abcc)^* + a$
(g) $(ba)^+(a^*b^* + a^*)$
(h) $(ba)^* ba^+(b^* + \varepsilon)$
(i) $b^+(a^*b^* + \varepsilon)b$
(j) $b(a^*b^* + \varepsilon)b+$
(k) $(a + \varepsilon)^*$
(l) $(a + b)^* b^*$
(m) $(a^* + ba^*)^*$
(n) $(b(a + \varepsilon)b^*)^*$
(o) $(a + b)^+$

Which of these expressions are equivalent?

1.6 Let E_1 and E_2 be any two regular expressions over an alphabet Σ such that $\varepsilon \notin L(E_1)$. Prove that there exists a regular expression E such that $L(E) = L(E_1)$ $L(E) \cup L(E_2)$.

1.7 If there exists a word that can be obtained from a given regular expression in two distinct ways, then this expression is *ambiguous*. For instance, $a^* ba^* + c^* bc^*$ is ambiguous because there exists a word b such that $a^* ba$ denotes b and, in addition, $c^* bc^*$ denotes b. Define ambiguous regular expressions formally. Present ten examples of ambiguous regular expressions over $\{a, b\}$.

1.8 Consider these regular expressions:
  (a) $ab(cc)^* + ab$
  (b) $a(aa)^* + (bb)^*a$
  (c) $((aa)^* + (aa + ab)^*)^*$
  (d) $(abba)^* + b^*aab^*$
  (e) $(ab + ba)^* + (abba)^*$
  (f) $(abba)^* + a^*bba^*$

  For each of these expressions, determine whether the expression is ambiguous. If the expression is ambiguous, construct an equivalent expression that is not ambiguous.

1.9 Complete the proof of Theorem 3.1.3

1.10 Complete the proof of Theorem 3.1.4

1.11 Besides the operations of union, concatenation and *, extended regular expressions allow the operations of complement, intersection and difference. Define extended regular expressions formally. Prove that extended regular expressions characterize the family of regular languages.

2 Finite automata

2.1 Give an example of a finite automaton, $M = (Q, \Sigma, R, s, F)$, and an input word, $w \in \Sigma^*$, such that for some $f \in F$, $sw \vdash^* f$ according to infinitely many rule words.

2.2 Consider each expression discussed in Exercises 1.2 and 1.3. Construct a finite automaton that accepts the language denoted by this expression. Give a proof that the automaton is correctly constructed.

2.3 Consider the finite automata:
  (a) 1: $sa \vdash s$
      2: $sb \vdash s$
      3: $sb \vdash q$
      4: $qb \vdash q$
      5: $qa \vdash q$
      6: $qa \vdash s$
      7: $s \vdash f$
  (b) 1: $sa \vdash q$
      2: $sb \vdash p$
      3: $qa \vdash q$
      4: $pb \vdash p$
      5: $qa \vdash s$
      6: $pb \vdash s$
      7: $s \vdash f$
  (c) 1: $sa \vdash q$
      2: $qa \vdash p$
      3: $pb \vdash q$
      4: $qb \vdash s$
      5: $sc \vdash f$
  (d) 1: $sa \vdash q$

$\quad\quad\quad$ 2: $sb \vdash p$
$\quad\quad\quad$ 3: $qc \vdash s$
$\quad\quad\quad$ 4: $pc \vdash s$
$\quad\quad\quad$ 5: $sc \vdash f$
$\quad$ (e) $\,$ 1: $sa \vdash q$
$\quad\quad\quad$ 2: $q \vdash p$
$\quad\quad\quad$ 3: $pa \vdash q$
$\quad\quad\quad$ 4: $sa \vdash f$
$\quad\quad\quad$ 5: $fb \vdash s$
$\quad\quad\quad$ 6: $fb \vdash f$
$\quad$ (f) $\,$ 1: $s \vdash f$
$\quad\quad\quad$ 2: $fa \vdash f$
$\quad\quad\quad$ 3: $fa \vdash p$
$\quad\quad\quad$ 4: $pb \vdash p$
$\quad\quad\quad$ 5: $pb \vdash q$
$\quad\quad\quad$ 6: $qa \vdash s$
$\quad$ (g) $\,$ 1: $sa \vdash s$
$\quad\quad\quad$ 2: $sb \vdash q$
$\quad\quad\quad$ 3: $q \vdash p$
$\quad\quad\quad$ 4: $pb \vdash p$
$\quad\quad\quad$ 5: $pb \vdash f$
$\quad\quad\quad$ 6: $fa \vdash f$
$\quad\quad\quad$ 7: $fa \vdash p$

For each of these automata, solve these tasks:
(A) give the finite state diagram of the automaton;
(B) give five words that the automaton accepts;
(C) give five words that the automaton does not accept;
(D) determine the language accepted by the automaton, and denote this language by a regular expression.

2.4 $\quad$ For each automaton in Exercise 2.3, construct an equivalent finite automaton that has fewer states or rules. If you claim that there exists no such automaton, justify your claim.

2.5 $\quad$ Return to the finite automaton M considered in Example 3.2.1.1. Based upon $\vdash^*$, give a detailed proof that $L(M) = \{a\}^*(\{b\}^+ \cup \{c\}^+)\{a\}^*$.

2.6 $\quad$ Let $M = (Q, \Sigma, R, s, F)$ be a finite automaton; $Q_1, Q_2 \subseteq Q$; $w_1, w_2 \in \Sigma^*$; $X_1 = Q_1\{w_1\}$; $X_2 = Q_2\{w_2\}$; and $X_1 \vdash^* X_2$ in M. Disprove that for all $q_1 \in Q_1$, $q_1 w_1 \vdash^* q_2 w_2$ in M for some $q_2 \in Q_2$.

2.7 $\quad$ Complete the proof of the following theorem.

Theorem
Let $M = (Q, \Sigma, R, s, F)$ be a finite automaton; $Q_1, Q_2 \subseteq Q$; $w_1, w_2 \in \Sigma^*$; $X_1 = Q_1\{w_1\}$; $X_2 = Q_2\{w_2\}$; and $X_1 \vdash^i X_2$ in M for some $i \geq 0$. Then, there exists a unique subset of Q_1, $Q'_1 \subseteq Q_1$, such that if $q_1 w_1 \vdash^i q_2 w_2$, where $q_1 \in Q_1$ and $q_2 \in Q_2$, then $q_1 \in Q'_1$.

Proof
This theorem is proved by induction on i in $X_1 \vDash^i X_2$, for $i \geq 0$.

Basis
Let $i = 0$. Then, $X_1 \vDash^0 X_2$, so $Q_1 = Q_2 \subseteq Q$, and $w_1 = w_2$. Set $Q_1' = Q_1$. At this point, if $q_1 w_1 \vdash^0 q_2 w_2$, where $q_1 \in Q_1$ and $q_2 \in Q_2$, then $q_1 \in Q_1'$ because Q_1, Q_2, and Q_1' are identical.

To demonstrate the uniqueness of Q_1', we prove that no proper subset of Q_1' satisfies this implication. Let Q_1'' be a proper subset of Q_1', $Q_1'' \subset Q_1'$. Consider any state, $p \in Q_1'' - Q_1'$. Set $p = q_1 = q_2$. At this point, we have $q_1 w_1 \vdash^0 q_2 w_2$, where $q_1 \in Q_1$ and $q_2 \in Q_2$; however, $q_1 \notin Q_1''$. We conclude that Q_1' is a unique subset of Q_1 such that if $q_1 w_1 \vdash^i q_2 w_2$, where $q_1 \in Q_1$ and $q_2 \in Q_2$, then $q_1 \in Q_1'$. Thus, the basis of this proof holds.

Induction hypothesis
Assume that this theorem holds for all $i = 0, \ldots, n$, for some $n \geq 0$.

Induction step
Consider

$$X_1 \vDash^{n+1} X_2$$

As $n + 1 \geq 1$, then $X_1 \vDash^{n+1} X_2$ can be expressed as

$$X_1 \vDash^n X_3 \vDash X_2$$

By the inductive hypothesis, there exists a unique subset of Q_1, $Q_1'' \subseteq Q_1$, such that if $q_1 w_1 \vdash^n q_3 w_3$, where $q_1 \in Q_1$ and $q_3 \in Q_3$, then $q_1 \in Q_1''$. Define

$Q_1' = \{ q_1 : q_1 \in Q_1''$ and there exists $q_3 \in Q_3$ such that
$\quad q_1 w_1 \vdash^n q_3 w_3 \vdash q_2 w_2$ for some $w_3 \in a w_2$, where $a \in \Sigma \cup \{\varepsilon\}\}$

By the definition of Q_1', if $q_1 w_1 \vdash^{n+1} q_2 w_2$, where $q_1 \in Q_1$ and $q_2 \in Q_2$, then $q_1 \in Q_1'$.

The completion of this proof requires proof of the uniqueness of Q_1' by demonstrating that there exists no set, $Q_1''' \subset Q_1'$, such that if $q_1 w_1 \vdash^{n+1} q_2 w_2$, where $q_1 \in Q_1$ and $q_2 \in Q_2$, then $q_1 \in Q_1'''$. ∎

Observe that this proof actually represents an algorithm that determines the greatest superconfiguration $X_1' \subseteq X_1$, satisfying the equivalence

$$\chi_1 \in X_1' \text{ if and only if } \chi_1 \vdash^* \chi_2 \text{ for some } \chi_2 \in X_2$$

Explain this observation in detail. Describe this algorithm by a Pascal-like notation.

2.8 For each finite automaton in Exercise 2.3, construct an equivalent ε-free finite automaton by using Algorithm 3.2.2.3 (Conversion of a finite automaton to an equivalent ε-free finite automaton).

2.9 Convert each ε-free finite automaton obtained in Exercise 2.6. to an equivalent deterministic finite automaton by using Algorithm 3.2.3.1 (Conversion of an ε-free finite automaton to an equivalent deterministic finite automaton – the subset method).

2.10 Convert each ε-free finite automaton obtained in Exercise 2.6 to an equivalent deterministic finite automaton by using Algorithm 3.2.3.4 (Conversion of an ε-free finite automaton to an equivalent deterministic finite automaton — the binary method).

2.11 Convert each ε-free finite automaton obtained in Exercise 2.6 to an equivalent well-specified finite automaton by using Algorithm 3.2.4.7 (Conversion of a deterministic finite automaton to an equivalent well-specified finite automaton).

2.12 Convert each ε-free finite automaton obtained in Exercise 2.11 to the equivalent minimum-state finite automaton by using Algorithm 3.2.5.1 (Well-specified finite automaton minimization).

2.13 Generalize the definition of a finite automaton by allowing a set of start states rather than a single start state. Formally define this generalization. Prove that this generalization does not increase the power of finite automata.

2.14 A *lazy finite automaton* reads a word, consisting of several symbols, in a move. Define the notion of a lazy finite automaton formally. Prove that this generalization does not increase the power of finite automata.

2.15 As its term indicates, a *two-head finite automaton* possesses two tape heads, H_0 and H_1, that may move independently, left to right, on the tape. Its state set Q is divided into two disjoint sets, Q_0 and Q_1. If the current state is in Q_i, for some $i \in \{0, 1\}$, the input symbol is read by H_i. The automaton accepts a word if it ends up in a final state after having read all the input word by both of the heads. Formalize the notion of a two-head finite automaton. Define the language accepted by a two-head finite automaton. Prove that finite automata are less powerful than two-head finite automata.

2.16 Consider the following language:
(a) $\{a^i b^i : i \geq 0\}$
(b) $\{ww : w \in \{a, b\}^+\}$
For each of these two languages, construct a two-head finite automaton that accepts the language.

2.17 By analogy with deterministic finite automata, define *deterministic two-head finite automata*. Prove or disprove that deterministic two-head finite automata and nondeterministic two-head finite automata have the same power.

2.18 A *two-tape finite automaton*, M, has two input tapes, T_0 and T_1, and two disjoint sets of states, Q_0 and Q_1. If M is in a state from Q_i, $i \in \{0, 1\}$, M reads the input symbol on T_i. M accepts pairs of words which are placed on T_0 and T_1. Formalize the notion of a two-tape finite automaton. Define the language accepted by a two-tape finite automaton. Introduce the notion of a deterministic two-tape finite automaton.

2.19 Consider these sets of pairs of words:
(a) $\{(a^i b, a^i b^j): i, j \geq 0\}$
(b) $\{(a^i b, a^j b^i): i, j \geq 0\}$
(c) $\{(c_1 \ldots c_n, d_1 \ldots d_n) : c_i, d_i \in \{a, b\}, c_i = a$ if and only if $d_i = b, 1 \leq i \leq n$, for $n \geq 1\} \cup \{(\varepsilon, \varepsilon)\}$

For each of these sets, construct a deterministic two-tape finite automaton that accept the set.

2.20 A *two-way finite automaton* moves either way on its tape. Formalize the notion of a two-way finite automaton. Define the language accepted by a two-way finite automaton. Introduce the notion of a deterministic two-way finite automaton. Prove that the deterministic two-way finite automata and the deterministic finite automata have the same power.

2.21 Complete Example 3.2.1.1 Part 9.
2.22 Prove Lemma 3.2.2.2 in detail.
2.23 Complete Example 3.2.2.1 Part 3.
2.24 Complete the proof of Lemma 3.2.2.4.
2.25 Discuss Example 3.2.2.1 Part 6 in detail.
2.26 Prove that Algorithm 3.2.2.7 is correct.
2.27 Complete the proof of Lemma 3.2.3.2
2.28 Discuss Example 3.2.3.1 Part 2 in detail.
2.29 Complete the proof of Lemma 3.2.3.5
2.30 Prove Lemma 3.2.4.2
2.31 Prove Lemma 3.2.4.4
2.32 Modify Algorithms 3.2.3.1 and 3.2.3.4 for state diagrams underlying the deterministic finite automata.
2.33 Prove Lemma 3.2.4.6
2.34 Complete the proof of Lemma 3.2.4.8
2.35 Prove that Algorithm 3.2.4.11 is correct.
2.36 Discuss Example 3.2.5.1 Part 1 in detail.
2.37 Return to Algorithm 3.2.5.1 (Well-specified finite automaton minimization). Design some other algorithms that minimize well-specified finite automata in a more efficient way.
2.38* Consider a well-defined finite automaton, M, as the input of Algorithm 3.2.5.1. (Well-specified finite automaton minimization). This algorithm converts M to the finite automaton, $M_{min} = (Q_{min}, \Sigma, R_{min}, s_{min}, F_{min})$, which represents a minimum-state finite automaton equivalent to M. Prove that if M' is a well-specified finite automaton that accepts $L(M)$, then M contains at least card(Q_{min}) states.
2.39 Consider the following definition.

Definition — state word

Let $M = (Q, \Sigma, R, s, F)$ be a finite automaton and $\chi \vdash^* \chi'\ [\rho]$ in M. The state word corresponding to ρ, sw(ρ), is defined as follows:

(1) if $\rho = \varepsilon$, then $\mathrm{sw}(\rho) = \varepsilon$;
(2) if $\rho = r_1...r_n$ with r_i: $q_i a_i \vdash q_{i+1}$ in R, for some $n \geq 1$, then $\mathrm{sw}(\rho) = q_1...q_{n+1}q_{n+1}$.

Let $M = (Q, \Sigma, R, s, F)$ be a deterministic finite automaton. Construct a finite automaton M' accepting the set of all state words corresponding to the accepting computation in M; that is,
$$L(M') = \{\mathrm{sw}(\rho): \mathrm{sw} \vdash^* f[\rho] \text{ in } M \text{ for some } w \in \Sigma^*, \rho \in R^*, f \in F\}$$

2.40 Using the notion of a state word, introduced in Exercise 2.39 to simplify the proof of Lemma 3.3.2.2.

3 Finite automata and regular expressions

3.1 Convert each regular expression discussed in Exercise 1.2 and Exercise 1.3 to an equivalent finite automata by Algorithm 3.3.1.11. Then, convert the resulting finite automaton M to the equivalent minimum-state finite automaton by using the algorithms presented in Section 3.2.

3.2 Construct a regular expression that denotes the language consisting of all lexemes of your favourite programming language. Convert this expression to an equivalent finite automaton by Algorithm 3.3.1.11. Then, convert the resulting finite automaton M to the equivalent minimum-state finite automaton by using the algorithms presented in Section 3.2.

3.3 Convert the minimum-state finite automata obtained in Exercise 2.10 to equivalent regular expressions by Algorithm 3.3.2.1. Simplify the resulting expressions.

3.4 Complete the proof of Lemma 3.3.1.5.

3.5 Prove Lemma 3.3.1.8

3.6 Complete the proof of Lemma 3.3.1.10

3.7 Complete the proof of Lemma 3.3.1.12

3.8 Complete Example 3.3.1.1

3.9 Section 3.3.1.2 informally described several COLA scanner components, including Concatenate, Digits, Empty, Symbol, GetSymbol, Empty, Letters, Lexeme, LexemeType, UnGetSymbol. Specify these components in Pascal.

3.10 Consider lexemes of type 7 through 16 in Section 3.3.1.2. By analogy with procedure P6, corresponding to lexemes of type 6, describe procedures P7 through P16, corresponding to lexemes of type 7 through 16.

3.11 Complete Example 3.3.2.1

Programming projects

1 Regular expressions

1.1 Design a data structure that represents regular expressions.

1.2 Write a program to check that a given regular expression is well formed.
1.3 Write a program that reads a natural number n and a fully parenthesized regular expression E to generate all words x such that $|x| \leq n$ and $x \in L(E)$.
1.4 Section 3.1 has explained how to simplify fully parenthesized regular expression by removing some parentheses from them. Write a program that simplifies fully parenthesized regular expressions in this way.
1.5 Write a program that converts a given extended regular expression (see Exercise 1.11) to an equivalent regular expression.

2 Finite automata

2.1 Write a program that checks if a given finite automaton is ε-free.
2.2 Write a program that checks if a given finite automaton is deterministic.
2.3 Write a program that checks if a given finite automaton is well specified.
2.4 Write a program that checks if a given finite automaton is minimum-state.
2.5 Write a program that simulates an ε-free finite automaton. Base the program on Algorithm 3.2.2.6 (ε-free finite automaton implementation).
2.6 Write a program that simulates an ε-free finite automaton. Base the program on Algorithm 3.2.2.7 (ε-free finite automaton implementation based on set operations).
2.7 Write a program that simulates a well-specified finite automaton. Base the program on Algorithm 3.2.4.9 (well-specified finite automaton implementation — the tabular method).
2.8 Write a program that simulates a well-specified finite automaton. Base the program on Algorithm 3.2.4.10 (well-specified finite automaton implementation — the case method).
2.9 Write a program that translates a set of rules, which define a well-specified finite automaton M, to a program that simulates M; in other words, write a *well-specified finite automaton compiler*.
2.10 Write programs implementing the algorithms given in Section 3.2.

3 Finite automata and regular expressions

3.1 Write a program that implements Algorithm 3.3.1.11 (conversion of a regular expression to an equivalent finite automata). That is, this program reads a regular expression and produces an equivalent finite automaton.
3.2 Write a program that implements the COLA scanner GetLexeme, described in Section 3.3.1.2.
3.3 Write a program that implements Algorithm 3.3.2.1 (conversion of a deterministic finite automaton to an equivalent regular expression). That is, this program converts a deterministic finite automaton to an equivalent regular expression.

4 Properties of Regular Languages

This chapter studies fundamental properties of regular languages. Section 4.1 establishes a crucial result — the pumping lemma for regular languages. Typically, this lemma is used to prove that a language is not regular. Section 4.2 studies closure properties of the regular languages. Finally, Section 4.3 discusses some decidable problems concerning these languages.

4.1 Pumping lemma

When examining a language L, it is useful to know whether L is regular. By constructing a finite automaton that accepts L, it can be demonstrated that L is regular. As a rule, it is more difficult to prove that L is not regular because this requires a proof that none of all possible finite automata accepts L. Fortunately, it is frequently possible to simplify such a proof by making use of a condition that all regular languages satisfy; indeed, proving that L does not satisfy the condition actually demonstrates that L is not a regular language. The pumping lemma for regular languages — the subject of this section — represents a condition of this kind.

Pumping lemma and its proof

The pumping lemma for regular languages states that if a regular language L contains a sufficiently long word $z \in L$, then z contains a nonempty subword v such that $z = uvw$ and for all $m \geq 0$, $uv^m w \in L$. This statement results from a relationship between $|z|$ and the sequence of moves that a deterministic finite automaton, $M = (Q, \Sigma, R, s, F)$, makes with z on the input tape. More precisely, let $L = L(M)$ and $z \in L(M)$ so $|z| \geq \text{card}(Q)$. As M reads a symbol on every move, M accepts z by making a sequence of $|z|$ moves; therefore, M visits a state $q \in Q$ twice when accepting z. These two visits of q determine the decomposition of z as $z = uvw$ so that:

1. u takes M from the start state to the first visit of q;
2. v takes M from the first visit of q to the second visit of q;
3. w takes M from the second visit of q to a final state f.

Automaton M can iterate the computation between the two visits of q m times, for all $m \geq 0$, and during each of these iteration, M reads v. Consequently, M accepts every word of the form $uv^m w$ (see Figure 4.1.1).

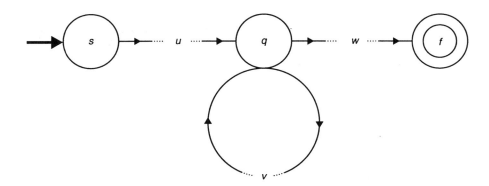

Figure 4.1.1 M accepts $uv^m w$, for all $m \geq 0$.

Lemma 4.1.1 Pumping lemma for regular languages

Let L be a regular language. Then, there exists a natural number k such that every word, $z \in L$, satisfying $|z| \geq k$ can be expressed as

$$z = uvw$$

where

1. $v \neq \varepsilon$;
2. $|uv| \leq k$;
3. $uv^m w \in L$, for all $m \geq 0$.

Proof

Let L be a regular language, and let $M = (Q, \Sigma, R, s, F)$ be a deterministic finite automaton such that $L(M) = L$. Set

$$k = \text{card}(Q)$$

Let $z \in L$ with $|z| \geq k$. Then,

$$sz \vdash^* f[\rho]$$

for some rule word ρ and $f \in F$ in M. Because M makes no ε-moves and, thus, reads a symbol on every move,

$$|\rho| = |z|$$

As $|z| \geq k$ and $k = \text{card}(Q)$, $|\rho| \geq \text{card}(Q)$. Therefore, some states appear in ρ more than once. Let us express $sz \vdash^* f[\rho]$ as

$$suvw \vdash^* qvw \qquad [\rho_1]$$
$$\vdash^* qw \qquad [\rho_2]$$
$$\vdash^* f \qquad [\rho_3]$$

where $\rho = \rho_1\rho_2\rho_3$, $q \in Q$, $|\rho_2| \geq 1$, q appears in $\rho_1\rho_2$ twice, and any other state, $p \in Q - \{q\}$, appears in $\rho_1\rho_2$ i times, for some $i \in \{0, 1\}$; less formally, $\rho_1\rho_2$ is the shortest prefix of ρ that contains two appearances of the same state, q.

The following three claims verify conditions 1 through 3 in Lemma 4.1.1.

Claim A
Condition 1 holds; that is, $v \neq \varepsilon$.

Proof
Because $|v| = |\rho_2|$ and $\rho_2 \neq \varepsilon$, then $v \neq \varepsilon$.
□

Claim B
Condition 2 holds; that is, $|uv| \leq k$.

Proof
Recall that during the computation according to $\rho_1\rho_2$, M enters q twice and any other state at most once. Consequently, $|\rho_1\rho_2| \leq \text{card}(Q)$. As $|uw| = |\rho_1\rho_2|$ and $\text{card}(Q) = k$, $|uv| \leq k$, so Claim B holds.
□

Claim C
Condition (3) holds; that is, $uv^m w \in L$, for all $m \geq 0$.

Proof
1. Consider $uv^m w \in L$ with $m \geq 1$. M accepts this word by repeating the computation according to ρ_2 m times; that is,

$$suv^m w \vdash^* qv^m w \qquad [\rho_1]$$
$$\vdash^* qv^{m-1} w \qquad [\rho_2]$$
$$\vdash^* qv^{m-2} w \qquad [\rho_2]$$
$$\cdots$$
$$\vdash^* qvw \qquad [\rho_2]$$
$$\vdash^* qw \qquad [\rho_2]$$
$$\vdash^* f \qquad [\rho_3]$$

In brief,

$$suv^m w \vdash^* qv^m w \qquad [\rho_1]$$
$$\vdash^* qw \qquad [\rho_2^m]$$
$$\vdash^* f \qquad [\rho_3]$$

2. Consider $uv^m w \in L$ with $m \geq 0$; that is, $uv^0 w = uw$. At this point, M accepts uw so it omits the computation according to ρ_2; indeed,

$$suw \vdash^* qw \qquad [\rho_1]$$
$$\vdash^* f \qquad [\rho_3]$$

Consequently, Claim C holds.

□

Having verified conditions 1 through 3, it is concluded that Lemma 4.1.1 holds.

■

Example 4.1.1 Illustration of the proof of lemma 4.1.1

To illustrate the technique used in the proof of Lemma 4.1.1, consider the regular language

$$L = \{a\}\{\{b\}\{c\}\}^*\{b\}$$

In addition, consider the deterministic finite automaton M with these three rule

1: $sa \vdash p$
2: $pb \vdash f$
3: $fc \vdash p$

where s is the start state, and f is the final state (Figure 4.1.2). Observe that $L = L(M)$.

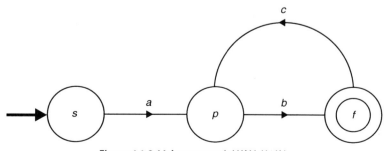

Figure 4.1.2 M that accepts $\{a\}\{\{b\}\{c\}\}^*\{b\}$.

As M has three states (s, p, and f), set

$$k = 3$$

Let $z = abcb$. Notice that $z \in L$. Because $|abcb| = 4$ and $k = 3$, $|z| \geq k$. M accepts z by making these four moves:

$$\begin{aligned} sabcb &\vdash pbcb & [1] \\ &\vdash fcb & [2] \\ &\vdash pb & [3] \\ &\vdash f & [2] \end{aligned}$$

Breaking this computation at the two appearances of p gives these three partial computations:

A. $sabcb \vdash pbcb$ [1]
B. $pbcb \vdash fcb$ [2]
       $\vdash pb$ [3]
C. $pb \vdash f$ [2]

Because M reads a, bc and b during computations A, B and C, respectively, decompose z as

$$z = uvw$$

where

$$u = a, v = bc \text{ and } w = b$$

Observe that $v \neq \varepsilon$ and that $|uv| \leq k$ ($k = 4$), so the first two conditions of Lemma 4.1.1 hold. As $a(bc)^m b \in L$, for all $i \geq 0$, the third condition is satisfied as well. To illustrate the third condition in greater detail, consider $m = 2$ in $a(bc)^m b$; that is, $a(bc)^2 b = abcbcb$. M accepts $abcbcb$ by iterating the partial computation according to 23 twice; formally,

$$\begin{aligned} sabcbcb &\vdash pbcbcb & [1] \\ &\vdash fcbcb & [2] \\ &\vdash pbcb & [3] \\ &\vdash fcb & [2] \\ &\vdash pb & [3] \\ &\vdash f & [2] \end{aligned}$$

▲

Applications

As already noted, the pumping lemma is usually used to prove that a given language L is not regular. A proof of this kind is made by contradiction, and its typical structure follows next:

1. Assume that L is regular.
2. Consider the constant k from the pumping lemma, and select a word $z \in L$ whose length depends on k so $|z| \geq k$ is surely true.
3. Consider all possible decompositions of z into uvw, satisfying $|uv| \leq k$ and $v \neq \varepsilon$; for each of these decompositions, demonstrate that there exists $m \geq 0$ such that $uv^m w \notin L$ — a contradiction of the third condition in Lemma 4.1.1.
4. Conclude that L is not regular.

Example 4.1.2 Simple application of the pumping lemma
Consider

$$L = \{a^n b^n : n \geq 0\}$$

The proof that L is not regular by Lemma 4.1.1 is as follows. Assume that L is regular. Then, there exists a natural number k satisfying Lemma 4.1.1. Set

$$z = a^k b^k$$

Notice that $z \in L$. As $|z| = 2k$ and $2k > k$, $|z| \geq k$. Then, by Lemma 4.1.1, z can be written as $z = uvw$ so the three conditions of the pumping lemma hold. As $|v| \geq 1$,

$$v \in \{a\}^+ \cup \{b\}^+ \cup \{a\}^+ \{b\}^+$$

1. Suppose $v \in \{a\}^+$. Consider $uv^0 w = uw$. Then, $uw = a^j b^k$, for some $j \leq k - 1$, so $uw \notin L$. By the third condition of the pumping lemma, however, $uw \in L$ which is a contradiction.

2. Suppose $v \in \{b\}^+$. Consider $uv^0 w = uw$. Then, $uw = a^k b^j$, for some $j \leq k - 1$, so $uw \notin L$. By the third condition of the pumping lemma, $uw \in L$ — a contradiction.

3. Suppose that $v \in \{a\}^+ \{b\}^+$. Consider $uv^2 w = uvvw$. Because $v \in \{a\}^+ \{b\}^+$, $uvvw \in \{a\}^* \{a\}^+ \{b\}^+ \{a\}^+ \{b\}^+ \{b\}^*$, so $uvvw \notin L$. By the third condition of the pumping lemma, however, $uvvw \in L$ — a contradiction.

For each of the three decompositions, there exists $m \geq 0$ such that $uv^m w \notin L$; in other words, all these decompositions lead to a contradiction. Therefore, L is not regular.

▲

Properties of regular languages

Example 4.1.2 illustrated a straightforward application of Lemma 4.1.1. The following example uses this lemma in a more ingenious way.

Example 4.1.3 More difficult application of the pumping lemma
Consider

$$L = \{a^n : n \text{ is prime}\}$$

(a natural number n is prime if its only positive divisors are 1 and n). By Lemma 4.1.1, this example demonstrates that L is not regular. Assume that L is regular. Then, there exists a natural number k satisfying the pumping lemma. As L is infinite, there exists a word $z \in L$ such that $|z| \geq k$. By Lemma 4.1.1, z can then be written as $z = uvw$, so the three conditions of the pumping lemma hold. Consider $uv^m w$ with

$$m = |uw| + 2|v| + 2$$

Observe that $|uv^m w| = |uw| + m|v| = |uw| + (|uw| + 2|v| + 2)|v| = (|uw| + 2|v|) + (|uw| + 2|v|)|v| = (|uw| + 2|v|)(1 + |v|)$, so $|uv^m w|$ is not prime and, thus, $uv^m w \notin L$. By the third condition of the pumping lemma, however, $uv^m w \in L$, which is a contradiction. Thus, L is not regular.

The present example can be used to demonstrate how to interpret a result concerning languages in terms of computation. As L is not regular, no finite automaton accepts L. Consequently, no finite automaton can represent a model behind a computer program that reads a natural number n and decides whether n is prime.

▲

Although the pumping lemma for regular languages is primarily used to disprove that some languages are regular, this important lemma has some other applications in the study of regular languages. Specifically, algorithms that decide problems concerning these languages make often use of this lemma, such as Algorithms 4.3.4 and 4.3.7.

Nonapplicability of the pumping lemma

As the previous two examples have illustrated, the pumping lemma is useful in disproving that a language is regular. However, this lemma is of no use in proving that a language is regular because, in addition to all regular languages, some nonregular languages satisfy the pumping-lemma conditions as well. That is, proving that a language satisfies these conditions does not necessarily imply that the language is regular. The next example presents a nonregular language satisfying the conditions of the pumping lemma.

Example 4.1.4 Nonregular language satisfying the pumping lemma conditions

Consider

$$L = \{a^m b^n c^n : m \geq 1 \text{ and } n \geq 0\} \cup \{b^m c^n : m, n \geq 0\}$$

This example proves the following two statements:

1. L satisfies the pumping lemma conditions;
2. L is not regular.

Pumping lemma conditions
Set

$$k = 1$$

Consider any word z satisfying $z \in L$ and $|z| \geq k$. By the definition of L, $z \in \{a^m b^n c^n : m \geq 1 \text{ and } n \geq 0\} \cup \{b^m c^n : m, n \geq 0\}$.

1. Let $z \in \{a^m b^n c^n : m \geq 1 \text{ and } n \geq 0\}$. That is,

$$z = a^m b^n c^n$$

for some $m \geq 1$ and $n \geq 0$. Decompose z as

$$z = uvw$$

where

$$u = \varepsilon, v = a, \text{ and } w = a^{m-1} b^n c^n$$

Notice that $v \neq \varepsilon$ and $|uv| \leq k$ ($k = 1$), so the first two conditions of the pumping lemma hold. In addition, observe that L contains $a^m b^n c^n$, for all $m \geq 0$; in other words, $uv^m w \in L$, for all $m \geq 0$. Therefore, the third condition holds as well.

2. Let $z \in \{b^m c^n : m, n \geq 0\}$. That is,

$$z = b^m c^n$$

for some $m, n \geq 0$. Decompose z as

$$z = uvw$$

where $u = \varepsilon$, v is the leftmost symbol of z, and w is the remaining suffix of z.

A. If $m = 0$, then $v = c$, and $w = c^{n-1}$. At this point, the first two conditions of the pumping lemma are true: $|v| > 0$ and $|uv| \leq 1$. Observe that $uv^i w \in L$, for all $i \geq 0$, so all three conditions hold.

B. If $m > 0$, then $v = b$ and $w = b^{m-1}c^n$. By analogy with the case when $m = 0$, prove that the conditions of the pumping lemma hold.

Non-Regularity
Consider

$$\{a^m b^n c^n : m \geq 1 \text{ and } n \geq 0\} \subseteq L$$

By analogy with the first part of Example 2.1.3 in Section 2.1, prove that there exists no finite automaton that accepts $\{a^m b^n c^n : m \geq 1$ and $n \geq 0\}$. Then, however, no finite automaton accepts L, so L is not regular by Theorem 3.3.3.2.

It is thus concluded that L represents a nonregular language that satisfies the three conditions of the pumping lemma.

▲

Exercise 1.6 modifies the pumping lemma for regular languages so the modified lemma is useful in both proving and disproving that some languages are regular.

4.2 Closure properties

The family of regular languages is closed under a language operation o if this family contains every language that results from o applied to any regular languages. This section proves that the family of regular languages is closed under the following operations:

1. union
2. concatenation
3. closure
4. complement
5. intersection
6. regular substitution
7. finite substitution
8. homomorphism.

The discussion below demonstrates most of these closure properties *effectively*. That is, to prove that a given operation o preserves the family of regular languages, an algorithm is presented that converts any finite automaton to a finite automaton that accepts the language resulting from o applied to the languages accepted by the input finite automaton.

Union, concatenation, and closure

Theorem 4.2.1
The family of regular languages is closed under union, concatenation and closure.

Proof
The definition of regular languages and Theorem 3.3.3.2 imply this theorem. ∎

An effective demonstration of the three closure properties stated by Theorem 4.2.1 is based on Algorithms 3.3.1.4, 3.3.1.7 and 3.3.1.9. Algorithm 3.3.1.4 constructs a finite automaton M from two finite automata M_0 and M_1, so $L(M) = L(M_0) \cup L(M_1)$. Algorithm 3.3.1.7 constructs a finite automaton M from two finite automata M_0 and M_1, so $L(M) = L(M_0)L(M_1)$. Finally, Algorithm 3.3.1.9 constructs a finite automaton M from a finite automaton M_0, so $L(M) = L(M_0)^*$. Consequently, these algorithms demonstrate the three closure properties effectively.

Complement and intersection

To prove that the family of regular languages is closed under complement, consider an alphabet Σ and any regular language, $L \subseteq \Sigma^*$. By Theorem 3.3.3.2, there exists a well-specified finite automaton, $M = (Q, \Sigma, R, s, F)$, such that $L = L(M)$. Complement the final states of M by making every nonfinal state final and every final state nonfinal; more formally, introduce the well-specified final automaton

$$M' = (Q, \Sigma, R, s, Q - F)$$

Observe that M' accepts precisely the words that M rejects. In other words, M' accepts the complement of $L(M)$; that is,

$$L(M') = \Sigma^* - L(M)$$

Note that the requirement that M represents a well-specified finite automaton is essential. Indeed, this requirement guarantees that M reads every $w \in \Sigma^*$, so M' accepts all $\Sigma^* - L(M)$, not a proper subset of $\Sigma^* - L(M)$.

The following algorithm formally describes the construction of M' from M so that M' accepts the complement of $L(M)$, then Lemma 4.2.3 proves that this construction is correct.

Algorithm 4.2.2: Construction of a finite automaton for the complement of the language accepted by a well-specified finite automaton

Input: A well-specified finite automaton $M = (Q, \Sigma, R, s, F)$.

Output: A well-specified finite automaton $M' = (Q, \Sigma, R, s, F')$, satisfying $L(M') = \Sigma^* - L(M)$.

Method

begin
 $F' := Q - F$
end.

Lemma 4.2.3
Algorithm 4.2.2 halts and correctly converts any well-specified finite automaton to a well-specified finite automaton M', satisfying $L(M') = \Sigma^* - L(M)$.

Proof

Termination
Clearly, Algorithm 4.2.2 always terminates.

Correctness
Let $M = (Q, \Sigma, R, s, F)$ be a well-specified finite automaton. Algorithm 4.2.2 converts M to a well-specified finite automaton $M' = (Q, \Sigma, R, s, F')$ with $F' = Q - F$. As M is well-specified, for all words $w \in \Sigma^*$, $sw \vdash^* p$ in M for some $p \in Q$; that is,

$$\Sigma^* = \{\, w: sw \vdash^* p \text{ in } M, \text{ where } p \in Q \,\}$$

For every word, $w \in \Sigma^*$,

$$w \notin L(M) \text{ if and only if } sw \vdash^* p \text{ in } M \text{ with } p \in Q - F$$

Because $F' = Q - F$,

$$sw \vdash^* p \text{ in } M \text{ with } p \in Q - F \text{ if and only if } sw \vdash^* p \text{ in } M' \text{ with } p \in F'$$

Clearly,

$$sw \vdash^* p \text{ in } M' \text{ with } p \in F' \text{ if and only if } w \in L(M')$$

These three equivalences imply that for every word $w \in \Sigma^*$,

$$w \notin L(M) \text{ if and only if } w \in L(M')$$

Thus,

$$L(M') = \Sigma^* - L(M)$$

This concludes that Lemma 4.2.2 holds. ∎

Theorem 4.2.4
The family of regular languages is closed under complement.

Proof
This theorem follows from Algorithm 4.2.1. and Lemma 4.2.2. ∎

Theorem 4.2.5
The family of regular languages is closed under intersection.

Proof
Let L_1 and L_2 be two regular languages. By Theorems 4.2.1 and 4.2.3, $\overline{L_1} \cup \overline{L_2}$ is regular. Therefore, $L_1 \cap L_2$ also represents a regular language because

$$L_1 \cap L_2 = \overline{\overline{L_1} \cup \overline{L_2}}$$

by DeMorgan's law. We conclude that the family of regular languages is closed under intersection. ∎

Boolean algebra of languages

The algebraic view of the closure properties of regular languages is now considered.

Definition — Boolean algebra
Let a family of languages be closed under union, intersection, and complementation. Then, this family is a *Boolean algebra of languages*. ◆

Corollary 4.2.6
The family of regular languages is a Boolean algebra of languages.

Properties of regular languages

Proof
This corollary follows from Theorems 4.2.1, 4.2.4 and 4.2.5. ∎

Regular substitution

Next, regular substitution is defined and it is proved that the family of regular languages is closed under this substitution (see Section 1.3 for the definition of a substitution). In addition to a detailed proof of this closure property in terms of finite automata, it is shown how to achieve this result in terms of regular expressions. This important closure property represents a powerful result, which implies several other closure properties, as demonstrated subsequently.

Definition — regular substitution
Let Σ and Ω be two alphabets, and let η be a substitution from Σ^* to Ω^* such that for all $a \in \Sigma$, $\eta(\{a\})$ represents a regular language. Then, η is a *regular substitution*.

◆

To prove that the family of regular languages is closed under regular substitution, the present section next demonstrates that if L is a regular language, and η is a regular substitution such that $L \subseteq \Sigma^*$, then $\eta(L)$ is a regular language as well. More precisely, the following algorithm considers a regular language L such that $L = L(M_0)$, where $M_0 = (Q_0, \Sigma_0, R_0, s_0, F_0)$ is an ε-free finite automaton. Let η be a regular substitution such that for each $a \in \Sigma_0$, $\eta(a) = L(M_a)$, where $M_a = (Q_a, \Sigma_a, R_a, s_a, F_a)$ is a finite automaton. Observe that for every word $a_1 a_2 \ldots a_n \in L(M_0)$, where $a_i \in \Sigma_0$, $i = 1, \ldots, n$, for some $n \geq 0$, the following equivalence holds:

$$w_1 w_2 \ldots w_n \in \eta(a_1 a_2 \ldots a_n) \text{ if and only if } w_i \in L(M_{a_i})$$

(Note that the case when $n = 0$ implies $a_1 a_2 \ldots a_n = w_1 w_2 \ldots w_n = \varepsilon$.) The next algorithm constructs a finite automaton $M = (Q, \Sigma, R, s, \{f\})$ satisfying

$$w \in L(M_0) \text{ if and only if } w' \in L(M)$$

where $w = a_1 a_2 \ldots a_n \in \Sigma_0^*$, $a_i \in \Sigma_0$; $w' = w_1 w_2 \ldots w_n \in \Sigma^*$, $w_i \in L(M_{a_i})$, $i = 1, \ldots, n$; for some $n \geq 0$. As $\eta(a) = L(M_a)$, for all $a \in \Sigma_0$,

$$L(M) = \eta(L)$$

By Theorem 3.3.3.2, the finite automata characterize the family of regular languages, so $\eta(L)$ is regular. Thus, the family of regular languages is closed under regular substitution as formally established next.

The following algorithm requires that

1. $Q_0 \cap Q_a = \emptyset$, for all $a \in \Sigma_0$;
2. $Q_b \cap Q_c = \emptyset$, for all $b, c \in \Sigma_0$ such that $b \neq c$.

Note that this requirement is without any loss of generality; indeed, if two sets contain some common states, they are renamed (in either of the two sets) to satisfy this requirement.

Algorithm 4.2.7: Construction of a finite automaton for a regular substitution

Input: An ε-free finite automaton $M_0 = (Q_0, \Sigma_0, R_0, s_0, F_0)$ and a regular substitution η such that for each $a \in \Sigma_0$, $\eta(a) = L(M_a)$, where $M_a = (Q_a, \Sigma_a, R_a, s_a, F_a)$ is a finite automaton. In addition, these two conditions are true:

1. $Q_0 \cap Q_a = \emptyset$, for all $a \in \Sigma_0$;
2. $Q_b \cap Q_c = \emptyset$, for all $b, c \in \Sigma_0$ such that $b \neq c$.

Output: A finite automaton $M = (Q, \Sigma, R, s_0, \{f\})$, satisfying $L(M) = \eta(L(M_0))$.

Method

begin
  $Q := \{q : q \in Q_0\} \cup \{<pq> : p \in Q_0, q \in Q_a, a \in \Sigma_0\} \cup \{f\}$
  $\{f$ is the final state of $M\}$;
  $\Sigma := \bigcup_{a \in \Sigma_0} \Sigma_a$;

  $R := \quad \{q_0 \vdash <q_0 s_a> : a \in \Sigma_0, q_0 \in Q_0\}$
  $\cup \{<q_0 q> b \vdash <q_0 q'> : q_0 \in Q_0, qb \vdash q' \in R_a$ for some $a \in \Sigma_0\}$
  $\cup \{<q_0 f_a> \vdash p_0 : a \in \Sigma_0, q_0, p_0 \in Q_0, f_a \in F_a, q_0 a \vdash p_0 \in R_0\}$
  $\cup \{f_0 \vdash f : f_0 \in F_0\}$
end.

The equation

$$L(M) = \eta(L(M_0))$$

follows from

$$w \in L(M_0) \text{ if and only if } w' \in L(M)$$

where $w = a_1 a_2 \ldots a_n \in \Sigma_0^*$, $a_i \in \Sigma_0$, $w' = w_1 w_2 \ldots w_n \in \Sigma^*$, $w_i \in L(M_{a_i})$, $i = 1, \ldots, n$, for some $n \geq 0$. To justify this equivalence, observe the behaviour of M (see Figure 4.2.1).

Properties of regular languages

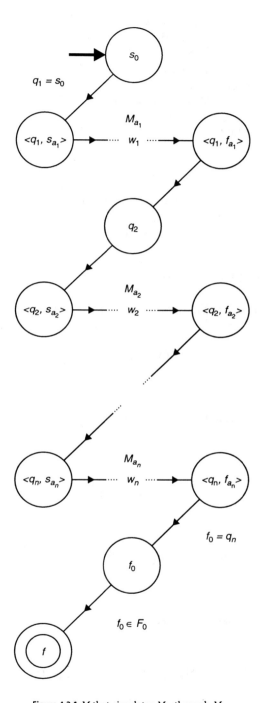

Figure 4.2.1 M that simulates M_{a_1} through M_{a_n}.

First, M simulates a finite automaton M_{a_1}. When M enters a final state of M_{a_1} during this simulation, M has read a word w_1 such that $w_1 \in L(M_{a_1})$; then, M simulates another finite automaton, M_{a_2}. Assume that M simulates $M_{a_1}, M_{a_2}, \ldots, M_{a_n}$ in this way; during these n simulations, M reads $w_1 \ldots w_n$ so $w_i \in L(M_{a_i})$, for $i = 1, \ldots, n$, and after these simulations, M occurs in a final state of M_{a_n}. From this state, M makes an ε-move to f_0 and, from f_0, M makes another ε-move to f. At this point, M accepts w', where $w' = w_1 w_2 \ldots w_n$, $w_i \in L(M_{a_i})$, $a_1 a_2 \ldots a_n = w$, $w \in L(M_0)$; in other words, the above equivalence holds.

Lemma 4.2.8

Let $M_0 = (Q_0, \Sigma_0, R_0, s_0, F_0)$ be an ε-free finite automaton, and let η be a regular substitution such that for each $a \in \Sigma_0$, $\eta(a) = L(M_a)$, where $M_a = (Q_a, \Sigma_a, R_a, s_a, F_a)$ is a finite automaton. In addition, let the two following conditions be satisfied:

1. $Q_0 \cap Q_a = \emptyset$, for all $a \in \Sigma_0$;
2. $Q_b \cap Q_c = \emptyset$, for all $b, c \in \Sigma_0$ such that $b \neq c$.

With M_0 and M_a, for all $a \in \Sigma_0$, Algorithm 4.2.7 halts and correctly constructs a finite automaton $M = (Q, \Sigma, R, s, \{f\})$, satisfying

$$L(M) = \eta(L(M_0))$$

Proof

Termination
This part of the proof is left to the exercises.

Correctness
To demonstrate

$$L(M) = \eta(L(M_0)),$$

establish the equivalence

$$w \in L(M_0) \text{ if and only if } w' \in L(M)$$

where $w = a_1 a_2 \ldots a_n \in \Sigma_0^*$, $a_i \in \Sigma_0$, $w' = w_1 w_2 \ldots w_n \in \Sigma^*$, $w_i \in L(M_{a_i})$, $i = 1, \ldots, n$, for some $n \geq 0$.

First, the following claim is proved.

Claim
Let $w = a_1 a_2 \ldots a_n \in \Sigma_0^*$, $a_i \in \Sigma_0$, $w_i \in L(M_{a_i})$, $i = 1, \ldots, n$ for some $n \geq 0$. Then,

$$s_0 a_1 a_2 \ldots a_n \vdash^* q_0 \text{ in } M_0$$

Properties of regular languages

if and only if

$$s_0 w_1 w_2 \ldots w_n \vdash^* q_0 \text{ in } M$$

where $q_0 \in Q_0$.

Proof
Only if
Assume that $w = a_1 a_2 \ldots a_n \in \Sigma_0^*$, $a_i \in \Sigma_0$, $w_i \in L(M_{a_i})$, $i = 1, \ldots, n$ for some $n \geq 0$. By induction on n, it is proved that $s_0 a_1 a_2 \ldots a_n \vdash^* q_0$ in M_0 implies $s_0 w_1 w_2 \ldots w_n \vdash^* q_0$ in M where $q_0 \in Q_0$.

Basis
Let $n = 0$. Then, $a_1 a_2 \ldots a_n = w_1 w_2 \ldots w_n = \varepsilon$. As M_0 is ε-free, M_0 reads ε by making this 0-move computation $s_0 \vdash^* s_0 [\varepsilon]$. Because $s_0 \vdash^* s_0 [\varepsilon]$ in M, it is concluded that the basis holds.

Induction hypothesis
Assume that the 'only if' part of the claim holds for all words consisting of the symbol k, where $k = 0, \ldots, n$, for some $n \geq 0$.

Induction step
Let $a_1 a_2 \ldots a_n a_{n+1}$ be a word consisting of $n + 1$ symbol, denoted as a_1 through a_{n+1}, where $a_i \in \Sigma_0$, $i = 1, \ldots, n + 1$. Now consider the computation

$$s_0 a_1 a_2 \ldots a_n a_{n+1} \vdash^* q_0$$

in M_0. In greater detail, express $s_0 a_1 a_2 \ldots a_n a_{n+1} \vdash^* q_0$ as

$$s_0 a_1 a_2 \ldots a_n a_{n+1} \vdash^* p_0 a_{n+1}$$
$$\vdash q_0 \quad [r]$$

in M, where $r: p_0 a_{n+1} \vdash q_0 \in R_0$, because $n + 1 \geq 1$ and M_0 is ε-free. By the induction hypothesis,

$$s_0 w_1 w_2 \ldots w_n \vdash^* p_0$$

in M, where $w_i \in L(M_{a_i})$, $i = 1, \ldots, n$. Let $w_{n+1} \in L(M_{a_{n+1}})$. Then,

$$s_{a_{n+1}} w_{n+1} \vdash^* f_{a_{n+1}}$$

in $M_{a_{n+1}}$, for some $f_{a_{n+1}} \in F_{a_{n+1}}$. By Algorithm 4.2.6,

$$\{p_0 \vdash <p_0, s_{a_{n+1}}>, <p_0, f_{a_{n+1}}> \vdash q_0\} \subseteq R$$

because $p_0 a_{n+1} \vdash q_0 \in R_0$. In addition, observe that

$$\{ <p_0, q>b \vdash <p_0, q'> : b \in \Sigma_{a_{n+1}} \text{ and } qb \vdash q' \in R_{a_{n+1}} \} \subseteq R$$

Thus,

$$p_0 w_{n+1} \vdash <p_0, s_{a_{n+1}}> w_{n+1} \quad [\, p_0 \vdash <p_0, s_{a_{n+1}}> \,]$$
$$\vdash^* <p_0, f_{a_{n+1}}>$$
$$\vdash q_0 \quad [\, <p_0, f_{a_{n+1}}> \vdash q_0 \,]$$

in M. Consequently,

$$s_0 w_1 w_2 \ldots w_n w_{n+1} \vdash^* p_0 w_{n+1}$$
$$\vdash <p_0, s_{a_{n+1}}> w_{n+1}$$
$$\vdash^* <p_0, f_{a_{n+1}}>$$
$$\vdash q_0$$

in M. That is, the 'only if' part of the proof has been demonstrated.

If
Assume that $w = a_1 a_2 \ldots a_n \in \Sigma_0^*$, $a_i \in \Sigma_0$, $w_i \in L(M_{a_i})$, $i = 1, \ldots, n$ for some $n \geq 0$. The 'if' part of the proof states that

$$s_0 a_1 a_2 \ldots a_n \vdash^* q_0 \text{ in } M_0$$

provided that

$$s_0 w_1 w_2 \ldots w_n \vdash^* q_0 \text{ in } M$$

for some $q_0 \in Q_0$. Recall the assumptions

1. $Q_0 \cap Q_a = \emptyset$, for all $a \in \Sigma_0$;
2. $Q_b \cap Q_c = \emptyset$, for all $b, c \in \Sigma_0$ such that $b \neq c$.

Under these assumptions, the 'if' part can be demonstrated by analogy with the proof of the 'only if' part. This demonstration is left to the exercises.

Thus the claim holds.

□

Consider the claim for $q_0 = f_0$, where $f_0 \in F_0$. That is, let $w = a_1 a_2 \ldots a_n \in \Sigma_0^*$, $a_i \in \Sigma_0$, $w_i \in L(M_{a_i})$, $i = 1, \ldots, n$ for some $n \geq 0$; then,

$$s_0 a_1 a_2 \ldots a_n \vdash^* f_0 \text{ in } M_0$$

if and only if

$$s_0 w_1 w_2 \ldots w_n \vdash^* f_0 \text{ in } M$$

Observe that

$$s_0 w_1 w_2 \ldots w_n \vdash^* f_0 \text{ in } M$$

if and only if

$$s_0 w_1 w_2 \ldots w_n \vdash^* f_0$$
$$\vdash f \quad [f_0 \vdash f]$$

in M. By these two equivalences,

$$w \in L(M_0) \text{ if and only if } w' \in L(M)$$

where $w = a_1 a_2 \ldots a_n \in \Sigma_0^*$, $a_i \in \Sigma_0$, $w' = w_1 w_2 \ldots w_n \in \Sigma^*$, $w_i \in L(M_{a_i})$, $i = 1, \ldots, n$, for some $n \geq 0$. As η is a regular substitution such that for each $a \in \Sigma_0$, $\eta(a) = L(M_a)$, this gives

$$L(M) = \eta(L(M_0))$$

This concludes that Lemma 4.2.8 holds. ∎

Theorem 4.2.9
The family of regular languages is closed under regular substitution.

Proof
This theorem follows from Algorithm 4.2.7 and Lemma 4.2.8. ∎

The above reasoning has established the property that the family of regular languages is closed under regular substitution in terms of finite automata. However, this property can be proved in terms of regular expressions as well. Indeed, consider a regular substitution η and a regular language L. To prove that $\eta(L)$ is regular, define L and η by regular expressions. More precisely, consider a regular language L such that $L = L(E_0)$, where E_0 is a regular expression over an alphabet Σ_0. Let η be a regular substitution η such that for each $a \in \Sigma_0$, $\eta(a) = L(E_a)$, where E_a is a regular expression. Observe that for every word $a_1 a_2 \ldots a_n \in L(E_0)$, where $a_i \in \Sigma_0$, $i = 1, \ldots, n$, for some $n \geq 0$, the following equivalence holds

$w_1w_2...w_n \in \eta(a_1a_2...a_n)$ if and only if $w_i \in L(E_{a_i})$

(Note that the case when $n = 0$ implies $a_1a_2...a_n = w_1w_2...w_n = \varepsilon$.) Construct a regular expression E satisfying

$$w \in L(E_0) \text{ if and only if } w' \in L(E)$$

where $w = a_1a_2...a_n \in \Sigma_0^*$, $a_i \in \Sigma_0$, $w' = w_1w_2...w_n$ with $w_i \in L(E_{a_i})$, $i = 1, ..., n$, for some $n \geq 0$. As $\eta(a) = L(E_a)$, for all $a \in \Sigma_0$,

$$L(M) = \eta(L(M_0)) = \eta(L)$$

and, thus, $\eta(L)$ is regular. In this alternative way, based on regular expressions, the exercises work out a detailed proof that the family of regular languages is closed under regular substitution.

Finite substitution and homomorphism

Theorem 4.2.9, stating that the family of regular languages is closed under regular substitution, implies some other closure properties concerning this family. Specifically, by this theorem, the family of regular languages is also closed under two special cases of regular substitution – finite substitution and homomorphism – as demonstrated next.

Definition — finite substitution
Let Σ and Ω be two alphabets, and let η be a substitution from Σ^* to Ω^* such that for all $a \in \Sigma$, $\eta(a)$ is a finite language. Then, η is a *finite substitution*.
◆

Theorem 4.2.10
The family of regular languages is closed under finite substitution.

Proof
By Theorem 3.1.1, every finite language is regular. Thus, if η is a finite substitution, then η is also a regular substitution. Therefore, Theorem 4.2.10 follows from Theorem 4.2.9.
■

Recall that if η is a substitution from Σ^* to Ω^* such that η represents a function from Σ^* to Ω^*, then η is a homomorphism (see Section 1.3).

Theorem 4.2.11
The family of regular languages is closed under homomorphism.

Proof
Let η be a homomorphism from Σ^* to Ω^*. As η represents a function from Σ^* to Ω^*, card($\eta(a)$) $\in \{0, 1\}$, so η is also a finite substitution. Therefore, Theorem 4.2.11 follows from Theorem 4.2.10.

■

The exercises establish several other closure properties concerning the family of regular languages.

Applications of closure properties

It is often possible to simplify a proof that a language L is regular by using closure properties. Indeed, rather than prove that L is regular by designing a complex finite automaton, L can be defined by several simple regular languages and operations that preserve regular languages.

Example 4.2.1 Use of closure properties to prove that a language is regular
Consider the language

$$L = \{a^i b^j c^k d^l : i, k \geq 0 \text{ and } j, l \geq 1\}$$

This example uses closure properties for regular languages to prove that L is regular.
Express L as

$$L = \eta(\{a\})\{b\}\eta(\{c\})\{d\}$$

where η is a regular substitution defined by

$$\eta(a) = \{a\}^*\{b\}^* \text{ and } \eta(c) = \{c\}^*\{d\}^*$$

The four one-symbol languages — $\{a\}, \{b\}, \{c\}$, and $\{d\}$ — are finite; therefore, by Theorem 3.1.1, they are regular. By Theorems 4.2.1 and 4.2.8, the family of regular languages is closed under concatenation and regular substitution. Thus, $\eta(\{a\})\{b\}\eta(\{c\})\{d\}$ is regular. This concludes that L represents a regular language.

▲

Together with the pumping lemma for regular languages, closure properties are frequently used to prove that a language L is not regular. Typically, such a proof is made by contradiction in the following way:

1. Assume that L is regular.
2. From L and some regular languages, construct a new language L' by using operations preserving regular languages.
3. Prove that L' is not regular by the pumping lemma for regular languages; however, by the closure properties concerning the operations used in step 2, L' is regular — a contradiction.
4. Conclude that L is not regular.

Example 4.2.2 Use of closure properties to disprove that a language is regular
Consider the language

$$L = \{a^n b^m : m, n \geq 0 \text{ and } n \neq m\}$$

This example uses closure properties for regular languages to disprove that L is regular.

Obviously, $\{a\}^*\{b\}^*$ represents a regular language. Consider

$$\overline{L} \cap \{a\}^*\{b\}^* = \{a^n b^n : n \geq 0\}$$

By using the pumping lemma for regular languages, Example 4.1.1 proves that $\{a^n b^n : n \geq 0\}$ is not regular. However, Theorems 4.2.2 and 4.2.3 state that the family of regular languages is closed under complement and intersection, so $\{a^n b^n : n \geq 0\}$ is regular — a contradiction. It is therefore concluded that L is not a regular language.
▲

4.3 Decidable problems

As stated in Section 2.3, this book views a problem as consisting of two components — a question and an instance. The question formulates the problem. The set of problem instances forms the collection of all allowable values for the problem unknowns.

This section introduces and discusses the following problems:

1. membership problem
2. emptiness problem
3. infiniteness problem
4. finiteness problem
5. equivalence problem.

The following discussion presents algorithms to solve these problems for regular languages, as defined by finite automata. Recall that Sections 3.2.2 through 3.2.5 introduce several restricted variants of finite automata and prove their equivalence

Properties of regular languages

to the basic model of finite automata, defined in Section 3.2.1. Therefore, without any loss of generality, each of the present algorithms uses the variant that allows the algorithm to decide a given problem in the simplest way.

Membership problem for finite automata

Instance: A finite automaton $M = (Q, \Sigma, R, s, F)$ and a word $w \in \Sigma^*$.
Question: Is w a member of $L(M)$?

The following algorithm decides the membership problem for deterministic finite automata (see Section 3.2.3). More precisely, with a word w and a deterministic finite automaton M on its input, this algorithm decides whether $w \in L(M)$.

Algorithm 4.3.1: Membership problem decision for finite automata

Input: A deterministic finite automaton $M = (Q, \Sigma, R, s, F)$ and a word $w \in \Sigma^*$.

Output: **YES** if $w \in L(M)$, or **NO** if $w \notin L(M)$.

Method

begin
   if $sw \vdash^* q$ with $q \in F$
   then write ('YES')
   else write ('NO')
end.

Lemma 4.3.2
Let $M = (Q, \Sigma, R, s, F)$ be a deterministic finite automaton, and let $w \in \Sigma^*$. With M and w on its input, Algorithm 4.3.1 halts and correctly decides the membership problem for M and w; that is, this algorithm writes **YES** if $w \in L(M)$, otherwise it writes **NO**.

Proof
Termination
As M is deterministic, w causes M to make precisely $|w|$ moves. Therefore, the determination of $sw \vdash^* q$ requires a simulation of $|w|$ moves in M. Thus, this algorithm always halts.

Correctness
By the definition of $L(M)$,

$$w \in L(M) \text{ if and only if } sw \vdash^* q \text{ in } M \text{ and } q \in F$$

By the **if-then-else** statement of Algorithm 4.3.1, it is concluded that this algorithm correctly decides the membership problem for M and w; indeed, Algorithm 4.3.1 writes **YES** if $w \in L(M)$, and it writes **NO** if $w \notin L(M)$.

∎

Theorem 4.3.3
The membership problem for finite automata is decidable.

Proof
This theorem follows from Algorithm 4.3.1 and Lemma 4.3.2.

∎

Emptiness problem for finite automata

Instance: A finite automaton $M = (Q, \Sigma, R, s, F)$.
Question: Is $L(M)$ empty?

Assume that $M = (Q, \Sigma, R, s, F)$ represents a well-specified finite automaton (see Section 3.2.4). Observe that

$$L(M) = \emptyset \text{ if and only if } F = \emptyset$$

Consequently, a decision about the emptiness problem for M requires finding out whether $F = \emptyset$. If so, $L(M) = \emptyset$; otherwise $L(M) \neq \emptyset$.

The following algorithm decides this problem by using the pumping lemma (4.1.1) for regular languages.

Algorithm 4.3.4: Emptiness problem decision for finite automata

Input: A deterministic finite automaton $M = (Q, \Sigma, R, s, F)$.

Output: **YES** if $L(M) = \emptyset$, or **NO** if $L(M) \neq \emptyset$.

Method

begin
  $k := \text{card}(Q)$ { k is set according to the proof of Lemma 4.1.1};
  if $\{ x : x \in \Sigma^*, x \in L(M), \text{ and } |x| < k \} = \emptyset$
  then write ('YES')
  else write ('NO')
end.

Lemma 4.3.5
Let $M = (Q, \Sigma, R, s, F)$ be a deterministic finite automaton. With M as its input, Algorithm 4.3.4 halts and correctly decides the emptiness problem for M; that is, this algorithm writes **YES** if $L(M) = \emptyset$, and it writes **NO** if $L(M) \neq \emptyset$.

Proof

Termination
By using Algorithm 4.3.1, it is possible to decide whether $x \in L(M)$, for all $x \in \Sigma^*$. To make this decision for all $x \in \Sigma^*$ with $|x| < k$, where $k = \text{card}(Q)$, invoke Algorithm 4.3.1 a finite number of times. Thus, we can effectively construct the finite set

$$\{ x : x \in \Sigma^*, x \in L(M), \text{ and } |x| < k \}$$

in a finite number of steps and, therefore, guarantee the termination of Algorithm 4.3.4.

Correctness
The correctness of Algorithm 4.3.4 follows from the following claim.

Claim
Given a deterministic finite automaton $M = (Q, \Sigma, R, s, F)$,

$$L(M) = \emptyset \text{ if and only if } \{ x : x \in \Sigma^*, x \in L(M), \text{ and } |x| < k \} = \emptyset$$

Proof

If
This part of the proof states that

$$\{ x : x \in \Sigma^*, x \in L(M), \text{ and } |x| < k \} = \emptyset \text{ implies } L(M) = \emptyset$$

This implication is established by contradiction, as follows. Assume that $\{ x : x \in \Sigma^*, x \in L(M), \text{ and } |x| < k \} = \emptyset$ and $L(M) \neq \emptyset$; that is, all words of $L(M)$ are longer than $k - 1$. Let z be the shortest word in $L(M)$. As $z \in L(M)$ and $|z| \geq k$, then by Lemma 4.1.1 (the pumping lemma for regular languages),

$$z = uvw$$

so

1. $v \neq \varepsilon$;
2. $|uv| \leq k$;
3. $uv^m w$, for all $m \geq 0$.

Consider $z' = uw$. From the third condition for $m = 0$,

$$z' \in L(M)$$

Observe that $|z'| = |z| - |v|$. From the first condition, $v \ne \varepsilon$, so $v \ge 1$ and, thus,

$$|z| > |z'|$$

Because $z' \in L(M)$ and $|z| > |z'|$, z is not the shortest word in $L(M)$ — a contradiction. It is concluded that $L(M) = \varnothing$ if $\{x : x \in \Sigma^*, x \in L(M), \text{ and } |x| < k\} = \varnothing$.

Only if
The 'only if' part states that

$$L(M) = \varnothing \text{ implies } \{x : x \in \Sigma^*, x \in L(M), \text{ and } |x| < k\} = \varnothing$$

As $\{x : x \in \Sigma^*, x \in L(M), \text{ and } |x| < k\} \subseteq L(M)$, this implication surely holds.

This concludes that the claim holds.

□

By this claim, with M as its input, Algorithm 4.3.4 writes YES if $L(M) = \varnothing$, and it writes NO if $L(M) \ne \varnothing$. In other words, Algorithm 4.3.4 correctly decides the emptiness problem for M.

Thus Lemma 4.3.5 holds.

■

Theorem 4.3.6
The emptiness problem for finite automata is decidable.

Proof
This theorem follows from Algorithm 4.3.4 and Lemma 4.3.5.

■

Infiniteness problem for finite automata

Instance: A finite automaton $M = (Q, \Sigma, R, s, F)$.
Question: Is $L(M)$ infinite?

Assume that $M = (Q, \Sigma, R, s, F)$ represents a well-specified finite automaton. If $F = \varnothing$, the decision of the infiniteness problem for M represents a trivial task: $F = \varnothing$ implies $L(M) = \varnothing$, so $L(M)$ is finite. Suppose that $F \ne \varnothing$. Observe at this point that

Properties of regular languages

$L(M)$ is infinite if and only if the state diagram of M contains a cycle (see Section 0.3 for the definition of a cycle). Consequently, to decide the infiniteness problem for M with $F \neq \emptyset$, it is necessary to find out whether there exists a cycle in the state diagram corresponding to M. If so, $L(M)$ is infinite; otherwise $L(M)$ is finite.

The following algorithm decides the infiniteness problem using an alternative method. By analogy with Algorithm 4.3.4, this method makes use of the pumping lemma for regular languages.

Algorithm 4.3.7: Infiniteness problem decision for finite automata

Input: A deterministic finite automaton $M = (Q, \Sigma, R, s, F)$.

Output: YES if $L(M)$ is infinite, or NO if $L(M)$ is finite.

Method

begin
    $k := \text{card}(Q)$ {k is the pumping lemma constant};
    if $\{ x : x \in \Sigma^*, x \in L(M), \text{ and } k \leq |x| < 2k \} \neq \emptyset$
    then write('YES')
    else write('NO')
end.

Lemma 4.3.8

Let $M = (Q, \Sigma, R, s, F)$ be a deterministic finite automaton. With M on its input, Algorithm 4.3.7 halts and correctly decides the infiniteness problem for M; that is, this algorithm writes YES if $L(M)$ is infinite, and it writes NO if $L(M)$ is finite.

Proof
Termination
This part of the proof is left to the exercises.

Correctness
Consider the following claim.

Claim
Given a deterministic finite automaton $M = (Q, \Sigma, R, s, F)$, $L(M)$ is infinite if and only if $\{ x : x \in \Sigma^*, x \in L(M), \text{ and } k \leq |x| < 2k \} \neq \emptyset$

Proof
If
This part of the proof states that if $\{ x : x \in \Sigma^*, x \in L(M), \text{ and } k \leq |x| < 2k \} \neq \emptyset$, then $L(M)$ is infinite

Let $z \in \{x : x \in \Sigma^*, x \in L(M), \text{ and } k \leq |x| < 2k\}$. As $z \in L(M)$ and $|z| \geq k$, the pumping lemma for regular languages gives

$$z = uvw$$

so

1. $v \neq \varepsilon$;
2. $|uv| \leq k$;
3. $uv^m w$, for all $m \geq 0$.

From conditions 1 and 3, $L(M)$ is infinite.

Only if
This part of the proof states that

if $L(M)$ is infinite, then $\{x : x \in \Sigma^*, x \in L(M), \text{ and } k \leq |x| < 2k\} \neq \varnothing$

This implication is proved by contradiction. Assume that L is infinite and $\{x : x \in \Sigma^*, x \in L(M), \text{ and } k \leq |x| < 2k\} = \varnothing$. Let z be the shortest word such that $z \in L(M)$ and $|z| \geq k$. As $\{x : x \in \Sigma^*, x \in L(M), \text{ and } k \leq |x| < 2k\} = \varnothing$,

$$|z| \geq 2k$$

As $z \in L(M)$, $|z| \geq 2k$, and $2k \geq k$, Lemma 4.1.1 implies that

$$z = uvw$$

so

1. $v \neq \varepsilon$;
2. $|uv| \leq k$;
3. $uv^m w$, for all $m \geq 0$.

Set $z' = uw$. By the third condition for $m = 0$, $z' \in L(G)$. Observe that

$$|z'| = |z| - |v|$$

As $v \neq \varepsilon$,

$$|z'| < |z|$$

Because $|uv| \leq k$ and, thus, $|v| \leq k$,

$$|z| - k \leq |z'|$$

As $|z| \geq 2k$ implies $k \leq |z| - k$,

$$k \leq |z'|$$

As $z' \in L(G)$ and $k \leq |z'| < |z|$, z is not the shortest word satisfying $z \in L(M)$ and $|z| \geq k$ — a contradiction. It is concluded that if $L(M)$ is infinite, then $\{ x : x \in \Sigma^*, x \in L(M), \text{ and } k \leq |x| < 2k \} \neq \emptyset$.

Therefore, the claim holds.

By this claim, Algorithm 4.3.7 writes **YES** if $L(M)$ is infinite; otherwise, it writes **NO**. That is, Algorithm 4.3.7 correctly decides the infiniteness problem for M.

This concludes that Lemma 4.3.8 holds. ∎

Theorem 4.3.9
The infiniteness problem for regular grammars is decidable.

Proof
This theorem follows from Algorithm 4.3.7 and Lemma 4.3.8. ∎

Finiteness problem for finite automata

Instance: A finite automaton $M = (Q, \Sigma, R, s, F)$.
Question: Is $L(M)$ finite?

Corollary 4.3.10
The finiteness problem for finite automata is decidable.

Proof
This corollary follows from Theorem 4.3.9. ∎

Equivalence problem for finite automata

Instance: Two finite automata M_0 and M_1.

Question: Is M_0 equivalent to M_1?

Assume that M_0 and M_1 are minimum-state finite automata (see Section 3.2.5). Consider their state diagrams, and remove all states, labeling nodes from these diagrams. If the resulting diagrams represent identical graphs, then $L(M_0) = L(M_1)$; otherwise, $L(M_0) \neq L(M_1)$.

The following algorithm decides the equivalence problem by using another method, which uses deterministic finite automata.

Algorithm 4.3.11: Equivalence problem decision for finite automata

Input: Two deterministic finite automata $M_0 = (Q_0, \Sigma_0, R_0, s_0, F_0)$ and $M_1 = (Q_1, \Sigma_1, R_1, s_1, F_1)$, such that $Q_1 \cap Q_0 = \emptyset$.

Output: YES if $L(M_0) = L(M_1)$, or NO if $L(M_0) \neq L(M_1)$.

Method

begin
  construct a finite automaton M such that

$$L(M) = (L(M_0) \cap \overline{L(M_1)}) \cup (\overline{L(M_0)} \cap L(M_1))$$

  by using Algorithm 3.3.1.4 (construction of a finite automaton for the union of two languages accepted by finite automata) Algorithm 4.2.2 (construction of a finite automaton for the complement of the language accepted by a well-specified finite automaton) and the proof of Theorem 4.2.5;

  if $L(M) = \emptyset$
  then write('YES')
  else write('NO')
end.

Lemma 4.3.12

Let $M_0 = (Q_0, \Sigma_0, R_0, s_0, F_0)$ and $M_1 = (Q_1, \Sigma_1, R_1, s_1, F_1)$ be two deterministic finite automata such that $Q_1 \cap Q_0 = \emptyset$. With M_0 and M_1 as its input, Algorithm 4.3.11 halts and correctly decides the equivalence problem for M_0 and M_1; that is, this algorithm writes YES if $L(M_0) = L(M_1)$, and it writes NO if $L(M_0) \neq L(M_1)$.

Proof
Termination
The termination of Algorithm 4.3.11 follows from the termination of Algorithm 3.3.1.4, the termination of Algorithm 4.2.2, and the technique used in the proof of Theorem 4.2.5. A detailed proof that Algorithm 4.3.11 always halts is left to the exercises.

Correctness

Claim
Let M_0 and M_1 be two deterministic finite automata. Then,

$$L(M_0) = L(M_1) \text{ if and only if } (L(M_0) \cap \overline{L(M_1)}) \cup (\overline{L(M_0)} \cap L(M_1)) = \emptyset$$

Proof
This claim is proved in the exercises.

□

By Algorithm 4.3.11, $L(M) = (L(M_0) \cap \overline{L(M_1)}) \cup (\overline{L(M_0)} \cap L(M_1))$ so, by the previous claim, $L(M) = \emptyset$ if and only if $L(M_0) = L(M_1)$. Therefore, with M_0 and M_1 on its input, Algorithm 4.3.11 writes YES if $L(M_0) = L(M_1)$, and it writes NO if $L(M_0) \neq L(M_1)$. In other words, Algorithm 4.3.11 correctly decides the equivalence problem for M_0 and M_1.

This concludes that the lemma holds.

■

Theorem 4.3.13
The equivalence problem for finite automata is decidable.

Proof
This theorem follows from Algorithm 4.3.12 and Lemma 4.3.13.

■

Exercises

1 Pumping Lemma

1.1 Consider each of these languages:
  (a) $\{a^i b a^i : i \geq 1\}$
  (b) $\{a^i b^j : 1 \leq i \leq j\}$
  (c) $\{a^{2i} : i \geq 0\}$
  (d) $\{w : w \in \{a, b\}^* \text{ and } \#_a w = \#_b w\}$
  (e) $\{a^i b^j c^k : i, j, k \geq 0 \text{ and } i = k + j\}$
  (f) $\{a^i b^i c^j : i, j \geq 0 \text{ and } i \leq j \leq 2i\}$
  (g) $\{a^i b^j c^k : i, j, k \geq 0, i \neq j, k \neq i, \text{ and } j \neq k\}$
  (h) $\{a^i b^j c^j d^i : i, j \geq 0 \text{ and } j \leq i\}$
  (i) $\{a^i b^{2i} : i \geq 0\}$
  (j) $\{w \text{ reversal }(w) : w \in \{a, b\}^*\}$
  (k) $\{w : w \in \{a, b\}^*, \text{ and } \#_a w \neq \#_b w\}$ Using Lemma 4.1.1, the pumping lemma for regular languages, demonstrate that the languages are not regular.

1.2 Consider each regular language L discussed in Exercise 1.3 of Chapter 3. Determine a nonregular language L' such that $L' \subseteq L$. Prove that L' is not regular by Lemma 4.1.1.

To illustrate this exercise, set $L = \{a\}\{a,b\}^*\{b\} \cup \{\varepsilon\}$ (see Exercise 1.3 of Chapter 3). Let $L' = \{a^n b^n : n \geq 0\}$. Observe that $L' \subseteq L$. Recall that by using Lemma 4.1.1, Example 4.1.1 has proved that L' is not regular.

1.3 Lemma 4.1.1 in terms of regular expressions.

1.4 The following modified version of the pumping lemma for regular languages.

Lemma

Let L be a regular language. Then, there is a natural number k such that if $xzy \in L$ and $|z| \geq k$, then z can be written as

$$z = uvw$$

where

1. $|v| \geq 1$;
2. $xuv^m wy \in L$, for all $m \geq 0$.

1.5 Use the lemma discussed in Exercise 1.4 to prove that $\{a^i b^j c^j : i, j \geq 1\}$ is not regular. Can this proof be based on Lemma 4.1.1?

1.6** Prove the following lemma

Lemma

A language L over an alphabet Σ is regular if and only if there exists a natural number k satisfying the following statement:

Let $z \in \Sigma^*$ and $|z| \geq k$. Then, z can be written as $z = uvw$, where $v \neq \varepsilon$ and

$$zx \in L \text{ if and only if } uv^m wx \in L$$

for all $m \geq 0$ and $x \in \Sigma^*$.

Explain how to use this lemma to prove that a language is regular. Then, explain how to use this lemma to disprove that a language is regular.

1.7 Complete Example 4.1.4.

2 Closure properties

2.1 Complete the proof of Lemma 4.2.8.
2.2 Give a proof of Theorem 4.2.9 based on regular expressions.
2.3 Let L be a language over an alphabet Σ. Consider prefix(L), defined in Section 1.1. Prove that if L is regular, then prefix(L) is regular as well. Conclude that the family of regular languages is closed under prefix.
2.4 Let L be a language over an alphabet Σ. Consider suffix(L), defined in Section 1.1. Prove that if L is regular, then suffix(L) is regular as well. Conclude that the family of regular languages is closed under suffix.
2.5 Let Σ be an alphabet, and let $x \in \Sigma^*$. Consider subword(x), introduced in Section 1.1. For a language L over an alphabet Σ, define Sub(L) as

$$\text{Sub}(L) = \{\text{subword}(x) : x \in L\}$$

Prove that the family of regular languages is closed under Sub.

2.6 Let L be a language over an alphabet Σ. Recall that Section 1.1 defines the reversal of L, reversal(L), as

$$\text{reversal}(L) = \{\text{reversal}(x) : x \in L\}$$

Prove that the family of regular languages is closed under reversal.

2.7 For languages L_1 and L_2, L_1/L_2 is defined as

$$L_1/L_2 = \{w : wx \in L_1 \text{ for some } x \in L_2\}$$

Prove that the family of regular languages is closed under this operation.

2.8 For a language L min(L) is defined as

$$\min(L) = \{w : w \in L \text{ and } (\text{prefix}(w) - \{w\}) \cap L = \emptyset\}$$

Prove that the family of regular languages is closed under min.

2.9 For a language L over an alphabet Σ, max(L) is defined as

$$\max(L) = \{w : w \in L \text{ and } \{w\}\Sigma^+ \cap L = \emptyset\}$$

Prove that the family of regular languages is closed under max.

2.10 For a language L over an alphabet Σ, sqrt(L) is defined as

$$\text{sqrt}(L) = \{x : xy \in L \text{ for some } y \in \Sigma^*, \text{ and } |y| = |x|^2\}$$

Prove that the family of regular languages is closed under sqrt.

2.11 For a language L over an alphabet Σ, log(L) is defined as

$$\log(L) = \{x: xy \in L \text{ for some } y \in \Sigma^*, \text{ and } |y| = 2^{|x|}\}$$

Prove that the family of regular languages is closed under log.

2.12* Prove that the family of regular languages is closed under inverse homomorphism, introduced in Section 1.3.

2.13 Is the family of regular languages closed under inverse substitution, introduced in Section 1.3?

2.14 For a language L over an alphabet Σ, cycle(L) is defined as

$$\text{cycle}(L) = \{vw: wv \in \text{ for some } v, w \in \Sigma^*\}$$

Is the family of regular languages closed under cycle?

2.15 Let $L_1 \subseteq \Sigma_1^*$ and $L_2 \subseteq \Sigma_2^*$ be two languages; shuffle(L_1, L_2) is defined as

$$\text{shuffle}(L_1, L_2) = \{v_1 w_1 ... v_n w_n: v_1 ... w_1 \in L_1, w_1 ... w_n \in L_2,$$

$$v_i \in \Sigma_1^*, w_i \in \Sigma_2^*, \text{ for } i = 1, ..., n, \text{ where } n \geq 0\}$$

Informally, shuffle(L_1, L_2) equals the set of words formed by shuffling a word of L_1 with a word of L_2.

Is the family of regular languages closed under shuffle?

2.16 For a language L over an alphabet Σ and a symbol $a \in \Sigma$, eraser$_a$(L) denotes the language obtained by removing all occurrences of a from the words of L. Formalize eraser$_a$(L). Is the family of regular languages closed under this operation?

2.17 For a language L over an alphabet Σ, half(L) is defined as

$$\text{half}(L) = \{w: wv \in L \text{ for some } v \in \Sigma^*, \text{ and } |w| = |v|\}$$

Is the family of regular languages closed under half?

2.18 For a language L over an alphabet Σ, inv(L) is defined as

$$\text{inv}(L) = \{xwy: x\text{reversal}(w)y \in L \text{ for some } x, y, w \in \Sigma^*\}$$

Is the family of regular languages closed under inv?

2.19 Consider these three languages:

(a) $\{w: w \in \{a, b\}^* \text{ and } \#_a w = 2\#_b w\}$
(b) $\{0^i 10^i: i \geq 1\}$
(c) $\{w\text{creversal}(w): w \in \{a, b\}^*\}$

Use the closure properties of regular languages to demonstrate that these languages are not regular.

2.20 Consider each language L discussed in Exercise 1.1 of this chapter. Use the closure properties of regular languages to demonstrate that L is not regular.

2.21 Consider each language L discussed in Exercise 1.3 in Chapter 3. Use the closure properties of the regular languages to demonstrate that L is regular.

3 Decidable problems

3.1 Complete the proof of Lemma 4.3.8.

3.2 Complete the proof of Lemma 4.3.12.

3.3 Consider the fundamental definition of finite automata in Section 3.2.1. Adapt all algorithms given in Section 3.3 for finite automata defined in this way.

3.4 Reformulate all decision problems discussed in Section 3.3 in terms of regular expressions. Design algorithms that decide these reformulated problems.

3.5 Return to the equivalence problem for finite automata:

Instance: Two finite automata M_0 and M_1.
Question: Is M_0 equivalent to M_1?

Let M_0 and M_1 be two minimum-state finite automata (see Section 3.2.5). Consider their state diagrams. Remove all states, labelling nodes, from these diagrams. Section 4.3 has stated that if the resulting diagrams represent identical graphs, $L(M_0) = L(M_1)$; otherwise, $L(M_0) \neq L(M_1)$. Justify this statement in detail.

3.6 Consider the equivalence problem for finite automata and regular expressions.

Instance: A finite automaton M and a regular expression E.
Question: Is M equivalent to E?

Design an algorithm that decides this problem.

3.6 Consider the computational multiplicity problem for finite automata.

Instance: A finite automaton $M = (Q, \Sigma, R, s, F)$ and $w \in \Sigma^*$.
Question: Can M compute $sw \vdash^* f[\rho]$ and $sw \vdash^* f'[\rho']$ so $f, f' \in F$ and $\rho \neq \rho'$?

Design an algorithm that decides this problem.

3.7 Consider the rejection problem for two finite automata.

Instance: A word, w, and two finite automata, $M_0 = (Q_0, \Sigma_0, R_0, s_0, F_0)$ and $M_1 = (Q_1, \Sigma_1, R_1, s_1, F_1)$.
Question: Does $x \notin (L(M_0) \cup L(M_1))$ hold?

Design an algorithm that decides this problem.

3.8 Consider the suffix membership problem for finite automata.

Instance: A finite automaton $M = (Q, \Sigma, R, s, F)$ and $w \in \Sigma^*$.
Question: Does there exist $v \in \Sigma^*$ such that $vw \in L(M)$?

Design an algorithm that decides this problem.

3.9 Consider the prefix membership problem for finite automata.

Instance: A finite automaton $M = (Q, \Sigma, R, s, F)$ and $w \in \Sigma^*$.
Question: Does there exist $v \in \Sigma^*$ such that $wv \in L(M)$?

Design an algorithm that decides this problem.

3.10 Consider the subword membership problem for finite automata.

Instance: A finite automaton $M = (Q, \Sigma, R, s, F)$ and $w \in \Sigma^*$.
Question: Does Σ^* contain two words, u and v, such that $uwv \in L(M)$?

Design an algorithm that decides this problem.

Bibliographical notes

Regular expressions

Regular expressions are defined in Kleene (1956). Brzozowski (1962, 1964), McCarthy and Painter (1967), McNaughton and Yamada (1960), McWhirter (1971) and Thompson (1968) are important early papers about regular expressions.

Beigel and Floyd (1994), Brookshear (1989), Carroll and Long (1989), Harrison (1978), Hopcroft and Ullman (1979), Kelley (1995), Linz (1990), Martin (1991), McNaughton (1982), Revesz (1983), Sudkamp (1988) and Wood (1987) cover regular expressions in detail.

Finite automata

Originally, McCulloch and Pitts (1943) introduced finite automata as formal models of neural nets. Mealy (1955) and Moore (1956) demonstrated several properties and applications of finite automata. Kleene (1956) proved their equivalence to regular expressions. Rabin and Scott (1959) established the equivalence between nondeterministic finite automata and deterministic finite automata. Bar-Hillel, Perles and Shamir (1961) demonstrated the pumping lemma for regular languages.

Barnes (1970), Elgot and Mezei (1965), Hopcroft (1971), Johnson *et al.* (1968), McNaughton and Yamada (1960), Myhill (1957), Scott (1967), Shannon and McCarthy (1956), Shepherdson (1959), and Thatcher (1967) are crucial early papers in the theory of finite automata. Beigel and Floyd (1994), Berstel (1979), Book (1980), Brookshear (1989), Bucher and Maurer (1984), Carroll and Long (1989), Eilenberg (1974, 1976), Harrison (1965, 1978), Hopcroft and Ullman (1979), Kelley (1995), Kuich and Salomaa (1985), Linz (1990), Martin (1991), McNaughton (1982), Revesz (1983), Salomaa (1969), Sudkamp (1988), Salomaa (1985) and Wood (1987) discuss finite automata in depth.

Finite automata underlie some other important automata, including cellular automata, systolic automata and tree automata.

A *cellular automaton* consists of an infinite array of finite automata. These automata work simultaneously so that each of them takes the states of its neighboring automata as its input. The game of life is a famous example of these automata. For more information about cellular automata, consult Hayes (1984) and Wolfram *et al.* (1984).

A *systolic automaton* works on a tree, whose leaves are associated with the symbols of the input word. On this tree, the automaton proceeds in a bottom-up manner. During a move, it goes from one level to the next level in parallel and determines states of the entered nodes. In this way, the automaton works until it reaches the root. If the root's state is final, the input is accepted; otherwise, it is rejected. Salomaa (1985) discusses systolic automata and their variants (Section 8.3).

The input of a *tree automaton* is a tree, not a word. On the tree, the automaton descends down in parallel. During this descent, it determines the states of the nodes visited. If a node occurs in a final state, the input tree is accepted. Gesceg and Steinby (1984) is a good introduction to tree automata.

Part III
Context-Free Languages

This part studies context-free languages and their two basic models — context-free grammars and pushdown automata. Chapter 5 formalizes both models, demonstrates their equivalence, and illustrates their practical use by constructing a compiler's parser based on these models. Chapter 6 states fundamental properties of context-free languages. These properties include a pumping lemma, closure properties, and several results concerning decision problems. Finally, Chapter 7 studies some special types of context-free languages.

5 Models for Context-Free Languages

Sections 1.2.2 and 2.1 explain that context-free languages and their models are central to this book. This chapter formalizes context-free grammars and pushdown automata, which represent the fundamental models for context-free languages, and establishes their equivalence.

This chapter has three sections: Section 5.1 defines the notion of a context-free grammar, Section 5.2 formalizes the notion of a pushdown automaton, and Section 5.3 proves that these two models have the same power.

5.1 Context-free grammars

Recall that Section 1.2.2 has introduces some grammatically based specification tools for the description of programming language syntax. Specifically, these specification tools are the Backus-Naur form, the extended Backus-Naur form, and syntax graphs. Section 1.2.2 also explains that these tools represent the most widely used specification methods for the syntactic structure of programming languages. All these tools are equivalent to the formal notion of a context-free grammar, which is the current topic of interest. Consequently, by using this formal notion, computational theory can rigorously model and study the pragmatically oriented specification tools, discussed in Section 1.2.2.

5.1.1 Basic definitions

Definition — context-free grammar
A *context-free grammar* is a quadruple

$$G = (N, T, P, S)$$

where

N is an alphabet of *nonterminals*;
T is an alphabet of *terminals* such that $N \cap T \neq \emptyset$;
$P \subseteq N \times (N \cup T)^*$ is a finite relation;
$S \in N$ is the start symbol.   ◆

Hereafter, the member of P are called *productions*; accordingly, P is known as the *set of productions*. A production, $(A, x) \in P$, is customarily written as

$$A \to x$$

Example 5.1.1.1 Part 1 Context-free grammar
Consider the context-free grammar

$$G = (\{S\}, \{a, b\}, P, S)$$

with

$$P = \{S \to aSb, S \to \varepsilon\}$$

G has one nonterminal, S, and two terminals, a and b. P contains two productions, $S \to aSb$ and $S \to \varepsilon$. S represents the start symbol of G.

△

For brevity, this book often labels productions and uses these labels to refer to the corresponding productions. To declare that a label p denotes the production $A \to x$, this is written as

$$p: A \to x$$

The nonterminal A is the left-hand side of p, denoted by lhs(p). The word x is the right-hand side of p, denoted by rhs(p).

A production, p, is called an *ε-production* if rhs(p) = ε.

Conventions
To describe a context-free grammar $G = (N, T, P, S)$ concisely, following conventions are used:

1. A, B, C, D, E, F and S represent nonterminals, where S represents the start symbol;
2. a, b, c and d represent terminals;
3. U, V, W, X, Y and Z represent members of $N \cup T$;
4. u, v, w, x, y and z represent members of $(N \cup T)^*$;
5. productions of P are labelled as $p_1, p_2, \ldots p_n$, where $n = \text{card}(P)$; if $n \leq 9$, these productions are sometimes labelled by $1, 2, \ldots, n$;
6. π represents a sequence of productions.

●

Subscripts and superscripts do not change these conventions; for instance, A_1 represents a nonterminal. Except when explicitly stated otherwise, these conventions are used throughout. The next example illustrates their use.

Example 5.1.1.1 Part 2 Simplified specification of a context-free grammar

Return to the context-free grammar G introduced in Part 1 of this example. Under the previous conventions, specify G as

1: $S \to aSb$
2: $S \to \varepsilon$

Consider the first production and observe that lhs(1) = S and rhs(1) = aSb.
Notice that the second production represents an ε-production because rhs(2) = ε.

△

By using its productions, a context-free grammar $G = (N, T, P, S)$ derives words from other words. Consider a word xAy and a production, $p: A \to w \in P$. By using p, G makes a derivation step from xAy to xwy by replacing A, which equals lhs(p), with w, which equals rhs(p); similarly, G makes a derivation step from $x$lhs(p)y to $x$rhs(p)y acording to p.

Definition — direct derivation

Let $G = (N, T, P, S)$ be a context-free grammar, $p \in P$, and $x, y \in (N \cup T)^*$. Then, $x$lhs(p)y *directly derives* $x$rhs(p)y according to p in G, denoted by

$$x\text{lhs}(p)y \Rightarrow x\text{rhs}(p)y \; [p]$$

or, briefly,

$$x\text{lhs}(p)y \Rightarrow x\text{rhs}(p)y$$

◆

Example 5.1.1.1 Part 3 Direct derivation

Return to the context-free grammar G discussed in the previous two parts of this example. Consider $x$lhs(1)y with $x = aa$ and $y = bb$. In other words, $x$lhs(1)$y = aaSbb$ because production 1 has the form

1: $S \to aSb$

and, thus, lhs(1) = S. At this point,

$$aaSbb \Rightarrow aaaSbbb \; [1]$$

in G.

In addition, consider $x$lhs(2)y with $x = aaa$ and $y = bbb$; that is, $x$lhs(2)$y = aaaSbbb$. Observe that

$$aaaSbbb \Rightarrow aaabbb \; [2]$$

in G because, by the ε-production 2: $S \to \varepsilon$, G replaces S with ε and, in effect, erases S.

If the specification of the used production in a derivation step is immaterial, this specification is omitted; to illustrate,

$$aaSbb \Rightarrow aaaSbbba \ [2]$$

is abbreviated to

$$aaSbb \Rightarrow aaaSbbb$$

by using this omission.

△

The following definition generalizes a derivation step to a sequence of n derivation steps for $n \geq 0$.

Definition — derivation, part 1
Let $G = (N, T, P, S)$ be a context-free grammar.

1. For any $u \in (N \cup T)^*$, G makes a *zero-step derivation* from u to u according to ε, which is written as

$$u \Rightarrow^0 u \ [\varepsilon]$$

2. Let $u_0, ..., u_n \in (N \cup T)^*$, for some $n \geq 1$, such that

$$u_{i-1} \Rightarrow u_i \ [p_i]$$

where $p_i \in P$, for $i = 1, ..., n$; that is,

$$\begin{aligned}u_0 &\Rightarrow u_1 \ [p_1] \\ &\Rightarrow u_2 \ [p_2] \\ &\vdots \\ &\Rightarrow u_n \ [p_n]\end{aligned}$$

Then, G makes an *n-step derivation* from u_0 to u_n according to $p_1 ... p_n$, written as

$$u_0 \Rightarrow^n u_n \ [p_1 ... p_n]$$

◆

Consider a context-free grammar $G = (N, T, P, S)$ and $v \Rightarrow^n w \ [\pi]$ in G, where π consists of n productions from P ($\pi = \varepsilon$ if $n = 0$). Observe that π, called the *production word* corresponding to $v \Rightarrow^n w$, actually represents the sequence of productions according to which G makes the n direct derivations from v to w. If this representation is immaterial, $v \Rightarrow^n w\ [\pi]$ is abbreviated to $v \Rightarrow^n w$.

Mathematically, $\Rightarrow^n$ represents the n-fold product of $\Rightarrow$. Based on $\Rightarrow^n$, the following definition introduces two other notions, $\Rightarrow^+$ and $\Rightarrow^*$. The former denotes the transitive closure of $\Rightarrow$, and the latter denotes the transitive and reflexive closure of $\Rightarrow$.

Definition — derivation, part 2

Let $G = (N, T, P, S)$ be a context-free grammar, and let $v, w \in (N \cup T)^*$.

1. If there exists $n \geq 1$ so $v \Rightarrow^n w\ [\pi]$ in G, then v properly derives w according to π in G, written as

$$v \Rightarrow^+ w\ [\pi]$$

2. If there exists $n \geq 0$ so $v \Rightarrow^n w\ [\pi]$ in G, then v derives w according to π in G, written as

$$v \Rightarrow^* w\ [\pi]$$

◆

This book frequently simplifies $v \Rightarrow^+ w\ [\pi]$ and $v \Rightarrow^* w\ [\pi]$ to $v \Rightarrow^+ w$ and $v \Rightarrow^* w$, respectively.

Example 5.1.1.1 Part 4 Derivations

Return to the context-free grammar G defined in Part 2 of this example, and observe that

$$\begin{aligned}
aSb &\Rightarrow aaSbb & [1] \\
&\Rightarrow aaaSbbb & [1] \\
&\Rightarrow aaaaSbbbb & [1] \\
&\Rightarrow aaaaaSbbbbb & [1] \\
&\Rightarrow aaaaabbbbb & [2]
\end{aligned}$$

Therefore,

$$aSb \Rightarrow^5 aaaaabbbbb \quad [11112]$$

or, simply,

$$aSb \Rightarrow^5 aaaaabbbbb$$

As $aSb \Rightarrow^5 aaaaabbbbb$, it also holds that

$$aSb \Rightarrow^+ aaaaabbbbb \text{ and } aSb \Rightarrow^* aaaaabbbbb$$

Observe that $aSb \Rightarrow^0 aSb$, so $aSb \Rightarrow^* aSb$. However, $aSb \Rightarrow^n aSb$ does not hold for any $n \geq 1$, so $aSb \Rightarrow^+ aSb$ is not true.

△

Based on $\Rightarrow^*$, the following definition introduces the language $L(G)$ generated by a context-free grammar G.

Definition — generated language
Let $G = (N, T, P, S)$ be a context-free grammar. If $S \Rightarrow^* w$ in G, then w is a *sentential form* of G. A sentential form w, such that $w \in T^*$ is a *sentence* generated by G. The *language generated* by G, $L(G)$, is the set of all sentences that G generates; formally,

$$L(G) = \{w : w \in T^* \text{ and } S \Rightarrow^* w \text{ in } G\}$$

◆

Example 5.1.1.1 Part 5 Sentential forms and sentences
Return to G as specified in Part 2 of this example. As $S \Rightarrow^* aSb$ in G, aSb is a sentential form; however, as $aSb \notin T^*$, S is not a sentence. Consider the word ab. This word is a sentence because $S \Rightarrow^* ab$ and $ab \in T^*$.

△

The following two parts of Example 5.1.1.1 explain how to determine $L(G)$ for a given context-free grammar G. Part 6 describes this determination informally, whereas Part 7 carries out this task rigorously.

Example 5.1.1.1 Part 6 Determination of the generated language: an intuitive approach
Recall that the previous parts of this example discuss the context-free grammar G defined as

1: $S \to aSb$
2: $S \to \varepsilon$

Any derivation commences with the start symbol, S. By using production 1, G replaces S with aSb. By applying production 2, G erases S. Consequently, G makes every derivation of a sentence according to a production word that has the form

$$1^k 2$$

for some $k \geq 0$. If $k = 0$, the production word equals 2, which gives rise to tion of ε as follows

$$S \Rightarrow^* \varepsilon \; [2]$$

If $k = 1$, the production word equals 12, which leads to

$$S \Rightarrow^* ab \; [12]$$

If $k = 2$, the production word equals 112, which leads to

$$S \Rightarrow^* aabb \; [112]$$

More generally, if $k = n$, for some $n \geq 0$, then the production word equals $1^n 2$, according to which G makes

$$S \Rightarrow^* a^n b^n \; [1^n 2]$$

From this observation, a word $w \in \{a, b\}^*$ belongs to $L(G)$ if and only if w consists of n as followed by n bs, for some $n \geq 0$; that is,

$$L(G) = \{a^n b^n : n \geq 0\}$$

△

Example 5.1.1.1 Part 7 Determination of the generated language: a rigorous approach

The previous part of this example outlined a proof that

$$L(G) = \{a^n b^n : n \geq 0\}$$

The present part verifies this equation rigorously. First, Claim A is proved, which gives an insight into the relationship between the length of derivations and the sentential forms that G produces by these derivations.

Claim A
Let $x \in \{a, b, S\}^*$. For all $m \geq 1$, $f S \Rightarrow^m x$ in G, then $x \in \{a^m S b^m, a^{m-1} b^{m-1}\}$.

Proof
We prove this implication by induction on m.

Basis
Let $m = 1$. At this point, $S \Rightarrow^m x$ represents a direct derivation of the form

$$S \Rightarrow x \ [p]$$

...re $p \in \{1, 2\}$. If $p = 1$, $x = aSb$, and if $p = 2$, $x = \varepsilon$. In both cases, x satisfies the ...quired form, so the basis holds.

Induction hypothesis
Assume that the claim holds for all i-step derivations, where $i = 1, \ldots, m$, for some $m \geq 1$.

Induction step
Consider a derivation of the form

$$S \Rightarrow^{m+1} x$$

Express $S \Rightarrow^{m+1} x$ as

$$S \Rightarrow^m y \Rightarrow x \ [p]$$

where $p \in \{1, 2\}$. By the induction hypothesis, $y \in \{a^m Sb^m, a^{m-1}b^{m-1}\}$. As $y \Rightarrow x \ [p]$, y contains lhs(p), so $y = a^m Sb^m$. Next, this proof distinguishes the two cases $p = 1$ and $p = 2$.

1. If $p = 1$, then $S \Rightarrow^m a^m Sb^m \Rightarrow a^{m+1}Sb^{m+1}$ [1]
2. If $p = 2$, then $S \Rightarrow^m a^m Sb^m \Rightarrow a^m b^m$ [2]

In both cases x has the required form, so the inductive step is completed. Therefore, Claim A holds.

□

Consider Claim A for $x \in \{a, b\}^*$. That is,

if $S \Rightarrow^m x$ in G with $x \in \{a, b\}^*$, then $x = a^{m-1}b^{m-1}$

for $m = 1, 2, \ldots$. Consequently,

$$x \in L(G) \text{ implies } x = a^n b^n$$

for some $n \geq 0$; therefore,

$$L(G) \subseteq \{a^n b^n : n \geq 0\}$$

Claim B, given next, states that for every word of the form $a^n b^n$, there exists a derivation of the form $S \Rightarrow^{n+1} a^n b^n$ in G, for $n = 0, 1, \ldots$.

Claim B
Let $x = a^n b^n$ for some $n \geq 0$. Then, $S \Rightarrow^{n+1} a^n b^n \ [1^n 2]$ in G.

Proof
This proof is made by induction on $n \geq 0$.

Basis
Let $n = 0$. That is, $x = a^0 b^0 = \varepsilon$. Observe that $S \Rightarrow \varepsilon$ [2] or, equivalently, $S \Rightarrow^1 \varepsilon$ [$1^0 2$] in G. Thus, the basis holds.

Induction hypothesis
Assume the claim holds for all $x = a^k b^k$, where $k = 0, \ldots, n$, for some $n \geq 0$.

Induction step
Consider $x = a^{n+1} b^{n+1}$. For $x = a^n b^n$, $S \Rightarrow^{n+1} a^n b^n$ [$1^n 2$] in G by the induction hypothesis. In greater detail, this derivation can be expressed as

$$\begin{aligned} S &\Rightarrow^n a^n S b^n && [1^n] \\ &\Rightarrow a^n b^n && [2] \end{aligned}$$

Therefore,

$$\begin{aligned} S &\Rightarrow^n a^n S b^n && [1^n] \\ &\Rightarrow a^{n+1} S b^{n+1} && [1] \\ &\Rightarrow a^{n+1} b^{n+1} && [2] \end{aligned}$$

That is,

$$S \Rightarrow^{n+2} a^{n+1} b^{n+1} \quad [1^{n+1} 2]$$

in G.
We have proved the claim for $n+1$ and, thus, completed the induction step.

Consequently, Claim B holds. □

By Claim B,

$$\{a^n b^n : n \geq 0\} \subseteq L(G)$$

Having proved that $L(G) \subseteq \{a^n b^n : n \geq 0\}$ and $\{a^n b^n : n \geq 0\} \subseteq L$, it is concluded that

$$L(G) = \{a^n b^n : n \geq 0\}$$

▲

Informally, this book has already used the notion of a context-free language several times. The following definition formalizes this important feature.

Definition — context-free language
A language L, is a *context-free language* if there exists a context-free grammar G such that $L = L(G)$.

◆

The previous part of Example 5.1.1.1 demonstrates that $\{a^n b^n : n \geq 0\}$ represents a context-free language by proving that the context-free grammar discussed throughout all parts of Example 5.1.1.1 generates this language. The following example presents another demonstration of this kind. Specifically, this example considers the language L that consists of all nonempty words containing an equal number of *a*s and *b*s and proves that L is context-free by defining a context-free grammar G so that $L(G) = L$.

Example 5.1.1.2 Part 1 Context-free language
Consider the language L that contains all nonempty words consisting of an equal number of *a*s and *b*s; formally,

$$L = \{ w : w \in \{a, b\}^+ \text{ and } \#_a w = \#_b w \}$$

To prove that L is context-free, this example demonstrates that

$$L = L(G),$$

where G is the context-free grammar defined as

1: $S \to aB$
2: $S \to bA$
3: $A \to a$
4: $A \to aS$
5: $A \to bAA$
6: $B \to b$
7: $B \to bS$
8: $B \to aBB$

To verify $L(G) = L$, this example first establishes the following claim, consisting of three equivalences.

Claim
For all $w \in T^+$, where $T = \{a, b\}$, these three equivalences hold

Equivalence 1: $S \Rightarrow^* w$ if and only if $\#_a w = \#_b w$
Equivalence 2: $A \Rightarrow^* w$ if and only if $\#_a w = \#_b w + 1$
Equivalence 3: $B \Rightarrow^* w$ if and only if $\#_a w + 1 = \#_b w$

Proof
This proof is made by induction on $|w|$.

Basis
Let $w \in T^+$ such that $|w| = 1$.

Equivalence 1
S does not derive any word w with $|w| = 1$, and there exists no word $w \in T^+$ such that $|w| = 1$ and $\#_a w = \#_b w$. Thus, in this case, the basis holds trivially.

Equivalence 2
Only if
Observe that if $A \Rightarrow^* w$ with $|w| = 1$, then $w = a$.

If
Let $w = a$. Then, $A \Rightarrow a$ [3].

This concludes that Equivalence 2 holds.

Equivalence 3
Prove this equivalence by analogy with the proof of Equivalence 2. Thus the basis holds.

Induction hypothesis
Assume that the claim holds for all words, $w \in T^+$, satisfying $|w| \leq n$, for some $n \geq 1$.

Induction step
Let $w \in T^+$ with $|w| = n + 1$.

Equivalence 1
Only if
Consider a derivation of the form

$$S \Rightarrow^* w\ [\pi]$$

This derivation starts from S, and lhs(p) = S for p =1, 2; therefore, $\pi = p\pi'$, where $p \in \{1, 2\}$.

A. If $p = 1$, $S \Rightarrow^* w\ [1\pi']$, where 1: $S \to aB$. At this point, $w = av$, and $B \Rightarrow^* v$, where $|v| = n$. By the induction hypothesis, Equivalence 3 holds for v, so $\#_a v + 1 = \#_b v$. Therefore, $\#_a w = \#_b w$.

B. If $p = 2$, $S \Rightarrow^* w\ [2\pi']$, where 2: $S \to bA$. At this point, $w = bv$, where $A \Rightarrow^* v$ and $|v| = n$. Hence, by induction hypothesis, Equivalence 2 holds for v. Thus, $\#_b v + 1 = \#_a v$, and $\#_a w = \#_b w$.

It is concluded that the 'only if' part of the inductive step concerning Equivalence 1 holds.

If
Let $\#_a w = \#_b w$. Notice that $w \in \{a, b\}\{a, b\}^n$.

A. Let $w = av$. Then, $|v| = n$ and $\#_a v + 1 = \#_b v$. By the induction hypothesis (see Equivalence 3), $B \Rightarrow^* v$, so

$$S \Rightarrow aB \quad [1]$$
$$\Rightarrow^* av$$

That is, $S \Rightarrow^* w$.

B. Let $w = bv$. Then, $|v| = n$ and $\#_b v + 1 = \#_a v$. By the induction hypothesis (see Equivalence 2), $A \Rightarrow^* v$, so

$$S \Rightarrow bA \quad [2]$$
$$\Rightarrow^* bv$$

That is, $S \Rightarrow^* w$.

Consequently, the 'if' part of the inductive step concerning Equivalence 1 holds.

This concludes that the inductive step concerning Equivalence 1 holds.

Equivalence 2
Only if
Consider a derivation of the form

$$A \Rightarrow^* w \; [\pi]$$

Observe that this derivation starts from A and that $\mathrm{lhs}(p) = A$ for $p = 3, 4, 5$. Therefore, $\pi = p\pi'$, where $p \in \{3, 4, 5\}$.

A. Let $p = 3$. Then, $w = a$.

B. Let $p = 4$. Then, $A \Rightarrow^* w \; [4\pi']$, where $4: A \to aS$. Therefore, $w = av$ so $S \Rightarrow^* v$ and $|v| = n$. By the induction hypothesis (Equivalence 1), $\#_a v = \#_b v$, so $\#_a w = \#_b w + 1$.

C. Let $p = 5$. Then $w = buv$ such that $A \Rightarrow^* u, A \Rightarrow^* v, |u| \le n$, and $|v| \le n$. By the induction hypothesis (Equivalence 2), $\#_a u = \#_b u + 1$, and $\#_a v = \#_b v + 1$. Consequently, $\#_a w = \#_a uv = \#_b uv + 2$. As $\#_b uv = \#_b w - 1$, $\#_a w = \#_b w + 1$.

Consequently, the 'only if' part of the inductive step concerning Equivalence 2 holds.

Models for context-free languages

If
Consider w such that $\#_a w = \#_b w + 1$. Obviously, $w \in \{a, b\}\{a, b\}^n$.

A. Let $w = av$. Then, $|v| = n$ and $\#_a v = \#_b v$. By the induction hypothesis (Equivalence 1), $S \Rightarrow^* v$, so

$$A \Rightarrow aS \quad [4]$$
$$\Rightarrow^* av$$

That is, $A \Rightarrow^* w$.

B. Let $w = bv$. Then $|v| = n$ and $\#_a v = \#_b v + 2$. Express v as $v = uz$ so $\#_a u = \#_b u + 1$ and $\#_a z = \#_b z + 1$. As $|v| = n$, $|u| \leq n$ and $|z| \leq n$. By the induction hypothesis (Equivalence 2), $A \Rightarrow^* u$ and $A \Rightarrow^* v$. Hence,

$$A \Rightarrow bAA \quad [5]$$
$$\Rightarrow^* buA$$
$$\Rightarrow^* buz$$

Thus, $A \Rightarrow^* w$.

Consequently, the 'if' part of the inductive step concerning Equivalence 1 holds.

This concludes that the inductive step concerning Equivalence 2 holds.

Equivalence 3
Establish the inductive step concerning Equivalence 3 by analogy with the proof of the inductive step concerning Equivalence 2.

Therefore, the claim holds.

□

By the definition of the language generated by a context-free grammar,

$$w \in L(G) \text{ if and only if } S \Rightarrow^* w \text{ and } w \in T^*$$

As G contains no ε-production $\varepsilon \notin L(G)$; therefore,

$$w \in L(G) \text{ if and only if } S \Rightarrow^* w \text{ and } w \in T^+$$

By Equivalence 1 in the claim, for all $w \in T^+$,

$$S \Rightarrow^* w \text{ if and only if } \#_a w = \#_b w$$

Consequently,

$$L(G) = L,$$

where

$$L = \{ w: w \in T^+ \text{ and } \#_a w = \#_b w \}$$

Therefore, L is context-free.

△

Different derivations that generate the same word

As its name indicates, a context-free grammar $G = (N, T, P, S)$ uses its productions to rewrite nonterminals regardless of the context in which these nonterminals appear. Indeed, G can apply any production $p \in P$ to any appearance of lhs(p) in the current sentential form x; in other words, G can make several different derivation steps from x. Consequently, G can generate the same sentence in many different ways.

Conventions
Underlining indicates nonterminals that are rewritten in a given derivation step.

●

Example 5.1.1.2 Part 2 Different derivations generating the same sentence

Returning to the context-free grammar G discussed in the previous part of this example, consider $aabbab \in L(G)$. From S, G generates this sentence by the following four derivations.

1. $\underline{S} \Rightarrow a\underline{B}$ [1]
    $\Rightarrow aa\underline{B}B$ [8]
    $\Rightarrow aab\underline{S}B$ [7]
    $\Rightarrow aab\underline{S}b$ [6]
    $\Rightarrow aabb\underline{A}b$ [2]
    $\Rightarrow aabbab$ [3]

That is,

$$S \Rightarrow^* aabbab \ [187623]$$

2. $\underline{S} \Rightarrow a\underline{B}$ [1]
    $\Rightarrow aa\underline{B}B$ [8]
    $\Rightarrow aa\underline{B}b$ [6]
    $\Rightarrow aab\underline{S}b$ [7]
    $\Rightarrow aabb\underline{A}b$ [2]
    $\Rightarrow aabbab$ [3]

In brief,

$$S \Rightarrow^* aabbab \ [186723]$$

3.
$$\begin{aligned}
\underline{S} &\Rightarrow a\underline{B} & [1] \\
&\Rightarrow aa\underline{B}B & [8] \\
&\Rightarrow aab\underline{S}B & [7] \\
&\Rightarrow aabb A\underline{B} & [2] \\
&\Rightarrow aabb\underline{A}b & [6] \\
&\Rightarrow aabbab & [3]
\end{aligned}$$

Consequently,

$$S \Rightarrow^* aabbab \; [187263]$$

4.
$$\begin{aligned}
\underline{S} &\Rightarrow a\underline{B} & [1] \\
&\Rightarrow aa\underline{B}B & [8] \\
&\Rightarrow aab\underline{S}B & [7] \\
&\Rightarrow aabb\underline{A}B & [2] \\
&\Rightarrow aabba\underline{B} & [3] \\
&\Rightarrow aabbab & [6]
\end{aligned}$$

Thus,

$$S \Rightarrow^* aabbab \; [187236]$$

To summarize this example, G generates *aabbab* according to four different production words – 187623, 186723, 187263 and 187236. However, observe that during these four derivations, G applies the same productions to the same occurrences of the same nonterminals. In other words, except for production words, these four derivations coincide.

△

The rest of this section introduces some formal notation, and uses this to reduce the multiplicity of context-free derivations, demonstrated in the previous example. Specifically, these include

1. leftmost derivations
2. rightmost derivations
3. derivation trees.

Leftmost derivations

If in each derivation step, a context-free grammar G applies a production to the leftmost nonterminal appearing in the current sentential form, then the resulting derivation is leftmost.

Definition — leftmost direct derivation

Let $G = (N, T, P, S)$ be the context-free grammar, $p \in P$, $x \in T^*$ and $y \in (N \cup T)^*$. Then, $x\text{lhs}(p)y$ *directly derives* $x\text{rhs}(p)y$ according to p in G in the *leftmost* way, as denoted by

$$x\text{lhs}(p)y \Rightarrow_{\text{lm}} x\text{rhs}(p)y \; [p]$$

or, more briefly, by

$$x\text{lhs}(p)y \Rightarrow_{\text{lm}} x\text{rhs}(p)y$$

♦

Extend $\Rightarrow_{\text{lm}}$ to $\Rightarrow_{\text{lm}}^n$, $\Rightarrow_{\text{lm}}^+$ and $\Rightarrow_{\text{lm}}^*$ by analogy with the extension of $\Rightarrow$ to $\Rightarrow^n$, $\Rightarrow^+$ and $\Rightarrow^*$, respectively.

Example 5.1.1.2 Part 3 Leftmost derivations

Derivation 4 in the previous part of Example 5.1.1.2 represents a leftmost derivation. In symbols,

$$\begin{aligned}
\underline{S} &\Rightarrow_{\text{lm}} a\underline{B} & [1] \\
&\Rightarrow_{\text{lm}} aa\underline{B}B & [8] \\
&\Rightarrow_{\text{lm}} aab\underline{S}B & [7] \\
&\Rightarrow_{\text{lm}} aabb\underline{A}B & [2] \\
&\Rightarrow_{\text{lm}} aabba\underline{B} & [3] \\
&\Rightarrow_{\text{lm}} aabbab & [6]
\end{aligned}$$

Thus,

$$S \Rightarrow_{\text{lm}}^* aabbab \; [187236]$$

The other three derivations discussed in the previous part of this example are not leftmost.

△

The following theorem ensures that attention is restricted to leftmost derivations when determining $L(G)$ for a context-free grammar $G = (N, T, P, S)$. Indeed, this theorem guarantees that G can generate every sentence in $L(G)$ by a leftmost derivation.

Theorem 5.1.1.1

Let $G = (N, T, P, S)$ be a context-free grammar, and $w \in T^*$. Then,

$$w \in L(G) \text{ if and only if } S \Rightarrow_{\text{lm}}^* w \text{ in } G.$$

Models for context-free languages

Proof

If

The 'only if' part of this proof states that for all $w \in T^*$,

$$S \Rightarrow^*_{lm} w \text{ in } G \text{ implies } w \in L(G)$$

If $S \Rightarrow^*_{lm} w$ in G, then $S \Rightarrow^* w$ in G. As $w \in T^*$, $w \in L(G)$. Thus, the 'if' part of this proof holds.

Only if

The 'if' part of this proof states that for all $w \in T^*$,

$$w \in L(G) \text{ implies } S \Rightarrow^*_{lm} w \text{ in } G$$

The proof of this part first establishes the following claim.

Claim

For all $w \in T^*$ and $n \geq 1$,

$$S \Rightarrow^n w \text{ implies } S \Rightarrow^n_{lm} w$$

Proof

Let $w \in T^*, n \geq 1$, and

$$S \Rightarrow^n w \, [p_1 \ldots p_n]$$

where $p_i \in P$, for $i = 1, \ldots, n$.

If $S \Rightarrow^n w \, [p_1 \ldots p_n]$ represents a leftmost derivation, the implication holds. Assume that $S \Rightarrow^n w \, [p_1 \ldots p_n]$ is not leftmost. Then, there exists $i \in \{2, \ldots, n-1\}$ such that

$$S \Rightarrow^*_{lm} w_{i-1} \, [p_1 \ldots p_{i-1}]$$

and

$$w_{i-1} \Rightarrow w_i \quad [p_i]$$
$$\Rightarrow^* w_n \quad [p_{i+1} \ldots p_n]$$

where $w_n = w$, and G does not make $w_{i-1} \Rightarrow w_i \, [p_i]$ in the leftmost way. Let $A \in N$ be the leftmost non-terminal appearing in w_{i-1}. Express $w_{i-1} = v_1 A v_2 \text{lhs}(p_i) v_3$, $w_i = v_1 A v_2 \text{rhs}(p_i) v_3$, and

$$v_1 A v_2 \underline{\text{lhs}(p_i)} v_3 \Rightarrow v_1 A v_2 \text{rhs}(p_i) v_3 \quad [p_i]$$

where $v_1 \in T^*$. As $w \in T^*$, there exists p_j, for some $j \in \{i+1, \ldots, n\}$, such that $A = \text{lhs}(p_j)$, $w_{j-1} = v_1 \underline{\text{lhs}(p_j)} u$, $w_j = v_1 \text{rhs}(p_j) u$, and

$$v_1\underline{\text{lhs}(p_j)}u \Rightarrow v_1\text{rhs}(p_j)u \quad [p_j]$$

Rearrange the use of the production in $S \Rightarrow^n w$ $[p_1 \ldots p_n]$ so that p_j is used in the ith derivation step and p_i is used in the $(i+1)$th derivation step; formally,

$$\begin{aligned}
S &\Rightarrow^*_{\text{lm}} v_1\underline{\text{lhs}(p_j)}v_2\text{lhs}(p_i)v_3 & [p_1 \ldots p_{i-1}] \\
&\Rightarrow_{\text{lm}} v_1\text{rhs}(p_j)v_2\underline{\text{lhs}(p_i)}v_3 & [p_j] \\
&\Rightarrow v_1\text{rhs}(p_j)v_2\text{rhs}(p_i)v_3 & [p_i] \\
&\Rightarrow^* w & [p_{i+1} \ldots p_{j-1}p_{j+1} \ldots p_n]
\end{aligned}$$

If this derivation represents a leftmost derivation, the claim is proved. If this derivation is not leftmost, rearrange this derivation by analogy with the rearrangement of $S \Rightarrow^n w$ $[p_1 \ldots p_n]$. By repeating k rearrangements of this kind, for some $k \le n-2$, a leftmost derivation of the form $S \Rightarrow^n_{\text{lm}} w$ is surely obtained. Therefore, this claim holds.

□

Observe that $w \in L(G)$ implies $S \Rightarrow^n w$, for some $n \ge 1$. This observation and the claim imply that Theorem 5.1.1.1 holds.

■

Recall that Theorem 5.1.1.1 requires $w \in T^*$. Notice that this requirement cannot be generalized to $w \in (N \cup T)^*$. Indeed, consider the following two-production context-free grammar, G,

1: $S \to AA$
2: $A \to a$

Observe that $\underline{S} \Rightarrow A\underline{A} \Rightarrow Aa$; however, G cannot derive Aa in the leftmost way. Therefore, Theorem 5.1.1.1 holds only under the assumption that $w \in T^*$.

Rightmost derivations

If in every derivation step, a context-free grammar G applies a production to the rightmost nonterminal appearing in the current sentential form, then the resulting derivation is rightmost.

Definition — rightmost direct derivation

Let $G = (N, T, P, S)$ be a context-free grammar $p \in P, x \in (N \cup T)^*$ and $y \in T^*$. Then, $x\text{lhs}(p)y$ *directly derives* $x\text{rhs}(p)y$ according to p in G in the *rightmost* way, denoted by

$$x\text{lhs}(p)y \Rightarrow_{\text{rm}} x\text{rhs}(p)y \quad [p]$$

or, simply,

$$x\mathrm{lhs}(p)y \Rightarrow_{rm} x\mathrm{rhs}(p)y$$

◆

Extend $\Rightarrow_{rm}$ to $\Rightarrow_{rm}^{n}$, $\Rightarrow_{rm}^{+}$ and $\Rightarrow_{rm}^{*}$ by analogy with the extension of $\Rightarrow$ to $\Rightarrow^{n}$, $\Rightarrow^{+}$ and $\Rightarrow^{*}$, respectively.

Example 5.1.1.2 Part 4 Rightmost derivations

Derivation 2 in Part 2 of Example 5.1.1.2 represents a rightmost derivation. In terms of $\Rightarrow_{rm}$, this derivation is written as

$$\begin{align}
\underline{S} &\Rightarrow_{rm} a\underline{B} & [1] \\
&\Rightarrow_{rm} aaB\underline{B} & [8] \\
&\Rightarrow_{rm} aa\underline{B}b & [6] \\
&\Rightarrow_{rm} aab\underline{S}b & [7] \\
&\Rightarrow_{rm} aabb\underline{A}b & [2] \\
&\Rightarrow_{rm} aabbab & [3]
\end{align}$$

That is,

$$S \Rightarrow_{rm}^{*} aabbab\ [186723]$$

The other three derivations discussed in Part 2 of this example are not rightmost.

△

Consider a context-free grammar $G = (N, T, P, S)$. The following theorem guarantees that G can generate each sentence in the leftmost way.

Theorem 5.1.1.2

Let $G = (N, T, P, S)$ be a context-free grammar, and $w \in T^{*}$. Then,

$$w \in L(G) \text{ if and only if } S \Rightarrow_{rm}^{*} w \text{ in } G.$$

Proof

As demonstrated in the exercises, this proof is analogous to the proof of Theorem 5.1.1.1.

■

Derivation trees

A derivation tree t graphically represents the structure of a derivation in a context-free grammar G so that t specifies the productions together with the nonterminals that these productions rewrite. However, t suppresses the order in which G uses these productions during the derivation because this order represents an inessential piece of information.

The following definition, which makes use of several notions described in Section 0.3, introduces a production tree, which bases the definition of a derivation tree, given subsequently.

Definition — production tree

Let $G = (N, T, P, S)$ be a context-free grammar, and $p \in P$. The *production tree*, pt(p), corresponding to p is a labelled elementary tree such that lhs(p) labels root(t) and fr(pt(p)) is defined as follows:

1. if $|\text{rhs}(p)| = 0$ (that is, p is an ε-production),
   then fr(t) consists of one node labelled ε;
2. if $|\text{rhs}(p)| \geq 1$,
   then fr(t) consists of $|\text{rhs}(p)|$ nodes that are labelled with the symbols appearing in rhs(p) from left to right.

◆

Consider a production p of the form

$$p: A \rightarrow X_1 X_2 \ldots X_n$$

where $n \geq 1$. The production tree corresponding to p, pt(p), is depicted in Figure 5.1.1.1.

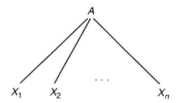

Figure 5.1.1.1 The production tree, pt(p), corresponding to $p: A \rightarrow X_1 X_2 \ldots X_n$.

Example 5.1.1.2 Part 5 Production trees

Return to the definition of the eight-production context-free grammar G given in the first part of this example. Consider the first production,

$$1: S \rightarrow aB$$

The production tree, pt(1), corresponding to 1 is displayed in Figure 5.1.1.2.

Models for context-free languages

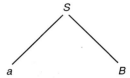

Figure 5.1.1.2 The production tree pt(1) corresponding to 1: $S \to aB$.

Also, consider the eighth production of G,

$$8: B \to aBB$$

The production tree pt(8) corresponding to this production is depicted in Figure 5.1.1.3.

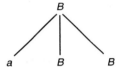

Figure 5.1.1.3 The production tree pt(8) corresponding to 8: $B \to aBB$.

△

Based on production trees, the next definition introduces derivation trees.

Definition — derivation tree

Let $G = (N, T, P, S)$ be a context-free grammar. A *derivation tree* of G is a labelled tree t satisfying two conditions:

1. root(t) is labelled with a nonterminal $A \in N$;
2. each elementary subtree t' appearing in t represents the production tree pt(p) corresponding to a production, $p \in P$.

♦

Example 5.1.1.2 Part 6 Derivation trees

Figure 5.1.1.4 depicts a derivation tree of G, as defined in Part 1 of this example.

△

Consider a context-free grammar $G = (N, T, P, S)$. Recall that every production tree pt(p) corresponds to a production $p \in P$ that is graphically specified by pt(p). Analogously, every derivation tree graphically describes the structure of a derivation in G, as the next definition explains.

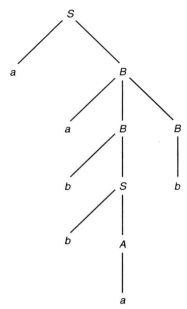

Figure 5.1.1.4 Derivation tree.

Definition — derivation tree corresponding to derivation

Let $G = (N, T, P, S)$ be a context-free grammar. The correspondence between derivation trees and the derivations that these trees represent is defined recursively as follows:

1. Let t be a one-node derivation tree t such that root(t) is labelled A, where $A \in N$. Then, t corresponds to $A \Rightarrow^* A\ [\varepsilon]$ in G.
2. Let t be the derivation tree corresponding to $A \Rightarrow^* x\text{lhs}(p)y\ [\pi]$ in G. The derivation tree corresponding to

$$A \Rightarrow^* x\text{lhs}(p)y\ [\pi]$$
$$\Rightarrow x\text{rhs}(p)y\ [p]$$

is constructed by attaching pt(p) to the $|x|+1$st leaf appearing in fr(t) (Figure 5.1.1.5). ◆

Models for context-free languages

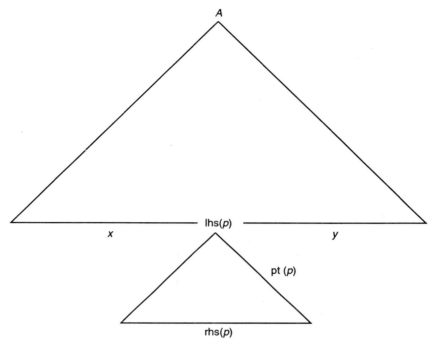

Figure 5.1.1.5 The derivation tree corresponding to:
$A \Rightarrow^* x\,lhs(p)\,y \quad [\pi]$
$\Rightarrow x\,rhs(p)\,y \quad [p]$

Example 5.1.1.2 Part 7 Derivation tree corresponding to a derivation

Return to the first derivation in Part 2 of Example 5.1.1.2; that is,

$$\begin{aligned}
S &\Rightarrow aB & [1] \\
&\Rightarrow aaBB & [8] \\
&\Rightarrow aabSB & [7] \\
&\Rightarrow aabbAB & [6] \\
&\Rightarrow aabb\underline{A}b & [2] \\
&\Rightarrow aabbab & [3]
\end{aligned}$$

This example now constructs the derivation tree corresponding to this derivation. The construction begins with the one-node derivation tree corresponding to $S \Rightarrow^0 S\ [\varepsilon]$ (Figure 5.1.1.6).

S

Figure 5.1.1.6 The derivation tree corresponding to $S \Rightarrow^0 S\ [\varepsilon]$.

As the derivation begins $\underline{S} \Rightarrow aB$ [1], append pt(1) to the one-node tree in Figure 5.1.1.6 to obtain the derivation tree corresponding to $S \Rightarrow aB$ (Figure 5.1.1.7).

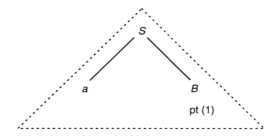

Figure 5.1.1.7 The derivation tree corresponding to $S \Rightarrow aB$ [1].

The second derivation step is $a\underline{B} \Rightarrow aaBB$ [8], so attach pt(8) to B in the tree described in Figure 5.1.1.7. The resulting derivation tree corresponds to

$$S \Rightarrow aB \quad [1]$$
$$\Rightarrow aaBB \quad [8]$$

(see Figure 5.1.1.8).

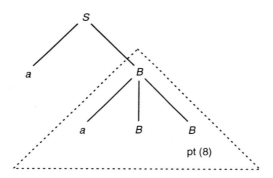

Figure 5.1.1.8 The derivation tree corresponding to
$S \Rightarrow aB \quad [1]$
$\Rightarrow aaBB \quad [8]$

As the third derivation step equals $aa\underline{B}B \Rightarrow aabSB$ [7], attach pt(7) to the leaf labelled by the first B appearing in the frontier of the tree in Figure 5.1.1.8. The resulting derivation tree, depicted in Figure 5.1.1.9, corresponds to

$$S \Rightarrow aB \quad [1]$$
$$\Rightarrow aaBB \quad [8]$$
$$\Rightarrow aabSB \quad [7]$$

Models for context-free languages

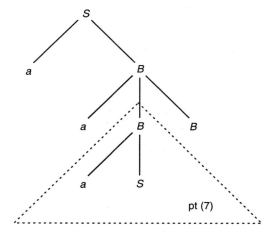

Figure 5.1.1.9 The derivation tree corresponding to
$S \Rightarrow aB$ [1]
$\Rightarrow aaBB$ [8]
$\Rightarrow aabSB$ [7]

Figures 5.1.1.10 through 5.1.1.12 pictorially describe the rest of the construction of the derivation tree corresponding to $S \Rightarrow^* aabbab$ [187623].

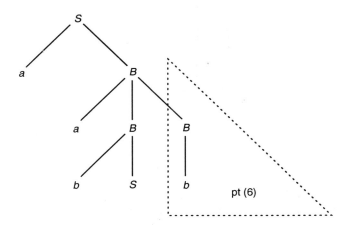

Figure 5.1.1.10 The derivation tree corresponding to
$S \Rightarrow aB$ [1]
$\Rightarrow aaBB$ [8]
$\Rightarrow aabSB$ [7]
$\Rightarrow aabSb$ [6]

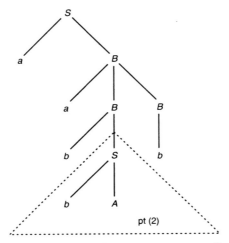

Figure 5.1.1.11 The derivation tree corresponding to
$S \Rightarrow aB$ [1]
$\Rightarrow aaBB$ [8]
$\Rightarrow aabSB$ [7]
$\Rightarrow aabSb$ [6]
$\Rightarrow aabbAb$ [2]

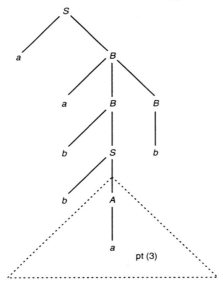

Figure 5.1.1.12 The resulting derivation tree corresponding to
$S \Rightarrow aB$ [1]
$\Rightarrow aaBB$ [8]
$\Rightarrow aabSB$ [7]
$\Rightarrow aabSb$ [6]
$\Rightarrow aabbAb$ [2]
$\Rightarrow aabbab$ [3]

Notice that the derivation tree displayed in Figure 5.1.1.12 corresponds to all four derivations discussed in the second part of Example 5.1.1.2.

△

Given a derivation in G, the previous example has illustrated how to construct the derivation tree that corresponds to the derivation. Conversely, there exists an algorithm that constructs a derivation from a given derivation tree t, so that t corresponds to the derivation. This algorithm forms a part of the next theorem's proof.

Theorem 5.1.1.3
Let $G = (N, T, P, S)$ be a context-free grammar, and $x \in (N \cup T)^*$. Then, $A \Rightarrow^* x$ in G if and only if there exists a derivation tree t such that A labels root(t) and x consists of symbols that label the nodes representing fr(t).

Proof
Only if
The 'only if' part of the equivalence, given in Theorem 5.1.1.3, states that if $A \Rightarrow^* x$ in G, then there exists a derivation tree, t, such that A labels root(t) and x consists of symbols that label the nodes of fr(t). The previous part of Example 5.1.1.2 illustrates how to obtain t from $A \Rightarrow^* x$. A general proof of this is left to the exercises.

If
The 'if' part of the equivalence states that if t is a derivation tree in G such that A labels root(t) and x represents the word of symbols that label the nodes of fr(t), then $A \Rightarrow^* x$ in G. This proof is made by induction on depth(t).

Basis
Let t be a derivation trees with depth(t) = 0. At this point, t is a tree consisting of one node, labelled by a nonterminal, $A \in N$. Observe that $A \Rightarrow^* A$ [ε] in G, so the basis holds.

Induction hypothesis
Suppose that there exists n, $n \geq 0$, such that all derivation trees t with depth(t) $\leq n$ satisfy the following implication: if t is a derivation tree in G such that A labels root(t) and x represents the word of symbols that label the nodes of fr(t), then $A \Rightarrow^* x$ in G.

Induction step
Let t be a derivation tree with depth(t) = $n + 1$. Let root(t) be labelled by A, where $A \in N$. Consider the production tree, pt(p), whose root coincides with root(t) (Figure 5.1.1.13).

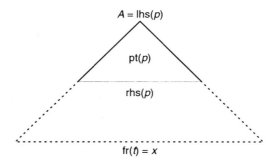

Figure 5.1.1.13 The production tree pt(p) whose root equals root(t).

1. Let $|\text{rhs}(p)| = 0$. Then, p has the form $p: A \to \varepsilon$. At this point,

$$\text{fr}(t) = \text{fr}(\text{pt}(p)) = \text{rhs}(p) = \varepsilon$$

(see Figure 5.1.1.14). Then, $A \Rightarrow^* \varepsilon\ [p]$ in G.

Figure 5.1.1.14 The derivation tree t such that root(t) = lhs(p), where $p: A \to \varepsilon$.

2. Let $|\text{rhs}(p)| = m$ with $m \geq 1$, so p represents a production that has the form

$$p: A \to X_1 \ldots X_m$$

(see Figure 5.1.1.15).

For $i = 1, \ldots, m$, this proof next distinguishes two cases:

(A) X_i labels a node that is not a leaf;
(B) X_i labels a leaf.

A. Let X_i label a node that is not a leaf in t. Then, X_i labels a node that represents root(t_i), where t_i is another derivation tree of G such that depth(t_i) < depth(t). Let x_i represent the word of symbols that label the nodes of fr(t_i) (see Figure 5.1.1.15). As depth(t_i) < depth(t), depth(t_i) $\leq n$; so, by the induction hypothesis, $X_i \Rightarrow^* x_i$ [π_i] in G for some production word π_i.

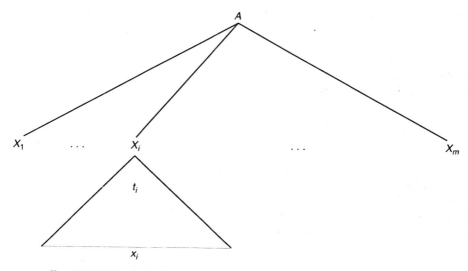

Figure 5.1.1.15 The derivation tree t such that root$(t) = $ lhs(p), where $p: A \rightarrow X_1...X_m$.

B. Let X_i label a leaf in t. Set $X_i = x_i$ and $\pi_i = \varepsilon$. In terms of this notation, $X_i \Rightarrow^* x_i\ [\pi_i]$.

By A and B, for all $i = 1, ..., m$,

$$X_i \Rightarrow^* x_i\ [\pi_i]$$

in G, where $x_1...x_n = x$. By using $X_i \Rightarrow^* x_i$, for $i = 1, ..., m$, construct the derivation

$$\begin{aligned}
\underline{A} &\Rightarrow \underline{X_1}...X_m & [p] \\
&\Rightarrow^* x_1...X_m & [\pi_1] \\
&\vdots \\
&\Rightarrow^* x_1...\underline{X_m} & [\pi_{m-1}] \\
&\Rightarrow^* x_1...x_m & [\pi_m]
\end{aligned}$$

As $x_1...x_n = x$,

$$A \Rightarrow^* x \quad [\pi]$$

in G, where $\pi = p\pi_1...\pi_{m-1}\pi_m$, so the 'if' part of the equivalence, given in Theorem 5.1.1.3, holds.

Thus, Theorem 5.1.1.3 is true. ∎

Consider a context-free grammar $G = (N, T, P, S)$. By Theorem 5.1.1.3 with $S = A$, x is a sentential form of G if and only if there exists a derivation tree t such that S

labels root(t) and x consists of symbols that label the nodes representing fr(t). The next theorem states an analogous statement in terms of sentences, which belong to $L(G)$.

Corollary 5.1.1.4
Let $G = (N, T, P, S)$ be a context-free grammar and $x \in T^*$. Then, $x \in L(G)$ if and only if there exists a derivation tree t such that S labels root(t) and x consists of symbols that label the nodes representing fr(t).

Proof
Let $G = (N, T, P, S)$ be a context-free grammar and $x \in T^*$. Set A to S in Theorem 5.1.1.3. Then, $S \Rightarrow^* x$ in G if and only if there exists a derivation tree t such that A labels root(t) and x consists of symbols that label the nodes representing fr(t). In other words, $x \in L(G)$ if and only if there exists a derivation tree t such that S labels root(t) and x consists of symbols that label the nodes representing fr(t). Thus, this corollary holds.
∎

The next theorem represents a modification of Theorem 5.1.1.3 in terms of leftmost derivations.

Theorem 5.1.1.5
Let $G = (N, T, P, S)$ be a context-free grammar and $x \in T^*$. Then, $S \Rightarrow^*_{lm} x$ in G if and only if there exists a derivation tree t such that S labels root(t) and x consists of symbols that label the nodes representing fr(t).

Proof
Establish this theorem by analogy with the proof of Theorem 5.1.1.3 and the proof of Corollary 5.1.1.4. A detailed proof is left to the exercises.
∎

The next theorem modifies Theorem 5.1.1.3 in terms of rightmost derivations.

Theorem 5.1.1.6
Let $G = (N, T, P, S)$ be a context-free grammar and $x \in T^*$. Then, $S \Rightarrow^*_{lm} x$ in G if and only if there exists a derivation tree t such that S labels root(t) and x consists of symbols that label the nodes representing fr(t).

Proof
This proof is left to the exercises.
∎

The following corollary represents the main results of Section 5.1.1.

Corollary 5.1.1.7
Let $G = (N, T, P, S)$ be a context-free grammar and $x \in T^*$. Then, these four equivalences hold:

1. $x \in L(G)$ if and only if $S \Rightarrow^* x$
2. $x \in L(G)$ if and only if $S \Rightarrow^*_{lm} x$
3. $x \in L(G)$ if and only if $S \Rightarrow^*_{rm} x$
4. $x \in L(G)$ if and only if there exists a derivation tree t such that S labels root(t) and x consists of symbols that label the nodes representing fr(t).

Proof
The first equivalence follows from the definition of the language generated by a context-free grammar. Corollary 5.1.1.4 and Theorem 5.1.1.5 imply the second equivalence. Analogously, Corollary 5.1.1.4 and Theorem 5.1.1.6 imply the third equivalence. Finally, the fourth equivalence holds by Corollary 5.1.1.4.
∎

Consider a context-free grammar $G = (N, T, P, S)$. By Corollary 5.1.1.7, without any loss of generality, it is always possible to solve problems concerning $L(G)$ in terms of any of these three notions:

1. leftmost derivations
2. rightmost derivations
3. derivation trees.

Many discussions concerning context-free languages make use of these notions, which significantly simplify the study of these languages.

5.1.2 Ambiguity

This section discusses ambiguous context-free grammars, which generate the same sentence by several different leftmost derivations. This ambiguity presents considerable problems to all pragmatically oriented computer science areas that use context-free grammars. By way of illustration, this section explores some of the problems that arise from ambiguity in the specification of programming languages.

Grammatical ambiguity

Definition — ambiguity
Let $G = (N, T, P, S)$ be a context-free grammar. If there exists a sentence $x \in L(G)$ such that $S \Rightarrow^*_{lm} x\ [\pi_1]$ and $S \Rightarrow^*_{lm} x\ [\pi_2]$ with $\pi_1 \neq \pi_2$, then G is *ambiguous*; otherwise, G is *unambiguous*.

◆

Equivalently, in terms of rightmost derivations, G is ambiguous provided that there exists a sentence $x \in L(G)$ such that $S \Rightarrow^*_{rm} x \ [\pi_1]$ and $S \Rightarrow^*_{rm} x \ [\pi_2]$ with $\pi_1 \neq \pi_2$. In terms of derivation trees, G is ambiguous if there exists a sentence $x \in L(G)$ such that $S = \text{root}(t) = \text{root}(t')$ and $x = \text{fr}(t) = \text{fr}(t')$, where t and t' represent two different derivation trees of G.

The following example discusses an ambiguous specification of the **if-then-else** statement; this ambiguity occurred in the original description of the programming language ALGOL 60, an ancestor of Pascal.

Example 5.1.2.1 Part 1 Ambiguous context-free grammar
Consider the following context-free grammar G:

1: $S \to$ **if** b **then** S **else** S
2: $S \to$ **if** b **then** S
3: $S \to a$

where the start symbol S is a nonterminal, and the other symbols are terminals. Observe that

$$\text{if } b \text{ then if } b \text{ then } a \text{ else } a \in L(G)$$

However, G makes these two different leftmost derivations:

$\underline{S} \Rightarrow_{lm}$ **if** b **then** $\underline{S}$ **else** S [1]
$\Rightarrow_{lm}$ **if** b **then if** b **then** $\underline{S}$ **else** S [2]
$\Rightarrow_{lm}$ **if** b **then if** b **then** a **else** $\underline{S}$ [3]
$\Rightarrow_{lm}$ **if** b **then if** b **then** a **else** a [3]

and

$\underline{S} \Rightarrow_{lm}$ **if** b **then** $\underline{S}$ [2]
$\Rightarrow_{lm}$ **if** b **then if** b **then** $\underline{S}$ **else** S [1]
$\Rightarrow_{lm}$ **if** b **then if** b **then** a **else** $\underline{S}$ [3]
$\Rightarrow_{lm}$ **if** b **then if** b **then** a **else** a [3]

In brief,

$S \Rightarrow^*_{lm}$ **if** b **then if** b **then** a **else** a [1233]

$S \Rightarrow^*_{lm}$ **if** b **then if** b **then** a **else** a [2133]

where

$$1233 \neq 2133$$

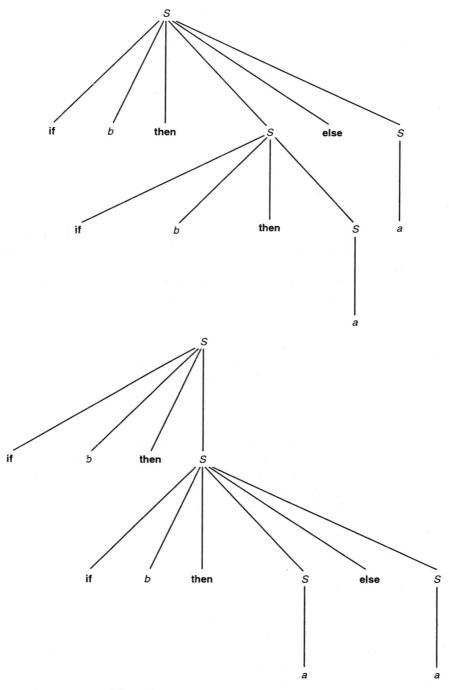

Figure 5.1.2.1 Two different derivation trees corresponding to **if** b **then if** b **then** a **else** a.

In terms of rightmost derivations, G generates if b then if b then a else a as follows:

$$S \Rightarrow^*_{rm} \text{if } b \text{ then if } b \text{ then } a \text{ else } a \ [2133]$$

$$S \Rightarrow^*_{rm} \text{if } b \text{ then if } b \text{ then } a \text{ else } a \ [1323]$$

where

$$2133 \neq 1323$$

Finally, in terms of derivation trees, Figure 5.1.2.1 presents two different derivation trees, whose frontier nodes are labelled by symbols of if b then if b then a else a.

Consequently, G represents an ambiguous context-free grammar, and this ambiguity makes G unusable in practice. Indeed, consider the two derivation trees corresponding to if b then if b then a else a (see Figure 5.1.2.1). The first tree associates the **else** part of this statement with the first **then**, whereas the other tree associates the **else** part with the other **then**. That is, G ambiguously associates the same **else** with two different **then**s – a gross practical drawback of G.

△

As the next example illustrates, for some ambiguous context-free grammars, there exist equivalent unambiguous context-free grammars.

Example 5.1.2.1 Part 2 Unambiguous context-free grammar

The previous part of this example discusses the ambiguous context-free grammar G for the **if-then-else** statement. Recall that G ambiguously associates the same **else** with two different **then**s. To specify this statement unambiguously, the **if-then-else** statement is redefined by the new context-free grammar G',

1: $S \rightarrow$ if b then S
2: $S \rightarrow$ if b then A else S
3: $S \rightarrow a$
4: $A \rightarrow$ if b then A else A
5: $A \rightarrow a$

where S and A are nonterminals, and the other symbols are terminals. In essence, G' uses the new nonterminal, A, to attach each **else** to the last proceeded unmatched **then** (see Figure 5.1.2.2). Consequently, G' represents an unambiguous context-free grammar equivalent to G, as verified in the exercises.

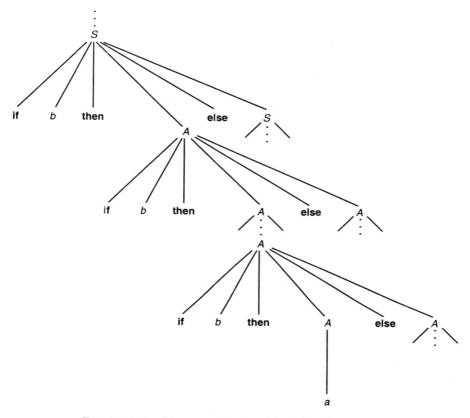

Figure 5.1.2.2 Unambiguous specification of the **if-then-else** statement.

△

Inherent ambiguity

As demonstrated by the previous example, for some languages generated by ambiguous context-free grammars, there also exist unambiguous context-free grammars that generate these languages. However, there exist context-free languages generated only by ambiguous context-free grammars.

Definition — inherent ambiguity
Let L be a context-free language. If every context-free grammar G satisfying $L(G) = L$ is ambiguous, then L is *inherently ambiguous*.

◆

The following example presents an inherently ambiguous language.

Example 5.1.2.2 Inherently ambiguous language

The context-free language

$$L = \{a^i b^j c^k : i, j, k \geq 1, \text{ and } i = j \text{ or } j = k\}$$

represents an inherently ambiguous context-free language. Express L as

$$L = L_1 \cup L_2$$

where

$$L_1 = \{a^i b^j c^k : i, j, k \geq 1 \text{ and } i = j\}$$

and

$$L_2 = \{a^i b^j c^k : i, j, k \geq 1 \text{ and } j = k\}$$

Observe that any context-free grammar G_1 such that $L(G_1) = L_1$ needs to match as and bs to guarantee the same number of these symbols, so G_1 is defined as

$$p_1: S \to AB$$
$$p_2: A \to aAb$$
$$p_3: A \to ab$$
$$p_4: B \to cB$$
$$p_5: B \to c$$

By analogy with G_1, any context-free grammar G_2 such that $L(G_2) = L_2$ is defined as

$$q_1: S \to CD$$
$$q_2: C \to aC$$
$$q_3: C \to a$$
$$q_4: D \to bDc$$
$$q_5: D \to bc$$

Let G be the context-free grammar consisting of productions p_1 through p_5 and q_1 through q_5. Observe that

$$L(G) = L(G_1) \cup L(G_2) = L_1 \cup L_2 = L$$

Consider $a^n b^n c^n \in L$, for some $n \geq 1$. G generates this sentence by making two distinct leftmost derivations so one derivation begins with p_1, and the other derivation begins with q_1:

$$S \Rightarrow_{lm} AB \quad [p_1]$$
$$\Rightarrow^*_{lm} a^n b^n c^n$$

and

$$S \Rightarrow_{lm} CD \quad [q_1]$$
$$\Rightarrow^*_{lm} a^n b^n c^n$$

Thus, G is ambiguous.

As formally proved in the exercises, all context-free grammars that generate L essentially resemble G. In other words, every context-free grammar that generates L necessarily contains four distinct nonterminals and 10 productions of the form coinciding with the form of G's productions. Consequently, every context-free grammar that generates L is ambiguous, so L represents an inherently ambiguous context-free language.

▲

5.1.3 Simplification

A context-free grammar G may contain some components that are of no use regarding the generation of $L(G)$. Because these useless components unnecessarily increase the size of G, this section explains how to remove them from G. First, Section 5.1.3.1 eliminates all useless symbols, that G cannot use to generate any sentence of $L(G)$. Then, Section 5.1.3.2 demonstrates how to eliminate all ε-productions from G. Section 5.1.3.3 eliminates all unit productions, that is, productions of the form $A \to B$. Finally, Section 5.1.3.4 summarizes these results and uses them to convert G to an equivalent context-free grammar containing no useless components.

5.1.3.1 Elimination of useless symbols

A context-free grammar G may contain symbols that are of no use in the generation of $L(G)$. This section detects and eliminates these useless symbols from G.

Nonterminating symbols

Using nonterminating symbols, G can derive no word consisting of terminals, so the removal of all nonterminating symbols from G does not disturb $L(G)$.

Definition — terminating symbol

Let $G = (N, T, P, S)$ be a context-free grammar, and $A \in N \cup T$. A is *terminating* if there exists $w \in T^*$ such that $A \Rightarrow^* w$ in G; otherwise, A is *nonterminating*. ◆

The following algorithm determines all terminating symbols in any context-free grammar.

Algorithm 5.1.3.1.1: Determination of terminating symbols

Input: A context-free grammar $G = (N, T, P, S)$.

Output: The set V that consists of all terminating symbols in G.

Method

begin
   $V := T \cup \{ \text{lhs}(p): p \in P \text{ and rhs}(p) \in T^* \}$;
   repeat
      $U := V$;
      for all $p \in P$ such that $\text{lhs}(p) \notin U$ **do**
         if $\text{rhs}(p) \in U^+$
         then $V := V \cup \{\text{lhs}(p)\}$
   until $U = V$
end.

Observe that every terminal $a \in T$ is terminating because $a \Rightarrow^0 a$ [ε] in G. Furthermore, if $p \in P$ with $\text{rhs}(p) \in T^*$, then $\text{lhs}(p) \Rightarrow \text{rhs}(p)$ [p] in G, so $\text{lhs}(p)$ is terminating as well. Therefore, Algorithm 5.1.3.1.1 initializes V with $T \cup \{ \text{lhs}(p): p \in P \text{ and rhs}(p) \in T^* \}$. Then, for all $p \in P$ with $\text{lhs}(p) \notin V$, this algorithm tests whether $\text{rhs}(p)$ consists of symbols currently contained in V; if so, Algorithm 5.1.3.1.1 adds $\text{lhs}(p)$ to V because $\text{lhs}(p)$ is also terminating. Algorithm 5.1.3.1.1 repeats this test until V contains all terminating symbols in G.

Lemma 5.1.3.1.2

Let $G = (N, T, P, S)$ be a context-free grammar. With G as its input, Algorithm 5.1.3.1.1 terminates and correctly produces the set V of all terminating symbols in G.

Proof

Throughout this proof, V_i denotes the current containment of V after Algorithm 5.1.3.1.1 has executed i iterations of its **repeat** loop and before this algorithm starts the execution of the $(i+1)$th iteration of the **repeat** loop, for $i = 0, 1, \ldots$.

Models for context-free languages

Termination
No performance of the **repeat** loop causes Algorithm 5.1.3.1.1 to remove any nonterminals from V, so

$$V_i \subseteq V_{(i+1)}$$

for all $i \geq 0$. Furthermore, Algorithm 5.1.3.1.1 executes this loop provided $V_i \subset V_{(i+1)}$; in other words, if $V_i = V_{(i+1)}$, then this algorithm exits from the **repeat** loop. Thus, this algorithm terminates after performing no more than card(N) iterations of the **repeat** loop.

Correctness
To establish the correctness of Algorithm 5.1.3.1.1, this proof first demonstrates two claims, Claim A and Claim B. By Claim A if Algorithm 5.1.3.1.1 adds a nonterminal $A \in N$ to V during an iteration of the **repeat** loop, then G makes a derivation from A to a word over T.

Claim A
Let $A \in N \cap V_i$, where $i = 0, \ldots,$ card(N). Then, $A \Rightarrow^+ w$ in G, for some $w \in T^*$.

Proof
Claim A is proved by induction on i.

Basis
Let $i = 0$. Consider $A \in N \cap V_0$. Then, there exists a production $p \in P$ with lhs(p) = A and rhs(p) $\in T^*$, so G makes the one-step derivation

$$A \Rightarrow^* \text{rhs}(p)\ [p]$$

Therefore, the basis holds.

Induction hypothesis
Assume that Claim A holds for all V_j with $j = 0, \ldots, i$, for some $i <$ card(N).

Induction step
Let $A \in N \cap V_{i+1}$.

1. Assume that $A \in V_j$, for some $j = 0, \ldots, i$. Then, this inductive step follows from the induction hypothesis.

2. Assume that $A \notin V_j$, for all $j = 0, \ldots, i$. That is, $A \in V_{(i+1)} - V_i$.

By the description of the **repeat** loop, P contains

$$p: A \rightarrow X_1 X_2 \ldots X_n,$$

for some $n \geq 1$, such that for each $k = 1, \ldots, n$,

$$X_k \in V_m$$

where $m = 0, \ldots, i$. By the induction hypothesis,

$$X_k \Rightarrow^* w_k \ [\pi_k]$$

where π_k is a production word and $w_k \in T^*$. Thus,

$$\begin{aligned} A &\Rightarrow \underline{X_1}X_2\ldots X_n & [p] \\ &\Rightarrow^* w_1\underline{X_2}\ldots X_n & [\pi_1] \\ &\Rightarrow^* w_1 w_2 \ldots X_n & [\pi_2] \\ &\vdots \\ &\Rightarrow^* w_1 w_2 \ldots w_n & [\pi_n] \end{aligned}$$

in G with $w_k \in T^*$ for all $k = 1, \ldots, n$. Set $w = w_1 w_2 \ldots w_n$. Conclude that

$$A \Rightarrow^+ w$$

in G with $w \in T^*$, so the inductive step holds.

Therefore, Claim A is true. □

Claim B, presented next, states that if $A \Rightarrow^+ w$ in G with $w \in T^*$, then Algorithm 5.1.3.1.1 adds A to V during an iteration of the **repeat** loop.

Claim B
Let $A \Rightarrow^{i+1} w$ in G, where $i \geq 0$ and $w \in T^*$. Then, Algorithm 5.1.3.1.1 produces V so that $A \in V$.

Proof
Claim B is proved by induction on i.

Basis
Let $i = 0$. That is,

$$A \Rightarrow w \ [p]$$

in G, where $p: A \to w \in P$ and $w \in T^*$. Therefore, Algorithm 5.1.3.1.1 adds A to V before this algorithm enters the **repeat** loop; that is, $A \in V_0$. Thus, $A \in V$. As a result, the basis holds.

Induction hypothesis
Assume that the claim is true for all k-step derivations, where $k = 1, \ldots, i$, for some $i \geq 1$.

Induction step
Let

$$A \Rightarrow^{i+1} w$$

in G, where $w \in T^*$. Express $A \Rightarrow^{i+1} w$ as

$$A \Rightarrow X_1 X_2 \ldots X_k \quad [p]$$
$$\Rightarrow w_1 w_2 \ldots w_k \quad [\pi]$$

where $X_j \in N \cup T$, $w = w_1 w_2 \ldots w_k$, $\pi = \pi_1 \pi_2 \ldots \pi_k$, for some $k \geq 1$, and

$$X_j \Rightarrow^* w_j [\pi_j]$$

for all $j = 1, \ldots, k$.

1. Let $X_j \in T$; that is, $X_j = w_j$ and $\pi_j = \varepsilon$. Thus, $X_j \in V_0$, so $X_j \in V$.
2. Let $X_j \in N$. As $p\pi$ consists of $i + 1$ productions, $X_j \Rightarrow^* w_j [\pi_j]$ represents an m-step derivation, for some $m \leq i$. By the inductive hypothesis, $X_j \in V$.

Using 1 and 2, $X_j \in V$, for all $j = 1, \ldots, k$. Then, from the definition of the **repeat** loop, $A \in V$. Thus, the inductive step holds.

Therefore, Claim B is true.

□

The rest of this proof, demonstrating Lemma 5.1.3.1.2, first considers nonterminals and, then, terminals.

Nonterminals
From the definition of terminating symbols, a nonterminal $A \in N$, is terminating if and only if $A \Rightarrow^+ w$ in G with $w \in T^*$. From Claims A and B, $A \Rightarrow^+ w$ in G with $w \in T^*$ if and only if Algorithm 5.1.3.1.1 includes A in V.

Terminals
From the definition of terminating symbols, every terminal is terminating. Observe that Algorithm 5.1.3.1.1 produces V, so V contains each $a \in T$.

Thus, V consists of all terminating symbols in G.

To summarize all proof, with G as its input, Algorithm 5.1.3.1.1 terminates and correctly produces the set V of all terminating symbols in G. Therefore, Lemma 5.1.3.1.2 holds.

∎

Example 5.1.3.1.1 Part 1 Application of Algorithm 5.1.3.1.1
Conider the context-free grammar G defined as

1: $S \rightarrow A + S$
2: $S \rightarrow A - S$
3: $S \rightarrow A$
4: $A \rightarrow a$
5: $B \rightarrow B + S$
6: $B \rightarrow S$
7: $C \rightarrow C - S$

Thus, according to the conventions introduced in the beginning of Section 5.1.1, G has the four nonterminals A, B, C and S, where S is the start symbol. Furthermore, G possesses the three terminals a, +, and −.

This example uses Algorithm 5.1.3.1.1 with G as its input to determine the set V containing all terminating symbols in G.

Before Algorithm 5.1.3.1.1 enters the **repeat** loop, it initializes V with G's terminals and, in addition, A because A forms the left-hand side of 4: $A \rightarrow a$, where a is a terminal. In brief, this algorithm initializes V as

$$V = \{+, -, a, A\}$$

Observe that for the production 3: $S \rightarrow A$, lhs(3) = S and rhs(3) = A, which belongs to V. Therefore, the first iteration of the **repeat** loop adds S to V, so

$$V = \{+, -, a, A, S\}$$

Notice that for the production 6: $B \rightarrow S$, lhs(6) = B, rhs(6) = S, and $S \in V$. Hence, the second iteration of the **repeat** loop adds B to V and, therefore, produces

$$V = \{+, -, a, A, B, S\}$$

The third iteration of this loop adds no new symbol to V, so Algorithm 5.1.3.1.1 exits this loop with

$$V = \{+, -, a, A, B, S\}$$

as the resulting set of all terminating symbols in G. The following table summarize the iterations of the **repeat** loop that Algorithm 5.1.3.1.1 executes with G on its input.

Iteration	V
0	$\{+, -, a, A\}$
1	$\{+, -, a, A, S\}$
2	$\{+, -, a, A, B, S\}$
3	$\{+, -, a, A, B, S\}$

Here, Iteration 0 indicates the initial containment of V (that is, V contains $+$, $-$, a and A before Algorithm 5.1.3.1.1 executes the first iteration of the **repeat** loop).

Notice that the resulting set V does not contain C, because C is nonterminating; indeed, G makes no derivation from C to a word over $\{+, -, a\}$.

△

Consider a context-free grammar $G = (N, T, P, S)$. By the definition of $L(G)$, $L(G) = \emptyset$ if and only if S is nonterminating. As this book mainly deals with nonempty context-free languages, the following convention is introduced.

Convention
Given a context-free grammar $G = (N, T, P, S)$, S is terminating unless explicitly stated otherwise.

●

The next algorithm converts any context-free grammar to an equivalent context-free grammar that contains only terminating symbols.

Algorithm 5.1.3.1.3: Conversion of a context-free grammar to an equivalent context-free grammar without nonterminating symbols

Input: A context-free grammar $G = (N, T, P, S)$.

Output: A context-free grammar $G_{term} = (N_{term}, T, P_{term}, S)$ such that $L(G) = L(G_{term})$ and $N_{term} \cup T$ contains only terminating symbols.

Method

begin
    use Algorithm 5.1.3.1.1 to determine the set V of all terminating symbols in G;
    $N_{term} := \{A : A \in N \cap V\}$;
    $P_{term} := \{p : p \in P, \text{lhs}(p) \in N_{term}, \text{ and rhs}(p) \in V^*\}$;
    produce $G_{term} = (N_{term}, T, P_{term}, S)$
end.

Theorem 5.1.3.1.4

Let $G = (N, T, P, S)$ be a context-free grammar. With G as its input, Algorithm 5.1.3.1.3 terminates and correctly produces an equivalent context-free grammar $G_{term} = (N_{term}, T, P_{term}, S)$ such that $L(G) = L(G_{term})$, and $N_{term} \cup T$ contains only terminating symbols.

Proof

Termination
Lemma 5.1.3.1.2 proves that Algorithm 5.1.3.1.1 terminates. Therefore, Algorithm 5.1.3.1.3 always halts, too.

Correctness

Terminating Symbols
As Lemma 5.1.3.1.2 has verified, Algorithm 5.1.3.1.1 correctly constructs the set V of all terminating symbols in G, so $N_{term} \cup T$ contains only terminating symbols.

Equivalence
To establish the equivalence of G and G_{term}, this proof first demonstrates that $L(G_{term}) \subseteq L(G)$ and, then, $L(G) \subseteq L(G_{term})$.

$L(G_{term}) \subseteq L(G)$
As $P_{term} \subseteq P$, $A \Rightarrow^* x \, [\pi]$ in G_{term} implies $A \Rightarrow^* x \, [\pi]$ in G, so $L(G_{term}) \subseteq L(G)$.

$L(G) \subseteq L(G_{term})$
By contradiction, this proof demonstrates that $x \in L(G)$ implies $x \in L(G_{term})$. Assume that there exists a word $x \in L(G)$ such that $x \notin L(G_{term})$. That is, $S \Rightarrow^* x \, [\pi]$ in G; however, G_{term} does not make a derivation from S to x. Consequently, π can be expressed as

$$\pi = \pi_1 p \pi_2$$

where $p \in (P - P_{term})$. By the definition of P_{term}, p contains a nonterminating symbol. Therefore, G can use p in no derivation of a sentence in $L(G)$ – a statement contradictory to $S \Rightarrow^* x \, [\pi]$ in G with $x \in L(G_{term})$. This contradiction implies $L(G) \subseteq L(G_{term})$.

Because $L(G_{term}) \subseteq L(G)$ and $L(G) \subseteq L(G_{term})$, $L(G_{term}) = L(G)$. Thus, Algorithm 5.1.3.1.3 correctly produces an equivalent context-free grammar, $G_{term} = (N_{term}, T, P_{term}, S)$, such that $L(G) = L(G_{term})$, and $N_{term} \cup T$ contains only terminating symbols. In other words, Theorem 5.1.3.1.3 holds. ∎

Example 5.1.3.1.1 Part 2 Application of Algorithm 5.1.3.1.3

Return to the seven-production context-free grammar G discussed in Part 1 of Example 5.1.3.1.1. Recall that Algorithm 5.1.3.1.1 determines

$$\{+, -, a, A, B, S\}$$

as the set of terminating symbols in G. Algorithm 5.1.3.1.3 converts G to the following six-production context-free grammar G_{term}:

1: $S \to A + S$
2: $S \to A - S$
3: $S \to A$
4: $A \to a$
5: $B \to B + S$
6: $B \to S$

Observe that Algorithm 5.1.3.1.3 does not include 7: $C \to C - S$ in G_{term} because $C \notin \{+, -, a, A, B, S\}$.

△

Inaccessible symbols

In addition to nonterminating symbols, a context-free grammar G may contain inaccessible symbols, which are also useless because they appear in no sentential form derived by G.

Definition — accessible symbol
Let $G = (N, T, P, S)$ be a context-free grammar and $X \in N \cup T$. X is *accessible* if $S \Rightarrow^* uXv$ in G, for some $u, v \in (N \cup T)^*$; otherwise, X is *inaccessible*.

♦

Alternatively, X is accessible if X appears in a sentential form of G; however, X is inaccessible if X appears in no sentential form of G.

The following algorithm determines the set of all accessible symbols in any context-free grammar.

Algorithm 5.1.3.1.5: Determination of accessible symbols

Input: A context-free grammar $G = (N, T, P, S)$.

Output: The set W of all accessible symbols in G.

Method

begin
   $W := \{S\}$;
   OLD := ∅;
   repeat

```
      NEW := W - (OLD ∪ T);
      OLD := W - T;
      for all A ∈ NEW do
        for each p ∈ P with lhs(p) = A do
          W := W ∪ {alph(rhs(p))}
    until W - T = OLD
end.
```

Observe that S is surely accessible because $S \Rightarrow^* S[\varepsilon]$ in G, so Algorithm 5.1.3.1.5 initially sets $W := \{S\}$. Then, for all $p \in P$ with $\text{lhs}(p) \in W$, this algorithm adds $\text{alph}(\text{rhs}(p))$ to W because, at this point, all symbols in $\text{alph}(\text{rhs}(p))$ appear in a sentential form and, thus, represent accessible symbols. In this way, Algorithm 5.1.3.1.5 adds symbols to W until W contains all accessible symbols in G.

Lemma 5.1.3.1.6
Let $G = (N, T, P, S)$ be a context-free grammar. With G as its input, Algorithm 5.1.3.1.5 terminates and correctly produces the set W containing all accessible symbols in G.

Proof
This proof resembles the proof of Lemma 5.1.3.1.2. Therefore, only the fundamental ideas behind the proof are given and its completion is left to the exercises.

Termination
If during an iteration of the **repeat** loop Algorithm 5.1.3.1.5 adds a new symbol to W, this algorithm remains in the loop and executes another iteration; otherwise, it exits from the loop. Therefore, Algorithm 5.1.3.1.5 performs no more than $\text{card}(N)$ iterations of this loop. As N is finite, the algorithm always terminates.

Correctness
To demonstrate that Algorithm 5.1.3.1.5 correctly produces the set W of all accessible symbols in G, this proof first establishes Claims A and B.

Claim A
For all $X \in N \cup T$, if Algorithm 5.1.3.1.5 includes X into W, then X is accessible in G.

Proof
This proof is by induction on n, where n denotes the number of iterations of the **repeat** loop.

Basis
Let $n = 0$. Before Algorithm 5.1.3.1.5 enters the **repeat** loop, it initializes W with $\{S\}$. S is surely accessible because $S \Rightarrow^* S[\varepsilon]$ in G, so the basis holds.

Induction hypothesis
Assume that after m iterations of the **repeat** loop, all symbols included in V_{access} are accessible in G, for $m = 0, \ldots, n$, where n is a nonnegative integer.

Induction step
Suppose that Algorithm 5.1.3.1.5 adds a symbol, $X \in N \cup T$, to W during the $(n+1)$th

iteration of the **repeat** loop. Then, there exists $p \in P$ so $X \in \mathrm{alph}(\mathrm{rhs}(p))$ and Algorithm 5.1.3.1.5 has included $\mathrm{lhs}(p)$ into W during the previous iteration of the **repeat** loop. By the induction hypothesis, $\mathrm{lhs}(p)$ is accessible, so

$$S \Rightarrow^* u\mathrm{lhs}(p)v$$

in G, for some $u, v \in (N \cup T)^*$. Therefore,

$$\begin{aligned} S &\Rightarrow^* x\mathrm{lhs}(p)y \\ &\Rightarrow x\mathrm{rhs}(p)y \quad [p] \end{aligned}$$

Thus, X is accessible, and the induction step is completed.

Consequently, Claim A holds.

□

Claim B
For all $n \geq 0$ and $X \in N \cup T$, if $S \Rightarrow^n uXv$, where $u, v \in (N \cup T)^*$, then Algorithm 5.1.3.1.5 includes X in W.

Proof
This proof is by induction on n.

Basis
Let $n = 0$. That is, $S \Rightarrow^* S$ [ε] in G. As Algorithm 5.1.3.1.5 initializes W with $\{S\}$, this basis holds.

Induction hypothesis
Suppose that for all $m = 0, \ldots, n$ and $X \in N \cup T$, if $S \Rightarrow^n uXv$, where $u, v \in (N \cup T)^*$, then Algorithm 5.1.3.1.5 includes X in W, where n is an integer such that $n \geq 0$.

Induction step
Consider

$$\begin{aligned} S &\Rightarrow^* u\mathrm{lhs}(p)v \\ &\Rightarrow u\mathrm{rhs}(p)v \quad [p] \end{aligned}$$

in G, where $u, v \in (N \cup T)^*$, and $X \in \mathrm{alph}(\mathrm{rhs}(p))$.

1. If $X \in W$, then the induction step is completed.

2. If $X \notin W$, then the previous iteration of the **repeat** loop has added $\mathrm{lhs}(p)$ to W, so the succeeding iteration adds X to W; thus, the induction step is completed in this case as well.

Therefore, Claim B holds.

□

By Claim A, for each $X \in N \cup T$, if Algorithm 5.1.3.1.5 includes X into W, then X is accessible in G. By Claim B, if X is accessible in G, then Algorithm 5.1.3.1.5 includes X in W. Therefore, Algorithm 5.1.3.1.5 includes X in W if and only if X is accessible in G. Consequently, with G as its input, Algorithm 5.1.3.1.5 correctly produces the set W containing all accessible symbols in G.

Thus, Lemma 5.1.3.1.6 holds.

■

Example 5.1.3.1.1 Part 3 Application of Algorithm 5.1.3.1.5

Recall that Part 2 of this example obtains the context-free grammar G_{term}, defined as

1: $S \rightarrow A + S$
2: $S \rightarrow A - S$
3: $S \rightarrow A$
4: $A \rightarrow a$
5: $B \rightarrow B + S$
6: $B \rightarrow S$

This example uses Algorithm 5.1.3.1.5 to determine the set W containing all terminating symbols in G_{term}. With G_{term} on its input, this algorithm initially sets W as follows

$$V_{access} = \{S\}$$

Observe that A, $+$ and $-$ appear on the right-hand sides of productions 1, 2 and 3, whose left-hand sides are equal to S. Therefore, the first iteration of the **repeat** loop adds A, $+$ and $-$ to W and, thus, produces W as

$$W = \{+, -, A, S\}$$

Consider the production 4: $A \rightarrow a$. Because lhs(4) $\in W$, the second iteration of the **repeat** loop adds a to W, so

$$W = \{+, -, a, A, S\}$$

Observe that a represents a terminal, so this iteration adds no new nonterminal to W and, therefore, Algorithm 5.1.3.1.5 exits from the **repeat** loop. The following table summarizes the iterations of the **repeat** loop that Algorithm 5.1.3.1.1 performs with G_{term} as its input.

Iteration	W
0	$\{S\}$
1	$\{+, -, A, S\}$
2	$\{+, -, a, A, S\}$

Consequently, $+$, $-$, a, A and S represent all accessible symbols in G_{term}. Notice that B is inaccessible; indeed, G makes no derivation from S to a sentential form containing B.

△

The next algorithm makes use of Algorithm 5.1.3.1.5 to convert any context-free grammar to an equivalent context-free grammar that contains only accessible symbols.

Algorithm 5.1.3.1.7: Conversion of a context-free grammar to an equivalent context-free grammar without inaccessible symbols

Input: A context-free grammar $G = (N, T, P, S)$.

Output: A context-free grammar $G_{\text{access}} = (N_{\text{access}}, T_{\text{access}}, P_{\text{access}}, S)$, such that $L(G) = L(G_{\text{access}})$, and $(N_{\text{access}} \cup T_{\text{access}})$ contains only terminating symbols.

Method

begin
  use Algorithm 5.1.3.1.5 to determine the set W containing all accessible symbols in G;
  $N_{\text{access}} := \{A : A \in N \cap W\}$;
  $T_{\text{access}} := \{a : a \in T \cap W\}$;
  $P_{\text{access}} := \{p : p \in P, \text{lhs}(p) \in N_{\text{access}}, \text{rhs}(p) \in W^*\}$;
  produce $G_{\text{access}} = (N_{\text{access}}, T_{\text{access}}, P_{\text{access}}, S)$
end.

Theorem 5.1.3.1.8

Let $G = (N, T, P, S)$ be a context-free grammar. With G as its input, Algorithm 5.1.3.1.7 terminates and correctly produces a context-free grammar $G_{\text{access}} = (N_{\text{access}}, T_{\text{access}}, P_{\text{access}}, S)$, such that $L(G) = L(G_{\text{access}})$ and $(N_{\text{access}} \cup T_{\text{access}})$ contains only accessible symbols.

Proof
Termination
Lemma 5.1.3.1.6 proves that Algorithm 5.1.3.1.5 terminates. Therefore, Algorithm 5.1.3.1.7 halts, too.

Correctness
Accessible symbols
Lemma 5.1.3.1.6 proves that Algorithm 5.1.3.1.5 correctly constructs the set W containing all accessible symbols in G. Thus, $N_{access} \cup T_{access}$ contains only accessible symbols.

Equivalence
To establish the equivalence of G and G_{term}, this proof demonstrates that $L(G_{access}) \subseteq L(G)$ and $L(G) \subseteq L(G_{access})$.

$L(G_{access}) \subseteq L(G)$
As $P_{access} \subseteq P, A \Rightarrow^* x\ [\pi]$ in G_{access} implies $A \Rightarrow^* x\ [\pi]$ in G, so $L(G_{access}) \subseteq L(G)$.

$L(G) \subseteq L(G_{access})$
This proof demonstrates that $x \in L(G)$ implies $x \in L(G_{access})$ by contradiction. Assume that there exists a word $x \in L(G) - L(G_{access})$. Consequently, $S \Rightarrow^* x\ [\pi]$ in G; however, G_{access} does not generate x from S. Thus, there exists $p \in (P - P_{access})$ so

$$\pi = \pi_1 p \pi_2$$

As $p \notin P_{access}$, p contains an inaccessible symbol. Therefore, G cannot use p in any derivation from S to a word from $L(G)$. Thus, there exists no derivation of the form $S \Rightarrow^* x\ [\pi]$ in G, where $\pi = \pi_1 p \pi_2$, which is a contradiction. Consequently, $L(G) \subseteq L(G_{access})$.
As $L(G_{access}) \subseteq L(G)$ and $L(G) \subseteq L(G_{access})$,

$$L(G_{access}) = L(G)$$

Thus, with G on its input, Algorithm 5.1.3.1.7 terminates and correctly produces a context-free grammar, $G_{access} = (N_{access}, T_{access}, P_{access}, S)$, such that $L(G) = L(G_{access})$, and $(N_{access} \cup T_{access})$ contains only accessible symbols. Therefore, Theorem 5.1.3.1.8 holds.

∎

Example 5.1.3.1.1 Part 4 Application of Algorithm 5.1.3.1.7

Now return to the six-production context-free grammar G_{term} discussed in Example 5.1.3.1.1 Part 2. Recall that Algorithm 5.1.3.1.5 determines

$$\{+, -, a, A, S\}$$

as the set of terminating symbols in G (see Part 3 of this example). Assume that G_{term} represents the input grammar of Algorithm 5.1.3.1.7. At this point, Algorithm 5.1.3.1.7 produces G_{access}, defined by the four productions

1: $S \to A + S$
2: $S \to A - S$
3: $S \to A$
4: $A \to a$

Observe that Algorithm 5.1.3.1.7 has not included 5: $B \to B + S$ or 6: $B \to S$ into G_{access} because these productions contain B, and $B \notin \{+, -, a, A, S\}$.

△

Useless Symbols

Definition — useful symbol
Let $G = (N, T, P, S)$ be a context-free grammar, and let $X \in N \cup T$. X is *useful* if $S \Rightarrow^* uXv \Rightarrow^* uxv$ in G, for some $u, v \in (N \cup T)^*$ and $x \in T^*$; otherwise, X is *useless*.

♦

Equivalently, if X is accessible and terminating, X is useful; otherwise, X is useless.

The next algorithm converts any context-free grammar to an equivalent context-free grammar that contains only useful symbols. This conversion uses Algorithms 5.1.3.1.3 and Algorithm 5.1.3.1.7.

Algorithm 5.1.3.1.9: Conversion of a context-free grammar to an equivalent context-free grammar without useless symbols

Input: A context-free grammar $G = (N, T, P, S)$.

Output: A context-free grammar, $G_{useful} = (N_{useful}, T_{useful}, P_{useful}, S)$, such that $L(G) = L(G_{useful})$ and $(N_{term} \cup T)$ contains only useful symbols.

Method

begin
    use Algorithm 5.1.3.1.3 to convert $G = (N, T, P, S)$ to $G_{term} = (N_{term}, T, P_{term}, S)$;
    use Algorithm 5.1.3.1.7 to convert $G_{term} = (N_{term}, T, P_{term}, S)$ to
    $G_{access} = (N_{access}, T_{access}, P_{access}, S)$;
    $N_{useful} := N_{access}$;
    $T_{useful} := T_{access}$;
    $P_{useful} := P_{access}$;
    produce $G_{useful} = (N_{useful}, T_{useful}, P_{useful}, S)$
end.

Theorem 5.1.3.1.10

Let $G = (N, T, P, S)$ be a context-free grammar. With G as its input, Algorithm 5.1.3.1.9 terminates and correctly produces a context-free grammar, $G_{\text{useful}} = (N_{\text{useful}}, T_{\text{useful}}, P_{\text{useful}}, S)$, such that $L(G) = L(G_{\text{useful}})$, and $(N_{\text{term}} \cup T)$ contains only useful symbols.

Proof

Termination
Theorem 5.1.3.1.4 proves that Algorithm 5.1.3.1.3 terminates, and Theorem 5.1.3.1.8 proves that Algorithm 5.1.3.1.7 terminates. Therefore, Algorithm 5.1.3.1.9 always halts.

Correctness
This section only sketches out the proof, and leaves its completion to the exercises.

Useful symbols
Theorem 5.1.3.1.4 demonstrates that Algorithm 5.1.3.1.3 correctly converts any context-free grammar to an equivalent context-free grammar without any nonterminating symbols; therefore, G_{term} contains only terminating symbols. Theorem 5.1.3.1.8 verifies that Algorithm 5.1.3.1.7 correctly converts any context-free grammar to an equivalent context-free grammar without any inaccessible symbols, so G_{access} contains only accessible symbols. In addition, observe that if the input grammar of Algorithm 5.1.3.1.7 contains only terminating symbols, then this algorithm produces an output grammar that also possesses only terminating symbols. Thus, G_{access} contains only accessible and terminating symbols. As G_{useful} coincides with G_{access}, G_{useful} contains only useful symbols.

Equivalence
Theorem 5.1.3.1.4 implies that

$$L(G) = L(G_{\text{term}})$$

Theorem 5.1.3.1.8 implies that

$$L(G_{\text{term}}) = L(G_{\text{access}})$$

Because G_{useful} coincides with G_{access},

$$L(G_{\text{access}}) = L(G_{\text{useful}})$$

From these three equations,

$$L(G) = L(G_{\text{useful}})$$

Therefore, with G as its input, Algorithm 5.1.3.1.9 terminates and correctly produces a context-free grammar, $G_{\text{useful}} = (N_{\text{useful}}, T_{\text{useful}}, P_{\text{useful}}, S)$, such that

$L(G) = L(G_{useful})$, and $(N_{term} \cup T)$ contains only useful symbols. Thus, Theorem 5.1.3.1.10 holds.

∎

Algorithm 5.1.3.1.9 applies Algorithm 5.1.3.1.3, then Algorithm 5.1.3.1.7. This sequence represents an important property of Algorithm 5.1.3.1.9. Reversal of this sequence may cause the resulting context-free grammar to contain some useless symbols because Algorithm 5.1.3.1.3 may produce an output grammar with some inaccessible symbols, as illustrated by the next example.

Example 5.1.3.1.2 Incorrect use of Algorithm 5.1.3.1.7 before Algorithm 5.1.3.1.3
Consider the context-free grammar G,

1: $S \rightarrow a$
2: $A \rightarrow a$
3: $S \rightarrow AB$

As G contains only accessible symbols, with G as its input, Algorithm 5.1.3.1.7 produces G_{access} that coincides with G. Then, with G_{access} as its input, Algorithm 5.1.3.1.3 produces

1: $S \rightarrow a$
2: $A \rightarrow a$

Observe that this grammar contains the useless symbol A.

▲

5.1.3.2 Elimination of ε-productions

This section explains how to eliminate ε-productions from any context-free grammar. This elimination usually significantly simplifies the exploration of a given context-free grammar G, both theoretically and practically. From a theoretical point of view, the assumption that G contains no ε-productions considerably simplifies the achievement of some results concerning G's properties, as frequently demonstrated hereafter. From a practical point of view, the elimination of ε-investigation from G often makes the application of G simpler. To give an insight into this practical simplification, consider a compiler's parser whose main task is the decision of whether a word w, representing a program, belongs to $L(G)$ (see Sections 5.3.1.2 and 9.3.2). To demonstrate that $w \in L(G)$, this parser constructs the derivation that G makes from its start symbol to w. If G possesses ε-productions, G can make a derivation step, $u \Rightarrow v$, with $|u| > |v|$; at this point, the lengths of the derived sentential forms vary with respect to one another, and this variation complicates the construction of a derivation for w. However, if G possesses no ε-productions, $u \Rightarrow v$ in G implies $|u| \leq |v|$, so the lengths of derived sentential forms monotonically increases, and this monotonic increase simplifies the construction of a derivation for w. Consequently, the elimination of ε-productions fulfils a crucial role in later discussions.

ε-Nonterminals

To eliminate all ε-productions from a context-free grammar G, this section first determines the nonterminals from which G can derive ε.

Definition — ε-nonterminal
Let $G = (N, T, P, S)$ be a context-free grammar and $A \in N$. A is an *ε-nonterminal* if $A \Rightarrow^* \varepsilon$ in G.

◆

The following algorithm determines the set of all ε-nonterminals in a given context-free grammar $G = (N, T, P, S)$.

Algorithm 5.1.3.2.1: Determination of ε-nonterminals

Input: A context-free grammar $G = (N, T, P, S)$.

Output: The set N_ε that contains all ε-nonterminals in G, $N_\varepsilon = \{ A : A \in N,$ and $A \Rightarrow^* \varepsilon$ in $G\}$.

Method

begin
   $N_\varepsilon := \{ \text{lhs}(p) : p \in P \text{ and rhs}(p) = \varepsilon \}$;
   repeat
      $W := N_\varepsilon$;
      for all $p \in P$ with $\text{lhs}(p) \in N - W$ **do**
         if $\text{rhs}(p) \in W^*$
         then $N_\varepsilon := N_\varepsilon \cup \{\text{lhs}(p)\}$
   until $W = N_\varepsilon$
end.

Observe that if $p \in P$ with $\text{rhs}(p) = \varepsilon$, then $\text{lhs}(p) \Rightarrow \varepsilon$ $[p]$ in G, so $\text{lhs}(p)$ represents an ε-nonterminal; therefore, Algorithm 5.1.3.2.1 initializes W with $\{ \text{lhs}(p) : p \in P$ and $\text{rhs}(p) = \varepsilon\}$. Then, for all $p \in P$ with $\text{lhs}(p) \notin W$, this algorithm tests whether $\text{rhs}(p)$ consists of symbols currently contained in W; if so, Algorithm 5.1.3.2.1 adds $\text{lhs}(p)$ to V because $\text{lhs}(p) \Rightarrow^* \varepsilon$ in G. Algorithm 5.1.3.2.1 repeats this test until W contains all ε-nonterminals in G.

Lemma 5.1.3.2.2

Let $G = (N, T, P, S)$ be a context-free grammar. With G on its input, Algorithm 5.1.3.2.1 terminates and correctly produces the set W of all ε-nonterminals in G.

Proof

Throughout this proof, W_i denotes the current containment of W after Algorithm 5.1.3.2.1 has executed i iterations of the **repeat** loop and before this algorithm starts the execution of the $(i+1)$th iteration of this loop, for $i = 0, 1, \ldots$.

Termination
Observe that

$$W_i \subseteq W_{i+1}$$

for all $i \geq 0$. Furthermore, Algorithm 5.1.3.1.1 executes this loop provided $W_{i+1} - W_i \neq \varnothing$; otherwise, this algorithm exits from the **repeat** loop. Thus, this algorithm terminates after performing no more than card(N) iterations of the **repeat** loop.

Correctness
To verify the correctness of Algorithm 5.1.3.2.1, this proof first establishes Claims A and B. By Claim A, if Algorithm 5.1.3.2.1 adds a nonterminal $A \in N$ to W during an iteration of the **repeat** loop, then lhs(p) $\Rightarrow^*$ ε in G.

Claim A

Let $A \in W_i$, where $i = 0, \ldots,$ card(N). Then, lhs(p) $\Rightarrow^+ \varepsilon$ in G.

Proof

Claim A is proved by induction on i.

Basis
Let $i = 0$. Assume that $A \in W_0$ with lhs(p) = A and rhs(p) = ε. Then,

$$A \Rightarrow^* \varepsilon \, [p]$$

Hence, the basis holds.

Induction hypothesis
Assume that Claim A holds for all W_j with $j = 0, \ldots, i$, for some $i \leq$ card(N) $- 1$.

Induction step
Let $A \in W_{i+1}$.

1. Assume that $A \in W_j$, for some $j = 0, \ldots, i$. Then, this inductive step follows from the induction hypothesis.

2. Assume that $A \notin W_j$, for all $j = 0, \ldots, i$. That is, $A \in W_{i+1} - W_i$. From the description of the **repeat** loop, P contains

$$p: A \to A_1 A_2 \ldots A_n$$

for some $n \geq 1$ so for $k = 1, \ldots, n$,

$$A_k \in W_j$$

where $j = 0, \ldots, i$. By the induction hypothesis, for all $k = 1, \ldots, n$,

$$A_k \Rightarrow^* \varepsilon \quad [\pi_k]$$

for a production word π_k. Thus,

$$\begin{aligned} \underline{A} & \Rightarrow & A_1 A_2 \ldots A_n & \quad [p] \\ & \Rightarrow^* & A_2 \ldots A_n & \quad [\pi_1] \\ & \vdots & \\ & \Rightarrow^* & \varepsilon & \quad [\pi_n] \end{aligned}$$

in G. Hence, the inductive step holds.

Consequently, Claim A is true. □

Claim B states that if $A \Rightarrow^+ \varepsilon$ in G, then Algorithm 5.1.3.2.1 adds A to W during an iteration of the **repeat** loop.

Claim B
Let $A \Rightarrow^{i+1} \varepsilon$ in G, where $i \geq 0$. Then, Algorithm 5.1.3.2.1 includes A into W.

Proof
Claim B is proved by induction on i.

Basis
Let $i = 0$. That is,

$$A \Rightarrow \varepsilon \, [p]$$

in G, where $p: A \to \varepsilon \in P$. Therefore, Algorithm 5.1.3.2.1 adds A to W before this algorithm enters the **repeat** loop; that is, $A \in W_0$. As a result, the basis holds.

Induction hypothesis
Assume that the claim holds for all k-step derivations, where $k = 1, \ldots, i$, for some $i \geq 1$.

Induction step
Let

$$A \Rightarrow^{i+1} \varepsilon$$

in G.

1. Let $A \in W_j$, for some $j = 0, \ldots, i$. Then, the induction step follows from the induction hypothesis.

2. Let $A \notin W_j$, for all $j = 0, \ldots, i$. Express $A \Rightarrow^{i+1} \varepsilon$ as

$$\begin{aligned} A &\Rightarrow A_1 A_2 \ldots A_k & [p] \\ &\Rightarrow \varepsilon & [\pi] \end{aligned}$$

where $A_j \in N$, $\pi = \pi_1 \pi_2 \ldots \pi_k$, for some $k \geq 0$ ($k = 0$ implies $\pi = \varepsilon$), and

$$A_j \Rightarrow^* \varepsilon \quad [\pi_j]$$

for all $j = 1, \ldots, k$. As $|p\pi| = i + 1$, $|\pi_j| \leq i$ for all $j = 1, \ldots, k$. By the induction hypothesis, $A_j \in W_m$, for some $m \leq i$. By the definition of the **repeat** loop, $A \in W$. Thus, the inductive step holds.

Therefore, Claim B is true.

□

From Claims A and B, Algorithm 5.1.3.2.1 includes a nonterminal, $A \in N$, to W if and only if $A \Rightarrow^+ \varepsilon$ in G. Thus, for each $A \in N$,

$A \in W$ if and only if A is an ε-nonterminal in G

Thus, Algorithm 5.1.3.2.1 correctly produces the set W containing all ε-nonterminals in G.

Therefore, Lemma 5.1.3.2.2 holds.

■

Example 5.1.3.2.1 Part 1 Application of Algorithm 5.1.3.2.1
Consider the context-free grammar G,

1: $S \to A$
2: $S \to B$
3: $S \to C$
4: $A \to aAb$

5: $B \to cBd$
6: $A \to \varepsilon$
7: $B \to \varepsilon$
8: $C \to \varepsilon$

Observe that

$$L(G) = \{a^n b^n : n \geq 0\} \cup \{c^n d^n : n \geq 0\}$$

This example uses Algorithm 5.1.3.2.1 to determine the set N_ε of all ε-nonterminals in G. Initially, this algorithm sets

$$N_\varepsilon = \{A, B, C\}$$

because G possesses ε-productions 6, 7 and 8 such that lhs(6) = A, lhs(7) = B and lhs(8) = C. Consider productions 1 through 3. Observe that each of these productions has its left-hand side equal to S and its right-hand side formed by a symbol from $\{A, B, C\}$. Therefore, during the first iteration of the **repeat** loop, Algorithm 5.1.3.2.1 adds S to N_ε and, thereby, obtains

$$N_\varepsilon = \{A, B, C, S\}$$

During the second iteration of the **repeat** loop, Algorithm 5.1.3.2.1 adds no new nonterminals to N_ε. As a result, Algorithm 5.1.3.2.1 exits from this loop and determines $\{A, B, C, S\}$ as the resulting set N_ε, containing all ε-nonterminals in G. The following table sums up the iterations of the **repeat** loop that Algorithm 5.1.3.1.1 performs with G on its input.

Iteration	N_ε
0	$\{A, B, C\}$
1	$\{A, B, C, S\}$
2	$\{A, B, C, S\}$

△

Algorithm 5.1.3.2.1 fulfils a crucial role in the elimination of all ε-productions from a context-free grammar, the topic for the rest of the section.

ε-Free context-free grammar

Definition — ε-free context-free grammar
Let $G = (N, T, P, S)$ be a context-free grammar. G is an *ε-free context-free grammar* if rhs(p) ≠ ε, for all $p \in P$.

◆

Equivalently, a context-free grammar $G = (N, T, P, S)$ is ε-free if P contains no ε-production. Observe that no ε-free context-free grammar generates ε; in other words, if G is an ε-free context-free grammar, then $\varepsilon \notin L(G)$. The following algorithm converts any context-free grammar G to an ε-free context-free grammar $G_{\varepsilon\text{-free}}$ that generates $L(G) - \{\varepsilon\}$; formally,

$$L(G_{\varepsilon\text{-free}}) = L(G) - \{\varepsilon\}$$

Therefore, in terms of the next definition, $G_{\varepsilon\text{-free}}$ and G are equivalent modulo ε because $L(G_{\varepsilon\text{-free}})$ and $L(G)$ contain the same nonempty words.

Definition — equivalence modulo ε

Let L_1 and L_2 be two context-free languages. If $L_1 - \{\varepsilon\} = L_2 - \{\varepsilon\}$, L_1 and L_2 are *equal modulo ε*, denoted by $L_1 =_\varepsilon L_2$. If G_1 and G_2 are two context-free grammars such that $L(G_1) =_\varepsilon L(G_2)$, then G_1 and G_2 are *equivalent modulo ε*.

◆

Notice that Algorithm 5.1.3.2.3 requires that the input context-free grammar G contains only useful symbols; from Algorithm 5.1.3.1.9 and Theorem 5.1.3.1.10, this requirement is without any loss of generality. Algorithm 5.1.3.2.3 produces its output ε-free context-free grammar, $G_{\varepsilon\text{-free}}$, so that $L(G_{\varepsilon\text{-free}}) = L(G) - \{\varepsilon\}$ and, in addition, $G_{\varepsilon\text{-free}}$ contains only useful symbols.

Algorithm 5.1.3.2.3: Conversion of a context-free grammar to an equivalent ε-free context-free grammar

Input: A context-free grammar $G = (N, T, P, S)$ such that $(N \cup T)$ contains only useful symbols.

Output: An ε-free context-free grammar, $G_{\varepsilon\text{-free}} = (N_{\varepsilon\text{-free}}, T, P_{\varepsilon\text{-free}}, S)$, satisfying these two properties:

1. $L(G_{\varepsilon\text{-free}}) = L(G) - \{\varepsilon\}$
2. $(N_{\varepsilon\text{-free}} \cup T)$ contains only useful symbols

Method

begin
    use Algorithm 5.1.3.2.1 to determine the set N_ε that contains all ε-nonterminals in G;
    $P' := P - \{p: p \text{ is an } \varepsilon\text{-production in } P\}$;

    for each $p \in P$ such that $\text{rhs}(p) = x_0 A_1 x_1 \ldots A_n x_n$ and

$x_0 x_1 \ldots x_n \neq \varepsilon$, where $A_i \in N_\varepsilon$ and $x_i \in (N \cup T)^*$,
for all $i = 1, \ldots, n$, and where $n \in \{1, \ldots, |\mathrm{rhs}(p)| - 1\}$ **do**
    $P' := P' \cup \{\mathrm{lhs}(p) \to x_0 x_1 x_2 \ldots x_n\}$;

use Algorithm 5.1.3.1.3 to convert $G' = (N, T, P', S)$ to the context-free grammar, $G_{\mathrm{term}} = (N_{\mathrm{term}}, T, P_{\mathrm{term}}, S)$, such that $L(G) = L(G')$ and $N_{\mathrm{term}} \cup T$ contains only terminating symbols;
$N_{\varepsilon\text{-free}} := N_{\mathrm{term}}$;
$P_{\varepsilon\text{-free}} := P_{\mathrm{term}}$;
produce $G_{\varepsilon\text{-free}} = (N_{\varepsilon\text{-free}}, T, P_{\varepsilon\text{-free}}, S)$
end.

Algorithm 5.1.3.2.3 first calls Algorithm 5.1.3.2.1 to determine the set N_ε that contains all ε-nonterminals in G. It then constructs the set of productions P' so that for each

$$B \to Y_1 Y_2 \ldots Y_n \in P$$

Algorithm 5.1.3.2.3 adds the set of productions,

$$\{B \to X_1 X_2 \ldots X_n : X_i = Y_i \text{ if } Y_i \in N - N_\varepsilon, X_i \in \{Y_i, \varepsilon\} \text{ if } Y_i \in N_\varepsilon, \text{ and } |X_1 X_2 \ldots X_n| \geq 1\}$$

to P'. Finally, Algorithm 5.1.3.1.3 is used to obtain the resulting grammar, $G_{\varepsilon\text{-free}}$, such that $L(G_{\varepsilon\text{-free}}) = L(G) - \{\varepsilon\}$ and $G_{\varepsilon\text{-free}}$ contains only useful symbols.

Theorem 5.1.3.2.4
Let $G = (N, T, P, S)$ be a context-free grammar such that $N \cup T$ contains only useful symbols. With G as its input, Algorithm 5.1.3.2.3 terminates and correctly produces an ε-free context-free grammar, $G_{\varepsilon\text{-free}} = (N_{\varepsilon\text{-free}}, T, P_{\varepsilon\text{-free}}, S)$, such that $L(G_{\varepsilon\text{-free}}) = L(G) - \{\varepsilon\}$, and $N_{\varepsilon\text{-free}} \cup T$ contains only useful symbols.

Proof
Termination
P is a finite set of productions, so Algorithm 5.1.3.2.3 repeats its **for** loop finitely many times. As Theorem 5.1.3.1.4. and Lemma 5.1.3.2.2 prove the termination of Algorithm 5.1.3.1.3 and Algorithm 5.1.3.2.1, respectively, Algorithm 5.1.3.2.3 surely terminates.

Correctness
This part of the proof demonstrates the following three properties concerning $G_{\varepsilon\text{-free}}$:

A. $P_{\varepsilon\text{-free}}$ contains no ε-production, so $G_{\varepsilon\text{-free}}$ represents an ε-free context-free grammar.
B. $N_{\varepsilon\text{-free}} \cup T$ contains only useful symbols.
C. $L(G_{\varepsilon\text{-free}}) = L(G) - \{\varepsilon\}$.

Models for context-free languages

Property A — no ε-productions
Algorithm 5.1.3.2.3 includes no ε-production into P'. Then, Algorithm 5.1.3.2.3 calls Algorithm 5.1.3.2.1, which does not introduce any ε-production either. As a result, Algorithm 5.1.3.2.3 produces $G_{\varepsilon\text{-free}} = (N_{\varepsilon\text{-free}}, T, P_{\varepsilon\text{-free}}, S)$ with $P_{\varepsilon\text{-free}}$ containing no ε-production. Therefore, $G_{\varepsilon\text{-free}}$ represents an ε-free context-free grammar, so Property A holds.

Property B — no useless symbols
Algorithm 5.1.3.2.3 assumes that its input context-free grammar, $G = (N, T, P, S)$, contains only useful symbols. Thus, $G_{\varepsilon\text{-free}} = (N_{\varepsilon\text{-free}}, T, P_{\varepsilon\text{-free}}, S)$ contains only useful terminals. To prove that $G_{\varepsilon\text{-free}}$ also contains only useful nonterminals, consider any nonterminal $A \in N$, and distinguish the following two cases.

1. There exists a nonempty word $w \in T^+$ such that $A \Rightarrow^* w$ in G. At this point, observe that A surely represents a useful symbol contained in $N_{\varepsilon\text{-free}}$.

2. There exists no nonempty word $w \in T^+$ such that $A \Rightarrow^* w$ in G. In other words, $A \Rightarrow^* w$ in G implies $w = \varepsilon$. Observe that when Algorithm 5.1.3.2.3 exits from the **for** loop, A becomes nonterminating and, thus, useless; however, after this exit, Algorithm 5.1.3.2.3 calls Algorithm 5.1.3.1.3, which removes all nonterminating symbols, including A.

Therefore, $N_{\varepsilon\text{-free}} \cup T$ contains only useful symbols, so Property B holds.

Property C — equivalence modulo ε
To demonstrate

$$L(G_{\varepsilon\text{-free}}) = L(G) - \{\varepsilon\}$$

this proof first establishes Claims A and B.

Claim A
Let $A \in N$. For all $i \geq 1$, if $A \Rightarrow^i w$ in G with $w \in T^+$, then $A \Rightarrow^+ w$ in $G_{\varepsilon\text{-free}}$.

Proof
This proof is made by induction on i, where $i \geq 1$.

Basis
Let $i = 1$. That is, $A \Rightarrow w\ [p]$ in G with $w \in T^+$, where $p: A \rightarrow w \in P$. At this point, Algorithm 5.1.3.2.3 produces $G_{\varepsilon\text{-free}} = (N_{\varepsilon\text{-free}}, T, P_{\varepsilon\text{-free}}, S)$ with $p \in P_{\varepsilon\text{-free}}$, so $A \Rightarrow w\ [p]$ in $G_{\varepsilon\text{-free}}$. Thus, the basis holds.

Induction hypothesis
Assume that the claim holds for all m-step derivations, where $m = 1, \ldots, i$, for some $i \geq 1$.

Induction step
Consider

$$A \Rightarrow^{i+1} w \text{ in } G \text{ with } w \in T^+$$

Express this derivation as

$$A \Rightarrow X_1 X_2 \ldots X_n \quad [p]$$
$$\Rightarrow_* w_1 w_2 \ldots w_k \quad [\pi]$$

where $p: A \rightarrow X_1 X_2 \ldots X_n \in P$, for some $n \geq 1$; $w = w_1 w_2 \ldots w_n$; $\pi = \pi_1 \pi_2 \ldots \pi_n$, for some $k \geq 0$, so that

$$X_j \Rightarrow^* w_j \quad [\pi_j]$$

for all $j = 1, \ldots, k$. Concerning w_j, this proof distinguishes the following two cases.

1. Assume that $w_j = \varepsilon$. Then, $X_j \in N_\varepsilon$ — that is, X_j represents an ε-nonterminal in G.

2. Assume that $w_j \neq \varepsilon$.

2.1. Let $X_j \in T$. Then, $X_j \Rightarrow^* w_j [\pi_j]$ in G, where $X_j = w_j$ and $\pi_j = \varepsilon$. At this point, $X_j \Rightarrow^* w_j$ in $G_{\varepsilon\text{-free}}$, too.
2.2. Let $X_j \in N$. As $|p\pi| = i + 1$, $|\pi_j| \leq i$. By the induction hypothesis, $X_j \Rightarrow^* w_j$ in $G_{\varepsilon\text{-free}}$, too.

As $p: A \rightarrow X_1 X_2 \ldots X_n \in P$, $P_{\varepsilon\text{-free}}$ contains

$$p': A \rightarrow Y_1 Y_2 \ldots Y_n$$

then for $j = 1, \ldots, n$,

$$Y_j = X_j \text{ if } w_j \neq \varepsilon; \text{ otherwise, } Y_j = \varepsilon.$$

Consequently,

$$A \Rightarrow Y_1 Y_2 \ldots Y_n \quad [p']$$
$$\Rightarrow^* w_1 w_2 \ldots w_n$$

in $G_{\varepsilon\text{-free}}$, where if $w_j \neq \varepsilon$, then $Y_j = X_j$ and $Y_j \Rightarrow^* w_j$ in $G_{\varepsilon\text{-free}}$, and if $w_j = \varepsilon$, then $Y_j = \varepsilon$. As $w_1 w_2 \ldots w_n = w$,

$$A \Rightarrow^* w$$

in $G_{\varepsilon\text{-free}}$.

Thus, the induction step is completed.

Therefore, Claim A holds.

□

Claim B
Let $A \in N_{\varepsilon\text{-free}}$. For all $i \geq 1$, if $A \Rightarrow^i w$ in $G_{\varepsilon\text{-free}}$ with $w \in T^+$, then $A \Rightarrow^+ w$ in G.

Proof
This proof is made by induction on i, where $i \geq 1$.

Basis
Let $i = 1$. That is, $A \Rightarrow w$ $[p]$ in $G_{\varepsilon\text{-free}}$ with $w \in T^+$, where $p: A \to w \in P_{\varepsilon\text{-free}}$. Then, P contains

$$p': A \to w_1 Y_2 w_2 \ldots Y_n w_n$$

in G, where $w = w_1 w_2 \ldots w_n$, and $Y_j \Rightarrow^* \varepsilon\, [\pi_j]$ for all $j = 1, \ldots, n$ (that is, Y_j represents an ε-nonterminal in G). Thus,

$$\begin{aligned} A &\Rightarrow w_1 Y_1 w_2 Y_2 \ldots wn Y_n \quad [p'] \\ &\Rightarrow^* w_1 w_2 \ldots w_n \end{aligned}$$

in G. Therefore, the basis holds.

Induction hypothesis
Assume that the claim holds for all m-step derivations, where $m = 1, \ldots, i$, for some $i \geq 1$.

Induction step
Consider

$A \Rightarrow^{i+1} w$ in $G_{\varepsilon\text{-free}}$ with $w \in T^+$

Express $A \Rightarrow^{i+1} w$ as

$$\begin{aligned} A &\Rightarrow X_1 X_2 \ldots X_n \quad [p] \\ &\Rightarrow w_1 w_2 \ldots w_n \quad [\pi] \end{aligned}$$

in $G_{\varepsilon\text{-free}}$, for some $n \geq 1$, where $p: A \to X_1 X_2 \ldots X_n \in P_{\varepsilon\text{-free}}$, $w = w_1 w_2 \ldots w_n$, $\pi = \pi_1 \pi_2 \ldots \pi_n$, and for all $j = 1, \ldots, n$,

$$Y_j \Rightarrow^* w_j \quad [\pi_j]$$

in $G_{\varepsilon\text{-free}}$. As $p: A \to X_1 X_2 \ldots X_n \in P_{\varepsilon\text{-free}}$, P contains

$$p': A \to y_1 X_1 y_2 X_2 \ldots y_n X_n$$

with $y_j \in N_\varepsilon^*$ for all $j = 1, \ldots, n$; therefore, $y_j \Rightarrow^* \varepsilon$ in G. Furthermore, for each $Y_j \Rightarrow^* w_j [\pi_j]$, where $j = 1, \ldots, n$, $|\pi_j| \le i$ because $|p\pi| = i + 1$ and π_j is a part of π. Thus, by the induction hypothesis, $Y_j \Rightarrow^* w_j$ in G. Consequently,

$$A \Rightarrow y_1 Y_1 y_2 Y_2 \ldots y_n Y_n \quad [p']$$
$$\Rightarrow^* w_1 w_2 \ldots w_n$$

in G. Because $w = w_1 w_2 \ldots w_n$, the induction step is completed.
Therefore, Claim B holds. □

Set A to S in Claims A and B to establish the equivalence

$$S \Rightarrow^+ w \text{ in } G_{\varepsilon\text{-free}} \text{ if and only if } S \Rightarrow^+ w \text{ in } G.$$

for all $w \in T^+$. From this equivalence,

$$L(G_{\varepsilon\text{-free}}) - \{\varepsilon\} = L(G) - \{\varepsilon\}$$

As $G_{\varepsilon\text{-free}}$ represents an ε-free context-free grammar, $\varepsilon \notin L(G_{\varepsilon\text{-free}})$, so

$$L(G_{\varepsilon\text{-free}}) = L(G) - \{\varepsilon\}$$

Therefore, Property C holds.
In summary, with G as its input, Algorithm 5.1.3.2.3 terminates and correctly produces an ε-free context-free grammar, $G_{\varepsilon\text{-free}} = (N_{\varepsilon\text{-free}}, T, P_{\varepsilon\text{-free}}, S)$, such that $L(G_{\varepsilon\text{-free}}) = L(G) - \{\varepsilon\}$, and $N_{\varepsilon\text{-free}} \cup T$ contains only useful symbols. Thus, Theorem 5.1.3.2.4 holds. ■

Corollary 5.1.3.2.5
Let $G = (N, T, P, S)$ be a context-free grammar. Then, there exists a context-free grammar G' satisfying the properties

1. G and G' are equivalent modulo ε;
2. G' has only useful symbols;
3. G' is ε-free.

Proof
This corollary follows from Algorithm 5.1.3.1.9, Theorem 5.1.3.1.10, Algorithm 5.1.3.2.3, and Theorem 5.1.3.2.4. ■

Example 5.1.3.2.1 Part 2 Application of Algorithm 5.1.3.2.3

The previous part of this example has discussed the following grammar G:

1: $S \rightarrow A$
2: $S \rightarrow B$
3: $S \rightarrow C$
4: $A \rightarrow aAb$
5: $B \rightarrow cBd$
6: $A \rightarrow \varepsilon$
7: $B \rightarrow \varepsilon$
8: $C \rightarrow \varepsilon$

This Example uses Algorithm 5.1.3.2.3 to convert G, containing only useful symbols, to an ε-free context-free grammar, $G_{\varepsilon\text{-free}}$, so $G_{\varepsilon\text{-free}}$ also contains only useful symbols and $L(G_{\varepsilon\text{-free}}) = L(G) - \{\varepsilon\}$.

Part 1 of this example determines the set N_ε that includes all ε-nonterminals in G as

$$N_\varepsilon = \{A, B, C, S\}.$$

According to its second statement, Algorithm 5.1.3.2.3 initializes P' with the set of all productions, p, satisfying rhs(p) $\neq \varepsilon$; specifically, this algorithm includes

$S \rightarrow A$
$S \rightarrow B$
$S \rightarrow C$
$A \rightarrow aAb$
$B \rightarrow cBd$

into P'. Then, Algorithm 5.1.3.2.3 executes its for loop. During this execution, $A \rightarrow aAb$ causes Algorithm 5.1.3.2.3 to add

$$A \rightarrow ab$$

to P', and $B \rightarrow cBd$ causes this algorithm to include

$$B \rightarrow cd$$

into P'. Having exited from its for loop, Algorithm 5.1.3.2.3 calls Algorithm 5.1.3.1.3, which determines C as a nonterminating symbol and, therefore, eliminates $S \rightarrow C$ from the current set of productions. Consequently, the resulting grammar $G_{\varepsilon\text{-free}}$ is defined as

1: $S \rightarrow A$
2: $S \rightarrow B$

3: $A \to aAb$
4: $B \to cBd$
5: $A \to ab$
6: $B \to cd$

Observe that

$$L(G_{\varepsilon\text{-free}}) = \{a^n b^n : n \geq 1\} \cup \{c^n d^n : n \geq 1\}$$

As $L(G) = \{a^n b^n : n \geq 0\} \cup \{c^n d^n : n \geq 0\}$,

$$L(G_{\varepsilon\text{-free}}) = L(G) - \{\varepsilon\}$$

In other words, the resulting grammar $G_{\varepsilon\text{-free}}$ and the input grammar G are equivalent modulo ε.

▲

5.1.3.3 Elimination of unit productions

Definition — unit production
Let $G = (N, T, P, S)$ be a context-free grammar. A production, $p \in P$, is a *unit production* if $\text{rhs}(p) \in N$.

◆

In other words, a unit production has the form

$$A \to B$$

where A and B are nonterminals of G.

This section explains how to eliminate all unit productions from any context-free grammar G, because these productions often complicate the exploration of G and its use. To see this complication observe that, by applying unit productions, G actually only renames nonterminals; otherwise, these productions fulfill no role. Besides, unit productions are undesirable because they underlie derivations, called cycles, that make G ambiguous, as explained next.

Unit derivations and cycles

If a context-free grammar, G repeatedly renames nonterminals by applying unit productions, then G makes a unit derivation. A unit derivation that begins and ends with the same nonterminal is a cycle.

Definition — unit derivation and cycle

Let $G = (N, T, P, S)$ be a context-free grammar. If $A \Rightarrow^* B$ in G, where $A, B \in N$, then $A \Rightarrow^* B$ represents a *unit derivation*. A *cycle* is a unit derivation of the form $A \Rightarrow^+ A$ in G, where $A \in N$.

♦

The following discussion explains why cycles make a context-free grammar ambiguous. Consider a context-free grammar $G = (N, T, P, S)$ which has only useful symbols. Consider a cycle,

$$A \Rightarrow^* A \; [\pi]$$

in G, where $\pi \neq \varepsilon$. Then,

$$A \Rightarrow^*_{lm} A \; [\pi^i]$$

for all $i \geq 0$. As A is useful,

$$S \Rightarrow^*_{lm} xAy \; [\pi_1]$$
$$\Rightarrow^*_{lm} xzy \; [\pi_2]$$

in G for some $x, y, z \in T^*$. Then, for all $i \geq 0$,

$$S \Rightarrow^*_{lm} xAy \; [\pi_1]$$
$$\Rightarrow^*_{lm} xAy \; [\pi^i]$$
$$\Rightarrow^*_{lm} xzy \; [\pi_2]$$

In other words, G produces infinitely many leftmost derivations from S to xzy. Therefore, G is ambiguous. To avoid problems of this kind, this section explains how to eliminate ε-productions, by which G produces cycles.

Before this explanation, however, the next algorithm describes how to determine the set of all nonterminals that G derives from a nonterminal, A, by a unit derivation.

Algorithm 5.1.3.3.1: Determination of nonterminals derived by unit derivations

Input: An ε-free context-free grammar $G = (N, T, P, S)$ without useless symbols, and $A \in N$.

Output: The set Unit(A), defined as Unit(A) = { B: B ∈ N and A ⇒* B in G}.

Method

begin
    Old(A) := ∅;
    Unit(A) := {A};
    repeat
        New(A) := Unit(A) - Old(A);
        Old(A) := Unit (A);
        for each B ∈ New(A) **do**
            if there exists p ∈ P such that B = lhs(p) and rhs(p) ∈ N
            then Unit(A) := Unit(A) ∪ {rhs(p)}
    until Unit(A) = Old(A)
end.

Observe that $A \Rightarrow^0 A$ [ε] in G, so Algorithm 5.1.3.3.1 initializes Unit(A) with {A}. Then, Algorithm 5.1.3.3.1 enters its **repeat** loop. For all $p \in P$ with rhs(p) ∉ Unit(A), the **repeat** loop tests whether lhs(p) is currently contained in Unit(A); if so, this loop adds rhs(p) to V because $A \Rightarrow^* $ rhs(p). Algorithm 5.1.3.3.1 exits from this loop when Unit(A) contains all nonterminals $B \in N$ satisfying $A \Rightarrow^* B$ in G.

Lemma 5.1.3.3.2
Let G = (N, T, P, S) be a context-free grammar without useless symbols and A ∈ N. With G and A as its input, Algorithm 5.1.3.3.1 terminates and correctly produces the set Unit(A), defined as Unit(A) = { B: B ∈ N and A ⇒* B in G}.

Proof
Throughout this proof, Unit(A)$_i$ denotes the current containment of Unit(A) after Algorithm 5.1.3.3.1 has executed *i* iterations of the repeat loop and before this algorithm starts the execution of the (*i*+1)th iteration of this loop, for *i* = 0, 1, ...

Termination
Algorithm 5.1.3.3.1 iterates the **repeat** loop provided that it has added a new nonterminal to Unit(A) during the previous iteration, so the algorithm surely halts because N is finite. More precisely, observe that the **repeat** loop does not remove any nonterminals from Unit(A), so

$$\text{Unit}(A)_i \subseteq \text{Unit}(A)_{i+1}$$

for all $i \geq 0$. Algorithm 5.1.3.3.1 iterates this loop if Unit(A)$_{i+1}$ − Unit(A)$_i$ ≠ ∅; otherwise, the algorithm exits from the **repeat** loop. Thus, the algorithm terminates after performing no more than card(N) iterations of the **repeat** loop.

Correctness

The correctness of Algorithm 5.1.3.3.1 follows from Claims A and B. By Claim A, if Algorithm 5.1.3.3.11 adds a nonterminal, $B \in N$, to Unit(A) during an iteration of the **repeat** loop, then G makes a derivation from A to B.

Claim A

Let $B \in \text{Unit}(A)_i$, where $B \in N$ and $i = 0, \ldots, \text{card}(N)$. Then, $A \Rightarrow^* B$ in G.

Proof

Claim A is proved by induction on i.

Basis

Let $i = 0$, and let $B \in \text{Unit}(A)_i$; then, $B = A$. Observe that

$$A \Rightarrow^* A \ [\varepsilon]$$

Therefore, the basis holds.

Induction hypothesis

Assume that Claim A holds for all $\text{Unit}(A)_j$ with $j = 0, \ldots, i$, for some $i \leq \text{card}(N) - 1$.

Induction step

Let $B \in N \cap \text{Unit}(A)_{i+1}$.

1. Assume that $B \in \text{Unit}(A)_j$, for some $j = 0, \ldots, i$. Then, this inductive step follows from the induction hypothesis.
2. Assume that $B \notin \text{Unit}(A)_j$, for all $j = 0, \ldots, i$. That is, $B \in \text{Unit}(A)_{i+1} - \text{Unit}(A)_i$. By the description of the **repeat** loop, P contains

$$p: C \rightarrow B$$

for some $C \in \text{Unit}(A)_i$. By the induction hypothesis,

$$A \Rightarrow^* C$$

Therefore,

$$\begin{aligned} A &\Rightarrow^* C \\ &\Rightarrow B \quad [p] \end{aligned}$$

in G. Hence,

$$A \Rightarrow^* B$$

in G, and the inductive step holds.

Therefore, Claim A is true. □

Claim B states that if $A \Rightarrow^* B$ in G with $B \in N$, then Algorithm 5.1.3.3.1 adds B to Unit(A) during an iteration of the repeat loop.

Claim B
Let $A \Rightarrow^i B$ in G, where $i \geq 0$ and $B \in N$. Then, Algorithm 5.1.3.3.1 adds A to $\text{Unit}(A)_i$.

Proof
Claim B is proved by induction on i.

Basis
Let $i = 0$. That is,

$$A \Rightarrow^0 A$$

in G. Observe that Algorithm 5.1.3.3.1 initializes Unit(A) with $\{A\}$ before this algorithm enters the **repeat** loop; formally,

$$A \in \text{Unit}(A)_0$$

As a result, the basis holds.

Induction hypothesis
Assume that the claim is true for all k-step derivations, where $k = 1, \ldots, i$, for some $i \geq 1$.

Induction step
Let

$$A \Rightarrow^{i+1} B$$

in G, where $B \in N$.

1. Let $B \in \text{Unit}(A)_j$, for some $j \leq i$. Then, $B \in \text{Unit}(A)_{i+1}$ as well.
2. Let $B \notin \text{Unit}(A)_j$, for all $j = 0, \ldots, i$. Express $A \Rightarrow^{i+1} B$ as

$$A \Rightarrow^i C \quad [\pi]$$
$$\Rightarrow B \quad [p]$$

where $C \in N$ and $p: C \to B \in P$. As $|\pi p| = i + 1$, $|\pi| = i$. By the induction hypothesis, $C \in \text{Unit}(A)_i$. By the definition of the **repeat** loop, $B \in \text{Unit}(A)_{i+1}$. Thus, the inductive step holds.

Therefore, Claim B is true.

□

From Claims A and B, Algorithm 5.1.3.1.1 includes a nonterminal, $B \in N$, to Unit(A) if and only if $A \Rightarrow^* B$ in G. Thus, Algorithm 5.1.3.3.1 correctly produces the set, Unit(A), defined as Unit(A) = { B: $B \in N$ and $A \Rightarrow^* B$ in G}.

Therefore, Lemma 5.1.3.3.2 holds.

■

Example 5.1.3.3.1 Part 1 Application of Algorithm 5.1.3.3.1

The present example illustrates the use of Algorithm 5.1.3.3.1. Recall that Part 2 of Example 5.1.3.2.1 constructs the following grammar, $G_{\varepsilon\text{-free}}$,

1: $S \to A$
2: $S \to B$
3: $A \to aAb$
4: $B \to cBd$
5: $A \to ab$
6: $B \to cd$

Consider $G_{\varepsilon\text{-free}}$ and S as the input to Algorithm 5.1.3.3.1. At this point, this algorithm initially sets

$$\text{Unit}(S) = \{S\}$$

Notice that lhs(1) = S and lhs(2) = S. Because rhs(1) = A and rhs(2) = B, the first execution of the **repeat** loop adds A and B to Unit(S), so

$$\text{Unit}(S) = \{A, B, S\}$$

As the second iteration of the **repeat** loop adds no nonterminal to Unit(S), $\{A, B, S\}$ represents the resulting set of all nonterminals that G derives from S by making a unit derivation. The following table summarizes the iterations of the **repeat** loop executed by Algorithm 5.1.3.3.1 with $G_{\varepsilon\text{-free}}$ and S as its input.

Iteration	Unit(S)	New	Old
0	$\{S\}$	$\{S\}$	∅
1	$\{S, A, B\}$	$\{A, B\}$	$\{S\}$
2	$\{S, A, B\}$	∅	$\{S, A, B\}$

With $G_{\varepsilon\text{-free}}$ and A on its input, Algorithm 5.1.3.3.1 produces

$$\text{Unit}(A) = \{A\}$$

With $G_{\varepsilon\text{-free}}$ and B on its input, this algorithm produces

$$\text{Unit}(B) = \{B\}$$

△

Unit-free context-free grammars

Having determined the set of all nonterminals that a context-free grammar G derives by making unit derivations, this section now explains how to remove all unit productions from G without affecting $L(G)$.

Definition — unit-free context-free grammar
Let $G = (N, T, P, S)$ be a context-free grammar. G is a *unit-free* context-free grammar if $\text{rhs}(p) \notin N$, for all $p \in P$.

◆

Algorithm 5.1.3.3.3: Conversion of an ε-free context-free grammar to an equivalent unit-free e-free context-free grammar

Input: An ε-free context-free grammar $G = (N, T, P, S)$ such that $N_{\varepsilon\text{-free}} \cup T$ contains only useful symbols.

Output: A unit-free ε-free context-free grammar $G_{\text{unit-free}} = (N_{\text{unit-free}}, T, P_{\text{unit-free}}, S)$ satisfying these two properties:

1. $L(G_{\text{unit-free}}) = L(G)$
2. $N_{\text{unit-free}} \cup T$ contains only useful symbols.

Method

begin
  $P_{\text{unit-free}} := \varnothing$;

  for each $A \in N$ **do**
    use Algorithm 5.1.3.3.1 with G and A on its input to produce the set, $\text{Unit}(A)$, defined as $\text{Unit}(A) = \{ B: B \in N \text{ and } A \Rightarrow^* B \text{ in } G\}$;

  for each $A \in N$ and each $p \in P$ such that $\text{lhs}(p) \in \text{Unit}(A)$ and $\text{rhs}(p) \notin N$ **do**

$P_{\text{unit-free}} := P_{\text{unit-free}} \cup \{A \to \text{rhs}(p)\};$

$N_{\text{unit-free}} := \{\text{lhs}(p): p \in P_{\text{unit-free}}\};$
produce $G_{\text{unit-free}} = (N_{\text{unit-free}}, T, P_{\text{unit-free}}, S)$
end.

For every nonterminal $A \in N$, Algorithm 5.1.3.3.3 uses Algorithm 5.1.3.3.1 to determine

$$\text{Unit}(A) = \{ B: B \in N \text{ and } A \Rightarrow^* B \text{ in } G\}$$

Then, for each $A \in N$ and each $p \in P$ satisfying $\text{lhs}(p) \in \text{Unit}(A)$ and $\text{rhs}(p) \notin N$, Algorithm 5.1.3.2.3 adds

$$A \to \text{rhs}(p)$$

to $P_{\text{unit-free}}$. Observe that the grammar $G_{\text{unit-free}}$, constructed in this way, contains no unit productions and that $L(G_{\text{unit-free}}) = L(G)$.

Theorem 5.1.3.3.4
Let $G = (N, T, P, S)$ be an ε-free context-free grammar such that $N_{\varepsilon\text{-free}} \cup T$ contains only useful symbols. With G on its input, Algorithm 5.1.3.3.3 terminates and correctly produces a unit-free ε-free context-free grammar, $G_{\text{unit-free}} = (N_{\text{unit-free}}, T, P_{\text{unit-free}}, S)$, satisfying these two properties:

1. $L(G_{\text{unit-free}}) = L(G)$
2. $N_{\text{unit-free}} \cup T$ contains only useful symbols.

Proof
Termination
Lemma 5.1.3.3.2 proves that Algorithm 5.1.3.3.1 always halts. N and P represent finite sets, so Algorithm 5.1.3.3.3 repeats both for loops finitely many times. Thus, Algorithm 5.1.3.3.3 terminates.

Correctness
As demonstrated in the exercises, $G_{\text{unit-free}}$ represents a unit-free ε-free context-free grammar such that $N_{\text{unit-free}} \cup T$ contains only useful symbols. Next, this proof only verifies that

$$L(G_{\text{unit-free}}) = L(G)$$

To make this verification, this proof first demonstrates Claims A and B.

Claim A

For all $i \geq 1$, if $S \Rightarrow_{lm}^{i} w$ in G with $w \in T^{+}$, then $S \Rightarrow_{lm}^{+} w$ in $G_{\text{unit-free}}$.

Proof
This proof is made by induction on i.

Basis
Let $i = 1$. That is, $S \Rightarrow_{lm} w$ $[p]$ in G with $w \in T^{+}$, where $p: A \to w \in P$. At this point, Algorithm 5.1.3.3.3 produces $G_{\text{unit-free}} = (N_{\text{unit-free}}, T, P_{\text{unit-free}}, S)$ with $p \in P_{\text{unit-free}}$, so $S \Rightarrow_{lm} w$ $[p]$ in $G_{\text{unit-free}}$. Thus, the basis holds.

Induction hypothesis
Assume that the claim holds for all m-step derivations, where $m = 1, \ldots, i$, for some $i \geq 1$.

Induction step
Consider

$$A \Rightarrow_{lm}^{*} w \quad [\pi]$$

in G with $|\pi| = i + 1$ and $w \in T^{+}$. Express this derivation as

$$\begin{aligned}
S = x_0 A_0 y_0 &\Rightarrow_{lm}^{*} x_0 \underline{\text{lhs}}(p_0) y_0 & [\pi_{\text{unit}_0}] \\
&\Rightarrow_{lm} x_0 \text{rhs}(p_0) y_0 & [p_0] \\
&\Rightarrow_{lm}^{*} x_1 A_1 y_1 & [\pi_{\text{unit-free}_0}] \\
&\Rightarrow_{lm}^{*} x_1 \underline{\text{lhs}}(p_1) y_1 & [\pi_{\text{unit}_1}] \\
&\Rightarrow_{lm} x_1 \text{rhs}(p_1) y_1 & [p_1] \\
&\Rightarrow_{lm}^{*} x_2 A_2 y_2 & [\pi_{\text{unit-free}_1}] \\
&\vdots \\
&\Rightarrow_{lm}^{*} x_n A_n y_n & [\pi_{\text{unit-free}_{n-1}}] \\
&\Rightarrow_{lm}^{*} x_n \underline{\text{lhs}}(p_n) y_n & [\pi_{\text{unit}_n}] \\
&\Rightarrow_{lm} x_n \text{rhs}(p_n) y_n & [p_n] \\
&\Rightarrow_{lm}^{*} w & [\pi_{\text{unit-free}_n}]
\end{aligned}$$

where n is a natural number, $S = x_0 A_0 y_0$ (that is, $S = A_0$, $x_0 = \varepsilon$, and $y_0 = \varepsilon$), and

$$\pi = \pi_{\text{unit}_0} p_0 \pi_{\text{unit-free}_0} \cdots \pi_{\text{unit}_n} p_n \pi_{\text{unit-free}_n}$$

so that, for $j = 0, \ldots, n$,

$$\pi_{\text{unit}_j} \in (P_{\text{unit}})^{*},\ p_j \in (P - P_{\text{unit}}),\ \pi_{\text{unit-free}_j} \in (P - P_{\text{unit}})^{*},\ \text{and}\ x_j \in T^{*}.$$

Because $p_j \pi_{\text{unit-free}_j}$ consists of nonunit productions and π_{unit_j} consists of unit productions, Algorithm 5.1.3.3.3 adds

$$A_j \to \mathrm{rhs}(p_j)$$

to $P_{\text{unit-free}}$ for all $j = 0, \ldots, n$. Thus,

$$\begin{aligned}
x_0 A_0 y_0 &\Rightarrow_{\text{lm}} x_0 \underline{\mathrm{rhs}}(p_0) y_0 & [A_0 \to \mathrm{rhs}(p_0)] \\
&\Rightarrow_{\text{lm}}^* x_1 \underline{A_1} y_1 & [\pi_{\text{unit-free}_0}] \\
&\Rightarrow_{\text{lm}} x_1 \underline{\mathrm{rhs}}(p_1) y_1 & [A_1 \to \mathrm{rhs}(p_1)] \\
&\Rightarrow_{\text{lm}}^* x_2 \underline{A_2} y_2 & [\pi_{\text{unit-free}_1}] \\
&\vdots \\
&\Rightarrow_{\text{lm}}^* x_n \underline{A_n} y_n & [\pi_{\text{unit-free}_{n-1}}] \\
&\Rightarrow_{\text{lm}} x_n \underline{\mathrm{rhs}}(p_n) y_n & [A_n \to \mathrm{rhs}(p_n)] \\
&\Rightarrow_{\text{lm}}^* w & [\pi_{\text{unit-free}_n}]
\end{aligned}$$

in $G_{\text{unit-free}}$ with $S = x_0 A_0 y_0$. Consequently,

$$S \Rightarrow_{\text{lm}}^+ w$$

in $G_{\text{unit-free}}$, so the induction step is completed. Therefore, Claim A holds. □

Claim B
If $x \Rightarrow y\ [p]$ in $G_{\text{unit-free}}$, where $x, y \in (N_{\text{unit-free}} \cup T)^*$, then $x \Rightarrow^* y$ in G.

Proof
Let $x, y \in (N_{\text{unit-free}} \cup T)^*$, and $x \Rightarrow y\ [p]$ in $G_{\text{unit-free}}$. Express

$$x = u\mathrm{lhs}(p)v \text{ and } y = u\mathrm{rhs}(p)v$$

for some $u, v \in (N_{\text{unit-free}} \cup T)^*$. As $G_{\text{unit-free}}$ represents a unit-free context-free grammar, $\mathrm{rhs}(p) \notin N_{\text{unit-free}}$. From Algorithm 5.1.3.3.3, there exists $B \in N$ so $\mathrm{lhs}(p) \Rightarrow^* B$ $[\pi]$ in G and $B \to \mathrm{rhs}(p) \in P$. Therefore,

$$\begin{aligned}
x &\Rightarrow^* uBv & [\pi] \\
&\Rightarrow u\mathrm{rhs}(p)v & [B \to \mathrm{rhs}(p)]
\end{aligned}$$

in G.

Therefore, Claim B holds. □

From Claim B, for all $w \in T^+$, $S \Rightarrow^* w$ in $G_{\text{unit-free}}$ implies $S \Rightarrow^* w$ in G. Thus,

$$L(G_{\text{unit-free}}) \subseteq L(G)$$

From Claim A and Theorem 5.1.1.1,

$$L(G) \subseteq L(G_{\text{unit-free}})$$

Therefore,

$$L(G) = L(G_{\text{unit-free}})$$

In summary, with G as its input, Algorithm 5.1.3.3.3 terminates and correctly produces a unit-free ε-free context-free grammar, $G_{\text{unit-free}} = (N_{\text{unit-free}}, T, P_{\text{unit-free}}, S)$, so $L(G_{\text{unit-free}}) = L(G)$ and $N_{\text{unit-free}} \cup T$ contains only useful symbols. Thus, Theorem 5.1.3.2.4 holds.

∎

The following corollary summarizes all the simplifications discussed throughout Section 5.1.3.

Corollary 5.1.3.3.5

Let $G = (N, T, P, S)$ be a context-free grammar. Then, there exists a context-free grammar G' satisfying these properties:

1. G and G' are equivalent modulo ε
2. G' has only useful symbols
3. G' is ε-free
4. G' is unit-free.

Proof
This corollary follows from Corollary 5.1.3.2.5, Algorithm 5.1.3.3.3 and Theorem 5.1.3.3.4.

Example 5.1.3.3.1 Part 2 Application of Algorithm 5.1.3.3.3

Part 1 of this example discusses the context-free grammar, $G_{\varepsilon\text{-free}}$,

1: $S \rightarrow A$
2: $S \rightarrow B$
3: $A \rightarrow aAb$
4: $B \rightarrow cBd$
5: $A \rightarrow ab$
6: $B \rightarrow cd$

The current part of this example uses Algorithm 5.1.3.3.3 to convert $G_{\varepsilon\text{-free}}$, which represents an ε-free context-free grammar containing only useful symbols, to a unit-free ε-free context-free grammar, $G_{\text{unit-free}}$, so $G_{\text{unit-free}}$ contains only useful symbols and $L(G_{\text{unit-free}}) = L(G_{\varepsilon\text{-free}})$. Consider the start symbol S. In the previous part of this example, Algorithm 5.1.3.3.1 determined

$$\text{Unit}(S) = \{S, A, B\}$$

Consider the production 3: $A \to aAb$. Notice that $A \in \text{Unit}(S)$ and $aAb \notin \{S, A, B\}$, so Algorithm 5.1.3.3.3 includes

$$S \to aAb$$

into $P_{\text{unit-free}}$. Analogously, based on productions 4 through 6, Algorithm 5.1.3.3.3 adds the productions

$$S \to bBc$$
$$S \to ab$$
$$S \to bc$$

to $P_{\text{unit-free}}$.
As $\text{Unit}(A) = \{A\}$, Algorithm 5.1.3.3.3 includes

$$A \to aAb$$
$$A \to ab$$

to $P_{\text{unit-free}}$.
Finally, as $\text{Unit}(B) = \{B\}$, Algorithm 5.1.3.3.3 includes

$$B \to cBd$$
$$B \to cd$$

to $P_{\text{unit-free}}$. As a result, Algorithm 5.1.3.3.3 produces the resulting grammar, $G_{\text{unit-free}}$, defined as

$$1: S \to aAb$$
$$2: S \to cBd$$
$$3: S \to ab$$
$$4: S \to cd$$
$$5: A \to aAb$$
$$6: A \to ab$$
$$7: B \to cBd$$
$$8: B \to cd$$

Observe that $G_{\text{unit-free}}$ represents a unit-free ε-free context-free grammar such that $L(G_{\text{unit-free}}) = L(G_{\varepsilon\text{-free}})$ and $G_{\text{unit-free}}$ contains only useful symbols. ▲

5.1.3.4 Proper context-free grammars

This section summarizes all key results concerning simplifications of context-free grammars, obtained in Sections 5.1.3.1 through 5.1.3.3.

Definition — proper context-free grammar
Let $G = (N, T, P, S)$ be a context-free grammar satisfying the following properties:

1. $N \cup T$ contains only useful symbols;
2. G is ε-free;
3. G is unit-free.

Then, G is a *proper context-free grammar*.

♦

Hereafter, this book assumes proper context-free grammars. The next theorem shows that this restriction is without any loss of generality.

Theorem 5.1.3.4.1
Let L be a context-free language. Then, there exists a proper context-free grammar G satisfying $L =_\varepsilon L(G)$.

Proof
This theorem follows from Corollary 5.1.3.3.5.

■

Example 5.1.3.4.1 Proper context-free grammar
Reconsider the context-free language

$$L = \{a^n b^n : n \geq 0\} \cup \{c^n d^n : n \geq 0\}$$

Initially, Part 1 of Example 5.1.3.2.1 generates L from the following context-free grammar G:

1: $S \rightarrow A$
2: $S \rightarrow B$
3: $S \rightarrow C$
4: $A \rightarrow aAb$
5: $B \rightarrow cBd$
6: $A \rightarrow \varepsilon$
7: $B \rightarrow \varepsilon$
8: $C \rightarrow \varepsilon$

Notice that G is not proper. Then, Examples 5.1.3.2.1 and 5.1.3.3.1 convert G to the following proper context-free grammar, $G_{\text{unit-free}}$:

1: $S \to aAb$
2: $S \to cBd$
3: $S \to ab$
4: $S \to cd$
5: $A \to aAb$
6: $A \to ab$
7: $B \to cBd$
8: $B \to cd$

(see Part 2 of Exercise 5.1.3.3.1). Observe that

$$L(G_{\text{unit-free}}) = \{a^n b^n : n \geq 1\} \cup \{c^n d^n : n \geq 1\}$$

That is, $L - \{\varepsilon\} = L(G_{\text{unit-free}})$, so

$$L =_\varepsilon L(G_{\text{unit-free}})$$

▲

5.1.4 Normal forms

This section explains how to transform any context-free grammar to an equivalent context-free grammar whose productions satisfy some normal forms. Transformations of this kind are central to the investigation of context-free grammars and their applications. Indeed, normal forms significantly simplify the demonstration of some properties concerning context-free grammars and languages. In addition, these forms make productions easy to implement and use in practice.

Specifically, the present section examines two normal forms of context-free productions:

1. Chomsky normal form
2. Greibach normal form.

A production in Chomsky normal form has on its right-hand side either a terminal or two nonterminals. A production in Greibach normal form has on its right-hand side a terminal followed by a word consisting of zero or more nonterminals.

5.1.4.1 Chomsky normal form

Definition — Chomsky normal form
Let $G = (N, T, P, S)$ be a context-free grammar. G is in *Chomsky normal form* if every production, $p \in P$, satisfies

$$\text{rhs}(p) \in (T \cup N^2)$$

♦

By this definition, a context-free grammar in Chomsky normal form has productions that satisfy these two forms:

1. $A \to BC$ with $B, C \in N$
2. $A \to a$ with $a \in T$.

The next algorithm transforms any context-free grammar G to a context-free grammar, G_{CNF}, so $L(G) = L(G_{\text{CNF}})$ and G_{CNF} is in Chomsky normal form. Note that without any loss of generality, this algorithm assumes that G is proper (see Theorem 5.1.3.4.1).

Algorithm 5.1.4.1.1: Conversion of a context-free grammar to an equivalent context-free grammar in Chomsky normal form.

Input: A proper context-free grammar $G = (N, T, P, S)$.

Output: A context-free grammar, $G_{\text{CNF}} = (N_{\text{CNF}}, T, P_{\text{CNF}}, S)$, satisfying these two properties:

1. $L(G_{\text{CNF}}) = L(G)$
2. G_{CNF} is in Chomsky normal form.

Method

begin
$P_{\text{CNF}} := \{p: p \in P \text{ and } \text{rhs}(p) \in (T \cup N^2)\}$;
$P' := \{p: p \in P, |\text{rhs}(p)| \leq 2, \text{ and } p \notin P_{\text{CNF}}\}$;
$N_{\text{CNF}} := N$;

    for each $p: \text{lhs}(p) \to X_1 X_2 ... X_n \in P$, where $X_i \in (N \cup T)$, $i = 1, ..., n$, for some $n \geq 3$ **do**

begin
  $P' := P'$
    $\cup \{\text{lhs}(p) \to X_1 \langle X_2 \ldots X_n \rangle,$
      $\langle X_2 \ldots X_n \rangle \to X_2 \langle X_3 \ldots X_n \rangle,$
      $\ldots$
      $\langle X_{n-2} \ldots X_n \rangle \to X_{n-2} \langle X_{n-1} \ldots X_n \rangle,$
      $\langle X_{n-1} X_n \rangle \to X_{n-1} X_n\};$

  $N_{\text{CNF}} = N_{\text{CNF}} \cup \{\langle X_i \ldots X_n \rangle : i = 2, \ldots, n-1\}$
    {each $\langle X_i \ldots X_n \rangle$ is a new nonterminal}
end;

for each $p \in P'$ such that $\text{alph}(\text{rhs}(p)) \cap T \neq \emptyset$ **do**
begin
  replace each terminal, $a \in T$,
    with a new nonterminal, a', in $\text{rhs}(p)$;
  $N_{\text{CNF}} := N_{\text{CNF}} \cup \{a'\};$
  $P_{\text{CNF}} := P_{\text{CNF}} \cup \{a' \to a\}$
end;

$P_{\text{CNF}} := P_{\text{CNF}} \cup \{p : p \in P' \text{ and } \text{rhs}(p) \in (T \cup N_{\text{CNF}}^2)\};$
produce $G_{\text{CNF}} = (N_{\text{CNF}}, T, P_{\text{CNF}}, S)$
end.

Algorithm 5.1.4.1.1 assumes that the input context-free grammar, $G = (N, T, P, S)$, is proper because this assumption very much simplifies the conversion of G to an equivalent context-free grammar G_{CNF} in Chomsky normal form. Specifically, as G is proper, P does not contain any ε-productions or unit productions, so if $p \in P$ and $|\text{rhs}(p)| = 1$, then $\text{rhs}(p) \in T$ and, at this point, p has the required form.

In the beginning, Algorithm 5.1.4.1.1 places all productions of P that satisfy the Chomsky normal form into P_{CNF}. Besides P_{CNF}, this algorithm uses a temporary set P' that initially contains all productions of P that have the form $A \to X_1 X_2$ with $\{X_1, X_2\} \cap T \neq \emptyset$. For each production,

$$A \to X_1 X_2 \ldots X_n \in P$$

with $n \geq 3$, the first for loop of Algorithm 5.1.4.1.1 adds to P' the $n - 1$ productions:

$$A \to X_1 \langle X_2 \ldots X_n \rangle,$$
$$\langle X_2 \ldots X_n \rangle \to X_2 \langle X_3 \ldots X_n \rangle,$$
$$\vdots$$
$$\langle X_{n-2} \ldots X_n \rangle \to X_{n-2} \langle X_{n-1} \ldots X_n \rangle,$$
$$\langle X_{n-1} X_n \rangle \to X_{n-1} X_n$$

where each $\langle X_i...X_n \rangle$ represent a new nonterminal. If there exits a terminal a appearing in rhs(p), where $p \in P'$, the second **for** loop replaces this terminal with a new nonterminal, a', in rhs(p), includes a' into N_{CNF}, and adds $a' \to a$ to P_{CNF}. Then, Algorithm 5.1.4.1.1 places all productions of P' that satisfy the Chomsky normal form into P_{CNF}. In this way, Algorithm 5.1.4.1.1 obtains the context-free grammar G_{CNF} such that $L(G_{\text{CNF}}) = L(G)$ and G_{CNF} is in Chomsky normal form.

Theorem 5.1.4.1.2

Let $G = (N, T, P, S)$ be a context-free grammar. With G as its input, Algorithm 5.1.4.1.1 halts and correctly constructs a context-free grammar, $G_{\text{CNF}} = (N_{\text{CNF}}, T, P_{\text{CNF}}, S)$, such that $L(G_{\text{CNF}}) = L(G)$, and G_{CNF} is in Chomsky normal form.

Proof

Termination
As P, P' and T are finite, Algorithm 5.1.4.1.1 repeats both **for** loops finitely many times. Therefore, Algorithm 5.1.4.1.1 surely halts.

Correctness
This part of the proof demonstrates that Algorithm 5.1.4.1.1 produces its output context-free grammar, $G_{\text{CNF}} = (N_{\text{CNF}}, T, P_{\text{CNF}}, S)$, so that G_{CNF} is in Chomsky normal form and $L(G_{\text{CNF}}) = L(G)$.

Chomsky normal form
Observe that if Algorithm 4.2.4.1.1 adds a production p to P_{CNF}, then rhs(p) $\in$ $(T \cup N_{\text{CNF}}^2)$. Thus, G_{CNF} is in Chomsky normal form.

Equivalence
To establish

$$L(G_{\text{CNF}}) = L(G),$$

this proof first presents Claims A and B. From Claim A for all $A \in N$ and $w \in T^+$, $A \Rightarrow^* w$ in G_{CNF} implies $A \Rightarrow^* w$ in G.

Claim A

Let $A \in N$ and $w \in T^+$. Then, for all $i \geq 1$, $A \Rightarrow^i w$ in G_{CNF} implies $A \Rightarrow^* w$ in G.

Proof
This claim is proved by induction on i.

Basis
Let $i = 1$. That is, $A \Rightarrow w$ $[p]$ in G_{CNF}, where $p: A \to w \in P_{\text{CNF}}$. At this point $w \in T$, so P also contains p. Thus, $A \Rightarrow w$ $[p]$ in G. Therefore, the basis holds.

Induction hypothesis
Assume that Claim A holds for all m-step derivations, where $m = 1, \ldots, k$, for some $k \geq 1$.

Induction step
Consider $A \Rightarrow^{k+1} w\ [p\pi]$ in G_{CNF}. As $k + 1 \geq 2$, p has the form $p: A \to B_1 B_2 \in P_{CNF}$ where $B_i \in N_{CNF}$, for $i = 1, 2$. Express $A \Rightarrow^{k+1} w\ [p\pi]$ as

$$A \Rightarrow B_1 B_2 \quad [p]$$
$$\Rightarrow^k w_1 w_2 \quad [\pi_1 \pi_2]$$

where $w = w_1 w_2$, $\pi = \pi_1 \pi_2$, and

$$B_i \Rightarrow^* w_i\ [\pi_i]$$

in G_{CNF}, for $i = 1, 2$.

Observe that although B_2 can represent a nonterminal, $B_2 \in N_{CNF} - N$, introduced by the first **for** loop contained in Algorithm 5.1.4.1.1, B_1 cannot. This observation underlies the rest of this proof, including the distinction of these three cases concerning B_2:

1. $B_2 \in N$.
2. B_2 represents a new nonterminal, $B_2 \in N_{CNF} - N$, introduced during the execution of the second **for** loop contained in Algorithm 5.1.4.1.1.
3. B_2 represents a new nonterminal, $B_2 \in N_{CNF} - N$, introduced during the execution of the first **for** loop contained in Algorithm 5.1.4.1.1.

Case 1
Let $B_2 \in N$. Observe that $|\pi_2| \in \{1, \ldots, k\}$, so by the inductive hypothesis,

$$B_2 \Rightarrow^* w_2$$

in G. In addition, as $B_2 \in N$, B_1 represents a nonterminal satisfying one of two conditions:

1.1 $B_1 \in N$, or
1.2 B_1 is a new nonterminal, $B_1 \in N_{CNF} - N$, introduced during the execution of the second **for** loop contained in Algorithm 5.1.4.1.1.

These conditions are considered individually:

1.1 Let $B_1 \in N$. Then by the inductive hypothesis,

$$B_1 \Rightarrow^* w_1$$

in G. Thus, $A \Rightarrow B_1 B_2 \Rightarrow^* w_1 w_2$ in G. As $w_1 w_2 = w$,

$$A \Rightarrow^* w$$

in G.

1.2 Let B_1 represent a new nonterminal, $B_1 \in N_{CNF} - N$, introduced during the execution of the second **for** loop contained in Algorithm 5.1.4.1.1; that is, $B_1 = a'$ where $a \in T$, so $a = w_1$. Because $B_2 \in N$, $A \to aB_2 \in P$. Then,

$$\begin{aligned} A &\Rightarrow aB_2 \quad [A \to aB_2] \\ &\Rightarrow^* aw_2 \end{aligned}$$

in G. As $aw_2 = w$,

$$A \Rightarrow^* w$$

in G.

Case 2

Assume that B_2 represents a new nonterminal introduced during the execution of the second **for** loop contained in Algorithm 5.1.4.1.1; in other words, $B_2 = a'$, where $a \in T$, so $a = w_2$. Then, B_1 represents a nonterminal satisfying one of two conditions:

2.1 $B_1 \in N$, or
2.2 B_1 is a new nonterminal, $B_1 \in N_{CNF} - N$, introduced during the execution of the second **for** loop contained in Algorithm 5.1.4.1.1.

These conditions are applied as follows:

2.1 Let $B_1 \in N$. Then, $A \to B_1 a \in P$. By the inductive hypothesis,

$$B_1 \Rightarrow^* w_1$$

in G. Thus,

$$\begin{aligned} A &\Rightarrow B_1 a \quad [A \to B_1 a] \\ &\Rightarrow^* w_1 a \end{aligned}$$

in G. As $w_1 a = w$,

$$A \Rightarrow^* w$$

in G.

2.2 Let B_1 represent a new nonterminal, $B_1 \in N_{CNF} - N$, introduced during the execution of the second **for** loop; that is, $B_1 = b'$, where $b \in T$, so $b = w_1$. Then, $A \to ba \in P$ and

Models for context-free languages

$$A \Rightarrow ba \ [A \to ba]$$

As $ba = w$,

$$A \Rightarrow^* w$$

in G.

Case 3

Assume that B_i represents a new nonterminal introduced during the execution of the first **for** loop contained in Algorithm 5.1.4.1.1. At this point, $A \in N$ implies $i = 2$, and p has the form

$$\text{lhs}(p) \to X_1 X_2 \ldots X_n \in P$$

with $B_1 = X_1$, $B_2 = \langle X_2 \ldots X_n \rangle$; in addition, $A \Rightarrow^* w \ [p\pi]$ can be expressed as

$$\begin{aligned}
\underline{A} &\Rightarrow C_1 \langle \underline{X_2 \ldots X_n} \rangle & [A \to C_1 \langle X_2 \ldots X_n \rangle] \\
&\Rightarrow C_1 C_2 \langle \underline{X_3 \ldots X_n} \rangle & [\langle X_2 \ldots X_n \rangle \to C_2 \langle X_3 \ldots X_n \rangle] \\
&\Rightarrow C_1 C_2 C_3 \langle \underline{X_4 \ldots X_n} \rangle & [\langle X_3 \ldots X_n \rangle \to C_3 \langle X_4 \ldots X_n \rangle] \\
&\vdots \\
&\Rightarrow C_1 C_2 C_3 \ldots C_{n-2} \langle \underline{X_{n-1} \ldots X_n} \rangle & [\langle X_{n-2} \ldots X_n \rangle \to C_{n-2} \langle X_{n-1} X_n \rangle] \\
&\Rightarrow C_1 C_2 C_3 \ldots C_n & [\langle X_{n-1} X_n \rangle \to C_{n-1} C_n] \\
&\vdots \\
&\Rightarrow z_1 z_2 z_3 \ldots z_n & [\pi_1 \pi_2 \ldots \pi_n]
\end{aligned}$$

where $w = z_1 z_2 z_3 \ldots z_n$, and

$$C_j \Rightarrow^* z_j \ [\pi_j]$$

for $j = 1, \ldots, n$. Observe that C_j represents a nonterminal satisfying one of these two conditions:

3.1 $C_j \in N$, or

3.2 C_j represents a new nonterminal introduced during the execution of the second **for** loop contained in Algorithm 5.1.4.1.1.

Consider these conditions

3.1 If $C_j \in N$, then by the induction hypothesis, $C_j \Rightarrow^* z_j$ in G because $|\pi_j| \in \{1, \ldots, k\}$.

3.2 If C_j represents a new nonterminal introduced during the execution of the second **for** loop, $C_j = a'$ with $a \in T$, so $a = z_j = X_j$. Therefore,

$$A \Rightarrow X_1 X_2 \ldots X_n \Rightarrow^* z_1 z_2 \ldots z_n$$

in G. As $w = z_1z_2z_3...z_n$,

$$A \Rightarrow^* w$$

in G.

Cases 1 through 3 actually cover all possible forms of this derivation

$$\begin{aligned} A &\Rightarrow B_1B_2 \\ &\Rightarrow^k w_1w_2 \end{aligned}$$

in G_{CNF}, where $w = w_1w_2$. In all these three cases,

$$A \Rightarrow^* w$$

in G, so the inductive step is completed.

Therefore, Claim A holds.

□

Claim B
Let $A \in N$ and $w \in T^+$. Then, for all $i \geq 1$, $A \Rightarrow^i w$ in G implies $A \Rightarrow^* w$ in G_{CNF}.

Proof
This proof is left to the exercises.

□

From Claims A and B, for all $w \in T^+$,

$$S \Rightarrow^* w \text{ in } G \text{ if and only if } S \Rightarrow^* w \text{ in } G_{\text{CNF}}$$

As G is proper, $\varepsilon \notin L(G)$. Notice that $\varepsilon \notin L(G_{\text{CNF}})$. Thus,

$$L(G_{\text{CNF}}) = L(G)$$

In summary of this proof, with G on its input, Algorithm 5.1.4.1.1 halts and correctly constructs a context-free grammar, G_{CNF}, such that $L(G_{\text{CNF}}) = L(G)$, and G_{CNF} is in Chomsky normal form. Thus, Theorem 5.1.4.1.2 holds.

■

Example 5.1.4.1.1 Application of Algorithm 5.1.4.1.1
Consider the proper context-free grammar G,

1: $S \rightarrow S + S$

Models for context-free languages

2: $S \to S * S$
3: $S \to (S)$
4: $S \to a$

in which G has one nonterminal, S. In addition, G contains the five terminals $+$, $*$, $($, $)$ and a. This example uses Algorithm 5.1.4.1.1 to convert G to a context-free grammar, $G_{CNF} = (N_{CNF}, T, P_{CNF}, S)$, such that $L(G_{CNF}) = L(G)$, and G_{CNF} is in Chomsky normal form.

Algorithm 5.1.4.1.1 initializes P_{CNF}, P' and N_{CNF} as follows:

$$P_{CNF} = \{S \to a\}$$
$$P' = \emptyset$$
$$N_{CNF} = \{S\}$$

From the production 1: $S \to S + S$, the first **for** loop produces

$$S \to S\langle +S \rangle$$
$$\langle +S \rangle \to +S$$

and adds these two productions to P'. Analogously, from the production 2: $S \to S * S$ and 3: $S \to (S)$, this loop constructs

$$S \to S\langle *S \rangle$$
$$\langle *S \rangle \to *S$$
$$S \to (\langle S \rangle)$$
$$\langle S \rangle) \to S)$$

and includes these productions into P'. The second **for** loop replaces $+$ with $+'$ in $\langle +S \rangle \to +S$, so the resulting production has the form

$$\langle +S \rangle \to +'S$$

In addition, the second **for** loop adds the new production

$$+' \to +$$

to P_{CNF}. Furthermore, this loop replaces $*$ with $*'$ in $\langle *S \rangle \to *S$ and, thereby, produces

$$\langle *S \rangle \to *'S$$

Moreover, this loop includes

$$*' \to *$$

into P_{CNF}. Then, this loop changes (to (' in $\langle (S \rangle \to (S$ and, thus, constructs

$$\langle (S \rangle \to ('S)$$

In addition, this loop includes

$$(' \to ($$

in P_{CNF}. Finally, the second **for** loop changes) to)' in $\langle S) \rangle \to S$) and, thus,

$$\langle S) \rangle \to S)'$$

Moreover, this loop adds

$$)' \to)$$

to P_{CNF}. Having exited from the second for loop, Algorithm 5.1.4.1.1 adds all Chomsky normal form productions of P' to P_{CNF}. Therefore, this algorithm produces $G_{CNF} = (N_{CNF}, T, P_{CNF}, S)$ so N_{CNF} contains these eight nonterminals

$$S, \langle +S \rangle, \langle *S \rangle, \langle S) \rangle, +', *', (',)'$$

and P_{CNF} consists of

$p_1: S \quad \to S\langle +S \rangle$
$p_2: S \quad \to S\langle *S \rangle$
$p_3: S \quad \to ('\langle S) \rangle)$
$p_4: \langle +S \rangle \to +'S$
$p_5: \langle *S \rangle \to *'S$
$p_6: \langle S) \rangle \to S\,)'$
$p_7: +' \quad \to +$
$p_8: *' \quad \to *$
$p_9: (' \quad \to ($
$p_{10}:)' \quad \to)$
$p_{11}: S \quad \to a$

To make G_{CNF} easier to understand, rename $\langle +S \rangle, \langle *S \rangle, \langle S) \rangle, +', *', (' $ and $)'$ to A, B, C, D, E, F and H, respectively; accordingly, change the previous eleven productions to

$p_1: S \quad \to SA$

$p_2: S \rightarrow SB$
$p_3: S \rightarrow FC$
$p_4: A \rightarrow DS$
$p_5: B \rightarrow ES$
$p_6: C \rightarrow SH$
$p_7: D \rightarrow +$
$p_8: E \rightarrow *$
$p_9: F \rightarrow ($
$p_{10}: H \rightarrow)$
$p_{11}: S \rightarrow a$

Observe that this context-free grammar, which satisfies Chomsky normal form, generates $L(G)$.

▲

The following statement represents the main result of this section.

Corollary 5.1.4.1.3
Let L be a context-free language. Then, there exists a context-free grammar G in Chomsky normal form such that $L =_\varepsilon L(G)$.

Proof
This corollary follows from Theorem 5.1.3.4.1, Algorithm 5.1.4.1.1 and Lemma 5.1.4.1.2.

■

5.1.4.2 Greibach normal form

Definition — Greibach normal form
Let $G = (N, T, P, S)$ be a context-free grammar. G is in *Greibach normal form* if every production $p \in P$ satisfies

$$\text{rhs}(p) \in TN^*$$

◆

From this definition, a context-free grammar in Greibach normal form has each production p of the form

$$A \rightarrow ax \text{ with } a \in T \text{ and } x \in N^*;$$

that is, $\text{rhs}(p)$ consists of a terminal a followed by zero or more nonterminals.

The present section demonstrates that, for any context-free language L, there exists a context-free grammar G in Greibach normal form so $L(G) =_\varepsilon L$. To prove this result, this section first treats the grammatical phenomenon of a left recursion and its elimination.

Directly left recursion

Definition — directly left recursion
Let $G = (N, T, P, S)$ be a context-free grammar. A production $p \in P$ represents a *left-recursive production* if

$$\mathrm{rhs}(p) \in \{\mathrm{lhs}(p)\}(N \cup T)^*$$

A nonterminal, $A \in N$, represents a *directly left-recursive nonterminal* in G if there exists a left-recursive production $p \in P$ such that $\mathrm{lhs}(p) = A$.
♦

By this definition, if p is a left-recursive production, $\mathrm{lhs}(p)$ represents a directly left-recursive nonterminal.

Example 5.1.4.2.1 Part 1 Directly left recursion
Example 5.1.4.1.1 considers the context-free grammar

1: $S \to S + S$
2: $S \to S * S$
3: $S \to (S)$
4: $S \to a$

Observe that productions 1 and 2 are directly left recursive: $\mathrm{lhs}(1) = S$ and $\mathrm{rhs}(1)$ begins with S, and $\mathrm{lhs}(2) = S$ and $\mathrm{rhs}(2)$ begins with S. Thus, S is a directly left-recursive nonterminal.
△

For a context-free grammar the following algorithm describes how to reduce the number of directly left-recursive nonterminals in G by one. Note that without any loss of generality, this algorithm requires that G is proper (see Theorem 5.1.3.4.1).

Algorithm 5.1.4.2.1: Elimination of a directly left-recursive nonterminal

Input: A proper context-free grammar $G = (N, T, P, S)$ and a nonterminal $A \in N$, such that G contains r directly left-recursive nonterminals, for some $r \geq 1$, and A is one of these r directly left-recursive nonterminals in G.

Output: A proper context-free grammar $G' = (N', T, P', S)$, satisfying these properties:

1. G' contains fewer than r directly left-recursive nonterminals;
2. A is not a properly left-recursive nonterminal in G';
3. $L(G) = L(G')$.

Method

begin
    $P'' := \{ p : p \in P \text{ and } \text{lhs}(p) \neq A\}$;
    $N'' := N \cup \{A'\}$ $\{A'$ is a new nonterminal$\}$;

    for each $p \in P$ such that
    $\text{lhs}(p) = A$ and $\text{rhs}(p) \notin \{A\}(N \cup T)^+$ **do**
        $P'' := P'' \cup \{A \to \text{rhs}(p), A \to \text{rhs}(p)A'\}$;

    for each $p: A \to Ax \in P$ with $x \in (N \cup T)^+$ **do**
        $P'' := P'' \cup \{A' \to x, A' \to xA'\}$;

    use Algorithm 5.1.3.3.3 with $G'' = (N'', T, P'', S)$ on its input to produce the resulting grammar, $G' = (N', T, P', S)$
end.

Initially, Algorithm 5.1.4.1.1 places all productions, $p \in P$, with $\text{lhs}(p) \neq A$ into a set of productions P''. Then, this algorithm introduces a new set of nonterminals defined as $N'' = N \cup \{A'\}$, where A' is a new nonterminal. The first **for** loop adds $A \to \text{rhs}(p)$ and $A \to \text{rhs}(p)A$ to P'' for all $p \in P$ with $\text{lhs}(p) = A$ and $\text{rhs}(p) \notin \{A\}(N \cup T)^*$. The second **for** loop adds $A' \to x$ and $A' \to xA'$ to P'' for all $p: A \to Ax \in P$ with $x \in (N \cup T)^+$. Because $A' \to x$ may represent a unit production, Algorithm 5.1.4.2.1 calls Algorithm 5.1.3.3.3 to produce the resulting proper grammar, $G' = (N', T, P', S)$, such that N' contains fewer than r directly left-recursive nonterminals, and $L(G) = L(G'') = L(G')$. To see how G' simulates G, consider

$$\begin{aligned} A &\Rightarrow Ax_n & [A \to Ax_n] \\ &\Rightarrow Ax_{n-1}x_n & [A \to Ax_{n-1}] \\ &\vdots \\ &\Rightarrow Ax_2 \ldots x_{n-1}x_n & [A \to Ax_2] \end{aligned}$$

$$\Rightarrow x_1 x_2 \ldots x_{n-1} x_n \quad [A \rightarrow x_1]$$

in G and observe that G' simulates this derivation in this way:

$$\begin{aligned} A &\Rightarrow x_1 A' & [A \rightarrow x_1 A'] \\ &\Rightarrow x_1 x_2 A' & [A' \rightarrow x_2 A'] \\ &\vdots \\ &\Rightarrow x_1 x_2 \ldots x_{n-1} A' & [A' \rightarrow x_{n-1} A'] \\ &\Rightarrow x_1 x_2 \ldots x_{n-1} x_n & [A' \rightarrow x_n] \end{aligned}$$

Theorem 5.1.4.2.2

Let $G = (N, T, P, S)$ be a context-free grammar such that N contains r directly left-recursive nonterminals, for some $r \geq 1$, and a left-recursive nonterminal, $A \in N$. With G and A as its input, Algorithm 5.1.4.2.1 halts and correctly constructs a proper context-free grammar, $G' = (N', T, P', S)$, such that $L(G) = L(G')$ and N' contains fewer than r directly left-recursive nonterminals.

Proof

Termination
As P is finite, Algorithm 5.1.4.2.1 repeats both **for** loops finitely many times. Therefore, Algorithm 5.1.4.2.1 halts.

Correctness
This part of the proof demonstrates that Algorithm 5.1.4.1.1 produces its output proper context-free grammar, $G' = (N', T, P', S)$, such that N' contains fewer than r directly left-recursive nonterminals and $L(G) = L(G')$.

Fewer directly left-recursive nonterminals
A is a directly left-recursive nonterminal in G; however, A is not a directly left-recursive nonterminal in G'. Notice that $\{A'\} = N'' - N$ and that A' is not a directly left-recursive nonterminal in G''. Furthermore, observe that with $G'' = (N'', T, P'', S)$ on its input, Algorithm 5.1.3.3.3 produces the resulting grammar, $G' = (N', T, P', S)$, so the number of directly left-recursive nonterminals in N' is less or equal to the number of directly left-recursive nonterminals in N''. Therefore, N' contains fewer than r directly left-recursive nonterminals. A detailed proof of this part of the proof is left to the exercises.

Equivalence
First, this proof demonstrates

$$L(G) = L(G'')$$

This equation follows from the following two claims, Claim A and Claim B. From

Models for context-free languages

Claim A for all $B \in N'' - \{A'\}$ and $w \in T^+$, $B \Rightarrow^* w$ in G'' implies $B \Rightarrow^* w$ in G.

Claim A
Let $B \in N'' - \{A'\}$ and $w \in T^+$. Then, for all $i \geq 1$, $B \Rightarrow^i w$ in G implies $B \Rightarrow^* w$ in G''.

Proof
This claim is proved by induction on i:

Basis
Let $i = 1$. That is,

$$B \Rightarrow w \ [p]$$

in G, where $p: B \to w \in P''$. At this point, $w \in T^+$ and P'' also contains p. Thus,

$$B \Rightarrow w \ [p]$$

in G''. Therefore, the basis holds.

Induction hypothesis
Assume that Claim A holds for all m-step derivations, where $m = 1, \ldots, i$, for some $i \geq 1$.

Induction step
Consider the $(i+1)$-step derivation

$$B \Rightarrow^*_{lm} w \ [\pi]$$

in G, where π consists of $i + 1$ productions that belong to P. Express this derivation as

$$\begin{aligned}
B &\Rightarrow^*_{lm} x_0 A y_0 & [\pi_{\text{non-}A_0}] \\
&\Rightarrow^*_{lm} x_0 u_0 y_0 & [\pi_{A_0}] \\
&\Rightarrow^*_{lm} x_1 A y_1 & [\pi_{\text{non-}A_1}] \\
&\Rightarrow^*_{lm} x_1 u_1 y_1 & [\pi_{A_1}] \\
&\vdots \\
&\Rightarrow^*_{lm} x_{n-1} A y_{n-1} & [\pi_{\text{non-}A_{n-1}}] \\
&\Rightarrow^*_{lm} x_{n-1} u_{n-1} y_{n-1} & [\pi_{A_{n-1}}] \\
&\Rightarrow^*_{lm} x_n u_n y_n & [\pi_{\text{non-}A_n}]
\end{aligned}$$

where $n \geq 0$, $w = x_n u_n y_n$, $\pi = \pi_{A_0} \pi_{\text{non-}A_0} \ldots \pi_{A_{n-1}} \pi_{\text{non-}A_n}$, and the following conditions, A and B, hold:

A. for $j = 1, \ldots, n$,

$$x_{j-1}u_{j-1}y_{j-1} \Rightarrow^*_{lm} x_j A y_j \qquad [\pi_{\text{non-}A_j}]$$

represents a derivation in G such that each production $p \in P$ appearing in $\pi_{\text{non-}A_j}$ satisfies $\text{lhs}(p) \neq A$;

B. for $j = 1, \ldots, n$,

$$x_j A y_j \Rightarrow^*_{lm} x_j u_j y_j \qquad [\pi_{A_j}]$$

represents a derivation during which A derives u_j according to π_{A_j} such that each production $p \in P$ appearing in $\pi_{\text{non-}A_j}$ is a left-recursive production $p \in P$ satisfying $\text{lhs}(p) = A$.

1. Consider $\pi_{\text{non-}A_j}$. Observe that $\pi_{\text{non-}A_j}$ also represents a production word in G''. Thus, if G makes a derivation according to $\pi_{\text{non-}A_j}$, then G'' makes this derivation according to $\pi_{\text{non-}A_j}$, too.

2. Consider π_{A_j} in

$$x_j A y_j \Rightarrow^*_{lm} x_j u_j y_j \qquad [\pi_{A_j}]$$

Less formally, A derives u_j according to π_{A_j}, where each production $p \in P$ appearing in $\pi_{\text{non-}A_j}$ represents a left-recursive production $p \in P$ satisfying $\text{lhs}(p) = A$. Let

$$\pi_{A_j} = p_m p_{m-1} \cdots p_2 p_1$$

for some $m \geq 1$. Then,

$$u_j = \text{rhs}(p_1)\text{rhs}(p_2)\ldots\text{rhs}(p_{m-1})\text{rhs}(p_m)$$

and

$$\begin{aligned}
A &\Rightarrow_{rm} \text{rhs}(p_1)A' & [A \to \text{rhs}(p_1)A'] \\
&\Rightarrow_{rm} \text{rhs}(p_1)\text{rhs}(p_2)A' & [A' \to \text{rhs}(p_2)A'] \\
&\vdots \\
&\Rightarrow_{rm} \text{rhs}(p_1)\text{rhs}(p_2)\ldots\text{rhs}(p_{m-1})A' & [A' \to \text{rhs}(p_{m-1})A'] \\
&\Rightarrow_{rm} \text{rhs}(p_1)\text{rhs}(p_2)\ldots\text{rhs}(p_{m-1})\text{rhs}(p_m) & [A' \to \text{rhs}(p_m)]
\end{aligned}$$

in G''. From 1 and 2, G' makes the derivation

$$\begin{aligned}
\underline{B} &\Rightarrow^*_{lm} x_0 \underline{A} y_0 \\
&\Rightarrow^*_{rm} x_0 u_0 y_0 \\
&\Rightarrow^*_{lm} x_1 \underline{A} y_1
\end{aligned}$$

Models for context-free languages

$$\Rightarrow^*_{rm} x_1 u_1 y_1$$
$$\vdots$$
$$\Rightarrow^*_{lm} x_{n-1} A y_{n-1}$$
$$\Rightarrow^*_{rm} x_{n-1} u_{n-1} y_{n-1}$$
$$\Rightarrow^*_{lm} x_n u_n y_n$$

where $w = x_n u_n y_n$. That is,

$$B \Rightarrow^* w$$

in G'', so the inductive step is completed.

Therefore, Claim A holds. □

Claim B
Let $B \in N'' - \{A'\}$ and $w \in T^+$. Then, for all $i \geq 1$, $B \Rightarrow^i w$ in G'' implies $B \Rightarrow^* w$ in G.

Proof
This proof is left to the exercises. □

From Claims A and B, for all $w \in T^+$,

$$S \Rightarrow^* w \text{ in } G \text{ if and only if } S \Rightarrow^* w \text{ in } G''$$

As G is proper, $\varepsilon \notin L(G)$. Observe that that $\varepsilon \notin L(G'')$. Thus,

$$L(G) = L(G'')$$

From Algorithm 5.1.3.3.3 and Theorem 5.1.3.3.4,

$$L(G'') = L(G')$$

To summarize this proof, with G and A as its input, Algorithm 5.1.4.2.1 halts and correctly constructs a proper context-free grammar $G' = (N', T, P', S)$ such that $L(G) = L(G')$ and N' contains fewer than r directly left-recursive nonterminals. Thus, Theorem 5.1.4.2.2 holds. ■

Example 5.1.4.2.1 Part 2 Application of Algorithm 5.1.4.2.1
Return to the context-free grammar G discussed in Part 1 of Example 5.1.4.2.1. Recall that G contains one directly left-recursive nonterminal, S. This part of Example

5.1.4.2.1 uses Algorithm 5.1.4.2.1 to convert G to a proper context-free grammar, $G' = (N', T, P', S)$, such that $L(G) = L(G')$, and no directly left-recursive nonterminal occurs in G'. Algorithm 5.1.4.2.1 initializes N'' and P'' as

$$N'' = \{S'\}$$

$$P'' = \varnothing$$

The first **for** loop adds $S \to (S)$, $S \to (S)S'$, $S \to a$, and $S \to aS'$ to P'', so

$$P'' = \{S \to (S), S \to (S)S', S \to a, S \to aS'\}$$

From $S \to S + S$, the second **for** loop constructs

$$S' \to + S$$

$$S' \to + SS'$$

and adds both productions to P''. Analogously, from $S \to S * S$, the second **for** loop constructs

$$S' \to * S$$

$$S' \to * SS'$$

and adds these two productions to P''. Having exited from the second for loop, Algorithm 5.1.4.2.1 calls Algorithm 5.1.3.3.3; however, as the input grammar G'' of Algorithm 5.1.3.3.3 contains no unit production, Algorithm 5.1.3.3.3 produces the output grammar G' that coincides with G''. Therefore,

$$G' = (N', T, P', S)$$

where

$$N' = \{S, S'\}$$

and P' contains the following productions:

$$S \to (S)$$
$$S \to (S)S'$$
$$S \to a$$
$$S \to aS'$$
$$S' \to + S$$

$$S' \to + SS'$$
$$S' \to * S$$
$$S' \to * SS'$$

To make both nonterminals clearly distinguishable in G', rename S' to A, so that $N' = \{S, A\}$; the eight productions of P' become:

$$p_1: S \to (S)$$
$$p_2: S \to (S)A$$
$$p_3: S \to a$$
$$p_4: S \to aA$$
$$p_5: A \to + S$$
$$p_6: A \to + SA$$
$$p_7: A \to * S$$
$$p_8: A \to * SA$$

Observe that G' has no directly left-recursive nonterminal.

Consider $a + a * a$. G makes the following leftmost derivation from S to $a + a * a$:

$$\underline{S} \Rightarrow_{lm} \underline{S} + S$$
$$\Rightarrow_{lm} a + \underline{S}$$
$$\Rightarrow_{lm} a + \underline{S} * S$$
$$\Rightarrow_{lm} a + a * \underline{S}$$
$$\Rightarrow_{lm} a + a * a$$

The corresponding leftmost derivation in G' has the form

$$\begin{array}{ll} \underline{S} \Rightarrow_{lm} a\underline{A} & [p_4] \\ \Rightarrow_{lm} a + \underline{S}A & [p_6] \\ \Rightarrow_{lm} a + a\underline{A} & [p_3] \\ \Rightarrow_{lm} a + a * \underline{S} & [p_7] \\ \Rightarrow_{lm} a + a * a & [p_3] \end{array}$$

Observe that

$$L(G) = L(G')$$

▲

In the above example, Algorithm 5.1.4.2.1 calls Algorithm 5.1.3.3.3 with G'' as its input, and Algorithm 5.1.3.3.3 produces the output grammar G' which coincides with G''.

In the following example, Algorithm 5.1.4.2.1 calls Algorithm 5.1.3.3.3 with G'', to produce G', which differs from G''.

Example 5.1.4.2.2 Another application of Algorithm 5.1.4.2.1
Consider the following proper context-free grammar G:

1: $S \to ASA$
2: $S \to AA$
3: $A \to AB$
4: $A \to a$
5: $B \to b$
6: $B \to c$

This grammar generates

$$L(G) = (\{a\}\{b,c\}^*\}^*)^2$$

Observe that G contains the directly left-recursive nonterminal A. The present example uses Algorithm 5.1.4.2.1 with G and A as its input, to obtain a proper context-free grammar G' containing no directly left-recursive nonterminal.

Algorithm 5.1.4.2.1 initializes N'' and P'' as

$$N'' = \{S, A, A', B\}$$
$$P'' = \{S \to ASA, S \to AA, B \to b, B \to c\}$$

The first **for** loop adds $A' \to a$ and $A' \to aA'$ to P'', so

$$P'' = \{S \to ASA, S \to AA, A' \to a, A' \to aA', B \to b, B \to c\}$$

From the production 3: $A \to AB$, the second **for** loop constructs

$$A' \to B$$
$$A' \to BA'$$

and adds both productions to P'', so

$$P'' = \{S \to ASA, S \to AA, A' \to a, A' \to aA', B \to b, B \to c,$$
$$A' \to B, A' \to BA'\}$$

Notice that P'' contains a unit production, $A' \to B$, so G'' is non-proper. Algorithm 5.1.4.2.1 calls Algorithm 5.1.3.3.3 with $G'' = (N'', T, P'', S)$ on its input and, in turn, Algorithm 5.1.3.3.3 produces the output proper context-free grammar,

$$G' = (N', T, P', S)$$

where

$$N' = \{S, A, A', B\}$$

and

$$P' = \{S \to ASA, S \to AA, A' \to a, A' \to aA', B \to b, B \to c,$$
$$A' \to b, A' \to c, A' \to BA'\}$$

Notice that G' differs from G''. Finally, observe that $L(G) = L(G'')$ and that G' represents a proper context-free grammar containing no directly left-recursive nonterminal.

▲

Left Recursion

Definition — left recursion
Let $G = (N, T, P, S)$ be a context-free grammar. A nonterminal, $A \in N$, represents a left-recursive nonterminal in G if

$$A \Rightarrow^+_{lm} Ay$$

in G, for some $y \in (N \cup T)^*$. If there exists a left-recursive nonterminal in G, then G is a *left-recursive context-free grammar*; otherwise, G is a *non-left-recursive context-free grammar*.

♦

By this definition, any directly left-recursive nonterminal also represents a left-recursive nonterminal. Indeed, if A is a directly left-recursive nonterminal, then P contains p of the form $A \to Ay$, for some $y \in (N \cup T)^*$, so $A \Rightarrow^+_{lm} Ay\ [p]$. Thus, A is a left-recursive nonterminal.

Left recursion is an undesirable grammatical phenomenon, which should be eliminated. In theory, this elimination simplifies the achievement of some results concerning context-free grammars. In fact, this section makes use of this elimination when demonstrating how to transform any context-free grammar G to a context-free grammar G' in Greibach normal form, so that $L(G) =_\varepsilon L(G')$ (see Algorithm 5.1.4.2.5). In practice, some parsing algorithms, including the recursive descent algorithm discussed in Sections 5.3.1.2 and 9.3.2, work only with non-left-recursive context-free grammars because left recursion makes these algorithms deadlocked. Consequently, the elimination of left recursion significantly simplifies the investigation of context-free grammars and their use.

Algorithm 5.1.4.2.5, given subsequently, describes the elimination of left recursion in detail. In its body, Algorithm 5.1.4.2.5 calls Algorithm 5.1.4.2.3, which performs a simple nonterminal substitution.

Algorithm 5.1.4.2.3: Nonterminal substitution

Input: A context-free grammar $G = (N, T, P, S)$; the nonterminal $B \in N$; and the production $p: A \to xBy \in P$ such that $A \neq B$ and $x, y \in (N \cup T)^*$.

Output: A context-free grammar $G' = (N, T, P', S)$ that satisfies the following three properties

(① replace B with its rhs's in all the non-B rules)

1. $p \notin P'$
2. $\{ A \to x\,\text{rhs}(p')\,y : p' \in P \text{ and lhs}(p') = B \} \subseteq P'$
3. $L(G) = L(G')$

Method

begin
    $P' := \{ A \to x\,\text{rhs}(p')\,y : p' \in P \text{ and lhs}(p') = B \}$;
    $P' := P' \cup (P - \{p\})$;
    produce $G' = (N, T, P', S)$
end.

Lemma 5.1.4.2.4
Let $G = (N, T, P, S)$ be a context-free grammar, $B \in N$, and $p: A \to xBy \in P$ such that $A \neq B$ and $x, y \in (N \cup T)^*$. With G, B and p as its input, Algorithm 5.1.4.2.3 halts and correctly constructs the context-free grammar $G' = (N, T, P', S)$, such that $p \notin P'$, $\{ A \to x\,\text{rhs}(p')\,y : p' \in P \text{ and lhs}(p') = B \} \subseteq P'$, and $L(G) = L(G')$.

Proof
Termination
Obviously, Algorithm 5.1.4.2.3 always halts.

Correctness
This part of the proof demonstrates Algorithm 5.1.4.1.3 produces its output context-free grammar $G = (N', T, P', S)$, such that $\{A \to x\,\text{rhs}(p')\,y : p' \in P \text{ and lhs}(p') = B\} \subseteq P'$, $p \notin P'$, and $L(G) = L(G')$. Notice this algorithm constructs P' by these two statements:

$$P' := \{ A \to x\,\text{rhs}(p')\,y : p' \in P \text{ and lhs}(p') = B \}$$
$$P' := P' \cup (P - \{p\})$$

Because $A \neq B$, the properties that $\{ A \rightarrow x\mathrm{rhs}(p')y : p' \in P$ and $\mathrm{lhs}(p') = B\} \subseteq P'$ and that $p \notin P'$ surely hold.

Equivalence
This part of the proof sketches how to demonstrate that

$$L(G) = L(G'');$$

a detailed proof of this identity is left to the exercises.

1. To demonstrate that $L(G') \subseteq L(G)$, consider $p' \in P'$.

   A. Assume that $p' \in P$. At this point, if G' makes a derivation step by p', G can simulate this step by using p' as well.

   B. Assume that $p': A \rightarrow x\mathrm{rhs}(p'')y \in P' - P$. Algorithm 5.1.4.2.3 constructs p' by replacing B with $\mathrm{rhs}(p'')$ in $p: A \rightarrow xBy$, where $p'' \in P$ and $\mathrm{lhs}(p'') = B$. At this point, if G' uses p', G can simulate this use as follows

   $$A \Rightarrow xBy \qquad [p]$$
   $$\Rightarrow x\mathrm{rhs}(p'')y \qquad [p'']$$

   in G. Therefore, $L(G') \subseteq L(G)$.

2. To demonstrate that $L(G) \subseteq L(G')$, consider $p' \in P$.

   A. Assume that $p' \in P'$. At this point, if G uses p', G' can simulate this use by p', too.

   B. Assume that $p' \in P - P'$, so p' equals $p: A \rightarrow xBy$. If G makes a derivation step by using p during the generation of a sentence, subsequently, G surely makes another derivation step during which G replaces B with $\mathrm{rhs}(p'')$ by a production, $p'' \in P$, such that $\mathrm{lhs}(p'') = B$. At this point, $A \rightarrow x\mathrm{rhs}(p'')y \in P' - P$, and G' can simulate these two steps by using $A \rightarrow x\mathrm{rhs}(p'')y$. Therefore, $L(G) \subseteq L(G')$. Consequently,

$$L(G) = L(G')$$

In summary, with G, B and p as its inputs, Algorithm 5.1.4.2.3 halts and correctly constructs a context-free grammar, $G' = (N, T, P', S)$, such that such that $p \notin P'$, $\{A \rightarrow x\mathrm{rhs}(p')y : p' \in P$ and $\mathrm{lhs}(p') = B\} \subseteq P'$, and $L(G) = L(G')$. Thus, Lemma 5.1.4.2.4 holds.

♦

The following algorithm converts any left-recursive context-free grammar G to an equivalent non-left-recursive proper context-free grammar. Without any loss of generality, this algorithm assumes that $G's$ nonterminals are called A_1 though A_n, for some $n \geq 1$. If G has nonterminals named in a different way, without affecting $L(G)$, G's nonterminals can be always renamed so this assumption is satisfied. By Corollary 5.1.4.1.3, without any loss of generality, this algorithm also assumes that G satisfies Chomsky normal form.

Algorithm 5.1.4.2.5: Elimination of left recursion

Input: A left-recursive context-free grammar, $G = (N, T, P, A_s)$, in Chomsky normal form such that $N = \{A_1, \ldots, A_n\}$, for some $n \geq 1$, and A_s is the start symbol of G, where $s \in \{1, \ldots, n\}$.

Output: A non-left-recursive proper context-free grammar, $G_{\text{NLR}} = (N_{\text{NLR}}, T, P_{\text{NLR}}, A_s)$, satisfying $L(G) = L(G')$.

Method

begin
  for $i:=1$ **to** n **do**
  begin
    for $j:=1$ **to** $i-1$ **do**
    begin
      for each $p: A_i \to A_j y \in P$ **do**
      begin
        use Algorithm 5.1.4.2.3 with $G = (N, T, P, A_s)$, A_j, and p on its input to obtain a context-free grammar, $G' = (N, T, P', S)$, so $p \notin P'$, $\{A_i \to \text{rhs}(p')y: p' \in P$ and $\text{lhs}(p') = A_j\} \subseteq P'$, and $L(G) = L(G')$;
        $P := P'$;
        $N := N'$;
      end;
    end;
    if A_i is a directly left-recursive nonterminal
    then
    begin
      use Algorithm 5.1.4.2.1 with G and A_i on its input to obtain a proper context-free grammar, $G' = (N', T, P', S)$, such that A_i is not a directly left-recursive nonterminal in G', G' has fewer left-recursive nonterminals than G has, and $L(G) = L(G')$;
      $P := P'$;
      $N := N'$;
    end
  end;

$P_{NLR} := P;$
$N_{NLR} := N;$
 produce $G_{NLR} = (N_{NLR}, T, P_{NLR}, A_s)$
end.

Consider a left-recursive context-free grammar $G = (N, T, P, A_s)$, in Chomsky normal form such that $N = \{A_1, ..., A_n\}$, for some $n \geq 1$. Algorithm 5.1.4.2.5 proceeds from A_1 to A_n, so for each nonterminal A_i this algorithm makes use of Algorithm 5.1.4.2.3 and Algorithm 5.1.4.2.1 as follows:

1. If $p: A_i \to A_j y \in P$ with $i > j$, Algorithm 5.1.4.2.5 calls Algorithm 5.1.4.2.3, which replaces A_j with rhs$(p')y$, for all $p' \in P$ with lhs$(p') = A_j$. As a result, after this call, $A_i \to A_k y \in P$ implies $k \in \{i, ..., n\}$.
2. If A_i represents a directly left-recursive nonterminal, Algorithm 5.1.4.2.5 calls Algorithm 5.1.4.2.1, which produces an equivalent proper context-free grammar in which A_i is not directly left-recursive. Therefore, after the call of Algorithm 5.1.4.2.1, $A_i \to A_k y \in P$ implies $k \in \{i+1, ..., n\}$.

Proceeding from A_1 to A_n, Algorithm 5.1.4.2.5 eventually produces the resulting proper context-free grammar, $G_{NLR} = (N_{NLR}, T, P_{NLR}, A_s)$, such that $L(G) = L(G_{NLR})$, and each production, $p \in P_{NLR}$, has the form

$$p: A_i \to A_k y$$

where i and k satisfy $1 \leq i < k \leq n$. Consequently, $G_{NLR} = (N_{NLR}, T, P_{NLR}, A_s)$ represents a non-left-recursive proper context-free grammar satisfying $L(G) = L(G')$ as desired.

Theorem 5.1.4.2.6
Let $G = (N, T, P, A_s)$ be a left-recursive context-free grammar in Chomsky normal form such that $N = \{A_1, ..., A_n\}$, for some $n \geq 1$, and A_s is the start symbol of G, where $s \in \{1, ..., n\}$. With G as its input, Algorithm 5.1.4.2.5 halts and correctly produces a non-left-recursive proper context-free grammar, $G_{NLR} = (N_{NLR}, T, P_{NLR}, A_s)$, satisfying $L(G) = L(G_{NLR})$.

Proof
Termination
Algorithm 5.1.4.2.5 contains Algorithm 5.1.4.2.1 and Algorithm 5.1.4.2.3, which always halt by Theorem 5.1.4.2.2 and Lemma 5.1.4.2.4, respectively. As N and P are finite, Algorithm 5.1.4.2.5 surely terminates.

Correctness
A detailed proof that Algorithm 5.1.4.1.5 produces its output grammar $G_{NLR} = (N_{NLR}, T, P_{NLR}, A_s)$, so G_{NLR} represents a proper context-free grammar that generates $L(G)$,

is left to the exercises. Next, this proof demonstrates that G_{NLR} is non-left-recursive. This demonstration consists of three claims. Claim A describes the form of productions contained in P_{NLR}.

Claim A
P_{NLR} contains these three kinds of productions:

1. $A_i \to A_j x$ with $j \in \{i+1, \ldots, n\}$ and $x \in N^*$
2. $A_i \to ax$ with $a \in T$ and $x \in N^*$
3. $A'_i \to y$ with $y \in (N \cup T)(N \cup \{A'_1, \ldots, A'_{i-1}\})^*$

where $i = 1, \ldots, n$.

Proof
This claim is proved by induction on $i = 1, \ldots, n$.

Basis
This part of the proof is left to the exercises.

Induction hypothesis
Assume that Claim A holds for all $i = 1, \ldots, m$, for some $m \in \{1, \ldots, n\}$.

Induction step
Let $i = m + 1$. Consider the ith iteration of the main **for** loop, Let $p \in P$ with $\text{lhs}(p) = A_i$. Then, $\text{rhs}(p)$ begins with a symbol from $N \cup T$. Based on the leftmost symbol of $\text{rhs}(p)$, distinguish the following two cases.

A. Let $\text{rhs}(p)$ begin with a symbol from $\{A_i + 1, \ldots, An\} \cup T$. Then, p has the required form.

B. Let p have the form

$$p: A_i \to A_j x$$

where $j \in \{1, \ldots, i-1\}$. At this point, Algorithm 5.1.4.2.5 calls Algorithm Algorithm 5.1.4.2.3, witch replaces A_j with $\text{rhs}(p')$, for all $p' \in P$ with $\text{lhs}(p') = A_j$. After repeating this call no more than $i-1$ times, Algorithm 5.1.4.2.5 obtains P so that if $p \in P$ with $\text{lhs}(p) = A_i$, then $\text{rhs}(p)$ begins with a symbol from $\{A_{i+1}, \ldots, A_n\} \cup T$. If $\text{rhs}(p)$ begins with a symbol from $\{A_{i+1}, \ldots, A_n\} \cup T$, p has the required form. Assume that $\text{rhs}(p)$ begins with A_i, so p has the form

$$p: A_i \to A_i y$$

As A_i represents a directly left-recursive nonterminal, Algorithm 5.1.4.2.5 calls

Algorithm 5.1.4.2.1, which introduces a new nonterminal, A'_i, and produces an equivalent proper context-free grammar in which A_i is not directly left-recursive. Observe that Algorithm 5.1.4.2.1 produces productions p' with $\mathrm{lhs}(p') = A'_i$ so p' has the form

$$A'_i \to y \text{ with } y \in (N \cup T)(N \cup \{A'_1, ..., A'_{i-1}\})^*,$$

which represents a production of the required form.

Thus, the induction step holds, so Claim A is true.

□

The following two claims demonstrate that G_{NLR} contains no left-recursive nonterminal.

Claim B
Let $A_i \in \{A_1, ..., A_n\}$. Then, A_i represents a non-left-recursive nonterminal in G_{NLR}.

Proof
Claim B is proved by contradiction. Assume that $A_i \in \{A_1, ..., A_n\}$ and A_i represents a non-left-recursive nonterminal in G_{NLR}. Thus,

$$A_i \Rightarrow^+_{\mathrm{lm}} A_i x$$

in G_{NLR}, for some $x \in (N_{\mathrm{NLR}} \cup T)^*$. Then, $A_i \Rightarrow^+_{\mathrm{lm}} A_i x$ can be expressed as

$$A_i \Rightarrow^*_{\mathrm{lm}} A_j y$$
$$\Rightarrow_{\mathrm{lm}} A_k z \; [p]$$
$$\Rightarrow^*_{\mathrm{lm}} A_i x$$

where $k \leq j$, and $y, z \in (N_{\mathrm{NLR}} \cup T)^*$. By Claim A, however, P_{NLR} cannot contain p such that $\mathrm{lhs}(p) = A_j$ and $\mathrm{rhs}(p)$ begins with A_k, where $k \leq j$ — a contradiction. Thus, Claim B holds.

□

Claim C
Let $A'_i \in N_{\mathrm{NLR}}$, where $i \in \{1, ..., n\}$. Then, A'_i represents a non-left-recursive nonterminal in G_{NLR}.

Proof
This part of the proof is left to the exercises.

□

Observe that Claims B and C imply that G_{NLR} is a non-left-recursive context-free grammar.

Consequently, with G as its input, Algorithm 5.1.4.2.5 halts and correctly produces a non-left-recursive proper context-free grammar $G_{NLR} = (N_{NLR}, T, P_{NLR}, A_s)$, satisfying $L(G) = L(G')$. Thus, Theorem 5.1.4.2.6 holds. ∎

Example 5.1.4.2.3 Part 1 Application of Algorithm 5.1.4.2.5

Consider the following context-free grammar G in Chomsky normal form:

1: $A_1 \rightarrow A_2A_3$
2: $A_2 \rightarrow A_3A_1$
3: $A_3 \rightarrow A_4A_5$
4: $A_4 \rightarrow A_3A_6$
5: $A_1 \rightarrow a$
6: $A_3 \rightarrow b$
7: $A_5 \rightarrow b$
8: $A_6 \rightarrow c$

G has nonterminals A_1 through A_4, where A_1 is the start symbol. G contains four terminals, a, b, c and d. Observe that

$$L(G) = \{ w: w \in K^n a K^n \text{ with } K = \{b\}\{cb\}^* \text{ and } n \geq 1 \}$$

Notice that A_3 is left-recursive because

$$A_3 \Rightarrow A_4A_5 \quad [3]$$
$$\Rightarrow A_3A_6A_5 \quad [4]$$

Thus, G is left-recursive. The present example uses Algorithm 5.1.4.2.5 with G as its input to obtain a non-left-recursive proper context-free grammar G_{NLR} satisfying $L(G) = L(G_{NLR})$.

Consider the production 1: $A_1 \rightarrow A_2A_3$. As $2 > 1$, the first iteration of the main for loop does not affect G. Analogously, the next two iterations do not change G. Consider the production 4: $A_4 \rightarrow A_3A_6$. As $3 < 4$, The fourth iteration of this loop calls Algorithm 5.1.4.2.3 to substitute rhs(3) for A_3 and, in addition, rhs(6) for A_3; therefore, after these substitutions, P contains the following productions:

$A_1 \rightarrow A_2A_3$
$A_2 \rightarrow A_3A_1$
$A_3 \rightarrow A_4A_5$
$A_4 \rightarrow A_4A_5A_6$
$A_4 \rightarrow bA_6$
$A_1 \rightarrow a$
$A_3 \rightarrow b$

$A_5 \to b$
$A_6 \to c$

As A_4 is directly left-recursive, Algorithm 5.1.4.2.5 calls Algorithm 5.1.4.2.1 with G and A_4 and, in turn, Algorithm 5.1.4.2.1 produces this grammar:

$p_1: A_1 \to A_2 A_3$
$p_2: A_2 \to A_3 A_1$
$p_3: A_3 \to A_4 A_5$
$p_4: A_4 \to b A_6 A_4'$
$p_5: A_4 \to b A_6$
$p_6: A_4' \to A_5 A_6 A_4'$
$p_7: A_4' \to A_5 A_6$
$p_8: A_1 \to a$
$p_9: A_3 \to b$
$p_{10}: A_5 \to b$
$p_{11}: A_6 \to c$

During the rest of its execution, Algorithm 5.1.4.2.5 makes no change; as a result, p_1 through p_{11} represent the output grammar, G_{NLR}, produced by Algorithm 5.1.4.2.5. Observe that G_{NLR} is a non-left-recursive proper context-free grammar G_{NLR} satisfying $L(G) = L(G_{NLR})$.

▲

Greibach normal form

Recall that a context-free grammar $G = (N, T, P, S)$, is in Greibach normal form if $p \in P$ implies $\mathrm{rhs}(p) \in TN^*$ — that is, p consists of a terminal followed by zero or more nonterminals. Algorithm 5.1.4.2.8 describes how to convert any context-free grammar G to an equivalent context-free grammar in Greibach normal form. Without any loss of generality, this algorithm assumes that its input grammar satisfies the propertied described by the next lemma.

Lemma 5.1.4.2.7

Let G' be a context-free grammar. Then, there exists a non-left-recursive proper context-free grammar $G = (N, T, P, S)$ satisfying the following properties:

1. $L(G') =_\varepsilon L(G)$
2. $N = N_A \cup N_B$ so $N_A \cap N_B = \emptyset, N_A = \{A_1, ..., A_n\}$, for some $n \geq 1$, and $N_B = \{B_1, ..., B_m\}$, for some $m \geq 0$ ($m = 0$ implies $N_B = \emptyset$)
3. P contains these three kinds of productions:
   A. $A_i \to A_j x$, where $i = 1, ..., n, j \in \{i+1, ..., n\}$, and $x \in N^*$
   B. $A_i \to ax$, where $i = 1, ..., n, a \in T$, and $x \in N^*$
   C. $B_i \to y$, where $i = 1, ..., n, y \in (\{A_1, ..., A_n\} \cup T)N^*$
4. $S = A_s$, for some $s \in \{1, ..., n\}$

Proof

Let G' be a context-free grammar. From Corollary 5.1.4.1.3, there exists a context-free grammar in Chomsky normal form such that $L =_\varepsilon L(G_{CNF})$. Use the method described by Algorithm 5.1.4.2.5 to convert G_{CNF} to a non-left-recursive proper context-free grammar G_{NLR} satisfying $L(G) = L(G_{NLR})$. By renaming each A'_i to B_i in G_{CNF}, produce the resulting context-free grammar, G. By analogy with Claim A contained in the proof of Theorem 5.1.4.2.6, demonstrate that G represents a non-left-recursive proper context-free grammar satisfying the properties of Lemma 5.1.4.2.7. A detailed proof of this lemma is left to the exercises. ∎

Algorithm 5.1.4.2.8: Conversion of a context-free grammar to an equivalent context-free grammar in Greibach normal form

Input: A non-left-recursive proper context-free grammar $G = (N, T, P, S)$ satisfying these properties:

1. $N = N_A \cup N_B$ so $N_A \cap N_B = \varnothing$, $N_A = \{A_1, ..., A_n\}$, for some $n \geq 1$, and $N_B = \{B_1, ..., B_m\}$, for some $m \geq 0$ ($m = 0$ implies $N_B = \varnothing$)
2. P contains these three kinds of productions:
   A. $A_i \to A_j x$, where $i = 1, ..., n, j \in \{i + 1, ..., n\}$, and $x \in N^*$
   B. $A_i \to ax$, where $i = 1, ..., n, a \in T$, and $x \in N^*$
   C. $B_i \to y$, where $i = 1, ..., n, y \in (\{A_1, ..., A_n\} \cup T)N^*$
   where $i = 1, ..., n$
3. $S = A_s$, for some $s \in \{1, ..., n\}$.

Output: A context-free grammar $G_{GNF} = (N_{GNF}, T, P_{GNF}, S)$ satisfying these two properties:

1. $L(G_{GNF}) = L(G)$
2. G_{GNF} is in Greibach normal form.

Method

begin
  for $i := n-1$ **downto** 1 **do**
    for each $p: A_i \to A_j x \in P$ with $A_j \in \{A_{i+1}, ..., A_n\}$
    and $x \in (\{A_1, ..., A_n\} \cup T)^*$ **do**
    begin
      use Algorithm 5.1.4.2.3 with $G = (N, T, P, A_s)$, A_j, and p on its input to obtain a context-free grammar, $G' = (N, T, P', S)$, so $p \notin P'$, $\{A_i \to \text{rhs}(p')y : p' \in P \text{ and } \text{lhs}(p') = A_j\} \subseteq P'$, and $L(G) = L(G')$;

         $P := P'$;
         $N := N'$;
      end;
   for $i := n\text{-}1$ downto 1 do
      for each p: $A_i \to A_j y \in P$ with $A_j \in \{A_{i+1}, \ldots, A_n\}$
      and $x \in (\{A_1, \ldots, A_n\} \cup T)^*$ do
      begin
         use Algorithm 5.1.4.2.3 with $G = (N, T, P, A_s)$, A_j, and p as its input to obtain a
         context-free grammar, $G' = (N, T, P', S)$, so $p \notin P'$, $\{A_i \to \text{rhs}(p')x: p' \in P$ and
         $\text{lhs}(p') = A_j\} \subseteq P'$ and $L(G) = L(G')$;
         $P := P'$;
         $N := N'$
      end;

   for $i := 1$ to m do
      for each p: $B_i \to A_j z \in P$ with $A_j \in \{A_1, \ldots, A_n\}$
      and $z \in N^*$ do
      begin
         use Algorithm 5.1.4.2.3 with $G = (N, T, P, A_s)$, A_j, and p on its input to obtain a
         context-free grammar, $G' = (N, T, P', S)$, so $p \notin P'$, $\{B_i \to \text{rhs}(p')y: p' \in P$ and
         $\text{lhs}(p') = A_j\} \subseteq P'$, and $L(G) = L(G')$;
         $P := P'$;
         $N := N'$;
      end;

   use Algorithm 5.1.3.1.7 with G as its input to obtain a context-free grammar,
   $G_{\text{access}} = (N_{\text{access}}, T, P_{\text{access}}, S)$, such that $L(G) = L(G_{\text{access}})$ and $(N_{\text{access}} \cup T)$ contains
   only terminating symbols;
   $N_{\text{GNF}} := N_{\text{access}}$;
   $P_{\text{GNF}} := P_{\text{access}}$;
   produce $G_{\text{GNF}} = (N_{\text{GNF}}, T, P_{\text{GNF}}, S)$
end.

Consider a non-left-recursive proper context-free grammar, $G = (N, T, P, S)$, satisfying the input requirements of Algorithm 5.1.4.2.8, and assume that G is on the input of this algorithm. Because n is the highest number in $\{1, \ldots, n\}$, $\text{rhs}(p) \in TN^*$ for all $p \in P$ with $\text{lhs}(p) = A_n$; in other words, if $p \in P$ with $\text{lhs}(p) = A_n$, then p satisfies the Greibach normal form.

Consider p: $A_{n-1} \to A_n y \in P$. At this point, Algorithm 5.1.4.2.8 calls Algorithm 5.1.4.2.3, which removes p and introduces $\{A_i \to \text{rhs}(p')y: p' \in P$ and $\text{lhs}(p') = A_n\}$. All productions in $\{A_i \to \text{rhs}(p')y: p' \in P$ and $\text{lhs}(p') = A_n\}$ satisfy the Greibach normal form because all productions, $p \in P$, with $\text{lhs}(p) = A_n$ satisfy the Greibach normal form. Analogously, proceeding from $A_{n-1}, \ldots, A_1$, Algorithm 5.1.4.2.8 transforms all productions, $p \in P$, with $\text{lhs}(p) \in \{A_1, \ldots, A_n\}$ so the resulting productions are in the Greibach normal form.

Then, for each $p: B_i \to A_j y \in P$ with $A_j \in \{A_1, \ldots, A_n\}$, Algorithm 5.1.4.2.3 removes p and introduces $\{B_i \to \text{rhs}(p')y: p' \in P \text{ and lhs}(p') = A_j\}$, whose productions satisfy the Greibach normal form because all productions, $p \in P$, with $\text{lhs}(p) = A_j$ are in this form. In this way, Algorithm 5.1.4.2.8 transforms all productions so they satisfy the Greibach normal form. After this transformation is completed, some nonterminals may be inaccessible, so Algorithm 5.1.3.1.7 removes these inaccessible nonterminals and produces the resulting context-free grammar, G_{GNF}, in Greibach normal form so that $L(G_{\text{GNF}}) = L(G)$.

Theorem 5.1.4.2.9
Let $G = (N, T, P, S)$ be a context-free grammar satisfying the properties stated in the input of Algorithm 5.1.4.2.8. With G as its input, Algorithm 5.1.4.2.8 halts and correctly constructs a context-free grammar $G_{\text{GNF}} = (N_{\text{GNF}}, T, P_{\text{GNF}}, S)$, such that $L(G_{\text{GNF}}) = L(G)$, and G_{GNF} is in Greibach normal form.

Proof
Termination
Algorithm 5.1.4.2.8 contains Algorithms 5.1.4.2.3 and 5.1.3.1.7 as its components. Algorithms 5.1.4.2.3 and Algorithm 5.1.3.1.7 halt by Theorem 5.1.3.1.8 and Lemma 5.1.4.2.4, respectively. As P is finite, Algorithm 5.1.4.2.8 surely halts as well.

Correctness
This part of the proof sketches a demonstration that Algorithm 5.1.4.2.8 produces its output context-free grammar, G_{GNF}, such that $L(G_{\text{GNF}}) = L(G)$, and G_{GNF} is in Greibach normal form.

Equivalence
Algorithm 5.1.4.2.3 and Algorithm 5.1.3.1.7 are correct from Theorem 5.1.3.1.8 and Lemma 5.1.4.2.4, respectively. Therefore,

$$L(G_{\text{GNF}}) = L(G)$$

Greibach normal form
This part of the proof is left to the exercises.

In summary, with G as its input, Algorithm 5.1.4.2.8 halts and correctly constructs a context-free grammar G_{GNF}, such that $L(G_{\text{GNF}}) = L(G)$, and G_{GNF} is in Greibach normal form. Thus, Theorem 5.1.4.2.9 holds. ∎

Example 5.1.4.3 Part 2 Application of Algorithm 5.1.4.2.8
Consider the non-left-recursive context-free grammar produced by the previous part of this example. Replace A_4' with B_1 in this grammar so that the resulting grammar G has the productions

$p_1: A_1 \to A_2 A_3$
$p_2: A_2 \to A_3 A_1$
$p_3: A_3 \to A_4 A_5$
$p_4: A_4 \to b A_6 B_1$
$p_5: A_4 \to b A_6$
$p_6: B_1 \to A_5 A_6 B_1$
$p_7: B_1 \to A_5 A_6$
$p_8: A_1 \to a$
$p_9: A_3 \to b$
$p_{10}: A_5 \to b$
$p_{11}: A_6 \to c$

This grammar satisfies all requirements that Algorithm 5.1.4.2.8 places on its input grammar.

The present part of Example 5.1.4.2.3 uses Algorithm 5.1.4.2.8 with G as its input to obtain a context-free grammar G_{GNF} such that $L(G_{\text{GNF}}) = L(G)$ and G_{GNF} is in Greibach normal form. Notice that A_6 forms $\text{lhs}(p_{11})$, which satisfies the Greibach normal form. Furthermore, each production with the left-hand side formed by A_5 or A_4 are in this form as well. Consider $p_3: A_3 \to A_4 A_5$. Algorithm 5.1.4.2.8 calls Algorithm 5.1.4.2.3, which removes p_3 and introduces $A_3 \to \text{rhs}(p_4)A_5$ and $A_3 \to \text{rhs}(p_5)A_5$ because $A_4 = \text{lhs}(p_4) = \text{lhs}(p_5)$. That is, these two new productions are

$$A_3 \to b A_6 B_1 A_5$$
$$A_3 \to b A_6 A_5$$

Analogously, Algorithm 5.1.4.2.3 removes p_2 and introduces

$$A_2 \to b A_1$$
$$A_2 \to b A_6 B_1 A_5 A_1$$
$$A_2 \to b A_6 A_5 A_1$$

In addition, Algorithm 5.1.4.2.3 removes p_1 and introduces

$$A_1 \to b A_1 A_3$$
$$A_1 \to b A_6 B_1 A_5 A_1 A_3$$
$$A_1 \to b A_6 A_5 A_1 A_3$$

At this point, Algorithm 5.1.4.2.8 has transformed all productions, $p \in P$, with $\text{lhs}(p) \in \{A_1, \ldots, A_6\}$ into the Greibach normal form.

Observe that $B_1 = \text{lhs}(p_6)$ and $B_1 = \text{lhs}(p_7)$. Therefore, Algorithm 5.1.4.2.8 first calls Algorithm 5.1.4.2.3 to remove $p_6: B_1 \to A_5 A_6 B_1$ and introduce

$$B_1 \to b A_6 B_1$$

Then, Algorithm 5.1.4.2.3 removes p_7: $B_1 \to A_5 A_6$ and introduces

$$B_1 \to bA_6$$

At this point, Algorithm 5.1.4.2.8 has transformed all productions into the Greibach normal form.

Finally, Algorithm 5.1.4.2.8 calls Algorithm 5.1.3.1.7; however, as all nonterminals are accessible, Algorithm 5.1.3.1.7 makes no change. Consequently, Algorithm 5.1.4.2.8 produces the following context-free grammar G_{GNF} in Greibach normal form:

$A_1 \to bA_1 A_3$
$A_1 \to bA_6 B_1 A_5 A_1 A_3$
$A_1 \to bA_6 A_5 A_1 A_3$
$A_2 \to bA_1$
$A_2 \to bA_6 B_1 A_5 A_1$
$A_2 \to bA_6 A_5 A_1$
$A_3 \to bA_6 B_1 A_5$
$A_3 \to bA_6 A_5$
$A_4 \to bA_6 B_1$
$A_4 \to bA_6$
$B_1 \to bA_6 B_1$
$B_1 \to bA_6$
$A_1 \to a$
$A_3 \to b$
$A_5 \to b$
$A_6 \to c$

As verified in the exercises G_{GNF} and G are equivalent.

▲

The main result of this section now follows.

Corollary 5.1.4.2.10
Let L be a context-free language. Then, there exists a context-free grammar G in Greibach normal form such that $L =_\varepsilon L(G)$.

Proof
This corollary follows from Lemma 5.1.4.2.7, Algorithm 5.1.4.2.8, and Theorem 5.1.4.2.9.

■

The last part of this section briefly discusses a special case of the Greibach normal form.

Definition — Greibach two-standard normal form
Let $G = (N, T, P, S)$ be a context-free grammar. G is in *Greibach two-standard normal form* if $p \in P$ implies $\text{rhs}(p) \in T(\{\varepsilon\} \cup N \cup N^2)$.

◆

From this definition, a context-free grammar in Greibach two-standard normal form has each production p such that $\text{rhs}(p)$ consists of a terminal followed by no more than two nonterminals.

Theorem 5.1.4.2.11
Let L be a context-free language. Then, there exists a context-free grammar G in Greibach two-standard normal form such that $L =_\varepsilon L(G)$.

Proof
This proof is left to the exercises.

■

Less formally, Theorem 5.1.4.2.11 states that the context-free grammars with each production p such that $\text{rhs}(p)$ consists of a terminal followed by no more than two nonterminals characterize the family of context-free languages. Notably, this result cannot be achieved for context-free grammars in which each production p has $\text{rhs}(p)$ formed by a terminal followed by no more than one nonterminal. Indeed, these grammars characterize the family of regular languages, and this family is properly included in the family of context-free languages (see Sections 7.2 and 7.3).

5.2 Pushdown automata

This section formalizes and investigates pushdown automata, which have the same power as context-free grammars. Section 5.2.1 introduces the basic model of a pushdown automaton, Section 5.2.2 generalizes this model, and Section 5.2.3 studies the deterministic model of a pushdown automaton.

5.2.1 Basic definitions

A pushdown automaton represents a finite automaton extended by a potentially unbounded pushdown store (see Figure 5.2.1.1).

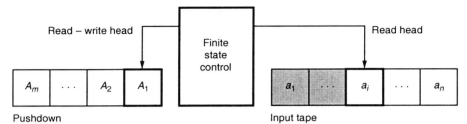

Figure 5.2.1.1 A Pushdown automaton.

Definition — pushdown automaton
A *pushdown automaton* is a quintuple

$$M = (Q, \Sigma, R, s, F)$$

where

Q is a finite set of *states*;
Σ is an alphabet such that $\Sigma \cap Q = \varnothing$ and $\Sigma = \Sigma_I \cup \Sigma_{PD}$, where Σ_I is an *input alphabet*, and Σ_{PD} is a *pushdown alphabet* containing S, the *start symbol*;
$R \subseteq \Sigma_{PD} Q (\Sigma_I \cup \{\varepsilon\}) \times \Sigma_{PD}^* Q$ is a finite relation;
$s \in Q$ is the *start state*;
$F \subseteq Q$ is a set of *final states*.

◆

Members of R are called *rules*, and thus, R is referred to as a finite *set of rules*. Consider a rule, $(Apa, wq) \in R$ with $A \in \Sigma_{PD}, p, q \in Q, a \in \Sigma_I \cup \{\varepsilon\}$, and $w \in \Sigma_{PD}^*$; instead of (Apa, wq), the following form is used:

$$Apa \vdash wq$$

Example 5.2.1.1 Part 1 Pushdown automaton
Consider the pushdown automaton

$$M = (\{s, q, f\}, \{a, b, S\}, R, s, \{f\})$$

M's input alphabet is $\{a, b\}$, and its pushdown alphabet is $\{a, b, S\}$, where S is the start symbol. The set of rules R is defined as

$$R = \{Ssa \vdash Sas, asa \vdash aas, asb \vdash q, aqb \vdash q, Sq \vdash f\}$$

△

If a label r denotes a rule, $Apa \vdash wq$, this is expressed as

$$r: Apa \vdash wq,$$

where Apa represents the left-hand side of r, lhs(r), and wq represents the right-hand side of r, rhs(r).

Conventions

Given a pushdown automaton, $M = (Q, \Sigma, R, s, F)$, Σ_I and Σ_{PD} denote the input alphabet of M and the pushdown alphabet of M, respectively. Also:

1. f, p, q and s represent states in Q where s is the start state, and f is a final state;
2. $a, ..., d$ represent symbols in Σ_I;
3. $A, ..., D$, and S represent symbols in Σ_{PD}, where S is the start symbol;
4. $u, ..., z$ represent words over Σ;
5. R's rules are labelled as $1, ..., 9$ or by $r_1, r_2, ...$;
6. ρ represents a sequence of rules from R.

●

Subscripts and superscripts do not change these conventions, which are used hereafter unless explicitly stated otherwise.

Example 5.2.1.1 Part 2 Simplified specification of a pushdown automaton

This part of Example 5.2.1.1 uses these conventions to specify M, as defined in Part 1 of this example, by simply listing its five rules:

1: $Ssa \vdash Sas$
2: $asa \vdash aas$
3: $asb \vdash q$
4: $aqb \vdash q$
5: $Sq \vdash f$

△

A pushdown automaton M works by making moves according to its computational rules. A move depends on the current state, the symbol on the top of the pushdown, and the input symbol. During a move, M changes the state, rewrites the top pushdown symbol with a word, and shifts the read head zero or one square right.

Definition — configuration

Let $M = (Q, \Sigma, R, s, F)$ be a pushdown automaton. A *configuration* of M is a word χ satisfying

$$\chi \in \Sigma_{PD}^* Q \Sigma_I^*$$

◆

Definition — move

Let $M = (Q, \Sigma, R, s, F)$ be a pushdown automaton. If $x\text{lhs}(r)y$ is a configuration of M, where $x \in \Sigma_{PD}^*$, $y \in \Sigma_I^*$, and $r \in R$, then M makes a *move from $x\text{lhs}(r)y$ to $x\text{rhs}(r)y$ according to r*, written as

$$x\text{lhs}(r)y \vdash x\text{rhs}(r)y \ [r]$$

◆

Convention

When the specification of the used rule r is immaterial, $x\text{lhs}(r)y \vdash x\text{rhs}(r)y \ [r]$ is simplified to

$$x\text{lhs}(r)y \vdash x\text{rhs}(r)y$$

●

Consider a pushdown automaton $M = (Q, \Sigma, R, s, F)$ and a configuration $\chi = x\text{lhs}(r)y$, where $x \in \Sigma_{PD}^*$, $y \in \Sigma_I^*$, and $r: Apa \vdash wq \in R$; that is,

$$\chi = xApay$$

Observe that χ actually represents an instantaneous description of M. This description consists of a word representing the contents of the pushdown, xA, followed by the current state, p, and the unread suffix of the input word, ay. In xA, the rightmost symbol A is the *top* of the pushdown, and the leftmost symbol of xA is the *bottom* of the pushdown. The current input symbol, scanned by the read head, is the leftmost symbol of ay.

Consider a move made by a pushdown automaton $M = (Q, \Sigma, R, s, F)$ according to a rule, $r: Apa \vdash wq \in R$, where $a \in \Sigma_I \cup \{\varepsilon\}$. If $a \in \Sigma_I$, M advances the read head; if $a = \varepsilon$, M keeps this head stationary. A detailed description of both moves follows next.

1. Let $r: Apa \vdash wq \in R$ with $a \in \Sigma_I$. According to this rule, M rewrites the pushdown top A with w, changes state q to p, reads a, and shifts the read head one square to the right (see Figure 5.2.1.2).

Models for context-free languages

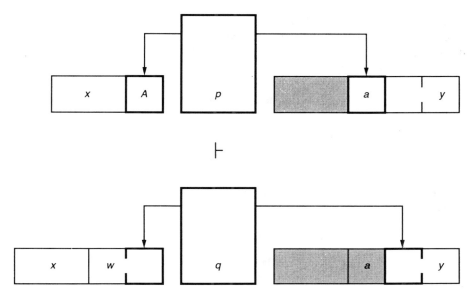

Figure 5.2.1.2 Move.

2. Let $r: Apa \vdash wq \in R$ with $a = \varepsilon$. At this point r called an ε-rule, has the form $Ap \vdash wq$. According to $Ap \vdash wq$, M makes an ε-move during which M rewrites the pushdown top A with w, changes state p to q, and keeps the read head stationary (see Figure 5.2.1.3); therefore, in the next move, M reads the same input symbol.

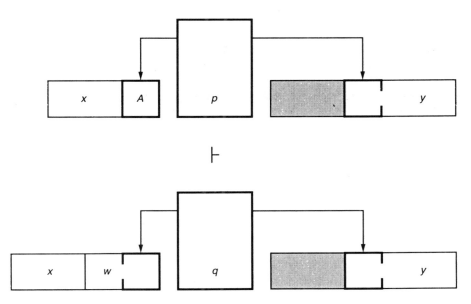

Figure 5.2.1.3 ε-Move.

Example 5.2.1.1 Part 3 Moves

Return to the pushdown automaton M discussed in the previous two parts of this example. Consider the configuration $x\text{lhs}(1)y$ such that $x = \varepsilon$ and $y = abb$. Recall that 1: $Ssa \vdash Sas$. Thus,

$$x\text{lhs}(1)y = Ssaabb$$

According to 1: $Ssa \vdash Sas$, M makes the move

$$Ssaabb \vdash Sasabb \ [1]$$

Consider another configuration, $Saasbb$. According to 3: $asb \vdash q$, M performs the move

$$Saasbb \vdash Saqb \ [3]$$

△

Conventions

Given a pushdown automaton M, χ_M denotes a configuration of M. When no confusion exists, simply use χ instead of χ_M.

●

The following definition extends a single move to a sequence of moves.

Definition — sequence of moves, part 1

Let $M = (Q, \Sigma, R, s, F)$ be a pushdown automaton.

1. Let χ be any configuration of M. M makes zero moves from χ to χ according to ε, written as

$$\chi \vdash^0 \chi \ [\varepsilon]$$

2. Let there exist a sequence of configurations

$$\chi_0, \ldots, \chi_n$$

for some $n \geq 1$ such that

$$\chi_{i-1} \vdash \chi_i \quad [r_i]$$

where $r_i \in R$, $i = 1, \ldots, n$; that is,

$$\chi_0 \vdash \chi_1 \ [r_1]$$
$$\vdash \chi_2 \ [r_2]$$
$$\vdots$$
$$\vdash \chi_n \ [r_n]$$

Then, M makes *n moves from χ_0 to χ_n according to $r_1\ldots r_n$*, written as

$$\chi_0 \vdash^n \chi_n \ [r_1\ldots r_n]$$

♦

Consider a pushdown automaton $M = (Q, \Sigma, R, s, F)$ and $\chi \vdash^n \chi' \ [\rho]$ in M, where ρ denotes a sequence of n rules ($\rho = \varepsilon$ if $n = 0$). Observe that ρ, called the *rule word* corresponding to $\chi \vdash^n \chi'$, represents the sequence of rules according to which M makes the n moves from χ to χ'. For brevity, ρ is sometimes omitted in $\chi \vdash^n \chi'$ $[\rho]$, thus: $\chi \vdash^n \chi'$.

Notice that $\vdash^n$ represents the n-fold product of $\vdash$. Based on $\vdash^n$ are two further notions, $\vdash^+$ and $\vdash^*$. Algebraically, $\vdash^+$ denotes the transitive closure of $\vdash$, and $\vdash^*$ denotes the transitive and reflexive closure of $\vdash$.

Definition — sequence of moves, part 2

Let $M = (Q, \Sigma, R, s, F)$ be a pushdown automaton, and let χ and χ' be two configurations of M:

1. If there exists $n \geq 1$ so $\chi \vdash^n \chi' \ [\rho]$ in M, then $\chi \vdash^+ \chi' \ [\rho]$.
2. If there exists $n \geq 0$ so $\chi \vdash^n \chi' \ [\rho]$ in M, then $\chi \vdash^* \chi' \ [\rho]$.

♦

For simplicity, it is common to use $\chi \vdash^+ \chi'$ and $\chi \vdash^* \chi'$ instead of $\chi \vdash^+ \chi' \ [\rho]$ and $\chi \vdash^* \chi' \ [\rho]$, respectively.

Example 5.2.1.1 Part 4 Sequences of moves

Return to the pushdown automaton M discussed in the previous parts of this example and consider these two configurations:

Sasaabbb and *Saqb*

M makes this four-move computation from *Sapaabbb* to *Saqb*:

$$Sasaabbb \vdash^4 Saqb$$

because

$$Sasaabbb \vdash Saasabbb$$
$$\vdash Saaasbbb$$
$$\vdash Saaqbb$$
$$\vdash Saqb$$

More precisely,

$$Sasaabbb \vdash^4 Saqb \; [2233]$$

because M computes $Sasaabbb \vdash^4 Saqb$ by using rules 2, 2, 3 and 3. Observe that $Sasaabbb \vdash^4 Saqb$ implies

$$Sasaabbb \vdash^+ Saqb \text{ and } Sasaabbb \vdash^* Saqb$$

in M.

△

A pushdown automaton $M = (Q, \Sigma, R, s, F)$ accepts a word w as follows. Initially, M is in its start state s with the pushdown and the input tape containing S and w, respectively. If from this initial configuration M can make a sequence of moves so M reads all w and enters a final state, M accepts w; otherwise, M rejects w. The collection of all words that M accepts forms the language accepted by M.

Definition — accepted language
Let $M = (Q, \Sigma, R, s, F)$ be a pushdown automaton and $w \in \Sigma_I^*$. If there exists an *accepting computation* of the form $Ssw \vdash^* zf$ in M, where $z \in \Sigma_{PD}^*$ and $f \in F$, then M accepts w. The *language accepted by M*, $L(M)$, is defined as

$$L(M) = \{w : w \in \Sigma_I^*, \text{ and } M \text{ accepts } w\}$$

That is,

$$L(M) = \{w : w \in \Sigma_I^*, \text{ and } Ssw \vdash^* zf \text{ in } M \text{ for some } z \in \Sigma_{PD}^* \text{ and } f \in F\}$$

◆

Example 5.2.1.1 Part 5 Accepted words
With *aabb*, M makes the following sequence of moves (see Figure 5.2.1.4):

$$Ssaabb \vdash Sasabb$$
$$\vdash Saasbb$$

⊢ $Saqb$
⊢ Sq
⊢ f

As f is final, M accepts $aabb$.

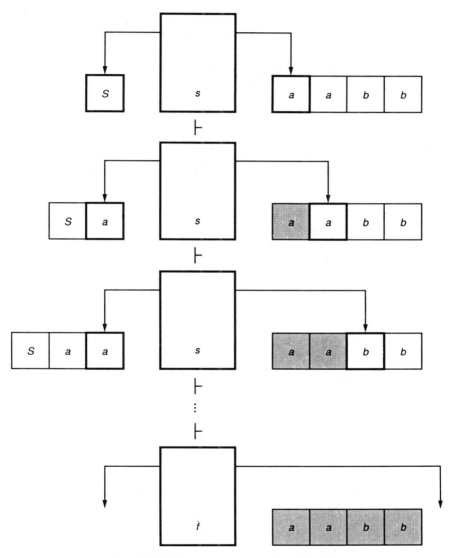

Figure 5.2.1.4 M's accepting computation with $aabb$.

△

To represent a pushdown automaton $M = (Q, \Sigma, R, s, F)$ graphically, this section introduces the *pushdown state diagram* of M. The nodes of this diagram are labelled with states of Q, where the start state is indicated by ⟶ and the final states are doubly circled. The edges have labels of the form $A/w, a$, where $A \in \Sigma_{PD}$, $w \in \Sigma_{PD}^*$ and $a \in \Sigma_I \cup \{\varepsilon\}$. Figure 5.2.1.5 describes how this diagram specifies a rule of the form $Apa \vdash wq$.

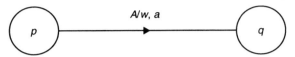

Figure 5.2.1.5 The graphical specification of $Apa \vdash wq$.

Example 5.2.1.1 Part 6 Pushdown state diagram

Figure 5.2.1.6 depicts the pushdown state diagram corresponding to M, examined in the previous parts of this example.

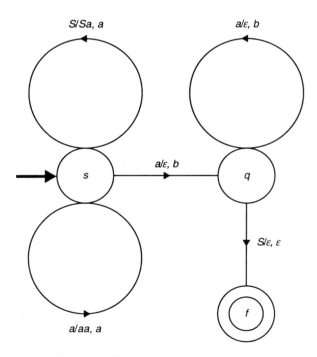

Figure 5.2.1.6 The pushdown state diagram of M.

△

The following two parts of Example 5.2.1.1 determine $L(M)$, where M is the pushdown automaton discussed in the previous parts of this example. Part 7 determines $L(M)$ informally, then Part 8 makes this determination rigorously.

Example 5.2.1.1 Part 7 Determination of the accepted language: an intuitive approach

To determine $L(M)$, where M is the pushdown automaton discussed throughout Example 5.2.1.1, observe how M works. As its graphical representation indicates (see Figure 5.2.1.6), M first pushes down as. When b appears, M begins to pop up as and pair them off with bs. If the number of as and bs coincide, M accepts the input word. These observations lead to the conjecture that M accepts an input word w if and only if w consists of n as followed by n bs, for some $n \geq 1$. To justify this conjecture in somewhat greater detail, recall that M is defined by these rules

1: $Ssa \vdash Sas$
2: $asa \vdash aas$
3: $asb \vdash q$
4: $aqb \vdash q$
5: $Sq \vdash f$

State changes
Rules 1: $Ssa \vdash Sas$ and 2: $asa \vdash aas$ imply that M remains in s while reading as. By 3: $asb \vdash q$, this automaton makes a move to q when b appears. As 4: $aqb \vdash q$ indicates, M remains in q while scanning bs. Finally, using 5: $Sq \vdash f$, M makes an ε-move to f when S appears on the pushdown top.

Pushdown changes
M first copies as from its input tape onto its pushdown by an application of rule 1 followed by several applications of rule 2. When reading the first b, M pops a from the pushdown according to rule 3. Then, M pops up as and pairs these as with bs by using rule 4. When the pushdown contains only S, M enters its final state, f, according to rule 5.

Determination of the accepted language
As these state and pushdown changes indicate, M accepts an input word w according to a rule word ρ such that

$$\rho = 12^n 34^n 5$$

for some $n \geq 0$. Therefore,

$$w = a^{n+1} b^{n+1}$$

For example, for $n = 0$, M accepts ab according to 135, and for $n = 2$, M accepts $aaabbb$

according to 1223445. Therefore, this part of of Example 5.2.1.1 makes a conjecture that

$$L(M) = \{a^n b^n : n \geq 1\}$$

△

Example 5.2.1.1 Part 8 Determination of the accepted language: a rigorous approach

The previous part of this example has sketched the reason why

$$L(M) = \{a^n b^n : n \geq 1\}$$

This identity is now rigorously identified. First Claim A is proved, which implies the inclusion

$$\{a^n b^n : n \geq 1\} \subseteq L(M)$$

Before this claim and its proof, recall that M has the five rules

1: $Ssa \vdash Sas$

2: $asa \vdash aas$

3: $asb \vdash q$

4: $aqb \vdash q$

5: $Sq \vdash f$

Claim A
For all $n \geq 0$,

$$Ssa^{n+1}b^{n+1} \vdash^* f[\rho]$$

in M, where $\rho = 12^n 34^n 5$.

Proof
This proofs established by induction on $n \geq 0$.

Basis
Let $n = 0$. Thus, $a^{n+1}b^{n+1} = ab$. Observe that

$Ssab$	$\vdash Sasb$	[1]
	$\vdash Sq$	[3]
	$\vdash f$	[5]

Hence,
$$Ssab \vdash^* f[\rho]$$
in M, where $\rho = 135 = 12^0 34^0 5$. Consequently, the basis holds.

Induction hypothesis
Assume that for all $k = 0, 1, \ldots, n$, where n is a nonnegative integer,
$$Ssa^{k+1}b^{k+1} \vdash^* f[\rho]$$
in M, where $\rho = 12^k 34^k 5$.

Induction step
Consider $a^{n+1}b^{n+1}$. By the induction hypothesis,
$$Ssa^n b^n \vdash^* f[\rho']$$
in M, where $\rho' = 12^{n-1} 34^{n-1} 5$. Then,

$$\begin{aligned}
S &\vdash^* a^n sab^n b & [12^{n-1}] \\
&\vdash aa^n qb^n b & [2] \\
&\vdash^* Saqb & [34^{n-1}] \\
&\vdash Sq & [4] \\
&\vdash f & [5]
\end{aligned}$$

That is,
$$Ssa^{n+1}b^{n+1} \vdash^* f[\rho]$$
in M, where $\rho = 12^n 34^n 5$, and the inductive step is completed.

Thus, Claim A holds. $\square$

Claim A implies that
$$\{a^n b^n : n \geq 1\} \subseteq L(M)$$

To verify
$$L(M) \subseteq \{a^n b^n : n \geq 1\},$$

this proof first establishes Claims B through D, which give an insight into the relationship between the length of words read by M and the number of moves that M makes with these words. Claim B states this relationship for computation during which M remains in state s (see Figure 5.2.1.7).

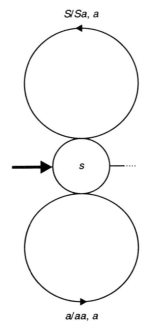

Figure 5.2.1.7 M's computation in state s.

Claim B
Let $Ssx \vdash^* ys\ [\rho]$ in M, where ρ represents a rule word consisting of n rules, for some $n \geq 1$. Then, $\rho = 12^{n-1}$, $x = a^n$, and $y = Sa^n$.

Proof
This proof is established by induction on $n \geq 0$.

Basis
Let $n = 0$. At this point,

$$Ssa \vdash Sas\ [1]$$

in M, where 1: $Ssa \vdash Sas$. Consequently, the basis holds.

Induction hypothesis
Assume that the claim holds for all computations according to ρ consisting of k rules, where $k = 1, \ldots, n$, for some $n \geq 1$.

Induction step
Consider

$$Ssx \vdash^* ys \ [\rho]$$

in M, where ρ represents a rule word consisting of $n + 1$ rules. In greater detail, express $Ssx \vdash^* ys \ [\rho]$ as

$$Ssx \vdash^* \chi \qquad [\rho']$$
$$\vdash ys \qquad [r]$$

where χ is a configuration of M, and $\rho = \rho' r$ so ρ' represents a rule word consisting of n rules and r is a rule such that $\text{rhs}(r) \in \{Sa, aa\}\{s\}$. As a result,

$$Ssx'a \vdash^* y'sa \qquad [\rho']$$
$$\vdash y'as \qquad [r],$$

where $x = x'a$ and $y = y'a$. Consider

$$Ssx' \vdash^* y's \ [\rho']$$

and recall that ρ' contains n rules. By the induction hypothesis,

$$\rho' = 12^{n-1}, x = a^n, \text{ and } y = Sa^n$$

These identities imply that r is the rule

$$2: asa \vdash aas$$

Thus, $\rho = \rho' r = 12^{n-1}2$, $x = a^n a$, and $y = Sa^n a$. That is,

$$\rho = 12^n, x = a^{n+1}, \text{ and } y = Sa^{n+1}$$

In other words, the inductive step is completed.

Consequently, Claim B holds.

$\square$

Claim B has explained the relationship between the length of words read by M in s and the number of moves that M makes with these words. Analogously, Claim C establishes the relationship between the length of words read by M in q and the number of moves that M makes with these words (see Figure 5.2.1.8).

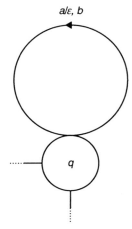

Figure 5.2.1.8 M's computation in state q.

Claim C
Let $wqx \vdash^* vq\ [\rho]$ in M, where ρ represents a rule word consisting of n rules, for some $n \geq 0$. Then, $\rho = 4^n$, $x = b^n$, and $w = va^n$.

Proof
This proof is established by induction on $n \geq 0$.

Basis
Let $n = 0$. Then,

$$wq \vdash^* wq\ [\varepsilon]$$

Consequently, the basis holds.

Induction hypothesis
Assume that the claim holds for all computations according to ρ consisting of k rules, where $k = 1, \ldots, n$, for some $n \geq 0$.

Induction step
Let

$$wqx \vdash^* vq\ [\rho]$$

in M, where ρ represents a rule word consisting of $n + 1$ rules. Express $wqx \vdash^* vq$ $[\rho]$ as

$$wqx \vdash^* \chi \quad [\rho']$$
$$\vdash vq \quad [r]$$

where χ is a configuration of M, and $\rho = \rho' r$ so ρ' represents a rule word consisting of n rules and r is a rule of M. Observe that $r = 4: aqb \vdash q$, so $x = x'b$ and $\chi = vaqb$. Consider

$$wqx' \vdash^* vaq \quad [\rho']$$

As ρ' consists of n rules, the induction hypothesis implies $\rho' = 4^n$, $x' = b^n$, and $w = vaa^n = va^{n+1}$. Therefore, $\rho = \rho' r = 4^n 4$, and $x = b^n b$. That is,

$$\rho = 4^{n+1}, x = b^{n+1}, \text{ and } w = va^{n+1}$$

Thus, the inductive step is completed, so Claim C holds.

□

Making use of Claims B and C, the following claim describes the form of Ms accepting computations.

Claim D
Every accepting computation in M has the form

$$Ssa^n b^n \vdash^* Sa^n sb^n \quad [\rho_1]$$
$$\vdash^* Sq \quad [\rho_2]$$
$$\vdash f \quad [5]$$

where $\rho_1 = 12^{n-1}$ and $\rho_2 = 34^{n-1}$.

Proof
Let

$$Ssx \vdash^* \chi_f [\rho]$$

be an accepting computation in M. Observe that this computation starts in s, goes through q, and ends in f (see Figure 5.2.1.6). From s to q, M makes a move according to 3: $asb \vdash q$. Express $Ssx \vdash^* \chi_f [\rho]$ as

$$Ssx \vdash^* ysv$$
$$\vdash \chi_{\text{first-}q} \quad [3]$$
$$\vdash^* \chi_f$$

so that during $Ssx \vdash^* ysv$, M remains in s, and thus $\chi_{\text{first-}q}$ denotes the first configuration in q. Assume that M makes $Ssx \vdash^* ys$ according to a rule word, ρ_1; symbolically,

$$Ssx \vdash^* ysv \quad [\rho_1]$$

Observe that ρ_1 surely begins with 1, so $\rho_1 \neq \varepsilon$. Let ρ_1 consist of n rules, for some $n \geq 1$. By Claim B, $\rho_1 = 12^{n-1}$, $x = a^n v$, and $y = Sa^n$, so

$$Ssa^n v \vdash^* Sa^n sv \quad [\rho_1]$$
$$\vdash \chi_{\text{first-}q} \quad [3]$$
$$\vdash^* \chi_f$$

The use of 3 causes M to pop a from the pushdown and read b. Thus, $v = bu$ and $\chi_{\text{first-}q} = Sa^{n-1}qu$. Consequently,

$$Ssa^n bu \vdash^* Sa^n sbu \quad [\rho_1]$$
$$\vdash Sa^{n-1}qu \quad [3]$$
$$\vdash^* \chi_f$$

From q to f, M makes a move according to 5: $Sq \vdash f$, so

$$Ssa^n bu \vdash^* Sa^n sbu \quad [\rho_1]$$
$$\vdash Sa^{n-1}qu \quad [3]$$
$$\vdash^* \chi_{\text{last-}q}$$
$$\vdash \chi_f \quad [5]$$

During $Sa^{n-1}qu \vdash^* \chi_{\text{last-}q}$, M remains in q; then, according to 5, M enters f and pops S from the pushdown. To have S on the pushdown top, M removes a^{n-1} from the pushdown during $Sa^{n-1}qu \vdash^* \chi_{\text{last-}q}$; therefore, $\chi_{\text{last-}q} = Sq$. Assume that M makes $Sa^{n-1}qu \vdash^* Sq$ according to a rule word, ρ_3; symbolically,

$$Sa^{n-1}qu \vdash^* Sq \ [\rho_3]$$

By Claim C, $\rho_3 = 4^{n-1}$ and $u = b^{n-1}$. Set $\rho_2 = 3\rho_3$ and observe that

$$Ssa^nb^n \vdash^* Sa^nsb^n \quad [\rho_1]$$
$$\vdash^* Sq \quad [\rho_2]$$
$$\vdash f \quad [5]$$

where $\rho_1 = 12^{n-1}$ and $\rho_2 = 34^{n-1}$; thus, Claim D holds.

□

Claim D implies

$$L(M) \subseteq \{a^nb^n : n \geq 1\}$$

To summarize, this part of Example 5.2.1.1 has proved

$$\{a^nb^n : n \geq 1\} \subseteq L(M) \text{ and } L(M) \subseteq \{a^nb^n : n \geq 1\}$$

Therefore,

$$L(M) = \{a^nb^n : n \geq 1\}$$

△

Three types of acceptance

Consider the language $L(M)$ accepted by a pushdown automaton, $M = (Q, \Sigma, R, s, F)$. Recall that

$$L(M) = \{w : w \in \Sigma^* \text{ and } Ssw \vdash^* zf \text{ in } M \text{ for some } z \in \Sigma^*_{PD} \text{ and } f \in F\}$$

To explain $Ssw \vdash^* zf$ informally, M accepts w if and only if after reading w, M enters a final state f; notice that z — the final content of the pushdown — is completely irrelevant to the acceptance of w. $L(M)_f$ is used instead of $L(M)$ to specifically indicate the final state.

Convention

For a pushdown automaton M, $L(M)_f$ and $L(M)$ are used interchangeably hereafter.

●

In addition to this type of acceptance is acceptance by empty pushdown and, then, the combination of acceptance by final state and acceptance by empty pushdown:

1. by final state;
2. by empty pushdown;
3. by final state and empty pushdown.

The following definition introduces acceptance by empty pushdown.

Definition — language accepted by empty pushdown

Let $M = (Q, \Sigma, R, s, F)$ be a pushdown automaton and $w \in \Sigma_I^*$. If $Ssw \vdash^* q$ in M, where $q \in Q$, M accepts w by empty pushdown. The *language accepted by M by empty pushdown*, denoted by $L(M)_\varepsilon$, is defined as

$$L(M)_\varepsilon = \{w : w \in \Sigma_I^*, \text{ and } M \text{ accepts } w \text{ by empty pushdown}\}$$

That is,

$$L(M)_\varepsilon = \{w : w \in \Sigma_I^* \text{ and } Ssw \vdash^* q \text{ in } M \text{ for some } q \in Q\}$$

♦

Example 5.2.1.1 Part 9 Language accepted by empty pushdown

Consider the pushdown automaton M discussed throughout the previous parts of this example. Recall that Part 8 of Example 5.2.1.1 proves that

$$L(M)_f = \{a^n b^n : n \geq 1\}$$

The exercises modify this proof to demonstrate that

$$L(M)_\varepsilon = \{a^n b^n : n \geq 1\}$$

Thus,

$$L(M)_f = L(M)_\varepsilon = \{a^n b^n : n \geq 1\}$$

△

Let $M = (Q, \Sigma, R, s, F)$ be a pushdown automaton. Observe that F does not affect $L(M)_\varepsilon$ at all. Specifically, set $F = \varnothing$ in $M = (Q, \Sigma, R, s, F)$; that is, confer $M' = (Q, \Sigma, R, s, \varnothing)$. Observe that

$$L(M)_\varepsilon = L(M')_\varepsilon$$

because M' accepts w by empty pushdown if and only if after reading w, M' empties its pushdown; the state in which M' ends up its computation with w is irrelevant. Therefore, when studying a pushdown automaton that accepts its language by empty pushdown, it can be assumed that this automaton has no final state. This assumption significantly simplifies the subsequent discussions concerning pushdown automata that accept by empty pushdown.

This section demonstrates how to convert any pushdown automaton, $M_f = (Q, \Sigma, R, s, F)$, to a pushdown automaton, $M_\varepsilon = (Q_\varepsilon, \Sigma_\varepsilon, R_\varepsilon, s_\varepsilon, \varnothing)$, so that $L(M_f)_f = L(M_\varepsilon)_\varepsilon$.

Algorithm 5.2.1.1: Conversion of a pushdown automaton accepting by final state to an equivalent pushdown automaton accepting by empty pushdown

Input: A pushdown automaton $M_f = (Q, \Sigma, R, s, F)$.

Output: A pushdown automaton, $M_\varepsilon = (Q_\varepsilon, \Sigma_\varepsilon, R_\varepsilon, s_\varepsilon, \varnothing)$, such that $L(M_f)_f = L(M_\varepsilon)_\varepsilon$.

Method

begin
    $Q_\varepsilon := Q \cup \{q_\varepsilon, s_\varepsilon\}$ {s_ε is the start state of M_ε};
    $\Sigma_{PD_\varepsilon} := \Sigma_{PD} \cup \{S_\varepsilon\}$ {Σ_{PD_ε} is the pushdown alphabet of M_ε, and S_ε is the start symbol
        of M_ε};
    $\Sigma_\varepsilon := \Sigma_{PD_\varepsilon} \cup \Sigma_I$;
    $R_\varepsilon := \{S_\varepsilon s_\varepsilon \vdash S_\varepsilon S s\} \cup R$;
    for each $f \in F$ and $A \in \Sigma_{PD_\varepsilon}$ **do**
        $R_\varepsilon := R_\varepsilon \cup \{Af \vdash q_\varepsilon, Aq_\varepsilon \vdash q_\varepsilon\}$;
    produce $M_\varepsilon = (Q_\varepsilon, \Sigma_\varepsilon, R_\varepsilon, s_\varepsilon, \varnothing)$
end.

Automaton M_ε, produced by Algorithm 5.2.1.1, simulates M_f move by move. In addition, when M_f occurs in a final state, M_ε can enter a special state, q_ε, in which M_ε empties its pushdown. Consider the special case when M_f reads an input word w, enters a nonfinal state q, and empties its pushdown so $w \notin L(M_f)_f$. When simulating this computation, M_ε also reads w and enters q; however, its pushdown contains the start symbol S_ε, which keeps M_ε from accepting w by empty pushdown at this point. Therefore, $L(M_f)_f = L(M_\varepsilon)_\varepsilon$.

Lemma 5.2.1.2
Let $M_f = (Q, \Sigma, R, s, F)$ be a pushdown automaton. With M_f as its input, Algorithm 5.2.1.1 halts and correctly constructs a pushdown automaton, $M_\varepsilon = (Q_\varepsilon, \Sigma_\varepsilon, R_\varepsilon, s_\varepsilon, \varnothing)$, so $L(M_f)_f = L(M_\varepsilon)_\varepsilon$.

Proof
Termination
Because F and Σ_{PD_ε} are finite, Algorithm 5.2.1.1 repeats its **for** loop finitely many times. Thus, Algorithm 5.2.1.1 surely terminates.

Correctness
To establish

$$L(M_f)_f = L(M_\varepsilon)_\varepsilon,$$

this proof first establishes two claims.

Claim A
For all $w \in \Sigma_I^*$,

$$Ssw \vdash^* zf \quad [\rho]$$

in M_f if and only if

$$S_\varepsilon S_\varepsilon w \vdash S_\varepsilon Ssw \quad [S_\varepsilon S_\varepsilon \vdash S_\varepsilon Ss]$$
$$\vdash^* zf \quad [\rho]$$
$$\vdash^* q_\varepsilon \quad [\rho_\varepsilon]$$

in M_ε, where $f \in F$, ρ consists of rules from R, and ρ_ε consists of rules from $(R_\varepsilon - (\{S_\varepsilon S_\varepsilon \vdash S_\varepsilon Ss\} \cup R))$.

Proof
The equivalence described in Claim A holds is only briefly given here; a formal proof is left to the exercises.

Only if
The 'only if' part of the equivalence states that for all $w \in \Sigma_I^*$,

$$Ssw \vdash^* zf \, [\rho]$$

in M_f implies

$$S_\varepsilon S_\varepsilon w \vdash S_\varepsilon Ssw \quad [S_\varepsilon S_\varepsilon \vdash S_\varepsilon Ss]$$
$$\vdash^* S_\varepsilon zf \quad [\rho]$$
$$\vdash^* q_\varepsilon \quad [\rho_\varepsilon]$$

in M_ε, where $f \in F$, ρ consists of rules from R, and ρ_ε consists of rules from $(R_\varepsilon - (\{S_\varepsilon S_\varepsilon \vdash S_\varepsilon Ss\} \cup R))$.

Let $w \in \Sigma_I^*$, and let $Ssw \vdash^* zf \, [\rho]$ in M_f. As $R \subseteq R_\varepsilon$,

$$Ssw \vdash^* zf \quad [\rho]$$

in M_ε. Consequently,

$$S_\varepsilon S_\varepsilon w \vdash S_\varepsilon Ssw \quad [S_\varepsilon S_\varepsilon \vdash S_\varepsilon Ss]$$
$$\vdash^* S_\varepsilon zf \quad [\rho]$$

in M_ε. By using rules from $R_\varepsilon - (\{S_\varepsilon s_\varepsilon \vdash S_\varepsilon Ss\} \cup R)$, M_ε can erase $S_\varepsilon z$, so

$$S_\varepsilon s_\varepsilon w \vdash S_\varepsilon Ssw \quad [S_\varepsilon s_\varepsilon \vdash S_\varepsilon Ss]$$
$$\vdash^* zf \quad [\rho]$$
$$\vdash^* q_\varepsilon \quad [\rho_\varepsilon]$$

in M_ε, where $f \in F$, ρ consists of rules from R, and ρ_ε consists of rules from $(R_\varepsilon - (\{S_\varepsilon s_\varepsilon \vdash S_\varepsilon Ss\} \cup R))$. Therefore, the 'only if' part of the equivalence holds.

If

The 'if' part of the equivalence states that for all $w \in \Sigma_I^*$,

$$S_\varepsilon s_\varepsilon w \vdash S_\varepsilon Ssw \quad [S_\varepsilon s_\varepsilon \vdash S_\varepsilon Ss]$$
$$\vdash^* S_\varepsilon zf \quad [\rho]$$
$$\vdash^* q_\varepsilon \quad [\rho_\varepsilon]$$

in M_ε implies

$$Ssw \vdash^* zf \quad [\rho]$$

in M_f, where $f \in F$, ρ consists of rules from R, and ρ_ε consists of rules from $R_\varepsilon - (\{S_\varepsilon s_\varepsilon \vdash S_\varepsilon Ss\} \cup R)$. This implication follows from $R \subseteq R_\varepsilon$, so the if part of the equivalence holds as well.

Consequently, Claim A holds. $\square$

Claim B

For all $w \in \Sigma_I^*$,

$$w \in L(M_\varepsilon)_\varepsilon$$

if and only if

$$S_\varepsilon s_\varepsilon w \vdash S_\varepsilon Ssw \quad [S_\varepsilon s_\varepsilon \vdash S_\varepsilon Ss]$$
$$\vdash^* zf \quad [\rho]$$
$$\vdash^* q_\varepsilon \quad [\rho_\varepsilon]$$

in M_ε, where $f \in F$, ρ consists of rules from R, and ρ_ε consists of rules from $R_\varepsilon - (\{S_\varepsilon s_\varepsilon \vdash S_\varepsilon Ss\} \cup R)$.

Proof
This section only gives a brief proof of Claim B, whose detailed verification is left to the exercises.

Only if
The 'only if' part of the equivalence states that for all $w \in \Sigma_I^*$,

$$w \in L(M_\varepsilon)_\varepsilon$$

implies

$$S_\varepsilon S_\varepsilon w \vdash S_\varepsilon Ssw \quad [S_\varepsilon S_\varepsilon \vdash S_\varepsilon Ss]$$
$$\vdash^* S_\varepsilon zf \quad [\rho]$$
$$\vdash^* q_\varepsilon \quad [\rho_\varepsilon]$$

in M_ε, where $f \in F$, ρ consists of rules from R, and ρ_ε consists of rules from $(R_\varepsilon - (\{S_\varepsilon S_\varepsilon \vdash S_\varepsilon Ss\} \cup R))$.

Let $w \in L(M_\varepsilon)_\varepsilon$. Then, $S_\varepsilon S_\varepsilon w \vdash^* q$ in M_ε for some $q \in Q_\varepsilon$. $S_\varepsilon S_\varepsilon \vdash S_\varepsilon Ss$ is the only rule with $S_\varepsilon S_\varepsilon$ on its left-hand side, so $S_\varepsilon S_\varepsilon w \vdash^* q$ begins by using $S_\varepsilon S_\varepsilon \vdash S_\varepsilon Ss$ as

$$S_\varepsilon S_\varepsilon w \vdash S_\varepsilon Ssw \quad [S_\varepsilon S_\varepsilon \vdash S_\varepsilon Ss]$$
$$\vdash^* q$$

M_ε can remove S_ε from its pushdown provided that M_ε occurs in q_ε, so $q = q_\varepsilon$. Furthermore, observe that once M_ε uses a rule from $R_\varepsilon - (\{S_\varepsilon S_\varepsilon \vdash S_\varepsilon Ss\} \cup R)$, it can never use a rule from $\{S_\varepsilon S_\varepsilon \vdash S_\varepsilon Ss\} \cup R$ and, for this reason, when M_ε enters q_ε it can never exit from this state. As a result,

$$S_\varepsilon S_\varepsilon w \vdash S_\varepsilon Ssw \quad [S_\varepsilon S_\varepsilon \vdash S_\varepsilon Ss]$$
$$\vdash^* \chi \quad [\rho]$$
$$\vdash^* q_\varepsilon \quad [\rho_\varepsilon]$$

in M_ε, where ρ consists of rules from R, and ρ_ε consists of rules from $R_\varepsilon - (\{S_\varepsilon S_\varepsilon \vdash S_\varepsilon Ss\} \cup R)$. Observe that all rules in $R_\varepsilon - (\{S_\varepsilon S_\varepsilon \vdash S_\varepsilon Ss\} \cup R)$ represent ε-rules and that M_ε enters q_ε according to a rule, whose left-hand side contains a state, f, satisfying $f \in F$. This observation implies that

$$S_\varepsilon S_\varepsilon w \vdash S_\varepsilon Ssw \quad [S_\varepsilon S_\varepsilon \vdash S_\varepsilon Ss]$$
$$\vdash^* S_\varepsilon zf \quad [\rho]$$
$$\vdash^* q_\varepsilon \quad [\rho_\varepsilon]$$

in M_ε, where $f \in F$, ρ consists of rules from R, and ρ_ε consists of rules from $(R_\varepsilon - (\{S_\varepsilon s_\varepsilon \vdash S_\varepsilon Ss\} \cup R))$. Therefore, the 'only if' part of the equivalence in Claim B holds.

If

The 'if' part of the equivalence states that for all $w \in \Sigma_I^*$,

$$S_\varepsilon s_\varepsilon w \vdash S_\varepsilon Ssw \quad [S_\varepsilon s_\varepsilon \vdash S_\varepsilon Ss]$$
$$\vdash^* S_\varepsilon z f \quad [\rho]$$
$$\vdash^* q_\varepsilon \quad [\rho_\varepsilon]$$

in M_ε implies

$$w \in L(M_\varepsilon)_\varepsilon$$

As $S_\varepsilon s_\varepsilon w \vdash^* q_\varepsilon$, M_ε accepts w by empty pushdown, so the 'if' part of the equivalence holds as well.

Consequently, Claim B holds. □

Observe that

$$w \in L(M_f)_f$$

if and only if

$$Ssw \vdash^* zf \quad [\rho]$$

in M_f, for some $f \in F$. By Claim A,

$$Ssw \vdash^* zf \quad [\rho]$$

in M_f if and only if

$$S_\varepsilon s_\varepsilon w \vdash S_\varepsilon Ssw \quad [S_\varepsilon s_\varepsilon \vdash S_\varepsilon Ss]$$
$$\vdash^* zf \quad [\rho]$$
$$\vdash^* q_\varepsilon \quad [\rho_\varepsilon]$$

in M_ε, where $f \in F$, ρ consists of rules from R, and ρ_ε consists of rules from $(R_\varepsilon - (\{S_\varepsilon s_\varepsilon \vdash S_\varepsilon Ss\} \cup R))$. By Claim B,

$$S_\varepsilon s_\varepsilon w \vdash S_\varepsilon Ssw \quad [S_\varepsilon s_\varepsilon \vdash S_\varepsilon Ss]$$
$$\vdash^* zf \quad [\rho]$$
$$\vdash^* q_\varepsilon \quad [\rho_\varepsilon]$$

if and only if

$$w \in L(M_\varepsilon)_\varepsilon$$

By these equivalences,

$$L(M_f)_f = L(M_\varepsilon)_\varepsilon$$

In summary, with M_f as its input, Algorithm 5.2.1.1 halts and correctly constructs a pushdown automaton $M_\varepsilon = (Q_\varepsilon, \Sigma_\varepsilon, R_\varepsilon, s_\varepsilon, \emptyset)$, so that $L(M_f)_f = L(M_\varepsilon)_\varepsilon$. Therefore, Lemma 5.2.1.2 holds. ∎

The following algorithm converts any pushdown automaton M_ε to a pushdown automaton M_f, so $L(M_f)_f = L(M_\varepsilon)_\varepsilon$.

Algorithm 5.2.1.3: Conversion of a pushdown automaton accepting by empty pushdown to an equivalent pushdown automaton accepting by final state

Input: A pushdown automaton $M_\varepsilon = (Q, \Sigma, R, s, \emptyset)$.

Output: A pushdown automaton $M_f = (Q_f, \Sigma_f, R_f, s_f, \{q_f\})$, such that $L(M_f)_f = L(M_\varepsilon)_\varepsilon$.

Method

begin
   $Q_f := Q \cup \{q_f, s_f\}$ {s_f is the start state of M_f};
   $\Sigma_{PD_f} := \Sigma_{PD} \cup \{S_f\}$ {Σ_{PD_f} is the pushdown alphabet of M_f, and S_f is the start symbol of M_f};

   $\Sigma_f := \Sigma_{PD_f} \cup \Sigma_I$;
   $R_f := \{S_f s_f \vdash S_f Ss\} \cup R$;
   for each $q \in Q$ **do**
     $R_f := R_f \cup \{S_f q \vdash q_f\}$;
   produce $M_f = (Q_f, \Sigma_f, R_f, s_f, \{q_f\})$
end.

Algorithm 5.2.1.3 produces M_f so M_f simulates M_ε move by move. During this simulation, however, M_f has its start pushdown symbol S_f placed on the pushdown bottom. Assume that M_ε reads an input word w and empties its pushdown, so M_ε accepts w by empty pushdown. When simulating this computation, M_f reads w with its pushdown containing one symbol, S_f, at this point, M_f enters its final state, q_f, and accepts w.

Lemma 5.2.1.4
Let $M_\varepsilon = (Q_\varepsilon, \Sigma_\varepsilon, R_\varepsilon, s_\varepsilon, \emptyset)$ be a pushdown automaton. With M_ε as its input, Algorithm 5.2.1.3 halts and correctly constructs a pushdown automaton $M_f = (Q_f, \Sigma_f, R_f, s_f, \{q_f\})$, such that $L(M_f)_f = L(M_\varepsilon)_\varepsilon$.

Proof
Termination
Because Q is finite, Algorithm 5.2.1.3 iterates its **for** loop finitely many times. Thus, Algorithm 5.2.1.3 surely terminates.

Correctness
To demonstrate

$$L(M_f)_f = L(M_\varepsilon)_\varepsilon,$$

this proof first establishes Claims A and B.

Claim A
For all $w \in \Sigma^*_I$,

$$Ssw \vdash^* q \quad [\rho]$$

in M_ε if and only if

$$S_f s_f w \vdash S_f Ssw \quad [S_f s_f \vdash S_f Ss]$$
$$\vdash^* S_f q \quad [\rho]$$
$$\vdash^* q_f \quad [S_f q \vdash q_f]$$

in M_f, where $q \in Q$ and ρ consists of rules from R.

Proof
Only an outline proof is given here; a detailed proof of Claim A is left to the exercises.

Only if
The 'only if' part of the equivalence states that for all $w \in \Sigma^*_I$,

$$Ssw \vdash^* q \quad [\rho]$$

in $M_{\bar{e}}$ implies

$$S_{f}s_{f}w \vdash S_{f}Ssw \quad [S_{f}s_{f} \vdash S_{f}Ss]$$
$$\vdash^{*} S_{f}q \quad [\rho]$$
$$\vdash^{*} q_{f} \quad [S_{f}q \vdash q_{f}]$$

in M_f, where $q \in Q$ and ρ consists of rules from R.
 Let $Ssw \vdash^{*} q \,[\rho]$ in $M_{\bar{e}}$, where $w \in \Sigma_{I}^{*}$. As $S_{f}s_{f} \vdash S_{f}Ss \in R_{f}$ and $R \subseteq R_f$,

$$S_{f}s_{f}w \vdash S_{f}Ssw \quad [S_{f}s_{f} \vdash S_{f}Ss]$$
$$\vdash^{*} S_{f}q \quad [\rho]$$

in M_f. Because $S_{f}q \vdash q_{f} \in R_f$,

$$S_{f}s_{f}w \vdash S_{f}Ssw \quad [S_{f}s_{f} \vdash S_{f}Ss]$$
$$\vdash^{*} S_{f}q \quad [\rho]$$
$$\vdash^{*} q_{f} \quad [S_{f}q \vdash q_{f}]$$

in M_f, where $q \in Q$ and ρ consists of rules from R. Therefore, the 'only if' part of the equivalence holds.

If
The if part of the equivalence given in Claim A states that for all $w \in \Sigma_{I}^{*}$,

$$S_{f}s_{f}w \vdash S_{f}Ssw \quad [S_{f}s_{f} \vdash S_{f}Ss]$$
$$\vdash^{*} S_{f}q \quad [\rho]$$
$$\vdash^{*} q_{f} \quad [S_{f}q \vdash q_{f}]$$

in M_f implies

$$Ssw \vdash^{*} q \quad [\rho]$$

in $M_{\bar{e}}$, where $q \in Q$ and ρ consists of rules from R.
 Let $w \in \Sigma_{I}^{*}$, and

$$S_{f}s_{f}w \vdash S_{f}Ssw \quad [S_{f}s_{f} \vdash S_{f}Ss]$$
$$\vdash^{*} S_{f}q \quad [\rho]$$
$$\vdash^{*} q_{f} \quad [S_{f}q \vdash q_{f}]$$

in M_f, where $q \in Q$ and ρ consists of rules from R. As $R \subseteq R_f$,

Models for context-free languages

$$S_sw \vdash^* q \quad [\rho]$$

in M_ε, so the 'if' part of the equivalence holds as well.

Consequently, Claim A holds. □

Claim B
For all $w \in \Sigma_I^*$,

$$w \in L(M_f)_f$$

if and only if

$$S_fs_fw \vdash S_fSsw \quad [S_fs_f \vdash S_fSs]$$
$$\vdash^* S_fq \quad [\rho]$$
$$\vdash^* q_f \quad [S_fq \vdash q_f]$$

in M_f, where $q \in Q$ and ρ consists of rules from R.

Proof
An outline proof is given here; a detailed demonstration is left to the exercises.

Only if
The 'only if' part of the equivalence states that for all $w \in \Sigma_I^*$,

$$w \in L(M_f)_f$$

implies

$$S_fs_fw \vdash S_fSsw \quad [S_fs_f \vdash S_fSs]$$
$$\vdash^* S_fq \quad [\rho]$$
$$\vdash^* q_f \quad [S_fq \vdash q_f]$$

in M_f, where $q \in Q$ and ρ consists of rules from R.

Let $w \in L(M_\varepsilon)_\varepsilon$. Then, $S_fs_fw \vdash^* q_f$ in M_f. As $S_fs_f \vdash S_fSs$ is the only rule with S_fs_f on its left-hand side,

$$S_fs_fw \vdash S_fSsw \quad [S_fs_f \vdash S_fSs]$$
$$\vdash^* q_f$$

M_f enters q_f by using $S_f q \vdash q_f$ with $q \in Q$ and, after this entrance, M_f can make no other moves: M_f has no rule with q_f on its left-hand side. Furthermore, observe that before M_f uses $S_f q \vdash q_f$ during $S_f S_f w \vdash^* q_f$, S_f appears on the pushdown bottom. Therefore,

$$S_f S_f w \vdash S_f S s w \quad [S_f S_f \vdash S_f S s]$$
$$\vdash^* S_f q \quad [\rho]$$
$$\vdash^* q_f \quad [S_f q \vdash q_f]$$

in M_f, where $q \in Q$ and ρ consists of rules from R. Therefore, the 'only if' part of the equivalence in Claim B holds.

If
The 'if' part of the equivalence states that for all $w \in \Sigma^*_I$,

$$S_f S_f w \vdash S_f S s w \quad [S_f S_f \vdash S_f S s]$$
$$\vdash^* S_f q \quad [\rho]$$
$$\vdash^* q_f \quad [S_f q \vdash q_f]$$

in M_f, where $q \in Q$ and ρ consists of rules from R, implies

$$w \in L(M_f)_f$$

As

$$S_f S_f w \vdash^* q_f \quad [S_f q \vdash q_f]$$

in M_f, M_f accepts w by final state, so the if part of the equivalence holds as well. Consequently, Claim B holds. □

Observe that

$$w \in L(M_\varepsilon)_\varepsilon$$

if and only if $Ssw \vdash^* q$ in M_ε, for some $q \in Q$. From Claim A, for all $w \in \Sigma^*_I$,

$$Ssw \vdash^* q \quad [\rho]$$

in M_ε if and only if

Models for context-free languages

$$S_f s_f w \vdash S_f S s w \quad [S_f s_f \vdash S_f S s]$$
$$\vdash^* S_f q \quad [\rho]$$
$$\vdash^* q_f \quad [S_f q \vdash q_f]$$

in M_f, where $q \in Q$ and ρ consists of rules from R. From Claim B,

$$S_f s_f w \vdash S_f S s w \quad [S_f s_f \vdash S_f S s]$$
$$\vdash^* S_f q \quad [\rho]$$
$$\vdash^* q_f \quad [S_f q \vdash q_f]$$

in M_f if and only if

$$w \in L(M_f)_f$$

From these equivalences,

$$L(M_f)_f = L(M_\varepsilon)_\varepsilon$$

In summary, with M_ε as its input, Algorithm 5.2.1.3 halts and correctly constructs a pushdown automaton M_f, so $L(M_f)_f = L(M_\varepsilon)_\varepsilon$. Therefore, Lemma 5.2.1.4 holds. ∎

Corollary 5.2.1.5
Let L be a language. Then, $L = L(M_f)_f$ for a pushdown automaton, M_f, if and only if $L = L(M_\varepsilon)_\varepsilon$ for a pushdown automaton, M_ε.

Proof
This corollary follows from Algorithm 5.2.1.1, Lemma 5.2.1.2, Algorithm 5.2.1.3 and Lemma 5.2.1.4. ∎

The following definition combines the acceptance by final state and acceptance by empty pushdown.

Definition — language accepted by final state and empty pushdown
Let $M = (Q, \Sigma, R, s, F)$ be a pushdown automaton and $w \in \Sigma_I^*$. If $Ssw \vdash^* f$ in M, where $f \in F$, M accepts w by final state and empty pushdown. The language that M accepts by final state and empty pushdown, denoted by $L(M)_{fe}$, is defined as

$L(M)_{f\varepsilon} = \{w: w \in \Sigma_I^*,$ and M accepts w by final state and empty pushdown$\}$

That is,

$L(M)_{f\varepsilon} = = \{w: w \in \Sigma_I^*,$ and $Ssw \vdash^* f$ in M for some $f \in F\}$

♦

Example 5.2.1.1 Part 10 Language accepted by final state and empty pushdown

Return to the pushdown automaton M discussed throughout the previous parts of Example 5.2.1.1. Part 8 of this example proves that

$$L(M)_f = \{a^n b^n : n \geq 1\}$$

The previous part of this example has states that

$$L(M)_\varepsilon = \{a^n b^n : n \geq 1\}$$

The exercises demonstrate

$$L(M)_{f\varepsilon} = \{a^n b^n : n \geq 1\}$$

Consequently,

$$L(M)_{f\varepsilon} = L(M)_f = L(M)_\varepsilon = \{a^n b^n : n \geq 1\}$$

△

Theorem 5.2.1.6

Let L be a language. Then, $L = L(M_\varepsilon)_\varepsilon$ for a pushdown automaton M_ε, if and only if $L = L(M_{f\varepsilon})_{f\varepsilon}$ for a pushdown automaton $M_{f\varepsilon}$.

Proof
Only the basics are given here; a detailed verification of this theorem is left to the exercises.

Only if
The 'only if' part of the equivalence given in Theorem 5.2.1.6 states that for every pushdown automaton M_ε there exists a pushdown automaton $M_{f\varepsilon}$, so $L(M_\varepsilon)_\varepsilon = L(M_{f\varepsilon})_{f\varepsilon}$.

Consider a pushdown automaton M_ε. Return to Algorithm 5.2.1.3 and observe that with M_ε as its input, this algorithm produces its output automaton $M_{f\varepsilon}$ such that $L(M_\varepsilon)_\varepsilon = L(M_{f\varepsilon})_{f\varepsilon}$. Therefore, the 'only if' part of the equivalence given in Theorem 5.2.1.6 holds.

If
The 'if' part of the equivalence given in Theorem 5.2.1.6 states that for every pushdown automaton $M_{f\varepsilon}$ there exists a pushdown automaton M_ε such that $L(M_\varepsilon)_\varepsilon = L(M_{f\varepsilon})_{f\varepsilon}$.

Consider a pushdown automaton $M_{f\varepsilon}$. Modify Algorithm 5.2.1.3 by substituting F for Q in the for loop of this algorithm. Observe that with $M_{f\varepsilon}$ on its input, the modified algorithm produces its output automaton M_ε so $L(M_\varepsilon)_\varepsilon = L(M_{f\varepsilon})_{f\varepsilon}$. Therefore, the 'if' part of the equivalence given in Theorem 5.2.1.6 holds, too.

Consequently, Theorem 5.2.1.6 holds. ∎

This section has discussed three types of acceptance:

1. by final state;
2. by empty pushdown;
3. by final state and empty pushdown.

The next result concludes this discussion by stating the equivalence of these three types.

Corollary 5.2.1.7
Let L be a language:

1. $L = L(M_f)_f$ for a pushdown automaton M_f if and only if $L = L(M_\varepsilon)_\varepsilon$ for a pushdown automaton M_ε.
2. $L = L(M_\varepsilon)_\varepsilon$ for a pushdown automaton M_ε if and only if $L = L(M_{f\varepsilon})_{f\varepsilon}$ for a pushdown automaton $M_{f\varepsilon}$.
3. $L = L(M_{f\varepsilon})_{f\varepsilon}$ for a pushdown automaton $M_{f\varepsilon}$ if and only if $L = L(M_f)_f$ for a pushdown automaton M_f.

Proof
Corollary 5.2.1.5 establishes the first equivalence. Theorem 5.2.1.6 has demonstrated the second equivalence. The third equivalence follows from the previous two equivalences. ∎

Nondeterminism

This section closes its discussion concerning pushdown automata by pointing out that in general, these automata work *nondeterministically*.

Example 5.2.1.1 Part 11 Nondeterministic pushdown automaton

Return to the pushdown automaton M defined in the first part of this example. Part 8 of Example 5.2.1.1 proves that $L(M) = \{a^n b^n : n \geq 1\}$, so $\varepsilon \notin L(M)$. To accept ε, extend M by adding a new rule of the form $Ss \vdash f$. This extension gives rise to a new pushdown automaton M' satisfying

$$L(M') = \{a^n b^n : n \geq 0\}$$

(see Figure 5.2.1.9).

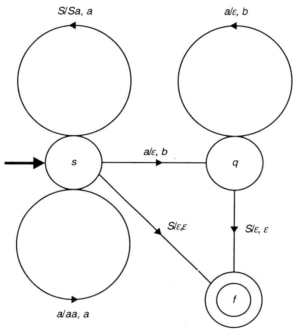

Figure 5.2.1.9 Pushdown automaton M' such that $L(M') = \{a^n b^n : n \geq 0\}$.

Although M' resembles M very much, there exists an essential difference between them: M works deterministically whereas M' does not. Indeed, M makes unique moves from any configuration. However, M' can carry out two different moves from a configuration. Specifically, assume that M' is in its start state s with the start symbol S on the pushdown top; furthermore, suppose that the current input symbol is a. From this configuration, M' can make two different moves:

1. M' uses $Ss \vdash f$, so it pops S and enter f_ε without reading a.
2. M' uses $Ssa \vdash Sas$, so it remains in s and moves the input symbol a onto the pushdown.

Consequently, M' works nondeterministically.

▲

Deterministic pushdown automata make a unique move sequence with any input, and this property makes them easy to use in practice. Sections 5.2.3, 5.3.1.2 and 7.1 study these automata and their applications in detail.

5.2.2 Extension

The previous section introduces the basic model of a pushdown automaton, which rewrites the top pushdown symbol during a move. The present section extends this model by permitting a pushdown automaton to rewrite a word, consisting of several symbols, on the pushdown top in a move (see Figure 5.2.2.1). This extension fulfils a crucial role in the investigation of pushdown automata and their applications. Theoretically, it simplifies the achievement of some results concerning pushdown automata, as frequently demonstrated later in this book. Practically, extended pushdown automata underlie bottom-up parsing (see Section 5.3.1.1).

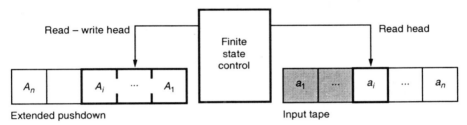

Figure 5.2.2.1 Extended pushdown automaton.

Definition — extended pushdown automaton
An *extended pushdown automaton* is a quintuple

$$M = (Q, \Sigma, R, s, F)$$

where

Q is a finite set of *states*;
Σ is an alphabet such that $\Sigma \cap Q = \Delta$ and $\Sigma = \Sigma_I \cup \Sigma_{PD}$, where Σ_I is an *input alphabet*, and Σ_{PD} is a *pushdown alphabet* containing S, the *start symbol*;
$R \subseteq \Sigma_{PD}^* Q(\Sigma_I \cup \{\varepsilon\}) \times \Sigma_{PD}^* Q$ is a finite relation;
$s \in Q$ is the *start state*;
$F \subseteq Q$ is a set of *final states*. ◆

By analogy with a pushdown automaton, this book refers to R's members as *rules*; accordingly, it calls R the *set of rules* in M. Furthermore, it writes

$$vpa \vdash wq$$

instead of $(vpa, wq) \in R$, where $v, w \in \Sigma_{PD}^*$, $p, q \in Q$, and $a \in \Sigma_I \cup \{\varepsilon\}$

The previous section commenced by introducing several conventions concerning the specification of pushdown automata. The present section specifies extended pushdown automata under these conventions as well.

Let M be an extended pushdown automaton. Define a configuration of M by analogy with the definition of a configuration of a pushdown automaton. In the same way, introduce $\vdash$, $\vdash n$, $\vdash^+$ and $\vdash^*$ for M. The language accepted by M, $L(M)$, is defined as

$$L(M) = \{w: w \in \Sigma_I^*, \text{ and } Ssw \vdash^* zf \text{ in } M \text{ for some } z \in \Sigma_{PD}^* \text{ and } f \in F\}$$

Notice that this definition is also analogous to the definition of the language accepted by a pushdown automaton, as presented in Section 5.2.

Example 5.2.2.1 Part 1 Extended pushdown automaton

Consider the following extended pushdown automaton M:

1: $sa \vdash as$
2: $sb \vdash bs$
3: $s \vdash Cs$
4: $aCsa \vdash Cs$
5: $bCsb \vdash Cs$
6: $SCs \vdash f$

Consider *Sasbba* as a configuration of M. According to rule 2, M computes

$$Sasbba \vdash Sabsba \quad [2]$$

M accepts *abba* as follows

$$\begin{aligned} Ssabba &\vdash Sasbba & [1] \\ &\vdash Sabsba & [2] \\ &\vdash SabCsba & [3] \\ &\vdash SaCsa & [5] \\ &\vdash SCs & [4] \\ &\vdash f & [6] \end{aligned}$$

△

Graphically, this section represents an extended pushdown automaton $M = (Q, \Sigma, R, s, F)$ by its *extended pushdown state diagram*, defined by analogy to a pushdown state diagram. Specifically, the extended pushdown state diagram of M represents a rule, $vpa \vdash wq \in R$, as depicted in Figure 5.2.2.2.

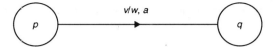

Figure 5.2.2.2 The graphical specification of $vpa \vdash wq$.

Example 5.2.2.1 Part 2 Extended pushdown state diagram

Figure 5.2.2.3 depicts the extended pushdown state diagram corresponding to M, examined in the previous part of this example.

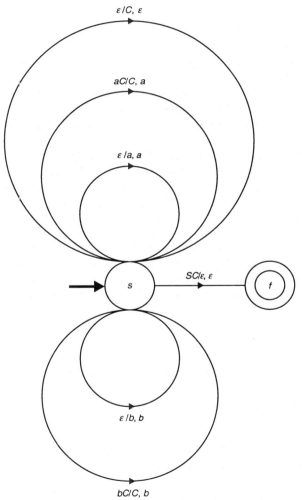

Figure 5.2.2.3 The extended pushdown state diagram of M.

△

Extended pushdown state diagrams simplify the presentation of various results concerning extended pushdown automata. The following part of Example 5.2.2.1 illustrates this use by referring to the extended pushdown diagram given in Figure 5.2.2.3.

Example 5.2.2.1 Part 3 Determination of the accepted language

This part determines $L(M)$, where M is the extended pushdown automaton discussed in Part 1. Consider a word $w \in \{a, b\}^*$. From the extended pushdown state diagram of M (see Figure 5.2.2.3), M works with w by performing these three computational phases:

1. M pushes down a prefix of w.
2. M places C on the pushdown top.
3. M pops up symbols from the pushdown against the same input symbols.

If in this way M empties its pushdown and reads all w, M enters f and accepts w; otherwise, M rejects w. Notice that S always appears on the pushdown bottom. In addition, observe that before M reads all symbols of w, this automation remains in the same state, s.

To explain these three computational phases in greater detail, observe how M uses its rules when performing of moves on w. M performs the first phase according to rules 1: $sa \vdash as$ and 2: $sb \vdash bs$, in which M stores a prefix of the input word, $w \in \{a, b\}^*$, onto the pushdown. To perform the second phase, M uses 3: $s \vdash Cs$ to place C, which acts as a center marker, on the pushdown top. Finally, M executes the third phase by applying rules 4 and 5 until S appears on the pushdown top. More precisely, by using 4: $aCsa \vdash Cs$, M replaces aC with C on the pushdown top and, simultaneously, reads a; analogously, by using rule 5: $bCsb \vdash Cs$, M replaces bC with C on the pushdown top and reads b. If $w \in L(M)$, M completes reading w with its pushdown containing only SC; at this point, M uses $SCs \vdash f$ and empties the pushdown, enters f, and accepts w.

Therefore, by the way M works with w, M accepts w if and only if w consists of a word v followed by reversal(v). Thus,

$$L(M) = \{v\text{reversal}(v): v \in \{a, b\}^*\}$$

The exercises reconsider this determination in greater detail.

△

Given an extended pushdown automaton M_{ext}, the following algorithm constructs a pushdown automaton M such that $L(M_{ext}) = L(M)$.

Algorithm 5.2.2.1: Conversion of an extended pushdown automaton to an equivalent pushdown automaton

Input: An extended pushdown automaton $M_{ext} = (Q_{ext}, \Sigma_{ext}, R_{ext}, s_{ext}, F_{ext})$.

Output: A pushdown automaton $M = (Q, \Sigma, R, s, F)$, such that $L(M_{ext}) = L(M)$.

Method

begin
    let m denote the greatest integer in $\{|v|: vpa \vdash wq \in R_{ext}\}$;
    $Q := \{\langle xq \rangle: x \in \Sigma^*_{PD_{ext}}, |x| \leq m, q \in Q_{ext}\}$;
    $\Sigma_{PD} := \Sigma^*_{PD_{ext}} \cup \{S\}$ {S is the start pushdown symbol of M};
    $\Sigma := \Sigma_{PD} \cup \Sigma^*_{I_{ext}}$;
    $s = \langle S^{m-1} S_{ext} s_{ext} \rangle$ {S_{ext} is the start pushdown symbol of M_{ext}};
    $F := \{\langle xq \rangle: q \in F_{ext}, \langle xq \rangle \in Q\}$;

    for each $vpa \vdash wq \in R_{ext}$ **do**
      if $|w| \geq |v|$
      then
        $R := R \cup \{A\langle xvp \rangle a \vdash Aw''\langle w'q \rangle: A \in \Sigma_{PD}, x \in \Sigma^*_{PD},$
          $|x| = m - |v|, w''w' = xw, |w'| = m\}$
      else
        $R := R \cup \{A\langle xvp \rangle a \vdash \langle Axwq \rangle: A \in \Sigma_{PD}, x \in \Sigma^*_{PD}, |x| = m - |v|\}$
          $\cup \{A\langle xwq \rangle \vdash \langle Axwq \rangle: A \in \Sigma_{PD}, x \in \Sigma^+_{PD}, |x| < |v| - |w|\}$;
    produce $M = (Q, \Sigma, R, s, F)$
end.

Algorithm 5.2.2.1 produces M that simulates M_{ext} by storing the top m symbols appearing on the pushdown of M_{ext} in M's states. Consider the move that M_{ext} makes according to $vpa \vdash wq$; during this move M_{ext} replaces the word v with w on its pushdown. M simulates this move by substituting wq for vp, which represents a suffix of the word stored in M's current state. Observe, however, that either $|v| \leq |w|$ or $|v| > |w|$; as a result, M performs this substitution of wq for vp in two different ways:

1. If $|v| \leq |w|$, then M substitutes wq for vp and, simultaneously, transfers $|w| - |v|$ symbols from its current state to M's pushdown. Denoting the $|w| - |v|$ transferred symbols by z, Figure 5.2.2.4 schematically depicts this move.

2. If $|v| > |w|$, then M substitutes wq for vp, pops the pushdown top symbol A and places A into the current state. Then, M executes $(|v| - |w| - 1)$ bookkeeping moves, during which M transfers the $(|v| - |w| - 1)$ top symbols from the pushdown into the state, which then contains the top m symbols appearing on the pushdown of M_{ext}. Denoting the $(|v| - |w| - 1)$ transferred symbols by z, Figure 5.2.2.5 depicts this move.

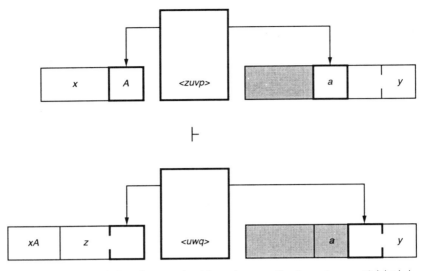

Figure 5.2.2.4 M's simulation of a move that M_{ext} makes according to $vpa \vdash wq$ with $|v| \le |w|$.

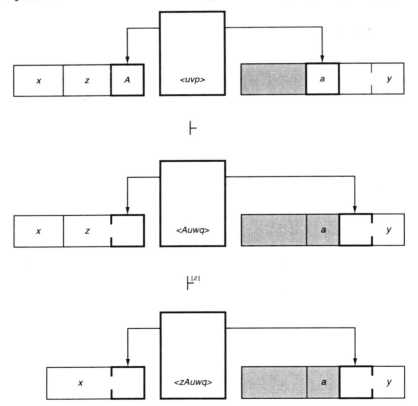

Figure 5.2.2.5 M's simulation of the move that M_{ext} makes according to $vpa \vdash wq$ with $|v| > |w|$.

Lemma 5.2.2.2

Let $M_{\text{ext}} = (Q_{\text{ext}}, \Sigma_{\text{ext}}, R_{\text{ext}}, s_{\text{ext}}, F_{\text{ext}})$ be an extended pushdown automaton. With M_{ext} as its input, Algorithm 5.2.2.1 halts and correctly produces a pushdown automaton $M = (Q, \Sigma, R, s, F)$, such that $L(M_{\text{ext}}) = L(M)$.

Proof

Termination

As R_{ext} is finite, Algorithm 5.2.2.1 repeats its **for** loop a finite number of times, so this algorithm surely terminates.

Correctness

To establish

$$L(M_{\text{ext}}) = L(M),$$

the present proof next demonstrates that

$$M_{\text{ext}} \text{ accepts a word } w \text{ if and only if } M \text{ accepts } w$$

To clarify this demonstration, break R into three subsets, defined as follows:

1. R_{longer} — contains the rules that Algorithm 5.2.2.1 introduces in the **then** part of its **if** statement.

2. $R_{\text{fill-up}}$ — contains the rules that Algorithm 5.2.2.1 introduces in the **else** part of its **if** statement, that fill up the state with symbols transferred from the pushdown.

3. R_{shorter} — contains the rules that Algorithm 5.2.2.1 introduces in the **else** part of its **if** statement and that do not belong to $R_{\text{fill-up}}$.

The following algorithm expresses this division of R into R_{longer}, R_{shorter}, and $R_{\text{fill-up}}$ in greater detail.

$R_{\text{longer}} := \emptyset;$
$R_{\text{shorter}} := \emptyset;$
$R_{\text{fill-up}} := \emptyset;$
for each $vpa \vdash wq \in R_{\text{ext}}$ **do**
  if $|w| \geq |v|$
  then
    $R_{\text{longer}} := R_{\text{longer}} \cup \{A\langle xvp\rangle a \vdash Aw''\langle w'q\rangle : A \in \Sigma_{\text{PD}},$
        $x \in \Sigma_{\text{PD}}^*, |x| = m - |v|, w''w' = xw, |w'| = m\}$
  else
    begin
      $R_{\text{shorter}} := R_{\text{shorter}} \cup \{A\langle xvp\rangle a \vdash \langle Axwq\rangle : A \in \Sigma_{\text{PD}}, x \in \Sigma_{\text{PD}}^*, |x| = m - |v|\};$
      $R_{\text{fill-up}} := R_{\text{fill-up}} \cup \{A\langle xwq\rangle \vdash \langle Axwq\rangle : A \in \Sigma_{\text{PD}}, x \in \Sigma_{\text{PD}}^*, |x| < |v| - |w|\}$
    end

Observe that

$$R = R_{\text{longer}} \cup R_{\text{shorter}} \cup R_{\text{fill-up}}$$

which implies

$$R_{\text{shorter}} \cup R_{\text{fill-up}} = R - R_{\text{longer}}$$

This proof next establishes Claims A through C, which refer to R_{longer}, R_{shorter} and $R_{\text{fill-up}}$.

Claim A
Let

$$\hat{y}\,\text{lhs}(r)z'' \vdash \hat{y}\,\text{rhs}(r)z''\ [r]$$

in M_{ext}, where $r: vpa \vdash wq \in R_{\text{ext}}$ such that $|v| \le |w|$, and let $y'', y' \in \Sigma_{\text{PD}}^+$ such that $\hat{y}\,v \in \text{suffix}(y''y')$ and $|y'| = m$. Then,

$$y''\langle y'p\rangle az'' \vdash u''\langle u'q\rangle z''\ [r']$$

in M where $r': A\langle xvp\rangle a \vdash Aw''\langle w'q\rangle \in R_{\text{longer}}$, $A \in \text{suffix}(y'')$, $y' = xv$, $|u'| = m$, $u'' = y''w''$, $u' = w'$, and $u''u' = y''xw$.

Proof
Let

$$\hat{y}\,\text{lhs}(r)z'' \vdash \hat{y}\,\text{rhs}(r)z''\ [r]$$

in M_{ext} where $r: vpa \vdash wq \in R_{\text{ext}}$, $|v| \le |w|$, and $y'', y' \in \Sigma_{\text{PD}}^+$ such that $\hat{y}\,v \in \text{suffix}(y''y')$ and $|y'| = m$. Then, for all $A \in \Sigma_{\text{PD}}$,

$$r': A\langle xvp\rangle a \vdash Aw''\langle w'q\rangle \in R_{\text{longer}}$$

where $xv = y'$ and $w''w' = xw$. Set $u' = w'$ and $u'' = y''w''$ to obtain

$$y''\langle y'p\rangle az'' \vdash u''\langle u'q\rangle z''\ [r']$$

in M, where $r': A\langle xvp\rangle a \vdash Aw''\langle w'q\rangle \in R_{\text{longer}}$, $A \in \text{suffix}(y'')$, $y' = xv$, $|u'| = m$, $u'' = y''w''$, $u' = w'$, and $u''u' = y''xw$. Thus, Claim A holds.

$\square$

Claim B
Let

$$\hat{y}\,\text{lhs}(r)z'' \vdash \hat{y}\,\text{rhs}(r)z''\ [r]$$

in M_{ext}, where $r\colon vpa \vdash wq \in R_{\text{ext}}$ such that $|v| > |w|$, and let $y'', y' \in \Sigma_{\text{PD}}^+$ such that $\hat{y}v \in \text{suffix}(y''y')$, $|y'| = m$, and $y'' = u''A_1\ldots A_{|v|-|w|}$. Then,

$$y''\langle y'p \rangle az'' \vdash^* u''\langle u'q \rangle z''\ [\rho]$$

in M, where $y' = xv$, $|u'| = m$, $u' = A_1\ldots A_{|v|-|w|}xw$, $u''u' = y''xw$, and $\rho = r_{|v|-|w|}r_{|v|-|w|-1}\ldots r_1$, where

$$r_{|v|-|w|}\colon A_{|v|-|w|}\langle xvp \rangle a \vdash \langle A_{|v|-|w|}xwq \rangle \in R_{\text{shorter}}$$

$$r_{|v|-|w|-1}\colon A_{|v|-|w|-1}\langle A_{|v|-|w|}xwq \rangle \vdash \langle A_{|v|-|w|-1}A_{|v|-|w|}xwq \rangle \in R_{\text{fill-up}}$$

$$\vdots$$

$$r_1\colon A_1\langle\ldots A_{|v|-|w|}xwq \rangle \vdash \langle A_1\ldots A_{|v|-|w|}xwq \rangle \in R_{\text{fill-up}}$$

Proof
Let

$$\hat{y}\,\text{lhs}(r)z'' \vdash \hat{y}\,\text{rhs}(r)z''\ [r\colon vpa \vdash wq]$$

in M_{ext} where $|v| > |w|$. In addition, suppose that $y'', y' \in \Sigma_{\text{PD}}^+$ such that $\hat{y}v \in \text{suffix}(y''y')$, $|y'| = m$, and $y'' = u''A_1\ldots A_{|v|-|w|}$. Then,

$$A_{|v|-|w|}\langle xvp \rangle a \vdash \langle A_{|v|-|w|}xwq \rangle \in R_{\text{shorter}}$$

and

$$\{\,A_i\langle xwq \rangle \vdash \langle A_i xwq \rangle \colon 1 \leq i < |v|-|w|\,\} \subseteq R_{\text{fill-up}}$$

Hence,

$$u''A_1\ldots A_{|v|-|w|-1}A_{|v|-|w|}\langle xvp \rangle az \vdash u''A_1\ldots A_{|v|-|w|-1}\langle A_{|v|-|w|}xwq \rangle z \quad [r_{|v|-|w|}]$$

$$\vdash u''A_1\ldots \langle A_{|v|-|w|-1}A_{|v|-|w|}xwq \rangle z \quad [r_{|v|-|w|-1}]$$

$$\vdots$$

$$\vdash u''\langle A_1\ldots A_{|v|-|w|-1}A_{|v|-|w|}xwq \rangle z \quad [r_1]$$

where

$$r_{|v|-|w|} : A_{|v|-|w|}\langle xvp\rangle a \vdash \langle A_{|v|-|w|}xwq\rangle \in R_{\text{shorter}}$$

$$r_{|v|-|w|-1} : A_{|v|-|w|-1}\langle A_{|v|-|w|}xwq\rangle \vdash \langle A_{|v|-|w|-1}A_{|v|-|w|}xwq\rangle \in R_{\text{fill-up}}$$

$$\vdots$$

$$r_1 : A_1\langle \ldots A_{|v|-|w|}xwq\rangle \vdash \langle A_1\ldots A_{|v|-|w|}xwq\rangle \in R_{\text{fill-up}}$$

Therefore,

$$y''\langle y'p\rangle az'' \vdash^* u''\langle u'q\rangle z'' \; [\rho]$$

in M, where $y' = xv$, $|u'| = m$, $u' = A_1\ldots A_{|v|-|w|}xw$, $u''u' = y''xw$, and $\rho = r_{|v|-|w|}r_{|v|-|w|-1}\ldots r_1$, where

$$r_{|v|-|w|} : A_{|v|-|w|}\langle xvp\rangle a \vdash \langle A_{|v|-|w|}xwq\rangle \in R_{\text{shorter}}$$

$$r_{|v|-|w|-1} : A_{|v|-|w|-1}\langle A_{|v|-|w|}xwq\rangle \vdash \langle A_{|v|-|w|-1}A_{|v|-|w|}xwq\rangle \in R_{\text{fill-up}}$$

$$\vdots$$

$$r_1 : A_1\langle \ldots A_{|v|-|w|}xwq\rangle \vdash \langle A_1\ldots A_{|v|-|w|}xwq\rangle \in R_{\text{fill-up}}$$

and, thus, Claim B holds.

Claim C
The following equivalence holds:

$$S_{\text{ext}}s_{\text{ext}}z'z'' \vdash^* uqz'' \; [\rho_{\text{ext}}]$$

in M_{ext}, where ρ_{ext} represents a rule word in M_{ext},

if and only if

$$S\langle S^{m-1}S_{\text{ext}}s\rangle z'z'' \vdash^* u''\langle u'q\rangle z'' \; [\rho]$$

in M, where ρ represents a rule word in M, $|u'| = m$, and $S^m u = u''u'$.

Proof
Only if
The 'only if' part of the equivalence is proved by induction on the number of rules appearing in ρ_{ext}.

Basis
Let $\rho_{\text{ext}} = \varepsilon$, so

$$S_{\text{ext}}s_{\text{ext}}z'z'' \vdash^* S_{\text{ext}}s_{\text{ext}}z'' \; [\varepsilon]$$

in M_{ext}. Hence, $z' = e$. Observe that

$$S\langle S^{m-1}S_{ext}S_{ext}\rangle z'' \vdash^* S\langle S^{m-1}S_{ext}S_{ext}\rangle z'' \ [\varepsilon]$$

in M, and this computation satisfied the required form.

Induction hypothesis

Assume that the claim holds for all rule words consisting of no more than n rules, for some $n \geq 0$.

Induction step
Consider

$$S_{ext}S_{ext}z'z'' \vdash^* uqz'' \ [\rho_{ext}r]$$

in M_{ext}, where ρ_{ext} is a rule word consisting of n rules, and $r: vpa \vdash wq \in R_{ext}$. Express $S_{ext}S_{ext}z'z'' \vdash^* uqz'' \ [\rho_{ext}r]$ as

$$S_{ext}S_{ext}z \vdash^* \chi \quad [\rho_{ext}]$$
$$\vdash uqz'' \quad [r]$$

where χ is a configuration χ of M_{ext} such that $\chi = ypaz'' = \hat{y}\,\text{lhs}(r)z''$, $uqz'' = \hat{y}\,\text{rhs}(r)z''$, so $y = \hat{y}v$ and $u = \hat{y}w$. By the induction hypothesis,

$$S\langle S^{m-1}S_{ext}s\rangle z'z'' \vdash^* y''\langle y'p\rangle az'' \ [\rho]$$

in M, where ρ represents a rule word in M, $|y'| = m$, and $S^m y = S^m \hat{y} v = y''y'$. Next, the present proof distinguishes two cases, $|w| \geq |v|$ and $|w| < |v|$.

1. Let $|w| \geq |v|$. From Claim A,

$$y''\langle y'p\rangle az'' \vdash u''\langle u'q\rangle z'' \ [r']$$

in M, where $r': A\langle xvp\rangle a \vdash Aw''\langle w'q\rangle \in R_{longer}$, $A \in \text{suffix}(y'')$, $y' = xv$, $|u'| = m$, $u'' = y''w''$, $u' = w'$, and $u''u' = y''xw$. As $S^m \hat{y} v = y''y' = y''xv$, $S^m \hat{y}$ equals $y''x$. Thus, $u''u' = y''xw = S\hat{y}w$. Hence,

$$S\langle S^{m-1}S_{ext}s\rangle z'z'' \vdash^* u''\langle u'q\rangle z'' \ [\rho'r']$$

where $S^m u = S^m w = u''u'$, and $\rho'r'$ is a rule word in M. In other words, for the case when $|w| \geq |v|$, the induction step is completed.
2. Let $|w| < |v|$. As $S^m \hat{y} v = y''y'$ and $|y'| = m$, $|y''| \geq |v| - |w|$. Express y'' as $y'' = u''A_1...A_{|v|-|w|}$. From Claim B,

$$y''\langle y'p\rangle az'' \vdash u''\langle u'q\rangle z'' \ [\rho]$$

in M where $y' = xv$, $|u'| = m$, $u' = A_1...A_{|v|-|w|}xw$, $u''u' = y''xw$, ρ represents a rule word such that the first rule in ρ belongs to R_{shorter} and the other rules belong to $R_{\text{fill-up}}$. As $S^m\hat{y}v = y''y' = u''A_1...A_{|v|-|w|}xv$, $S^m\hat{y} = u''A_1...A_{|v|-|w|}x$, so $S^m\hat{y}w = u''A_1...A_{|v|-|w|}xw = u''u'$. Consequently,

$$S\langle S^{m-1}S_{\text{ext}}s\rangle z'z'' \vdash^* u''\langle u'q\rangle z'' \ [\rho'\rho]$$

where $S^mu = S^m\hat{y}w = u''u'$, and $\rho'\rho$ is a rule word in M. That is, for the case when $|w| < |v|$, the induction step is completed, too.

Therefore, the 'only if' part of the equivalence, given in Claim C, holds.

If
The 'only if' part of the equivalence, stated in Claim C, is proved by induction on the number of rules appearing in ρ.

Basis
Let $\rho = \varepsilon$; that is,

$$S\langle S^{m-1}S_{\text{ext}}s\rangle z'z'' \vdash^* u''\langle u'q\rangle z'' \ [\varepsilon]$$

in M, where $u''u' = S^mu$ and $|u'| = m$. Thus, $z' = \varepsilon$, $u'' = S$, and $u' = S^{m-1}S_{\text{ext}}$. As $SS^{m-1}S_{\text{ext}} = S^mu$, $u = S_{\text{ext}}$. Observe that

$$S_{\text{ext}}s_{\text{ext}}z'' \vdash^* S_{\text{ext}}s_{\text{ext}}z'' \ [\rho_{\text{ext}}]$$

in M_{ext}, where $\varepsilon = \rho_{\text{ext}}$. Because this computation satisfied the required form, the basis holds.

Induction hypothesis
Assume that the claim holds for all rule words consisting of no more than n rules, for some $n \geq 0$.

Induction step
Consider

$$S\langle S^{m-1}S_{\text{ext}}s\rangle z'z'' \vdash^* u''\langle u'q\rangle z'' \ [\rho]$$

in M, where $|u'| = m$, and ρ is a rule word consisting of $n + 1$ rules. Express this computation as

$$S\langle S^{m-1}S_{\text{ext}}s\rangle z'z'' \vdash^* y''\langle y'p\rangle az'' \quad [\rho']$$
$$\vdash^+ u''\langle u'q\rangle z'' \quad [\rho'']$$

where $|y'| = m$, $S^m y = y''y'$, $a \in \{\varepsilon\} \cup \Sigma_I$ and, in addition, between $y''\langle y'p \rangle az''$ and $u''\langle u'q \rangle z''$, every configuration, $x''\langle x'q' \rangle az''$, satisfies $|x'| < m$. In other words, if

$$y''\langle y'p \rangle az'' \vdash^+ x''\langle x'q' \rangle bz'' \quad [\rho_1]$$
$$\vdash^+ u''\langle u'q \rangle z'' \quad [\rho_2]$$

where $\rho'' = \rho_1 \rho_2$, $b \in \{\varepsilon, a\}$, then $|x'| < m$. As ρ' is a rule word consisting of no more than n rules, the induction hypothesis implies

$$S_{ext}S_{ext}z \vdash^* ypaz'' \quad [\rho_{ext}]$$

in M_{ext}, where $S^m y = y''y'$ and ρ_{ext} is a rule word in M_{ext}. Recall that $|y'| = m$. Thus, by the definition of $R_{fill-up}$, ρ'' does not begin with a rule from $R_{fill-up}$, so ρ'' starts with a rule r'' such that $r'' \in R_{longer} \cup R_{shorter}$. Let $lhs(r'') = A\langle xvp \rangle a$ and $y' = xv$. Because S does not appear in v and $S^m y = y''y'$, y equals $\hat{y}v$ and $S^m \hat{y}$ equals $y''x$. This distinguishes two cases, $r'' \in R_{longer}$ and $r'' \in R_{shorter}$.

1. Let $r'' \in R_{longer}$. By examination of the rules in R_{longer}, r'' has the form r'': $A\langle xvp \rangle a \vdash Aw''\langle w'q \rangle$, for some $A \in \Sigma_{PD}$, $x \in \Sigma_{PD}^*$, and r: $vpa \vdash wq \in R_{ext}$ so $w''w' = xw$ and $|w'| = m$. Furthermore, $|w'| = m$ implies $|\rho''| = 1$, so $\rho'' = r''$. Set $u'' = y''w''$ and $u' = w'$. By using r, M_{ext} make the move

$$\hat{y} lhs(r)z'' \vdash \hat{y} rhs(r)z'' \quad [r]$$

where $\hat{y} rhs(r) = \hat{y} wq$. Set $u = \hat{y}w$. Observe that

$$S_{ext}S_{ext}z'z'' \vdash^* uqz'' \quad [\rho_{ext}r]$$

in M_{ext}, where $S^m u = S^m \hat{y}w = y''xw = y''w''w' = u''u'$. In other words, for the case when $r'' \in R_{longer}$, the induction step is completed.

2. Let $r'' \in R_{shorter}$. Examine the rules in R_{longer} to see that r'' has the form r'': $A\langle xvp \rangle a \vdash \langle Axwq \rangle$, for some $A \in \Sigma_{PD}$, and r: $vpa \vdash wq \in R_{ext}$ with $|v| > |w|$. After applying r'', M uses rules of $R_{fill-up}$ $|v|-|w|-1$ times to obtain u' such that $|u'| = m$. Because $m = |y'|$, $y'' = x''A_1...A_{|v|-|w|}$, for some $x'' \in \Sigma_{PD}^*$ and $A_1,...,A_{|v|-|w|} \in \Sigma_{PD}$ such that $A = A_{|v|-|w|}$, $A_1...A_{|v|-|w|-1}A_{|v|-|w|}xw$ equals u' and x'' equals u''; in addition, $\rho'' = r''r_{|v|-|w|-1}...r_1$, and

$$r_{|v|-|w|} : A_{|v|-|w|}\langle xvp \rangle a \vdash \langle A_{|v|-|w|}xwq \rangle,$$
$$r_{|v|-|w|-1} : A_{|v|-|w|-1}\langle A_{|v|-|w|}xwq \rangle \vdash \langle A_{|v|-|w|-1}A_{|v|-|w|}xwq \rangle,$$
$$\vdots$$
$$r_1 : A_1\langle ...A_{|v|-|w|}xwq \rangle \vdash \langle A_1...A_{|v|-|w|}xwq \rangle,$$

where $r_j \in R_{fill-up}$ for $j = |v|-|w|-1, ..., 1$. Then,

$$\hat{y}\,\text{lhs}(r)z'' \vdash \hat{y}\,\text{rhs}(r)z''\ [r'']$$

in M_{ext}, where $\hat{y}\,\text{rhs}(r) = \hat{y}\,wq$. Set $u = \hat{y}\,w$ and observe that

$$S_{\text{ext}}s_{\text{ext}}z'z'' \vdash^{*} uqz''\ [\rho_{\text{ext}}r]$$

in M_{ext}, where $S^m u = S^m \hat{y} w = y''xw = x''A_1 \ldots A_{|v|-|w|} xw = u''u'$. That is, for the case when $r'' \in R_{\text{shorter}}$, the induction step is completed, too.

Therefore, the if part of the equivalence, given in Claim C, holds.

Thus, the proof of Claim C is true. □

Consider Claim C for $z'' = \varepsilon$ and $q \in F$ to obtain this equivalence:

$$S_{\text{ext}}s_{\text{ext}}z' \vdash^{*} uq \text{ in } M_{\text{ext}}$$

if and only if

$$S\langle S^{m-1}S_{\text{ext}}s\rangle z' \vdash^{*} u''\langle u'q\rangle \text{ in } M$$

where $|u'| = m$, and $S^m u = u''u'$. By the definition of F, $\langle u'q\rangle \in F$. Consequently,

$$z' \in L(M_{\text{ext}}) \text{ if and only if } z' \in L(M)$$

and, thus,

$$L(M_{\text{ext}}) = L(M)$$

In summary, with M_{ext} as its input, Algorithm 5.2.2.1 halts and correctly produces a pushdown automaton $M = (Q, \Sigma, R, s, F)$ such that $L(M_{\text{ext}}) = L(M)$. Thus, Lemma 5.2.2.2 holds. ■

Example 5.2.2.1 Part 4 Application of Algorithm 5.2.2.1

Return to the extended pushdown automaton discussed in Part 1 of Example 5.2.2.1. Recall that this automaton is defined by these six rules:

1: $sa \vdash as$
2: $sb \vdash bs$
3: $s \vdash Cs$
4: $aCas \vdash Cs$

5: $bCbs \vdash Cs$
6: $SCs \vdash f$

The exercises use Algorithm 5.2.2.1 to convert this extended pushdown automaton to an equivalent pushdown automaton. The present part of this example only illustrates how the output pushdown automaton, produced by Algorithm 5.2.2.1, simulates the input extended pushdown automaton. Specifically, consider the computation made by the input automaton with *abba* (see Part 1 of Example 5.2.2.1). The output automaton simulates this computation as follows

$$
\begin{aligned}
S'\langle S'S'Ss\rangle abba &\vdash S'S'\langle S'Sas\rangle bba & [S'\langle S'S'Ss\rangle a \vdash S'S'\langle S'Sas\rangle] \\
&\vdash S'S'S'\langle Sabs\rangle ba & [S'\langle S'Sas\rangle b \vdash S'S'\langle Sabs\rangle] \\
&\vdash S'S'S'S\langle abCs\rangle ba & [S'\langle Sabs\rangle \vdash S'S\langle abCs\rangle] \\
&\vdash S'S'S'Sa\langle bCbs\rangle a & [S\langle abCs\rangle b \vdash Sa\langle bCbs\rangle] \\
&\vdash S'S'S'S\langle aCs\rangle a & [a\langle bCbs\rangle a \vdash \langle aCs\rangle] \\
&\vdash S'S'S'\langle SaCs\rangle a & [S\langle aCs\rangle a \vdash \langle SaCs\rangle] \\
&\vdash S'S'S'S\langle aCas\rangle & [S'\langle SaCs\rangle a \vdash S'S\langle aCas\rangle] \\
&\vdash S'S'S'\langle SCs\rangle & [S\langle aCas\rangle \vdash \langle SCs\rangle] \\
&\vdash S'S'\langle S'SCs\rangle & [S'\langle SCs\rangle \vdash \langle S'SCs] \\
&\vdash S'\langle S'S'f\rangle & [\langle S'SCs\rangle \vdash \langle S'S'f\rangle]
\end{aligned}
$$

where S' and $\langle S'S'Ss\rangle$ denote the start symbol and the start state, respectively.

△

Theorem 5.2.2.3
Let L be a language. Then, $L = L(M)$ for a pushdown automaton M if and only if $L = L(M_{ext})$ for an extended pushdown automaton, M_{ext}.

Proof
Only if
Any pushdown automaton represents a special case of an extended pushdown automaton, so the 'only if' part of the theorem holds.

If
The 'if' part of the theorem follows from Algorithm 5.2.2.1 and Lemma 5.2.2.2.

Thus, Theorem 5.2.2.3 holds. ∎

Three types of acceptance

For a pushdown automaton M, the previous section has introduced three types of acceptance:

1. by final state;
2. by empty pushdown;
3. by final state and empty pushdown.

Accordingly, M defines these three languages:

A. The language accepted by final state, denoted by $L(M)_f$.
B. The language accepted by empty pushdown, denoted by $L(M)_\varepsilon$.
C. The language accepted by final state and empty pushdown, denoted by $L(M)_{f\varepsilon}$.

Analogously, introduce $L(M)_f$, $L(M)_\varepsilon$ and $L(M)_{f\varepsilon}$ for the case when M represents an extended pushdown automata.

Example 5.2.2.1 Part 5 Three types of acceptance
Reconsider the extended pushdown automaton M defined in Part 1 of Example 5.2.2.1. From the proof given in Part 2

$$L(M)_f = \{w\text{reversal}(w): w \in \{a, b\}^*\}$$

The exercises modify this proof to demonstrate that

$$L(M)_f = L(M)_\varepsilon = L(M)_{f\varepsilon} = \{w\text{reversal}(w): w \in \{a, b\}^*\}$$

△

The next task is to generalize Algorithm 5.2.1.1 so its input automaton represents an extended pushdown automaton M_f. Observe that the resulting algorithm, generalized in this way, produces an extended pushdown automaton M_ε such that $L(M_f)_f = L(M_\varepsilon)_\varepsilon$. Analogously, modify Algorithm 5.2.1.3 so its input automaton is an extended pushdown automaton M_ε. At this point, the modified algorithm produces an extended pushdown automaton M_f satisfying $L(M_f)_f = L(M_\varepsilon)_\varepsilon$. These observations imply the following theorem.

Theorem 5.2.2.4
Let L be a language. Then, $L = L(M_f)_f$ for an extended pushdown automaton M_f if and only if $L = L(M_\varepsilon)_\varepsilon$ for an extended pushdown automaton M_ε.

Proof
A detailed proof of this theorem is left to the exercises. ∎

From Theorem 5.2.1.6, for every language L, $L = L(M_\varepsilon)_\varepsilon$ for a pushdown automaton M_ε if and only if $L = L(M_{f\varepsilon})_{f\varepsilon}$ for a pushdown automaton $M_{f\varepsilon}$. The following theorem reformulates this statement in terms of extended pushdown automata.

Theorem 5.2.2.5
Let L be a language. Then $L = L(M_\varepsilon)_\varepsilon$ for an extended pushdown automaton M_ε if and only if $L = L(M_{f\varepsilon})_{f\varepsilon}$ for a extended pushdown automaton $M_{f\varepsilon}$.

Proof
This proof is left to the exercises.

■

Corollary 5.2.2.6
Let L be a language.

1. $L = L(M_f)_f$ for an extended pushdown automaton M_f if and only if $L = L(M_\varepsilon)_\varepsilon$ for an extended pushdown automaton M_ε.
2. $L = L(M_\varepsilon)_\varepsilon$ for an extended pushdown automaton M_ε if and only if $L = L(M_{f\varepsilon})_{f\varepsilon}$ for an extended pushdown automaton $M_{f\varepsilon}$.
3. $L = L(M_{f\varepsilon})_{f\varepsilon}$ for an extended pushdown automaton $M_{f\varepsilon}$ if and only if $L = L(M_f)_f$ for an extended pushdown automaton M_f.

Proof
Theorem 5.2.2.4 and Theorem 5.2.2.5 state the first equivalence and the second equivalence, respectively. These two equivalences imply the third equivalence.

■

Nondeterminism

The conclusion of this section demonstrates that, in general, extended pushdown automata work nondeterministically.

Example 5.2.2.1 Part 6 Nondeterministic extended pushdown automaton
Reconsider the extended pushdown automaton M discussed in the previous parts of this example (see Figure 5.2.2.3). Part 3 of Example 5.2.2.1 determines

$$L(M) = \{v\text{reversal}(v): v \in \{a, b\}^*\}$$

For a word $w \in \{a, b\}^*$, M works so that it performs these three computational phases:

1. M pushes down a prefix of w;
2. M places C onto the pushdown top;
3. M pops up symbols from the pushdown against the same input symbols.

Notice, however, that M can end the first phase and begin the second phase at any time. More precisely, M ends the first phase based on its guess that it has reached the middle of w. Consequently, M can make different moves from the same configuration, so M works nondeterministically. More generally and importantly, *all* extended pushdown automata that accept $\{vreversal(v): v \in \{a, b\}^*\}$ work nondeterministically because there exists no deterministic way of detecting the middle of w. Therefore, deterministic extended pushdown automata are less powerful than nondeterministic extended pushdown automata.

Next, consider

$$\{vcreversal(v): v \in \{a, b\}^*\}$$

where c is a new symbol, appearing in the middle of every word in this language. At a glance, this language resembles $\{vreversal(v): v \in \{a, b\}^*\}$. However, there exists an important difference between both languages: $\{vreversal(v): v \in \{a, b\}^*\}$ cannot be accepted deterministically, whereas $\{vcreversal(v): v \in \{a, b\}^*\}$ can. Indeed, a deterministic pushdown automaton M' can accept $\{vcreversal(v): v \in \{a, b\}^*\}$, so M' pushes down as and bs until c appears; then, M' pops the pushdown against the remaining suffix of the input word. To obtain M' from M, replace the third rule, 3: $s \vdash Cs$, with $sc \vdash Cs$ in the definition of M; Figure 5.2.2.6, displaying M', points out this replacement by underlining.

5.2.3 Determinism

The previous two sections have pointed out that in general, pushdown automata, including their extended versions, work nondeterministically — that is, these automata can make many different move sequences with the same input word. Because this property significantly complicates the use of these automata, practically oriented computer science concentrates on deterministic pushdown automata, which make a unique move sequence with any input word.

The present section investigates deterministic pushdown automata, which are less powerful than their nondeterministic versions (see Part 6 of Example 5.2.2.1). It compares the power of deterministic pushdown automata with other types of automata, such as finite automata. The three types of acceptance are reconsidered — acceptance by final state, acceptance by empty pushdown and acceptance by final state and empty pushdown — in terms of deterministic pushdown automata. Finally, implementation of deterministic pushdown automata is explained.

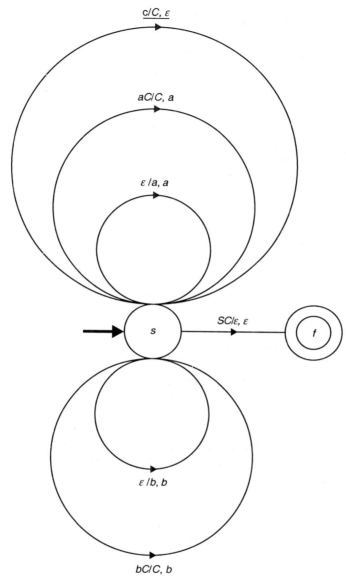

Figure 5.2.2.6 An extended pushdown automaton M' that accepts $\{v c \text{reversal}(v): v \in \{a, b\}^*\}$.

Deterministic extended pushdown automata

This section first explores deterministic extended pushdown automata. Then, it narrows attention to the determinism of ordinary pushdown automata.

Definition — deterministic extended pushdown automaton

Let $M = (Q, \Sigma, R, s, F)$ be an extended pushdown automaton. M is *deterministic* if each rule, $r \in R$, where $\mathrm{lhs}(r) = vpa$ with $a \in \Sigma_I \cup \{\varepsilon\}$, satisfies

$$\{r\} = \{r': r' \in R, vpa \in \mathrm{subword}(\mathrm{lhs}(r')) \text{ or } vp \in \mathrm{subword}(\mathrm{lhs}(r'))\}$$

♦

Equivalently, an extended pushdown automaton, $M = (Q, \Sigma, R, s, F)$, is deterministic if every rule, $r: vpa \vdash wq \in R$, satisfies

$$\{uvpb: u \in \Sigma_{PD}^* \text{ and } b \in \{a, \varepsilon\}\} \cap \{\mathrm{lhs}(r'): r' \in R - \{r\}\} = \Delta$$

This property guarantees that from any configuration M can make no more than one move. Consequently, for all $x \in \Sigma_I^*$, there exists a unique rule word ρ so $Ssw \vdash^* zq \,[\rho]$ in M, where $z \in \Sigma_{PD}^*$; less formally, with x, M makes a unique sequence of moves.

The previous section has investigated three types of acceptance (acceptance by final state, acceptance by empty pushdown and acceptance by final state and empty pushdown for extended pushdown automata). The present section reconsiders this investigation in terms of deterministic extended pushdown automata. Then, deterministic extended pushdown automata that accept by final state and empty pushdown are examined. The algorithm that follows returns to the notion of a deterministic finite automaton (see Section 3.2.3) and demonstrate how to convert any deterministic finite automaton M_f to a deterministic extended pushdown automaton M_{pd} so $L(M_f)_f = L(M_{pd})_{fe}$.

Algorithm 5.2.3.1: Conversion of a deterministic finite automaton to an equivalent deterministic extended pushdown automaton accepting by final state and empty pushdown

Input: A deterministic finite automaton $M_f = (Q, \Sigma, R, s, F)$.

Output: A deterministic extended pushdown automaton, $M_{pd} = (Q_{pd}, \Sigma_{pd}, R_{pd}, s_{pd}, F)$, such that $L(M_f)_f = L(M_{pd})_{fe}$.

Method

begin
$\quad Q_{pd} := Q \cup \{s_{pd}\}$ $\{s_{pd}$ is the start state of $M_{pd}\}$;
$\quad \Sigma_{I_{pd}} := \Sigma$;
$\quad \Sigma_{pd} := \{S_{pd}\} \cup \Sigma_{I_{pd}}$ $\{S_{pd}$ is the start symbol of $M_{pd}\}$;
$\quad R_{pd} := \{S_{pd} s_{pd} \vdash s\} \cup R$;
end.

Models for context-free languages

This algorithm produces the deterministic extended pushdown automaton M_{pd} so M_{pd} simulates the input deterministic finite automaton M_f move by move. During this simulation, M_{pd} keeps its pushdown empty. Because both automata have the same set of final states, $L(M_f)$ and $L(M_{pd})_{f\varepsilon}$ coincide.

Lemma 5.2.3.2

Let $M_f = (Q, \Sigma, R, s, F)$ be a deterministic finite automaton. With M_f on its input, Algorithm 5.2.3.1 halts and correctly constructs a deterministic extended pushdown automaton, $M_{pd} = (Q_{pd}, \Sigma_{pd}, R_{pd}, s_{pd}, F)$, such that $L(M_f)_f = L(M_{pd})_{f\varepsilon}$.

Proof

A detailed version of this proof is left to the exercises. The proof given here only outlines how to demonstrate that $L(M_f) = L(M_{pd})_{f\varepsilon}$ By using $S_{pd}s_{pd} \vdash s$, M_{pd} first removes S_{pd} from its pushdown. Then, keeping its pushdown empty, M_{pd} simulates M_f move by move. As M_f and M_{pd} have the same set of final states, F, M_f enters a final state, f, if and only if M_{pd} enters f, so $L(M_f) = L(M_{pd})_{f\varepsilon}$ Thus, with M_f as its input, Algorithm 5.2.3.1 halts and correctly constructs a deterministic extended pushdown automaton $M_{pd} = (Q_{pd}, \Sigma_{pd}, R_{pd}, s_{pd}, F)$ such that $L(M_f)_f = L(M_{pd})_{f\varepsilon}$. Thus, Lemma 5.2.3.2 holds. ∎

Theorem 5.2.3.3

The family of regular languages is properly contained in the family of languages accepted by deterministic extended pushdown automata by final state and empty pushdown.

Proof

From Theorem 3.3.3.2, deterministic finite automata characterize the family of regular languages. Thus, Algorithms 5.2.3.1 and Lemma 5.2.3.2 imply that the family of regular languages is contained in the family of languages accepted by deterministic extended pushdown automata by final state and empty pushdown.
Consider

$$L = \{a^n b^n : n \geq 1\}$$

Example 4.1.2 demonstrates that L is not regular. By analogy with Part 8 of Example 5.2.1.1, prove that L belongs to the family of languages accepted by deterministic extended pushdown automata by final state and empty pushdown. Therefore, L represents a nonregular language included in the family of languages accepted by deterministic extended pushdown automata by final state and empty pushdown.

Thus, the family of regular languages is properly contained in the family of languages accepted by deterministic extended pushdown automata by final state and empty pushdown. That is, Theorem 5.2.3.3 holds. ∎

From the third equivalence given in Corollary 5.2.2.6, for every language L, $L = L(M_{fe})_{fe}$ for an extended pushdown automaton M_{fe} if and only if $L = L(M_f)_f$ for a extended pushdown automaton M_f. Surprisingly, in terms of deterministic extended pushdown automata, this equivalence does not hold, as demonstrated next.

Lemma 5.2.3.4
There exists no deterministic extended pushdown automaton that accepts $\{a^n: n \geq 1\} \cup \{a^n b^n: n \geq 1\}$ by final state and empty pushdown.

Proof
This proof is made by contradiction. Consider

$$L = \{a^n: n \geq 1\} \cup \{a^n b^n: n \geq 1\}$$

and assume that there exists a deterministic extended pushdown automaton, $M = (Q, \Sigma, R, s, F)$, so $L(M)_{fe} = L$. Suppose that M has $a^m b^m$, for some $m > \text{card}(F)$, as its input. After reading any number of as in this word, M always empties its pushdown and enters a final state because M is deterministic and $\{a^n: n \geq 1\} \subseteq L(M)$. In addition, because $m > \text{card}(F)$, there exists a final state, $f \in F$, that M visits twice when reading as in $a^m b^m$. Let M read k as, where $k \geq 1$, between these two visits of f. Then, M also accepts $a^{m-k} b^m$; that is, $a^{m-k} b^m \in L(M)_{fe}$. However, because $L(M)_{fe} = L$ and $a^{m-k} b^m \notin L$, $a^{m-k} b^m \notin L(M)_{fe}$ — a contradiction. Therefore, there exists no deterministic extended pushdown automaton that accepts L by final state and empty pushdown. Thus, Lemma 5.2.3.4, whose detailed proof is left to the exercises, holds.
∎

Lemma 5.2.3.5
There exists a deterministic extended pushdown automata M such that $L(M)_f = \{a^n: n \geq 1\} \cup \{a^n b^n: n \geq 1\}$

Proof
Consider the deterministic extended pushdown automata M defined by these five rules

1: $Ssa \vdash Sas$
2: $asa \vdash aas$
3: $asb \vdash q$
4: $aqb \vdash q$
5: $sq \vdash f$

where s and f are the final states of M. As formally verified in the exercises, M accepts $\{a^n: n \geq 1\} \cup \{a^n b^n: n \geq 1\}$ by final state, so Lemma 5.2.3.5 holds.
∎

Lemma 5.2.3.6
Let M be a deterministic extended pushdown automaton. Then, there exists a deterministic extended pushdown automaton M' satisfying $L(M')_f = L(M)_{f\varepsilon}$.

Proof
Return to Algorithm 5.2.1.3 and modify it by replacing Q with F in the for loop. In addition, assume that this algorithm has a deterministic extended pushdown automaton M as its input. Observe that the algorithm modified in this way produces a deterministic extended pushdown automaton M' satisfying $L(M')_f = L(M)_{f\varepsilon}$. Therefore, Lemma 5.2.3.6 holds; a detailed proof of this lemma is left to the exercises.
∎

Theorem 5.2.3.7
The family of languages accepted by deterministic extended pushdown automata by final state and empty pushdown is properly contained in the family of languages accepted by deterministic extended pushdown automata by final state.

Proof
This theorem follows from Lemmas 5.2.3.4 through 5.2.3.6.
∎

In terms of deterministic extended pushdown automata, this section has investigated the acceptance by final state and the acceptance by final state and empty pushdown. The Exercises continue this investigation by examining the acceptance by empty pushdown.

Deterministic pushdown automata

So far, Section 5.2.3 has explored deterministic extended pushdown automata. The rest of this section narrows its attention to their special cases — deterministic pushdown automata.

As any pushdown automaton represents a special case of an extended pushdown automaton, the definition of a deterministic extended pushdown automaton, given in the beginning of this section, also covers the notion of a deterministic pushdown automaton. As opposed to an extended pushdown automata, however, every pushdown automaton, $M = (Q, \Sigma, R, s, F)$, satisfies lhs$(r) \in \Sigma_{PD}Q(\Sigma_I \cup \{\varepsilon\})$, for all $r \in R$. Taking advantage of this property, this section next defines a deterministic pushdown automaton in an alternative way.

Definition — deterministic pushdown automaton
Let $M = (Q, \Sigma, R, s, F)$ be a pushdown automaton. M is *deterministic* if each rule $r \in R$, where lhs$(r) = Apa$ with $a \in \Sigma_I \cup \{\varepsilon\}$, satisfies

$\{r\} = \{r': r' \in R, Apa = \text{lhs}(r') \text{ or } Ap = \text{lhs}(r')\}$

♦

According to the following theorem, deterministic pushdown automata have the same power as deterministic extended pushdown automata.

Theorem 5.2.3.8
Let L be a language. $L = L(M)$ for a deterministic pushdown automaton M if and only if $L = L(M_{ext})$ for a deterministic extended pushdown automaton M_{ext}.

Proof
Only if
As any deterministic pushdown automaton is a special case of a deterministic extended pushdown automaton, the 'only if' part of the equivalence given in Theorem 5.2.3.8 surely holds.

If
Consider Algorithm 5.2.2.1. As formally verified in the exercises, this algorithm preserves determinism; that is, if its input automaton M_{ext} represents a deterministic extended pushdown automaton, then Algorithm 5.2.2.1 produces a deterministic pushdown automaton M such that $L(M_{ext}) = L(M)$. Consequently, for any extended deterministic pushdown automaton, there exists an equivalent deterministic extended pushdown automaton. Hence, the if part of the equivalence given in Theorem 5.2.3.8 holds.

Thus, this theorem holds.

■

Deterministic pushdown automata are less powerful than their nondeterministic versions. Indeed, from Part 6 of Example 5.2.2.1, Theorem 5.2.2.3 and Theorem 5.2.3.8, there exists a pushdown automaton that accepts $\{v\text{reversal}(v): v \in \{a, b\}^*\}$; however, there is no deterministic pushdown automaton that accepts this language. As proved in Section 7.1, $\{a^i b^j c^k: i = j \text{ or } j = k\}$ represents another language of this kind. That is, there exist pushdown automata that accept $\{a^i b^j c^k: i = j \text{ or } j = k\}$; however, none of these automata work deterministically.

Implementation

The remainder of this section describes the implementation of a deterministic pushdown automaton M. For simplicity, this implementation assumes that M always completes reading its input word. This assumption represents no loss of generality: the following theorem explains how to transform any deterministic pushdown automaton to an equivalent deterministic pushdown automaton that satisfies this requirement.

Theorem 5.2.3.9

Let M be a deterministic pushdown automaton. Then, there exists a deterministic pushdown automaton M' such that $L(M) = L(M')$ and for all words, $w \in \Sigma_I^*$,

$$Ssw \vdash^* zq$$

in M, for some $q \in Q$ and $z \in \Sigma_{PD}^*$.

Proof

This proof sketches the conversion of a deterministic pushdown automaton $M = (Q, \Sigma, R, s, F)$ to a deterministic pushdown automaton M' such that $L(M) = L(M')$ and M' completes reading all input words. A detailed version of this proof is left to the exercises.

Observe that M cannot read all symbols of its input word if, during this reading, M enters a dead configuration or a looping configuration. From a *dead configuration*, M cannot make another move. In a *looping configuration*, M makes an infinitely many ε-moves; however, it never reads another input symbol. To rule out these two configurations, this proof modifies M to a deterministic pushdown automaton M' which never enters either of these configuration.

Dead configuration avoidance

This part of the proof transforms M to a deterministic pushdown automaton M'' such that $L(M) = L(M'')$ and M'' never enters a dead configuration. Observe that M occurs in a dead configuration if

1. M has its pushdown empty, or;
2. M has no rule to use.

1. To guarantee that M never erases its pushdown entirely, place a special pushdown symbol on the pushdown bottom.

2. To guarantee that M has always a rule to use, introduce a special nonfinal state t. If $\{Aqa, Aq\} \cap \{lhs(r): r \in R\} = \emptyset$, where $A \in \Sigma_{PD}, q \in Q, a \in \Sigma_I$, then add $Aqa \vdash t$ to R. In addition, for each $b \in \Sigma_I$, add a new rule of the form $tb \vdash t$.

Based on 1 and 2, construct the deterministic pushdown automaton M'' from M so that $L(M) = L(M'')$ and M'' never enters a dead configuration.

Looping configuration avoidance

The transformation of M'' to a deterministic pushdown automaton, M''', such that $L(M) = L(M')$ and M' never enters a looping configuration is left to the exercises.

The resulting automaton M' represents a deterministic pushdown automaton such that $L(M) = L(M')$ and M' completes reading any input words, so this theorem holds. ∎

Algorithm 5.2.3.10 describes the implementation of a deterministic pushdown automaton M. From Theorem 5.2.3.9, without any loss of generality, this algorithm assumes that M completes reading any input word. In addition, the present algorithm supposes that M has no ε-rules and leaves the implementation of a deterministic pushdown automaton with ε-rules as a programming project. Note that M's pushdown, which represents an unbounded data structure, is implemented as a linked list. A given input word w is followed by a special end-of-input symbol, #.

Algorithm 5.2.3.10: Deterministic pushdown automaton implementation

Input: A deterministic pushdown automaton M defined by its n rules, for some $n \geq 1$, as follows

$$1: A_1 p_1 a_1 \vdash w_1 q_1$$
$$\vdots$$
$$i: A_i p_i a_i \vdash w_i q_i$$
$$\vdots$$
$$n: A_n p_n a_n \vdash w_n q_n$$

where p_1 is the start state, and A_1 is the start symbol ($a_i \neq \varepsilon$ for $i = 1, \ldots, n$); in addition $w\#$, where w is an input word $w \in \Sigma^*$.

Output: **YES** if $w \in L(M)$; **NO** if $w \notin L(M)$.

Method

type
   States = $(p_1, q_1, \ldots, p_n, q_n)$;
   InputSymbols = $(a_1, \ldots, a_n)$;
   PushdownSymbols = $(A_1, \ldots, A_n)$;
   PushdownPointer = ^PushdownElement;
   PushdownElement = **record**
                   PushdownSymbol: PushdownSymbols;
                   NextPointer: PushdownPointer
                end {PushdownElement};

var
   PushdownTop: PushdownPointer;
   State: States;
   InputSymbol: InputSymbols;

begin

State := p_1 {p_1 is the start state};
PushdownTop^.PushdownSymbol := A_1 {the start symbol is pushed onto the (empty) pushdown};

read(InputSymbol) {M has been initialized};

while InputSymbol ≠ '#' **do** {move simulation}
  case PushdownTop^.PushdownSymbol **of**
    ⋮
    A_i: **case** State **of**
      ⋮
      p_i: **case** InputSymbol **of**
        ⋮
        a_i: simulate a move according to $A_i p_i a_i \vdash w_i q_i$
        {replace PushdownTop^.PushdownSymbol
        with w_i, State := q_i, and **read**(InputSymbol)};
        ⋮
      end{Symbol}
      ⋮
    end{State}
    ⋮
  end{Pushdown};

if State contains a final state of M
then write('YES')
else write('NO')

end.

This algorithm highlights the fundamental idea behind the implementation of a deterministic pushdown automaton. On the other hand, it only sketches the declarations of states, input symbols, and pushdown symbols. Furthermore, it suppresses the description of all common pushdown operations, such as creating, pushing and popping the pushdown. The addition of these routines is left as a programming project.

5.3 Pushdown automata and context-free grammars

This section demonstrates that the family of languages accepted by pushdown automata coincides with the family of context-free languages. Section 5.3.1 converts context-free grammars to pushdown automata. Then, Section 5.3.2 converts pushdown automata to context-free grammars. Finally, Section 5.3.3 states the equivalence between pushdown automata and context-free grammars.

5.3.1 From context-free grammars to pushdown automata

Section 5.3.1.1 presents several algorithms that convert context-free grammars to equivalent pushdown automata and demonstrates that these conversions actually represent the fundamental methodology behind the design of compiler parsers. Then, Section 5.3.1.2 approaches parsers more practically; indeed, this section constructs a parser for the programming language COLA (see Section 1.2.3).

5.3.1.1 Conversion of context-free grammars to pushdown automata

This section converts context-free grammars to equivalent pushdown automata by using several alternative algorithms. These algorithms are valuable not only theoretically but also practically because the resulting automata, represent basic techniques used in the design of compiler parsers.

Essentials of parsing

Consider a programming language L and a context-free grammar $G = (N, T, P, S)$ that specifies this language, so $L(G) = L$. Assume that a computer programmer has written a program in L and, then, translates this program by a compiler for L. During this translation, this compiler calls its parser, which decides the crucial problem of whether the input program is written in L correctly. To express this problem formally, the parser actually decides whether $w \in L(G)$, where w is a word representing the input program. To demonstrate that $w \in L(G)$, the parser constructs a derivation tree t for w in G. Concerning t, the parser has initially only these two pieces of information:

1. S labels root(t)
2. w labels fr(t).

where root(t) and fr(t) denote the root and frontier of t, respectively (see Section 0.3). The parser's main task is the construction of the rest of t by using production trees corresponding to productions in P (Figure 5.3.1.1.1).

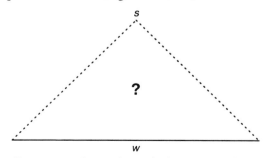

Figure 5.3.1.1.1 The initial part of a derivation tree for w.

If the parser constructs t so it starts at root(t) and proceeds down toward fr(t) from left to right, it represents a *top-down parser* (see Figure 5.3.1.1.2).

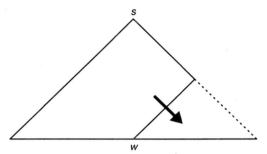

Figure 5.3.1.1.2 Top-down parsing.

Alternatively, if the parser constructs t so it starts at fr(t) and moves up toward root(t) from left to right, then it represents a *bottom-up parser* (see Figure 5.3.1.1.3).

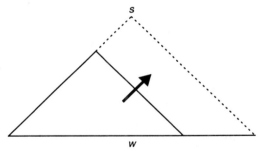

Figure 5.3.1.1.3 Bottom-up parsing.

This section presents three algorithms that convert any context-free grammar to an equivalent pushdown automata; as demonstrated later on, the resulting pushdown automata actually act as top-down parsers. Then, another algorithm is given that transforms any context-free grammars to an equivalent pushdown automaton, which works as a bottom-up parser.

Top-down parsers

Three algorithms are presented that convert context-free grammars to equivalent pushdown automata, and which act as top-down parsers.

Algorithm 5.3.1.1.1: Conversion of a context-free grammar in Greibach normal form to an equivalent pushdown automaton accepting by empty pushdown

Input: A context-free grammar $G = (N, T, P, S)$, in Greibach normal form.

Output: A pushdown automaton $M = (\{s\}, \Sigma, R, s, \varnothing)$, such that $L(G) = L(M)_\varepsilon$.

Method

begin
  $\Sigma_I := T$;
  $\Sigma := N \cup \Sigma_I$ $\{N = \Sigma_{PD}$, where S is the start pushdown symbol$\}$;
  for each $A \to aB_1B_2...B_n \in P$ **do**
    $R := R \cup \{Asa \vdash B_n...B_2B_1s\}$;
end.

This algorithm produces the output pushdown automaton M so M acts as a top-down parser, which simulates leftmost derivations in G. More precisely, as G is in Greibach normal form, by leftmost derivations, this grammar produces sentential forms consisting of a word of terminals followed by a word of nonterminals. Consider

$$S \Rightarrow^*_{lm} v\underline{A}y$$
$$\Rightarrow_{lm} vaB_1B_2...B_ny \; [A \to aB_1B_2...B_n]$$
$$\Rightarrow^*_{lm} w$$

where $v \in T^*, y \in N^*$, and $w = vaz$ with $z \in T^*$; Figure 5.3.1.1.4 depicts the derivation tree corresponding to this derivation (Figure 5.3.1.1.4.).

After reading v, M's pushdown contains reversal$(y)A$, and az represents the unread suffix of w, where a is the input symbol; therefore, M's configuration equals reversal$(y)Asaz$. From this configuration, M simulates

$$v\underline{A}y \Rightarrow_{lm} vaB_1B_2 ... B_ny \; [A \to aB_1B_2...B_n]$$

by using $Asa \vdash B_n...B_2B_1s$ as

$$\text{reversal}(y)Asaz \vdash \text{reversal}(y)B_n ... B_2B_1sz \; [Asa \vdash B_n ... B_2B_1s]$$

(see Figure 5.3.1.1.5).

Models for context-free languages

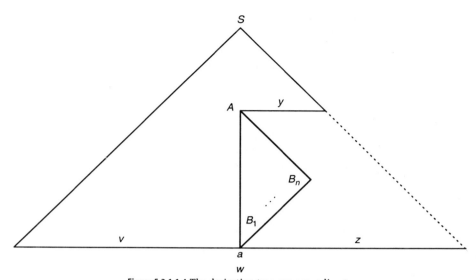

Figure 5.3.1.1.4 The derivation tree corresponding to
$$S \Rightarrow^*_{lm} v\underline{A}y$$
$$\Rightarrow_{lm} vaB_1B_2 \ldots B_n y \quad [A \to aB_1B_2\ldots B_n]$$
$$\Rightarrow^*_{lm} w$$

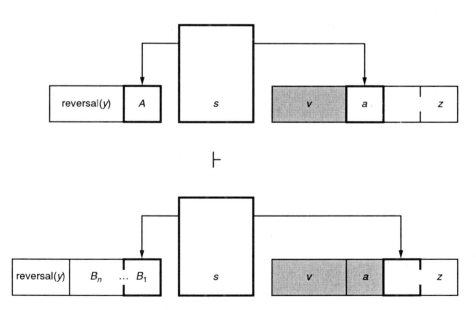

Figure 5.3.1.1.5 M's simulation of $v\underline{A}y \Rightarrow_{lm} vaB_1B_2 \ldots B_n y \quad [A \to aB_1B_2\ldots B_n]$

By simulating leftmost derivation steps in this way, M accepts w by empty pushdown if and only if $S \Rightarrow_{lm}^* w$ in G. Considering the derivation tree t corresponding to $S \Rightarrow_{lm}^* w$ in G and observe that M constructs t by working from $root(t)$ towards $fr(t)$, so M represents a top-down parser for $L(G)$.

Lemma 5.3.1.1.2
Let $G = (N, T, P, S)$ be a context-free grammar in Greibach normal form. With G as its input, Algorithm 5.3.1.1.1 halts and correctly constructs a pushdown automaton, $M = (\{s\}, \Sigma, R, s, \emptyset)$, such that $L(G) = L(M)_\varepsilon$.

Proof
Termination
As P is finite, Algorithm 5.3.1.1.1 repeats its **for** loop finitely many times, so this algorithm surely terminates.

Correctness
To demonstrate

$$L(G) = L(M)_\varepsilon$$

this proof first establishes the following claim.

Claim
For all $w \in T^*$ and $x \in N^*$,

$$S \Rightarrow_{lm}^* wx \text{ in } G \text{ if and only if } Ssw \vdash^* reversal(x)s \text{ in } M$$

Proof
Only if
By induction on $i \geq 0$, this part of the proof demonstrates that

$$S \Rightarrow_{lm}^i wx \text{ in } G \text{ implies } Ssw \vdash^* reversal(x)s$$

Basis
Let $i = 0$. Then,

$$S \Rightarrow_{lm}^* S \quad [\varepsilon]$$

in G. Observe that

$$Ss \vdash^* reversal(S)s \quad [\varepsilon]$$

in M. Thus, the basis holds.

Induction hypothesis
Assume that the claim is true for all k-step derivations, where $k = 0, \ldots, i$ for some $i \geq 0$.

Induction step
Consider

$$S \Rightarrow_{lm}^* wx \; [\pi p]$$

in G, where π is a production word consisting of i productions and $p \in P$; therefore, πp represents a production word consisting of $i + 1$ productions. As G is in Greibach normal form, p has the form

$$p: A \rightarrow aB_1B_2\ldots B_n$$

Express $S \Rightarrow_{lm}^* wx \; [\pi p]$ as

$$S \Rightarrow_{lm}^* vAy \qquad [\pi]$$
$$S \Rightarrow_{lm}^* vaB_1B_2\ldots B_ny \qquad [p]$$

where $w = va$ and $x = B_1B_2\ldots B_ny$. As π has i productions, the induction hypothesis implies

$$Ssv \vdash^* \text{reversal}(y)As$$

in M; thus,

$$Ssw \vdash^* \text{reversal}(y)Asa$$

in M. Because $p: A \rightarrow aB_1B_2\ldots B_n \in P$, the **for** loop of the algorithm includes $Asa \vdash B_n\ldots B_2B_1s$ into R, so

$$Ssw \vdash^* \text{reversal}(y)Asa$$
$$\vdash \text{reversal}(y)B_n\ldots B_2B_1s \qquad [Asa \vdash B_n\ldots B_2B_1s]$$

As $\text{reversal}(y)B_n\ldots B_2B_1 = \text{reversal}(x)$,

$$Ssw \vdash^* \text{reversal}(x)s$$

in M. In other words, the inductive step is completed.

Therefore, the 'only if' part of the equivalence holds.

If
By induction on $i \geq 0$, this part of the proof demonstrates that

$Ssw \vdash^i \text{reversal}(x)s$ in G implies $S \Rightarrow^*_{lm} wx$

Basis
Let $i = 0$. Then,

$$Ss \vdash^* \text{reversal}(S)s \; [\varepsilon] \text{ in } M$$

Notice

$$S \Rightarrow^*_{lm} S \; [\varepsilon]$$

in G. Thus, the basis of the claim.

Induction hypothesis
Assume that

$$Ssw \vdash^k \text{reversal}(x)s \text{ in } G \text{ implies } S \Rightarrow^*_{lm} wx$$

is true for all $k = 1, \ldots, i$, for some $i \geq 0$.

Induction step
Suppose that

$$Ssw \vdash^* \text{reversal}(x)s \; [\rho r]$$

in M, where ρ is a rule word consisting of i rules and $r \in R$, so ρr represents a rule word consisting of $i + 1$ rules. From the **for** loop of the algorithm, r has the form

$$Asa \vdash B_n \ldots B_2 B_1 s$$

where $a \in T$, and $A, B_1, \ldots, B_n \in N$. In greater detail, express $Ssw \vdash^* \text{reversal}(x)s \; [\rho r]$ as

$$Ssw \vdash^* \text{reversal}(y)Asa \qquad [\rho]$$
$$\vdash \text{reversal}(y)B_n \ldots B_2 B_1 s \qquad [Asa \vdash B_n \ldots B_2 B_1 s]$$

where $\text{reversal}(y)B_n \ldots B_2 B_1 = \text{reversal}(x)$. Hence,

$$Ssv \vdash^* \text{reversal}(y)As \qquad [\rho]$$

where $va = w$. As ρ represents a rule word consisting of i rules,

$$S \Rightarrow^*_{lm} vAy$$

in G by the induction hypothesis. Furthermore, $Asa \vdash B_n...B_2B_1s \in R$ implies

$$A \to aB_1B_2...B_n \in P$$

Thus,

$$S \Rightarrow^*_{lm} vAy \qquad [\pi]$$
$$\Rightarrow^*_{lm} vaB_1B_2...B_ny \qquad [A \to aB_1B_2...B_n]$$

Therefore,

$$S \Rightarrow^*_{lm} wx$$

in G. Consequently, the inductive step is completed, so the 'if' part of the equivalence holds.

Hence, the claim holds.

□

Consider the claim for $x = \varepsilon$. At this point,

$$S \Rightarrow^*_{lm} w \text{ in } G \text{ if and only if } Ssw \vdash^* s \text{ in } M$$

for all $w \in T^*$. Therefore,

$$L(G) = L(M)_\varepsilon$$

In summary, with G as its input, Algorithm 5.3.1.1.1 halts and correctly constructs a pushdown automaton $M = (\{s\}, \Sigma, R, s, \varnothing)$, such that $L(G) = L(M)_\varepsilon$. Therefore, this lemma holds.

■

Example 5.3.1.1.1 Application of algorithm 5.3.1.1.1

Consider the following context-free grammar G in Greibach normal form:

$p_1: S \to aSA$
$p_2: S \to bSB$
$p_3: S \to aA$
$p_4: S \to bB$
$p_5: A \to a$
$p_6: B \to b$

Observe that

$$L(G) = \{w\text{reversal}(w): w \in \{a, b\}^+\}$$

The present example uses Algorithm 5.3.1.1.1 to convert G to a pushdown automaton $M = (\{s\}, \Sigma, R, s, \varnothing)$, so $L(G) = L(M)_\varepsilon$. The first two steps of this algorithm define

$$\Sigma = \{S, B, a, b\}$$

where $\Sigma_I = \{a, b\}$ and, thus, $\Sigma_{PD} = \{S, B\}$. Then, Algorithm 5.3.1.1.1 computes its **for** loop. From the production $p_1: S \to aSA$, this algorithm constructs

$$Ssa \vdash ASs$$

and inserts this rule into R. Analogously, from $p_2: S \to bSB$, this algorithm constructs

$$Ssb \vdash BSs$$

From production $p_3: S \to aA$, it produces

$$Ssa \vdash As$$

From the other three productions ($p_4: S \to bB$, $p_5: A \to a$, and $p_6: B \to b$) Algorithm 5.3.1.1.1 produces

$Ssb \vdash Bs$
$Asa \vdash s$
$Bsb \vdash s$

As a result, M produces these six rules:

$r_1: Ssa \vdash ASs$
$r_2: Ssb \vdash BSs$
$r_3: Ssa \vdash As$
$r_4: Ssb \vdash Bs$
$r_5: Asa \vdash s$
$r_6: Bsb \vdash s$

Consider $babbab \in L(G)$. G derives this sentence in the following leftmost way:

$$\begin{aligned} S &\Rightarrow_{lm} b\underline{S}B & [p_2] \\ &\Rightarrow_{lm} ba\underline{S}AB & [p_1] \\ &\Rightarrow_{lm} bab\underline{B}AB & [p_4] \\ &\Rightarrow_{lm} babb\underline{A}B & [p_6] \end{aligned}$$

$$\Rightarrow_{lm} babba\underline{B} \quad [p_5]$$
$$\Rightarrow_{lm} babbab \quad [p_6]$$

That is,

$$S \Rightarrow_{lm}^* babbab \quad [p_2p_1p_4p_6p_5p_6]$$

M accepts $babbab$ by empty pushdown as follows:

$$Ssbabbab \vdash BSsabbab \quad [r_2]$$
$$\vdash BASsbbab \quad [r_1]$$
$$\vdash BABsbab \quad [r_4]$$
$$\vdash BAsab \quad [r_6]$$
$$\vdash Bsb \quad [r_5]$$
$$\vdash s \quad [r_6]$$

That is,

$$Ssbabbab \vdash^* s \quad [r_2r_1r_4r_6r_5r_6]$$

in M.

Reconsider $S \Rightarrow_{lm}^* babbab$ $[p_2p_1p_4p_6p_5p_6]$ in G and $Ssbabbab \vdash^* s$ $[r_2r_1r_4r_6r_5r_6]$ in M in somewhat greater detail. Specifically, notice the index correspondence between

$$r_2r_1r_4r_6r_5r_6$$

and

$$p_2p_1p_4p_6p_5p_6$$

As this correspondence indicates, M actually simulates the leftmost derivation, $S \Rightarrow_{lm}^* babbab$ $[p_2p_1p_4p_6p_5p_6]$, which represents the top-down parsing of $babbab$; indeed, the top-down left-to-right attachment of the corresponding production trees

$$\text{pt}(p_2), \text{pt}(p_1), \text{pt}(p_4), \text{pt}(p_6), \text{pt}(p_5), \text{pt}(p_6)$$

gives rise to the derivation tree for $babbab$ (see Figure 5.3.1.1.6). Consequently, M acts as a top-down parser of $L(G)$.

▲

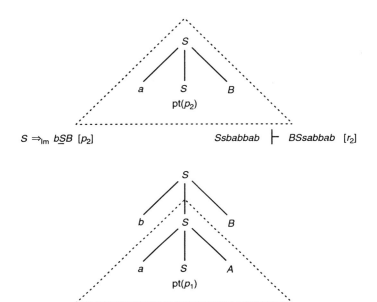

$S \Rightarrow_{lm} b\underline{S}B \ [p_2]$ $Ssbabbab \ \vdash \ BSsabbab \ [r_2]$

$b\underline{S}B \Rightarrow_{lm} baSAB \ [p_1]$ $BSsabbab \ \vdash \ BASsbbab \ [r_1]$

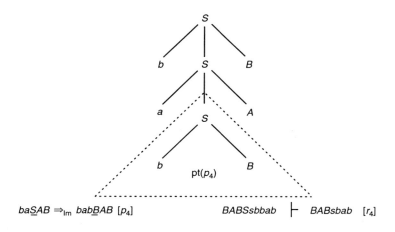

$ba\underline{S}AB \Rightarrow_{lm} bab\underline{B}AB \ [p_4]$ $BABSsbbab \ \vdash \ BABsbab \ [r_4]$

Models for context-free languages

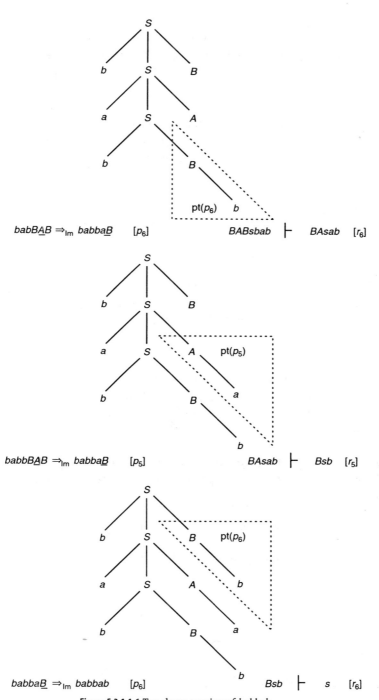

Figure 5.3.1.1.6 Top-down parsing of *babbab*.

Observe that Algorithm 5.3.1.1.1 produces its output pushdown automaton M without any ε-rules Therefore, given a context-free language L, there surely exists a pushdown automaton M without any ε-rules so that $L =_\varepsilon L(M)_\varepsilon$, as stated next.

Definition — ε-free pushdown automaton
Let $M = (Q, \Sigma, R, s, F)$ be a pushdown automaton. M is *ε-free* if R has no ε-rule.

◆

Theorem 5.3.1.1.3
For every context-free language L, there exists an ε-free pushdown automaton M such that $L =_\varepsilon L(M)_\varepsilon$.

Proof
Let L be a context-free language. By Corollary 5.1.4.2.10, there exists a context-free grammar G in Greibach normal form such that $L =_\varepsilon L(G)$. Consequently, Theorem 5.3.1.1.3 follows from Algorithm 5.3.1.1.1 and Lemma 5.3.1.1.2.

■

Algorithm 5.3.1.1 transforms any context-free grammar in Greibach normal form to an equivalent pushdown automaton accepting by empty pushdown. The next algorithm makes an analogical transformation except that its output pushdown automaton accepts by final state.

Algorithm 5.3.1.1.4: Conversion of a context-free grammar in Greibach normal form to an equivalent pushdown automaton accepting by final state

Input: A context-free grammar $G = (N, T, P, S)$ in Greibach normal form.

Output: A pushdown automaton $M = (\{s, f\}, \Sigma, R, s, \{f\})$ such that $L(G) = L(M)_f$.

Method

begin
  $\Sigma_I := T$;
  $N' := \{ A' : A \in N\}$;
  $\Sigma := N' \cup N \cup \Sigma_I$ $\{\Sigma_{PD} = N' \cup N$, where S' is the start pushdown symbol$\}$;
  for each $A \to aB_1B_2...B_n \in P$, where $n \geq 0$ **do**
    $R := R \cup \{Asa \vdash B_nB_{n-1}...B_2B_1s\}$;

for each $A \to aB_1B_2...B_n \in P$, where $n \geq 1$ **do**
  $R := R \cup \{A'sa \vdash B'_nB_{n-1}...B_2B_1s\}$;
for each $A \to a \in P$ **do**
  $R := R \cup \{A'sa \vdash f\}$
end.

Algorithm 5.3.1.1.4 represents a modification of Algorithm 5.3.1.1.1. As opposed to Algorithm 5.3.1.1.1, however, Algorithm 5.3.1.1.4 produces a pushdown automaton M, so that during its computation M has always its pushdown bottom symbol denoted by a prime. In addition, for each production of the form $A \to a \in P$, R contains a rule of the form $A'sa \vdash f$, where f is M's final state. Otherwise, M works by analogy with the output automaton produced by Algorithm 5.3.1.1.1. Observe that G always uses a production of the form $A \to a$ in the last derivation step of a derivation, $S \Rightarrow^*_{lm} w$, such that $w \in T^*$. Therefore, $L(G) = L(M)_f$.

Lemma 5.3.1.1.5

Let $G = (N, T, P, S)$ be a context-free grammar in Greibach normal form. With G as its input, Algorithm 5.3.1.1.4 halts and correctly constructs a pushdown automaton $M = (\{s, f\}, \Sigma, R, s, \{f\})$ such that $L(G) = L(M)_f$.

Proof
This proof is left to the exercises.

∎

Theorem 5.3.1.1.6

For every context-free language L, there exists an ε-free pushdown automaton M such that $L =_\varepsilon L(M)_f$.

Proof
Let L be any context-free language. From Corollary 5.1.4.2.10, there exists a context-free grammar G in Greibach normal form such that $L =_\varepsilon L(G)$. Thus, Theorem 5.3.1.1.3 follows from Algorithm 5.3.1.1.4 and Lemma 5.3.1.1.5.

∎

Observe that Algorithm 5.3.1.4 actually produces its output pushdown automaton M so that this automaton enters its final state f and, simultaneously, empties its pushdown; in other words, $L(G) = L(M)_f = L(M)_{f\varepsilon}$ as formally stated next.

Theorem 5.3.1.1.7
For every context-free language L, there exists an ε-free pushdown automaton M such that $L(G) =_\varepsilon L(M)_{f\varepsilon}$.

Proof
A detailed version of this proof is left to the Exercises. ∎

Corollary 5.3.1.1.8
Let L be a context-free language. Then, these three statements hold:

1. $L =_\varepsilon L(M_f)_f$, for an ε-free pushdown automaton M_f.
2. $L =_\varepsilon L(M_\varepsilon)_\varepsilon$, for an ε-free pushdown automaton M_ε.
3. $L =_\varepsilon L(M_{f\varepsilon})_{f\varepsilon}$, for an ε-free pushdown automaton $M_{f\varepsilon}$.

Proof
Corollary 5.3.1.1.8 follows from Theorems 5.3.1.1.3, 5.3.1.1.6, and 5.3.1.1.7. ∎

Algorithms 5.3.1.1.1 and 5.3.1.1.4 require their input context-free grammars to satisfy Greibach normal form. The following algorithm place no requirements on the input context-free grammar G, from which this algorithm constructs an equivalent pushdown automaton acting as a top-down parser of $L(G)$.

Algorithm 5.3.1.1.9: Conversion of a context-free grammar to an equivalent pushdown automaton accepting by empty pushdown

Input: A context-free grammar $G = (N, T, P, S)$.

Output: A pushdown automaton $M = (\{s\}, \Sigma, R, s, \varnothing)$, such that $L(G) = L(M)_\varepsilon$.

Method

begin
   $\Sigma_I := T$;
   $\Sigma := N \cup \Sigma_I \{\Sigma_{PD} = N,$ where S is the start pushdown symbol$\}$;
   for each $a \in T$ **do**
     $R := R \cup \{asa \vdash s\}$;
   for each $p \in P$ **do**
     $R := R \cup \{\text{lhs}(p)s \vdash \text{reversal}(\text{rhs}(p))s\}$
end.

Algorithm 5.3.1.1.9 produces the resulting pushdown automaton M that acts as a top-down parser of $L(G)$. The rule $asa \vdash s$, introduced in the first **for** loop of this algorithm, causes M to pop a from the pushdown and, simultaneously, read a on the input tape. The rule $\text{lhs}(p)s \vdash \text{reversal}(\text{rhs}(p))s$, introduced in the second **for** loop, causes M to simulate the use of p by G so M replaces $\text{lhs}(p)$, appearing on the pushdown top, with $\text{reversal}(\text{rhs}(p))$. By simulating leftmost derivation steps in this way, M accepts w by empty pushdown if and only if $S \Rightarrow^*_{\text{lm}} w$ in G.

Lemma 5.3.1.1.10
Let $G = (N, T, P, S)$ be a context-free grammar. With G as its input, Algorithm 5.3.1.1.9 halts and correctly constructs a pushdown automaton $M = (\{s\}, \Sigma, R, s, \emptyset)$ such that $L(G) = L(M)_\varepsilon$.

Proof
This proof is left to the exercises. ∎

Example 5.3.1.1.2 Application of Algorithm 5.3.1.1.9
Consider this context-free grammar G:

$$p_1: S \to SS$$
$$p_2: S \to (S)$$
$$p_3: S \to \varepsilon$$

where S is a nonterminal, and (and) are terminals. Observe that

$$L(G) = K^*$$

where

$$K = \{ \, (^n)^n : n \geq 0 \}$$

Less formally, L consists of the concatenations of well-balanced words of parentheses. For instance, $()(()) \in L(G)$, but $()() \notin L(G)$.

This example uses Algorithm 5.3.1.1.9 to convert G to a pushdown automaton $M = (\{s\}, \Sigma, R, s, \emptyset)$ so $L(G) = L(M)_\varepsilon$. The first two steps of this algorithm set

$$\Sigma := \{S, (,)\}$$

where $\Sigma_I := \{(,)\}$ and, thus, $\Sigma_{\text{PD}} := \{S\}$. The first **for** loop of Algorithm 5.3.1.1.9 produces the following two rules, which this example labels as $r_($ and $r_)$:

$$r_(: (s(\vdash s$$
$$r_):)s) \vdash s$$

From $p_1: S \to SS$, the second **for** loop produces

$$r_1: Ss \vdash SSs$$

From $p_2: S \to (S)$, this loop constructs

$$r_2: Ss \vdash)S(s$$

Finally, from $p_3: S \to \varepsilon$, this loop produces

$$r_3: Ss \vdash s$$

Therefore, M contains these five rules:

$$
\begin{aligned}
r_(&: \ (s(\vdash s \\
r_)&: \ )s) \vdash s \\
r_1&: \ Ss \vdash SSs \\
r_2&: \ Ss \vdash)S(s \\
r_3&: \ Ss \vdash s
\end{aligned}
$$

Consider $()(()) \in L(G)$. G generates $()(())$ by making the following leftmost derivation:

$$
\begin{aligned}
S &\Rightarrow_{lm} \underline{S}S & [p_1] \\
&\Rightarrow_{lm} (\underline{S})S & [p_2] \\
&\Rightarrow_{lm} ()\underline{S} & [p_3] \\
&\Rightarrow_{lm} ()(\underline{S}) & [p_2] \\
&\Rightarrow_{lm} ()((\underline{S})) & [p_2] \\
&\Rightarrow_{lm} ()(()) & [p_3]
\end{aligned}
$$

In brief,

$$S \Rightarrow_{lm}^* ()(()) \qquad [p_1 p_2 p_3 p_2 p_2 p_3]$$

M accepts $()(())$ by empty pushdown as follows:

$$
\begin{aligned}
Ss()(()) &\vdash SSs()(()) & [r_1] \\
&\vdash S)S(s()(()) & [r_2] \\
&\vdash S)Ss)(()) & [r_(] \\
&\vdash S)s)(()) & [r_3]
\end{aligned}
$$

$$\vdash Ss(()) \qquad [r_1]$$
$$\vdash)S(s(()) \qquad [r_2]$$
$$\vdash)Ss()) \qquad [r_1]$$
$$\vdash))S(s()) \qquad [r_2]$$
$$\vdash))Ss)) \qquad [r_1]$$
$$\vdash))s)) \qquad [r_3]$$
$$\vdash)s) \qquad [r_1]$$
$$\vdash s \qquad [r_1]$$

That is,

$$Ss()(()) \vdash^* s \qquad [r_1 r_2 r_{(} r_3 r_{)} r_2 r_{(} r_2 r_{(} r_3 r_{)} r_{)}]$$

Observe that M acts as a top-down parser of $L(G)$. Indeed, take a closer look at

$$S \Rightarrow^*_{lm} ()(()) \qquad [p_1 p_2 p_3 p_2 p_2 p_3]$$

in G and

$$Ss()(()) \vdash^* s \qquad [r_1 r_2 r_{(} r_3 r_{)} r_2 r_{(} r_2 r_{(} r_3 r_{)} r_{)}]$$

in M. By $r_{(}$ and $r_{)}$, M pairs off the current pushdown top and the input symbol; however, M does not use these two rules to simulate any production of P. Remove these two rules from $r_1 r_2 r_{(} r_3 r_{)} r_2 r_{(} r_2 r_{(} r_3 r_{)} r_{)}$, and notice the index correspondence between the resulting sequence of rules,

$$r_1 r_2 r_3 r_2 r_2 r_3$$

and the production word

$$p_1 p_2 p_3 p_2 p_2 p_3$$

Consider the sequence of production trees

$$\text{pt}(p_1), \text{pt}(p_2), \text{pt}(p_3), \text{pt}(p_2), \text{pt}(p_2) \text{ and } \text{pt}(p_3)$$

corresponding to $p_1 p_2 p_3 p_2 p_2 p_3$. If these production trees are put together in the top-down left-to-right way, the resulting tree (Figure 5.3.1.1.7) represents the derivation tree for $()(())$.

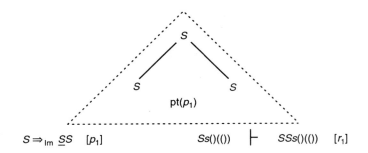

$S \Rightarrow_{lm} \underline{S}S \quad [p_1]$ $\qquad Ss()(()) \vdash SSs()(()) \quad [r_1]$

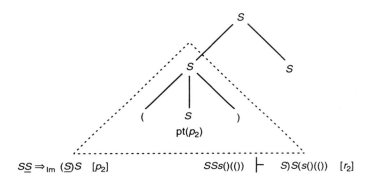

$S\underline{S} \Rightarrow_{lm} (\underline{S})S \quad [p_2]$ $\qquad SSs()(()) \vdash S)S(s()(()) \quad [r_2]$

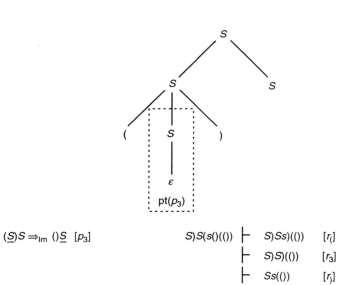

$(\underline{S})S \Rightarrow_{lm} ()\underline{S} \quad [p_3]$ $\qquad S)S(s()(()) \vdash S)Ss)(()) \quad [r_1]$
$\qquad\qquad\qquad\qquad\qquad \vdash S)S)(()) \quad [r_3]$
$\qquad\qquad\qquad\qquad\qquad \vdash Ss(()) \quad [r_j]$

Models for context-free languages

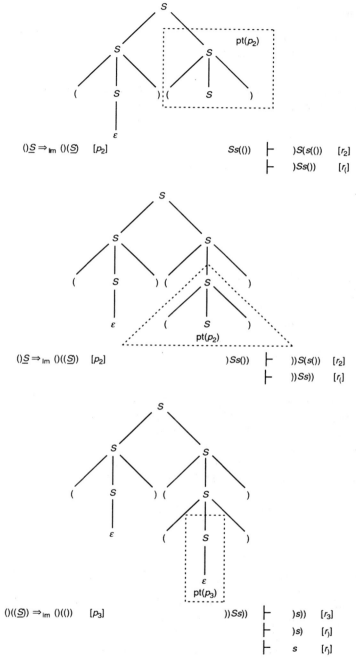

Figure 5.3.1.1.7 Top-down parsing of ()(()).

Bottom-up parsers

Algorithm 5.3.1.1.11 converts any context-free grammar to an equivalent pushdown automaton that acts as a top-down parser.

Algorithm 5.3.1.1.11: Conversion of a context-free grammar to an equivalent extended pushdown automaton

Input: A context-free grammar $G = (N, T, P, S)$.

Output: An extended pushdown automaton $M = (\{s, f\}, \Sigma, R, s, \{f\})$ such that $L(G) = L(M)$.

Method

begin
$\quad \Sigma_I := T;$
$\quad \Sigma := \{S_M\} \cup N \cup \Sigma_I \;\{\Sigma_{PD} = \{S_M\} \cup N$, where S_M is the start pushdown symbol$\};$
$\quad$**for** each $a \in T$ **do**
$\quad\quad R := R \cup \{sa \vdash as\};$
$\quad$**for** each $p \in P$ **do**
$\quad\quad R := R \cup \{\text{rhs}(p)s \vdash \text{lhs}(p)s\};$
$\quad R := R \cup \{S_M S s \vdash f\}$
end.

This algorithm produces its output extended pushdown automaton M that acts as a bottom-up parser for $L(G)$ so M, proceeding from w towards S, simulates G's rightmost derivations in reverse. From the rule, $sa \vdash as$, introduced in the first **for** loop of Algorithm 5.3.1.1.11, M shifts the input symbols a from the input tape onto the pushdown top. From the rule $\text{rhs}(p)s \vdash \text{lhs}(p)s$, introduced in the second **for** loop, M simulates the following rightmost derivation step in reverse:

$$x\text{lhs}(p)v \;\;\Rightarrow_{rm} x\text{rhs}(p)v \;\;\;[p]$$
$$\Rightarrow^*_{rm} w$$

where $x \in (N \cup T)^*$ and $v \in T^*$ (see Figure 5.3.1.1.8).

More precisely, after the simulation of $x\text{rhs}(p)v \Rightarrow^*_{rm} w$, M's pushdown contains $x\text{rhs}(p)$, its current state is s, and the unread suffix of the input word, w, equals v; that is, M's configuration is $x\text{rhs}(p)sv$. From this configuration, M simulates $x\text{lhs}(p)v \Rightarrow_{rm} x\text{rhs}(p)v \;[p]$ in reverse by the ε-move

$$x\text{rhs}(p)sv \vdash x\text{lhs}(p)sv \;\;\;[\text{rhs}(p)s \vdash \text{lhs}(p)s]$$

(see Figure 5.3.1.1.9).

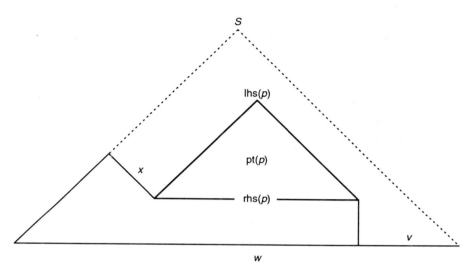

Figure 5.3.1.1.8 The derivation tree's path corresponding to
$x\mathrm{lhs}(p)v \Rightarrow_{\mathrm{rm}} x\mathrm{rhs}(p)v \quad [p]$
$\Rightarrow_{\mathrm{rm}}^{*} w$

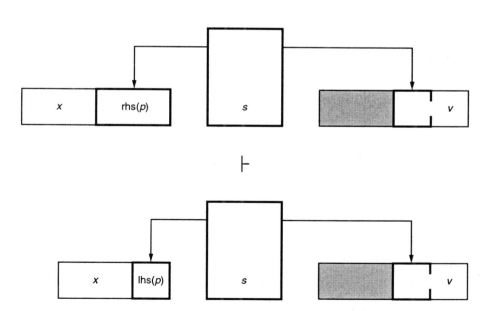

Figure 5.3.1.1.9 M's simulation of $x\mathrm{lhs}(p)v \Rightarrow_{\mathrm{rm}} x\mathrm{rhs}(p)v \quad [p]$.

When M completes the simulation of $S \Rightarrow_{rm}^* w$ in reverse, its configuration is $S_M S s$; at this point, M uses $S_M S s \vdash f$ to enter f and, thereby, accept w. Consequently, $S \Rightarrow_{rm}^* w$ in G if and only if $w \in L(M)$, so $L(G) = L(M)$. Observe that by simulating $S \Rightarrow_{rm}^* w$ in reverse, M actually constructs the derivation tree for w in a bottom-up left-to-right way (see Figure 5.3.1.1.8). In other words, M works as a bottom-up parser of $L(G)$.

Lemma 5.3.1.1.12

Let $G = (N, T, P, S)$ be a context-free grammar. With G as its input, Algorithm 5.3.1.1.11 terminates and correctly constructs an extended pushdown automaton, $M = (\{s, f\}, \Sigma, R, s, \{f\})$, such that $L(G) = {}_L(M)$.

Proof
Termination
As T and P are finite, Algorithm 5.3.1.1.11 repeats the two **for** loops finitely many times, so this algorithm surely terminates.

Correctness
To demonstrate

$$L(G) = L(M)$$

this proof first establishes Claims A and B.

Claim A
Let

$$S \Rightarrow_{rm}^* xv$$
$$\Rightarrow_{rm}^* uv \quad [\pi]$$

in G, where $v, u \in T^*$, $x \in (T \cup N)^*$, and π is a production word. Then,

$$S_M suv \vdash^* S_M xsv$$

in M.

Proof
This proof is made by induction on the number of productions appearing in π.

Basis
Let π contain no production; that is, $\pi = \varepsilon$ and

$$S \Rightarrow^*_{rm} xv \Rightarrow^*_{rm} uv \qquad [\varepsilon]$$

in G. Thus, $u = x$. Observe that

$$S_M suv \vdash^* S_M usv \qquad [\rho]$$

in M, where ρ consists of $|u|$ rules, introduced in the first **for** loop that cause M to shift u from the input tape onto the pushdown. Therefore, the basis holds.

Induction hypothesis
Assume that the claim is true for all production words consisting of k productions, $k = 0, \ldots, i$, for some $i \geq 0$.

Induction step
Consider

$$\begin{aligned} S &\Rightarrow^*_{rm} xv \\ &\Rightarrow^*_{rm} uv \end{aligned} \qquad [p\pi]$$

in G, where π consists of i productions, and $p \in P$, so πp consists of $i + 1$ productions. Express $xv \Rightarrow^*_{rm} uv$ $[p\pi]$ as

$$\begin{aligned} xv &\Rightarrow_{rm} y\mathrm{rhs}(p)v & [p] \\ &\Rightarrow^*_{rm} uv & [\pi] \end{aligned}$$

where $x = y\mathrm{lhs}(p)$. From the second **for** loop described in Algorithm 5.3.1.1.11, $p \in P$ implies $\mathrm{rhs}(p)s \vdash \mathrm{lhs}(p)s \in R$. This proof now distinguishes two cases — $y\mathrm{rhs}(p) \in T^*$ and $y\mathrm{rhs}(p) \notin T^*$:

1. Let $y\mathrm{rhs}(p) \in T^*$. Then, $y\mathrm{rhs}(p) = u$. By analogy with the basis of this inductive proof, construct

$$S_M suv \vdash^* S_M y\mathrm{rhs}(p)sv \qquad [\rho]$$

in M, where ρ consists of $|u|$ rules introduced in the first **for** loop. Consequently,

$$\begin{aligned} S_M suv &\vdash^* S_M y\mathrm{rhs}(p)sv \\ &\vdash^* S_M y\mathrm{lhs}(p)sv \qquad [\mathrm{rhs}(p)s \vdash \mathrm{lhs}(p)s] \end{aligned}$$

As $x = y\mathrm{lhs}(p)$,

$$S_M suv \vdash^* S_M xsv$$

in M, so for the case when $y\mathrm{rhs}(p) \in T^*$, the induction step is completed.

2. Let $\mathrm{yrhs}(p) \notin T^*$. Express $\mathrm{yrhs}(p)$ as

$$\mathrm{yrhs}(p) = zBv',$$

where B is the rightmost nonterminal appearing in $\mathrm{yrhs}(p)$, and $v' \in T^*$. Using the inductive hypothesis,

$$S \Rightarrow^*_{\mathrm{rm}} yzBv'v \Rightarrow^*_{\mathrm{rm}} uv \quad [\pi]$$

implies

$$S_M suv \vdash^* S_M yzBsv'v$$

in M. Then,

$$S_M yzBsv'v \vdash^* S_M yzBv'sv \quad [\rho]$$

in M, where ρ consists of $|v'|$ rules introduced in the first for loop. Hence,

$$S_M suv \vdash^* S_M \mathrm{yrhs}(p)sv$$
$$\vdash^* S_M \mathrm{ylhs}(p)sv \quad [\mathrm{rhs}(p)s \vdash \mathrm{lhs}(p)s]$$

As $x = y\mathrm{lhs}(p)$,

$$S_M suv \vdash^* S_M xsv$$

in M, then for the case when $\mathrm{yrhs}(p) \notin T^*$, the induction step is completed as well.

Consequently, Claim A holds. □

Claim B
Let

$$S_M suv \vdash^* S_M xsv \quad [\rho]$$

in M, where $v, u \in T^*$, $x \in (T \cup N)^*$, and ρ is a rule word. Then,

$$xv \Rightarrow^*_{\mathrm{rm}} uv$$

in G.

Proof
This proof is made by induction on the number of rules in ρ.

Models for context-free languages

Basis
Let $\rho = \varepsilon$, so $u = \varepsilon$, $x = \varepsilon$, and

$$S_M sv \vdash^* S_M sv \quad [\varepsilon]$$

in M. Observe that

$$v \Rightarrow^*_{rm} v \quad [\varepsilon]$$

in G. Therefore, the basis holds.

Induction hypothesis
Assume that the claim is true for all rule words consisting of k rules, $k = 0, \ldots, i$, for some $i \geq 0$.

Induction step
Consider

$$S_M suv \vdash^* S_M xsv \quad [\rho r]$$

in M, where $v, u \in T^*$, $x \in (T \cup N)^*$, ρ consists of i rules, and $r \in R$, so ρr consists of $i + 1$ rules. As $S_M xsv$ contains s, r differs from $S_M Ss \vdash f$. Then, by using algorithm 5.3.1.1.11, rhs(r) begins with a symbol from $(T \cup N)$, so $x \in (T \cup N)^*(T \cup N)$. This proof now distinguishes the two cases $x \in (T \cup N)^* N$ and $x \in (T \cup N)^* T$.

1. Let $x \in (T \cup N)^* N$. Then, the second **for** loop of the algorithm produces r, which has the form

$$r: \text{rhs}(p)s \vdash \text{lhs}(p)s$$

where $p \in P$. Express $S_M suv \vdash^* S_M xsv \quad [\rho r]$ as

$$S_M suv \vdash^* S_M y\text{rhs}(p)sv \quad [\rho]$$
$$\vdash S_M y\text{lhs}(p)sv \quad [r]$$

where $x = y\text{lhs}(p)$. From the inductive hypothesis,

$$y\text{rhs}(p)v \Rightarrow^*_{rm} uv$$

in G. As $x = y\text{lhs}(p)$,

$$xv \Rightarrow_{rm} y\text{rhs}(p)v \quad [p]$$
$$\Rightarrow^*_{rm} uv$$

in G

Therefore, for the case when $x \in (T \cup N)^*N$, the induction step is completed.

2. Let $x \in (T \cup N)^*T$. Then, the first **for** loop of the algorithm produces r, so r has the form

$$r: sa \vdash as$$

for some $a \in T$. Express

$$S_M suv \vdash^* S_M xsv \qquad [\rho r]$$

as

$$S_M suv \vdash^* S_M y\mathrm{rhs}(p)sv \qquad [\rho]$$
$$\vdash S_M y\mathrm{lhs}(p)sv \qquad [r]$$

where $x = ya$. From the inductive hypothesis,

$$yav \Rightarrow^*_{rm} uv$$

in G. As $x = ya$,

$$xv \Rightarrow^*_{rm} uv$$

in G, so for the case when $x \in (T \cup N)^*T$, the induction step is completed, too.

Consequently, Claim B holds.

□

Consider Claim A with $v = \varepsilon$ and $x = S$. At this point, for all $u \in T^*$, if

$$S \Rightarrow^*_{rm} u \text{ in } G,$$

then

$$S_M su \vdash^* S_M Ss \text{ in } M.$$

As $S_M Ss \vdash f \in R$,

$$S \Rightarrow^*_{rm} u$$

in G implies

$$S_M sv \vdash^* S_M Ss$$
$$\vdash f \quad [S_M Ss \vdash f]$$

in M. Hence,

$$L(G) \subseteq L(M)$$

Observe that if $u \in L(M)$, then M accepts u as follows

$$S_M su \vdash^* S_M Ss$$
$$\vdash f \quad [S_M Ss \vdash f]$$

Consider Claim B so $v = \varepsilon$ and $x = S$. At this point, for all $u \in T^*$, if

$$S_M su \vdash^* S_M Ss \quad [\rho]$$

in M, then

$$S \Rightarrow^*_{rm} u$$

in G. Therefore, $u \in L(M)$ implies $u \in L(G)$, so

$$L(M) \subseteq L(G)$$

Consequently,

$$L(G) = L(M)$$

because $L(G) \subseteq L(M)$ and $L(M) \subseteq L(G)$.

In summary, with G as its input, Algorithm 5.3.1.1.11 halts and correctly constructs an extended pushdown automaton, $M = (\{s, f\}, \Sigma, R, s, \{f\})$, such that $L(G) = L(M)$. Thus, Lemma 5.3.1.1.12 holds. ∎

Example 5.3.1.1.3 Application of Algorithm 5.3.1.1.11
Consider the following context-free grammar G:

$p_1: E \to E + T$
$p_2: E \to T$
$p_3: T \to T * F$
$p_4: T \to F$
$p_5: F \to (E)$
$p_6: F \to i$

Here, E, T and F are nonterminals, where E is the start symbol; the other symbols — $i, +, *, ($, and $)$ — are terminals. Intuitively, E, T, F and i stand for *expression, term, factor* and *identifier*, respectively. Observe that $L(G)$ consists of all legal arithmetic expressions over $\{i, +, *, (, \text{and })\}$.

Algorithm 5.3.1.1.11 converts G to an equivalent extended pushdown automaton $M = (\{s, f\}, \Sigma, R, s, \{f\})$, as follows. Initially, this algorithm sets

$$\Sigma := \{S_M, E, T, F, i, +, *, (,)\}$$

where $\Sigma_I := \{i, +, *, (,)\}$ and $\Sigma_{PD} = \{S_M, E, T, F\}$. Then, Algorithm 5.3.1.1.11 enters its first **for** loop. This loop produces the following five rules, labelled by $r_i, r_+, r_*, r_($ and $r_)$:

$r_i: si \vdash is$
$r_+: s+ \vdash +s$
$r_*: s* \vdash *s$
$r_(: s(\vdash (s$
$r_): s) \vdash)s$

Having exited the first **for** loop, Algorithm 5.3.1.1.11 enters its second **for** loop, which produces the six rules r_1 through r_6. From $p_1: E \to E + T$, this loop constructs

$$r_1: E + Ts \vdash Es$$

and adds r_1 to R. From $p_2: E \to T$, this loop constructs

$$r_2: Ts \vdash Es$$

and adds r_2 to R. From the remaining four productions,

$$p_3: T \to T * F, p_4: T \to F, p_5: F \to (E), p_6: F \to i,$$

this loop produces

$r_3: T*Fs \vdash Ts$
$r_4: Fs \vdash Ts$
$r_5: (E)s \vdash Fs$
$r_6: is \vdash Fs$

and adds these productions to R. Finally, Algorithm 5.3.1.1.11 adds $r_f: S_M Es \vdash f$ to R and completes the construction of R, which thus consists of the following rules:

$r_i: si \vdash is$
$r_+: s+ \vdash +s$
$r_*: s* \vdash *s$

Models for context-free languages

$r_(: s($ ⊢ $(s$
$r_): s)$ ⊢ $)s$
$r_1: E+Ts$ ⊢ Es
$r_2: Ts$ ⊢ Es
$r_3: T*Fs$ ⊢ Ts
$r_4: Fs$ ⊢ Ts
$r_5: (E)s$ ⊢ Fs
$r_6: is$ ⊢ Fs
$r_f: S_M Es$ ⊢ f

Consider

$$i*(i+i) \in L(G)$$

G generates this sentence by the following rightmost derivation:

$$\begin{array}{lll}
E \Rightarrow_{rm} \underline{T} & & [p_2] \\
\Rightarrow_{rm} T*\underline{F} & & [p_3] \\
\Rightarrow_{rm} T*(\underline{E}) & & [p_5] \\
\Rightarrow_{rm} T*(E+\underline{T}) & & [p_1] \\
\Rightarrow_{rm} T*(E+\underline{F}) & & [p_4] \\
\Rightarrow_{rm} T*(\underline{E}+i) & & [p_6] \\
\Rightarrow_{rm} T*(\underline{T}+i) & & [p_2] \\
\Rightarrow_{rm} T*(\underline{F}+i) & & [p_4] \\
\Rightarrow_{rm} \underline{T}*(i+i) & & [p_6] \\
\Rightarrow_{rm} \underline{F}*(i+i) & & [p_4] \\
\Rightarrow_{rm} i*(i+i) & & [p_6]
\end{array}$$

In summary,

$$S \Rightarrow^*_{rm} i*(i+i) \qquad [p_2 p_3 p_5 p_1 p_4 p_6 p_2 p_4 p_6 p_4 p_6]$$

Correspondingly, M accepts $i*(i+i)$ as follows:

$$\begin{array}{lll}
S_M si*(i+i) & \vdash S_M is*(i+i) & [r_i] \\
& \vdash S_M Fs*(i+i) & [r_6] \\
& \vdash S_M Ts*(i+i) & [r_4] \\
& \vdash S_M T*s(i+i) & [r_*] \\
& \vdash S_M T*(si+i) & [r_(] \\
& \vdash S_M T*(is+i) & [r_i]
\end{array}$$

$$\vdash S_M T^*(Fs+i) \quad [r_6]$$

$$\vdash S_M T^*(Ts+i) \quad [r_4]$$

$$\vdash S_M T^*(Es+i) \quad [r_2]$$

$$\vdash S_M T^*(E+si) \quad [r_+]$$

$$\vdash S_M T^*(E+is) \quad [r_i]$$

$$\vdash S_M T^*(E+Fs) \quad [r_6]$$

$$\vdash S_M T^*(E+Ts) \quad [r_4]$$

$$\vdash S_M T^*(Es) \quad [r_1]$$

$$\vdash S_M T^*(E)s \quad [r_)]$$

$$\vdash S_M TFs \quad [r_5]$$

$$\vdash S_M Ts \quad [r_3]$$

$$\vdash S_M Es \quad [r_2]$$

$$\vdash f \quad [r_f]$$

That is,

$$S_M si^*(i+i) \quad \vdash^* f \quad [r_i r_6 r_4 r_* r_(r_i r_6 r_4 r_2 r_+ r_i r_6 r_4 r_1 r_) r_5 r_3 r_2 r_f]$$

The rules subscripted with terminals cause M to push the input symbol onto the pushdown; however, they do not simulate any production of G. Their removal reduces $r_i r_6 r_4 r_* r_(r_i r_6 r_4 r_2 r_+ r_i r_6 r_4 r_1 r_) r_5 r_3 r_2 r_f$ to $r_6 r_4 r_6 r_4 r_2 r_6 r_4 r_1 r_5 r_3 r_2$. Consider

$$reversal(r_6 r_4 r_6 r_4 r_2 r_6 r_4 r_1 r_5 r_3 r_2) = r_2 r_3 r_5 r_1 r_4 r_6 r_2 r_4 r_6 r_4 r_6$$

Notice the correspondence between

$$r_2 r_3 r_5 r_1 r_4 r_6 r_2 r_4 r_6 r_4 r_6$$

and the production word

$$p_2 p_3 p_5 p_1 p_4 p_6 p_2 p_4 p_6 p_4 p_6$$

In other words, M simulates $\Rightarrow^*_{rm} i^*(i+i)$ in reverse, and this simulation represent the bottom-up parsing of $i^*(i+i)$ (see Figure 5.3.1.1.10).

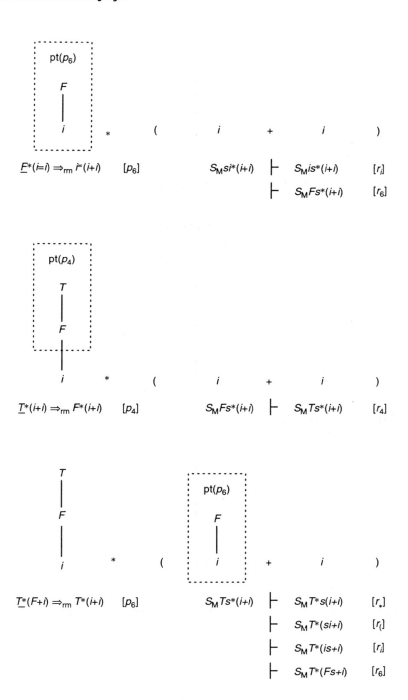

Figure 5.3.1.1.10(a) Bottom-up parsing of $i*(i+i)$.

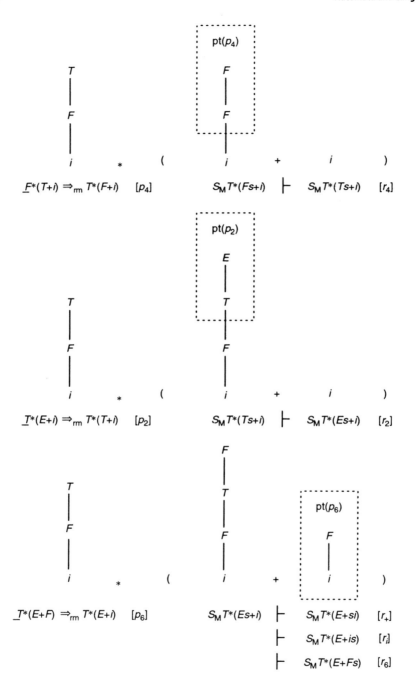

Figure 5.3.1.1.10(b) Bottom-up parsing of $i * (i + i)$.

Models for context-free languages

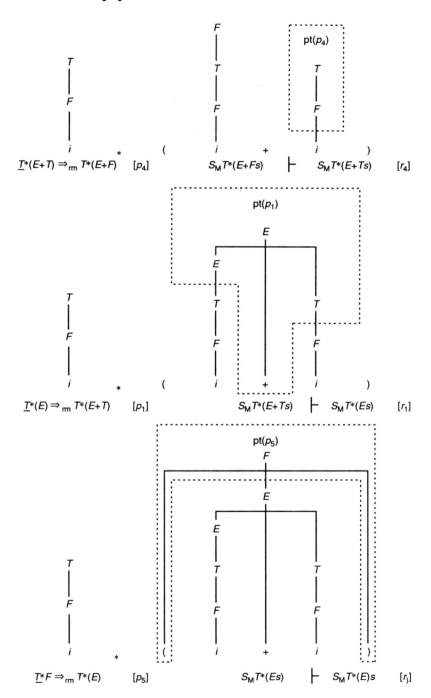

Figure 5.3.1.1.10(c) Bottom-up parsing of $i * (i + i)$.

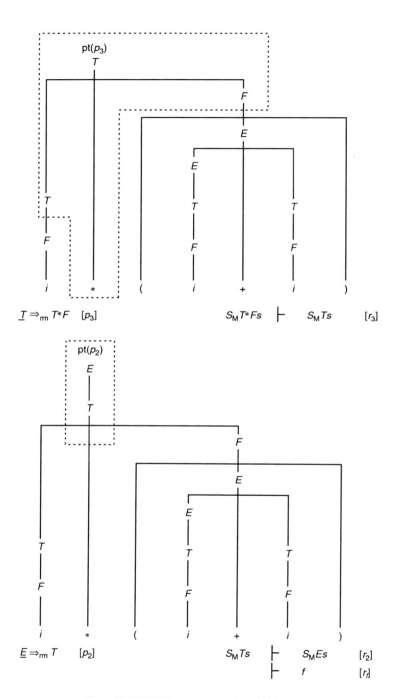

Figure 5.3.1.1.10(d) Bottom-up parsing of $i*(i+i)$.

Sections 5.3.1.2 and 9.2.1.1 reconsider this example in greater detail.

The following lemma states the most important result of this section.

▲

Lemma 5.3.1.1.13
Let L be a context-free language. Then, $L = L(M)$ for a pushdown automaton M.

Proof
This lemma follows from Algorithm 5.3.1.1.9 and Lemma 5.3.1.1.10.
■

Notice that Lemma 5.3.1.1.13 also follows from Theorem 5.2.2.3, Algorithm 5.3.1.1.11 and Lemma 5.3.1.1.12.

5.3.1.2 Parsing

The previous section explains the fundamental methodology of parsing in general. The present section gives a more realistic insight into parsing. Specifically, it describes a parsing method called *recursive descent*, which is often used in practice.

Essentials of recursive descent

Consider a programming language defined by a grammar G. Given an input program w the recursive-descent parsing method constructs a derivation tree for w by using G's productions, so it starts from the root and works down to the leaves in a left-to-right way. By looking at the next input lexeme occurring in w, this parser uniquely determines the production to use in each step of this parsing process. If the recursive-descent parser successfully constructs the tree for w, then w represents a well-formed program. However, if the parser encounters a situation when it has no production to use, it stops and indicates that w is incorrect.

Advantageously, the recursive-descent parsing method frees us from explicitly manipulating a pushdown list because the construction of a derivation tree is simulated by recursively calling boolean functions. More precisely, for each nonterminal A, there exists a boolean function f_A. This function simulates rewriting the leftmost nonterminal, A, according to a production with A on the left-hand side. If A forms the left-hand side of several productions, f_A determines the production to use by looking at the next lexeme occurring in the program.

Recursive-descent parser for COLA

To demonstrate the recursive-descent parsing method in detail, this section designs a parser for the programming language COLA (see Section 1.2). The following context-free grammar, G_{COLA}, defines this language:

1: ⟨program⟩ → **begin**⟨statement list⟩**end**
2: ⟨statement list⟩ → ⟨statement⟩; ⟨statement list⟩
3: ⟨statement list⟩ → ⟨statement⟩
4: ⟨statement⟩ → label
5: ⟨statement⟩ → **goto** label
6: ⟨statement⟩ → identifier := ⟨expression⟩
7: ⟨statement⟩ → **read**(⟨read list⟩)
8: ⟨statement⟩ → **write**(⟨write list⟩)
9: ⟨statement⟩ → **if**(⟨expression⟩ relational operator ⟨expression⟩ **goto** label
10: ⟨read list⟩ → identifier, ⟨read list⟩
11: ⟨read list⟩ → identifier
12: ⟨write list⟩ → ⟨write member⟩, ⟨write list⟩
13: ⟨write list⟩ → ⟨write member⟩
14: ⟨write member⟩ → identifier
15: ⟨write member⟩ → text literal
16: ⟨write member⟩ → new-line text literal
17: ⟨expression⟩ → ⟨term⟩+⟨expression⟩
18: ⟨expression⟩ → ⟨term⟩–⟨expression⟩
19: ⟨expression⟩ → ⟨term⟩
20: ⟨term⟩ → ⟨factor⟩*⟨term⟩
21: ⟨term⟩ → ⟨factor⟩/⟨term⟩
22: ⟨term⟩ → ⟨factor⟩
23: ⟨factor⟩ → (⟨expression⟩)
24: ⟨factor⟩ → identifier
25: ⟨factor⟩ → integer

G_{COLA} contains nine nonterminals — ⟨expression⟩, ⟨factor⟩, ⟨program⟩, ⟨read list⟩, ⟨statement⟩, ⟨statement list⟩, ⟨term⟩, ⟨write list⟩ and ⟨write member⟩, where ⟨program⟩ is the start symbol. Furthermore, G_{COLA} has 24 terminals — identifier; integer; label; text literal; new-line text literal; the arithmetic operators +, −, * and /; the relational operators =, ⟩ and ⟨; parentheses (and) ; assignment operator :=; reserved words **begin, end, goto, if, read, write**; and the separators , and ;. These terminals coincide with the lexemes of COLA. Section 3.3.1.2 constructs GetLexeme — the COLA scanner that accepts these lexemes. The COLA parser makes use of this scanner whenever the parser needs to obtain the next lexeme occurring in the COLA program and, moreover, the type of this lexeme (Section 3.3.1.2 classifies the COLA lexemes into 24 lexeme types).

At the heart of the COLA parser are the boolean functions corresponding to the nine nonterminals of G_{COLA}. The boolean function ColaProgram simulates the leftmost derivations starting from the start symbol ⟨program⟩. There exists a single production with ⟨program⟩ on its left-hand side, namely,

1: ⟨program⟩ → **begin**⟨statement list⟩**end**

This production implies that every well-formed COLA program begins with **begin** and ends with **end**; between these two reserved words, there occurs a word w derived from ⟨statement list⟩ (see Figure 5.3.1.2.1).

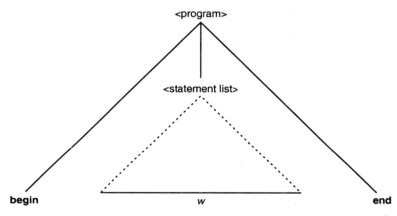

Figure 5.3.1.2.1 The structure of a COLA program

As a result, ColaProgram has the form:

function ColaProgram: **boolean**;
begin
    ColaProgram := **false**;
    GetLexeme;
    if LexemeType = 18 {18 is the lexeme type of **begin**}
    then if StatementList
        then if LexemeType = 19 {19 is the lexeme type of **end**}
            then ColaProgram := **true**
end

ColaProgram contains the function StatementList, which corresponds to ⟨statement list⟩. This nonterminal forms the left-hand side of the two productions

    2: ⟨statement list⟩ → ⟨statement⟩; ⟨statement list⟩
    3: ⟨statement list⟩ → ⟨statement⟩

These two productions imply that ⟨statement list⟩ derives a word w that consists of a sequence of subwords, separated by semicolons, so that each of these subwords is derived from ⟨statement⟩. More formally,

$$\langle \text{statement list} \rangle \Rightarrow^*_{\text{lm}} v_1; \ldots v_n$$

where $n \geq 1$, and

$$\langle \text{statement} \rangle \Rightarrow^*_{\text{lm}} v_i$$

for $i = 1, \ldots, n$ (see Figure 5.3.1.2.2). Notice that $n = 1$ actually means that

$$\langle \text{statement list} \rangle \Rightarrow_{\text{lm}} \langle \text{statement} \rangle \Rightarrow^*_{\text{lm}} v_1$$

with $w = v_1$.

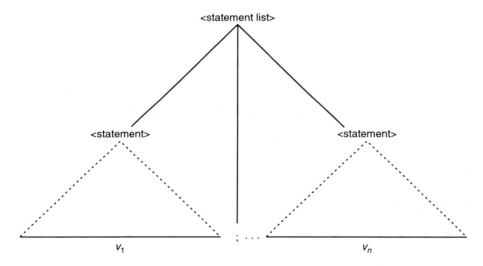

Figure 5.3.1.2.2 The structure of a COLA statement list.

The function StatementList begins by calling Statement. The true value of Statement means that the parser has successfully derived a word of lexemes from $\langle \text{statement} \rangle$, so StatementList calls GetLexeme to test whether the next lexeme represents a semicolon. If so, StatementList recursively calls itself; otherwise, StatementList is set to **true** because the simulation of $\langle \text{statement list} \rangle \Rightarrow^*_{\text{lm}} v_1; \ldots v_n$ has successfully been completed.

function StatementList:**boolean**;
begin
   StatementList := **false**;
   if Statement

```
        then
        begin
            if LexemeType = 16 {16 is the lexeme type of ;}
            then StatementList := StatementList
            else StatementList := true
        end
end
```

StatementList contains function Statement, which corresponding to nonterminal ⟨statement⟩. This nonterminal occurs on the left-hand side of the following six productions:

4: ⟨statement⟩ → label
5: ⟨statement⟩ → **goto** label
6: ⟨statement⟩ → identifier := ⟨expression⟩
7: ⟨statement⟩ → **read**(⟨read list⟩)
8: ⟨statement⟩ → **write**(⟨write list⟩)
9: ⟨statement⟩ → **if**(expression⟩ relational operator ⟨expression⟩ **goto** label

Thus, Statement needs to determine which of these six productions to use. Statement makes this determination by taking advantage of the property that the right-hand sides of these productions begin with different terminals. Indeed, by looking at the next lexeme appearing in the input program, Statement uniquely determines the production to apply. For instance, if the next lexeme is **if**, Statement simulates the application of production 9, which starts with **if**. Statement follows next.

function Statement:**boolean**;

procedure Success{This procedure sets Statement to **true** and reads the next lexeme. Some parts of the following **case** statement use Success before Statement exits for StatementList because the latter assumes that the next lexeme's type is in LexemeType.}
```
begin
    Statement := true;
    GetLexeme
end;

begin
    Statement := false;
    GetLexeme;
    case LexemeType of

        3:  {3 is the lexeme type of labels, so production 4 is simulated}
            Success;
```

20: {20 is the lexeme type of **goto**, so production 5 is simulated}
   begin
      GetLexeme;
      if LexemeType = 20 then Success
   end;

1: {1 is the lexeme type of identifiers, so production 6 is simulated}
   begin
      GetLexeme;
      if LexemeType = 17
      then if Expression
         then Statement := true
   end;

22: {22 is the lexeme type of **read**, so production 7 is simulated}
   begin
      GetLexeme;
      if LexemeType = 13
      then if ReadList
         then if LexemeType = 14
            then Success
   end;

23: {23 is the lexeme type of **write**, so production 8 is simulated}
   begin
      GetLexeme;
      if LexemeType = 13
      then if WriteList
         then if LexemeType = 14
            then Success
   end;

21: {21 is the lexeme type of **if**, so production 9 is simulated}
   begin
   if Expression
   then if LexemeType in [10, 11, 12] {10, 11, 12 are lexeme types of =, >, <, respectively}
      then if Expression
         then if LexemeType = 20 {20 is the lexeme type of **goto**}
            then
            begin
               GetLexeme;
               if LexemeType = 3 {3 is the lexeme type of labels}
               then Success
            end

```
        end
    end{of case}
end
```

ReadList is the function corresponding to ⟨read list⟩, which forms the left-hand side of the two productions

10: ⟨read list⟩ → identifier, ⟨read list⟩
11: ⟨read list⟩ → identifier

ReadList follows next.

```
function ReadList:boolean;
begin
    ReadList := false;
    GetLexeme;
    if LexemeType = 1 {1 is the lexeme type of identifiers}
    then
    begin
        GetLexeme;
        if LexemeType = 15 {15 is the lexeme type of ,}
        then ReadList := ReadList
        else ReadList := true
    end
end
```

The function WriteList corresponds to ⟨write list⟩, which occurs on the left-hand side of the following two productions:

12: ⟨write list⟩ → ⟨write member⟩, ⟨write list⟩
13: ⟨write list⟩ → ⟨write member⟩

WriteList follows next.

```
function WriteList:boolean;
begin
    WriteList := false;
    if WriteMember
    then
    begin
        GetLexeme;
        if LexemeType = 15 {15 is the lexeme type of ,}
        then WriteList := WriteList
        else WriteList := true
    end
end
```

WriteList contains WriteMember, which corresponds to the nonterminal ⟨write member⟩. This nonterminal occurs on the left-hand side of the three productions

14: ⟨write member⟩ → identifier
15: ⟨write member⟩ → text literal
16: ⟨write member⟩ → new-line text literal

The right-hand sides of these productions form three lexemes — identifier, text literal and new-line text literal. Consequently, WriteMember is defined in the following way.

function WriteMember:**boolean**;
begin
   GetLexeme;
   if LexemeType **in** [1, 4, 5] {1, 4, 5 are lexeme types of
   identifiers, text literals, and new-line text literals,
   respectively}
   then WriteMember := **true**
   else WriteMember := **false**
end

The function Expression corresponds to ⟨expression⟩, which forms the left-hand side of the three productions,

17: ⟨expression⟩ → ⟨term⟩+⟨expression⟩
18: ⟨expression⟩ → ⟨term⟩−⟨expression⟩
19: ⟨expression⟩ → ⟨term⟩

Expression follows next.

function Expression:**boolean**;
begin
   Expression := **false**;
   if Term
   then if LexemeType **in** [6, 7] {6 and 7 are lexeme types of + and −, respectively}
      then Expression := Expression
      else Expression := **true**
end

Expression calls Term, which corresponds to ⟨term⟩, occurring on the left-hand side of the productions

20: ⟨term⟩ → ⟨factor⟩*⟨term⟩
21: ⟨term⟩ → ⟨factor⟩/⟨term⟩
22: ⟨term⟩ → ⟨factor⟩

Term, constructed by analogy with Expression, is as follows.

function Term:**boolean**;
begin
  Term := **false**;
  if Factor
  then
  begin
    GetLexeme;
    if LexemeType **in** [8, 9] {8 and 9 are lexeme types of * and /, respectively}
    then Term := Term
    else Term := **true**
  end
end

The function Factor, contained in Term, corresponds to ⟨factor⟩, which occurs on the left-hand side of three productions:

23: ⟨factor⟩ → (⟨expression⟩)
24: ⟨factor⟩ → identifier
25: ⟨ factor ⟩ → integer

Factor is defined as follows.

function Factor:**boolean**;
begin
  Factor := **false**;
  GetLexeme;
  case LexemeType **of**
  1, 2 : {1 and 2 are the lexeme type of identifiers and integers, respectively}
    Factor := **true**;
  13   : {13 is the lexeme type of (, so production 23 is simulated}
    if Expression
    then if LexemeType = 14 {14 is the lexeme type of)}
        then Factor := **true**
  end
end

Having defined the Boolean function corresponding to all nine nonterminals occurring in G_{COLA}, this section completes the COLA parser by adding its main program body. Given an input COLA program, the main program first calls ColaProgram. If ColaProgram returns **true** and, in addition, the next lexeme is the end-of-file symbol, then the parser has successfully constructed a derivation tree for the input program, so the input program represents a well-formed COLA program. The program body is thus specified as follows:

begin
  if ColaProgram
    then if eof {eof is the end-of-file symbol}
       then writeln('successful parsing')
end

The parser for COLA is further discussed in the exercises and in Section 9.3.2.

5.3.2 From pushdown automata to context-free grammars

The following discussion demonstrates how to transform any pushdown automaton to an equivalent context-free grammar.

Algorithm 5.3.2.1: Conversion of a pushdown automaton to an equivalent context-free grammar

Input: A pushdown automaton $M = (Q, \Sigma, R, s, \emptyset)$.

Output: A context-free grammar $G = (N, T, P, S_G)$, such that $L(G) = L(M)_\varepsilon$.

Method
begin
  $N := \{\langle qAp \rangle: q, p \in Q, A \in \Sigma_{PD}\} \cup \{S_G\}$ {S_G is the start symbol of G};
  $T := \Sigma_I$;
  $P := \{S_G \rightarrow \langle sAp \rangle : p \in Q\}$;
  for each $Aq_0 a \vdash B_n...B_1 q_1 \in R$, where $a \in \Sigma_I \cup \{\varepsilon\}$),
  $A, B_1, ..., B_n \in \Sigma_{PD}, q_0, q_1 \in Q$, for some $n \geq 0$ **do**
    $P := P \cup \{\langle q_0 A q_{n+1}\rangle \rightarrow a\langle q_1 B_1 q_2\rangle\langle q_2 B_2 q_3\rangle...\langle q_n B_n q_{n+1}\rangle: q_2, ..., q_{n+1} \in Q\}$
    {$n = 0$ implies $\langle q_0 A q_1 \rangle \rightarrow a$}
end.

Algorithm 5.3.2.1 produces its output context-free grammar G so that, by making leftmost derivations, G simulates M accepting by empty pushdown. More precisely, $\langle qAp \rangle \Rightarrow^*_{lm} w$ in G, where $w \in T^*$, if and only if $Aqw \vdash^* p$ in M. Therefore, $S_G \Rightarrow_{lm} \langle sSp \rangle \Rightarrow^*_{lm} w$ if and only if M accepts w by empty pushdown; in other words, $L(G) = L(M)_\varepsilon$.

Models for context-free languages

Lemma 5.3.2.2
Let $M = (Q, \Sigma, R, s, \emptyset)$ be a pushdown automaton. With M as its input, Algorithm 5.3.2.1 halts and correctly constructs a context-free grammar $G = (N, T, P, S_G)$ such that $L(G) = L(M)_\varepsilon$.

Proof
Termination
As R is finite, Algorithm 5.3.2.1 repeats its **for** loop finitely many times, so this algorithm surely halts.

Correctness
To establish

$$L(G) = L(M)_\varepsilon$$

this proof first demonstrates the following claim.

Claim
For all $w \in T^*, A \in N$, and $q, q' \in Q$,

$$\langle qAq' \rangle \Rightarrow^*_{lm} w \text{ in } G \text{ if and only if } Aqw \vdash^* q' \text{ in } M$$

Proof

Only if
The 'only if' part of this claim states that for all $i \geq 0$,

$$\langle qAq' \rangle \Rightarrow^i_{lm} w \text{ in } G \text{ implies } Aqw \vdash^* q' \text{ in } M$$

This implication is proved by induction on i.

Basis
For $i = 0$, this implication holds vacuously, so the basis is true.

Induction hypothesis
Assume that the 'only if' part holds for all j-step derivations, where $j = 1, \ldots, i$, for some $i \geq 0$.

Induction step
Consider

$$\langle qAq' \rangle \Rightarrow^*_{lm} w \qquad [p\pi]$$

in G, where π represents a production word consisting of i productions, and $p \in P$. Thus, $\langle qAq' \rangle \Rightarrow_{\text{lm}}^* w\ [p\pi]$ is a derivation that has $i + 1$ steps. From Algorithm 5.3.2.1, p takes the form

$$p: \langle qAq' \rangle \to a \langle q_1 B_1 q_2 \rangle \langle q_2 B_2 q_3 \rangle \ldots \langle q_n B_n q_{n+1} \rangle$$

where

$$q' = q_{n+1}$$

Now express $\langle qAq' \rangle \Rightarrow_{\text{lm}}^* w\ [p\pi]$ as

$$\langle qAq' \rangle \Rightarrow_{\text{lm}} a \langle q_1 B_1 q_2 \rangle \langle q_2 B_2 q_3 \rangle \ldots \langle q_n B_n q_{n+1} \rangle \quad [p]$$
$$\Rightarrow_{\text{lm}}^* w \quad [\pi]$$

In greater detail,

$$\langle qAp \rangle \Rightarrow_{\text{lm}} a \langle q_1 B_1 q_2 \rangle \langle q_2 B_2 q_3 \rangle \ldots \langle q_n B_n q_{n+1} \rangle \quad [p]$$
$$\Rightarrow_{\text{lm}}^* aw_1 w_2 \ldots w_n$$

where $w = aw_1 w_2 \ldots w_n$, $\pi = \pi_1 \pi_2 \ldots \pi_n$, and

$$\langle q_j B_j q_{j+1} \rangle \Rightarrow_{\text{lm}}^* w_j \quad [\pi_j]$$

in G, for all $j = 1, \ldots, n$. As π_j consists of no more than i productions, the induction hypothesis implies

$$B_j q_j w_j \vdash^* q_{j+1}$$

in M, so

$$B_n \ldots B_{j+1} B_j q_j w_j \vdash^* B_n \ldots B_{j+1} q_{j+1}$$

in M. As $p: \langle qAq' \rangle \to a \langle q_1 B_1 q_2 \rangle \langle q_2 B_2 q_3 \rangle \ldots \langle q_n B_n q_{n+1} \rangle \in P$, R contains

$$r: Aqa \vdash B_n \ldots B_1 q_1$$

Thus,

$$Aqw \vdash B_n \ldots B_1 q_1 w_1 w_2 \ldots w_n \quad [r]$$

in M. Consequently,

$$Aqw \vdash B_n \ldots B_1 q_1 w_1 w_2 \ldots w_n \quad [r]$$

$$\vdash^* B_n...B_2q_2w_2...w_n$$
$$\vdots$$
$$\vdash^* B_nq_nw_n$$
$$\vdash^* q_{n+1}$$

in M. Because $q' = q_{n+1}$,

$$Aqw \vdash^* q'$$

in M, and the inductive step is completed.

Consequently, the 'only if' part of this claim holds.

If
The 'if' part of this claim states that for all $i \geq 0$,

$$Aqw \vdash^i q' \text{ in } M \text{ implies } \langle qAq' \rangle \Rightarrow^*_{\text{lm}} w \text{ in } G$$

This implication is proved by induction on i.

Basis
For $i = 0$, this implication holds vacuously. Thus, the basis is true.

Induction hypothesis
Assume that the if part of this claim holds for every j-move computation in M, where $j = 1, ..., i$, for some $i \geq 0$.

Induction step
Consider

$$Aqw \vdash^* q' \qquad [r\rho]$$

in M, where ρ represents a rule word consisting of i rules, and $r \in R$. Thus, $Aqw \vdash^{i+1} q' \ [r\rho]$ in M. From Algorithm 5.3.2.1, r has the form

$$r: Aqa \vdash B_n...B_1q_1$$

Now express $Aqw \vdash^* q' \ [r\rho]$ as

$$Aqav \vdash^* B_n...B_1q_1v \qquad [r]$$
$$\vdash^* q' \qquad [\rho]$$

In more detail,

$$Aqv \vdash B_n...B_1q_1v_1v_2...v_n \quad [r]$$
$$\vdash^* B_n...B_2q_2v_2...v_n \quad [\rho_1]$$
$$\vdots$$
$$\vdash^* B_nq_nv_n \quad [\rho_{n-1}]$$
$$\vdash^* q_{n+1} \quad [\rho_n]$$

where $q' = q_{n+1}$, $v = v_1v_2...v_n$, $\rho = \rho_1...\rho_{n-1}\rho_n$ and, for all $j = 1, ..., n$,

$$B_n...B_{j+1}B_jq_jv_jv_{j+1}...v_n \vdash^* B_n...B_{j+1}q_{j+1}v_{j+1}...v_n \quad [\rho_j]$$

As ρ_j consists of no more than i rules, the induction hypothesis implies

$$\langle q_jB_jq_{j+1}\rangle \Rightarrow^*_{lm} v_j \quad [\pi_j]$$

in G, for all $j = 1, ..., n$. As $r: Aqa \vdash B_n...B_1q_1 \in R$ and $q_2, ..., q_{n+1} \in Q$, P contains

$$p: \langle qAq_{n+1}\rangle \to a\langle q_1B_1q_2\rangle\langle q_2B_2q_3\rangle...\langle q_nB_nq_{n+1}\rangle$$

from the **for** loop of Algorithm 5.3.2.1. Consequently,

$$\langle qAp\rangle \Rightarrow_{lm} a\langle q_1B_1q_2\rangle\langle q_2B_2q_3\rangle...\langle q_nB_nq_{n+1}\rangle \quad [p]$$
$$\Rightarrow^*_{lm} av_1v_2...v_n \quad [\pi]$$

where $\pi = \pi_1\pi_2...\pi_n$. As $q' = q_{n+1}$ and $w = av_1v_2...v_n$, G makes this derivation

$$\langle qAp\rangle \Rightarrow^*_{lm} w$$

That is, the inductive step is completed.

Consequently, the 'if' part of this claim is true, so the claim holds. □

Consider this claim for $A = S$ and $q = s$. At this point, for all $w \in T^*$,

$$\langle sSq'\rangle \Rightarrow^*_{lm} w \text{ in } G \text{ if and only if } Ssw \vdash^* q' \text{ in } M$$

Therefore,

$$S_G \Rightarrow_{lm} \langle sSq'\rangle \Rightarrow^*_{lm} w \text{ if and only if } M \ Ssw \vdash^* q' \text{ in } M$$

In other words,

$$L(G) = L(M)_\varepsilon$$

Models for context-free languages

To summarize, with M as its input, Algorithm 5.3.2.1 halts and correctly produces its output context-free grammar $G = (N, T, P, S_G)$ satisfying $L(G) = L(M)_\varepsilon$. Thus, Lemma 5.3.2.2 holds.

■

Example 5.3.2.1 Application of Algorithm 5.3.2.1
Consider the pushdown automaton M

r_1: $Ssa \vdash Sas$

r_2: $asa \vdash aas$

r_3: $asb \vdash q$

r_4: $aqb \vdash q$

r_5: $Sq \vdash q$

By analogy with the proof given in Part 8 of Example 5.2.1.1, demonstrate that

$$L(M)_\varepsilon = \{a^n b^n : n \geq 1\}$$

From Algorithm 5.3.2.1, the present example converts M to a context-free grammar $G = (N, T, P, S_G)$ such that $L(G) = L(M)_\varepsilon$. This algorithm initially sets

$N := \{\langle sSs \rangle, \langle qSq \rangle, \langle sSq \rangle, \langle qSs \rangle, \langle sas \rangle, \langle qaq \rangle, \langle saq \rangle, \langle qas \rangle, S_G\}$

$T := \{a, b\}$

$P := \{S_G \to \langle sSs \rangle, S_G \to \langle sSq \rangle\}$

Then, Algorithm 5.3.2.1 enters its **for** loop. From r_1: $Ssa \vdash Sas$, this loop produces

$\langle sSs \rangle \to a\langle sas \rangle\langle sSs \rangle$

$\langle sSs \rangle \to a\langle saq \rangle\langle qSs \rangle$

$\langle sSq \rangle \to a\langle sas \rangle\langle sSq \rangle$

$\langle sSq \rangle \to a\langle saq \rangle\langle qSq \rangle$

and adds these four productions to P. Analogously, from r_2: $asa \vdash aas$, the **for** loop constructs

$\langle sas \rangle \to a\langle sas \rangle\langle sas \rangle$

$\langle sas \rangle \to a\langle saq \rangle\langle qas \rangle$

$$\langle saq \rangle \to a \langle sas \rangle \langle saq \rangle$$

$$\langle saq \rangle \to a \langle saq \rangle \langle qaq \rangle$$

and adds these four productions to P. Based on r_3: $asb \vdash q$, this loop adds

$$\langle saq \rangle \to b$$

to P. From r_4: $aqb \vdash q$, the **for** loop constructs

$$\langle qaq \rangle \to b$$

and includes this production in P. Finally, from r_5: $Sq \vdash q$, this loop produces

$$\langle qSq \rangle \to \varepsilon$$

and adds it to P. As a result, P consists of the following productions:

$$S_G \to \langle sSs \rangle,$$

$$S_G \to \langle sSq \rangle,$$

$$\langle sSs \rangle \to a\langle sas \rangle\langle sSs \rangle,$$

$$\langle sSs \rangle \to a\langle saq \rangle\langle qSs \rangle,$$

$$\langle sSq \rangle \to a\langle sas \rangle\langle sSq \rangle,$$

$$\langle sSq \rangle \to a\langle saq \rangle\langle qSq \rangle,$$

$$\langle sas \rangle \to a\langle sas \rangle\langle sas \rangle,$$

$$\langle sas \rangle \to a\langle saq \rangle\langle qas \rangle,$$

$$\langle saq \rangle \to a\langle sas \rangle\langle saq \rangle,$$

$$\langle saq \rangle \to a\langle saq \rangle\langle qaq \rangle,$$

$$\langle saq \rangle \to b,$$

$$\langle qaq \rangle \to b,$$

$$\langle qSq \rangle \to \varepsilon$$

For simplicity, remove all useless symbols from G by using Algorithm 5.1.3.1.9 to construct the equivalent grammar, G_{useful}, defined as

$p_0: S_G \rightarrow \langle sSq \rangle,$
$p_1: \langle sSq \rangle \rightarrow a\langle saq \rangle\langle qSq \rangle,$
$p_2: \langle saq \rangle \rightarrow a\langle saq \rangle\langle qaq \rangle,$
$p_3: \langle saq \rangle \rightarrow b,$
$p_4: \langle qaq \rangle \rightarrow b,$
$p_5: \langle qSq \rangle \rightarrow \varepsilon$

Observe that

$$L(G) = L(G_{\text{useful}}) = L(M)_\varepsilon = \{a^n b^n : n \geq 1\}$$

Consider $aaabbb \in L(M)_\varepsilon$. By empty pushdown, M accepts $aaabbb$ as follows:

$$
\begin{array}{lll}
Ssaaabbb & \vdash Sasaabbb & [r_1] \\
& \vdash Saasabbb & [r_2] \\
& \vdash Saaasbbb & [r_2] \\
& \vdash Saaqbb & [r_3] \\
& \vdash Saqb & [r_4] \\
& \vdash Ss & [r_4] \\
& \vdash q & [r_5]
\end{array}
$$

That is,

$$Ssbabbab \vdash^* s \qquad [r_1 r_2 r_2 r_3 r_4 r_4 r_5]$$

Accordingly, G generates $babbab$ by making this leftmost derivation

$$
\begin{array}{ll}
\underline{S_G} \Rightarrow_{\text{lm}} \langle \underline{sSq} \rangle & [p_0] \\
\Rightarrow_{\text{lm}} a\langle \underline{saq} \rangle\langle qSq \rangle & [p_1] \\
\Rightarrow_{\text{lm}} aa\langle \underline{saq} \rangle\langle qaq \rangle\langle qSq \rangle & [p_2] \\
\Rightarrow_{\text{lm}} aaa\langle \underline{saq} \rangle\langle qaq \rangle qaq \rangle\langle qSq \rangle & [p_2] \\
\Rightarrow_{\text{lm}} aaab\langle \underline{qaq} \rangle\langle qaq \rangle\langle qSq \rangle & [p_3] \\
\Rightarrow_{\text{lm}} aaabb\langle \underline{qaq} \rangle\langle qSq \rangle & [p_4] \\
\Rightarrow_{\text{lm}} aaabbb\langle \underline{qSq} \rangle & [p_4] \\
\Rightarrow_{\text{lm}} aaabbb & [p_5]
\end{array}
$$

That is,

$$S \Rightarrow^*_{lm} aaabbb \quad [p_0 p_1 p_2 p_2 p_3 p_4 p_4 p_5]$$

▲

The next lemma states the main result of Section 5.3.2.

Lemma 5.3.2.3
Let $L = L(M)$ where M is a pushdown automaton. Then, L is context-free.

Proof
This lemma follows from Corollary 5.2.1.5, Algorithm 5.3.2.1 and Lemma 5.3.2.2. ■

5.3.3 Equivalence of pushdown automata and context-free grammars

This section establishes the equivalence of pushdown automata and context-free grammars.

Theorem 5.3.3.1
Let L be a language. Then $L = L(M)$ for a pushdown automaton M if and only if $L = L(G)$, for a context-free grammar, G.

Proof
Theorem 5.3.3.3.1 follows from Lemmas 5.3.1.1.13 and 5.3.2.3. ■

The following theorem summarizes the main results of all Chapter 5.

Theorem 5.3.3.2
The following classes of computational models characterize the family of context-free languages:

1. context-free grammars;
2. pushdown automata that accept by final state;
3. pushdown automata that accept by empty pushdown;

4. pushdown automata that accept by final state and empty pushdown;
5. extended pushdown automata that accept by final state;
6. extended pushdown automata that accept by empty pushdown;
7. extended pushdown automata that accept by final state and empty pushdown.

Proof
This theorem follows from Corollary 5.2.1.7, Theorem 5.2.2.3, Corollary 5.2.2.7, Theorem 5.2.2.3 and Theorem 5.3.3.1.

■

Exercises

1 Context-free grammars

1.1 Consider these context-free grammars
(a) 1: $S \to abSba$
2: $S \to A$
3: $S \to cAc$
4: $A \to cc$
(b) 1: $S \to aSbSa$
2: $S \to \varepsilon$
(c) 1: $S \to ASB$
2: $S \to \varepsilon$
3: $A \to aSb$
4: $A \to \varepsilon$
5: $B \to aBb$
6: $B \to ba$
(d) 1: $S \to SS$
2: $S \to a_1 S a_2$
3: $S \to a_1 a_2$
4: $S \to a_3 S a_4$
5: $S \to a_3 a_4$
6: $S \to a_5 S a_6$
7: $S \to a_5 a_6$

For each of these context-free grammars,
(A) give five sentences that the grammar generates;
(B) describe a derivation for each of the sentences in (A);
(C) describe all leftmost derivations for each of the sentences in (A);
(D) describe all rightmost derivations for each of the sentences in (A);
(E) describe all derivation trees for each of the sentences in (A).

1.2 Consider these trees:

(a)
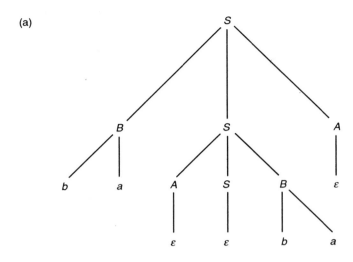

(b)
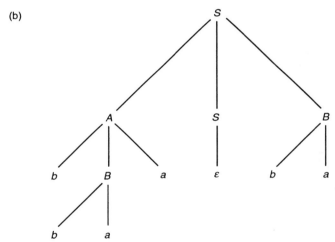

(c)
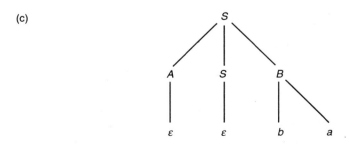

Models for context-free languages

Do any of these trees represent a derivation tree of a context-free grammar given in Exercise 1.1?

1.3 Consider the following context-free grammars:
(a) 1: $S \to aSa$
    2: $S \to bSb$
    3: $S \to \varepsilon$
(b) 1: $S \to aSa$
    2: $S \to bSb$
    3: $S \to a$
    4: $S \to b$
(c) 1: $S \to aS$
    2: $S \to Sb$
    3: $S \to a$
(d) 1: $S \to aS$
    2: $S \to Sb$
    3: $S \to a$
    4: $S \to SS$
(e) 1: $S \to aSa$
    2: $S \to bb$

For each of these context-free grammars, determine the language that the context-free grammar generates.

1.4 Consider these languages
(a) $\{a^i b^j c^k : i, j, k \geq 0 \text{ and } i = j + k\}$
(b) $\{a^i b^j c^k : i, j, k \geq 0 \text{ and } j = i + k\}$
(c) $\{a^i b^j c^k : i, j, k \geq 0 \text{ and } i \neq j + k\}$
(d) $\{a^i b^j c^k : i, j, k \geq 0 \text{ and } j \neq i\}$
(e) $\{a^i b^j c^k : i, j, k \geq 0 \text{ and } j \neq k\}$
(f) $\{a^i b^j c^k : i, j, k \geq 0 \text{ and } j \neq i + k\}$
(g) $\{a^i b^j c^k : i, j, k \geq 0 \text{ and } i = j \text{ or } j = k\}$
(h) $\{a^i b^j c^k : i, j, k \geq 0 \text{ and } i = j \text{ or } i = k\}$
(i) $\{a^i b^j c^k : i, j, k \geq 0 \text{ and } i < j \text{ or } j > k\}$
(j) $\{a^i b^j : i, j \geq 0 \text{ and } i \leq 2j\}$
(k) $\{a^i b^j : i, j \geq 0 \text{ and } i \leq j \leq 2i\}$
(l) $\{a^i b^i c^j : i, j \geq 0\}$
(m) $\{a^i b^i c^j d^j : i, j \geq 0\}$
(n) $\{a^i b^j c^k d^l : i, j, k, l \geq 0, i < l, \text{ and } j \neq k\}$
(o) $\{a^i b^j b^i a^j : i, j \geq 0\}$
(p) $\{a^i b^j c^j d^i : i, j \geq 0\}$
(q) $\{a^i b^j c^j d^i : i, j \geq 0\} \cup \{a^i b^i c^j d^j : i, j \geq 0\}$

For each of these languages, construct a context-free grammar that generates the language. Prove that this construction is correct.

1.5 Construct a context-free grammar that generates the language consisting of all numbers in FORTRAN. Describe how the grammar generates these numbers:
(a) 16
(b) −61
(c) −6.12
(d) −32.61E+04
(e) −21.32E−02

1.6 Construct a context-free grammar that generates the language consisting of the declaration statements in PL/I; for simplicity, ignore the precision attributes and the initial attributes. Describe how the grammar generates these declarations:
(a) DECLARE A FIXED BINARY, B FLOAT;
(b) DECLARE (A, B) FIXED;
(c) DECLARE (A(10), B(−1:2), C) FLOAT;

1.7 Construct a context-free grammar that generates Pascal.

1.8 Construct a context-free grammar that generates the language of parenthesized logical expressions consisting of the logical variable p and the logical operators **and**, **or**, and **not**. Describe how the grammar generates these expression:
(a) **not** p **or** p
(b) **not** (p **and** p) **or** p
(c) (p **or** p) **or** (p **and** (**not** p))

1.9 A *palindrome* is a word that is identical to itself when written backwards. A *binary palindrome* is a palindrome over $\{0, 1\}$. Define binary palindromes formally. Construct a context-free grammar that generates the language consisting of all binary palindromes.

1.10 Prove Theorem 5.1.1.2.

1.11 An E0S system is a context-free grammar that can rewrite terminals. More precisely, an *E0S system* is a quadruple

$$G = (N, T, P, S)$$

where
N is an alphabet of nonterminals;
T is an alphabet of terminals such that $N \cap T \neq \emptyset$;
$P \subseteq (N \cup T) \times (N \cup T)^*$ is a finite relationship;
$S \in N$ is the start symbol.

Let $G = (N, T, P, S)$ be an E0S system. Adapt $\Rightarrow$ and $\Rightarrow^*$ for G. Define the language $L(G)$ generated by G, as

$$L(G) = \{w : w \in T^* \text{ and } S \Rightarrow^* w\}$$

Prove that L is a context-free language if and only if there exists an E0S system G so that $L(G) = L$.

1.13 A pure context-free grammar has only terminals. More precisely, a *pure context-free grammar* is a triple

$$G = (T, P, S)$$

where
T is an alphabet;
$P \subseteq T \times T^*$ is a finite relationship;
$S \in T^+$ is the start symbol.

Adapt $\Rightarrow$ and $\Rightarrow^*$ for a pure context-free grammar, $G = (T, P, S)$; then, define the language $L(G)$ generated by G, as

$$L(G) = \{w: S \Rightarrow^* w\}$$

1.14 Consider the following languages:
  (a) $\{b, aa\}$
  (b) $\{a, aa\}$
  (c) $\{a^n c b^n : n \geq 1\}$
  (d) $\{a^n b^n : n \geq 1\}$
  For each of these languages, prove or disprove that there exists a pure context-free grammar that generates the language.

1.15 Prove that for every pure context-free grammar G there exists a context-free grammar G' such that $L(G) = L(G')$.

1.16 Prove that for every context-free grammar G there exists a pure context-free grammar G' such that

$$L(G') = \{x : x \text{ is a sentential form of } G\}$$

1.17 An operator context-free grammar represents an ε-free context-free grammar such that no production has two consecutive nonterminals on its right-hand side. That is, an ε-free context-free grammar, $G = (N, T, P, S)$, is an *operator context-free grammar* if for all $p \in P$, $\text{rhs}(p) \notin (N \cup T)^* NN(N \cup T)^*$. Define the notion of an operator context-free grammar formally. Prove that for every context-free grammar G there exists an operator context-free grammar, G', such that $L(G) = L(G')$.

1.18 Return to the Backus–Naur form (see Section 1.2.2). Prove that this form characterizes the family of context-free languages.

1.19 Return to the extended Backus–Naur form (see Section 1.2.2). Prove that this form characterizes the family of context-free languages.

1.20 Return to syntax graphs (see Section 1.2.2). Prove that these graphs characterize the family of context-free languages.

1.21 Perform these three tasks:
  (A) By analogy with the ambiguity of context-free grammars, introduce the ambiguity of the Backus–Naur form.

(B) The definition of the decimal digit calculator language, which performs arithmetic operations on integer arguments, was originally defined by the following Backus–Naur form:

⟨DDC expr⟩ → ⟨DDC term⟩ | ⟨DDC expr⟩⟨op1⟩⟨DDC expr⟩
⟨DDC term⟩ → ⟨decimal arg⟩ | ⟨DDC term⟩⟨op2⟩⟨DDC arg⟩
⟨DDC arg⟩ → ⟨digit⟩ | ⟨decimal arg⟩⟨digit⟩
⟨digit⟩ → 0 | 1 | 2 | 3 | 4 | 5 | 6 | 7 | 8 | 9
⟨op1⟩ → + | −
⟨op2⟩ → * | /

Demonstrate the ambiguity of this Backus–Naur form.

(C) Construct an unambiguous context-free grammar equivalent to the Backus–Naur form given in (B).

1.22 Consider this context-free grammar G:

1: $S \to S + S$
2: $S \to S * S$
3: $S \to (S)$
4: $S \to a$

Prove that $a + a * a \in L(G)$. Present two distinct derivation trees of $a + a * a$. Determine $L(G)$. Construct an unambiguous context-free grammar that generates $L(G)$.

1.23 Consider the following context-free grammars:

(a) 1: $S \to \varepsilon$
   2: $S \to aSb$
   3: $S \to SS$

(b) 1: $S \to \varepsilon$
   2: $S \to aSb$
   3: $S \to bSa$
   4: $S \to SS$

(c) 1: $S \to bS$
   2: $S \to Sb$
   3: $S \to \varepsilon$

(d) 1: $S \to SaSa$
   2: $S \to b$

(e) 1: $S \to Sb$
   2: $S \to aSb$
   3: $S \to Sa$
   4: $S \to a$

(f) 1: $S \to a$
   2: $S \to aaS$
   3: $S \to aaaS$

(g) 1: $S \to A$
   2: $S \to aSb$
   3: $S \to bS$
   4: $A \to Aa$
   5: $A \to a$

(h) 1: $S \to AA$
   2: $A \to AAA$
   3: $A \to bA$
   4: $A \to Ab$
   5: $A \to a$

For each of these grammars, prove or disprove that the grammar is ambiguous. If the grammar is ambiguous, prove or disprove that the language generated by this grammar is inherently ambiguous.

1.24** Consider the language

$$L = \{w\,\text{reversal}(w): w \in \{a, b\}^*\}$$

Prove that L^2 represents an inherently ambiguous context-free language.

1.25 Let $G = (N, T, P, S)$ be a context-free grammar. Let k be the length of the longest right-hand side of a production in P, and let $n = \text{card}(P')$, where $P' = \{\,p: p \in P,$ and $\text{rhs}(p) \neq \varepsilon\}$. Assume that G is on the input of Algorithm 5.1.3.3.3. Determine the maximum number of productions in the output ε-free context-free grammar $G_{\varepsilon\text{-free}}$ produced by this algorithm.

1.26 Consider the following context-free grammars:
(a) 1: $S \to ABB$
   2: $S \to CAC$
   3: $A \to a$
   4: $B \to Bc$
   5: $B \to ABB$
   6: $C \to bB$
   7: $C \to a$
(b) 1: $S \to aSASb$
   2: $S \to Saa$
   3: $S \to AA$
   4: $A \to caA$
   5: $A \to Ac$
   6: $A \to bca$
   7: $A \to \varepsilon$
(c) 1: $S \to AB$
   2: $S \to CA$
   3: $A \to a$
   4: $B \to BC$
   5: $B \to AB$
   6: $C \to aB$
   7: $C \to b$
(d) 1: $S \to AB$
   2: $S \to \varepsilon$
   3: $A \to aASb$
   4: $A \to a$
   5: $B \to bS$

(e) 1: $S \to ABA$
2: $A \to aA$
3: $A \to \varepsilon$
4: $B \to bB$
5: $B \to \varepsilon$

(f) 1: $S \to aSa$
2: $S \to bSb$
3: $S \to A$
4: $A \to aBb$
5: $A \to bBa$
6: $B \to aB$
7: $B \to bB$
8: $B \to \varepsilon$

For each of these grammars, determine the language L generated by the grammar. Then, construct a proper context-free grammar G, such that $L(G) =_\varepsilon L$.

1.26 Consider these context-free grammars:

(a) 1: $S \to aA$
2: $S \to abB$
3: $A \to bc$
4: $B \to c$

(b) 1: $S \to aSASb$
2: $S \to Saa$
3: $S \to b$
4: $A \to caA$
5: $A \to Ac$
6: $A \to bca$

(c) 1: $S \to cBA$
2: $S \to B$
3: $A \to cB$
4: $A \to AbbS$
5: $B \to aaa$

Convert each of these grammars to an equivalent context-free grammar in Chomsky normal form.

1.27 Let $G = (N, T, P, S)$ be a context-free grammar in Chomsky normal form, and let $w \in T^+$. Determine the number of steps in a derivation of the form $S \Rightarrow^* w$ in G.

1.28* Prove that for every context-free language L there exists a context-free grammar $G = (N, T, P, S)$, satisfying these four conditions:

(a) $L(G) =_\varepsilon L$
(b) G is in Chomsky normal form
(c) for all $p \in P$, $\text{rhs}(p) \notin \{A^2 : A \in N\}$
(d) for all $p, p' \in P$,

if $\text{rhs}(p) \in N\{A\}$ and $\text{rhs}(p') \in \{A\}N$, for some $A \in N$, then $\text{lhs}(p) \neq \text{lhs}(p')$

1.29 Consider the following context-free grammars:
  (a) 1: $S \to ASa$
      2: $S \to Ab$
      3: $A \to SA$
      4: $A \to c$
  (b) 1: $S \to BS$
      2: $S \to Aa$
      3: $A \to ba$
      4: $B \to Ac$
  (c) 1: $S \to SAc$
      2: $S \to dB$
      3: $A \to SS$
      4: $A \to a$
      5: $B \to Bb$

Convert each of these grammars to an equivalent context-free grammar in Greibach normal form.

1.30 Let $G = (N, T, P, S)$ be a context-free grammar in Greibach two-standard normal form, and let $w \in T^+$. Determine the number of steps in the derivation $S \Rightarrow^* w$ in G.

1.31* Prove that for every context-free language L there exists a context-free grammar $G = (N, T, P, S)$ satisfying these two conditions:
  (a) $L(G) =_\varepsilon L$
  (b) for all $p \in P$, $\mathrm{rhs}(p) \in T \cup T(N \cup T)^* T$

1.32 Complete the proof of Theorem 5.1.1.3.
1.33 Complete the proof of Theorem 5.1.1.5.
1.34 Give a detailed proof of Theorem 5.1.1.6.
1.35 Complete Example 5.1.2.1 Part 2.
1.36 Complete the proof of Lemma 5.1.3.1.6.
1.37 Complete the proof of Theorem 5.1.3.1.10.
1.38 Complete the proof of Theorem 5.1.4.2.6.
1.39 Complete the proof of Lemma 5.1.4.2.7.
1.40 Complete Part 2 of example 5.1.4.3.
1.41 Prove Theorem 5.1.4.2.11.

2 Pushdown automata

2.1 Consider the pushdown automaton
  r_1: $Ssa \vdash aq$
  r_2: $Ssa \vdash aaq$
  r_3: $Ssb \vdash bq$
  r_4: $Ssb \vdash bbq$
  r_5: $aqa \vdash aaq$
  r_6: $aqa \vdash aaaq$
  r_7: $bqb \vdash bbq$

r_8: $bqb \vdash bbbq$
r_9: $aqb \vdash f$
r_{10}: $bqa \vdash f$
r_{11}: $afb \vdash f$
r_{12}: $bfa \vdash f$

Perform the following tasks:
(A) give the pushdown state diagram of this automaton;
(B) give five words that this pushdown automaton accepts;
(C) for each of the words given in (B), present the rule word according to which this pushdown automaton accepts the word;
(D) give five words over $\{a, b\}$ that this automaton rejects.

2.2 Construct a pushdown automaton $M = (Q, \Sigma, R, s, F)$, such that for some $w \in \Sigma_I^*$ and $f \in F$, M computes

$$Ssw \vdash^* f$$

according to infinitely many rule words.

2.3 Consider the following pushdown automata:
(a) 1: $Ssa \vdash Sas$
    2: $asa \vdash aas$
    3: $asb \vdash q$
    4: $aqb \vdash q$
    5: $Sq \vdash Ss$
    6: $Sq \vdash s$
(b) 1: $Ss \vdash SSs$
    2: $Ssa \vdash Sas$
    3: $asa \vdash aas$
    4: $asb \vdash q$
    5: $aqb \vdash q$
    6: $Sq \vdash s$
(c) 1: $Ssa \vdash As$
    2: $Asa \vdash AAs$
    3: $Asc \vdash q$
    4: $Ssb \vdash As$
    5: $Asb \vdash AAs$
    6: $Aqc \vdash q$

For each of these automata, describe the corresponding pushdown state diagram; then, determine the language that the pushdown automaton accepts.

2.4 Consider the following pushdown automata:
(a) 1: $Ssa \vdash Sq$
    2: $aqa \vdash aas$
    3: $aqb \vdash q$
    4: $Sq \vdash f$
(b) 1: $Ssa \vdash Saaq$
    2: $bqb \vdash q$

3: $bqa \vdash q$
4: $bqa \vdash bq$
5: $Sq \vdash f$

For each of these automata, determine these three languages
(A) the language that the pushdown automaton accepts by final state;
(B) the language that the pushdown automaton accepts by empty pushdown;
(C) the language that the pushdown automaton accepts by final state and empty pushdown.

2.5 Reconsider each of the languages discussed in Exercises 1.4 through 1.10. Construct a pushdown automaton that accepts the language by empty pushdown.

2.6 Prove that for every language L, $L = L(M_{f\varepsilon})_{f\varepsilon}$ for an pushdown automaton $M_{f\varepsilon}$ if and only if $L = L(M_f)_f$ for a pushdown automaton M_f.

2.7 Let $M = (Q, \Sigma, R, s, F)$ be a pushdown automaton. Prove that

$$\{z: Ssw \vdash^* zq \text{ in } M\}$$

represents a regular language.

2.8* A language L has the prefix property if none of its words is a proper prefix of another word in L. Formally, L has the *prefix property* if $v \in L$ implies $v \notin$ prefix(w) for all $w \in L - \{v\}$. Prove or disprove that if $L = L(M)_\varepsilon$ for a pushdown automaton M, then L has the prefix property.

2.10 A *lazy pushdown automaton* reads a word, consisting of several symbols, during a move.
(A) Formalize this generalization.
(B) Prove that this generalization does not add to the power of pushdown automata.

2.11 A *two-way pushdown automaton* moves either way on its input.
(A) Formalize this generalization.
(B) Prove that $\{a^n b^n c^n : n \geq 1\}$ is accepted by a two-way pushdown automaton.
(C) Prove that $\{a^n b^n c^n : n \geq 1\}$ is accepted by no pushdown automaton.
NOTE: (B) and (C) imply that the pushdown automata are not as powerful as the two-way pushdown automata.

2.12 Let $M = (Q, \Sigma, R, s, F)$ be a pushdown automaton. M is a *counter pushdown automaton* if card$(\Sigma_{PD}) = 1$.
(A) Prove that for every counter pushdown automaton M there exists a counter pushdown automaton M' such that $L(M)_\varepsilon = L(M')_{f\varepsilon}$.
(B) Prove that

$$L(M)_\varepsilon \neq \{a^i b^j c : i \geq j \geq 0\}$$

for any counter pushdown automaton.
(C) Construct a counter pushdown automaton M such that

$$L(M)_{fe} = \{a^i b^j c : i \geq j \geq 0\}.$$

NOTE: (A), (B) and (C) imply that the family of languages accepted by counter pushdown automata by empty pushdown represents a proper subfamily of the family of languages accepted by counter pushdown automata by final state and empty pushdown.

2.13 Consider the family of languages accepted by counter pushdown automata by empty pushdown and the family of languages accepted by counter pushdown automata by final state. State the relationship between these two families.

2.14 Consider

$$L = \{a^i b^j a^j b^i : i \geq j \geq 0\}$$

(A) Prove that

$$L(M)_{fe} \neq L$$

for any counter pushdown automaton.

(B) Construct a pushdown automaton M' such that

$$L(M')_{fe} = L$$

NOTE: From (A) and (B), the counter pushdown automata are not as powerful as the pushdown automata.

2.15 Consider the extended pushdown automaton M discussed in Example 5.2.2.2.

(A) Give a rigorous proof that

$$L(M) = \{w \operatorname{reversal}(w) : w \in \{a, b\}^*\}$$

(B) Return to Algorithm 5.2.2.1 and convert M to an equivalent pushdown automaton by using this algorithm.

2.16 Consider each of the languages discussed in Exercises 1.4 through 1.10. Construct an extended pushdown automaton that accepts the language.

2.17 Consider each of the extended pushdown automata constructed in Exercise 2.16. Convert the automaton to an equivalent pushdown automaton by using Algorithm 5.2.2.1.

2.18 Give a formal proof that for every language L, $L = L(M_f)_f$ for an extended pushdown automaton, M_f, if and only if $L = L(M_{fe})_{fe}$ for an extended pushdown automaton, M_{fe}.

2.19 An *atomic pushdown automaton* is an extended pushdown automaton $M = (Q, \Sigma, R, s, F)$ such that any rule, $r \in R$, causes M to change the current state and, in addition, perform one of these three actions:
(a) popping a pushdown symbol
(b) pushing a pushdown symbol

(c) reading an input symbol.
(A) Formalize the notion of an atomic pushdown automaton.
(B) Prove that the power of atomic pushdown automata coincides with the power of extended pushdown automata.

2.20 Consider these languages
(a) $\{a^{2i}cb^i : i \geq 0\}$
(b) $\{a^{2i+1}cb^i : i \geq 0\}$
(c) $\{w : w \in \{a, b\}^*, \#_a w = \#_b w\}$
For each of these languages, construct a deterministic pushdown automaton that accepts the language.

2.21 Consider each of the languages discussed in Exercises 1.4 through 1.10. Prove or disprove that there exists a deterministic pushdown automaton that accepts the language.

2.22 Prove that for every deterministic pushdown automaton $M_f = (Q, \Sigma, R, s, F)$ and a symbol # such that #, $\notin \Sigma_I$, there exists a deterministic pushdown automaton M_ε such that $L(M_f)_f\{\#\} = L(M_\varepsilon)_\varepsilon$.

2.23 Prove that for every deterministic pushdown automaton M_ε there exists a deterministic pushdown automaton $M_{f\varepsilon}$ such that $L(M_\varepsilon)_\varepsilon = L(M_{f\varepsilon})_{f\varepsilon}$.

2.24 Prove that the family of languages accepted by deterministic pushdown automata by final state and empty pushdown is properly contained in the family of languages accepted by deterministic pushdown automata by final state.

2.25* Determine the relationships between the family of languages accepted by deterministic pushdown automata by final state and empty pushdown, the family of languages accepted by deterministic pushdown automata by final state, and the family of languages accepted by deterministic pushdown automata by empty pushdown.

2.26 Consider $L = \{a^i b^j c : i \geq j \geq 0\}$.
(A) Prove that

$$L(M)_{f\varepsilon} \neq L$$

for any ε-free deterministic pushdown automaton.
(B) Construct a deterministic pushdown automaton, M', such that

$$L(M')_{f\varepsilon} = L$$

NOTE: From (A) and (B), the deterministic pushdown automata that accept by final state and empty pushdown are more powerful than the ε-free deterministic pushdown automata that accept by final state and empty pushdown.

2.27* Prove that if $L = L(M)_\varepsilon$ for a deterministic pushdown automaton M, then L has the prefix property (see Exercise 2.8).

2.28** Prove that a language $L = L(M)_\varepsilon$ for a deterministic pushdown automaton, M, if and only if L has the prefix property and $L = L(M')_f$ for a deterministic pushdown automaton M'.

2.29 Complete Example 5.2.1.1 Part 9.

2.30   Complete Example 5.2.2.1 Part 5.
2.31   Prove Theorem 5.2.2.4.
2.32   Prove Theorem 5.2.2.5.
2.33   Complete the proof of Lemma 5.2.3.2.
2.34   Complete the proof of Lemma 5.2.3.4.
2.35   Return to Lemma 5.2.3.5. Give a rigorous proof that $L(M)_f = \{a^n : n \geq 1\} \cup \{a^n b^n : n \geq 1\}$.
2.36   Complete the proof of Lemma 5.2.3.6.
2.37   Section 5.1 has defined $\vdash$, $\vdash^n$, $\vdash^+$, and $\vdash^*$ for pushdown automata. Adapt these notions for extended pushdown automata.

3 Pushdown automata and context-free grammars

3.1   The context-free grammars resulting from Exercise 1.29 satisfy Greibach normal form. Convert them to equivalent pushdown automata that accept by empty pushdown by using Algorithm 5.3.1.1.1.
3.2   Prove Lemma 5.3.1.1.5.
3.3   Consider the context-free grammars in Exercise 1.3. Use Algorithm 5.3.1.1.9 to transform these grammars to equivalent pushdown automata that accept by empty pushdown.
3.4   Consider the pushdown automata given in Exercise 2.3. Convert them to equivalent context-free grammars by using Algorithm 5.3.2.1.
3.5   Prove Theorem 5.3.1.1.7.
3.6   Discuss Example 5.3.2.1 in detail.

Programming Projects

1 Context-free grammars

1.1   Design a data structure for representing context-free grammars.
1.2   Given a context-free grammar G and a natural number n, write a program that generates all leftmost k-step derivations, for $k = 1, \ldots, n$.
1.3   Write a program that checks whether a given context-free grammar satisfies the properties discussed in Sections 5.1.3 and 5.1.4.
1.4   Write programs that implement the algorithms presented in Sections 5.1.3 and 5.1.4.

2 Pushdown automata

2.1 Write a program that checks whether a given pushdown automaton is deterministic.
2.2 Write a program that simulates a deterministic pushdown automaton. Base this program on Algorithm 5.2.3.10.
2.3 Write a program that transforms a deterministic pushdown automaton M to a program that simulates M. M is specified by its rules. The output program, simulating M, has the form of Algorithm 5.2.3.10.
2.4 Write programs that implement the algorithms given in Section 5.2.

3 Context-free grammars and pushdown automata

3.1 Write a program that implements Algorithm 5.3.1.1.1.
3.2 Write a program that implements Algorithm 5.3.1.1.9.
3.3 Write a program that implements Algorithm 5.3.1.1.11.
3.4 Section 5.3.1.2 has defined a parser for the programming language COLA. Extend this parser by adding procedures that provide error detection and error recovery. Write a program that implements the parser extended in this way.
3.5 Write a program that implements Algorithm 5.3.2.1.

6 Properties of Context-free Languages

This chapter studies properties of context-free languages and their models. Section 6.1 establishes an important result, called the pumping lemma for context-free languages, which represents a useful tool for demonstrating that some languages are not context-free. Section 6.2 examines closure properties for the family of context-free languages. Finally, Section 6.3 studies algorithmically decidable problems concerning context-free grammars.

6.1 Pumping lemma

Section 4.1 has established a pumping lemma for the regular languages (see Lemma 4.1.1) and demonstrated how to use this lemma to prove that some languages are not regular. Analogously, the present section develops a pumping lemma for context-free languages. From the pumping lemma for context-free languages, if a context-free language L contains a sufficiently long word z, then z can be expressed as $z = uvwxy$, where $vx \neq \varepsilon$, so that for all $m \geq 0$, L contains $uv^m wx^m y$. Consequently, to prove that a language L' is not context-free, select a sufficiently long word, $z \in L'$, consider all possible decompositions of z into $uvwxy$ and, for each of these decompositions, demonstrate that $uv^n wx^n y \notin L'$ for some $n \geq 0$. In this way, the present section uses this lemma to prove that some languages are not context-free.

Preliminary results

To prove the pumping lemma for context-free languages, this section first establishes the following preliminary lemma concerning context-free grammars in Chomsky normal form (see Section 5.1.4.1). Note that this lemma and its proof use some notions, such as *depth*, defined in Section 0.3.

Lemma 6.1.1
Let $G = (N, T, P, S)$ be a context-free grammar in Chomsky normal form and $A \Rightarrow^* w$ in G with $w \in T^+$. If t is the derivation tree representing $A \Rightarrow^* w$, then $|w| \leq 2^{\text{depth}(t)-1}$.

Proof
This lemma is proved by induction on depth(t).

Basis
Let depth(t) = 1. Because G is in Chomsky normal form, $A \Rightarrow w$ in G according to $A \to w \in P$ with $w \in T$, and thus, t has the form described in Figure 6.1.1. Therefore, $1 = |w| \leq 2^{\text{depth}(t)-1} = 1$ as required.

Figure 6.1.1 The derivation tree corresponding to A fi w.

Induction hypothesis
Suppose that this lemma holds for all derivation trees of depth m, where $m = 1, \ldots, n$, for some $n \geq 1$.

Induction step
Let t be a derivation tree representing

$$A \Rightarrow^* w \ [\pi]$$

such that depth(t) = $n + 1$. As $n + 1 \geq 2$, π consists of j productions, where $j \geq 2$. Express $A \Rightarrow^* w \ [\pi]$ as

$$A \Rightarrow^* w \ [p\pi']$$

where $\pi = p\pi'$, $p \in P$, and π' consists of $j - 1$ productions. As $j - 1 \geq 1$ and G is in Chomsky normal form, p has the form

$$A \to B_1 B_2$$

for some $B_1, B_2 \in N$. In more detail, express $A \Rightarrow^* w \ [p\pi']$ as

$$\begin{aligned} A &\Rightarrow B_1 B_2 & [p] \\ &\Rightarrow^* w_1 w_2 & [\pi_1 \pi_2] \end{aligned}$$

where $w = w_1 w_2$, $\pi' = \pi_1 \pi_2$, and

Properties of context-free languages

$$B_i \Rightarrow^* w_i \quad [\pi_i]$$

in G for $i = 1,2$. Pictorially, t has the form given in Figure 6.1.2, where t_i represents $B_i \Rightarrow^* w_i \, [\pi_i]$.

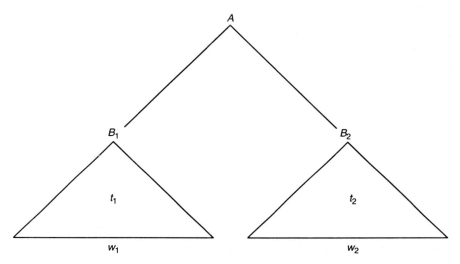

Figure 6.1.2 The derivation tree corresponding to
$A \Rightarrow B_1 B_2 \quad [p]$
$\Rightarrow^* w_1 w_2 \quad [\pi_1 \pi_2]$

As $\mathrm{depth}(t) = n + 1$, $\mathrm{depth}(t_i) \leq n$ for $i = 1, 2$. From the induction hypothesis, $|w_i| \leq 2^{\mathrm{depth}(t_i)-1} \leq 2^{n-1}$. As $|w| = |w_1| + |w_2|$, $|w| \leq 2^{n-1} + 2^{n-1}$. Hence, $|w| \leq 2^n$. Because $\mathrm{depth}(t) = n + 1$,

$$|w| \leq 2^{\mathrm{depth}(t)-1}$$

Thus, Lemma 6.1.1 holds. ∎

Corollary 6.1.2
Let $G = (N, T, P, S)$ be a context-free grammar in Chomsky normal form, and let t be a derivation tree such that t corresponds to $A \Rightarrow^+ w$ in G, where $w \in T^+$. If $|w| \geq 2^m$, for some $m \geq 0$, then $\mathrm{depth}(t) \geq m+1$.

Proof
This corollary follows from the contrapositive law (see Section A.4) and Lemma 6.1.1. ∎

The pumping lemma and its proof

Before this section states and proves the pumping lemma for context-free languages formally, an insight is given into this proof. The present lemma says that if a context-free language L contains a sufficiently long word $z \in L$ then $z = uvwxy$, where $vx \neq \varepsilon$ and $uv^m wx^m y \in L(G)$ for every $m \geq 0$. To see why this lemma holds, consider a context-free grammar G in Chomsky normal form so $L =_\varepsilon L(G)$. Choose a sentence $z \in L(G)$, so z labels the frontier of a derivation tree t that contains a path with two occurrences of the same nonterminal A. Decompose t at these two occurrences of A and, accordingly, divide z into $uvwxy$ (see Figure 6.1.1).

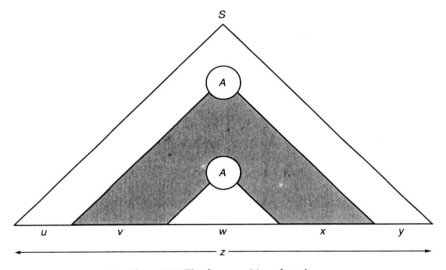

Figure 6.1.3 The decomposition of t and z.

Consider the shaded portion of t (see Figure 6.1.3). Construct a new derivation tree t_m by attaching this portion to itself m times (see Figure 6.1.4). Observe that the frontier of t_m is labeled by $uv^m wx^m y$. Consequently, $uv^m wx^m y \in L(G)$. As $L =_\varepsilon L(G)$, $uv^m wx^m y \in L$.

Lemma 6.1.3 Pumping lemma for context-free languages

Let L be a context-free language. Then, there exists a natural number k such that if $z \in L$ and $|z| \geq k$, then

$$z = uvwxy$$

so that

1. $vx \neq \varepsilon$;
2. $|vwx| \leq k$;
3. $uv^m wx^m y \in L$, for all $m \geq 0$.

Properties of context-free languages 515

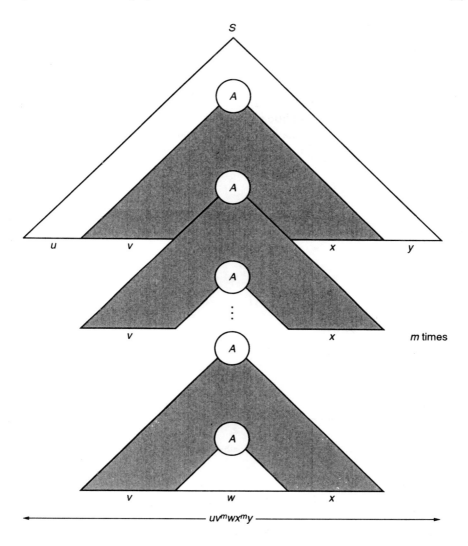

Figure 6.1.4 The derivation tree t_m for $uv^m wx^m y$.

Proof

Let L be a context-free language. From Corollary 5.1.4.1.3, there exists a context-free grammar $G = (N, T, P, S)$ in Chomsky normal form such that $L =_\varepsilon L(G)$. Set

$$k = 2^{\text{card}(N)}$$

Let $z \in L$ such that $|z| \geq k$. Then, $S \Rightarrow^* z$ in G. Let t be the derivation tree corresponding to $S \Rightarrow^* z$. From Corollary 6.1.2, $\text{depth}(t) \geq \text{card}(N)+1$. Select a root-to-frontier path of the longest length in t. Let this path contain n nodes,

$$A_1, \ldots, A_n$$

for some $n \geq \text{card}(N) + 2$, where $A_1, A_2, \ldots, A_{n-1} \in N$, $A_1 = S$, and $A_n \in T$ (see Figure 6.1.5). As $n - 1 \geq \text{card}(N) + 1$, there exist natural numbers i and j so that $n > j > i \geq 1$, $A_i = A_j$, and in addition, for any A_r and A_s appearing in $A_{i+1}, \ldots, A_{n-1}$, $r \neq s$ implies $A_r \neq A_s$ (less formally, no nonterminal appears two or more times in $A_{i+1}, \ldots, A_{n-1}$).

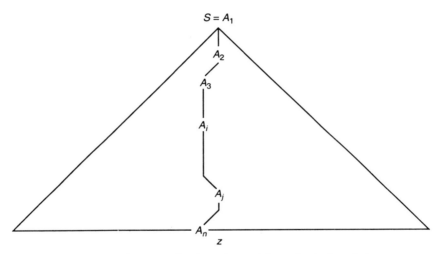

Figure 6.1.5 The root-to-frontier path containing nodes A_1 through A_n.

Decompose t into three subtrees – t_{A_j}, t_{A_i} and t_{A_1} – as shown in Figure 6.1.6.

1. t_{A_j} represents $A_j \Rightarrow^* w$ in G because A_j and w label $\text{root}(t_{A_j})$ and $\text{fr}(t_{A_j})$, respectively;
2. t_{A_i} represents $A_i \Rightarrow^* vA_jx$ $[\pi]$ in G for some production word $\pi \neq \varepsilon$, because A_i and vA_jx label $\text{root}(t_{A_i})$ and $\text{fr}(t_{A_i})$, respectively;
3. t_{A_1} represents $A_1 \Rightarrow^* uA_iy$ because A_1 and uA_iy label $\text{root}(t_{A_1})$ and $\text{fr}(t_{A_1})$, respectively.

The following Claims A through C verify the three conditions stated in Lemma 6.1.3.

Claim A
The condition that $vx \neq \varepsilon$ holds.

Properties of context-free languages

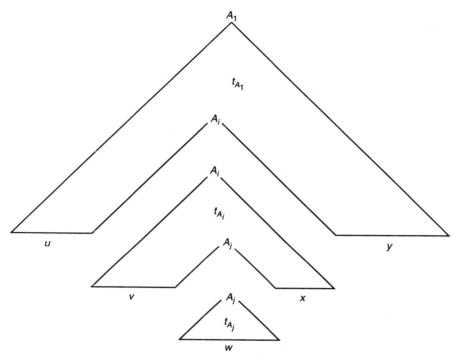

Figure 6.1.6 The decomposition of t into into t_{A_1}, t_{A_i} and t_{A_j}.

Proof
As G satisfies the Chomsky normal form, G has no ε-productions. Thus, $\pi \neq \varepsilon$ implies $vx \neq \varepsilon$.

□

Claim B
The condition that $|vwx| \leq k$ holds.

Proof
Consider t_{A_i} attached to t_{A_j} (see Figure 6.1.7).

As $A_1, \ldots, A_n$ represents a root-to-frontier path of the longest length in t, $A_i, \ldots, A_n$ is a path of the longest length in the subtree given in Figure 6.1.7, so the depth of this tree equals $|A_i \ldots A_n| - 1$. Observe that for any $r, s = i, \ldots, n$ such that $r \neq s$, $A_r \neq A_s$; therefore, $|A_i \ldots A_n| - 1 \leq \text{card}(N) + 1$. Thus, from Lemma 6.1.1, $|vwx| \leq 2^{\text{card}(N)}$. Because $2^{\text{card}(N)} = k$, $|vwx| \leq k$, so Claim B holds.

□

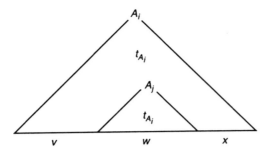

Figure 6.1.7 t_{A_i} attached to t_{A_j}.

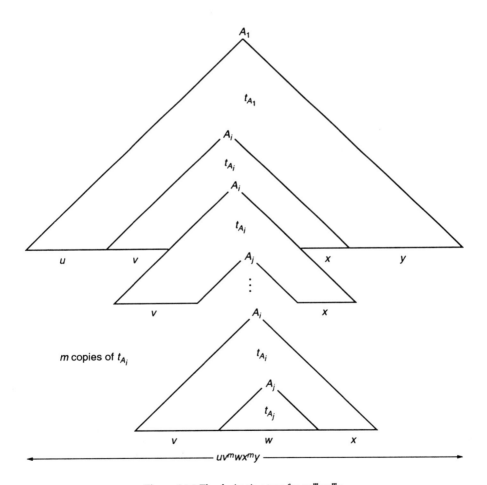

Figure 6.1.8 The derivation tree for $uv^m wx^m y$.

Claim C
For all $m \geq 0$, $uv^m wx^m y \in L$.

Proof
This proof establishes Claim C first in terms of derivation trees, then in terms of production words.

Proof of Claim C in terms of derivation trees
This proof distinguishes two cases, $m \geq 1$ and $m = 0$.

1. For $m \geq 1$, $uv^m wx^m y$ labels the frontier of the derivation tree displayed in Figure 6.1.8.

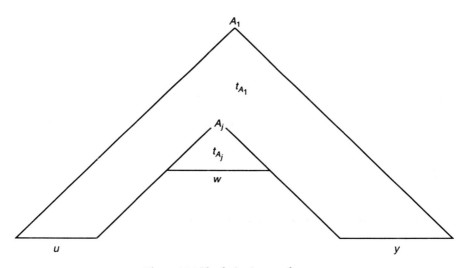

Figure 6.1.9 The derivation tree for uwy.

2. For $m = 0$, $z = uwy$. At this point, t_{A_i} is actually removed from t; in other words, t_{A_1} and t_{A_j} are put together without t_{A_i} (see Figure 6.1.9).

Proof of Claim C in terms of production words
Express $S \Rightarrow^* z$, where $z = uvwxy$, as

$$S \Rightarrow^* uAy$$
$$\Rightarrow^* uvAxy \quad [\pi]$$
$$\Rightarrow^* uvwxy$$

By analogy with the proof based on derivation trees, this following proof distinguishes two cases, $m \geq 1$ and $m = 0$.

1. Let $m \geq 1$. To generate $uv^m wx^m y$, repeat $A \Rightarrow^* vAx$ $[\pi]$ m times as

$$S \Rightarrow^* uAy$$
$$\Rightarrow^* v\underline{A}x \quad [\pi]$$
$$\Rightarrow^* vv\underline{A}xx \quad [\pi]$$
$$\vdots$$
$$\Rightarrow^* v^m \underline{A} x^m \quad [\pi]$$
$$\Rightarrow^* uv^m wx^m y$$

That is,

$$S \Rightarrow^* uAy$$
$$\Rightarrow^* v^m A x^m \quad [\pi^m]$$
$$\Rightarrow^* uv^m wx^m y$$

2. Let $m = 0$, so $z = uwy$. To generate uwy, construct

$$S \Rightarrow^* uAy$$
$$\Rightarrow^* uwy$$

Thus, Claim C holds. □

In summary, for any context-free language L there exists a natural number k such that if $z \in L$ and $|z| \geq k$, then

$$z = uvwxy$$

so that

1. $vx \neq \varepsilon$;
2. $|vwx| \leq k$;
3. $uv^m wx^m y \in L$, for all $m \geq 0$

Thus, Lemma 6.1.3 holds. ■

Example 6.1.1 Illustration of the proof of Lemma 6.1.1

This example illustrates the technique used to verify the pumping lemma for context-free languages. Consider

$$L = \{wbaw: w \in \{b\}^*\}$$

and the following context-free grammar G in Chomsky normal form:

1: $S \to BA$
2: $A \to SB$
3: $A \to a$
4: $B \to b$

Observe that

$$L(G) = L$$

Set

$$k = 8$$

because $2^{\text{card}(\{S, A, B\})} = 2^3$ and $2^3 = 8$. Furthermore, set

$$z = bbbbbabbbb$$

Notice that $z \in L$ and $10 = |z| \geq k = 8$. Figure 6.1.10 depicts the derivation tree t for z.

Select the dotted path in Figure 6.1.10, and notice that no other path is longer than this path. Carry out a frontier-to-root scan of the path to determine A as the first nonterminal appearing twice. The upper appearance of A and the lower appearance of A are denoted by A_{upper} and A_{lower}, respectively. Break t into three subtrees – t_S, $t_{A_{\text{upper}}}$, and $t_{A_{\text{lower}}}$ – at these two appearances of A (see Figure 6.1.11):

1. $t_{A_{\text{lower}}}$ represents $A \Rightarrow^* w$, where $w = a$.
2. $t_{A_{\text{upper}}}$ represents $A \Rightarrow^* vAx$, where $v = b$ and $x = b$.
3. t_S represents $S \Rightarrow^+ uAy$, where $u = bbbb$ and $y = bbb$

Thus,

$$z = uvwxy$$

where $u = bbbb, v = b, w = a, x = b$ and $y = bbb$. Observe that z satisfies the first pumping-lemma condition:

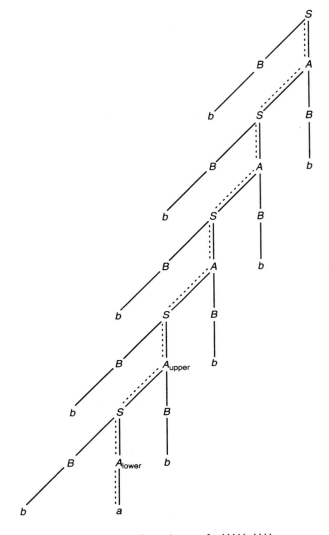

Figure 6.1.10 The derivation tree for *bbbbbabbbb*.

$$vx \neq \varepsilon$$

The second pumping-lemma condition also holds:

$$|vwx| \leq k$$

because $3 = |vwx|$ and $k = 8$. Finally, the third pumping-lemma condition is true as well. Indeed, for all $i \geq 0$,

Properties of context-free languages

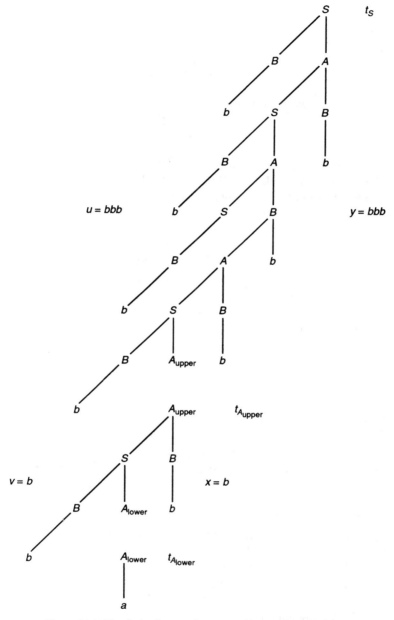

Figure 6.1.11 The derivation tree decomposed into t_S, $t_{A_{upper}}$, and $t_{A_{lower}}$

$$uv^m wx^m y \in L$$

or, equivalently,

$$bbbb^m ab^m bbb \in L$$

Consider, for instance, $m = 3$, where

$$bbbb^3 ab^3 bbb = bbbbbbbabbbbbb$$

Observe that $bbbbbbbabbbbbb \in L$. Indeed, to obtain a derivation tree for $bbbbbb$-$babbbbbb$, attach $t_{A_{upper}}$ to itself three times in t (see Figure 6.1.12).
To obtain a derivation from S to $bbbbbbbabbbbbb$, construct

$$S \Rightarrow^* bbbb\underline{A}bbb$$
$$\Rightarrow^* bbbbb\underline{A}bbbb$$
$$\Rightarrow^* bbbbbb\underline{A}bbbbb$$
$$\Rightarrow^* bbbbbbb\underline{A}bbbbbb$$
$$\Rightarrow^* bbbbbbbabbbbbb$$

by iterating $A \Rightarrow^* bAb$ three times.

▲

Applications

The pumping lemma for context-free languages is often used to prove that a language L is not context-free. Typically, a proof of this kind is made by contradiction as follows:

1. assume that L is context-free;
2. by using the constant k from the pumping lemma for context-free languages, select a word, $z \in L$, so $|z| \geq k$ is surely true;
3. consider all possible decompositions of z into $uvwxy$ so $vx \neq \varepsilon$ and $|vwx| \leq k$; for each of these decompositions, demonstrate that there exists $m \geq 0$ such that $uv^m wx^m y \notin L$, which contradicts the third pumping-lemma condition;
4. conclude that L is not context-free.

The following three examples present proofs using this methodology.

Properties of context-free languages

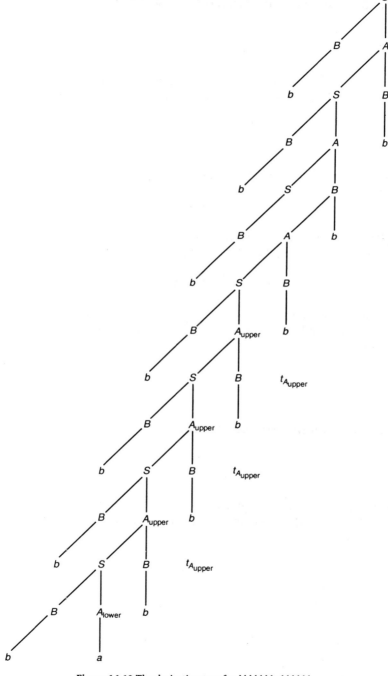

Figure 6.1.12 The derivation tree for *bbbbbbbabbbbbb*.

Example 6.1.1 Simple application of Lemma 6.1.1
Consider

$$L = \{a^{n^2}: n \geq 1\}$$

By contradiction, this example proves that L is not context-free. Assume that L is context-free. Then, there exists a natural number k satisfying Lemma 6.1.1. Set

$$z = a^{k^2}$$

Notice that $z \in L$. As $k^2 \geq k$, $|z| \geq k$. By Lemma 6.1.1,

$$z = uvwxy$$

so the three conditions of the pumping lemma hold. Observe that $(k + 1)^2 = k^2 + 2k + 1 > k^2 + k \geq |uv^2wx^2y| > k^2$ because $1 \leq |vx| \leq |vwx| \leq k$. That is,

$$k^2 < |uv^2wx^2y| < (k + 1)^2$$

L contains no word of length j satisfying $k^2 < j < (k + 1)^2$, so $uv^2wx^2y \notin L$. However, by the third pumping-lemma condition, $uv^2wx^2y \in L$ – a contradiction. Therefore, L is not context-free.

▲

Example 6.1.2 Another simple application of Lemma 6.1.1
Consider

$$L = \{a^n b^n c^n: n \geq 1\}$$

By using Lemma 6.1.1, this example demonstrates that L is not context-free.

Assume that L is context-free. Then, there exists a natural number k satisfying Lemma 6.1.1. Set

$$z = a^k b^k c^k$$

As $z \in L$ and $|z| = 3k \geq k$,

$$z = uvwxy$$

so that the three pumping-lemma conditions hold. Because $|vwx| \leq k$, $vwx \in \{a\}^*\{b\}^* \cup \{b\}^*\{c\}^*$.

1. Suppose that $vwx \in \{a,b\}^*$. Then, uwy contains k cs but fewer than k as or bs. Thus, $uwy \notin L$. However, by the pumping lemma, $uwy \in L$ – a contradiction.
2. Suppose $vwx \in \{b,c\}^*$. Then, uwy contains more as than bs or cs, so $uwy \notin L$. However, by the pumping lemma, $uwy \in L$ – a contradiction. Therefore, L is not context-free.

▲

Example 6.1.3 More difficult application of Lemma 6.1.1
Consider

$$L = \{a^i b^j a^i b^j : i, j \geq 1\}$$

This example uses Lemma 6.1.1 to demonstrates that L is not context-free.

Assume that L is context-free. Then, there exists a natural number k satisfying Lemma 6.1.1. Set

$$z_1 = z_3 = a^k \text{ and } z_2 = z_4 = b^k$$

and consider

$$z = z_1 z_2 z_3 z_4$$

Notice that $z \in L$ and $|z| = 4k \geq k$. Based on Lemma 6.1.1, express z as

$$z = uvwxy$$

so the three conditions of the pumping lemma hold. As $|vwx| \leq k$, $vwx \in$ subword($z_i z_{i+1}$), for some $i = 1, 2$ or 3:

1. If $i = 1$, then $vwx \in$ subword($z_1 z_2$). At this point, $|vx| > 0$ implies $uwy = a^r b^s a^k b^k$, where $r < k$ or $s < k$. Thus, $vwx \notin L$. However, by the third condition of the pumping lemma, $uwy \in L$ – a contradiction.
2. If $i = 2$, then $vwx \in$ subword($z_2 z_3$). As $|vx| > 0$, $uwy = a^k b^r a^s b^k$, where $r < k$ or $s < k$. Therefore, $vwx \notin L$; however, by the third condition of the pumping lemma, $uwy \in L$ – a contradiction.
3. If $i = 3$, then $vwx \in$ subword($z_3 z_4$). Because $|vx| > 0$, $uwy = a^k b^k a^r b^s$, where $r < k$ or $s <, k$, so $vwx \notin L$. By the third condition of the pumping lemma, $uwy \in L$ – a contradiction.

Therefore, L is not context-free.

▲

The three examples given above demonstrate how to use the pumping lemma to disprove that a language is context-free. Notice, however, that this lemma is of no use in proving that a language is context-free because, in addition to all context-free languages, some non-context-free languages also satisfy the pumping-lemma conditions. As the exercises demonstrate,

$$\{a^i b^j c^k d^l : i = 0 \text{ or } j = k = l\}$$

represents a language of this kind. Consequently, proving that a language satisfies these conditions does not necessarily imply that the language is context-free.

6.2 Closure properties

This section investigates whether the family of context-free languages is closed under various language operations, including

union
intersection
complement
context-free substitution
regular substitution
finite substitution
homomorphism
concatenation
closure.

In addition, this section explains how to use the results to decide whether some languages are context-free.

Union

Algorithm 6.2.1 transforms two context-free grammars, G_0 and G_1, into a context-free grammar, G, such that $L(G) = L(G_0) \cup L(G_1)$. This algorithm assumes that G_0 and G_1 have no nonterminal in common. This assumption represents no loss of generality: if G_0 and G_1 do not satisfy this requirement, rename nonterminals in either of these grammars so the generated language remains identical and the assumption holds.

Algorithm 6.2.1: Construction of a context-free grammar for the union of two context-free languages

Input: Two context-free grammars, $G_0 = (N_0, T_0, P_0, S_0)$ and $G_1 = (N_1, T_1, P_1, S_1)$, such that $N_0 \cap N_1 = \emptyset$.

Properties of context-free languages

Output: A context-free grammar, $G = (N, T_0 \cup T_1, P, S)$, such that $L(G) = L(G_0) \cup L(G_1)$.

Method

begin
$N := \{S\} \cup N_0 \cup N_1 \; \{S \notin N_0 \cup N_1\};$
$P := \{S \to S_0, S \to S_1\} \cup P_0 \cup P_1$
end.

From this algorithm, if $S_i \Rightarrow^* w$ and $w \in L(G_i)$, where $i \in \{0, 1\}$, then $S \Rightarrow S_i \Rightarrow^* w$ in G because $P_i \subseteq P$, so $L(G_0) \cup L(G_1) \subseteq L(G)$. Conversely, G generates every sentence, $w \in L(G)$ by a derivation of the form

$$S \Rightarrow S_i$$
$$\Rightarrow^* w \; [\pi]$$

for some $i \in \{0, 1\}$. As $N_0 \cap N_1 = \emptyset$, π consists of productions from P_i to P_{1-i}. Consequently, $S_i \Rightarrow^* w$ in G_i and $w \in L(G_i)$, so $L(G) \subseteq L(G_0) \cup L(G_1)$. Because $L(G_0) \cup L(G_1) \subseteq L(G)$ and $L(G) \subseteq L(G_0) \cup L(G_1)$,

$$L(G_0) \cup L(G_1) = L(G).$$

Lemma 6.2.2
Let $G_0 = (N_0, T_0, P_0, S_0)$ and $G_1 = (N_1, T_1, P_1, S_1)$ be two context-free grammars such that $N_0 \cap N_1 = \emptyset$. With G_0 and G_1 as its input, Algorithm 6.2.1 halts and correctly constructs a context-free grammar $G = (N, T, P, S)$ satisfying $L(G) = L(G_0) \cup L(G_1)$.

Proof
Termination
Clearly, Algorithm 6.2.1 terminates.

Correctness
To demonstrate

$$L(G) = L(G_0) \cup L(G_1)$$

this proof first establishes the following claim.

Claim

$$S \Rightarrow^+ w \text{ in } G \text{ if and only if } S_i \Rightarrow^* w \text{ in } G_i$$

for some $i \in \{0, 1\}$ and $w \in (N_i \cup T_i)^*$.

Proof

Only if
By induction on j, this proof next establishes the following implication:

$$\text{if } S \Rightarrow^j w \text{ in } G, \text{ where } j \geq 1, \text{ then } S_i \Rightarrow^* w \text{ in } G_i$$

for some $i \in \{0, 1\}$ and $w \in (N_i \cup T_i)^*$.

Basis
Let $j = 1$. That is,

$$S \Rightarrow w \, [p]$$

in G, where $p \in P$. By this algorithm, p is a production of the form

$$p: S \rightarrow S_i$$

for some $i \in \{0, 1\}$. Thus, $w = S_i$. Observe that

$$S_i \Rightarrow^* S_i \, [\varepsilon]$$

in G_i. Therefore, the basis holds.

Induction hypothesis
Assume that the 'only if' part is true for all q-step derivations, where $q = 1, \ldots, k$, for some $k \geq 1$.

Induction step
Consider a derivation

$$S \Rightarrow^* w \, [\pi p]$$

in G, where $p \in P$ and π is a production word consisting of k productions. Express $S \Rightarrow^* w \, [\pi p]$ as

$$S \Rightarrow^* v \qquad [\pi]$$
$$\Rightarrow w \qquad [p]$$

From the inductive hypothesis,

$$S_i \Rightarrow^* v$$

in G_i for some $i \in \{0, 1\}$. As $S \notin N_i$ and $k \geq 1$, $\text{lhs}(p) \neq S$, so p differs from $S \rightarrow S_i$, $i = 0, 1$. As $v \in (N_i \cup T_i)^*$ and $N_i \cap N_{1-i} = \emptyset$, $\text{lhs}(p) \in N_i$, so $p \in P_i$. Thus,

$$v \Rightarrow w \, [p]$$

in G_i. Consequently,

$$S_i \Rightarrow^* v \Rightarrow w$$

in G, and the inductive step is completed. Therefore, the 'only if' part holds.

If
By induction on j, this proof next establishes the following implication:

$$\text{if } S \Rightarrow^j w \text{ in } G_i, \text{ where } j \geq 1, \text{ then } S_i \Rightarrow^* w \text{ in } G$$

for some $i \in \{0, 1\}$ and $w \in (N_i \cup T_i)^*$.

Basis
Let $j = 0$. That is, $w = S_i$, and

$$S_i \Rightarrow^* S_i \ [\varepsilon]$$

in G_i, where $i \in \{0, 1\}$. Then, $p: S \rightarrow S_i \in P$, so

$$S \Rightarrow S_i \ [p]$$

in G. Therefore, the basis holds.

Induction hypothesis
Assume that the 'if' part is true for all q-step derivations, where $q = 0, \ldots, k$, for some $k \geq 0$.

Induction step
Consider a derivation

$$S_i \Rightarrow^* w \qquad [\pi p]$$

in G_i, for some $i \in \{0, 1\}$, such that $p \in P_i$, and π is a production word consisting of k productions. Express $S_i \Rightarrow^* w \ [\pi p]$ as

$$S_i \Rightarrow^* v \qquad [\pi]$$
$$\Rightarrow w \qquad [p]$$

From the inductive hypothesis,

$$S \Rightarrow^+ v$$

in G. As $P_i \subseteq P$, P contains p, so

$$S \Rightarrow^* v$$
$$\Rightarrow w \qquad [p]$$

in G. Therefore, the inductive step is completed, so the 'if' part of the claim holds. Consequently, the claim holds. □

Let $w \in T^*$. By this claim,

$$w \in L(G) \text{ if and only if } w \in L(G_i)$$

where $i \in \{0, 1\}$. Therefore,

$$L(G) = L(G_0) \cup L(G_1)$$

To summarize, with G_0 and G_1 on its input, Algorithm 6.2.1 halts and correctly constructs a context-free grammar, $G = (N, T, P, S)$, satisfying $L(G) = L(G_0) \cup L(G_1)$. Thus, Lemma 6.2.2 holds. ∎

Theorem 6.2.3
The family of context-free languages is closed under union.

Proof
Let L_0 and L_1 be two context-free languages. Let $G_i = (N_i, T_i, P_i, S_i)$ be a context-free grammar satisfying $L(G_i) = L_i$, where $i = 0, 1$. Without any loss of generality, assume that $N_0 \cap N_1 = \emptyset$. Use Algorithm 6.2.1 to construct a context-free grammar $G = (N, T, P, S)$ satisfying $L(G) = L(G_0) \cup L(G_1)$. Thus,

$$L_0 \cup L_1$$

is context-free. Therefore, the family of context-free languages is closed under union, so Theorem 6.2.3 holds. ∎

Intersection

From Theorem 4.2.5, the family of regular languages is closed under intersection. Concerning the family of context-free languages, however, this result does not hold.

Theorem 6.2.4
The family of context-free languages is not closed under intersection.

Proof
Consider

$$L_1 = \{a^i b^j c^k : i, j, k \geq 1 \text{ and } i = j\}$$

$$L_2 = \{a^i b^j c^k : i, j, k \geq 1 \text{ and } j = k\}$$

From Example 5.1.2.2, L_1 and L_2 are context-free. Observe that

$$L_1 \cap L_2 = \{a^n b^n c^n : n \geq 1\}$$

From Example 6.1.2, $\{a^n b^n c^n : n \geq 1\}$ is not context-free. Thus, the family of context-free languages is not closed under intersection, so Theorem 6.2.4 holds. ∎

From Theorem 6.2.4, there exist two context-free languages such that their intersection represents a non-context-free language. However, the intersection of a context-free language and a regular language is necessarily context-free as demonstrated next.

Algorithm 6.2.5: Construction of a pushdown automaton for the intersection of a context-free language and a regular language

Input: An ε-free pushdown automaton, $M_0 = (Q_0, \Sigma_0, R_0, s_0, F_0)$, and a deterministic finite automaton, $M_1 = (Q_1, \Sigma_1, R_1, s_1, F_1)$.

Output: A pushdown automaton, $M = (Q, \Sigma, R, \langle s_0 s_1 \rangle, F)$, such that $L(M) = L(M_0) \cap L(M_1)$.

Method

begin

$Q := \{\langle q_0 q_1 \rangle : q_0 \in Q_0, \text{ and } q_1 \in Q_1\}$;

$\Sigma := \Sigma_0 \cup \Sigma_1$, where the pushdown alphabet of M coincides with the pushdown alphabet of M_0, and the start pushdown symbol of M coincides with the start pushdown symbol of M_0;

for every $Ap_0 a \vdash xq_0 \in R_0$ and every $p_1 a \vdash q_1 \in R_0$ **do**
$\quad R := R \cup \{A \langle p_0 p_1 \rangle a \vdash x \langle q_0 q_1 \rangle\}$;

$F := \{\langle f_0 f_1 \rangle : f_0 \in F_0 \text{ and } f_1 \in F_1\}$
end.

This algorithm produces the output pushdown automaton M, so M simulates M_0 and M_1 simultaneously. More precisely, with an input symbol a, M simulates these two moves:

1. a move made by M_0 on a, and
2. a move made by M_1 on a.

M enters a final state if and only if M_0 enters a final state, and M_1 also enters a final state. Thus, $L(M) = L(M_0) \cap L(M_1)$.

Lemma 6.2.6
Let $M_0 = (Q_0, \Sigma_0, R_0, s_0, F_0)$ be an ε-free pushdown automaton, and let $M_1 = (Q_1, \Sigma_1, R_1, s_1, F_1)$ be a deterministic finite automaton. With M_0 and M_1 on its input, Algorithm 6.2.5 halts and correctly constructs a pushdown automaton, $M = (Q, \Sigma, R, \langle s_0 s_1 \rangle, F)$, such that $L(M) = L(M_0) \cap L(M_1)$.

Proof
Termination
As R_0 and R_1 are finite, this algorithm repeats its **for** loop a finite number of times. Thus, Algorithm 6.2.5 surely halts.

Correctness
To establish

$$L(M) = L(M_0) \cap L(M_1),$$

this proof first presents the following claim, which describes how M simulates M_0 and M_1.

Claim
This equivalence holds:

$$S\langle s_0 s_1 \rangle w \vdash^* z \langle q_0 q_1 \rangle \text{ in } M$$

if and only if

$$S_0 s_0 w \vdash^* z q_0 \text{ in } M_0 \text{ and } s_1 w \vdash^* q_1 \text{ in } M_1$$

Proof
Only if
By induction on j, where $j \geq 0$, this proof next establishes that if

$$S\langle s_0 s_1 \rangle w \vdash^j z \langle q_0 q_1 \rangle \text{ in } M$$

then

$$S_0s_0w \vdash^* zq_0 \text{ in } M_0 \text{ and } s_1w \vdash^* q_1 \text{ in } M_1$$

Basis
Let $j = 0$. Then,

$$S\langle s_0s_1\rangle w \vdash^* z\langle q_0q_1\rangle \quad [\varepsilon]$$

in M. Therefore, $S = z$, $w = \varepsilon$, and $s_i = q_i$ for $i = 0,1$. Notice that

$$S_0s_0 \vdash^* S_0s_0 \quad [\varepsilon]$$

in M_0 and

$$s_1 \vdash^* s_1 \quad [\varepsilon]$$

in M_1. Thus, the basis holds.

Induction hypothesis
Assume that the 'only if' part holds for all $j = 1, \ldots, n$, for some $n \geq 0$.

Induction step
Consider

$$S\langle s_0s_1\rangle w \vdash^* z\langle q_0q_1\rangle \quad [\rho r]$$

in M, where r is a rule word consisting of n rules, and $r: A\langle p_0p_1\rangle a \vdash x\langle q_0q_1\rangle \in R$. In more detail, express $S\langle s_0s_1\rangle w \vdash^* z\langle q_0q_1\rangle$ $[\rho r]$ as

$$S\langle s_0s_1\rangle va \vdash^* yA\langle p_0p_1\rangle a \quad [\rho]$$
$$\vdash yx\langle q_0q_1\rangle \quad [r]$$

where $w = va$ and $yx = z$. By the induction hypothesis,

$$S_0s_0v \vdash^* yAp_0$$

in M_0 and

$$s_1v \vdash^* p_1$$

in M_1. From the definition of R, $A\langle p_0p_1\rangle a \vdash x\langle q_0q_1\rangle \in R$ implies $Ap_0a \vdash xq_0 \in R_0$ and $p_1a \vdash q_1 \in R_0$. Therefore,

$$S_0s_0v \vdash^* yAp_0$$
$$\vdash yxq_0 \qquad [Ap_0a \vdash xq_0]$$

in M_0 and

$$s_1va \vdash^* p_1a$$
$$\vdash q_1 \qquad [p_1a \vdash q_1]$$

in M_1. As $w = va$ and $yx = z$,

$$S_0s_0w \vdash^* zq_0$$

in M_0 and

$$s_1w \vdash^* q_1$$

in M_1. Therefore, the induction step is completed.

Thus, the 'only if' part of the proof holds.

If
The 'if' part of this claim states that if

$$S_0s_0w \vdash^* zq_0 \text{ in } M_0 \text{ and } s_1w \vdash^* q_1 \text{ in } M_1$$

then

$$S\langle s_0s_1\rangle w \vdash^* z\langle q_0q_1\rangle \text{ in } M$$

This part of the proof is left to the exercises.

Consequently, the claim holds.

□

Consider the claim for $f_0 \in F_0$ and $f_1 \in F_1$ to see that

$$S\langle s_0s_1\rangle w \vdash^* z\langle f_0f_1\rangle \text{ in } M$$

if and only if

$$S_0s_0w \vdash^* zf_0 \text{ in } M_0 \text{ and } s_1w \vdash^* f_1 \text{ in } M_1$$

By the definition of F,

$w \in L(M)$ if and only if $w \in L(M_0) \cap L(M_1)$

Therefore,

$$L(M) = L(M_0) \cap L(M_1)$$

In summary, with M_0 and M_1 as its input, Algorithm 6.2.5 halts and correctly constructs a pushdown automaton, $M = (Q, \Sigma, R, \langle s_0 s_1 \rangle, F)$, such that $L(M) = L(M_0) \cap L(M_1)$. Therefore, Theorem 6.2.6 holds. ∎

Theorem 6.2.7
Let L_0 and L_1 be a context-free language and a regular language, respectively. Then, $L_0 \cap L_1$ is context-free.

Proof
Let L_0 and L_1 be a context-free language and a regular language, respectively. From Corollary 5.3.1.1.3, there exists an ε-free pushdown automaton M_0 such that $L_0 =_\varepsilon L(M_0)$. Let $L_1 = L(M_1)$ for a deterministic finite automaton M_1. By Theorem 6.2.6, with M_0 and M_1 on its input, Algorithm 6.2.5 constructs a pushdown automaton M such that $L(M) = L(M_0) \cap L(M_1)$. Define the context-free language L as

$$L = L(M) \cup \{\varepsilon\} \text{ if } \varepsilon \in L_0 \cap L_1; \text{ otherwise, } L = L(M).$$

As $L = L_0 \cap L_1$ and L is context-free, Theorem 6.2.7 is true. ∎

Complement

From Theorem 4.2.4, the family of regular languages is closed under intersection. However, the next theorem states that the family of context-free languages is not closed under this language operation.

Theorem 6.2.8
The family of context-free languages is not closed under complement.

Proof
This theorem is proved by contradiction. Assume that the family of context-free languages is closed under complement. Consider these two context-free languages:

$$L_1 = \{a^i b^j c^k : i, j, k \geq 1 \text{ and } i = j\}$$

$$L_2 = \{a^i b^j c^k : i, j, k \geq 1 \text{ and } j = k\}$$

From DeMorgan's law (see Exercise 1.26 in Section 1),

$$\overline{\overline{L_1} \cup \overline{L_2}} = L_1 \cap L_2$$

From Theorem 6.2.3, $L_1 \cap L_2$ is context-free. However,

$$L_1 \cap L_2 = \{a^n b^n c^n : n \geq 1\}$$

and Example 6.1.2 has proved that $\{a^n b^n c^n : n \geq 1\}$ is not context-free – a contradiction. Thus, the family of context-free languages is not closed under complement, so Theorem 6.2.8 holds.
∎

From Corollary 4.2.6, the family of regular languages is a Boolean algebra of languages because this family is closed under union, intersection and complement. However, from Theorems 6.2.4 and 6.2.8, the family of context-free languages does not represent a Boolean algebra of languages.

Context-free substitution

This section defines context-free substitution and proves that the family of context-free languages is closed under this substitution. This crucial property represents a powerful result, which implies several other closure properties, as demonstrated later on in this section.

Definition — context-free substitution
Let Σ and Ω be two alphabets, and let η be a substitution from Σ^* to Ω^* such that for all $x \in \Sigma$, $\eta(x)$ is a context-free language. Then, η is a context-free substitution.
♦

The following algorithm demonstrates that if η is a context-free substitution from Σ^* to Ω^*, where Σ and Ω are two alphabets and L is a context-free language such that $L \subseteq \Sigma^*$, then $\eta(L)$ is context-free, too. This algorithm defines L as

$$L = L(M_0)_\varepsilon$$

where $M_0 = (Q_0, \Sigma_0, R_0, s_0, \emptyset)$ is an ε-free pushdown automaton, whose input alphabet is denoted by Σ_{I_0}. Furthermore, this algorithm defines η so that for each $a \in \Sigma_{I_0}$, there exists a pushdown automaton, $M_a = (Q_a, \Sigma_a, R_a, s_a, \emptyset)$, satisfying

$$\eta(a) = L(M_a)_\varepsilon$$

As a result, for each word, $a_1 a_2 \ldots a_n \in L(M_0)_\varepsilon$,

$$w_1 w_2 \ldots w_n \in \eta(a_1 a_2 \ldots a_n) \text{ if and only if } w_i \in L(M_{a_i})_\varepsilon$$

The following algorithm constructs an extended pushdown automaton $M = (Q, \Sigma, R, s, \{f\})$ satisfying

$$w \in L(M_0)_\varepsilon \text{ if and only if } w' \in L(M)_{f\varepsilon}$$

where

1. $w = a_1 a_2 \ldots a_n \in \Sigma_{I_0}^*$ with $a_i \in \Sigma_{I_0}$ for $i = 1, \ldots, n$
2. $w' = w_1 w_2 \ldots w_n \in \Sigma_I^*$ with $w_i \in L(M_{a_i})_\varepsilon$ for $i = 1, \ldots, n$

where n is a natural number. As a result,

$$L(M)_{f\varepsilon} = \eta(L(M_0)_\varepsilon) = \eta(L)$$

Therefore, $\eta(L)$ is context-free.

Algorithm 6.2.9 assumes that if one of the input automata uses a state q or a pushdown symbol A then none of the other input automata contains q or A. This assumption is without any loss of generality: any of these sets can be renamed so this requirement is satisfied.

Algorithm 6.2.9: Construction of an extended pushdown automaton for a context-free substitution

Input: An ε-free pushdown automaton, $M_0 = (Q_0, \Sigma_0, R_0, s_0, \varnothing)$, and a context-free substitution η, defined by $\eta(a) = L(M_a)_\varepsilon$, where $M_a = (Q_a, \Sigma_a, R_a, s_a, F_a)$ is a pushdown automaton corresponding to a, $a \in \Sigma_{I_0}$, where Σ_{I_0} denotes the input alphabet of M_0. If one of these card $(\Sigma_{I_0}) + 1$ automata contains a state q or a pushdown symbol A, then none of the other automata contains q or A.

Output: An extended pushdown automaton $M = (Q, \Sigma, R, s, \{f\})$, satisfying

$$w \in L(M_0)_\varepsilon \text{ if and only if } w' \in L(M)_{f\varepsilon}$$

where

1. $w = a_1 a_2 \ldots a_n \in \Sigma_{I_0}^*$ with $a_i \in \Sigma_{I_0}$ for $i = 1, \ldots, n$
2. $w' = w_1 w_2 \ldots w_n \in \Sigma_I^*$ with $w_i \in L(M_{a_i})_\varepsilon$ for $i = 1, \ldots, n$

where n is a natural number; that is,

$$L(M)_{f\varepsilon} = \eta(L(M_0)_\varepsilon)$$

Method

begin
  $Q := \{q\colon q \in Q_a,\text{ where } a \in \Sigma_{I_0}\} \cup \{s, f\}$ {s is the start stateof M, and f is the final state of M};

  $\Sigma := \Sigma_{PD_0} \cup \bigcup_{a \in \Sigma_{I_0}} \Sigma_a \cup \{q\colon q \in Q_0\} \cup \{S\}$ $\{\Sigma_I = \bigcup_{a \in \Sigma_{I_0}} \Sigma_{I_a}$, and

  $\Sigma_{PD} = \Sigma - \Sigma_I$, where S is the start pushdown symbol of M};

  $R := \{Ss \vdash S_0 s_0 S_a s_a\}$

  $\cup \bigcup_{a \in \Sigma_{I_0}} R_a$

  $\cup \{q_0 q_a \vdash f\colon q_0 \in Q_0, q_a \in Q_a, a \in \Sigma_{I_0}\}$;

  for each $r\colon Ap_0 a \vdash xq_0 \in R_0$ **do**
    $R := R \cup \{Ap_0 q_a \vdash xq_0 S_b s_b\colon q_a \in Q_a, b \in \Sigma_{I_0}\}$
end.

Let $a_1 a_2 \ldots a_n$, where $a_i \in \Sigma_{I_0}$, be the input word of M_0. Then, the output extended pushdown automaton M simulates M_{a_1} through M_{a_n} as follows. Assume that M simulates M_{a_i} that empties its pushdown after reading a word w_i because $w_i \in \eta(a_i)$; at this point, M stops the simulation of M_{a_i} and begins to simulate $M_{a_{i+1}}$. If M_{a_n} empties its pushdown, M enters f and, thereby, accepts $w_1 w_2 \ldots w_n$ with $w_i \in \eta(a_i)$, for $i = 1, \ldots, n$; therefore, $w_1 w_2 \ldots w_n \in \eta(a_1 a_2 \ldots a_n)$. (see Figure 6.2.1).

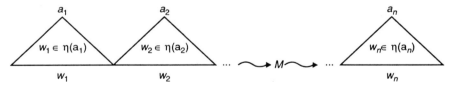

Figure 6.2.1 M that accepts $w_1 w_2 \ldots w_n \in \eta(a_1 a_2 \ldots a_n)$.

Lemma 6.2.10
Let $M_0 = (Q_0, \Sigma_0, R_0, s_0, \varnothing)$ be an ε-free pushdown automaton, and a context-free substitution η defined by $\eta(a) = L(M_a)_\varepsilon$, where $M_a = (Q_a, \Sigma_a, R_a, s_a, F_a)$ is a pushdown automaton corresponding to a, $a \in \Sigma_{I_0}$, where Σ_{I_0} denotes the input alphabet of M_0. In addition, if one of these card(Σ_{I_0}) + 1 automata contains a state q or a pushdown

Properties of context-free languages

symbol A, then none of the other automata contains q or A. With these automata as its input, Algorithm 6.2.9 halts and correctly constructs an extended pushdown automaton, $M = (Q, \Sigma, R, s, \{f\})$, so

$$w \in L(M_0)_\varepsilon \text{ if and only if } w' \in L(M)_{f\varepsilon}$$

where

1. $w = a_1 a_2 \ldots a_n \in \Sigma_{I_0}^*$ with $a_i \in \Sigma_{I_0}$ for $i = 1, \ldots, n$
2. $w' = w_1 w_2 \ldots w_n \in \Sigma_I^*$ with $w_i \in L(M_{a_i})_\varepsilon$ for $i = 1, \ldots, n$

where n is a natural number; that is, $L(M)_{f\varepsilon} = \eta(L(M_0)_\varepsilon)$.

Proof
Termination
As R_0 is finite, the for loop is iterated a finite number of times, so Algorithm 6.2.9 halts.

Correctness
This part of the proof demonstrates that

$$w \in L(M_0)_\varepsilon \text{ if and only if } w' \in L(M)_{f\varepsilon}$$

where

1. $w = a_1 a_2 \ldots a_n \in \Sigma_{I_0}^*$ with $a_i \in \Sigma_{I_0}$ for $i = 1, \ldots, n$
2. $w' = w_1 w_2 \ldots w_n \in \Sigma_I^*$ with $w_i \in L(M_{a_i})_\varepsilon$ for $i = 1, \ldots, n$

where n is a natural number.

Claim
Let $a_1 a_2 \ldots a_n \in \Sigma_{I_0}^*$, $a_i \in \Sigma_{I_0}$, $w_i \in L(M_{a_i})_\varepsilon$, $i = 1, \ldots, n$ for some $n \geq 1$. Then,

$$S_0 s_0 a_1 a_2 \ldots a_n \vdash^* z q_0 \text{ in } M_0$$

if and only if

$$S_0 s_0 S_{a_1} s_{a_1} w_1 w_2 \ldots w_n \vdash^* z q_0 q_{a_n} \text{ in } M$$

for some $z \in \Sigma_{PD_0}^*$, $q_0 \in Q_0$, and $q_{a_n} \in Q_{a_n}$.

Proof
Only if
Let $a_1 a_2 \ldots a_n \in \Sigma_{I_0}^*$, $a_i \in \Sigma_{I_0}$, $w_i \in L(M_{a_i})_\varepsilon$, $i = 1, \ldots, n$ for some $n \geq 1$. By induction

on n, this part of the proof demonstrates that

$$S_0 s_0 a_1 a_2 \ldots a_n \vdash^* z q_0 \text{ in } M_0$$

implies

$$S_0 s_0 S_{a_1} s_{a_1} w_1 w_2 \ldots w_n \vdash^* z q_0 q_{a_n} \text{ in } M$$

for some $z \in \Sigma_{PD_0}^*$, $q_0 \in Q_0$, and $q_{a_n} \in Q_{a_n}$.

Basis
This part of the proof is left to the exercises.

Induction hypothesis
Assume that if

$$S_0 s_0 a_1 a_2 \ldots a_k \vdash^* z q_0 \text{ in } M_0$$

then

$$S_0 s_0 S_{a_1} s_{a_1} w_1 w_2 \ldots w_k \vdash^* z q_0 q_{a_k} \text{ in } M$$

for some $z \in \Sigma_{PD_0}^*$, $q_0 \in Q_0$, and $q_{a_k} \in Q_{a_k}$, for all $k = 1, \ldots, n$, where n is a natural number.

Induction step
Consider

$$S_0 s_0 a_1 a_2 \ldots a_n a_{n+1} \vdash^* z q_0 \text{ in } M_0$$

As M_0 is ε-free, express $S_0 s_0 a_1 a_2 \ldots a_n a_{n+1} \vdash^* z q_0$ as

$$S_0 s_0 a_1 a_2 \ldots a_n a_{n+1} \vdash^* y A p_0 a_{n+1}$$
$$\vdash y x q_0 \quad [r]$$

in M, where $r: A p_0 a_{n+1} \vdash x q_0 \in R_0$, and $yx = z$. By the induction hypothesis,

$$S_0 s_0 S_{a_1} s_{a_1} w_1 w_2 \ldots w_n \vdash^* y A p_0 q_{a_n} \text{ in } M$$

with $w_i \in L(M_{a_i})_\varepsilon$, for $i = 1, \ldots, n$. Let

$$w_{n+1} \in L(M_{a_{n+1}})_\varepsilon$$

Then,

$$S_{a_{n+1}}s_{a_{n+1}}w_{n+1} \vdash^* q_{a_{n+1}}$$

in $M_{a_{n+1}}$. Observe that $R_{a_{n+1}} \subseteq R$ and $Ap_0q_{a_n} \vdash xq_0S_{a_{n+1}}s_{a_{n+1}} \in R$ because $r: Ap_0a_{n+1} \vdash xq_0 \in R_0$. Thus,

$$yAp_0 \vdash^* yxq_0S_{a_{n+1}}s_{a_{n+1}}$$
$$\vdash^* yxq_0q_{a_{n+1}}$$

in M. As a result,

$$S_0s_cS_{a_1}s_{a_1}w_1w_2\ldots w_nw_{n+1} \vdash^* yAp_0$$
$$\vdash^* zq_0S_{a_{n+1}}s_{a_{n+1}}$$
$$\vdash^* zq_0q_{a_{n+1}}$$

in M. To summarize this part of the proof, if

$$S_0s_0a_1a_2\ldots a_{n+1} \vdash^* zq_0 \text{ in } M_0$$

then

$$S_0s_0S_{a_1}s_{a_1}w_1w_2\ldots w_{n+1} \vdash^* zq_0q_{a_{n+1}}$$

in M for some $z \in \Sigma_{PD_0}^*$, $q_0 \in Q_0$, and $q_{a_{n+1}} \in Q_{a_{n+1}}$.

As a result, the 'only if' part of this claim holds.

If
The 'if' part of this claim is proved in the exercises.

Therefore, the claim holds.

□

Consider the claim for $z = \varepsilon$. That is, let $a_1a_2\ldots a_n \in \Sigma_{I_0}^*$, $a_i \in \Sigma_{I_0}$, $w_i \in L(M_{a_i})_\varepsilon$, $i = 1, \ldots, n$ for some $n \geq 1$; then,

$$S_0s_0a_1a_2\ldots a_n \vdash^* q_0 \text{ in } M_0$$

if and only if

$$S_0s_0S_{a_1}s_{a_1}w_1w_2\ldots w_n \vdash^* q_0q_{a_n} \text{ in } M$$

for some $q_0 \in Q_0$, and $q_{a_n} \in Q_{a_n}$. Observe that

$$S_0 s_0 S_{a_1} s_{a_1} w_1 w_2 \ldots w_n \vdash^* q_0 q_{a_n} \text{ in } M$$

if and only if

$$SsS_{a_1} s_{a_1} w_1 w_2 \ldots w_n \vdash S_0 s_0 S_{a_1} s_{a_1} w_1 w_2 \ldots w_n \quad [Ss \vdash S_0 s_0 S_{a_1} s_{a_1}]$$
$$\vdash^* q_0 q_{a_n}$$
$$\vdash f \quad\quad\quad\quad\quad\quad\quad\quad\quad\quad\quad\quad [q_0 q_{a_n} \vdash f]$$

in M. Therefore,

$$w \in L(M_0)_\varepsilon \text{ if and only if } w' \in L(M)_{f\varepsilon}$$

where

1. $w = a_1 a_2 \ldots a_n \in \Sigma_{I_0}^*$ with $a_i \in \Sigma_{I_0}$ for $i = 1, \ldots, n$
2. $w' = w_1 w_2 \ldots w_n \in \Sigma_I^*$ with $w_i \in L(M_{a_i})_\varepsilon$ for $i = 1, \ldots, n$

where n is a natural number. In other words,

$$L(M)_{f\varepsilon} = \eta(L(M_0)_\varepsilon)$$

To summarize this proof, Algorithm 6.2.9 halts and correctly constructs an extended pushdown automaton $M = (Q, \Sigma, R, s, \{f\})$ so

$$w \in L(M_0)_\varepsilon \text{ if and only if } w' \in L(M)_{f\varepsilon}$$

where

1. $w = a_1 a_2 \ldots a_n \in \Sigma_{I_0}^*$ with $a_i \in \Sigma_{I_0}$ for $i = 1, \ldots, n$
2. $w' = w_1 w_2 \ldots w_n \in \Sigma_I^*$ with $w_i \in L(M_{a_i})_\varepsilon$ for $i = 1, \ldots, n$

where n is a natural number; thus,

$$L(M)_{f\varepsilon} = \eta(L(M_0)_\varepsilon)$$

Therefore, Lemma 6.2.10 holds. ∎

Theorem 6.2.11
The family of context-free languages is closed under context-free substitution.

Proof
Let η be a context-free substitution from Σ^* to Ω^*, where Σ and Ω are two alphabets, and let L be a context-free language such that $L \subseteq \Sigma^*$. From Corollary 5.3.1.1.8, there exists an ε-free pushdown automaton that accepts $L - \{\varepsilon\}$. From Theorem 3.3.3.2, Algorithm 6.2.9 and Lemma 6.2.10, $\eta(L - \{\varepsilon\})$ is context-free. Set $L' = \eta(L(M)_\varepsilon) \cup \{\varepsilon\}$ if $\varepsilon \in L$; otherwise, set $L' = \eta(L(M))$. As $\eta(L) = L'$ and L' is context-free, Theorem 6.2.11 is true. ∎

Regular substitution, finite substitution, homomorphism, concatenation and closure

Theorem 6.2.11 is a powerful result, which is now used to demonstrate that the family of context-free languages is closed under regular substitution, finite substitution, homomorphism, concatenation and closure.

Corollary 6.2.12
The family of context-free languages is closed under regular substitution, finite substitution and homomorphism.

Proof
Regular substitution, finite substitution, and homomorphism represent special cases of context-free substitution. Therefore, Corollary 6.2.12 follows from Theorem 6.2.11. ∎

Theorem 6.2.13
The family of context-free languages is closed under concatenation.

Proof:
Let L_a and L_b be two context-free languages. Consider the context-free substitution η defined by $\eta(a) = L_a$ and $\eta(b) = L_b$. Clearly, $\{ab\}$ is context-free. Thus, from Theorem 6.2.11, $h(\{ab\}) = L_a L_b$ is context-free, so Theorem 6.2.13 holds. ∎

Theorem 6.2.14
The family of context-free languages is closed under closure.

Proof
Let L_a be a context-free language. Set

$$L = \{a\}^*$$

Observe that L is context-free. Define the context-free substitution η as $\eta(a) = L_a$. From Theorem 6.2.11, $h(L) = L_a^*$ is context-free. Therefore, Theorem 6.2.14 holds.
■

Theorem 6.2.11 implies several other closure properties, some of which this section has already established in a different way. To illustrate this, return to Theorem 6.2.3, stating that the family of context-free languages is closed under union. Consider any two context-free languages, L_a and L_b, and define the context-free substitution η as $\eta(a) = L_a$ and $\eta(b) = L_b$. Observe that $\eta(\{a, b\}) = L_a \cup L_b$, which is context-free by Theorem 6.2.11. Thus, the family of context-free languages is closed under union. Based on Theorem 6.2.11, the Exercises establish many more closure properties concerning the family of context-free languages.

Applications of closure properties

Closure properties are often used to decide whether a given language L is context-free. First, assume that L is a context-free language. If L is syntactically complex, a direct proof, designing a complicated context-free grammar that generates L, usually represents a difficult task. To simplify this task, use closure properties under which the family of context-free languages is closed to combine several simple context-free languages so that the resulting language coincides with L, thus L is surely context-free. In this way, the following three examples easily prove that some rather complex languages are context-free.

Example 6.2.1 Proof that a language is context-free
Consider

$$L = \{a^i b^j c^k : i, j, k \geq 0 \text{ and } j \geq i + k\}$$

Express L as

$$L = \{a^n b^n : n \geq 0\}\{b\}^* \{b^m c^m : m \geq 0\}$$

where $\{a^n b^n : n \geq 0\}$, $\{b\}^*$, and $\{b^m c^m : m \geq 0\}$ are context-free. From Theorem 6.2.13, stating that the family of context-free languages is closed under concatenation, L is context-free as well.

▲

Example 6.2.2 Proof that the complement of a non-context-free language is context-free

Example 6.1.2 has demonstrated that

$$L = \{a^n b^n c^n : n \geq 1\}$$

is not context-free. However, its complement

$$\bar{L} = \{a, b, c\}^* - L$$

is context-free as the present example proves by using Theorem 6.2.3. Express $\bar{L}$ as

$$\bar{L} = L_0 \cup L_1 \cup L_2$$

where

$$L_0 = \{a, b, c\}^* - \{a\}^+\{b\}^+\{c\}^+$$

$$L_1 = \{a^i b^j c^k : i, j, k \geq 0 \text{ and } j \neq i\}$$

$$L_2 = \{a^i b^j c^k : i, j, k \geq 0 \text{ and } j \neq k\}$$

Observe that $\{a\}^+\{b\}^+\{c\}^+$ is regular. Thus, by Theorem 4.2.4, L_0 is regular, and therefore, from Theorems 5.2.3.3 and 3.3.3.2, L_0 is context-free. Furthermore, the exercises demonstrate that L_1 and L_2 are context-free, too. From Theorem 6.2.3, $\bar{L}$ is context-free.

▲

Example 6.2.3 Part 1 Another proof that the complement of a language is context-free

Consider

$$L = \{ww : w \in \{a, b\}^+\}$$

This example demonstrates that its complement

$$\bar{L} = \{a, b\}^* - L$$

is context-free. Observe that

$$\bar{L} = L_1 \cup L_2 \cup \{\varepsilon\}$$

where

$$L_1 = (\{a, b\}\{a, b\})^*\{a, b\}$$

$$L_2 = \{ucvu'c'v': u, v, u', v' \in \{a,b\}^*, c,c' \in \{a,b\}, c \neq c', |u| = |u'|, |v| = |v'|\}$$

Notice that L_1 is regular. As demonstrated in the exercises, it has this grammar

1: $S \to AB$
2: $S \to BA$
3: $A \to CAC$
4: $A \to a$
5: $B \to CBC$
6: $B \to b$
7: $C \to a$
8: $C \to b$

As L_1 and L_2 are context-free, Theorem 6.2.3 implies that $\bar{L}$ is context-free.

△

Up until now, this section has used closure properties to prove that a language is context-free. Combined with the pumping lemma, the closure properties can also be used to prove that a language L is not context-free. A proof of this kind is made by contradiction. A typical structure is:

1. Assume that L is context-free.
2. From L and some context-free languages, construct a new language L' by using closure operations under which the family of context-free languages is closed.
3. Prove that L' is not context-free by the pumping lemma for context-free languages; however, by the closure properties concerning the operations used in step 2, L' is context-free – a contradiction.
4. Conclude that L is not context-free.

Example 6.2.3 Part 2 Proof that a language is not context-free

Recall that the first part of this example defines $L = \{ww: w \in \{a, b\}^+\}$ and, then, proves that its complement is context-free. However, L is not context-free, as demonstrated here.

Assume that L is context-free. Consider

$$L \cap \{a\}^+\{b\}^+\{a\}^+\{b\}^+ = \{a^i b^j a^i b^j: i, j \geq 1\}$$

As $\{a\}^+\{b\}^+\{a\}^+\{b\}^+$ is regular, $\{a^ib^ja^ib^j: i,j \geq 1\}$ is context-free by Theorem 6.2.8. However, Example 6.1.3 has proved that $\{a^ib^ja^ib^j: i,j \geq 1\}$ is not context-free – a contradiction. Thus, L is not context-free.

▲

The closure properties established in this section have also quite practical consequences. Based on these properties, the next example demonstrates that Pascal is not context-free.

Example 6.2.4 Proof that Pascal is not context-free

Let Pascal be the language consisting of all well-formed Pascal programs. Assume that Pascal is context-free. Consider the following regular language, L:

$\{\text{program}\}\{\square\}\{p\}\{\square\}\{(\}\{\text{input}\}\{)\}\{;\}\{\text{var}\}\{\square\}\{X,Y\}^+\{:\text{integer}\}\{;\}$
$\{\text{begin}\}\{\square\}\{X,Y\}^+\{:=0\}\{\square\}\{\text{end}\}\{.\}$

where $\square$ represents a blank. Let η be the homomorphism defined by

$$\eta(X) = X, \eta(Y) = Y, \text{ and } \eta(Z) = \varepsilon$$

for all $Z \in \text{alph}(L) - \{X, Y\}$. The programming language Pascal requires that all identifiers are declared; however, it places no restriction on the length of identifiers. As a result,

$$\eta(\text{Pascal} \cap L) = \{ww: w \in \{X,Y\}^+\}$$

Let γ be the homomorphism defined by

$$\gamma(X) = a \text{ and } \gamma(Y) = b$$

Then,

$$\gamma(\{ww: w \in \{X, Y\}^+\}) = \{ww: w \in \{a, b\}^+\}$$

By Theorems 6.2.7 and 6.2.12, $\{ww: w \in \{a, b\}^+\}$ is context-free; however, the previous example proved that $\{ww: w \in \{a, b\}^+\}$ is not context-free – a contradiction. Therefore, Pascal is not a context-free language.

▲

More generally, the argument described in the above example implies that every programming language that requires the declaration of all identifiers, whose length is unbounded, is a non-context-free language. In fact, there exist some other programming language features that context-free grammars fail to capture. For instance, these grammars cannot guarantee that the number of formal parameters coincides with the number of corresponding actual parameters; also, they even fail to detect the reference to an undeclared identifier. Despite these failures, context-free grammars represent widely used specification tools for programming languages because these grammars can capture most common features of these languages. More importantly, context-free grammars are easy to use in practice, so they underlie most compilers (see Sections 5.3.1. and 9.3). If a programming language has a non-context-free feature, then the compiler for this language contains a special routine that handles this feature.

After these considerations concerning non-context-free features of programming languages, it come as no surprise that most natural languages, such as English, are not context-free either.

Example 6.2.5 Proof that English is not context-free

Assume that English is a context-free language. Consider the following regular language, L:

$$L = (M\{,\})^* M\{and\} M\{are\} (N\{,\})^* N\{and\} N\{, \text{respectively.}\}$$

where $M = \{Abraham\} \cup \{Agatha\}$, and $N = \{a\ girl\} \cup \{a\ boy\}$. Consider

$$\text{English} \cap L$$

For instance, this intersection contains the sentence

$$\text{Abraham and Agatha are a boy and a girl, respectively.}$$

Let η be the homomorphism defined by

$$\eta(b) = b \text{ and } \eta(g) = a;$$

in addition, η maps all other symbols to ε. Observe that

$$\eta(\text{English} \cap L) \cup \{aa, bb\} = \{ww: w \in \{a, b\}^+\}$$

From Theorems 6.2.3, 6.2.7 and 6.2.12, $\{ww: w \in \{a, b\}^+\}$ is context-free; however, the second part of Example 6.2.5 has proved that $\{ww: w \in \{a, b\}^+\}$ is not context-free – a contradiction. Therefore, English is not a context-free language. ▲

6.3 Decidable problems

This section describes algorithms that solve the following problems concerning context-free grammars:

1. membership
2. emptiness
3. infiniteness
4. finiteness.

Membership problem for context-free grammars

Instance: A context-free grammar $G = (N, T, P, S)$, and a word $w \in T^*$.
Question: Is w a member of $L(G)$?

Section 5.3.1 has already solved this problem by several parsing algorithms, which decide whether $w \in L(G)$ for a given context-free grammar G and a word w. The following two algorithms represent other methods that solve this problem. Algorithm 6.3.1 decides the membership problem for context-free grammars in Chomsky normal form (see Section 5.1.4). As the context-free grammars in this form do not generate ε, the next algorithm requires that its input word w differs from ε.

Algorithm 6.3.1: Membership problem decision for context-free grammars in Chomsky normal form

Input: A context-free grammar $G = (N, T, P, S)$ in Chomsky normal form, and a word $w \in T^+$.

Output: **YES** if $w \in L(G)$, and **NO** if $w \notin L(G)$.

Method

begin
    if $w \in \{ w' : w' \in T^+, S \Rightarrow^i w'$ in G, where $i = 1, \ldots, 2|w| - 1\}$
    then write('YES')
    else write('NO')
end.

Lemma 6.3.2

Let $G = (N, T, P, S)$ be a context-free grammar in Chomsky normal form, and let $w \in T^+$. With G and w on its input, Algorithm 6.3.1 halts and correctly decides the membership problem for G and w – that is, this algorithm writes **YES** if $w \in L(G)$; otherwise, it writes **NO**.

Proof
Termination
As $\{w': w' \in T^+, S \Rightarrow^i w'$ in G, where $i = 1, \ldots, 2|w| - 1\}$ is finite, this algorithm surely halts.

Correctness
To verify the correctness of Algorithm 6.3.1, this proof first establishes the following claim.

Claim
Let $G = (N, T, P, S)$ be a context-free grammar in Chomsky normal form. If $A \Rightarrow^i w$ in G, where $i \geq 1$, $A \in N$, and $w \in T^+$, then $i \leq 2|w| - 1$.

Proof
This claim is proved by induction on $|w|$.

Basis
Let $|w| = 1$; that is, $w \in T$. As G is in Chomsky normal form, A derives w by making the one-step derivation

$$A \Rightarrow^1 w \ [A \to w]$$

where $A \to w \in P$. As $1 \leq 2|w| - 1 = 2 - 1 = 1$, the basis holds.

Induction hypothesis
Suppose that the claim holds for all w satisfying $|w| \leq n$, for some $n \geq 1$.

Induction step
Consider

$$A \Rightarrow^i w$$

where $|w| = n + 1$ and $i \geq 1$. Because G satisfies Chomsky normal form, in greater detail, $A \Rightarrow^* w$ has the form

$$A \Rightarrow B_1 B_2$$
$$\Rightarrow^{j+k} w_1 w_2$$

where $i = 1 + j + k$, $w = w_1 w_2$, $B_1 \Rightarrow^j w_1$ in G for some $j \geq 1$, and $B_2 \Rightarrow^k w_2$ in G for some $k \geq 1$. As G has no ε-productions, $1 \leq |w_i|$ for $i = 1, 2$. Furthermore, $|w_i| \leq n$

because $|w_1 w_2| = |w| = n + 1$ and $w_i \neq \varepsilon$. By the induction hypothesis, $j \leq 2|w_1| - 1$ and $k \leq 2|w_2| - 1$. Hence, $i = 1 + j + k \leq 1 + 2|w_1| - 1 + 2|w_2| - 1 = 2|w_1| + 2|w_2| - 1 = 2(|w_1| + |w_2|) - 1 = 2|w| - 1$. Thus, the claim holds.

□

Let $w \in T^+$. Consider the claim for $A = S$; that is, if $S \Rightarrow^i w$ in G, for some $i \geq 1$, then $i \leq 2|w| - 1$. In other words, $w \in L(G)$ implies $w \in \{ w' : w \in T^*,$ and $S \Rightarrow^i w'$ in G, where $i = 1, \ldots, 2|w| - 1\}$. Therefore, Algorithm 6.3.1 correctly decides the membership problem for G and w.

Therefore, with G and w as its input, Algorithm 6.3.1 halts and correctly decides the membership problem for G and w – that is, this algorithm writes YES if $w \in L(G)$; otherwise, it writes NO. Thus, Lemma 6.3.2 holds.

■

Algorithm 6.3.1 requires that its input context-free grammars satisfies the Chomsky normal form. It plays a crucial role in the following algorithm, which decides the membership problem without any requirement placed on the input context-free grammar. As a result, the next algorithm permits ε as its input word.

Algorithm 6.3.3: Membership problem decision for context-free grammars

Input: A context-free grammar $G = (N, T, P, S)$ and a word $w \in T^*$.

Output: YES if $w \in L(G)$, and NO if $w \notin L(G)$.

Method

begin

    use Algorithm 5.1.3.2.1 to determine the set N_ε defined as $N_\varepsilon = \{A : A \in N,$ and $A \Rightarrow^* \varepsilon$ in $G\}$;

    use Algorithms 5.1.3.3.3 and 5.1.4.1.1 to convert G to a context-free grammar G_{CNF} in Chomsky normal form such that $L(G) =_\varepsilon L(G_{\text{CNF}})$;

if $w = \varepsilon$
then
begin
  if $S \in N_\varepsilon$
    then write('YES')
    else write('NO')
end

```
      else
      begin
         use Algorithm 6.3.1 with G_CNF and w as its input to decide whether w ∈ L(G_CNF);
         if w ∈ L(G_CNF)
         then write('YES')
         else write('NO')
      end

   end.
```

Lemma 6.3.4

Let $G = (N, T, P, S)$ be a context-free grammar, and let $w \in T^*$. With G and w as its input, Algorithm 6.3.3 halts and correctly decides the membership problem for G and w; that is, this algorithm writes YES if $w \in L(G)$; otherwise, it writes NO.

Proof

Termination
Lemma 5.1.3.2.2 and Theorem 5.1.3.3.4 prove that Algorithm 5.1.3.2.1 and Algorithm 5.1.3.3.3 terminate, respectively. Therefore, Algorithm 6.3.3 terminates as well.

Correctness
This part of the proof distinguishes two cases, $w = \varepsilon$ and $w \neq \varepsilon$:

1. Let $w = \varepsilon$. Observe that $\varepsilon \in L(G)$ if and only if $S \Rightarrow^* \varepsilon$ in G. Furthermore, $S \Rightarrow^* \varepsilon$ in G if and only if Algorithm 5.1.3.2.1 includes S in N_ε, where $N_\varepsilon = \{A: A \in N,$ and $A \Rightarrow^* \varepsilon$ in $G\}$. If $S \in N_\varepsilon$, then Algorithm 6.3.3 writes YES; otherwise, it writes NO. Consequently, Algorithm 6.3.3 correctly decides the membership problem for G and ε.

2. Let $w \neq \varepsilon$. Algorithm 6.3.3 converts G to a context-free grammar G_{CNF} in Chomsky normal form such that $L(G) =_\varepsilon L(G_{CNF})$. As $w \neq \varepsilon$, $w \in L(G)$ if and only if $w \in L(G_{CNF})$. Therefore, Algorithm 6.3.3 uses Algorithm 6.3.1 to decide whether $w \in L(G_{CNF})$. If $w \in L(G_{CNF})$, Algorithm 6.3.3 writes YES; otherwise, it writes NO. Consequently, Algorithm 6.3.3 correctly decides the membership problem for G and w, where $w \neq \varepsilon$.

Therefore, with G and w as its input, Algorithm 6.3.3 halts and correctly decides the membership problem for G and w – that is, this algorithm writes YES if $w \in L(G)$; otherwise, it writes NO. In other words, Theorem 6.3.4 holds. ∎

Theorem 6.3.5
The membership problem for context-free grammars is decidable.

Proof
This theorem follows from Algorithm 6.3.3 and Lemma 6.3.4.

■

Emptiness problem for context-free grammars

Instance: A context-free grammar $G = (N, T, P, S)$.
Question: Is $L(G)$ empty?

Algorithm 6.3.6: Emptiness problem decision for context-free grammars

Input: A context-free grammar $G = (N, T, P, S)$.

Output: **YES** if $L(G) = \emptyset$, and **NO** if $L(G) \neq \emptyset$.

Method

begin
  use Algorithm 5.1.3.1.1 with G as its input to determine the set V that contains all terminating symbols in G;
  if $S \notin V$
  then write('YES')
  else write('NO')
end.

Lemma 6.3.7
Let $G = (N, T, P, S)$ be a context-free grammar. With G as its input, Algorithm 6.3.6 halts and correctly decides the emptiness problem for G – that is, it writes **YES** if $L(G) = \emptyset$, otherwise it writes **NO**.

Proof
Termination
Lemma 5.1.3.1.2 proves that Algorithm 5.1.3.1.1 terminates, so Algorithm 6.3.6 terminates as well.

Correctness
Observe that $L(G) \neq \emptyset$ if and only if there exists a word $w \in T^*$, such that $S \Rightarrow^* w$. In other words, $L(G) \neq \emptyset$ if and only if S is terminating. Therefore, Algorithm 6.3.6 uses Algorithm 5.1.3.1.1 with G as its input to determine the set V that contains all

terminating symbols in G. If $S \notin V$, then $L(G) = \emptyset$, so Algorithm 6.3.6 writes **YES**; if $S \in V$, then $L(G) \neq \emptyset$, so Algorithm 6.3.6 writes **NO**.

In other words, Lemma 6.3.7 holds.

∎

Theorem 6.3.8
The emptiness problem for context-free grammars is decidable.

Proof
This theorem follows from Algorithm 6.3.6 and Lemma 6.3.7.

∎

Finiteness problem for context-free grammars

Instance: A context-free grammar $G = (N, T, P, S)$.
Question: Is $L(G)$ finite?

Algorithm 6.3.9: Finiteness problem decision for context-free grammars

Input: A context-free grammar $G = (N, T, P, S)$.

Output: **YES** if $L(G)$ is finite, and **NO** if $L(G)$ is infinite.

Method

begin
   $k := 2^{\text{card}(N)}$;
   if $\{x : x \in L(G) \text{ and } k \leq |x| < 2k\} = \emptyset$
   then write('**YES**')
   else write('**NO**')
end.

Lemma 6.3.10
Let $G = (N, T, P, S)$ be a context-free grammar. With G as its input, Algorithm 6.3.9 halts and correctly decides the finiteness problem for G – that is, it writes **YES** if $L(G)$ is finite, otherwise it writes **NO**.

Proof
Termination
As $\{x : x \in L(G) \text{ and } k \leq |x| < 2k\}$ is finite, this algorithm always halts.

Properties of context-free languages

Correctness
Return to Lemma 6.1.3, the pumping lemma for context-free languages, and observe that the proof of this lemma sets

$$k = 2^{\text{card}(N)}$$

In other words, Algorithm 6.3.9 sets k by analogy with the proof of Lemma 6.1.3. This observation plays an important role in the proof of the following claim.

Claim

Let $G = (N, T, P, S)$ be a context-free grammar, and let $k = 2^{\text{card}(N)}$. $L(G)$ is finite if and only if $\{x : x \in L(G) \text{ and } k \le |x| < 2k\}$ is empty.

Proof
If
The 'if' part of the equivalence states that $\{x : x \in L(G) \text{ and } k \le |x| < 2k\} = \varnothing$ implies that $L(G)$ is finite. This part is proved by contradiction.

Assume that $\{x : x \in L(G) \text{ and } k \le |x| < 2k\} = \varnothing$ and that $L(G)$ is infinite. Let z be the shortest word that satisfies $z \in L(G)$ and $|z| \ge 2k$. As $z \in L$ and $|z| \ge k$, Lemma 6.1.3 implies that

$$z = uvwxy$$

so that

1. $vx \ne \varepsilon$;
2. $|vwx| \le k$;
3. $uv^m wx^m y \in L$, for all $m \ge 0$.

Then, $uwy \in L(G)$ and $k \le |uwy| < 2k$, so $\{x : x \in L(G) \text{ and } k \le |x| < 2k\} \ne \varnothing$ – a contradiction. Thus, L is finite.

Only if
The 'only if' part of the equivalence states that if $L(G)$ is finite, then $\{x : x \in L(G) \text{ and } k \le |x| < 2k\} = \varnothing$. This part of the proof is left to the exercises.

Therefore, the claim holds.

$\square$

The claim shows that $L(G)$ is finite if and only if $\{x : x \in L(G) \text{ and } k \le |x| < 2k\} = \varnothing$. Therefore, Algorithm 6.3.9 writes **YES** if $\{x : x \in L(G) \text{ and } k \le |x| < 2k\}$ is empty; it writes **NO** if $\{x : x \in L(G) \text{ and } k \le |x| < 2k\} \ne \varnothing$.

In summary, with G as its input, Algorithm 6.3.9 halts and correctly decides the finiteness problem for G – it writes **YES** if $L(G)$ is finite, otherwise it writes **NO**. In other words, Lemma 6.3.10 holds. ∎

Theorem 6.3.11
The finiteness problem for context-free grammars is decidable.

Proof
This theorem follows from Algorithm 6.3.9 and Lemma 6.3.10. ∎

Infiniteness problem for context-free grammars

Instance: A context-free grammar $G = (N, T, P, S)$.
Question: Is $L(G)$ infinite?

Theorem 6.3.12
The infiniteness problem for context-free grammars is decidable.

Proof
This theorem follows from Theorem 6.3.11. ∎

The exercises decide several other features about context-free grammars. However, Section 10.3 demonstrates that some problems concerning these grammars cannot be solved algorithmically.

Exercises

1 Pumping lemma

1.1 Consider the following languages:
(a) $\{a^i b^j c^k : i, j, k \geq 0 \text{ and } i < j < k\}$
(b) $\{a^i b^j : i, j \geq 0 \text{ and } j = i^2\}$
(c) $\{a^i : i \text{ is a prime}\}$
(d) $\{w : w \in \{a, b, c\}^* \text{ and } \#_a w = \#_b w = \#_b w\}$

(e) $\{a^i b^i c^j : i, j \geq 0 \text{ and } j \leq i\}$
(f) $\{a^i b^i c^j : i, j \geq 0 \text{ and } i \leq j \leq 2i\}$
(g) $\{a^i b^j c^k : i, j, k \geq 0, i \neq j, k \neq i, \text{ and } j \neq k\}$
(h) $\{a^i b^j c^j d^i : i, j \geq 0 \text{ and } j \leq i\}$
(i) $\{a^i b^{2i} c^i : i \geq 0\}$
(j) $\{ww : w \in \{a, b\}^*\}$
(k) $\{wvw : w \in \{a, b\}^* \text{ and } v = reversal(w)\}$

Use the pumping lemma to demonstrate that none of these languages is context-free.

1.2 Consider each of the context-free languages discussed in Exercise 1.4 of Chapter 5. Select a non-context-free subset of the language. Prove that the selected subset is not context-free by the pumping lemma. For instance, consider $\{a^i b^j c^k : i, j, k \geq 0 \text{ and } i = j \text{ or } j = k\}$. Observe that this language contains $\{a^n b^n c^n : n \geq 1\}$ as its subset. By using the pumping lemma, Example 6.1.2 has already proved that $\{a^n b^n c^n : n \geq 1\}$ represents a non-context-free language.

1.3 Based on the Greibach two-standard normal form, give an alternative proof of the pumping lemma.

1.4 Prove the pumping lemma based on context-free grammars that do not satisfy any normal form, such as the Chomsky normal form or the Greibach normal form.

1.5 Based on pushdown automata, give an alternative proof of the pumping lemma.

1.6 Prove a pumping lemma for the family of languages accepted by the counter pushdown automata (see Exercise 2.12 in Chapter 5).

1.7 Let $G = (N, T, P\ S)$ be a proper context-free grammar. A nonterminal $A \in N$ is *recursive* if $A \Rightarrow^* uAv$, for some $uv \in T^+$. Give a formal proof of the following theorem.

Theorem

Let $G = (N, T, P\ S)$ be a proper context-free grammar. Then, $L(G)$ is infinite if and only if N contains a recursive nonterminal.

1.8** Prove the following generalization of the pumping lemma:

Ogden's lemma

Let L be a context-free language over an alphabet T. Then, there exists a natural number k such that

if for some $n \geq k$,

$$z_0 a_1 z_1 a_2 z_2 \ldots a_n z_n \in L$$

where $z_i \in T^*$ for all $i = 0, \ldots, n$, and $a_j \in T$ for all $j = 0, \ldots, n$,

then $z_0 a_1 z_1 a_2 z_2 \ldots a_n z_n$ can be written as

$$z_0 a_1 z_1 a_2 z_2 \ldots a_n z_n = uvwxy$$

where

1. for some $t = 1, \ldots, n$, a_t appears in vx;
2. if vwx contains $a_r, \ldots, a_s$, for some $r = 1, \ldots, n$, and

$$s = r, \ldots, n,$$

then $s - r \leq k - 1$
3. $uv^m wx^m y \in L$, for all $m \geq 0$

1.9* Consider the following languages
  (a) $\{a^i b^j c^k d^l : i, j, k, l \geq 0,$ and either $i = 0$ or $j = k = l\}$
  (b) $\{a^i b^j c^k : i, j, k \geq 0, i \neq j, k \neq i,$ and $j \neq k\}$
  Use Ogden's lemma to prove that neither of these languages is context-free. Explain why this proof cannot be based on Lemma 6.1.3.

2 Closure properties

2.1 Complete the proof of Lemma 6.2.6.
2.2 Complete the proof of Lemma 6.2.10.
2.3 Adapt Algorithm 6.2.9 for context-free grammars.
2.4 Complete Example 6.2.2.
2.5 Let M' and M'' be two pushdown automata. Design an algorithm that converts M' and M'' to a pushdown automaton, M, such that $L(M) = L(M')L(M'')$.
2.6 Let G' and G'' be two context-free grammars. Design an algorithm that converts G' and G'' to a context-free grammar G such that $L(G) = L(G')L(G'')$.
2.7 Let M' be a pushdown automaton. Design an algorithm that converts M' to a pushdown automaton M such that $L(M) = L(M')^*$.
2.8 Let G' be a context-free grammar. Design an algorithm that converts G' to a context-free grammar G such that $L(G) = L(G')^*$.
2.9 Recall that for a language L

$$\text{Prefix}(L) = \{w : wx \in L \text{ for some } x \in T^*\}$$

Prove that if L is a context-free language, then $\text{Prefix}(L)$ is context-free as well.
2.10 Recall that for a language L

$$\text{Suffix}(L) = \{w : xw \in L \text{ for some } x \in T^*\}$$

Prove that if L is a context-free language, then $\text{Suffix}(L)$ is context-free as well.
2.11 Recall that for a language L

Properties of context-free languages

$$\mathrm{Sub}(L) = \{\mathrm{subword}(x): x \in L\}$$

Prove that if L is a context-free language, then $\mathrm{Sub}(L)$ is context-free as well.

2.12 Recall that for a language L

$$\mathrm{Reversal}(L) = \{\mathrm{reversal}(w): w \in L\}$$

Prove that if L is a context-free language, then $\mathrm{Reversal}(L)$ is context-free as well.

2.13 Recall that for a language L over an alphabet T

$$\mathrm{Cycle}(L) = \{vw: wv \in L, \text{ where } v, w \in T^*\}$$

Prove that if L is a context-free language, then $\mathrm{Cycle}(L)$ is context-free as well.

2.14 Recall that for two languages L_1 and L_2,

$$L_1/L_2 = \{w: wx \in L_1, \text{ for some } x \in L_2\}$$

Prove that if L_1 is context-free and L_2 is regular, then L_1/L_2 is context-free, too.

2.15 Let $L_1 \subseteq T_1^*$ and $L_2 \subseteq T_2^*$ be two languages. Define $\mathrm{Shuffle}(L_1, L_2)$ as

$$\mathrm{Shuffle}(L_1,L_2) = \{\, v_1 w_1 \ldots v_n w_n : v_i \in T_1^*, w_i \in T_2^*, i = 1, \ldots, n \\ (\text{for some } n \geq 0), v_1 \ldots v_n \in L_1, w_1 \ldots w_n \in L_2\};$$

less formally, $\mathrm{Shuffle}(L_1,L_2)$ is the set of words formed by shuffling a word of L_1 with a word of L_2. Prove that if L_1 is context-free and L_2 is regular, then L_1/L_2 is context-free, too.

2.16 Prove the family of context-free languages is closed under inverse homomorphism.

2.17 For a language L over an alphabet T and a symbol $a \in T$, define $\mathrm{Eraser}_a(L)$ as

$$\mathrm{Eraser}_a(L) = \{\, b_1 \ldots b_n : \{a\}^* \{b_1\}\{a\}^* \ldots \{a\}^* \{b_n\}\{a\}^* \cap L \neq \emptyset, \\ b_i \in (T - \{a\}), i = 1, \ldots, n, \text{ for some } n \geq 0 \ (n = 0 \text{ implies} \\ b_1 \ldots b_n = \varepsilon)\};$$

less formally, $\mathrm{Eraser}_a(L)$ is the language obtained by removing all occurrences of a from words of L. Prove that if L is a context-free language, then $\mathrm{Eraser}_a(L)$ is context-free as well.

2.18 Consider the following languages:
(a) $\{w: w \in \{a, b, c\}^*, \#_a w = 2\#_b w, \text{ and } \#_c w = 3\#_b w\}$
(b) $\{0^i 10^i 10^i 10^i : i \geq 1\}$
(c) $\{wcv: v, w \in \{a, b\}^* \text{ and } |w| = 2^{|v|}\}$
(d) $\{wcw^R cw: w \in \{a, b\}^*\}$
Use the closure properties obtained in Section 6.2 to demonstrate that none of these languages is context-free.

2.19 Return to the languages defined in Exercise 1.1 of this section. Prove that none of these languages is context-free by using Lemma 6.1.3 combined with the closure properties obtained in Section 6.2.

2.20 Return to the languages defined in Exercise 1.4 of this section. Prove that all these languages are context-free by using the closure properties obtained in Section 6.2

2.21 Recall that for a language L

$$\text{Min}(L) = \{w : w \in L \text{ and } \{\text{prefix}(w) - \{w\}\} \cap L = \varnothing\}$$

Give a context-free language L such that $\text{Min}(L)$ is not context-free.

2.22 Recall that for a language L

$$\text{Max}(L) = \{w : w \in L, \text{ and } \{w\}T^+ \cap L = \varnothing\}$$

Give a context-free language L such that $\text{Max}(L)$ is not context-free.

2.23 Give two context-free languages, L_1 and L_2, such that $\text{Shuffle}(L_1, L_2)$ is not context-free.

2.24 For a language L over an alphabet T, define $\text{Half}(L)$ as

$$\text{Half}(L) = \{w : wv \in L, \text{ for some } v \in T^* \text{ and } |w| = |v|\}$$

Give a context-free language L such that $\text{Half}(L)$ is not context-free.

2.25 Recall that for a language L

$$\text{Inv}(L) = \{xwy : xw^R y \in L, \text{ for some } x, y, w \in T^*\}$$

Give a context-free language L such that $\text{Inv}(L)$ is not context-free.

2.26 Consider a common programming language such as C. Prove or disprove that the language under consideration is context-free.

2.27 Consider a natural language such as French. Prove or disprove that the language under consideration is context-free.

3 Decidable problems

3.1 Complete the proof of Lemma 6.3.11.

3.2 Consider the recursive nonterminal problem for context-free grammars:

Instance: A context-free grammar $G = (N, T, P, S)$ and $A \in N$.
Question: Is A recursive?

Design an algorithm that decides this problem.

3.3 Consider the emptiness problem for pushdown automata:

Instance: A pushdown automaton $M = (Q, \Sigma, R, s, F)$.
Question: Is $L(M)$ empty?

Design an algorithm that decides this problem.

3.4 Consider the derivation problem for context-free grammars:

Instance: A context-free grammar $G = (N, T, P, S)$ and $v, w \in (N \cup T)^*$.
Question: Is it true that $v \Rightarrow^* w$ in G?

Design an algorithm that decides this problem.

3.5 Consider the leftmost derivation problem for context-free grammars:

Instance: A context-free grammar $G = (N, T, P, S)$ and $v, w \in (N \cup T)^*$.
Question: Is it true that $v \Rightarrow^*_{lm} w$ in G?

Design an algorithm that decides this problem.

3.6 Consider the rightmost derivation problem for context-free grammars:

Instance: A context-free grammar $G = (N, T, P, S)$ and $v, w \in (N \cup T)^*$.
Question: Is it true that $v \Rightarrow^*_{rm} w$ in G?

Design an algorithm that decides this problem.

3.7 Modify the algorithms presented in Section 6.3 so that they work more efficiently.

7 Special Types of Context-Free Languages and Their Models

This chapter investigates special types of context-free languages, resulting from some restricted models of pushdown automata and context-free grammars. Most importantly, the relationships between the context-free language subfamilies defined by these restricted models are studied. Section 7.1 examines the family of deterministic context-free languages, defined by deterministic pushdown automata. Section 7.2 reconsiders the family of regular languages and characterizes this family by three restricted variants of context-free grammars. Additionally, linear grammars are introduced, which define a proper superfamily of regular languages.

7.1 Deterministic context-free languages

This section examines the family of languages accepted by deterministic pushdown automata.

Definition — deterministic context-free language
Let L be a language. If there exists a deterministic pushdown automaton M such that $L = L(M)$, then L is a *deterministic context-free language*.

◆

This section establishes fundamental properties of deterministic context-free languages, including closure properties investigated next.

Closure properties

From Theorem 6.2.8, the family of context-free languages is not closed under complement. As demonstrated next, however, the family of deterministic context-free languages is closed under complement. For simplicity, the following algorithm assumes that its input deterministic pushdown automaton always completes reading its input word. From Theorem 5.2.3.1, this assumption represents no loss of generality.

Algorithm 7.1.1: Construction of a deterministic pushdown automaton for the complement of a deterministic context-free language

Input: A deterministic pushdown automaton $M = (Q, \Sigma, R, s, F)$ such that for all words $w \in \Sigma_1^*$, $Ssw \vdash^* zq$ in M for some $q \in Q$ and $z \in \Sigma_{PD}^*$.

Output: A deterministic pushdown automaton $M' = (Q', \Sigma, R', s', F')$, such that

$$L(M') = \overline{L(M)}$$

Method

begin
  $Q' := \{ [q, k] : q \in Q \text{ and } k \in \{1, 0, @\}\}$;
  $F' := \{ [q, @] : q \in Q\}$;

  if $s \in F$
  then $s' = [s, 1]$
  else $s' = [s, 0]$;

  for each $r: Aq \vdash xp \in R$ and $k = 0, 1$ **do**
    if $p \in F$ or $k = 1$
    then $R' := R' \cup \{ A[q, k] \vdash x[p, 1]\}$
    else $R' := R' \cup \{ A[q, k] \vdash x[p, 0]\}$;

  for each $r: Aqa \vdash xp \in R$ **do**
  begin
    $R' := R' \cup \{ A[q, 0] \vdash A[q, @]\}$;
    if $p \in F$
    then $R' := R' \cup \{ A[q, 1]a \vdash x[p, 1], A[q, @]a \vdash x[p, 1]\}$
    else $R' := R' \cup \{ A[q, 1]a \vdash x[p, 0], A[q, @]a \vdash x[p, 0]\}$
  end

end.

Automaton M', produced by Algorithm 7.1.1, simulates M as follows. Consider the following n-move computation made by M, for some $n \geq 2$:

A during move 1, M reads the rightmost symbol of a word w;

B. during moves 2 through $n-1$, M makes ε-moves;

C. during move n, M reads an input symbol a by using a rule of the form $Aqa \vdash xp$.

Depending on moves 1 through $n-1$, M' simulates move n in these two distinct ways:

1. Assume that during moves 1 through $n-1$, M has entered a final state, so $w \in L(M)$. When M' simulates move n, its state is $[q, 1]$. At this point, M' simulates this move without entering $[q, @]$, which is a final state of M'. Therefore, $w \notin L(M')$.
2. Assume that during moves 1 through $n-1$, M has never entered a final state, so $w \notin L(M)$. When M' simulates move n, its state is $[q, 0]$. At this point, before M' simulates move n, M' enters $[q, @]$ and, thus, $w \in L(M')$.

Consequently, M accepts w if and only if M' does not accept w. As M completes reading every input word,

$$L(M') = L(M)$$

Lemma 7.1.2
Let $M = (Q, \Sigma, R, s, F)$ be a deterministic pushdown automaton such that for all words $w \in \Sigma_I^*$, $Ssw \vdash^* zq$ in M, for some $q \in Q$ and $z \in \Sigma_{PD}^*$. With M as its input, Algorithm 7.2.1 halts and correctly constructs a deterministic pushdown automaton M' such that $L(M') = L(M)$.

Proof
This proof is left to the exercises. ■

Theorem 7.1.3
The family of deterministic context-free languages is closed under complement.

Proof
This theorem follows from Algorithm 7.1.1 and Lemma 7.1.2. ■

Observe that Algorithm 7.1.1 produces its output deterministic pushdown automaton so this automaton makes no ε-moves from any final states. This observation gives rise to the next corollary.

Corollary 7.1.4
Every deterministic context-free language is accepted by a deterministic pushdown automaton that makes no ε-move from any of its final states.

Proof
Let L be a deterministic context-free language. From Theorem 7.1.3, its complement $\overline{L}$ also represents a deterministic context-free language. In other words, there exists a deterministic pushdown automaton M such that $\overline{L} = L(M)$. From Theorem 5.2.3.9, without any loss of generality, assume that M satisfies the input requirements of

Algorithm 7.1.1. By using this algorithm, transform M to a deterministic pushdown automaton that accepts L and that makes no ε-move from any of its final states. As a result, Corollary 7.1.4 holds. ∎

Theorem 7.1.5
The family of deterministic context-free languages is not closed under intersection.

Proof
Consider these two languages

$L_1 = \{a^i b^j c^k : i, j, k \geq 1 \text{ and } i = j\}$
$L_2 = \{a^i b^j c^k : i, j, k \geq 1 \text{ and } j = k\}$

Here, L_1 and L_2 are context-free (see Example 5.1.2.2); in fact, the exercises demonstrates that both languages represent deterministic context-free languages. Consider

$$\overline{L_1} \cap \overline{L_2} = \{a^n b^n c^n : n \geq 1\}$$

From Example 6.1.2, $\{a^n b^n c^n : n \geq 1\}$ is not context-free. Consequently, L_1 and L_2 represent two deterministic context-free languages, whose intersection is not a deterministic context-free language. Therefore, Theorem 7.1.5 holds. ∎

Theorem 7.1.6
The family of deterministic context-free languages is not closed under union.

Proof
This theorem is proved by contradiction. Assume that the family of deterministic context-free languages is closed under union. Consider

$L_1 = \{a^i b^j c^k : i, j, k \geq 1 \text{ and } i = j\}$
$L_2 = \{a^i b^j c^k : i, j, k \geq 1 \text{ and } j = k\}$

As stated in the proof of Theorem 7.1.5, L_1 and L_2 represent two deterministic context-free languages. By DeMorgan's law (see Exercise 1.26 in Section 1),

$$\overline{L_1} \cup \overline{L_2} = L_1 \cap L_2$$

From Theorem 7.1.3, $L_1 \cap L_2$ is a deterministic context-free language. However,

$$L_1 \cap L_2 = \{a^n b^n c^n : n \geq 1\}$$

and Example 6.1.2 has proved that $\{a^n b^n c^n : n \geq 1\}$ is not context-free – a contradiction. Thus, the family of deterministic context-free languages is not closed under union, so Theorem 7.1.6 holds. ∎

Family relationships

From Part 6 of Example 5.2.2.1,

$$\{v\text{reversal}(v) : v \in \{a, b\}^*\}$$

represents a context-free language accepted by no deterministic pushdown automata. In other words, this language belongs to the family of context-free languages; however, it does not belong to the family of deterministic context-free languages. Examples 7.1.1 and 7.1.2 present two other languages of this kind.

Example 7.1.1 Non-deterministic context-free language
Consider

$$L = \{a, b, c\}^* - \{a^n b^n c^n : n \geq 1\};$$

that is, L represents the complement of $\{a^n b^n c^n : n \geq 1\}$. Example 6.2.2 has proved that L is context-free. On the other hand, Example 6.1.2 has demonstrated that $\{a^n b^n c^n : n \geq 1\}$ is not context-free. From Theorem 7.1.3, L represents a context-free language, which is not a deterministic context-free language, however. ▲

Example 7.1.2 Another non-deterministic context-free language
Consider

$$L = \{a^i b^j c^k : i = j \text{ or } j = k\}$$

From Example 5.1.2.2, L is context-free. By contradiction, this example demonstrates that L is not a deterministic context-free language.

Assume that L represents a deterministic context-free language. Then, Theorem 7.1.3 shows that its complement, $\overline{L}$, is a deterministic context-free language as well. Consider

$$\overline{L} \cap \{a\}^* \{b\}^* \{c\}^* = \{a^i b^j c^k : i \neq j \text{ or } j \neq k\}$$

As $\{a\}^*\{b\}^*\{c\}^*$ is regular, Theorem 6.2.7 implies that $\{a^i b^j c^k: i \neq j \text{ or } j \neq k\}$ is context-free. As proved in the exercises, however, $\{a^i b^j c^k: i \neq j \text{ or } j \neq k\}$ is not context-free – a contradiction. Thus, L is a context-free language that is not a deterministic context-free language.

▲

Theorem 7.1.7
The family of context-free languages properly contains the family of deterministic context-free languages.

Proof
By the definition of a deterministic context-free language, every deterministic context-free language is accepted by a pushdown automaton. Thus, by Theorem 5.3.3.1, every deterministic context-free language is a context-free language. Furthermore, the previous two examples have presented context-free languages that are not deterministic context-free languages. Thus, Theorem 7.1.7 holds.

■

According to Theorem 7.1.7, the family of deterministic context-free languages represents a proper subfamily of the family of context-free languages. The family of finite languages and the family of regular languages are properly included in the family of context-free languages as well. Theorem 7.1.8, given next, explains the relationships between these subfamilies.

Theorem 7.1.8
The following three statements are true.

1. The family of finite languages is properly contained in the family of regular languages.
2. The family of regular languages is properly contained in the family of deterministic context-free languages.
3. The family of deterministic context-free languages is properly contained in the family of context-free languages.

Proof
The first statement follows from Theorem 3.1.1. The second statement follows from Lemma 5.2.3.4 and Theorems 5.2.3.3, 5.2.3.7 and 5.2.3.8. Finally, the third statement actually represents Theorem 7.1.7, formulated in a slightly different way. Thus, Theorem 7.1.8 holds.

■

Informally, from the third statement of this theorem, the power of pushdown automata that work nondeterministically is greater than the power of pushdown automata that work deterministically. For instance, there exists a nondeterministic pushdown automaton that accepts $\{a^i b^j c^k : i = j \text{ or } j = k\}$; however, there is no deterministic pushdown automaton that accepts this language. As finite automata characterize the family of regular languages, the second statement actually means that the power of deterministic pushdown automata is greater than the power of finite automata. For example, there exists a deterministic pushdown automaton that accepts $\{a^i b^i : i \geq 0\}$; however, no finite automaton accepts $\{a^i b^i : i \geq 0\}$.

Decidable problems

This section discusses algorithmically decidable problems concerning deterministic pushdown automata. First, recall that Section 6.3 algorithmically solves the following four context-free grammars problems:

1. membership
2. emptiness
3. infiniteness
4. finiteness.

Concerning pushdown automata, these four problems are also algorithmically decidable because Algorithm 5.3.2.1 transforms any pushdown automaton to an equivalent context-free grammar. Consequently, regarding deterministic pushdown automata, which represent special cases of pushdown automata, these four problems are decidable, too.

The present section next adds five other algorithmically decidable problems concerning deterministic pushdown automata. By contrast, in terms of nondeterministic pushdown automata, none of these problems is algorithmically decidable.

Equivalence problem for deterministic finite automata and deterministic pushdown automata

Instance: A deterministic pushdown automaton M and a deterministic finite automaton M' such that M and M' have the same input alphabet.
Question: Is $L(M)$ equal to $L(M')$?

Theorem 7.1.9
The equivalence problem for deterministic finite automata and deterministic pushdown automata is decidable.

Proof

Let M be a deterministic pushdown automaton, and let M' be a deterministic finite automaton. Suppose that M and M' have the same input alphabet. Observe that

$$L(M) = L(M') \text{ if and only if } ((L(M) \cap \overline{L(M')}) \cup (\overline{L(M)} \cap L(M'))) = \varnothing$$

From Theorem 7.1.3 $\overline{L(M)}$ is a deterministic context-free language, and from Theorem 4.2.4 $\overline{L(M')}$ is regular. Theorem 6.2.7 implies that both $L(M) \cap \overline{L(M')}$ and $\overline{L(M)} \cap L(M')$ are context-free. Thus, from Theorem 6.2.3,

$$((L(M) \cap \overline{L(M')}) \cup (\overline{L(M)} \cap L(M')))$$

represents a context-free language as well. Consequently, Theorem 7.1.8 follows from Theorem 6.3.8, stating that the emptiness problem for context-free grammars is decidable. ∎

Containment problem for deterministic finite automata and deterministic pushdown automata

Instance: A deterministic pushdown automaton M and a deterministic finite automaton M' such that M and M' have the same input alphabet.
Question: Does $L(M)$ contain $L(M')$?

Theorem 7.1.10
The containment problem for deterministic finite automata and deterministic pushdown automata is decidable.

Proof

Let M be a deterministic pushdown automaton, and let M' be a deterministic finite automaton. Assume that M and M' have the same input alphabet. Observe that

$$L(M') \subseteq L(M) \text{ if and only if } \overline{L(M)} \cap L(M') = \varnothing$$

From Theorem 7.1.3, $\overline{L(M)}$ is a deterministic context-free language, so $\overline{L(M)}$ is context-free. Theorem 6.2.7 implies that $\overline{L(M)} \cap L(M')$ is context-free. Theorem 6.3.8, imples that it is decidable whether $\overline{L(M)} \cap L(M') = \varnothing$. Therefore, Theorem 7.1.10 holds. ∎

Emptiness problem for the complement of deterministic context-free languages

Instance: A deterministic pushdown automaton M.
Question: Is $\overline{L(M)}$ empty?

Theorem 7.1.11
The emptiness problem for the complement of deterministic context-free languages is decidable.

Proof
From Theorem 7.1.3, $\overline{L(M)}$ is a deterministic context-free language, so $\overline{L(M)}$ is context-free. From Theorem 6.3.8, the problem of whether $\overline{L(M)} = \emptyset$ is decidable. Therefore, Theorem 7.1.11 holds. ∎

Context-freeness problem for the complement of deterministic context-free languages

Instance: A deterministic pushdown automaton M.
Question: Is $\overline{L(M)}$ context-free?

Theorem 7.1.12
The context-freeness problem for the complement of deterministic context-free languages is decidable.

Proof
From Theorem 7.1.3, $\overline{L(M)}$ is a deterministic context-free language, so $\overline{L(M)}$ is context-free; therefore, Theorem 7.1.12 holds. ∎

Regularness problem for deterministic context-free languages

Instance: A deterministic pushdown automaton M.
Question: Is $L(M)$ regular?

Theorem 7.1.13
The regularness problem for the deterministic context-free languages is decidable.

Proof
This proof is left to the exercises.
∎

As already noted, if the previous five problems are reformulated in terms of nondeterministic pushdown automata, then none of them is algorithmically decidable. Even in terms of deterministic pushdown automata, however, there exist some important problems that are algorithmically undecidable. To illustrate, the crucial question as to whether there is a deterministic pushdown automaton that accepts a given context-free language is undecidable. (Undecidable problems are discussed in Section 10.3.)

7.2 Linear and regular grammars

This section introduces four restricted versions of context-free grammars:

1. right-linear grammars
2. regular grammars
3. left-linear grammars
4. linear grammars.

Right-linear grammars, regular grammars and left-linear grammars characterize the family of regular languages. The family of linear languages, defined by linear grammars, properly contains the family of regular languages. However, the family of linear language is properly included in the family of context-free languages.

Right-linear grammars

A context-free grammar is right-linear if the right-hand side of each production consists of terminals followed by zero or one nonterminals.

Definition — right-linear grammar
Let $G = (N, T, P, S)$ be a context-free grammar. G is *right-linear* if, for all $p \in P$,

$$\text{rhs}(p) \in T^*(N \cup \{\varepsilon\})$$

◆

Example 7.2.1 Part 1 Right-linear grammar

Consider the right-linear grammar

1: $S \rightarrow abS$
2: $S \rightarrow \varepsilon$

Observe that

$$L(G) = \{\,(ab)^i : i \geq 0\}$$

△

The next algorithm converts any right-linear grammar to an equivalent finite automaton.

Algorithm 7.2.1: Conversion of a right-linear grammar to an equivalent finite automaton

Input: A right-linear grammar $G = (N, T, P, S)$.

Output: A finite automaton $M = (Q, T, R, \langle S \rangle, \{\langle \varepsilon \rangle\})$, such that $L(G) = L(M)$.

Method

begin
  $Q := \{\,\langle x \rangle : x \in \{S\} \cup \text{suffix}(\text{rhs}(p)), \text{ where } p \in P\}$;
  for each $p \in P$ **do**
    $R := R \cup \{\langle \text{lhs}(p) \rangle \vdash \langle \text{rhs}(p) \rangle\}$;
  for each $\langle ay \rangle \in Q$ with $a \in T$ and $y \in T^*(N \cup \{\varepsilon\})$ **do**
    $R := R \cup \{\langle ax \rangle a \vdash \langle x \rangle\}$
end

Algorithm 7.2.1 converts G to M so the following equivalence holds

$$\langle S \rangle w \vdash^+ \langle z \rangle \text{ in } M$$

if and only if

$$\begin{aligned} S &\Rightarrow^* u\text{lhs}(p) \\ &\Rightarrow u\text{rhs}(p) \quad [p] \text{ in } G, \end{aligned}$$

where $\text{rhs}(p) = vz$ and $uv = w$. As $\langle \varepsilon \rangle$ is the final state of M,

$w \in L(M)$ if and only if $\langle S \rangle w \vdash^* \langle \varepsilon \rangle$ in M

Furthermore,

$\langle S \rangle w \vdash^+ \langle \varepsilon \rangle$ in M if and only if $S \Rightarrow^+ w$ in G

Consequently,

$L(M) = L(G)$

Lemma 7.2.2
Let $G = (N, T, P, S)$ be a right-linear grammar. With G as its input, Algorithm 7.2.1 halts and correctly constructs a finite automaton $M = (Q, T, R, \langle S \rangle, \{\langle \varepsilon \rangle\})$ such that

$L(G) = L(M).$

Proof
Termination
As P and Q are finite sets, Algorithm 7.2.1 repeats both **for** loops a finite number of times, so this algorithm surely terminates.

Correctness
To establish the identity

$L(G) = L(M)$

this proof first demonstrates the following claim.

Claim
For all $u, w \in T^*$ and $z \in T^*(N \cup \{\varepsilon\})$,

$S \Rightarrow^* u\text{lhs}(p) \Rightarrow u\text{rhs}(p)$ in G

if and only if

$\langle S \rangle w \vdash^+ \langle z \rangle$ in M

where $\text{rhs}(p) = vz$ and $uv = w$, for some $v \in T^*$.

Proof
Only if
By induction on i, where $i \geq 0$, this part of the proof demonstrates that for all u, $w \in T^*$ and $z \in T^*(N \cup \{\varepsilon\})$, if

$$S \Rightarrow^i u\mathrm{lhs}(p) \Rightarrow u\mathrm{rhs}(p) \text{ in } G$$

then

$$\langle S \rangle w \vdash^+ \langle z \rangle \text{ in } M$$

where $\mathrm{rhs}(p) = vz$ and $uv = w$, for some $v \in T^*$.

Basis
Let $i = 0$. At this point,

$$\mathrm{lhs}(p) \Rightarrow \mathrm{rhs}(p) \qquad [p]$$

in G, where $p \in P$, $\mathrm{lhs}(p) = S$, and $\mathrm{rhs}(p) = vz = wz$ because $u = \varepsilon$. From the present algorithm,

$$\{\langle S \rangle\} \cup \{\langle yz \rangle : y \in \mathrm{suffix}(w)\} \subseteq Q$$

and

$$\{\langle \mathrm{lhs}(p) \rangle \vdash \langle \mathrm{rhs}(p) \rangle\} \cup \{\langle axz \rangle a \vdash \langle xz \rangle : ax \in \mathrm{suffix}(w), a \in T, \text{ and } x \in T^*\} \subseteq Q$$

Therefore,

$$\langle S \rangle w \vdash \langle wz \rangle w \; [\langle \mathrm{lhs}(p) \rangle \vdash \langle \mathrm{rhs}(p) \rangle]$$
$$\vdash^* \langle z \rangle$$

in M, so the basis holds.

Induction hypothesis
Assume that the 'only if' part of the claim is true for all derivations of the form

$$S \Rightarrow^i u\mathrm{lhs}(p) \Rightarrow u\mathrm{rhs}(p) \text{ in } G$$

where $p \in P$ and $i = 0, \ldots, n$, for some $n \geq 0$.

Induction step
Consider

$$S \Rightarrow^{n+1} u\mathrm{lhs}(p) \Rightarrow u\mathrm{rhs}(p) \qquad [p]$$

in G, where $\mathrm{rhs}(p) = vz$, $u, v \in T^*$, and $z \in T^*(N \cup \{\varepsilon\})$. In greater detail, express $S \Rightarrow^{n+1} u\mathrm{lhs}(p)$ as

$$S \Rightarrow^n u'\mathrm{lhs}(p') \Rightarrow u'\mathrm{rhs}(p')$$

where $\mathrm{rhs}(p') = v'\mathrm{lhs}(p)$, $u'v' = u$ for some $p' \in P$ and $v' \in T^*$. By the inductive hypothesis,

$$\langle S \rangle u \vdash^+ \langle \mathrm{lhs}(p) \rangle$$

in M. As

$$\{\langle yz \rangle : y \in \mathrm{suffix}(v)\}\} \subseteq Q$$

and

$$(\{\langle \mathrm{lhs}(p) \rangle \vdash \langle \mathrm{rhs}(p) \rangle\} \cup \{\langle axz \rangle a \vdash \langle xz \rangle : ax \in \mathrm{suffix}(v), a \in T, \text{ and } x \in T^*\}) \subseteq R,$$

M computes

$$\langle \mathrm{lhs}(p) \rangle v \vdash \langle vz \rangle v \qquad [\langle \mathrm{lhs}(p) \rangle \vdash \langle \mathrm{rhs}(p) \rangle]$$
$$\vdash^* \langle z \rangle$$

Therefore,

$$\langle S \rangle uv \vdash^+ \langle \mathrm{lhs}(p) \rangle v$$
$$\vdash \langle vz \rangle v \qquad [\langle \mathrm{lhs}(p) \rangle \vdash \langle \mathrm{rhs}(p) \rangle]$$
$$\vdash^* \langle z \rangle$$

In brief,

$$\langle S \rangle w \vdash^+ \langle z \rangle$$

in M where $w = uv$. Thus, the inductive step holds.
Consequently, the 'only if' part of the claim is true.

If
By induction on i, where $i \geq 0$, this part of the proof demonstrates that for all u, $w \in T^*$ and $z \in T^*(N \cup \{\varepsilon\})$, if

$$\langle S \rangle w \vdash^i \langle z \rangle \text{ in } M$$

then

$$S \Rightarrow^i u\mathrm{lhs}(p) \Rightarrow u\mathrm{rhs}(p) \text{ in } G$$

where $\mathrm{rhs}(p) = vz$ and $uv = w$, for some $v \in T^*$.

Basis
Let $i = 0$. At this point,

$$\langle S \rangle w \vdash \langle z \rangle$$

in M, where $w = \varepsilon$, $\mathrm{lhs}(p) = S$, $\mathrm{rhs}(p) = z$ for some $p \in P$. Then,

$$S \Rightarrow \mathrm{rhs}(p)\ [p]$$

in G. Thus, the basis holds.

Induction hypothesis
Assume that the 'if' part of the claim is true for all i-move computations of the form $\langle S \rangle w \vdash^i \langle z \rangle$ in M, where $i = 1, \ldots, n$, for some $n \geq 1$.

Induction step
Consider

$$\langle S \rangle w \vdash^{n+1} \langle z \rangle$$

in M, where $w \in T^*$ and $z \in T^*(N \cup \{\varepsilon\})$. Express $\langle S \rangle w \vdash^{n+1} \langle z \rangle$ as

$$\langle S \rangle uv \vdash^* \langle \mathrm{lhs}(p) \rangle v$$
$$\vdash \langle vz \rangle v \qquad [\langle \mathrm{lhs}(p) \rangle \vdash \langle \mathrm{rhs}(p) \rangle]$$
$$\vdash^* \langle z \rangle$$

where $uv = w$, $vz = \mathrm{rhs}(p)$, for some $v \in T^*$ and $p \in P$. Notice that $\langle S \rangle uv \vdash^* \langle \mathrm{lhs}(p) \rangle v$ represents an m-move computation, for some $m = 1, \ldots, n$. By the induction hypothesis,

$$S \Rightarrow^* u'\mathrm{lhs}(p') \Rightarrow u'\mathrm{rhs}(p')$$

where $w = uv$ and $vz = \mathrm{rhs}(p)$. Consequently,

$$S \Rightarrow^* u\mathrm{lhs}(p)$$
$$\Rightarrow u\mathrm{rhs}(p) \qquad [p]$$

in G, where $\mathrm{rhs}(p) = vz$ and $uv = w$. Thus, the inductive step holds.

Consequently, the 'if' part of the claim is true.

As a result, the claim holds. □

As $\langle S \rangle$ is a nonfinal state, M accepts every word by making one or more moves; that is, for all $w \in L(M)$,

$$\langle S \rangle w \vdash^+ \langle z \rangle$$

in M. Furthermore, G generates every sentence by making one or more derivation steps; formally, for all $w \in L(G)$,

$$S \Rightarrow^+ w$$

in G. Consider the above claim for the final state $\langle \varepsilon \rangle$. Under this consideration,

$$\begin{aligned} S &\Rightarrow^* u\mathrm{lhs}(p) \\ &\Rightarrow u\mathrm{rhs}(p) \quad [p] \text{ in } G \end{aligned}$$

if and only if

$$\langle S \rangle w \vdash^+ \langle \varepsilon \rangle \text{ in } M$$

where $u\mathrm{rhs}(p) = w$, and $w \in T^*$. That is,

$$S \Rightarrow^+ w \text{ in } G$$

if and only if

$$\langle S \rangle w \vdash^+ \langle \varepsilon \rangle \text{ in } M$$

Therefore,

$$L(G) = L(M)$$

In summary, with G as its input, Algorithm 7.2.1 halts and correctly constructs a finite automaton $M = (Q, T, R, \langle S \rangle, \{\langle \varepsilon \rangle\})$ such that $L(G) = L(M)$. Thus, Lemma 7.2.2 holds. ∎

Example 7.2.1 Part 2 Application of Algorithm 7.2.1

Part 1 of Example 7.2.1 defines this right-linear grammar

1: $S \to abS$
2: $S \to \varepsilon$

This part of Example 7.2.1 uses Algorithm 7.2.1 to convert this grammar to a nondeterministic finite automaton, $M = (Q, T, R, \langle S \rangle, \{\langle \varepsilon \rangle\})$, satisfying $L(G) = L(M)$. First, Algorithm 7.2.1 defines

$$Q := \{ \langle S \rangle, \langle abS \rangle, \langle bS \rangle, \langle \varepsilon \rangle \}$$

The first **for** loop produces the following rules:

$\langle S \rangle \vdash \langle abS \rangle$
$\langle S \rangle \vdash \langle \varepsilon \rangle$

The second **for** loop produces

$\langle abS \rangle a \vdash \langle bS \rangle$
$\langle bS \rangle b \vdash \langle S \rangle$

Therefore, the resulting automaton M is defined by the four rules

$r_1 : \langle S \rangle \vdash \langle abS \rangle$
$r_2 : \langle S \rangle \vdash \langle \varepsilon \rangle$
$r_3 : \langle abS \rangle a \vdash \langle bS \rangle$
$r_4 : \langle bS \rangle b \vdash \langle S \rangle$

(see Figure 7.2.1).

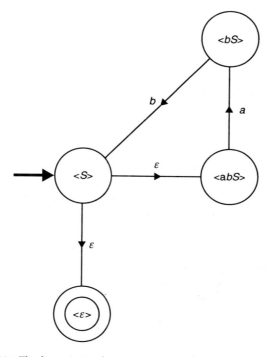

Figure 7.2.1 The deterministic finite automaton produced by Algorithm 7.2.1.

Consider $abab \in L(G)$. G generates the sentence

$$S \Rightarrow abS \quad [1]$$
$$\Rightarrow ababS \quad [1]$$
$$\Rightarrow abab \quad [2]$$

In brief,

$$S \Rightarrow^* abab \quad [112]$$

Automaton M, produced by Algorithm 7.2.1, accepts $abab$ in the following way:

$$\langle S \rangle abab \vdash \langle abS \rangle abab \quad [r_1]$$
$$\vdash \langle bS \rangle bab \quad [r_3]$$
$$\vdash \langle S \rangle ab \quad [r_4]$$
$$\vdash \langle abS \rangle ab \quad [r_1]$$
$$\vdash \langle bS \rangle b \quad [r_3]$$
$$\vdash \langle S \rangle \quad [r_4]$$
$$\vdash \langle \varepsilon \rangle \quad [r_2]$$

That is,

$$\langle S \rangle abab \vdash^* \langle \varepsilon \rangle \quad [r_1 r_3 r_4 r_1 r_3 r_4 r_2]$$

A rigorous proof that $L(M) = L(G)$ is left to the exercises.

▲

Regular grammars

A right-linear grammar is regular if the right-hand side of each production consists of one terminal followed by zero or one nonterminal.

Definition — regular grammar
Let $G = (N, T, P, S)$ be a right-linear grammar. G is *regular* if, for all $p \in P$,

$$\text{rhs}(p) \in T(N \cup \{\varepsilon\})$$

◆

Algorithm 7.2.3 Conversion of a deterministic finite automaton to an equivalent regular grammar

Input: A deterministic finite automaton $M = (Q, \Sigma, R, s, F)$.

Output: A regular grammar $G = (Q, \Sigma, P, s)$, satisfying

$$L(G) =_\varepsilon L(M)$$

Method

begin
  for each $qa \vdash q' \in R$, where $q, q' \in Q$ and $a \in Q$ **do**
    $P := P \cup \{q \to aq'\}$;
  for each $qa \vdash f \in R$, where $q \in Q, a \in Q$, and $f \in F$ **do**
    $P := P \cup \{q \to a\}$
end

The present algorithm produces G that simulates M so that

$$qw \vdash^* q' \text{ in } M \text{ if and only if } q \Rightarrow^* wq' \text{ in } G$$

Furthermore, because for each $qa \vdash f \in R$ with $f \in F$, P contains $q \to a$. Hence, the previous equivalence actually implies that

$$sw \vdash^* f \text{ in } M \text{ if and only if } s \Rightarrow^* w \text{ in } G$$

Consequently,

$$L(M) =_\varepsilon L(G)$$

Lemma 7.2.4

Let $M = (Q, \Sigma, R, s, F)$ be a deterministic finite automaton. With M on its input, Algorithm 7.2.3 halts and correctly constructs a regular grammar $G = (Q, \Sigma, P, s)$, such that $L(G) =_\varepsilon L(M)$.

Proof
Termination
As R is a finite set, Algorithm 7.2.3 repeats both **for** loops a finite number of times. Therefore, this algorithm surely halts.

Correctness
To establish

$$L(G) =_\varepsilon L(M),$$

this proof first demonstrates the following claim.

Claim
For every $w \in T^*$ and $q, q' \in Q$,

$$q \Rightarrow^* wq' \text{ in } G \text{ if and only if } qw \vdash^* q' \text{ in } M$$

Proof

Only if

By induction on i, where $i \geq 0$, this part of the proof demonstrates that for every $w \in T^*$ and $q, q' \in Q$,

$$q \Rightarrow^i wq' \text{ in } G \text{ implies } qw \vdash^* q' \text{ in } M$$

Basis
Let $i = 0$; that is,

$$q \Rightarrow^0 wq'$$

in G. Then, $q = q'$ and $w = \varepsilon$. Notice that

$$q \vdash^0 q$$

in M. Consequently, the basis holds.

Induction hypothesis
Assume that the 'only if' part of the claim is true for $i = 1, \ldots, n$, for some $n \geq 0$.

Induction step
Consider

$$q \Rightarrow^{n+1} wq'$$

where $w \in \Sigma^*$. Express this derivation as

$$q \Rightarrow^n vq'' \\ \Rightarrow vaq' \qquad [\, q'' \to aq'\,]$$

where $w = va$ and $q'' \to aq' \in P$. By the inductive hypothesis,

$$qv \vdash^* q''$$

in M. As $q'' \to aq' \in P$, R contains $q''a \vdash q'$. Therefore,

$$q''a \vdash q' \qquad [q''a \vdash q']$$

in M. Hence,

$$qva \vdash^* q''a$$
$$\vdash q'$$

In brief,

$$qw \vdash^* q'$$

The inductive step is completed, so the 'only if' part of the claim holds.

If
By induction on j, where $j \geq 0$, this part of the proof demonstrates that for every $w \in T^*$ and $q, q' \in Q$,

$$qw \vdash^j q' \text{ in } M \text{ implies } q \Rightarrow^* wq' \text{ in } G$$

Basis
Let $j = 0$. That is,

$$qw \vdash^0 q'$$

in M, so $q = q'$ and $w = \varepsilon$. Notice that

$$q \Rightarrow^0 q$$

in G. Consequently, the basis holds.

Induction hypothesis
Assume that the if part of the claim is true for all $j = 1, \ldots, n$, for some $n \geq 0$.

Induction step
Consider

$$qw \vdash^{n+1} q'$$

in M, where $w \in \Sigma^*$. In greater detail, express $qw \vdash^{n+1} q'$ as

$$qva \vdash^n q''a$$
$$\vdash q' \qquad [q''a \vdash q']$$

where $w = va$ and $q''a \vdash q' \in R$. By the inductive hypothesis,

$$q \Rightarrow^* vq''$$

in G. Furthermore, $q''a \vdash q' \in R$ implies $q'' \to aq' \in P$; therefore,

$$q'' \Rightarrow aq' \qquad [q'' \to aq']$$

in G. Consequently,

$$q \Rightarrow^* vq'' \Rightarrow vaq'$$

in G, so

$$q \Rightarrow^* wq'$$

and the inductive step is completed.

Thus, the 'if' part of the claim holds. Therefore, the claim holds. □

Consider the claim for $q = s$. At this point,

$$s \Rightarrow^* vq' \text{ in } G$$

if and only if

$$sv \vdash^* q' \text{ in } M$$

where $v \in T^*$ and $q' \in Q$. By the second for loop of Algorithm 7.2.3, $q' \to a \in P$ if and only if $q'a \vdash f \in R$, for some $f \in F$
Thus,

$$s \Rightarrow^* vq'$$
$$\Rightarrow va \qquad [q' \to a] \text{ in } G$$

if and only if

$$sva \vdash^* q'a$$
$$\vdash f \qquad [q'a \to f] \text{ in } M$$

That is,

$$s \Rightarrow^+ w \text{ in } G \text{ if and only if } sw \vdash^+ f \text{ in } M$$

where $f \in F$. Observe that M accepts every word by making one or more moves; in other words, for all $w \in L(M)$,

$$\langle s \rangle w \vdash^+ \langle z \rangle$$

in M. Furthermore, G generates every sentence by making one or more derivation steps; that is, for all $w \in L(G)$,

$$S \Rightarrow^+ w$$

in G. Therefore, the previous equivalence implies

$$L(G) =_\varepsilon L(M)$$

Summarizing, with M on its input, Algorithm 7.2.3 halts and correctly constructs a regular grammar $G = (Q, \Sigma, P, s)$ such that $L(G) =_\varepsilon L(M)$. Thus, Lemma 7.2.4 holds. ∎

Observe that no regular grammar generates ε; therefore, Algorithm 7.2.3 converts any deterministic finite automaton M' to a regular grammar G', so $L(G) =_\varepsilon L(M)$. A right-linear grammar, however, can generate ε, so this section explains how to transform any deterministic finite automaton M to a right-linear grammar G, so $L(G) = L(M)$.

Algorithm 7.2.5: Conversion of a deterministic finite automaton to an equivalent right-linear grammar

Input: A deterministic finite automaton $M = (Q, \Sigma, R, s, F)$.

Output: A right-linear grammar $G = (Q \cup \{S\}, \Sigma, P, S)$ satisfying $L(G) = L(M)$.

Method

begin
　　use Algorithm 7.2.3 to transform M to a regular grammar $G' = (Q, \Sigma, P, s)$ satisfying $L(G') =_\varepsilon L(M)$;
　　$P := P \cup \{S \to s\}$ {S is the start symbol of G};
　　if $s \in F$ **then** $P := P \cup \{S \to \varepsilon\}$;
　　produce $G = (Q \cup \{S\}, \Sigma, P, S)$
end

Algorithm 7.2.5 first uses Algorithm 7.2.3 to transform its input deterministic finite automaton $M = (Q, \Sigma, R, s, F)$ to a regular grammar $G' = (Q, \Sigma, P, s)$, satisfying $L(G') =_\varepsilon L(M)$. Observe that

$$\varepsilon \in L(M) \text{ if and only if } s \in F$$

Therefore, if $s \in F$, Algorithm 7.2.5 adds $S \to s$ and $S \to \varepsilon$ to P; otherwise, this algorithm adds only $S \to s$ to P. Thus G, where $G = (Q \cup \{S\}, \Sigma, P, S)$, generates $L(M)$. In addition, observe that for all $p \in P$, $\mathrm{rhs}(p) \in T(N \cup \{\varepsilon\}) \cup \{s\} \cup \{\varepsilon\}$, so G represents a right-linear grammar.

Lemma 7.2.6
Let $M = (Q, \Sigma, R, s, F)$ be a deterministic finite automaton. With M on its input, Algorithm 7.2.5 halts and correctly constructs a right-linear grammar $G = (Q \cup \{S\}, \Sigma, P, S)$, such that $L(G) = L(M)$.

Proof
This proof is left to the exercises.

■

Example 7.2.2 Application of Algorithm 7.2.5
Consider the deterministic finite automaton M,

r_1: $q_0 b \vdash q_1$
r_2: $q_1 a \vdash q_1$
r_3: $q_1 a \vdash q_2$
r_4: $q_2 b \vdash q_0$

where q_0 is both the start state and the final state of M (see Figure 7.2.2). Observe that

$$L(M) = \{\{b\}\{a\}^+\{b\}\}^*$$

This example uses Algorithm 7.2.5 to transform M to a right-linear grammar, $G = (Q \cup \{S\}, \Sigma, P, S)$, satisfying $L(G) = L(M)$.

First, Algorithm 7.2.5 calls Algorithm 7.2.3 to transform M to the regular grammar, $G' = (\{q_0, q_1, q_2\}, \{a, b\}, P, \{q_0\})$, where P contains these productions:

$q_0 \to b q_1$
$q_1 \to a q_1$
$q_1 \to a q_2$
$q_2 \to b q_0$

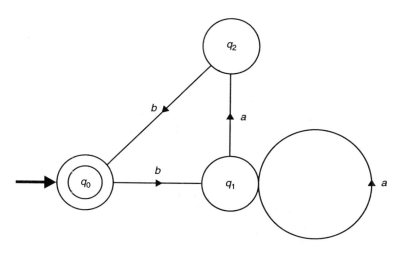

Figure 7.2.2 The deterministic finite automaton of Example 7.2.2.

Notice that

$$L(G') =_\varepsilon L(M)$$

As q_0 represents M's final state, Algorithm 7.2.5 also constructs two productions:

$S \to \varepsilon$
$S \to q_0$

The resulting right-linear grammar thus has these six productions

$p_1: S \to \varepsilon$
$p_2: S \to q_0$
$p_3: q_0 \to bq_1$
$p_4: q_1 \to aq_1$
$p_5: q_1 \to aq_2$
$p_6: q_2 \to bq_0$

A formal proof that $L(G) = L(M)$ is left to the exercises. ▲

The results established so far imply the next two theorems, concerning regular grammars and right-linear grammars.

Theorem 7.2.7
Let L be a language. Then, L is regular if and only if $L = L(G)$, for a right-linear grammar G.

Proof
Only if
Let L be a regular language. From Theorem 3.3.3.2, there exists a deterministic finite automaton, M, so $L = L(M)$. Then, from Algorithm 7.2.5 and Lemma 7.2.6, there also exists a right-linear grammar G such that $L(G) = L(M)$, so the 'only if' part of the theorem holds.

If
Let G be a right-linear grammar. From Algorithm 7.2.1 and Lemma 7.2.2, there exists a nondeterministic finite automaton, M, such that $L(M) = L(G)$. Hence, L is regular and the 'if' part of the theorem is true.
Thus, the present theorem holds. ∎

Theorem 7.2.8
Let L be a language. Then, L is regular if and only if $L =_\varepsilon L(G)$, for a regular grammar G.

Proof
Only if
Let L be a regular language. From Theorem 3.3.3.2, $L = L(M)$ for a deterministic finite automaton M. Then, from Algorithm 7.2.3 and Lemma 7.2.4, there exists a regular grammar G such that $L(G) =_\varepsilon L(M)$, so the 'only if' part of the theorem holds.

If
Let G be a regular grammar. Because any regular grammar represents a special case of a right-linear grammar, Theorem 7.2.7 implies that $L(G)$ is regular. Therefore, the 'if' part of the theorem is true.

Thus, Theorem 7.2.8 holds. ∎

Left-linear grammars

A context-free grammar is left-linear if the right-hand side of each production consists of terminals preceded by zero or one nonterminal.

Definition — left-linear grammar

Let $G = (N, T, P, S)$ be a context-free grammar. G is *left-linear* if, for all $p \in P$,

$$\text{rhs}(p) \in (N \cup \{\varepsilon\})T^*$$

◆

The next algorithm reverses the right-hand sides of the productions in a right-linear grammar G and, thereby, produces a left-linear grammar that generates reversal($L(G)$).

Algorithm 7.2.9: Construction of a left-linear grammar that generates the reversal of the language generated by a right-linear grammar

Input: A right-linear grammar $G = (N, T, P, S)$.

Output: A left-linear grammar $G' = (N, T, P', S)$ such that $L(G') = $ reversal($L(G)$).

Method

begin
   for each $p \in P$ do
      $P' := P' \cup \{\text{lhs}(p) \rightarrow \text{reversal}(\text{rhs}(p))\}$
end

Lemma 7.2.10

Let G be a right-linear grammar. With G as its input, Algorithm 7.2.9 halts and correctly constructs a left-linear grammar $G' = (N, T, P', S)$ such that $L(G') = $ reversal($L(G)$).

Proof
Termination
As P is finite, this algorithm surely terminates.

Correctness
To demonstrate

$$L(G') = \text{reversal}(L(G)),$$

this proof first establishes the following claim.

Claim

$$S \Rightarrow^* \text{lhs}(p)u$$
$$\Rightarrow \text{rhs}(p)u \quad [p] \quad \text{in } G'$$

if and only if

$$S \Rightarrow^* \text{reversal}(u)\text{lhs}(p)$$
$$\Rightarrow \text{reversal}(u)\text{reversal}(\text{rhs}(p)) \quad \text{in } G$$

where $u \in T^*$ and $p \in P'$.

Proof
Only if
By induction on i, where $i \geq 0$, this proof next establishes that

$$S \Rightarrow^* \text{lhs}(p)u$$
$$\Rightarrow \text{rhs}(p)u \quad [p] \quad \text{in } G'$$

implies

$$S \Rightarrow^* \text{reversal}(u)\text{lhs}(p)$$
$$\Rightarrow \text{reversal}(u)\text{reversal}(\text{rhs}(p)) \quad \text{in } G$$

Basis
Let $i = 0$. Then,

$$S \Rightarrow \text{rhs}(p)u \quad [p]$$

in G', where $u = \varepsilon$, $S = \text{lhs}(p)$, and $p \in P'$. From the present algorithm, $p \in P'$ implies $\text{lhs}(p) \to \text{reversal}(\text{rhs}(p)) \in P$. Therefore,

$$S \Rightarrow \text{reversal}(\text{rhs}(p)) \quad [\text{lhs}(p) \to \text{reversal}(\text{rhs}(p))]$$

in G. Thus, the basis holds.

Induction hypothesis
Assume that the 'only if' part is true for all $i = 1, \ldots, n$, for some $n \geq 0$.

Induction step
Consider

$$S \Rightarrow^{n+1} \text{lhs}(p)u$$
$$\Rightarrow \text{rhs}(p)u \quad [p]$$

in G', where $p \in P'$. Express $S \Rightarrow^{n+1} \text{lhs}(p)u$ as

$$S \Rightarrow^n \text{lhs}(p')u'$$
$$\Rightarrow \text{rhs}(p')u'$$

where $\text{rhs}(p')u' = \text{lhs}(p)u$, for some $p' \in P$. From the inductive hypothesis,

$$S \Rightarrow^* \text{reversal}(u')\text{lhs}(p')$$
$$\Rightarrow \text{reversal}(u')\text{reversal}(\text{rhs}(p'))$$

in G. Notice that

$$\text{reversal}(u')\text{reversal}(\text{rhs}(p')) = \text{reversal}(\text{rhs}(p')u') = \text{reversal}(\text{lhs}(p)u) = \text{reversal}(u)\text{lhs}(p)$$

As $\text{lhs}(p) \to \text{reversal}(\text{rhs}(p)) \in P$,

$$S \Rightarrow^* \text{reversal}(u)\text{lhs}(p)$$
$$\Rightarrow \text{reversal}(u)\text{reversal}(\text{rhs}(p))$$

in G. Thus, the inductive step holds.

Consequently, the 'only if' part of the claim is true.

If

The 'if' part of the claim is proved in the exercises. □

Consider the claim for all p with $\text{rhs}(p) \in T^*$ and all $u \in T^*$; that is,

$$S \Rightarrow^+ \text{rhs}(p)u \quad [p] \text{ in } G'$$

if and only if

$$S \Rightarrow^+ \text{reversal}(u)\text{reversal}(\text{rhs}(p)) \text{ in } G$$

As

$$\text{reversal}(u)\text{reversal}(\text{rhs}(p)) = \text{reversal}(\text{rhs}(p)u),$$

the following equivalence holds:

$$S \Rightarrow^+ w \text{ in } G \text{ if and only if } S \Rightarrow^+ \text{reversal}(w) \text{ in } G'$$

for all $w \in T^*$. Therefore,

$$L(G) = \text{reversal}(L(G'))$$

In summary, with G as its input, Algorithm 7.2.9 halts and correctly constructs a left-linear grammar $G' = (N, T, P', S)$, such that $L(G') = \text{reversal}(L(G))$. Thus, Lemma 7.2.10 holds. ∎

Example 7.2.3 Application of Algorithm 7.2.9

Part 1 of Example 7.2.1 introduces the following right-linear grammar G:

1: $S \to abS$
2: $S \to \varepsilon$

Recall that

$$L(G)) = \{(ab)^i : i \geq 0\}$$

With G as its input, Algorithm 7.2.9 produces the following left-linear grammar G':

$1'$: $S \to Sba$
$2'$: $S \to \varepsilon$

Observe that

$$L(G') = \{(ba)^i : i \geq 0\}$$

That is,

$$L(G') = \text{reversal}(L(G))$$

▲

By analogy with Algorithm 7.2.9, the following algorithm converts any left-linear grammar G to an right-linear grammar that generates $\text{reversal}(L(G))$.

Algorithm 7.2.11: Construction of a right-linear grammar that generates the reversal of the language generated by a left-linear grammar

Input: A left-linear grammar $G = (N, T, P, S)$.

Output: A right-linear grammar $G' = (N, T, P', S)$, such that $L(G') = \text{reversal}(L(G))$.

Method

begin
   for each $p \in P$ **do**
      $P' := P' \cup \{\, \text{lhs}(p) \rightarrow \text{reversal}(\text{rhs}(p))\}$
end

Lemma 7.2.12
Let G be a left-linear grammar. With G on its input, Algorithm 7.2.11 halts and correctly constructs a right-linear grammar $G' = (N, T, P', S)$, such that $L(G') = \text{reversal}(L(G))$.

Proof
By analogy with the proof of Lemma 7.2.10, the exercises establishe this lemma.
∎

According to the next lemma, for any deterministic finite automaton M there exists a left-linear grammar G such that $L(G) = L(M)$.

Lemma 7.2.13
For every deterministic finite automaton M there exists a left-linear grammar G such that $L(G) = L(M)$.

Proof
Let M be a deterministic finite automaton. Consider $\text{reversal}(L(M))$, which surely represents a regular language (see Exercise 2.6 in Chapter 4). Theorem 3.3.3.2 implies that there exists a deterministic finite automaton that accepts $\text{reversal}(L(M))$. From Algorithm 7.2.5 and Lemma 7.2.6, there is a right-linear grammar, G', that generates $\text{reversal}(L(M))$. Use Algorithm 7.2.9 with G' as its input to produce a left-linear grammar G such that

$$L(G) = \text{reversal}(\text{reversal}(L(M))).$$

As $\text{reversal}(\text{reversal}(L(M))) = L(M)$,

$$L(G) = L(M).$$

Thus, the present lemma holds.
∎

Theorem 7.2.14
Let L be a language. Then, L is regular if and only if $L = L(G)$, for a left-linear grammar G.

Proof
Only if
Let L be a regular language. From Theorem 3.3.3.2, there exists a deterministic finite automaton M so $L = L(M)$. Then, by the previous theorem, there exists a left-linear grammar G such that $L(G) = L(M)$, so the 'only if' part of the theorem holds.

If
Let G be a left-linear grammar. From Algorithm 7.2.11 and Lemma 7.2.12, there exists a right-linear grammar G' such that $L(G') = \text{reversal}(L(G))$. Consider reversal($L(G')$), which is a regular language (see Exercise 2.6 in Chapter 4). Observe that

$$\text{reversal}(L(G')) = \text{reversal}(\text{reversal}(L(G))) = L(G) = L(M))$$

Hence, $L(G)$ is regular. Therefore, the if part of the theorem is true.
Thus, the present theorem holds. ∎

Grammatical characterization of the family of regular languages

The algorithms and the lemmas that this section has established so far underlie the next two theorems concerning regular and right-linear grammars.

Theorem 7.2.15
The class of right-linear grammars and the class of left-linear grammars characterize the family of regular languages.

Proof
This theorem follows from Theorems 7.2.7 and 7.2.14. ∎

Theorem 7.2.16
The class of regular grammars characterizes the family of regular languages without ε.

Proof
This theorem follows from Theorem 7.2.8.

∎

Linear grammars

A context-free grammar is linear if the right-hand side of each production contains zero or one nonterminal. As a result, the notion of a linear grammar generalizes both the notion of a right-linear grammar and the notion of a left-linear grammar.

Definition — linear grammar
Let $G = (N, T, P, S)$ be a context-free grammar. G is a *linear grammar* if, for all $p \in P$,

$$\text{rhs}(p) \in T^*(N \cup \{\varepsilon\})T^*$$

◆

Definition — linear language
Let L be a language. L is a *linear language* if there exists a linear grammar G such that $L(G) = L$.

◆

Example 7.2.4
Reconsider the context-free grammar G defined in Example 5.1.1.1. Recall that

$$G = (\{S\}, \{a, b\}, P, S)$$

where P contains the productions

1: $S \to aSb$
2: $S \to \varepsilon$

Observe that G is a linear grammar. As

$$L(G) = \{a^i b^i : i \geq 0\},$$

$\{a^i b^i : i \geq 0\}$ is a linear language.

▲

Theorem 7.2.17
The family of linear languages properly contains the family of regular languages.

Proof
As already noted, right-linear grammars represent special cases of linear grammars. Therefore, from Theorem 7.2.15, the family of linear languages contains the family of regular languages. Example 7.2.4 presents a linear grammar G such that

$$L(G) = \{a^i b^i : i \geq 0\}$$

Example 4.1.2 proves that $\{a^i b^i : i \geq 0\}$ is not regular. Therefore, the family of family of linear languages properly contains the family of regular languages, so Theorem 7.2.17 holds. ∎

From Theorem 7.2.17, the family of linear languages represents a proper superfamily of the family of regular languages. However, the family of linear languages is a proper subfamily of the family of context-free languages. The following pumping lemma remarkably simplifies most proofs, demonstrating that some context-free languages are not linear.

Lemma 7.2.18 Pumping lemma for linear languages
Let L be a linear language. Then, there exists a natural number k such that if $z \in L$ and $|z| \geq k$, then z can be expressed as

$$z = uvwxy$$

so that

1. $|vx| \geq 1$;
2. $|uvxy| \leq k$;
3. $uv^m w x^m y \in L$, for all $m \geq 0$.

Proof
This lemma is demonstrated by modifying the proof of Lemma 6.1.3 in terms of linear grammars. The details of this modification are left to the exercises. ∎

By using Lemma 7.2.18, the exercises prove that the context-free language $\{a^i b^i c^j d^j : i \geq 1 \text{ and } j \geq 1\}$ is not linear.

Theorem 7.2.19

The family of context-free languages properly contains the family of linear languages.

Proof

Linear grammars represent special cases of context-free grammars, so the family of context-free languages contains the family of linear languages. Furthermore, $\{a^ib^ic^jd^j: i \geq 1 \text{ and } j \geq 1\}$ is a context-free language that is not linear. Thus, Theorem 7.2.19 holds.

∎

Exercises

1 Deterministic context-free languages

1.1 Consider these two context-free languages
(a) $\{a^ib^i: i \geq 1\} \cup \{a^ib^{2i}: i \geq 1\}$
(b) $\{w\text{reversal}(w): w \in \{a, b\}^*\}$
Prove that neither of them represents a deterministic context-free language.

1.2 Recall that for a language L over an alphabet T, Max(L) is defined as

$$\text{Max}(L) = \{ w : w \in L \text{ and } \{w\}T^+ \cap L = \emptyset\}$$

Prove that if L is a deterministic context-free language, then Max(L) is a deterministic context-free language. In other words, demonstrate that the family of deterministic context-free languages is closed under Max. Observe that this closure property does not hold for the family of all context-free languages (see Exercise 2.22 in Chapter 6).

1.3 Recall that for a language L, Min(L) is defined as

$$\text{Min}(L) = \{w: w \in L \text{ and } (\text{prefix}(w) - \{w\}) \cap L = \emptyset\}$$

Prove that if L is a deterministic context-free language, then Min(L) is a deterministic context-free language. In other words, demonstrate that the family of deterministic context-free languages is closed under Min. Observe that this closure property does not hold for the family of all context-free languages (see Exercise 2.21 in Chapter 6).

1.4 Let L_1 and L_2 be two languages. Recall that L_1/L_2 is defined as

$$L_1/L_2 = \{w: wx \in L_1 \text{ for some } x \in L_2\}$$

Prove that if L_1 is a deterministic context-free language and L_2 is a regular language, then L_1/L_2 is a deterministic context-free language. That is, demonstrate that the family of deterministic context-free languages is closed under the right quotient with respect to regular languages. Observe that this closure property also holds for the family of all context-free languages (see Exercise 2.14 in Chapter 6).

1.5* Prove that the family of deterministic context-free languages is closed under inverse homomorphism. Observe that this closure property also holds for the family of all context-free languages (see Exercise 2.16 in Chapter 6).

1.6 Prove that the family of deterministic context-free languages is not closed under union. Observe that by contrast, the family of all context-free languages is closed under union (see Theorem 6.2.3).

1.7 Prove that the family of deterministic context-free languages is not closed under concatenation. Observe that by contrast, the family of all context-free languages is closed under concatenation (see Theorem 6.2.13).

1.8 Prove that the family of deterministic context-free languages is not closed under closure. Observe that as opposed to this result, the family of all context-free languages is closed under closure (see Theorem 6.2.14).

1.9 Prove that the family of deterministic context-free languages is not closed under homomorphism. Observe that the family of all context-free languages is closed under homomorphism (see Corollary 6.2.12).

1.10* Let L_1 and L_2 be two languages. Prove that if L_1 is a deterministic context-free language and L_2 is a regular language, then $L_1 - L_2$ and $L_2 - L_1$ are deterministic context-free languages.

1.11 Let L_1 and L_2 be two languages. Prove that if L_1 is a deterministic context-free language and L_2 is a regular language, then $L_1 \cup L_2$ is a deterministic context-free language. Consequently, although the family of deterministic context-free languages is not closed under union (see Exercise 1.6 in this section), this family is closed under union with regular languages.

1.12 Consider the following definition.

Definition — marked union
Let T be an alphabet, let L_1 and L_2 be two languages such that $L_1, L_2 \subseteq T^*$, and let $ and @ be two special symbols such that $\{\$, @\} \cap T = \varnothing$. Then, $\$L_1 \cup @L_2$ is the *marked union* of L_1 and L_2.

◆

Prove that the family of deterministic context-free languages is closed under marked union. Notice that this family is not closed under union (see Exercise 1.6 in this section).

1.13 Consider the following definition.

Definition — marked concatenation
Let T be an alphabet, let L_1 and L_2 be two languages such that $L_1, L_2 \subseteq T^*$, and let $ and @ be two special symbols such that $@ \notin T$. Then, $L_1 @ L_2$ is the *marked concatenation* of L_1 and L_2.

◆

Prove that the family of deterministic context-free languages is closed under marked concatenation. Notice that this family is not closed under union (see Exercise 1.7 in this section).

1.14 Consider the following definition.

Definition — marked closure

Let T be an alphabet, L be a language such that $L \subseteq T^*$, and @ be a symbol such that @ $\notin T$. Then, $(L\{@\})^*$ is the *marked closure* of L.

◆

Prove that the family of deterministic context-free languages is closed under marked closure. Notice that this family is not closed under closure (see Exercise 1.8 in this section)

1.15 Prove Lemma 7.1.2.
1.16 Complete the proof of Theorem 7.1.5.
1.17 Complete Example 7.1.2
1.18 Prove Theorem 7.1.12

2. Linear and regular grammars

2.1 Complete Part 2 of Example 7.2.1
2.2 Prove Lemma 7.2.6.
2.3 Complete Example 7.2.2
2.4 Complete the proof of Lemma 7.2.10
2.5 Complete the proof of Lemma 7.2.12
2.6 Lemma 7.2.18 states that for every linear language L there exists a natural number k such that if $z \in L$ and $|z| \geq k$, then z can be expressed as

$$z = uvwxy$$

where

(1) $|vx| \geq 1$;
(2) $|uvxy| \leq k$;
(3) $uv^m wx^m y \in L$, for all $m \geq 0$.

Prove this lemma.

2.7 Let $L = \{a^i b^i c^j d^j : i \geq 1 \text{ and } j \geq 1\}$. Demonstrate that L is context-free. Then, prove that L is not linear by using Lemma 7.2.18.
2.8 A *one-turn pushdown automaton*, $M = (Q, \Sigma, R, s, F)$, first writes symbols on its pushdown and then pops these symbols from the pushdown. Most importantly, after M starts popping symbols from the pushdown, it can then never write any symbol on its pushdown. Formalize the notion of a one-turn pushdown automaton.

2.9 Prove that the class of one-turn pushdown automata characterizes the family of linear languages.

2.10 State the relationship between the family of linear languages and the family of deterministic context-free languages.

2.11 Consider this definition.

Definition — k-linear context-free grammar
Let k be a natural number, and let $G = (N, T, P, S)$ be a context-free grammar. G is *k-linear* if each production, $p \in P$, satisfies these conditions:

(1) if lhs(p) = S, then rhs(p) $\in (T^*((N - \{S\}) \cup \{\varepsilon\})T^*)^k$
(2) if lhs(p) $\neq$ S, then rhs(p) $\in (T^*((N - \{S\}) \cup \{\varepsilon\})T^*)$

◆

Intuitively, these two conditions imply the following three properties:

(A) S does not appear on rhs(p)
(B) if lhs(p) = S, then rhs(p) contains no more than k nonterminal;
(C) if lhs(p) $\neq$ S, then rhs(p) contains zero or one nonterminal.

Prove that L is a linear language if and only if there exists a 1-linear grammar such that $L(G) = L$.

2.12 Consider this language

$$L = \{a^i b^i c^j d^j : i \geq 1 \text{ and } j \geq 1\}$$

Construct a 2-linear grammar G, so $L(G) = L$.

2.13 Consider the language

$$L = \{a^n b a^n c : n \geq 1\}$$

Prove that the following implication holds for all $k \geq 2$: if a language L' satisfies

$$\{(a^n b a^n c)^k : n \geq 1\} \subseteq L' \subseteq L^*$$

then there exists no $(k-1)$-linear grammar that generates L'.

2.14* Consider this definition.

Definition — k-linear language
Let L be a language, and let $k \geq 1$. L is a *k-linear* language if there exists a k-linear grammar G such that $L(G) = L$.

◆

Prove that for every $k \geq 1$, the family of $(k+1)$-linear languages properly contains the family of k-linear languages.

2.15 Consider these definitions.

Definition — metalinear grammar
Let G be a k-linear grammar, for some $k \geq 1$. Then, G is a *metalinear grammar*.
♦

Definition — metalinear language
Let L be a language. L is a metalinear language if there exists a metalinear grammar G such that $L(G) = L$.
♦

Prove that the family of metalinear languages properly contains the family of linear languages.

2.16 Prove that the family of metalinear languages is closed under concatenation.
2.17 Prove that the family of metalinear languages is closed under union.
2.18 Prove that the family of metalinear languages is not closed under intersection.
2.19 Prove that the family of metalinear languages is not closed under complement.
2.20 Prove that the family of metalinear languages is not closed under closure.
2.21 Consider the following definition.

Definition — linear substitution
Let Σ and Ω be two alphabets, and let η be a substitution from Σ^* to Ω^* such that for all $x \in \Sigma$, $\eta(x)$ is a linear language. Then, η is a *linear substitution*.
♦

Prove that the family of linear languages is not closed under linear substitution.

2.22 Prove that the family of metalinear languages is properly contained in the family of context-free languages.

2.23 Consider the following definition.

Definition — Dyck language
Let k be a natural number, and

$$G = (\{S\}, T, P, S)$$

be a context-free grammar satisfying these properties:

(1) $T = \{a_i : i = 1, ..., k\} \cup \{b_i : 1\ i = 1, ..., k\}$

(2) for all $p \in P$,

$$\text{rhs}(p) \in (\{S^2\} \\ \cup \{aSb : a \in \{a_i : i = 1, ..., k\}, b \in \{b_i : i = 1, ..., k\}\} \\ \cup \{\varepsilon\})$$

Then, $L(G)$ is a *Dyck language*. ◆

Explain this definition informally.

2.23** Let T be an alphabet. Introduce an alphabet T', a Dyck language L_{Dyck}, and a homomorphism η from $(T')^*$ to T^*, so the following implication holds:

If L is a context-free language such that $L \subseteq T^*$,
then there exists a regular language L_{reg} satisfying

$$\eta(L_{\text{Dyck}} \cap L_{\text{reg}}) = L$$

Bibliographic Notes

Context-free grammars

Context-free grammars were introduced by Chomsky (1956). Chomsky (1959) studied various properties and normal forms of these grammars. Backus (1959) and Naur (1960) introduced pragmatically oriented notation, resembling context-free grammars, and explained how to specify the syntax of programming languages by this notation; Ginsburg and Rice (1962) established the equivalence between this notation and context-free grammars. Bar-Hillel, Perles and Shamir (1961) has proved the pumping lemma for context-free languages. Floyd (1962) discussed the problem of ambiguity in context-free grammars.

Bar-Hillel (1964), Berstel (1979), Ginsburg (1966), Chomsky (1962), Chomsky and Schutzenberger (1963), Ginsburg and Spanier (1963), Greibach (1965), Greibach (1973), Gruska (1971), Hartmanis (1967), Harrison (1978), Kasami (1965), Lewis et al. (1965), Parikh (1966), Scheinberg (1963), Schutzenberger (1963), Thatcher (1967), Valiant (1975), Wise (1976), Yentema (1971) and Younger (1976) are important early papers about context-free grammars. Beigel and Floyd (1994), Berstel (1979), Book (1980), Brainerd and Landweber (1974), Brookshear (1989), Bucher and Maurer (1984), Carroll and Long (1989), Denning et al. (1978), Hopcroft and Ullman (1979), Kelley (1995), Kuich and Salomaa (1985), Linz (1990), Martin (1991), McNaughton (1982), Pagan (1981), Prather (1976), Revesz (1983), Rozenberg and Salomaa (1997), Salomaa (1973), Sudkamp (1988), Salomaa (1985), Savitch (1982) and Wood (1987) are useful complements to the discussion of context-free grammars given in Part III.

Based on context-free productions, modern language theory has also introduced some modified versions of context-free grammars, including regulated grammars, E0L systems, scattered context grammars, selective substitution grammars and grammars over word monoids.

In general, context-free grammars can use any production in any derivation step, so they work in a rather nondeterministic way.

Regulated grammars reduce nondeterminism by using additional mechanisms that regulate the derivation process. These grammars are also more powerful than context-free grammars, so it comes as no surprise that literally hundreds various types of regulated grammars were introduced over the past three decades. Dassow and Paun (1989) and Rozenberg and Salomaa (1997) discuss most of them.

E0L systems are, in essence, context-free grammars that work in parallel. By analogy with a context-free grammar, an E0L system G is a quadruple consisting of four components, which are very similar to the components of a context-free grammar. First, G has an alphabet of nonterminals. Second, it contains an alphabet of terminals. Third, G possesses a finite set of productions of the form $a \to x$, where a is a symbol and x is a word. Finally, G has its start symbol. Unlike a context-free grammar, however, an E0L system rewrites all symbols appearing in a word during a derivation step. More precisely, if x and y are words such that $x = a_1 a_2 \ldots a_n$ and $y = y_1 y_2 \ldots y_n$, where a's are symbols and y's are words, and $a_1 \to y_1, a_2 \to y_2, \ldots, a_n \to y_n$ are G's productions, then x directly derives y. Given two words, v and u, u derives v provided that there exists a sequence of direct derivations transforming u to v. If u derives v, u equals G's start symbol, and v contains only terminals, then v is a sentence generated by G. The generated language consists of the set of all sentences. Rozenberg and Salomaa (1980) contains a detailed exposition of E0L systems and their variants.

Besides purely sequential grammars and purely parallel grammars, language theory has also introduced semiparallel grammars, such as *scattered context grammars* (Greibach and Hopcroft, 1969; Meduna, 1993b, 1995a, 1995b, 1997a, 1998b). During a derivation step, these grammars rewrite some symbols in parallel while leaving the other symbols unrewritten.

Selective substitution grammars are very powerful grammars because they can simulate any type of rewriting, including sequential, parallel, and semiparallel rewriting (Rozenberg, 1977). Roughly speaking, a selective substitution grammar consists of a base and a selector. The base is a slightly modified context-free grammar that can rewrite any symbols, including terminals. The selector is a language over an alphabet, consisting of the original symbols of the base alphabet and their barred versions. A word x can be rewritten provided that the selector contains a word y equal to x when the bars over symbols are ignored; at this point, the barred symbols appearing in x are rewritten while the other symbols remain unchanged. Consequently, to simulate context-free grammars by a selective substitution grammar, each word of the selector would have precisely one occurrence of a barred symbol; to simulate an E0L systems, each word of the selector would have all occurrence of all symbols barred. Dassow and Paun (1989, chapter 10) discusses selective substitution grammars and their variants.

Meduna (1990a) defined *context-free grammars over word monoids*, and Meduna (1992) introduced *E0L systems over word monoids*. These grammars and systems are very strong; in fact, they characterize the family of recursively enumerable languages even if the generators of the word monoids consist of no more than two symbols (Meduna, 1996).

Pushdown automata

Pushdown automata were introduced by Oettinger (1961). Chomsky (1962) proved the equivalence between these automata and context-free grammars. Schutzenberger (1963) discussed deterministic pushdown automata, and Ginsburg and Greibach (1966) studied their properties. Aho and Ullman (1972) investigated extended pushdown automata. Aho and Ullman (1969a), Evey (1963) and van Leewen (1974b) are significant early papers about pushdown automata. Beigel and Floyd (1994), Berstel (1979), Brookshear (1989), Bucher and Maurer (1984), Carroll and Long (1989), Hopcroft and Ullman (1979), Kelley (1995), Kuich and Salomaa (1985), Linz (1990), Martin (1991), McNaughton (1982), Revesz (1983), Salomaa (1969), Sudkamp (1988), Salomaa (1985) and Wood (1987) constitute excellent references concerning pushdown automata.

Part IV
Beyond Context-Free Languages

The previous two parts of this book primarily deal with three computational models — finite automata, pushdown automata, and context-free grammars. Recall that finite automata are less powerful than the other two models, whose power is restricted to the family of context-free languages. To increase the power of these models, this part, consisting of a single chapter, generalizes finite automata, pushdown automata and context-free grammars to Turing machines, two-pushdown automata and unrestricted grammars, respectively. It demonstrates that these three generalized models have the same power, which significantly exceeds the family of context-free languages.

8 Generalized Models

This chapter generalizes the finite automaton, the pushdown automaton, and the context-free grammar. Section 8.1 generalizes the finite automaton to the *Turing machine*. The tape of the Turing machine is potentially infinite to the right. The tape head shifts in either direction on the tape, and during these shifts, the head not only reads but also writes symbols. The Turing machine represents a central model used in computational theory, including all the crucial topics discussed in Chapter 10. Section 8.2 generalizes the pushdown automaton to the *two-pushdown automaton*. As its name indicates, the two-pushdown automaton possesses two, rather than one, pushdowns. Section 8.3 generalizes the context-free grammar to the *unrestricted grammar*. The left-hand side of every production in the unrestricted grammar is a word, consisting of several symbols. Section 8.4 demonstrates that these three generalized models characterize the family of recursively enumerable languages, which properly contains the family of context-free languages.

8.1 Turing machines

Section 8.1.1 introduces the basic model of a Turing machine, then Sections 8.1.2 through 8.1.4 present its equivalent variants. Sections 8.1.5 discusses a universal Turing machine, which can simulate every Turing machine. Finally, Sections 8.1.6 and 8.1.7 place some power-decreasing restrictions on Turing machines.

8.1.1 Basic definitions

Like a finite automaton, a Turing machine M consists of these three components:

1. a tape, divided into squares
2. a read-write tape head
3. a finite state control.

Unlike a finite automaton, however, M's tape is semi-infinite; that is, the tape has its leftmost square, but its squares may extend infinitely to the right. These squares contain symbols, which M rewrites by using its tape head. The finite state control is represented by a finite set of states together with a finite relationship, which is customarily specified as a finite set of computational rules. According to these rules, M makes moves. During a move, M changes its current state, rewrites the scanned symbol with another tape symbol, and either keeps its head stationary or shifts its head one square to the right or left. To decide whether a given input word $a_1...a_n$ is accepted, M has one state defined as the start state and some states designated as final states. Initially, M's tape contains $a_1...a_n$ followed by Bs, where B denotes a blank symbol, and M's tape head is over a_1 (see Figure 8.1.1.1). If starting from the start state, M can make a sequence of moves so it enters a final state, then M accepts $a_1...a_n$; otherwise, M rejects $a_1...a_n$. The collection of all words that M accepts in this way represents the language accepted by M.

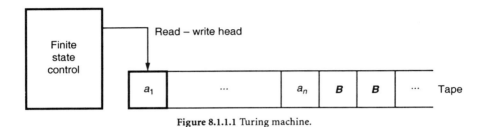

Figure 8.1.1.1 Turing machine.

Example 8.1.1.1 Part 1 Intuitive design of a Turing machine
Consider

$$L = \{a^n b^n : n \geq 0\}$$

This example constructs a Turing machine M accepting L by repeating the following six-step cycle (see Figure 8.1.1.2).

1. If M reads a, M replaces a with B and shifts the tape head a square right.
2. Skipping over as and bs, M keeps shifting the tape head right until it reads B.
3. M shifts the tape head a square left.
4. If M reads b, M replaces b with B and shifts the tape head a square left.
5. Skipping over as and bs, M keeps shifting the tape head left until it reads B.
6. M shifts the tape head a square right.

If in the first step of this cycle M reads B, then M accepts its input word.

To give a more precise insight into the way M works, suppose that M's tape initially contains

$$a^n b^n B...$$

for some $n \geq 1$. M begins its computation by scanning the leftmost a in $a^n b^n B...$. During the first iteration of the cycle, M replaces the leftmost a with B and the rightmost b with B, so it changes the tape contents from $a^n b^n B$ to

Generalized models

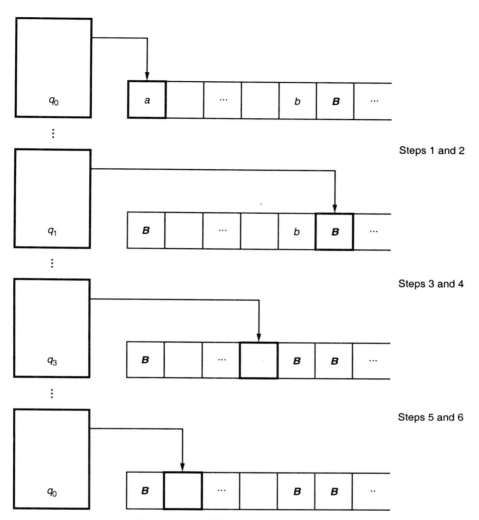

Figure 8.1.1.2 The six-step cycle repeated by M.

$$Ba^{n-1}b^{n-1}BB\ldots$$

During the second iteration, M changes $Ba^{n-1}b^{n-1}BB\ldots$ to

$$BBa^{n-2}b^{n-2}BBB\ldots$$

M makes n iterations of this kind and, during these iterations, M changes the tape contents as follows:

Iteration 1: $Ba^{n-1}b^{n-1}B\ldots$
Iteration 2: $BBa^{n-2}b^{n-2}B\ldots$
$\vdots$

Iteration i: $B^i a^{n-i} b^{n-i} B\ldots$
$\vdots$

Iteration $n-1$: $B^{n-1}abB\ldots$
Iteration n: $B^n BB\ldots$

After these n iterations, M occurs in the first step of the cycle with B under the tape head, so M accepts $a^n b^n$.

Consider the special case when the input word equals $a^n b^n$ with $n = 0$; that is

$$a^n b^n = \varepsilon$$

At this point, M actually repeats the computational cycle zero times; in other words, it accepts ε by making no move at all.

In greater detail, M's input alphabet is $\{a, b\}$. Besides a and b, M uses B, so Ms complete tape alphabet is

$$\{a, b, B\}$$

M has five states,

$$q_0, q_1, q_2, q_3, \text{ and } q_4$$

where q_0 is the start state and q_4 is the final state. M begins its computation cycle in q_0 so it scans the leftmost symbol of the input word. If the scanned symbol equals a and M occurs in q_0, M replaces a with B, changes q_0 to q_1, and shifts the tape head one square right. From q_1, depending on the scanned symbol, M makes two different moves:

1. If M scans a or b, M shifts the tape head right while remaining in q_1.
2. If M scans B, M shifts the tape head left and enters q_2.

If in q_2, M scans b, then it replaces b with B, changes q_2 to q_3, and shifts the tape head a square left. From q_3, M makes two different moves depending on the scanned symbol:

1. If M scans b, M shifts the tape head a square left and remains in q_3.
2. If M scans B, M shifts the tape head a square left and enters q_0.

If M scans B in q_0, M enters q_4, keeping the tape head stationary; at this point, M accepts its input word. M makes the following moves according to the following computational rules:

Generalized models

Rule 1: change q_0 to q_1, rewrite a with B, and shift the tape head a square right
Rule 2: change q_1 to q_1, rewrite a with a, and shift the tape head a square right
Rule 3: change q_1 to q_1, rewrite b with b, and shift the tape head a square right
Rule 4: change q_1 to q_2, rewrite B with B, and shift the tape head a square left
Rule 5: change q_2 to q_3, rewrite b with B, and shift the tape head a square left
Rule 6: change q_3 to q_3, rewrite a with a, and shift the tape head a square left
Rule 7: change q_3 to q_3, rewrite b with b, and shift the tape head a square left
Rule 8: change q_3 to q_0, rewrite B with B, and shift the tape head a square right
Rule 9: change q_0 to q_4,, rewrite B with B, and do not shift the tape head.

△

Definition — Turing machine

A *Turing machine* is a quintuple,

$$M = (Q, \Sigma, R, s, F)$$

where

Q is a finite set of *states*;
Σ is a *tape alphabet* such that $\Sigma \cap Q = \varnothing$ and $\Sigma_I \subseteq \Sigma$, where Σ_I is an *input alphabet*, and $\Sigma - \Sigma_I$ contains B, called the *blank*;
$R \subseteq Q\Sigma \times Q\Sigma$ is a finite relation containing subrelations

$$R_{\text{stationary-move}}, R_{\text{right-move}}, \text{ and } R_{\text{left-move}}$$

so that

$$R = R_{\text{stationary-move}} \cup R_{\text{right-move}} \cup R_{\text{left-move}};$$

$s \in Q$ is the *start state*;
$F \subseteq Q$ is a set of *final states*.

◆

Members of R are called *rules*, and thus R is referred to as a finite *set of rules*. Let $(qX, pY) \in R$, where $q, p \in Q$ and $X, Y \in \Sigma$. If $(qX, pY) \in R_{\text{stationary-move}}$, then (qX, pY) is symbolically written as

$$qX \vdash pY\downarrow$$

If $(qX, pY) \in R_{\text{right-move}}$, then (qX, pY) is written as

$$qX \vdash pY \hookrightarrow$$

Finally, if $(qX, pY) \in R_{\text{left-move}}$, then (qX, pY) is written as

$$qX \vdash pY\lhd$$

Example 8.1.1.1 Part 2 Formal specification of a Turing machine

Return to the Turing machine M informally described in part 1 of this example. Formally, M is specified as follows:

$$M = (\{q_0, q_1, q_2, q_3, q_4\}, \{a, b, B\}, R, q_0, \{q_4\}),$$

where $\{a, b\}$ is the input alphabet of M. Reconsider Rule 1: change q_0 to q_1, rewrite a with B, and shift the tape head a square right.

Symbolically, this rule is specified as

$$q_0 a \vdash q_1 B \hookrightarrow$$

In this way, formalize all rules of M to obtain R, defined as,

$$\begin{aligned} R = \{ & q_0 a \vdash q_1 B \hookrightarrow, q_1 a \vdash q_1 a \hookrightarrow, q_1 b \vdash q_1 b \hookrightarrow, q_1 B \vdash q_2 B \lhd, \\ & q_2 b \vdash q_3 B \lhd, q_3 a \vdash q_3 a \lhd, q_3 b \vdash q_3 b \lhd, q_3 B \vdash q_0 B \hookrightarrow, \\ & q_0 B \vdash q_4 B \downarrow \}, \end{aligned}$$

where $R_{\text{stationary-move}}$, $R_{\text{right-move}}$, and $R_{\text{left-move}}$ are specified as

$$R_{\text{stationary-move}} = \{q_0 B \vdash q_4 B \downarrow\}$$

$$R_{\text{right-move}} = \{q_0 a \vdash q_1 B \hookrightarrow, q_1 a \vdash q_1 a \hookrightarrow, q_1 b \vdash q_1 b \hookrightarrow, q_3 B \vdash q_0 B \hookrightarrow\}$$

$$R_{\text{left-move}} = \{q_1 B \vdash q_2 B \lhd, q_2 b \vdash q_3 B \lhd, q_3 a \vdash q_3 a \lhd, q_3 b \vdash q_3 b \lhd\}$$

Notice that

$$R = R_{\text{stationary-move}} \cup R_{\text{right-move}} \cup R_{\text{left-move}}$$

△

For simplicity, this book frequently applies labels the rules of a Turing machine so that these labels to refer to the rules in a succinct way. For example, if a label r denotes a rule $qX \vdash pYt$, for some $t \in \{\hookrightarrow, \lhd, \downarrow\}$, then this is written as

$$r: qX \vdash pYt,$$

where qX represents the *left-hand side* of r, denoted lhs(r), and pYt represents the *right-hand side* of r, denoted rhs(r).

Conventions

Given a Turing machine $M = (Q, \Sigma, R, s, F)$, Σ_I denotes the input alphabet of M. Furthermore,

1. f, p, q and s represent states in Q, where s is the start state, and f is a final state;
2. U, V, W, X, Y, Z represent symbols from Σ;
3. $a, \ldots, c$ represent symbols in Σ_I;
4. $A, \ldots, C,$ and S represent symbols in $\Sigma - \Sigma_I$;
5. $u, \ldots, z$ represent words over Σ;
6. t represents an element of $\{\downarrow, \hookrightarrow, \lrcorner\}$;
7. R's rules are labelled by $1, \ldots, 9$ or by $r_1, r_2, \ldots$;
8. ρ represents a sequence of rules from R.

●

Subscripts and superscripts do not change these conventions, which are used hereafter unless explicitly stated otherwise.

Example 8.1.1.1 Part 3 Simplified specification of a Turing machine

Reconsider the Turing machine M defined in Part 2 of this example. Label M's rules with 1 through 9, and then, specify the whole machine by its rules as

1: $q_0 a \vdash q_1 B \hookrightarrow$
2: $q_1 a \vdash q_1 a \hookrightarrow$
3: $q_1 b \vdash q_1 b \hookrightarrow$
4: $q_1 B \vdash q_2 B \lrcorner$
5: $q_2 b \vdash q_3 B \lrcorner$
6: $q_3 a \vdash q_3 a \lrcorner$
7: $q_3 b \vdash q_3 b \lrcorner$
8: $q_3 B \vdash q_0 B \hookrightarrow$
9: $q_0 B \vdash q_4 B \downarrow$

where q_4 is the final state.

△

A Turing machine M works by making moves according to its computational rules. A move depends on the current state of M and the symbol scanned by the tape head of M. During a move, M changes the current state and rewrites the scanned symbol; in addition, M either keeps its tape head stationary or shifts it one square to the right or left.

Definition — configuration
Let $M = (Q, \Sigma, R, s, F)$ be a Turing machine. A *configuration* of M is a word χ satisfying

$$\chi \in \Sigma^* Q(\Sigma^*(\Sigma - \{B\}) \cup \{B\})$$

◆

Definition — move
Let $M = (Q, \Sigma, R, s, F)$ be a Turing machine, and let χ and χ' be two configurations of M. M makes a *move* from χ to χ' according to r, written as

$$\chi \vdash \chi' \, [r]$$

if at least one of the following three conditions holds:

1. *Stationary move*

$$\chi = xpUy, \chi' = xqVy, \text{ and } r: pU \vdash qV\downarrow \in R$$

2. *Right move*

$$\chi = xpUy, \chi' = xVqy', \text{ and } r: pU \vdash qV\hookrightarrow \in R$$

where $y' = y$ if $y \neq \varepsilon$, and $y' = B$ if $y = \varepsilon$.

3. *Left move*

$$\chi = xXpUy, \chi' = xqXy', \text{ and } r: pU \vdash qV\lrcorner \in R$$

where $y' = Vy$ if $V \neq B$ or $y \neq B$, and $y' = \varepsilon$ if $V = B$ and $y = B$.

◆

Conventions
Given a Turing machine M χ_M denotes a configuration of M; when no confusion exists, χ_M is simplified to χ. Whenever in $\chi \vdash \chi' \, [r]$, r represents an immaterial piece of information, this is written as $\chi \vdash \chi'$.

●

Consider a Turing machine M. Suppose that M's configuration is

$$\chi = xqy$$

Generalized models

where $x \in \Sigma^*, q \in Q, y \in \Sigma^*(\Sigma - \{B\}) \cup \{B\})$. Notice that xqy represents an instantaneous description of M because it specifies these three pieces of information:

1. M's current state is q;
2. M's tape currently contains xy, followed by Bs;
3. M's tape head scans the leftmost symbol of y.

As $y \in \Sigma^*(\Sigma - \{B\}) \cup \{B\})$, y ends with no more than one B, informally y contains no trailing blanks.

The previous definition describes three kinds of moves — a stationary move, a right move and a left move. These moves are now explained in greater detail.

Consider a stationary move that a Turing machine M makes from its current configuration $xpUy$, by using $pU \vdash qV\downarrow \in R$. During this move, M leaves p for q, rewrites U with V, and keeps its tape head stationary (see Figure 8.1.1.3).

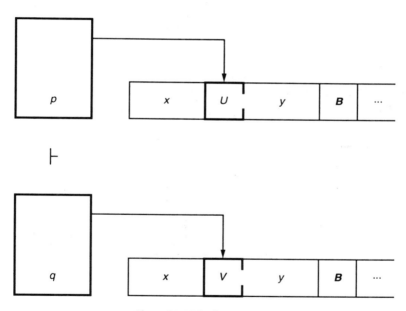

Figure 8.1.1.3 Stationary move.

Consider a right move that M makes from $xpUy$ by using $pU \vdash qV\hookrightarrow \in R$. During this move, M leaves p for q, rewrites U with V, and shifts the tape head one square right (see Figure 8.1.1.4). Therefore, in the next move, M scans Y; that is, the symbol right of V. Notice that M can make a right move even if all symbols following U are Bs.

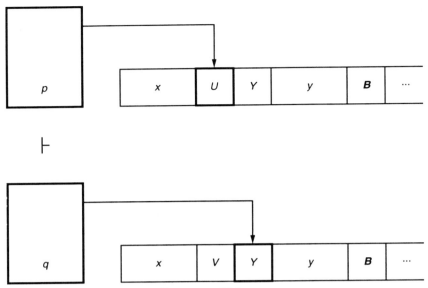

Figure 8.1.1.4 Right move.

Finally, consider a left move that M makes from its current configuration $xXpUy$ by using $pU \vdash qV\lrcorner \in R$. During this move, M leaves p for q, rewrites U with V, and shifts the tape head one square left (see Figure 8.1.1.5). Notice that if $x = \varepsilon$ and $X = \varepsilon$, then U is located in the leftmost tape square, from which M can make no left move.

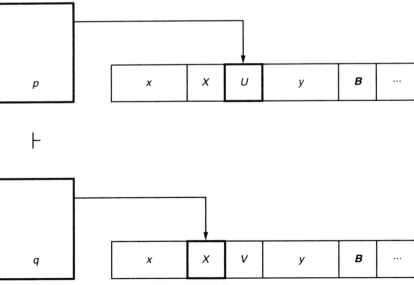

Figure 8.1.1.5 Left move.

Example 8.1.1.1 Part 4 Left, right and stationary moves

Consider the Turing machine M. Let q_0aabb be its current configuration. By using 1: $q_0a \vdash q_1B \hookrightarrow$, M makes the right move

$$q_0abba \vdash Bq_1bba \qquad [1]$$

Next, assume that $Babbq_1B$ is M's configuration. From this configuration, by using $q_1B \vdash q_2B\lhook$, M makes the left move

$$Babbq_1B \vdash Babq_2b \qquad [5]$$

Finally, suppose that BBq_0B is M's configuration. By using 9: $q_0B \vdash q_4B\downarrow$, M makes the following move, during which the tape head's position remains unchanged:

$$BBq_0B \vdash BBq_4B \qquad [9]$$

$\triangle$

The next definition extends a single move to a sequence of moves.

Definition — sequence of moves, part 1

Let $M = (Q, \Sigma, R, s, F)$ be a Turing machine.

1. Let χ be any configuration of M. M makes *zero moves* from χ to χ according to ε, written as

$$\chi \vdash^0 \chi \qquad [\varepsilon]$$

2. Let there exist a sequence of configurations

$$\chi_0, ..., \chi_n$$

for some $n \geq 1$ such that

$$\chi_{i-1} \vdash \chi_i \qquad [r_i]$$

where $r_i \in R$, $i = 1, ..., n$; that is,

$$\chi_0 \vdash \chi_1 \qquad [r_1]$$
$$\vdash \chi_2 \qquad [r_2]$$
$$\vdots$$
$$\vdash \chi_n \qquad [r_n]$$

Then, M makes n moves from χ_0 to χ_n according to $r_1\ldots r_n$, written as

$$\chi_0 \vdash^n \chi_n \qquad [r_1\ldots r_n]$$

♦

Consider a Turing machine $M = (Q, \Sigma, R, s, F)$. Let $\chi \vdash^n \chi'$ $[\rho]$ in M, where ρ denotes a sequence of n rules ($\rho = \varepsilon$ if $n = 0$). Observe that ρ, called the *rule word* corresponding to $\chi \vdash^n \chi'$, represents the sequence of rules according to which M makes the n moves from χ to χ'. For simplicity, this book frequently omits ρ in $\chi \vdash^n \chi'$ $[\rho]$ and writes $\chi \vdash^n \chi'$.

Mathematically, $\vdash^n$ represents the n-fold product of $\vdash$. Based on $\vdash^n$, the following definition introduces $\vdash^+$ and $\vdash^*$, where $\vdash^+$ denotes the transitive closure of $\vdash$ and $\vdash^*$ denotes the transitive and reflexive closure of $\vdash$.

Definition — sequence of moves, part 2
Let $M = (Q, \Sigma, R, s, F)$ be a Turing machine, and let χ and χ' be two configurations of M:

1. If there exists $n \geq 1$ so $\chi \vdash^n \chi'$ $[\rho]$ in M, then $\chi \vdash^+ \chi'$ $[\rho]$.
2. If there exists $n \geq 0$ so $\chi \vdash^n \chi'$ $[\rho]$ in M, then $\chi \vdash^* \chi'$ $[\rho]$.

♦

For brevity, write $\chi \vdash^+ \chi'$ and $\chi \vdash^* \chi'$ instead of $\chi \vdash^+ \chi'$ $[\rho]$ and $\chi \vdash^* \chi'$ $[\rho]$, respectively.

Example 8.1.1.1 Part 5 Sequences of moves
Return to the Turing machine M discussed in previous parts of this Example (M's rules are listed in Part 3 of this example). By using rules 1, 2, 3, 3 and 4, M computes

$$q_0aabb \vdash^5 Babq_2b \qquad [12334]$$

because

$$\begin{aligned}
q_0aabb &\vdash Bq_1abb & [1] \\
&\vdash Baq_1bb & [2] \\
&\vdash Babq_1b & [3] \\
&\vdash Babbq_1B & [3] \\
&\vdash Babq_2b & [4]
\end{aligned}$$

As $q_0aabb \vdash^5 Babq_2b$ $[12334]$,

$$q_0aabb \vdash^+ Babq_2b \ [12334] \text{ and } q_0aabb \vdash^* Babq_2b \quad [12334]$$

Notice that the rule word 12335 specifies the rules according to which M computes $q_0aabb \vdash^5 Babq_2b$. If this specification is unimportant, $q_0aabb \vdash^* Babq_2b$ [12334] is written more briefly as $q_0aabb \vdash^5 Babq_2b$. Analogously, $q_0aabb \vdash^+ Babq_2b$ [12334] and $q_0aabb \vdash^* Babq_2b$ [12334] are simplified to $q_0aabb \vdash^+ Babq_2b$ and $q_0aabb \vdash^* Babq_2b$, respectively.

△

A Turing machine $M = (Q, \Sigma, R, s, F)$ accepts a word w as follows. Initially, M's tape contains wBs, M's state is s, and M's tape head scans the leftmost symbol of w. If from this initial configuration, M can make a sequence of moves that end in a final state, M accepts w. The collection of all words that M accepts forms the language accepted by M.

Definition — accepted language
Let $M = (Q, \Sigma, R, s, F)$ be a Turing machine.

1. M accepts ε if

$$sB \vdash^* ufv$$

in M, for some $f \in F$, $u \in \Sigma^*$, and $v \in \Sigma^*(\Sigma - \{B\}) \cup \{B\}$.

2. Let $w \in \Sigma_I^+$. M accepts w if

$$sw \vdash^* ufv$$

in M, for some $f \in F$, $u \in \Sigma^*$, and $v \in \Sigma^*(\Sigma - \{B\}) \cup \{B\}$.

The *language accepted by* M, $L(M)$, is defined as

$$L(M) = \{w: w \in \Sigma_I^*, \text{ and } M \text{ accepts } w\}$$

◆

Example 8.1.1.1 Part 6 Acceptance
Return to the Turing machine M discussed throughout the previous parts of this example. With ab, M makes the following sequence of moves (see Figure 8.1.1.6):

$$
\begin{aligned}
q_0ab &\vdash Bq_1b & [1] \\
&\vdash Bbq_1B & [3] \\
&\vdash Bq_2b & [4] \\
&\vdash q_3B & [5] \\
&\vdash Bq_0B & [8] \\
&\vdash Bq_4B & [9]
\end{aligned}
$$

In brief,
$$q_0 ab \vdash^* B q_4 B$$

As q_4 is final, M accepts ab.

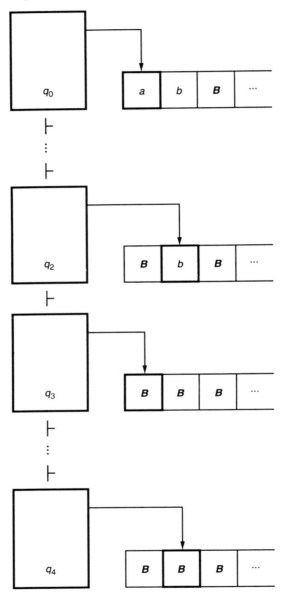

Figure 8.1.1.6 M's acceptance of ab.

△

Generalized models

Graphically, a Turing machine $M = (Q, \Sigma, R, s, F)$, is represented by its *Turing state diagram*. The nodes of this diagram are labelled with states of Q; an arrow points to the start state, and the final states are doubly circled. The edges have labels of the form $X/Y, t$, where $X, Y \in \Sigma$ and $t \in \{\downarrow, \hookrightarrow, \lrcorner\}$. Figure 8.1.1.7 explains how this diagram specifies a rule of the form $pX \vdash qYt$.

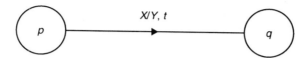

Figure 8.1.1.7 The graphical specification of $pX \vdash qYt$.

Example 8.1.1.1 Part 7 Turing state diagram

Figure 8.1.1.7 presents the Turing state diagram corresponding to the Turing machine M examined in the previous parts of this example.

△

The following, final, part of Example 8.1.1.1 rigorously verifies that the Turing machine M, discussed throughout the previous parts accepts $L(M) = \{a^n b^n : n \geq 0\}$. Notice that this verification makes use of several formal notations, such as rule words, introduced earlier in this section.

Example 8.1.1.1 Part 8 Accepted language

Return to the Turing machine M informally designed in the first part of Example 8.1.1.1 so that

$$L(M) = \{a^n b^n : n \geq 0\}$$

The present part of Example 8.1.1.1 formally verifies this identity. First, it establishes the inclusion

$$\{a^n b^n : n \geq 0\} \subseteq L(M)$$

To verify $\{a^n b^n : n \geq 0\} \subseteq L(M)$, requires the computation by which M accepts $a^n b^n$, where $n \geq 0$. Distinguish the two cases $n = 0$ and $n \geq 1$.

1. Let $n = 0$. Then, $a^n b^n = \varepsilon$, so M's tape is completely blank. At this point, by using 9: $q_0 B \vdash q_4 B \downarrow$, M enters its final state, q_4, and accepts ε.
2. Let $n \geq 1$. Then, M's tape initially contains

$$a^n b^n B \ldots$$

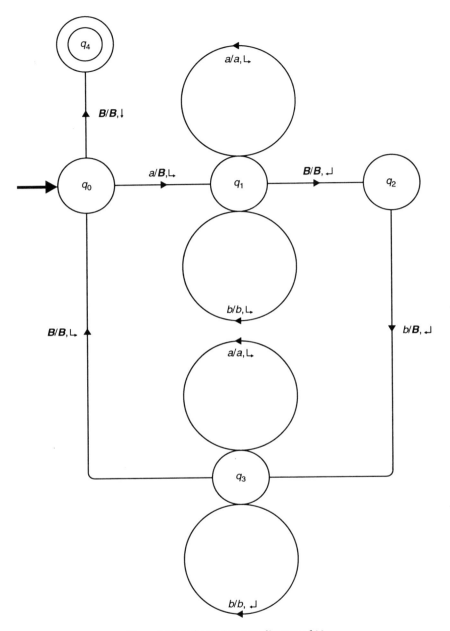

Figure 8.1.1.8 The Turing state diagram of M.

Starting from q_0 with its tape head scanning the leftmost a, M makes a right move according to rule 1: $q_0 a \vdash q_1 B \hookrightarrow$; as a result, it replaces a with B, changes q_0 to q_1, and shifts the tape head one square right. Then, by using 2: $q_1 a \vdash q_1 a \hookrightarrow$ and 3: $q_1 b$

Generalized models

$\vdash q_1 b \hookrightarrow$, M skips all as and 's until M scans B; at this point, M's configuration equals $Ba^{n-1}b^n q_1 B$. From this configuration, M shifts the tape head left and enters q_2 by applying 4: $q_1 B \vdash q_2 B \dashv$. After this move, M uses 5: $q_2 b \vdash q_3 B \dashv$, according to which M replaces the rightmost b with B, changes q_2 to q_3, and shifts the tape head one square left. Proceeding from right to left, M then skips all bs and as by using 7: $q_3 b \vdash q_3 b \dashv$ and 6: $q_3 a \vdash q_3 a \dashv$ until it scans B, preceding $a^{n-1}b^{n-1}$; at this point, M's configuration is $q_3 B a^{n-1} b^{n-1}$. From $q_3 B a^{n-1} b^{n-1}$, M makes a right move according to 8: $q_3 B \vdash q_0 B \hookrightarrow$ and, thereby, completes the first computational cycle made according to the rule word

$$12^{n-1}3^n 457^{n-1}6^{n-1}8$$

M then executes the second iteration according to

$$12^{n-2}3^{n-1}457^{n-2}6^{n-2}8$$

After n cycles, M's configuration is $B^n q_0 B$, from which M enters its final state, q_4, by using 9: $q_0 B \vdash q_4 B \downarrow$.

In summary, with $a^n b^n$ on its tape, M makes a move sequence according to the rule word

$$\rho_n \rho_{n-1} \ldots \rho_1 9$$

where

$$\rho_i = 12^{i-1}3^i 457^{i-1}6^{i-1}8$$

for $i = 1, \ldots, n$. To illustrate, consider $n = 2$ and notice that M accepts $aabb$ according to 123345768134589.

These preliminary observations lead to the following claim and its proof.

Claim A
For all $n \geq 0$,

$$q_0 a^n b^n \vdash^* q_4 B \quad [\rho]$$

in M, where

$$\rho = \rho_n \rho_{n-1} \ldots \rho_1 9$$

with

$$\rho_i = 12^{i-1}3^i 456^{i-1}7^{i-1}8$$

for $i = 1, \ldots, n$.

Proof
This claim is established by induction on n.

Basis
Let $n = 0$. Then,
$$a^n b^n = \varepsilon \text{ and } \varepsilon = \rho_n \rho_{n-1} \cdots \rho_1$$

Thus, $\rho = 9$. Observe that
$$q_0 B \vdash^* q_4 B \qquad [9]$$

in M, so the basis holds.

Induction hypothesis
Assume that the claim holds for all $n = 0, \ldots, m$, for some $m \geq 0$.

Induction step
Consider
$$w = a^{m+1} b^{m+1}$$

Express w as
$$w = a a^m b^m b$$

From the induction hypothesis,
$$q_0 a^m b^m \vdash^* q_4 B \qquad [\rho]$$

where $\rho = \rho_m \rho_{m-1} \cdots \rho_1 9$ with $\rho_i = 12^{i-1} 3^i 456^{i-1} 7^{i-1} 8$ for $i = 1, \ldots, m$. Furthermore, notice that
$$q_0 a a^m b^m b \vdash^* q_0 a^m b^m \qquad [\rho_{m+1}]$$

in M, where $\rho_{m+1} = 12^m 3^{m+1} 457^m 6^m 8$. Therefore,
$$q_0 a a^m b^m b \vdash^* q_0 a^m b^m \qquad [\rho_{m+1}]$$
$$\vdash^* q_4 B \qquad [\rho_m \rho_{m-1} \cdots \rho_1 9]$$

Hence,
$$q_0 a^{m+1} b^{m+1} \vdash^* q_4 B \qquad [\rho]$$

in M, where

$$\rho = \rho_{m+1}\rho_m \cdots \rho_1 9$$

with

$$\rho_i = 12^{i-1}3^i 456^{i-1}7^{i-1}8$$

for $i = 1, \ldots, m+1$. Thus, the induction step is completed.

Therefore, Claim A holds.

□

Claim A implies

$$\{a^n b^n : n \geq 0\} \subseteq L(M)$$

To establish

$$L(M) \subseteq \{a^n b^n : n \geq 0\},$$

this example presents two other claims. Claim B, given next, demonstrates that if M accepts a word w according to a rule word that satisfies the form described in Claim A, then

$$w \in \{a^n b^n : n \geq 0\}$$

Claim B
Let

$$q_0 w \vdash^* q_4 B \quad [\rho]$$

in M, where $w \in \{a, b\}^*$. Then, for all $n \geq 0$, if

$$\rho = \rho_n \rho_{n-1} \cdots \rho_1 9$$

where for $i = 1, \ldots, n$,

$$\rho_i = 12^{i-1}3^i 456^{i-1}7^{i-1}8$$

then

$$w = a^n b^n$$

Proof
This proof is established by induction on n.

Basis
Let $n = 0$. Then,

$$\rho_n \rho_{n-1} \ldots \rho_1 = \varepsilon$$

That is,

$$\rho = 9$$

Then, $q_0 w \vdash^* q_4 B \,[\rho]$ actually has the form

$$q_0 B \vdash q_4 B \qquad [9]$$

Thus,

$$w = \varepsilon \text{ and } \varepsilon = a^0 b^0$$

Therefore, the basis of the claim holds.

Induction hypothesis
Assume that the claim holds for all $n = 0, \ldots, m$, for some $m \geq 0$.

Induction step
Let

$$q_0 w \vdash^* q_4 B \qquad [\rho]$$

in M, where $w \in \{a, b\}^*$, and let

$$\rho = \rho_{m+1} \rho_m \ldots \rho_1 9$$

where for $i = 1, \ldots, m+1$,

$$\rho_i = 12^{i-1} 3^i 4 5 6^{i-1} 7^{i-1} 8$$

Express

$$q_0 w \vdash^* q_4 B \qquad [\rho]$$

as

Generalized models

$$q_0 w \vdash^* \chi \qquad [\rho_{m+1}]$$
$$\vdash^* q_4 B \qquad [\rho_m \rho_{m-1} \cdots \rho_1 9]$$

Consider

$$q_0 w \vdash^* \chi \qquad [\rho_{m+1}]$$

where $\rho_{m+1} = 12^m 3^{m+1} 457^m 6^m 8$. As proved in the exercises, this form of ρ_{m+1} implies

1. $w = aw'b$
2. $q_0 w \vdash^* B q_0 w' \qquad [\rho_{m+1}]$

That is,

$$q_0 w \vdash^* B q_0 w' B \qquad [\rho_{m+1}]$$
$$\vdash^* q_4 B \qquad [\rho_m \rho_{m-1} \cdots \rho_1 9]$$

From the induction hypothesis,

$$q_0 w' \vdash^* q_4 B \qquad [\rho_m \rho_{m-1} \cdots \rho_1 9]$$

implies

$$w' = a^n b^n$$

Thus,

$$w = aw'b = aa^m b^m b = a^{m+1} b^{m+1}$$

Consequently, the induction step is completed.

Therefore, Claim B holds.

$\square$

Claim C states that M accepts every word by a computation described in Claim B.

Claim C

M accepts every word, $w \in L(M)$, as follows:

$$q_0 w \vdash^* q_4 B \qquad [\rho]$$

where for some $n \geq 1$,

with
$$\rho = \rho_n \rho_{n-1} \cdots \rho_1 9$$

$$\rho_i = 12^{i-1} 3^i 456^{i-1} 7^{i-1} 8$$

for all $i = 1, \ldots, n$.

Proof
This proof is left to the exercises. □

Recall that Claim A implies
$$\{a^n b^n : n \geq 0\} \subseteq L(M)$$

On the other hand, Claims B and C imply
$$L(M) \subseteq \{a^n b^n : n \geq 0\}$$

As a result,
$$L(M) = \{a^n b^n : n \geq 0\}.$$
▲

The notion of a Turing machine fulfils an extremely important role, and one that is central to all computational theory.

Church's thesis

The notion of a procedure is equivalent to the notion of a Turing machine.

Undoubtedly, every Turing machine constitutes a procedure. More surprisingly, Church's thesis also asserts that every procedure can be formalized by a Turing machine. Observe that this thesis cannot be verified. Indeed, a verification of this kind requires formalizing the intuitive notion of a procedure and, then, comparing this formalized notion with the notion of a Turing machine. At this point, there arises a problem of whether the new formalized notion is equivalent to the intuitive notion of a procedure. Consequently, any attempt of verifying Church's thesis necessarily involves another thesis that is analogous to Church's thesis, so this verification ends up with an infinite regression. However, the evidence supporting Church's thesis is overwhelming: throughout its history, computer science has introduced many other formalizations of procedures, and all of them are equivalent to the notion of a Turing machine. Hereafter, the investigation concerning Turing machines frequently takes advantage of Church's thesis, so this investigation presents its results in terms of Pascal-like procedures rather than Turing machines, whose formal descriptions are usually tedious.

By Church's thesis, a language L is accepted by a Turing machine if and only if a procedure enumerates all words in L. This equivalence leads to the following definition, which concludes this section.

Definition — recursively enumerable language
A language L is a *recursively enumerable language* if there exits a Turing machine such that $L(M) = L$.

◆

8.1.2 Determinism

In general, the Turing machine works nondeterministically because it can make several different moves from the same configuration. As a result, with the same input word, it can make many different sequences of moves.

Example 8.1.2.1 Part 1 Nondeterminism
Consider

$$L' = \{xy : x \in \{a, c\}^*, y \in \{b, c\}^*, |x| = |y|\}$$

Notice that L' represents a superset of the language L defined in the first part of Example 8.1.1.1 as

$$L = \{a^n b^n : n \geq 0\}$$

By extending the Turing machine M defined in the second part of Example 8.1.1.1, the present example constructs a Turing machine M' that accepts L'. To explain the fundamental idea underlying M', consider

$$xy$$

where $x \in \{a, c\}^*, y \in \{b, c\}^*$, and $|x| = |y|$. With xy on its tape, M' first replaces all cs appearing in x with as, then replaces all cs appearing in y with bs and, after this replacement, M' acts as M. More precisely, M' makes the initial replacement of cs by the rules

$p_0B \vdash q_0B\downarrow$
$p_0a \vdash p_1B\hookrightarrow$
$p_0c \vdash p_1B\hookrightarrow$
$p_1a \vdash p_1a\hookrightarrow$
$p_1c \vdash p_1a\hookrightarrow$
$p_1b \vdash p_2b\hookrightarrow$
$p_1c \vdash p_2b\hookrightarrow$
$p_2b \vdash p_2b\hookrightarrow$
$p_2c \vdash p_2b\hookrightarrow$
$p_2B \vdash p_3B\hookleftarrow$
$p_3a \vdash p_3a\hookleftarrow$
$p_3b \vdash p_3b\hookleftarrow$
$p_3c \vdash p_3c\hookleftarrow$
$p_3B \vdash q_0a\downarrow$

where p_0 is the start state of M'. As well as these new rules, M' contains all rules of M. Proceeding from left to right, M' uses the new rules to replace all cs appearing in x with as and all cs appearing in y with bs. After this replacement, M' returns to the leftmost tape square, enters q_0, and acts as M by using rules of M. In this way, M' accepts L' as formally verified in the exercises.

Assume that M' is in state p_1 with c under its tape head. At this point, M' can use two rules:

$$p_1c \vdash p_1a \hookrightarrow \text{ or } p_1c \vdash p_2b \hookrightarrow$$

In other words, from this configuration, M' can make two different moves. Consequently, M' works nondeterministically.

△

The deterministic Turing machine is now introduced, which disallows two different rules with the same left-hand side.

Definition — deterministic Turing machine
Let $M = (Q, \Sigma, R, s, F)$ be a Turing machine. M is a *deterministic Turing machine* if every rule $r \in R$ satisfies

$$\text{lhs}(r) \notin \{\text{lhs}(r'): r' \in (R - \{r\})\}$$

◆

Implementation

Using the definition of a deterministic Turing machine $M = (Q, \Sigma, R, s, F)$, qa forms the left-hand side of no more than one rule in R, for every $q \in Q$ and every $a \in \Sigma$. Therefore, from the same configuration, M cannot perform two different moves. Consequently, M makes a unique move sequence with any input word, and this property makes M easy to implement. The following algorithm describes an implementation of the deterministic Turing machine discussed in Example 8.1.1.1.

Algorithm 8.1.2.1 Deterministic Turing machine implementation

Input: The deterministic Turing machine of Example 8.1.1.1 (see Figure 8.1.1.7).

Output: YES if $w \in L(M)$, and NO if $w \notin L(M)$.

Method

var
  Symbol denotes the currently scanned symbol
  {initially the leftmost symbol is scanned};

begin
  while Symbol $\neq B$ **do**
  begin
    if Symbol $= a$
    then rewrite Symbol with B and move right
    else write('NO') and stop;
    while Symbol $\neq B$ **do**
        move right;
    move left;
    if Symbol $= b$
    then rewrite Symbol with B and move left
    else write('NO') and stop;
    while Symbol $\neq B$ **do**
        move left;
    move right;
  end;
  write('YES')
end.

Transformation of a Turing machine to an equivalent deterministic Turing machine

The following text explains how to convert any Turing machine

$$M = (Q, \Sigma, R, s, F)$$

to an equivalent deterministic Turing machine

$$D$$

D works so that it explores all nonempty sequences of moves that M can make. (This exploration excludes the empty sequence. This exclusion represents no loss of generality because for every Turing machine, there exists an equivalent Turing machine that accepts every word by making one or more moves, as demonstrated in the exercises.)

To explain how D explores all nonempty move sequences made by M, recall that M accepts a word, w, if and only if there exists a rule word ρ such that $sw \vdash^* ufv \; [\rho]$ in M, for some $f \in F$. Therefore, D systematically generates all rule words consisting of rules contained in R and, according to each of these words, D simulates M's computation with w. If there exists a rule word according to which M accepts w, D eventually generates this rule word and, thus, accepts w. However, if M does not accept w according to any rule word, then D never generates a rule word according to which D accepts w.

To describe D more precisely, for all natural numbers, m and n, introduce the function

$$\text{Next}_{m,n}$$

over the set of sequences

$$\{ i_1, \ldots, i_m : i_k \text{ is an integer such that } 0 \leq i_k < n, \text{ where } k = 1, \ldots, m \}$$

as follows:

1. for all $i_1, \ldots, i_m$ such that $n^{m-1}i_m + n^{m-2}i_{m-1} + \ldots n i_2 + i_1 < n^m - 1$:

$$\text{Next}_{m,n}(i_1, \ldots, i_m) = j_1, \ldots, j_m$$

if and only if

$$(n^{m-1}i_m + n^{m-2}i_{m-1} + \ldots + n i_2 + i_1) + 1 = n^{m-1}j_m + n^{m-2}j_{m-1} + \ldots + n j_2 + j_1$$

2. for $i_1, \ldots, i_m$ such that $n^{m-1}i_m + n^{m-2}i_{m-1} + \ldots n i_2 + i_1 = n^m - 1$:

Generalized models

$$\text{Next}_{m,n}(i_1, \ldots, i_m) \text{ is undefined}$$

Notice that the set

$$\{j_1, \ldots, j_m : \text{Next}_{m,n}(i_1, \ldots, i_m) = j_1, \ldots, j_m, \text{ where } 0 \le i_k < n, \\ k = 1, \ldots, m, \text{ and } n^{m-1}i_m + n^{m-2}i_{m-1} + \ldots + i_1 < n^m - 1\}$$

contains all m-element sequences consisting of n-ary digit numbers. The exercises constructs an algorithm enumerating all members of this set.

Example 8.1.2.1 Part 2 Function Next

Suppose that m and n equal 4 and 16, respectively. Then,

$\text{Next}_{4,16}(15, 0, 12, 14) = 0, 1, 12, 14$
$\text{Next}_{4,16}(15, 15, 15, 0) = 0, 0, 0, 1$
$\text{Next}_{4,16}(15, 15, 15, 15)$ is undefined.

For $m = 4$ and $n = 16$,

$$\{j_1, \ldots, j_m : \text{Next}_{m,n}(i_1, \ldots, i_m) = j_1, \ldots, j_m, \text{ where } 0 \le i_k < n, \\ k = 1, \ldots, m, \text{ and } n^{m-1}i_m + n^{m-2}i_{m-1} + \ldots + i_1 < n^m - 1\}$$

consists of these sequences

0, 0, 0, 0
1, 0, 0, 0
⋮
15, 0, 0, 0
0, 1, 0, 0
1, 1, 0, 0
⋮
15, 15, 15, 15

Convention

$\text{Next}_{m,n}$ is simplified to Next whenever m and n are understood.

Having defined Next, this section now describes the transformation of $M = (Q, \Sigma, R, s, F)$ to D. Suppose that R consists of these n rules:

$$0: q_0 U_0 \vdash p_0 V_0 t_0$$
$$\vdots$$
$$i: q_i U_i \vdash p_i V_i t_i$$
$$\vdots$$
$$n{-}1: q_{n-1} U_{n-1} \vdash p_{n-1} V_{n-1} t_{n-1}$$

for some $n \geq 1$. Then, the tape alphabet of D contains B and the set of all symbols that have the form described in Figure 8.1.2.1, where $a \in \Sigma_I \cup \{B\}, i \in \{0, ..., n-1\} \cup \{B\}, q \in Q \cup \{B\}$, and $U \in \Sigma$.

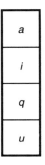

Figure 8.1.2.1 The form of a tape symbol in D.

When D works, its tape always contains k four-component symbols of the form described in Figure 8.1.2.1, for some $k \geq 1$, these k symbols are followed by Bs. Concatenate the first components of the k symbols and denote this concatenation by TRACK[1]; furthermore, for $i = 1, ..., k$, use TRACK[1, i] to refer to the ith symbol of TRACK[1]. Analogously, introduce TRACK[j] and TRACK[j, i] for $j = 2, ..., 4$ (see Figure 8.1.2.2).

D initializes its tape as described in Figure 8.1.2.3. During D's computation, TRACK[1] always holds the input word. On TRACK[2], D systematically generates M's rule words, which D subsequently uses to simulate M. More precisely, D produces the shortest words first, and it generates the words of equal length by using Next. In other words, D produces the rule words in this order:

$0, 1, ..., n-1,$

$00, 01, ..., nn,$

$000, 001, ..., nnn,$

$\vdots$

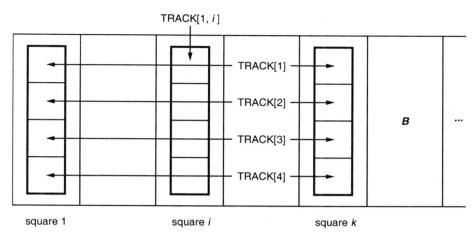

Figure 8.1.2.2 The four tracks on D's tape.

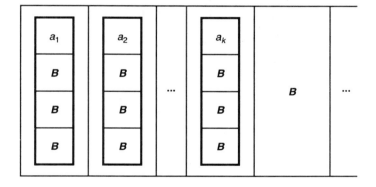

Figure 8.1.2.3 The initialization of D's tape.

Before D begins to simulate every computation made by M according to a rule word, D places s into TRACK[3, 1] and copies TRACK[1] onto TRACK[4]. D starts the first simulation with the tape displayed in Figure 8.1.2.4. Because TRACK[2] = 0, D simulates the one-move computation according to rule 0. If this move causes D to enter a final state, D accepts $a_1\ldots a_n$; otherwise, D generates the next rule word, 1, according to which D then performs another simulation. If there exists a rule word by which M accepts $a_1\ldots a_n$, D eventually generates this rule word on TRACK[2] and, thus, accepts $a_1\ldots a_n$ as well. If, however, no rule word causes M to accept its input, D never accepts.

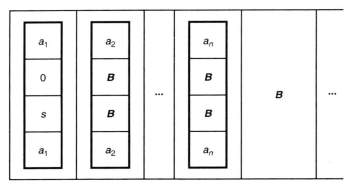

Figure 8.1.2.4 D's tape before the simulation of M according to 0.

Figure 8.1.2.5 pictorially explains how D simulates a right move that M makes according to $qU \vdash pV \hookrightarrow \; \in R$. Similarly, D simulates a left move and a stationary move in M.

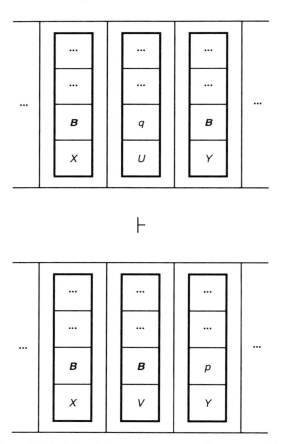

Figure 8.1.2.5 D's simulation of N's move according to $qU \vdash pV \hookrightarrow$.

Generalized models

The following discussion describes D in more detail using

function DTM(InputWord): boolean

which simulates M by InputWord on the tape. This function exits with DTM = **true** if and only if M accepts InputWord. However, this function never exits if and only if M does not accept InputWord.

DTM contains two simple procedures, Max and BlankTrack. Max determines the greater of two integers; that is, for two integers i and j, Max$(i, j) = i$ if and only if $i > j$; otherwise, Max$(i, j) = j$. BlankTrack(i), where i is a natural number, places a four-component blank symbol of the form described by Figure 8.1.2.6 into square i.

Figure 8.1.2.6 Four-component blank symbol used on D's tape.

DTM follows next.

function DTM(InputWord): **boolean**;

type

    Acceptance = (YES, NO, MAYBE);

var

    Accepted: Acceptance;
    Last: **integer** {Last indicates the position of the right most symbol of the rule word on TRACK[2]};

procedure Simulation(**var** Accepted: Acceptance)
{this procedure generates the next rule word on TRACK[2] and, then, simulates the computation according to this rule word};

begin

{the generation of the next rule word on TRACK[2]}
if (TRACK[2,1] = B) {the first call of Simulation}
  or (TRACK[2,j] = n − 1 for all j = 1, ..., Last) {all rule words of length Last have been examined}
then
begin {the generation of $0^{(Last + 1)}$ on TRACK[2]}
  Last := Last + 1;
  if square Last contains B
  then BlankTrack(Last);
  for k := 1 **to** Last **do**
    TRACK[2, k] := 0
end
else {Not all rule words of length Last have been examined, so generate another rule word}
  if Next $_{Last,n}$(TRACK[2,1], ..., TRACK[2, Last]) = $j_1, ..., j_{Last}$
  then
  for k := 1 **to** Last **do**
    TRACK[2, j] := j_k;

{Initialization of TRACK[3]}
TRACK[3, 1] := s {the leftmost element of TRACK[3] is s};
for j := 2 **to** Max(|InputWord|, Last) **do**
  TRACK[3, j] := B {The leftmost element of TRACK[3] is s, and the others are blank};

{Initialization of TRACK[4]}
for j := 1 **to** |InputWord| **do**
  TRACK[4, j] := TRACK[1, j] {InputWord is copied from TRACK[1] onto TRACK[4]};

{If Max(|InputWord|, Last) = k, then square k is the rightmost square that should be occupied with a symbol different from B before the simulation according to TRACK[2] begins. However, during the previous call of Simulation, some symbols different from B may have been placed in the squares following square k. Therefore, the following **while** loop replaces each of these symbols with B.}
j := Max(|InputWord|, Last) + 1;
while square j does not contain B **do**
  begin
    place B into square j;
    j := j + 1
  end;
{Simulation according to TRACK[2]}
i_2 := 0 {index of TRACK[2]};

$i_3 := 1$ {index of TRACK[3]};
Accepted := MAYBE;
while Accepted = MAYBE do
  if TRACK[3, i_3] in F
  then
    Accepted := YES
  else
  begin
    $i_2 := i_2 + 1$;
    if $i_2 >$ Last
    then
      Accepted := NO {the computation according to the rule word on TRACK[2] was completed; however, InputWord was not accepted}
    else
      if TRACK[2, i_2] = i for some $i \in \{0, ..., n-1\}$ {the simulation of a move according to i: $q_i U_i \vdash p_i V_i t_i$}
      then
      begin
        if TRACK[3, t_3]TRACK[4, t_3] $\neq q_i U_i$
        then
          Accepted := NO {InputWord is rejected because i: $q_i U_i \vdash p_i V_i t_i$ is not applicable}
        else
        begin
          TRACK[4, i_3] := V_i;
          case t_i of
          $\downarrow$: {stationary move}
              TRACK[3, i_3] := p_i;

          $\llcorner$: {left move}
            if $i_3 = 1$
            then
              Accepted := NO {from the leftmost square, no left move can be made}
            else
            begin
              TRACK[3, i_3] := B;
              $i_3 := i_3 - 1$;
              TRACK[3, i_3] := p_i
            end{else};

            $\hookrightarrow$: {right move}
              begin
                TRACK[3, i_3] := B;
                $i_3 := i_3 + 1$;

```
                    if square i₃ contains B
                    then BlankTrack(i₃);
                         TRACK[3, t₃] := pᵢ
                 end{ ↪ };
              end{case};
           end{else};
        end{then};
     end{else};
end;

begin {the main program}

   {Initialization of TRACK[1] with InputWord}
   if InputWord = ε
   then
      BlankTrack(1)
   else
      for j = 1 to |InputWord| do
      begin
         BlankTrack(j);
         place the jth symbol of InputWord into TRACK[1, j];
      end;

   Last := 0;
   repeat
      Simulation (Accepted)
   until Accepted = YES;

   DTM := true
end.
```

DTM's **repeat** loop calls Simulation until Accepted = YES. More precisely, if the rule word on TRACK[2] causes Simulation to obtain a final state on TRACK[3], Simulation exits with Accepted = YES; at this point, DTM exits with DTM = **true**, and this exit means that D accepts its input. If, however, the rule word on TRACK[2] never causes Simulation to obtain a final state on TRACK[3], Simulation exits with Accepted = NO; then, the **repeat** loop calls Simulation again with the next rule word. If there exists a rule word ρ causing M to accept its input, ρ eventually appears on TRACK[2]; at this point, Simulation exits with Accepted = YES and, thus, D accepts its input. However, if no rule word causes Simulation to set Accepted = YES, **function** DTM never exits; therefore, D never accepts its input.

Theorem 8.1.2.2
Let L be a language. Then, $L = L(M)$ for a Turing machine M if and only if $L = L(D)$ for a deterministic Turing machine D.

Proof

If

Any deterministic Turing machine represents a special case of a Turing machine, so the 'if' part of this theorem surely holds.

Only if

Let L be a language, and let $L = L(M)$ for a Turing machine. This section has already described how to convert M to an equivalent deterministic Turing machine D. A full technical demonstration of the 'only if' part is left to the exercises.

Therefore, the present theorem holds.

■

Hereafter, when investigating Turing machines, attention is frequently restricted to deterministic Turing machines; from Theorem 8.1.2.2, this restriction represents no loss of generality.

8.1.3 Simplification

This section simplifies deterministic Turing machines by reducing the size of their components. First, is explained how to reduce the number of tape symbols. More precisely, any deterministic Turing machine M is coverted to an equivalent deterministic Turing machine T that has only one non-input tape symbol B. Then, the reduction of states is discussed. Finally, it is pointed out that both reductions cannot be attained simultaneously; that is, a reduction of both the number of tape symbols and the number of states in the deterministic Turing machines results in a decrease in machine power.

Tape symbol reduction

Consider how to convert any deterministic Turing machine $M = (Q, \Sigma, R, s, F)$ to an equivalent deterministic Turing machine T that contains the single non-input tape symbol B. That is, the alphabet of T is

$$\Sigma_I \cup \{B\},$$

where Σ_I is the input alphabet of M. Without any loss of generality, suppose that $card(\Sigma_I) \geq 2$ because if $card(\Sigma_I) = 1$, a new symbol is added to Σ_I. Furthermore, assume that

$$\{0, 1\} \subseteq \Sigma_I$$

This assumption represents no loss of generality either: if Σ_I does not contain 0 or 1, then the following tape symbol reduction can be easily modified by using any other two symbols, a and b, that appear in Σ_I, as the exercises demonstrate.

Recall that Section 3.2.3 introduces the bijection Binary_n, where $n \geq 0$, from $\{0, 1, \ldots, 2^n - 1\}$ to $\{x : x \in \{0, 1\}^*, |x| = n\}$; Binary_n is defined by the equivalence

$$\text{Binary}_n(i) = b_n \ldots b_1 \text{ if and only if } 2^{n-1}b_n + 2^{n-2}b_{n-1} + \ldots + 1b_1 = i$$

for $i = 0, \ldots, 2^n - 1$. This bijection is used to encode symbols of Σ in binary. More precisely, number the elements of Σ by 0 through $\text{card}(\Sigma)$, and set n to the natural number satisfying

$$2^{n-1} < \text{card}(\Sigma) \leq 2^n$$

Then, encode each symbol in Σ as an n–bit word by using Binary_n so if i denotes X, where $i \in \{0, \ldots, \text{card}(\Sigma)\}$ and $X \in \Sigma$, then $\text{Binary}_n(i)$ encodes X; symbolically,

$$\text{Code}(X) = \text{Binary}_n(i)$$

Throughout the rest of this section, $\text{Code}(X)$ represents this n-bit word encoding X.

To describe how T works, consider an input word

$$a_1 \ldots a_m$$

Initially, T replaces this word with

$$\text{Code}(a_1) \ldots \text{Code}(a_m)$$

Notice that $\text{Code}(a_1) \ldots \text{Code}(a_m)$ occupies mn squares. After this replacement, T shifts its tape head to the leftmost square, and enters M's start state, s. From now on, working with the binary word $\text{Code}(a_1) \ldots \text{Code}(a_m)$, T simulates the moves that M makes on $a_1 \ldots a_m$. Before the simulation of a move, T makes three tests:

A. T tests whether the current state corresponds to a final state in M, and if so T accepts and halts.
B. T tests whether its tape head scans B. If so, the tape head appears over a square that has never been scanned before; that is, the head is one square to the right of the encoded portion of the tape. In this case, T extends this encoded tape portion by $\text{Code}(B)$ as depicted in Figure 8.1.3.1, where $\text{Code}(X_1) \ldots \text{Code}(X_k)$ denotes the encoded portion of the tape;

Generalized models

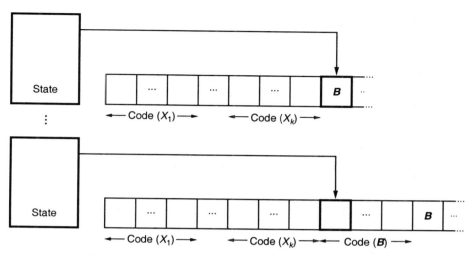

Figure 8.1.3.1 The extension of the encoded tape portion by Code(B).

C. T tests whether M has a rule according to which T can perform the simulation of the next move. More precisely, to simulate a move that M makes from state q with tape symbol U, T needs a rule, $r \in R$, with lhs(r) = Uq; if no such rule appears in R, T rejects and halts. If there exists a rule of the form

$$qU \vdash pVt \in R$$

T simulates the next move that M makes according to $qU \vdash pVt$.

T performs the simulation of a move according to $qU \vdash pVt$ so it replaces Code(U) with Code(V), and enters state p; in addition, depending on t, where $t \in \{\hookrightarrow, \dashv, \downarrow\}$, T shifts its tape head. To describe this shift in greater detail, if $t = \hookrightarrow$, T shifts the tape head n squares to the right (see Figure 8.1.3.2). If $t = \dashv$, T shifts the tape head n squares to the left. Finally, if $t = \downarrow$, T does not shift the tape head at all.

Notice that there exist three types of computation that T can produce, when simulating M:

1. T eventually enters a final state, accepts the input word, and halts.
2. T never enters a final state and, after making finitely many moves, T reaches a configuration from which it cannot simulate another move in M; at this point, T rejects the input word and halts.
3. T never halts; that is, T never enters a final state. However, it can always simulate another move.

Now consider in greater detail T described as

function OneTapeSymbolDTM(InputWord): **boolean**

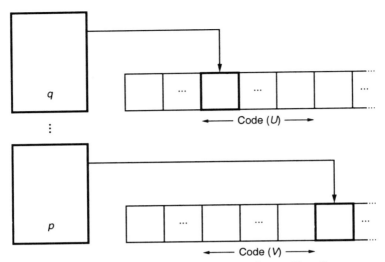

Figure 8.1.3.2 The simulation of a move according to $qU \vdash pV \hookrightarrow$.

InputWord contains M's input word, $a_1\ldots a_m$. In other words, OneTapeSymbolDTM simulates M whose tape initially contains $a_1\ldots a_m B\ldots$. This function exits with OneTapeSymbolDTM = **true** if and only if M accepts $a_1\ldots a_m$. The following description of OneTapeSymbolDTM uses SQUARES[i,j] to refer to the word of symbols contained in the tape squares i through j, where i and j satisfy $1 \leq i \leq j$. For brevity, SQUARES[i, i] is simplified to SQUARE[i] in this description.

function OneTapeSymbolDTM(InputWord): **boolean**;

type

    Acceptance = (YES, NO, MAYBE);
    States = **set of** Q {Q is the set of M's states};

var

    Accepted: Acceptance;
    HeadPosition: **integer**;
    State: States;

begin

    {InputWord in binary}
    if InputWord = $a_1\ldots a_m$ for some $m \geq 0$
    then SQUARES[1,mn] := Code (a_1)... Code (a_m) {n denotes the integer satisfying
        $2^{m-1} < \text{card}(\Sigma) \leq 2^m$};

Generalized models

```
{Initialization}
HeadPosition := 1;
State := s;
Accepted := MAYBE;

while Accepted = MAYBE do
    if State in F {F is the set of final states of M}
    then Accepted := YES
    else
    begin
        if SQUARE[HeadPosition] = B
        then SQUARES[HeadPosition, HeadPosition+n−1] := Code (B)
        {SQUARE[HeadPosition] has not been scanned previously. That is,
        SQUARE[HeadPosition] represents the square that follows the encoded tape
        portion. Therefore, this encoded portion is extended by Code(B)};

        if there exists a rule of the form qU ⊢ pVt ∈ R
            where q = State and
            Code (U) = SQUARES[HeadPosition, HeadPosition+n−1]
        then
        begin
            SQUARES[HeadPosition, HeadPosition+ n−1] := Code (V);
            State := p;
            case t of

            ↓: {stationary move};

            ↵: {left move}
                if HeadPosition = 1
                then Accepted := NO {from the leftmost tape square, no left move can
                        be made}
                else HeadPosition := HeadPosition − n;

            ↪: {right move}
                HeadPosition := HeadPosition + n;

            end{case}
        end{then}

        else Accepted := NO {no rule applicable}

    end{else};

if Accepted = YES
then OneTapeSymbolDTM := true
else OneTapeSymbolDTM := false

end.
```

To explain this function, assume that

$$\text{InputWord} = a_1 \ldots a_m$$

for some $m \geq 0$. Initially, OneTapeSymbolDTM replaces $a_1 \ldots a_m$ with its encoding

$$\text{Code}(a_1) \ldots \text{Code}(a_m)$$

which occupies mn squares, where n denotes the integer satisfying

$$2^{n-1} < \text{card}(\Sigma) \leq 2^n$$

Then, OneTapeSymbolDTM sets

$$\text{HeadPosition} := 1;$$

that is, it places the tape head over the leftmost square. In addition, OneTapeSymbolDTM sets State to the start state of M by

$$\text{State} := s$$

Then, OneTapeSymbolDTM simulates M's moves. The simulation of a move is performed by an iteration of the **while** loop, which begins by making the three tests (A, B and C) outlined earlier in this section. This section now explains these tests in somewhat greater detail.

A. The **while** loop tests whether State corresponds to a final state of M, and if so, OneTapeSymbolDTM sets

$$\text{Accepted} := \text{YES};$$

as a result, this function exits so OneTapeSymbolDTM = **true**.

B. If State contains a non-final state, the **while** loop examines whether SQUARE[HeadPosition] = B. If so, SQUARE[HeadPosition] is the square that follows the encoded tape portion, so this loop computes

$$\text{SQUARES}[\text{HeadPosition}, \text{HeadPosition} + n - 1] := \text{Code}(B)$$

and, thereby, extends this encoded portion by Code(B).

C. Assume that HeadPosition points at the leftmost bit of Code(U) and State = q. At this point, the **while** loop examines whether M has a rule whose left-hand side equals Uq. If not, OneTapeSymbolDTM sets

$$\text{Accepted} := \text{NO};$$

Generalized models

therefore, OneTapeSymbolDTM exits so OneTapeSymbolDTM = **false**. However, if R contains a rule of the form

$$qU \vdash pVt,$$

then the simulation of a move according to this rule occurs.

The simulation of a move according to $qU \vdash pVt$ replaces Code(U) with Code(V), sets State to p, and determines the new value of HeadPosition depending on t, where $t \in \{\downarrow, \dashv, \hookrightarrow\}$, as follows.

I. If $t = \downarrow$, HeadPosition remains unchanged because according to $qU \vdash pVt$, M makes a move without shifting its tape head.
II. If $t = \dashv$, the function sets HeadPosition := HeadPosition $- n$ because according to $qU \vdash pV\dashv$, M makes a left move.
III. If $t = \hookrightarrow$, the function sets HeadPosition := HeadPosition $+ n$ because, according to $qU \vdash pV\hookrightarrow$, M makes a right move.

The function OneTapeSymbolDTM can make the following three types of computation corresponding to the computation types 1, 2 and 3 outlined earlier in this section:

1. OneTapeSymbolDTM exits so OneTapeSymbolDTM = **true** if and only if M eventually reaches a final state and, therefore, accepts its input word.
2. OneTapeSymbolDTM exits so OneTapeSymbolDTM = **false** if and only if M never reaches a final state, and after making finitely many moves, it reaches a configuration from which it can make no other move.
3. T's **while** loop never exits if and only if M makes infinitely many moves, none of which, however, causes M to enter a final state.

Theorem 8.1.3.1
Let L be a langauge. Then, $L = L(M)$, where M is a deterministic Turing machine, if and only if $L = L(T)$, where $T = (Q, \Sigma, R, s, F)$ is a deterministic Turing machine satisfying $\Sigma = \Sigma_I \cup \{B\}$.

Proof
If
The 'if' part of the equivalence stated in the present theorem is trivial.

Only if
This section has already described how to transform any deterministic Turing machine M to an equivalent deterministic Turing machine satisfying $\Sigma = \Sigma_I \cup \{B\}$. A detailed proof of this part is left to the exercises.

Consequently, Theorem 8.1.3.1 holds. ∎

Corollary 8.1.3.2

Let Σ_I be an alphabet, and let $L \subseteq \Sigma_I^*$ be a language. Then, L represents a recursively enumerable language if and only if there exists a deterministic Turing machine $T = (Q, \Sigma_I \cup \{B\}, R, s, F)$, satisfying $L(T) = L$.

Proof
Let Σ_I be an alphabet. Consider a language $L \subseteq \Sigma_I^*$.

If
Assume that there exists a deterministic Turing machine $T = (Q, \Sigma_I \cup \{B\}, R, s, F)$, satisfying $L(T) = L$. As defined in the conclusion of Section 8.1.1, a language is recursively enumerable if and only if there exits a Turing machine that accepts the language. Thus, L surely represents a recursively enumerable language, so the 'if' part of the theorem holds.

Only if
Let L represent a recursively enumerable language. By the definition of a recursively enumerable language, there exists a Turing machine M' satisfying $L(M') = L$. From Theorem 8.1.2.1, $L = L(M)$ for a deterministic Turing machine. Finally, from Theorem 8.1.3.1, $L = L(T)$, where $T = (Q, \Sigma, R, s, F)$ is a deterministic Turing machine satisfying $\Sigma = \Sigma_I \cup \{B\}$. Thus, the 'only if' part of the theorem holds.

Therefore, Corollary 8.1.3.2 holds. ∎

Corollary 8.1.3.3

Let L be a language such that $L \subseteq \{0, 1\}^*$. Then, L represents a recursively enumerable language if and only if there exists a deterministic Turing machine $T = (Q, \{0, 1, B\}, R, s, F)$, satisfying $L(T) = L$.

Proof
Consider Corollary 8.1.3.2 with $\Sigma_I = \{0, 1\}$. Under this consideration, Corollary 8.1.3.2 implies Corollary 8.1.3.3. Thus, Corollary 8.1.3.3 holds. ∎

State reduction

The discussion that follows demonstrates how to transform any deterministic Turing machine to an equivalent deterministic Turing machine that contains only one final state.

Algorithm 8.1.3.4: Conversion of a deterministic Turing machine to an equivalent deterministic Turing machine with one final state

Input: A deterministic Turing machine $M = (Q, \Sigma, R, s, F)$.

Output: A deterministic Turing machine, $M_f = (Q_f, \Sigma, R_f, s, F_f)$, such that $\text{card}(F) = 1$ and $L(M) = L(M_f)$.

Method

begin
    $Q_f := Q - F$;
    $F_f := \{f\}$ {f is a new state, which represents the final state of M_f};
    for all $qU \vdash pVt \in R$ with $q \in Q - F$ do
        if $p \in F$
        then $R_f := R_f \cup \{qU \vdash fVt\}$
        else $R_f := R_f \cup \{qU \vdash pVt\}$
end.

Algorithm 8.1.3.4 is based on the idea that once a deterministic Turing machine accepts, it may as well halt. Therefore, the for loop considers only rules of the form $qU \vdash pVt \in R$ with $q \in Q - F$ so that if p is final, this loop replaces p with f, the only final state of M_f; otherwise, this loop does not modify $qU \vdash pVt$ at all. As a result, the output deterministic Turing machine produced by Algorithm 8.1.3.3 accepts $L(M)$ and contains one final state, f.

Lemma 8.1.3.5
Let $M = (Q, \Sigma, R, s, F)$ be a deterministic Turing machine. With M on its input, Algorithm 8.1.3.4 halts and correctly constructs a deterministic Turing machine $M_f = (Q_f, \Sigma, R_f, s, F_f)$, such that $\text{card}(F) = 1$ and $L(M) = L(M_f)$.

Proof
A detailed proof of this lemma is left to the exercises. ∎

The following theorem fulfils a crucial role later on in Section 8.1.5.

Theorem 8.1.3.6
Let L be a language such that $L \subseteq \{0, 1\}^*$. Then, L represents a recursively enumerable language if and only if there exists a deterministic Turing machine $M = (Q, \{0, 1, B\}, R, s, \{f\})$ satisfying $L(M) = L$.

Proof
This theorem follows from Corollary 8.1.3.3, Algorithm 8.1.3.4 and Lemma 8.1.3.5.   ■

The following theorem states that every recursively enumerable language can be accepted by a deterministic Turing machine that has no more than four states, one of which is final.

Theorem 8.1.3.7
Let L be a language. Then, L is a recursively enumerable language if and only if there exists a deterministic Turing machine $M = (Q, \Sigma, R, s, F)$ satisfying $L(M) = L$, $card(Q) \leq 4$ and $card(F) = 1$.

Proof
The 'if' part of the equivalence stated in Theorem 8.1.3.7 is trivial. The exercises prove the 'only if' part. Consequently, Theorem 8.1.3.7 holds.   ■

From Corollary 8.1.3.2, deterministic Turing machines with one non-input tape symbol B characterize the family of recursively enumerable languages. Analogously, from Theorem 8.1.3.7, the deterministic Turing machines with four states characterize this family. However, deterministic Turing machines with a limited number of tape symbols and, in addition, a limited number of states do not characterize all this family. In other words, a simultaneous reduction of the number of tape symbols and the number of states in deterministic Turing machines results in a decrease of machine power, as demonstrated in the exercises.

8.1.4 Extension

This section extends the basic model of a Turing machine, as defined in Section 8.1.1, in several ways. As all these extended models can be viewed as procedures by Church's thesis, they are equivalent to the basic model of a Turing machine. This section by explaining how to convert each of these extended models to an equivalent Turing machine.

k-Tape Turing machines

A k-tape Turing machine, where $k \geq 1$, represents a Turing machine with k tapes, each of which has its read-write tape head (see Figure 8.1.4.1).

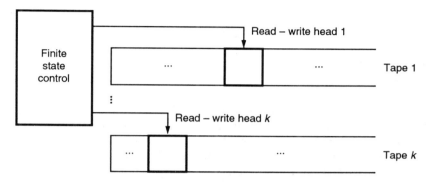

Figure 8.1.4.1 k-Tape Turing machine.

A move made by a k-tape Turing machine M depends on the current state and on the k symbols scanned by the tape heads. During a move, M changes the current state, rewrites the k scanned symbols, and shifts each of its k heads zero or one squares to the right or left. Initially, the first tape contains the input word, the other tapes are blank, each read-write head scans the leftmost tape square, and M occurs in its start state. If from this initial configuration, M can make a sequence of moves that ends in a final state, then M accepts the input word. The collection of all words that M accepts represents the language accepted by M.

Definition — k-tape Turing machine
Let k be a natural number. A k-tape Turing machine is a quintuple

$$M = (Q, \Sigma, R, s, F)$$

where Q, Σ, s and F have the same meaning as for a Turing machine and R is the set of rules of the form

$$qX_1...X_k \vdash pY_1t_1...Y_kt_k$$

where $q, p \in Q, X_i \in \Sigma$, and $t_i \in \{\downarrow, \hookrightarrow, \lrcorner\}$ for $i = 1, ..., k$.

♦

Definition — configuration

Let k be a natural number, $M = (Q, \Sigma, R, s, F)$ be a k-tape Turing machine, $q \in Q$,

$$\chi = \chi_1 | \ldots | \chi_k,$$

where $|$ is a special symbol such that $| \notin \Sigma^*$, and for $j = 1, \ldots, k$,

$$\chi_j \in \Sigma^* \{q\} (\Sigma^* (\Sigma - \{B\}) \cup \{B\})$$

Then, χ is a configuration of M. ◆

Consider a k-tape Turing machine $M = (Q, \Sigma, R, s, F)$. Let $\chi_1 | \ldots | \chi_k$ be a configuration of M. According to the previous definition, the same state, q, appears in every χ_j, for $j = 1, \ldots, k$. The fundamental reason for this repetition is that each of these k occurrences of q actually specifies the position of the read-write head on the corresponding tape as follows from the next definition.

Definition — move

Let k be a natural number, $M = (Q, \Sigma, R, s, F)$ be a k-tape Turing machine, and

$$qX_1 \ldots X_k \vdash pY_1 t_1 \ldots Y_k t_k \in R$$

Furthermore, let

$$\chi = \chi_1 | \ldots | \chi_k \text{ and } \chi' = \chi'_1 | \ldots | \chi'_k$$

be two configurations of M. For $j = 1, \ldots, k$, let M_j be the Turing machine defined as

$$M_j = (Q, \Sigma, R_j, s, F)$$

where

$$R_j = \{qX_i \vdash pY_i t_i : qX_1 \ldots X_j \ldots X_k \vdash pY_1 t_1 \ldots Y_j t_j \ldots Y_k t_k \in R\}.$$

M makes a *move* from χ to χ' according to r, written as

$$\chi \vdash \chi' \quad [r]$$

if for all $j = 1, \ldots, k$,

in M_j.

$$\chi_j \vdash \chi'_j \, [qX_j \vdash pY_j t_j]$$

◆

Convention
If in $\chi \vdash \chi' [r]$, r represents an immaterial piece of information, $\chi \vdash \chi' [r]$ is simplified to $\chi \vdash \chi'$.

●

Return to the definition of $\vdash^+$ and $\vdash^*$ for the Turing machine in Section 8.11. By analogy with this definition, define $\vdash^+$ and $\vdash^*$ for a k-tape Turing machine.

Definition — accepted language
Let k be a natural number, $M = (Q, \Sigma, R, s, F)$ be a k-tape Turing machine, and $w \in \Sigma_I^*$. M accepts w if

$$sw(sB)^{k-1} \vdash^* \chi$$

in M with

$$\chi = \chi_1 | \ldots | \chi_k$$

so that for a final state $f \in F$,

$$\chi_j \in \Sigma^* \{f\} (\Sigma^*(\Sigma - \{B\}) \cup \{B\})$$

where $j = 1, \ldots, k$. The *language accepted by* M, $L(M)$, is defined as

$$L(M) = \{w \colon w \in \Sigma_I^*, \text{ and } M \text{ accepts } w\}$$

◆

Observe that for $k = 1$, the notion of a k-tape Turing machine coincides with the notion of a Turing machine (see Section 8.1.1).

Definition — deterministic k-tape Turing machine
Let $M = (Q, \Sigma, R, s, F)$ be a k-tape Turing machine. M is a *deterministic k-tape Turing machine* if every rule, $r \in R$, satisfies

$$\text{lhs}(r) \notin \{\text{lhs}(r') \colon r' \in (R - r)\}$$

◆

Theorem 8.1.4.1

Let L be a language, and let k be a natural number. Then, $L = L(M)$ for a k-tape Turing machine M if and only if $L = L(D)$ for a deterministic k-tape Turing machine, D.

Proof
Let k be a natural number, and let L be a language.

If
Assume that $L = L(D)$, where D is a deterministic k-tape Turing machine. Because any deterministic k-tape Turing machine represents a special case of a k-tape Turing machine, the 'if' part of the equivalence stated in this theorem surely holds.

Only if
Let $L = L(M)$ for a k-tape Turing machine. Section 8.1.2 has explained how to convert any Turing machine M to a deterministic Turing machine D satisfying $L(M) = L(D)$. By analogy with this conversion, transform any k-tape Turing machine to an equivalent deterministic k-tape Turing machine; the exercises describes this transformation in detail. Thus, the 'only if' part of the equivalence holds.

Therefore, Theorem 8.1.4.1 holds. ∎

Undoubtedly, any deterministic k-tape Turing machine

$$M = (Q, \Sigma, R, s, F)$$

can be seen as a procedure. Therefore, Church's thesis and Theorem 8.1.2.1 guarantee that there exists a Turing machine equivalent to M. This section now describes a method that converts M to an equivalent deterministic Turing machine D.

By analogy with the conversion described in Section 8.1.2.2, the following construction of D is based on a tape with tracks. More precisely, the tape alphabet of D contains B and the set of all symbols that have the form described in Figure 8.1.4.2, where $q_i \in Q \cup \{B\}$ and $X_i \in \Sigma \cup \{B\}$ for $i = 1, \ldots, k$. As a result, the tape of D has $2k$ tracks. Denote these tracks H-TRACK[1], T-TRACK[1], ..., H-TRACK[k], T-TRACK[k] so H-TRACK[j] and T-TRACK[j] correspond to head j and tape j, respectively. For $j = 1, \ldots, k$, H-TRACK[j, i] denotes the ith symbol of H-TRACK[j], and T-TRACK[j, i] denotes the ith symbol of T-TRACK[j].

H-TRACK[j] is always completely blank except for one occurrence of the current state q of the simulated machine, M; this state appears in the square corresponding to the symbol scanned by the jth head of M. Consequently, the entire tape holds k occurrences of q (see Figure 8.1.4.3).

Generalized models

Figure 8.1.4.2 The form of a tape symbol in D.

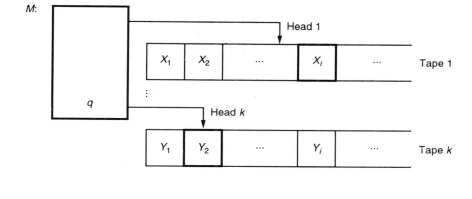

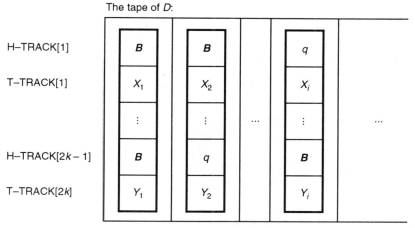

Figure 8.1.4.3 M together with the corresponding tape of D.

Initially, the tape head of D occurs at the leftmost square, whose head tracks contain M's start state, s. T-TRACK[1], corresponding to the first tape of M, and contains a given input word w; the other tape tracks, T-TRACK[2] through T-TRACK[k], are blank (see Figure 8.1.4.4). Starting from this initial configuration, D simulates moves made by M. If D simulates a move that causes M to enter a final state, D accepts w, and halts; therefore, $w \in L(D)$ if and only if $w \in L(M)$.

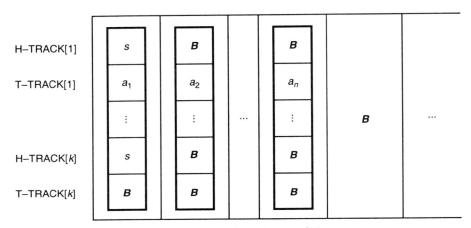

Figure 8.1.4.4 The initial containment of D's tape.

D performs the simulation of a move made by M from a non-final state q, as follows. To determine the k occurrences of q on M's tapes, D sweeps right on its tape, and if q appears at H-TRACK[j, i], where $j = 1, \ldots, k$ and $i \geq 1$, D records [j, i]. After D records all k occurrences of q in this way, D finds out whether R has a rule of the form

$$qX_1\ldots X_k \vdash pY_1t_1\ldots Y_kt_k$$

so that for $j = 1, \ldots, k$,

$$\text{T-TRACK}[j, i] = X_j \text{ and H-TRACK}[j, i] = q$$

(Note that D has recorded [j, i] during its determination of the k occurrences of q.) If R lacks a rule of this form, M cannot move from the non-final state q, so $w \notin L(M)$; therefore, D rejects w and halts. However, if $qX_1\ldots X_k \vdash pY_1t_1\ldots Y_kt_k \in R$, then for $j = 1, \ldots, k$, D changes T-TRACK[j, i] from X_j to Y_j; in addition, depending on t_j, D changes H-TRACK[j] in the following way:

1. if $t_j = \downarrow$, then H-TRACK[j, i] = p;
2. if $t_j = \lrcorner$, then H-TRACK[j, i] = B and H-TRACK[$j, i-1$] = p;
3. if $t_j = \hookrightarrow$, then H-TRACK[j, i] = B and H-TRACK[$j, i+1$] = p.

Generalized models

Figure 8.1.4.5 describes the changes corresponding to the case when $t_j = \hookrightarrow$.

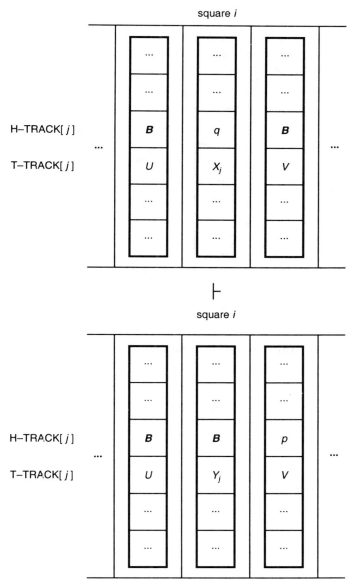

Figure 8.1.4.5 Changes of T-TRACK[j] and H-TRACK[j] corresponding to $qX_1\ldots X_j\ldots X_k \vdash pY_1t_1\ldots Y_j \hookrightarrow \ldots Y_kt_k$.

In greater detail, this section describes D as

function OneTapeDTM(InputWord): **boolean**

which simulates M with InputWord on the tape. The function exits with OneTapeDTM = **true** if and only if M accepts InputWord.

OneTapeDTM uses a procedure called BlankTrack(i), which places a tape symbol of the form described in Figure 8.1.4.6 into square i, where $i \geq 1$.

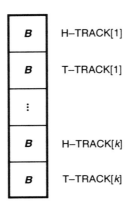

Figure 8.1.4.6 A $2k$-component blank symbol used on D's tape.

function OneTapeDTM(InputWord): **boolean**;

type

Acceptance = (YES, NO, MAYBE);
States = **set of** Q;

var

Accepted: Acceptance;
Position: **array** $[1..k]$ **of** **integer**;
Counter: $0..k$;
State: States;

begin

{Initialization of T-TRACK[1] with InputWord}
if InputWord = ε
then
  BlankTrack(1)

Generalized models

```
else
  for j = 1 to |InputWord| do
  begin
    BlankTrack(j) ;
    TRACK[1, j] := a_j, where a_j is the jth symbol of InputWord
  end;

{Initialization of H-TRACK[1, 1]] through H-TRACK[k, 1] with s}
for j = 1 to k do
    H-TRACK[j, 1] := s;

State := s;
Accepted := MAYBE;

while Accepted = MAYBE do
  if State in F
  then Accepted := YES
  else
  begin

    {Recording the track positions of the k state occurrences}
    i := 0;
    Counter := 0;
    while Counter < k do
    begin
      i := i + 1;
      for j = 1 to k do
          if H-TRACK[j, i] = State
          then
          begin
             Counter := Counter + 1;
             Position[j] := i
          end{then};
    end{while};
```

if there exists a rule of the form $qX_1...X_k \vdash pY_1t_1...Y_kt_k$ in R so that for $j = 1$, ..., k,
1. State = q
2. $X_j = $ T-TRACK[j, Position[j]]

```
    then {The simulation of a move according to qX_1...X_k ⊢ pY_1t_1...Y_kt_k}
      for j = 1 to k do
        begin
          T-TRACK[ j, Position[j] ] := Y_j;
```

```
              case t_j of
              ↓:  {stationary move}
                  H-TRACK[ j, Position[j] ] := p;

              ⌐:  {left move }
                  if Position[j] = 1
                  then Accepted := NO {from the leftmost tape square, no left
                                       move can be made}
                  else
                  begin
                    H-TRACK[j, Position[j] ] := B;
                    H-TRACK[j, Position[j] – 1] := p
                  end {else};

              ↪:  {right move}
                  begin
                    if square Position[j] + 1 contains B
                    then BlankTrack(Position[j] + 1])
                    {the track portion of the tape is extended};
                    H-TRACK[j, Position[j]] := B;
                    H-TRACK[j, Position[j] + 1] := p;
                  end;
              end{case};

         end{for};

         else Accepted := NO {no applicable rule};

      end;

  if Accepted = YES
  then OneTapeDTM := true
  else OneTapeDTM := false

end.
```

Theorem 8.1.4.2

Let k be a natural number, and let L be a language. Then, $L = L(M)$ where M is a k-tape deterministic Turing machine if and only if $L = L(D)$, where D is a deterministic Turing machine.

Proof

Let k be a natural number, and let L be a language.

Generalized models

If
Any deterministic Turing machine actually represents a k-tape deterministic Turing machine with $k = 1$, so the 'if' part of the equivalence stated in Theorem 8.1.4.2 surely holds.

Only if
Let k be a natural number, and let $L = L(M)$ for a k-tape deterministic Turing machine. This section has already explained how OneTapeDTM represents a deterministic Turing machine equivalent to M; a detailed proof of this proof part is left to the exercises.

Therefore, Theorem 8.1.4.2 holds.
∎

k-Head Turing machines

A *k-head Turing machine*, where $k \geq 1$, represents a Turing machine with k tape heads moving over a single tape (see Figure 8.1.4.7).

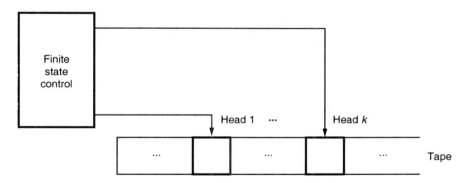

Figure 8.1.4.7 k-Head Turing machine.

A move made by a k-head Turing machine M depends on the current state and the k symbols scanned by M's tape heads. During a move, M changes its state and rewrites the k scanned symbols; in addition, M may shift any of its heads a square left or right. Consider the special case when n tape heads occur over the same square, for some $n = 2, \ldots, k$; at this point, M makes the next move so all these n tape heads writes the same symbol into this square. Initially, the tape contains the input word, each of the k heads scans the leftmost square of this tape, and M is in its start state. If from this initial configuration, M can make a sequence of moves that ends in a final state, then M accepts the input word. The language accepted by M consists of all words that M accepts in this way. The exercises formalizes the notion of a k-head Turing machine in detail.

Practically oriented computer science frequently uses a k-head Turing machine to verify that a word w satisfies a condition. Typically, a verification of this kind is carried out so some of the k heads keep a finger on particular squares whereas the other heads synchronously read some subwords of w and, thereby, verify the given condition. The following example illustrates this use.

Example 8.1.4.1 Three-head Turing machine
Consider

$$\{a^n b^n c^n : n \geq 0\},$$

which represents a non-context-free language (Example 6.1.2). The present example designs a three-head Turing machine M such that

$$L(M) = \{a^n b^n c^n : n \geq 0\}$$

M works by performing the following three computational phases (see Figure 8.1.4.8).

1. Keeping head 1 stationary over the leftmost tape square, M shifts heads 2 and 3 right until heads 2 and 3 simultaneously scan b and c, respectively.
2. M computes a sequence of right moves so that during each of these moves, heads 1, 2 and 3 read a, b and c, respectively.
3. M accepts its input when heads 1, 2 and 3 simultaneously scan b, c and B, respectively.

M is formalized in the exercises.

▲

Definition — deterministic k-head Turing machine
Let $M = (Q, \Sigma, R, s, F)$ be a k-head Turing machine, for some $k \geq 1$. M is a *deterministic k-head Turing machine* if every rule, $r \in R$, satisfies

$$\text{lhs}(r) \notin \{\text{lhs}(r') : r' \in (R - r)\}$$

◆

Theorem 8.1.4.3
Let L be a language, and let k be a natural number. Then, $L = L(M)$ for a k-head Turing machine M if and only if $L = L(D)$ for a deterministic k-head Turing machine D.

Generalized models

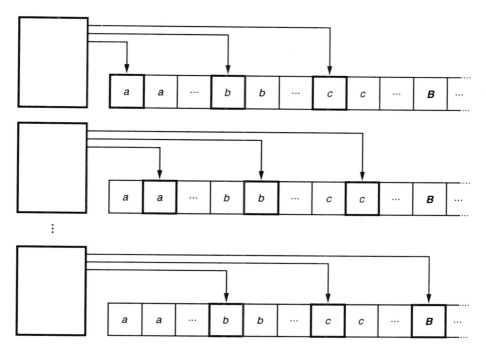

Figure 8.1.4.8 M's computation.

Proof
Let k be a natural number, and let L be a language.

If
Let $L = L(D)$, where D is a deterministic k-head Turing machine. As any deterministic k-head Turing machine represents a special case of a k-head Turing machine, the 'if' part of the equivalence stated in this theorem holds.

Only if
Section 8.1.2 has explained how to convert any Turing machine N to a deterministic Turing machine D satisfying $L(N) = L(D)$. By analogy with this conversion, transform any k-head Turing machine M to an equivalent deterministic k-head Turing machine; the exercises describes this transformation in detail. Thus, the 'only if' part of the equivalence holds.

Therefore, Theorem 8.1.4.3 holds. ∎

A method is now given that converts any deterministic k-head Turing machine M to an equivalent deterministic Turing machine D. D has a tape with $k + 1$ tracks. The first track, denoted by T-TRACK, corresponds to the original tape of M. The other tracks, denoted by H-TRACK[1] through H-TRACK[k], correspond to the k heads. For each j, H-TRACK[j] is completely blank, except for a single occurrence of a state placed in the square corresponding to the symbol scanned by the jth head of M. Consequently, the entire tape holds k state occurrences, all of which indicate the same state — the current state of the simulated machine, M. Figure 8.1.4.9 displays M together with the corresponding tape of D.

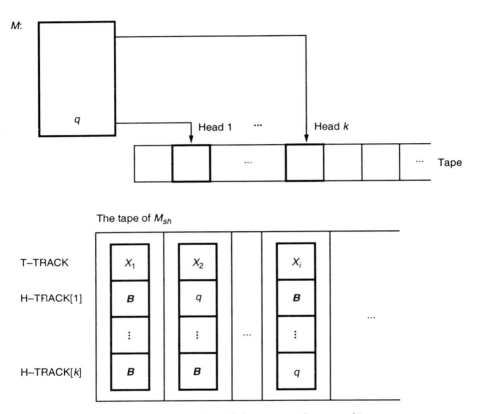

Figure 8.1.4.9 M together with the corresponding tape of D.

Initially, D's head scans the leftmost square, whose k head tracks contain s; T-TRACK contains the input word of M. To determine the k occurrences of s, D sweeps right on its tape, and if q appears at position i on H-TRACK[j], D records [j, i]. After D records all k occurrences of s, D finds out whether R has a rule applicable in the current configuration. If not, D rejects. If R contains an applicable rule, D updates all tracks according to this rule. Then, D accepts and halts provided that the new state, q, which appears on H-TRACK[1] through H-TRACK[k], is final; otherwise, D simulates another move from the new state.

Theorem 8.1.4.4
Let k be a natural number, and let L be a language. Then, $L = L(M)$ for a k-head deterministic Turing machine M if and only if $L = L(D)$ for a deterministic Turing machine D.

Proof

If
Any deterministic Turing machine actually represents a k-head deterministic Turing machine with $k = 1$, so the 'if' part of this theorem surely holds.

Only if
Let k be a natural number, and let $L = L(M)$ for a k-head deterministic Turing machine. This section has already shown how to convert M to an equivalent deterministic Turing machine, and the exercises discuss this conversion in detail. Thus, the 'only if' part of the proof holds.

Consequently, Theorem 8.1.4.4 holds.

∎

Turing machines with two-way infinite tapes

As its name indicates, a Turing machine with two-way infinite tapes has its tapes infinite both to the right and to the left (see Figure 8.1.4.10).

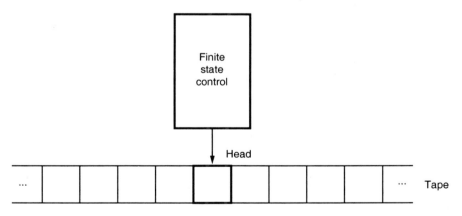

Figure 8.1.4.10 Turing machine with a two-way infinite tape.

Initially, a Turing machine M with a two-way infinite tape occurs in its start state with an input word w placed in $|w|$ contiguous squares; the other squares are blank. M's tape head occurs over the leftmost symbol of w. Starting from this initial configuration, M works by analogy with the basic model of a Turing machine (see Section 8.1.1). As opposed to this basic model, M can always make a left move because its tape is infinite to both directions, and this difference leads to the following modifications of some notions, such as the configuration.

Definition — configuration

Let $M = (Q, \Sigma, R, s, F)$ be a Turing machine with a two-way infinite tape. A *configuration* of M is a word χ satisfying

$$\chi \in ((\Sigma - \{B\})\Sigma^* \cup \{B\})Q(\Sigma^*(\Sigma - \{B\}) \cup \{B\})$$

♦

Notice that for a Turing machine $M = (Q, \Sigma, R, s, F)$, with a two-way infinite tape, a word of the form

$$qx$$

where $q \in Q$ and $x \in (\Sigma^*(\Sigma - \{B\}) \cup \{B\})$, represents no configuration. By contrast, if M is seen as a Turing machine with a semi-infinite tape, qx is a valid configuration of M.

Definition — move

Let $M = (Q, \Sigma, R, s, F)$ be a Turing machine with a two-way infinite tape, and let χ and χ' be two configurations of M. M makes a *move* from χ to χ' according to r, written as

$$\chi \vdash \chi' \quad [r]$$

if at least one of the following three conditions holds:

1. *Stationary move*

$$\chi = xpUy, \chi' = xqVy, \text{ and } r: pU \vdash qV\!\downarrow\, \in R;$$

2. *Right move*

$$\chi = xpUy, \chi' = x'Vqy', \text{ and } r: pU \vdash qV \hookrightarrow\, \in R,$$

where y' and x' are defined as

$y' = y$ if $y \neq \varepsilon$, and $y' = B$ if $y = \varepsilon$
$x' = x$ if $V \neq B$ or $x \neq B$, and $x' = \varepsilon$ if $V = B$ and $x = B$

3. *Left move*

$$\chi = xXpUy, \chi' = x'qXy', \text{ and } r: pU \vdash qV \lrcorner \in R,$$

where y' and x' are defined as

$y' = Vy$ if $V \neq B$ or $y \neq B$, and $y' = \varepsilon$ if $V = B$ and $y = B$
$x' = x$ if $x \neq \varepsilon$, and $x' = B$ if $x = \varepsilon$

◆

Although this definition resembles the definition of $\vdash$ for a Turing machine with a semi-infinite tape, there are two differences between these definitions:

1. Consider a Turing machine $M = (Q, \Sigma, R, s, F)$ with a two-way infinite tape. Let $BpUy$ be the current configuration of M. By using $pU \vdash qB \hookrightarrow \in R$, M makes this move

$$xpUy \vdash Bqy$$

However, if M is viewed as a Turing machine with a semi-infinite tape, then

$$xpUy \vdash BBqy \quad [pU \vdash qB \hookrightarrow]$$

in M.

2. From the description of a left move in the previous definition, a Turing machine with a two-way infinite tape can always make a left move. By contrast, if a Turing machine with a semi-infinite tape has its head over the leftmost tape square, then this machine can make no left move.

Return to the definition of $\vdash^*$ for a Turing machine in Section 8.11 by analogy with this definition, define $\vdash^*$ for a Turing machine with a two-way infinite tape.

Definition — accepted language

Let $M = (Q, \Sigma, R, s, F)$ be a Turing machine with a two-way infinite tape, and let $w \in \Sigma_I^*$. If $Bsw \vdash^* ufv$ in M, for some $f \in F$ and $u,v \in \Sigma^*$, then M accepts w. The *language accepted by* M, $L(M)$, is defined as

$$L(M) = \{w: w \in \Sigma_I^*, \text{ and } M \text{ accepts } w\}$$

That is,

$$L(M) = \{w: w \in \Sigma_I^* \text{ and } Bsw \vdash^* ufv \text{ for some } f \in F \text{ and } u,v \in \Sigma^*\}$$

◆

Definition — deterministic Turing machine with a two-way infinite tape
A Turing machine $M = (Q, \Sigma, R, s, F)$ with a two-way infinite tape is *deterministic* if every rule $r \in R$ satisfies

$$\text{lhs}(r) \notin \{\text{lhs}(r'): r' \in (R - \{r\})\}$$

♦

Theorem 8.1.4.5
Let L be a language. Then, $L = L(M)$ for a Turing machine M with a two-way infinite tape if and only if $L = L(D)$ for a deterministic Turing machine D with a two-way infinite tape.

Proof
Let L be a language.

If
Let $L = L(D)$, where D is a deterministic Turing machine D with a two-way infinite tape. Because D is a special case of a Turing machine with a two-way infinite tape, the 'if' part of the equivalence stated in the present theorem holds.

Only if
Section 8.1.2 describes a method that converts every Turing machine to an equivalent deterministic Turing machine. By analogy with this conversion, transform any Turing machine with a two-way infinite tape to an equivalent deterministic Turing machine with a two-way infinite tape; the exercises describe this transformation in detail. Thus, the 'only if' part of the equivalence holds.

Therefore, Theorem 8.1.4.5 holds.
■

The following description provides a simple method that transforms any deterministic Turing machine, having a semi-infinite tape, to an deterministic Turing machine with a two-way infinite tape. Consider a deterministic Turing machine, D. Construct a deterministic Turing machine M with a two-way infinite tape so M first uses a special symbol # to mark the square to the left of its initial head position and, then, acts as D. As M has no rule for #, M halts without acceptance if it reaches the square marked. As a result, M represents a deterministic Turing machine with a two-way infinite tape satisfying $L(M) = L(D)$.

Generalized models

Lemma 8.1.4.6
Let D be a deterministic Turing machine. Then, there exists a deterministic Turing machine, M, with a two-way infinite tape so $L(D) = L(M)$.

Proof
Let D be a deterministic Turing machine. This section has outlined the construction of a deterministic Turing machine M with a two-way infinite tape so $L(D) = L(M)$; the details of this construction are left to the axercises.

Therefore, Lemma 8.1.4.6 holds.

∎

A somewhat more difficult method is now given, with which to convert any deterministic Turing machine M with a two-way infinite tape to an equivalent deterministic Turing machine, D, which has a semi-infinite tape. Let $a_1...a_n$ be the input word of M, whose tape has its squares numbered as shown in Figure 8.1.4.11.

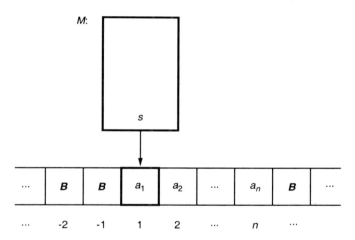

Figure 8.1.4.11 The initialization of M's tape together with the integers denoting the squares of this tape.

Machine D uses a two-track tape. Initially, D places two special symbols, ↘ and ↗, into the leftmost square's upper and lower track (neither of these two symbols appear anywhere else on the tape during D's computation). The input word, $a_1...a_n$, is placed into the n upper-track components following ↘ whereas the n lower-track components following ↗ are filled with Bs. The other squares are blank. This initialization is depicted in Figure 8.1.4.12, which also shows how the track components of Ds tape are numbered.

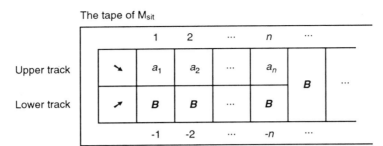

Figure 8.1.4.12 The initialization of D's tape together with integers denoting the components of this tape's tracks.

For every integer i, track component i on D's tape corresponds to square i on M's tape. That is, if M makes a move with its tape head scanning square j, where $j \geq 1$, then D simulates this move by using the upper track's component j. If M makes a move with its tape head scanning square k, where $k \leq -1$, then D simulates this move by using the lower track's component j (on the lower track, D moves in the direction opposite to the direction in which M moves). When simulating a move of M, D may need to shift its tape head to the right of the tape's two-track portion. At this point, before this shift, D first extends the two-track portion of the tape by rewriting the B that is adjacent to the right end of the two-track portion with a new two-track symbol, whose tracks contain B. The leftmost square of D's tape fulfils a special role: D uses this square to simulate either M's left move from square 1 to square -1 or M's right move from square -1 to square 1, as follows.

1. Assume that D simulates M's left move from square 1 to square -1. At this point, D shifts its tape head from the upper track's component 1 to the left, scans ↘, and, therefore, shifts the tape head down and to the right in order to reach component -1 (see Figure 8.1.4.13).

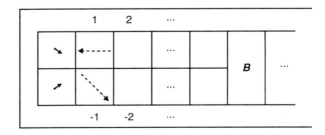

Figure 8.1.4.13 D's simulation of M's left move from square 1 to square -1.

2. Assume that D simulates M's right move from square -1 to square 1. Then, it shifts its tape head from the lower track's component -1 to the left, scans ⤢, and shifts the tape head up and to the right in order to reach component 1 (see Figure 8.1.4.14).

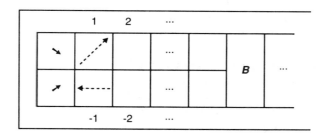

Figure 8.1.4.14 D's simulation of M's right move from square -1 to square 1.

Naturally, D accepts $a_1...a_n$ if and only if M accepts $a_1...a_n$; as a result, M represents a deterministic Turing machine with a two-way infinite tape satisfying $L(M) = L(D)$.

Lemma 8.1.4.7
Let M be a deterministic Turing machine M with a two-way infinite tape. Then, there exists a deterministic Turing machine D such that $L(D) = L(M)$.

Proof
Let M be a deterministic Turing machine with a two-way infinite tape. This section has already explained how to construct a deterministic Turing machine M, so $L(D) = L(M)$; the details of this constructions are left to the exercises.
Therefore, Lemma 8.1.4.7 holds.
■

Theorem 8.1.4.8
Let L be a language. Then, $L = L(M)$ for a deterministic Turing machine M with a two-way infinite tape if and only if $L = L(D)$ for a deterministic Turing machine D.

Proof
Theorem 8.1.4.8 follows from Lemmas 8.1.4.6 and 8.1.4.7.
■

The next theorem summarizes all the Turning machine variants covered so far.

Theorem 8.1.4.9
The following classes of computational models characterize the family of recursively enumerable languages.

1. Turing machines;
2. deterministic Turing machines;
3. deterministic Turing machines with one non-input tape symbol;
4. deterministic four-state Turing machines;
5. k-tape Turing machines, where $k \geq 1$;
6. deterministic k-tape Turing machines, where $k \geq 1$;
7. k-head Turing machines, where $k \geq 1$;
8. deterministic k-head Turing machines, where $k \geq 1$;
9. Turing machines with two-way infinite tape;
10. deterministic Turing machines with two-way infinite tape.

Proof
This theorem follows from Theorems 8.1.2.1 and 8.1.3.1, Corollary 8.1.3.2, and Theorems 8.1.3.7, 8.1.4.1, 8.1.4.2, 8.1.4.3, 8.1.4.4, 8.1.4.5 and 8.1.4.8. ■

8.1.5 Universality

A deterministic Turing machine defined by its rules resembles a program encoded by rudimentary instructions of a machine language. A program encoded in this way is executed by a computer, which actually acts as a universal machine that can compute every program written in the machine language. Analogously, the present section constructs a universal Turing machine U that can simulate every deterministic Turing machine M. More precisely, U reads the description of M together with an input word w and then simulates the moves that M makes with w (see Figure 8.1.5.1). U accepts if and only if $w \in L(M)$.

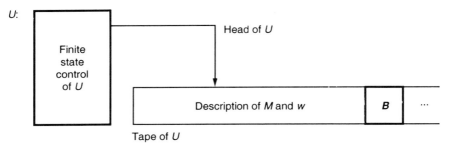

Figure 8.1.5.1 A universal Turing machine U.

In addition to the construction of U, this section defines a language that no Turing machine accepts and, thereby, proves that not all languages are recursively enumerable.

Turing machine description

Before the construction of U, it is necessary to describe any deterministic Turing machine M in binary. Assume that M has the form

$$M = (Q, \Sigma_I \cup \{B\}, R, q_0, \{q_1\})$$

Less formally, M has only one non-input tape symbol, B. Furthermore, M contains one final state, q_1, and its start state is denoted by q_0. From Corollary 8.1.3.2, Algorithm 8.1.3.4 and Lemma 8.1.3.5, this assumption represents no loss of generality. Concerning Q and $\Sigma_I \cup \{B\}$, the following conventions introduce a fixed notation.

Conventions

1. $Q \subseteq \Theta$, where

$$\Theta = \{q_0, q_1, q_2, \ldots\}$$

2. $(\Sigma_I \cup \{B\}) \subseteq I$, where

$$I = \{a_0, a_1, a_2, \ldots\}$$

so that $B = a_0$.

●

Notice that neither of these two conventions represent any loss of generality. Indeed, the states of any deterministic Turing machine can be always renamed so the first convention holds and the language accepted by the machine remains unchanged. Furthermore, as I is infinite, the assumption that I contains all symbols that can ever appear as an input symbol of a deterministic Turing machine is also without any loss of generality, so the second convention does not represent any loss of generality either.

The following definition explains how to describe every deterministic Turing machine in binary.

Definition — binary description of a deterministic Turing machine

Let δ be the function from

$$(\Theta \cup I \cup \{B, \hookrightarrow, \dashv, \downarrow\}) \text{ to } \{0, 1\}^*$$

defined as

$\delta(\downarrow) = 01$

$\delta(\lrcorner) = 001$
$\delta(\hookrightarrow) = 0001$
$\delta(q_i) = \delta(a_i) = 0^{i+1}1$, for all $i \geq 0$

Let

$$M = (Q, \Sigma_I \cup \{B\}, R, q_0, \{q_1\})$$

be a deterministic Turing machine. For every $r: pU \vdash qVt \in R$, define

$$\delta(r) = \delta(p)\delta(U)\delta(q)\delta(V)\delta(t)1$$

Let $R = \{r_0, r_1, \ldots, r_m\}$, where $m = \text{card}(R)$; then,

$$\delta(M) = 111\delta(r_0)\delta(r_1)\ldots\delta(r_m)1$$

is the *description* of M, denoted by $\delta(M)$.

◆

From the definition of δ, any binary word, $w \in \{0, 1\}^*$, describes no more than one deterministic Turing machine. In addition, the exercises design a simple algorithm that finds out whether w describes a deterministic Turing machine, and if so, then this algorithm converts w to the deterministic Turing machine described by w. More formally, if $w = \delta(M)$, where M is a deterministic Turing machine, then this algorithm converts $\delta(M)$ to M.

Example 8.1.5.1 Part 1 Binary description of a deterministic Turing machine

Consider the following deterministic Turing machine M:

1: $q_0 a_1 \vdash q_4 B \hookrightarrow$
2: $q_4 a_1 \vdash q_4 a_1 \hookrightarrow$
3: $q_4 a_2 \vdash q_4 a_2 \hookrightarrow$
4: $q_4 B \vdash q_2 B \lrcorner$
5: $q_2 a_2 \vdash q_3 B \lrcorner$
6: $q_3 a_1 \vdash q_3 a_1 \lrcorner$
7: $q_3 a_2 \vdash q_3 a_2 \lrcorner$
8: $q_3 B \vdash q_0 B \hookrightarrow$
9: $q_0 B \vdash q_1 B \downarrow$

Generalized models

Observe that M satisfies all conventions introduced by this section. (Notice that M resembles the Turing machine discussed in Example 8.1.1.1. Indeed, M renamed q_4 to q_1 and vice versa; in addition, M uses a_1 and a_2 instead of a and b, respectively. Otherwise, both machines coincide.)

The present example converts M to its binary description $\delta(M)$. From the definition of δ,

$\delta(\downarrow) = 01$
$\delta(\lrcorner) = 001$
$\delta(\hookrightarrow) = 0001$

The states are described as

$\delta(q_0) = 01$
$\delta(q_1) = 001$
$\delta(q_2) = 0001$
$\delta(q_3) = 00001$
$\delta(q_4) = 000001$

From the definition of δ,

$\delta(B) = 01$
$\delta(a_1) = 001$
$\delta(a_2) = 0001$

Consider the first rule,

$$1: q_0 a_1 \vdash q_4 B \hookrightarrow$$

Observe that

$$\delta(1) = \delta(q_0)\delta(a_1)\delta(q_4)\delta(B)\delta(\hookrightarrow)1 = 010010000010100011$$

Analogously, transform the other rules into their binary description. Then, determine $\delta(M)$ as

$\delta(M) = 111\delta(1)\delta(2)\delta(3)\delta(4)\delta(5)\delta(6)\delta(7)\delta(8)\delta(9)1$

$\quad = \delta(q_0)\delta(a_1)\delta(q_4)\delta(B)\delta(\hookrightarrow)1\delta(q_4)\delta(a_1)\delta(q_4)\delta(B)\delta(\hookrightarrow)1$
$\quad \delta(q_4)\delta(a_2)\delta(q_4)\delta(a_2)\delta(\hookrightarrow)1\delta(q_4)\delta(B)\delta(q_2)\delta(B)\delta(\lrcorner)1$
$\quad \delta(q_2)\delta(a_2)\delta(q_3)\delta(B)\delta(\lrcorner)1\delta(q_3)\delta(a_1)\delta(q_3)\delta(a_1)\delta(\lrcorner)1$
$\quad \delta(q_3)\delta(a_2)\delta(q_3)\delta(a_2)\delta(\lrcorner)1\delta(q_3)\delta(B)\delta(q_0)\delta(B)\delta(\hookrightarrow)1$
$\quad \delta(q_0)\delta(B)\delta(q_1)\delta(B)\delta(\downarrow)11$

= 11101001000001010001100000100100000010100011
0000010001000001000100011000001010001010011
000100010000101001100001001000010010011
000010001000010001001100001010101000011
0101001010111

This binary word thus represents $\delta(M)$, the description of M in binary. △

The next definition uses δ to describe words in binary.

Definition — binary description of word

Let δ be the function introduced in the previous definition, K be an alphabet such that $K \subseteq I$, and $w \in K^*$. The *description* of w, denoted $\delta(w)$, is defined as follows:

1. if $w = \varepsilon$, then $\delta(w) = \varepsilon$;
2. if $w = a_1\ldots a_n$, where $n \geq 1$, and for $i = 1, \ldots, n$, $a_i \in K$, then $\delta(w) = \delta(a_1)\ldots\delta(a_n)$. ◆

Example 8.1.5.1 Part 2 Binary description of a word

As already stated in the previous part of this example,

$$\delta(a_1) = 001 \text{ and } \delta(a_2) = 0001$$

Consider $a_1 a_1 a_2 a_2$. Observe that

$$\delta(a_1 a_1 a_2 a_2) = \delta(a_1)\delta(a_1)\delta(a_2)\delta(a_2) = 00100100010001$$

△

Three-tape universal Turing machine

A deterministic three-tape Turing machine T is now constructed which acts as a universal Turing machine. That is, for any deterministic Turing machine M and any input word w, T reads $\delta(M)\delta(w)$, simulates moves that M makes with w, and accepts w if and only if M accepts w.

Generalized models

Example 8.1.5.1 Part 3 Binary description of a deterministic Turing machine and a word

Return to the deterministic Turing machine M and its description $\delta(M)$, discussed in Part 1 of Example 8.1.5.1. The second part of this example considers $a_1a_1a_2a_2$ and produced its description as $\delta(a_1a_1a_2a_2)$. Observe that $\delta(M)\delta(a_1a_1a_2a_2)$ equals

11101001000001010001100000100100000101000110000100010000010001000110000
10100010100110001000100001010011000010010000100100110000100010000010001001
1000010101010001101010010101110010010001000010001

This binary word represents a typical example of an input supplied to T — the deterministic three-tape Turing machine, whose construction follows next.

▲

Assume that T has its three tapes denoted by $TAPE_1$, $TAPE_2$ and $TAPE_3$. Initially, $TAPE_1$ contains a binary word x while $TAPE_2$ and $TAPE_3$ are blank. T verifies that x is of the form $\delta(M)\delta(w)$, for a deterministic Turing machine M and an input word w; if not, T rejects its input and halts. Figure 8.1.5.2 depicts T with x satisfying the required form; that is, $x = \delta(M)\delta(w)$.

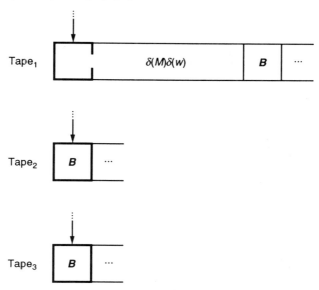

Figure 8.1.5.2 The initial configuration of T.

During the simulation of moves made by M on w, T uses its three tapes as follows:

1. $TAPE_1$ fulfills the role of M's tape, so it contains $\delta(w)$;
2. $TAPE_2$ contains $\delta(M)$;
3. $TAPE_3$ contains $\delta(q)$, where q represents the current state of M.

Therefore, to begin this simulation, T changes the initial containment of its tapes, displayed in Figure 8.1.5.2, as follows:

A. $\delta(M)$ is moved from $TAPE_1$ to $TAPE_2$;
B. $\delta(w)$ is shifted to the left so it begins at the leftmost square of $TAPE_1$;
C. 01 is placed onto $TAPE_3$ because $01 = \delta(q_0)$, where q_0 is the start state of M.

Figure 8.1.5.3 describes T's configuration after these changes. Starting from this configuration, T simulates moves made by M on w. T accepts and halts if and only if 001 appears on $TAPE_3$ because $001 = \delta(q_1)$ and q_1 represents the final state of M. Consequently, T accepts $\delta(M)\delta(w)$ if and only if M accepts w.

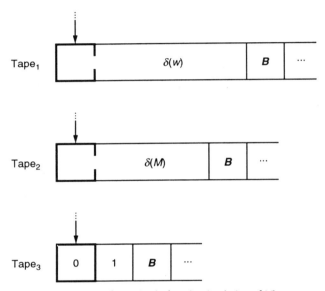

Figure 8.1.5.3 T's configuration before the simulation of M's moves.

To explain how T simulates a move made by M, suppose that $TAPE_3$ contains $\delta(q_j) = 0^{j+1}1$, for some $j \geq 0$, where q_j is a state of M. As already noted, if $j = 1$, M_u accepts and stops the simulation because q_1 is the final state of M. Assume that $j \neq 1$, meaning that q_j represents a non-final state of M. Let $TAPE_1$ contain

$$\delta(ya_iz)B\ldots$$

where the leftmost symbol of $\delta(a_i)$ is currently scanned by the $TAPE_1$ head. To simulate a move that M makes with a_i, T scans $\delta(M)$ on $TAPE_2$ to find out whether M has an applicable rule; that is, a rule r with

$$\mathrm{lhs}(r) = q_j a_i$$

Generalized models

If M possesses no rule satisfying this condition, T halts and rejects because $w \notin L(M)$. However, if M has a rule of the form

$$r: q_j a_i \vdash q_l a_k \hookrightarrow,$$

T simulates this right move in M.

$$y q_j a_i z \vdash y a_k q_l z \qquad [r]$$

T performs this simulation by changing $TAPE_1$ and $TAPE_3$ as follows:

1. on $TAPE_1$, T replaces $\delta(a_i)$ with $\delta(a_k)$ and, in addition, shifts the $TAPE_1$ head k squares to the right in order to scan the leftmost symbol of $\delta(z)$ in the next move;
2. on $TAPE_3$, T replace $\delta(q_j)$ with $\delta(q_l)$ on $TAPE_3$.

Analogously, T simulates a left move in M except that during this simulation, T shifts the $TAPE_1$ head to the left. Finally, T simulates a stationary move in M without shifting the $TAPE_1$ head at all.

Next T is described by

function UTM(Description): boolean

where Description contains T's input word. This function exits with UTM = **true** if and only if $w \in L(M)$.

UTM uses $TAPE_k[i,j]$ to refer to the word of symbols contained in $TAPE_k$'s squares i through j, where i, j and k are natural numbers satisfying $1 \leq i \leq j$ and $k \in \{1, 2, 3\}$; $TAPE_k[i, i]$ is simplified to $TAPE_k[i]$. Furthermore, UTM contain

function Transformation (Description): boolean

and

procedure Replace($TAPE_k[i,j]$, $TAPE_l[m, n]$)

The functions Transformation and Replace are briefly outlined here; their detailed description is left to the exercises.

The Transformation function reads the word x contained in Description and then verifies that

$$x = \delta(M)\delta(w)$$

for a deterministic Turing machine M and an input word w. If $x = \delta(M)\delta(w)$, Transformation transforms $TAPE_1$ through $TAPE_3$ as shown in Figure 8.1.5.3; then it exits with Transformation = **true**. If x has an improper form, this function exits with Transformation = **false**.

In greater detail, to exit with Transformation = **true**, this function first examines whether

$$x = vu$$

where v is the prefix satisfying $111 \in \text{suffix}(v)$ and $111 \notin \text{subword}(v) - v$. If so, Transformation finds out whether $u = \delta(M)$, for a deterministic Turing machine. Then, Transformation tests whether $u = \delta(w)$ for an input word w. Having verified that $x = \delta(M)\delta(w)$, Transformation copies $\delta(M)$ onto TAPE_2, moves $\delta(w)$ to the leftmost square on TAPE_1, and fills the two leftmost squares of TAPE_3 with 0 and 1. Then, this function sets Transformation = **true** and exits.

With Replace($\text{TAPE}k[i,j]$, $\text{TAPE}l[m,n]$), UTM replaces $\text{TAPE}_k[i,j]$ with $\text{TAPE}_l[m,n]$. If $|\text{TAPE}_l[m,n]| = |\text{TAPE}_k[i,j]|$, then $\text{TAPE}_k[i,j]$ can be replaced by $\text{TAPE}_l[m,n]$ without any prearrangement of TAPE_k. If, however, $|\text{TAPE}_l[m,n]| \neq |\text{TAPE}_k[i,j]|$, Replace shifts the non-blank suffix following $\text{TAPE}_k[j]$ before the replacement occurs. Depending on the difference between $|\text{TAPE}_l[m,n]|$ and $|\text{TAPE}_k[i,j]|$, Replace makes two kinds of this shift:

1. Let $|\text{TAPE}_k[i,j]| - |\text{TAPE}_l[m,n]| = h > 0$. At this point, Replace shifts the non-blank suffix following $\text{TAPE}_k[j]$ to the left by h squares and, then, replaces $\text{TAPE}_k[i, j-h]$ with $\text{TAPE}_l[m,n]$.

2. Let $|\text{TAPE}_l[m,n]| - |\text{TAPE}_k[i,j]| = h > 0$. Then, Replace shifts the non-blank suffix following $\text{TAPE}_k[j]$ to the right by h squares before it replaces $\text{TAPE}_k[i, j+h]$ with $\text{TAPE}_l[m,n]$.

UTM follows next.

function UTM(Description): **boolean**;

type
    Acceptance = (YES, NO, MAYBE);

var

    Accepted: Acceptance;
    Counter: $0..k$;
    Head1, Head2: **integer**;
    W1, W2, W3, W4, W5, W6, W7, W8: **integer** {W1 through W8 act as temporary counters and tape pointers};

begin

Generalized models

```
if Transformation (Description) = false
then Accepted := NO
else Accepted := MAYBE;

Head1 := 1;

while Accepted = MAYBE do
  if TAPE₃[1,3] = 001 {001 = δ(q₁), where q₁ is the final state}
  then Accepted := YES
  else
  begin
    W1 := 1;
    while TAPE₃[W1] ≠ 1 do
      W1 := W1 + 1    {if TAPE₃ contains 0^{j+1}1 = δ(qⱼ), then
                        W1 = |δ(qⱼ)| = j + 2};
    W2 := Head1 {Head1 points to the beginning of δ(aᵢ), written as 0^{i+1}1 on
                  TAPE₁, aᵢ is the currently scanned symbol};
    while TAPE₁[W2] ≠ 1 do
      W2 := W2 + 1 {W2 points to 1 in 0^{i+1}1};

    Head2 := 2;

    {The following loop searches TAPE₂ for a rule whose left-hand side coincides
    with the current state and the currently scanned symbol, which are
    described in TAPE₃[1, W1] and TAPE₁[Head1, W2], respectively}
    repeat
      while TAPE₂[Head2, Head2+1] ≠ 11 do
        Head2 := Head2 + 1;
    until

      (TAPE₂[Head2+2] = 1)

    or

      ((TAPE₃[1,W1] = TAPE₂[Head2 + 2, Head2 + W1 + 1]) and
      (TAPE₁[Head1, W2] = TAPE₂[Head2+W1+2, Head2+W1+2+(W2-Head1)]))
      {if TAPE₂[Head2+2] = 1, this search has reached 111, meaning that there
      exists no applicable rule; otherwise, this search ends when it finds an applic-
      able rule};

    if TAPE₂[Head2+2] = 1
    then Accepted := NO {no applicable rule}
    else
      begin
```

Head2 := Head2 + 2
   {Head2 points to the leftmost symbol of $\delta(r)$, where

$$r: q_j a_i \vdash q_l a_k t,$$

written as

$$\delta(q_j)\delta(a_i)\delta(q_l)\delta(a_k)\delta(t)$$

on $TAPE_2$. The next move is simulated according to this rule.};

W3 := Head2+W1+ (W2-Head1) + 1
   {W3 points to the beginning position of $\delta(q_l)$};

W4 := W3;
while $TAPE_2[W4] \neq 1$ **do**
   W4 := W4 + 1 {W4 points to the end of $\delta(q_l)$};

W5 := W4 + 1 {W5 points to the beginning of $\delta(a_k)$};

W6 := W5;
while $TAPE_2[W6] \neq 1$ **do**
   W6 := W6 + 1 {W6 points to the end position of $\delta(a_k)$};

Replace($TAPE_1$[Head1, W2], $TAPE_2$[W5, W6]);
Replace($TAPE_3$[1, W1], $TAPE_2$[W3, W4]);

W7 := W6 + 1 {W7 points to the beginning position of $\delta(t)$};

W8 := W6 + 3;

case $TAPE_2$[W7, W8] **of** {$\delta(t) \in \{01, 001, 001\}$, so $TAPE_2$[W7, W8] = 011 or 001 or 000, describing $\downarrow$ or $\dashv$ or $\hookrightarrow$, respectively}

011: {stationary move};

001: {left move}
   if Head1 = 1
   then Accepted := NO {from the leftmost square, no left move can be made}
   else
   begin
      Head1 := Head1 − 3;
      while $TAPE_1$[Head1] $\neq$ 1 **and** Head1 > 1 **do**
         Head1 := Head1 − 1;

```
                        if Head1 > 1
                          then Head1 := Head1 + 1;
                        end;

              000: {right move}
                    Head1 := Head1 + (W5 - W6) + 1;
                    if TAPE₁[Head1] = B
                      then TAPE₁[Head1, Head1 + 1] := 01 {the binary tape portion is
                            extended by replacing BB, following the right end of the
                            binary portion, with δ(B) = 01}
                  end{case};
                end{else};
              end{else};

      if Accepted = YES
        then UTM := true
        else UTM := false

end.
```

Theorem 8.1.5.1

There exists a deterministic three-tape Turing machine T such that for every deterministic Turing machine, $M = (Q, \Sigma_I \cup \{B\}, R, q_0, \{q_1\})$ with $Q \subseteq \Theta$ and $\Sigma_I \subseteq I$, and every $w \in \Sigma_I^*$, the following equivalence holds:

$$w \in L(M) \text{ if and only if } \delta(M)\delta(w) \in L(T)$$

Proof

UTM acts as a deterministic three-tape Turing machine T satisfying this theorem, which is formally verified in the exercises.

∎

Universal Turing machine

Section 8.1.4 explains how to convert a k-tape deterministic Turing machine to an equivalent deterministic Turing machine. Analogously, the deterministic three-tape Turing machine T specified by UTM, can be transformed to an equivalent deterministic universal Turing machine U.

Theorem 8.1.5.2

There exists a deterministic Turing machine U such that for every deterministic Turing machine, $M = (Q, \Sigma_I \cup \{B\}, R, q_0, \{q_1\})$ with $Q \subseteq \Theta$ and $\Sigma_I \subseteq I$, and every $w \in \Sigma_I^*$, this equivalence holds:

$$w \in L(M) \text{ if and only if } \delta(M)\delta(w) \in L(U)$$

Proof
A detailed proof of this theorem is left to the exercises. ∎

The machine U is universal in that it can simulate every deterministic Turing machine.

Beyond recursively enumerable languages

Based on δ, the remainder of this section defines a language that no Turing machine accepts and, thereby, demonstrates that some languages are not recursively enumerable.

Consider the binary language

$L_{\text{SelfAcceptance}} = \{\ \delta(M): M = (Q, \{0, 1, B\}, R, q_0, \{q_1\})$ is a deterministic Turing machine, where $\Sigma_I = \{0, 1\}$ and $Q \subseteq \Theta$, and $\delta(M) \in L(M)\}$

Less formally, $L_{\text{SelfAcceptance}}$ contains $\delta(M)$ if and only if M is a deterministic Turing machine, $M = (Q, \{0, 1, B\}, R, q_0, \{q_1\})$, that accepts its description, $\delta(M)$. The complement of $L_{\text{SelfAcceptance}}$ is $L_{\text{NonSelfAcceptance}}$; that is,

$$L_{\text{NonSelfAcceptance}} = \{0, 1\}^* - L_{\text{SelfAcceptance}}$$

It is now proved that whereas $L_{\text{SelfAcceptance}}$ is recursively enumerable, $L_{\text{NonSelfAcceptance}}$ does not represent a recursively enumerable language. To prove that $L_{\text{SelfAcceptance}}$ is recursively enumerable, first consider

$L_{\text{Acceptance}} = \{\delta(M)\delta(w): M = (Q, \{0, 1, B\}, R, q_0, \{q_1\})$ is a deterministic Turing machine, where $\Sigma_I = \{0, 1\}$, $Q \subseteq \Theta$, and $w \in L(M)\}$

In other words, $L_{\text{Acceptance}}$ contains a binary word x if and only if $x = \delta(M)\delta(w)$, where M is a deterministic Turing machine $M = (Q, \{0, 1, B\}, R, q_0, \{q_1\})$, and w is a binary word accepted by M.

Lemma 8.1.5.3
$L_{\text{Acceptance}}$ is recursively enumerable.

Proof
This section constructs the universal Turing machine U so

$$\delta(M)\delta(w) \in L(U) \text{ if and only if } w \in L(M)$$

where $M = (Q, \Sigma, R, q_0, \{q_1\})$ is a deterministic Turing machine, $Q \subseteq \Theta$, and $(\Sigma_I \cup \{B\}) \subseteq I$. In other words,

$$L(U) = L_{\text{Acceptance}}$$

Thus, $L_{\text{Acceptance}}$ is recursively enumerable. ∎

Lemma 8.1.5.4
$L_{\text{SelfAcceptance}}$ is recursively enumerable.

Proof
Based on U, this proof constructs a deterministic Turing machine V that accepts $L_{\text{SelfAcceptance}}$. Given an input word w, V first checks whether

$$w = \delta(M)$$

for a deterministic Turing machine, $M = (Q, \{0, 1, B\}, R, q_0, \{q_1\})$, where $\Sigma_I = \{0, 1\}$ and $Q \subseteq \Theta$. If not, V rejects w and halts; otherwise, V places $\delta(M)\delta(M)$ on its tape and then works as U. Observe that V satisfies

$$V \text{ accepts } \delta(M) \text{ if and only if } U \text{ accepts } \delta(M)\delta(M)$$

for every deterministic Turing machine, $M = (Q, \Sigma, R, q_0, \{q_1\})$, where $Q \subseteq \Theta$ and $(\Sigma_I \cup \{B\}) \subseteq I$. That is,

$$\delta(M) \in L(V) \text{ if and only if } \delta(M)\delta(M) \in L(U)$$

As $L(U) = L_{\text{Acceptance}}$,

$$\delta(M)\delta(M) \in L(U) \text{ if and only if } \delta(M)\delta(M) \in L_{\text{Acceptance}}$$

From the definition of $L_{\text{Acceptance}}$,

$$\delta(M)\delta(M) \in L_{\text{Acceptance}} \text{ if and only if } \delta(M) \in L(M)$$

These equivalences imply that

$$\delta(M) \in L(V) \text{ if and only if } \delta(M) \in L(M)$$

From the definition of $L_{\text{SelfAcceptance}}$,

$$\delta(M) \in L(V) \text{ if and only if } \delta(M) \in L_{\text{SelfAcceptance}}$$

That is,

$$L(V) = L_{\text{SelfAcceptance}}$$

Therefore, $L_{\text{SelfAcceptance}}$ is recursively enumerable. The details of this proof are left to the exercises. ∎

The proof of the next lemma, stating that $L_{\text{NonSelfAcceptance}}$ is not recursively enumerable, includes an enumeration

$$M_1, M_2, \ldots$$

of all deterministic Turing machines that have the form

$$M = (Q, \{0, 1, B\}, R, q_0, \{q_1\})$$

where $\Sigma_I = \{0, 1\}$ and $Q \subseteq \Theta$. To obtain this enumeration, for every deterministic Turing machine M satisfying this form, consider the word

$$\text{lhs}(r_0)\text{rhs}(r_0)\text{lhs}(r_1)\text{rhs}(r_1)\ldots\text{lhs}(r_m)\text{rhs}(r_m)$$

where $\{r_0, r_1, \ldots, r_m\}$ is the set of rules in M; notice that this word completely determines M. To obtain $M_1, M_2, \ldots$, enumerate all these words according to length and alphabetic order; the details of this simple method are left to the exercises.

Lemma 8.1.5.5

$L_{\text{NonSelfAcceptance}}$ is not recursively enumerable.

Generalized models

Proof

Let

$$M_1, M_2, \ldots$$

be an enumeration of all deterministic Turing machines that satisfy the form

$$M = (Q, \{0, 1, B\}, R, q_0, \{q_1\})$$

with $\Sigma_I = \{0, 1\}$ and $Q \subseteq \Theta$. Consider an infinite binary matrix B whose rows are denoted by $M_1, M_2, \ldots$ and whose columns are denoted by $\delta(M_1), \delta(M_2), \ldots$. B's entry in row M_i and column $\delta(M_j)$ equals 1 if and only if $\delta(M_j) \in L(M_i)$; more formally,

$$B[M_i, \delta(M_j)] = 1 \text{ if and only if } \delta(M_j) \in L(M_i)$$

Consequently, the entry in row i and column j equals 0 if and only if $\delta(M_j) \notin L(M_i)$; formally,

$$B[M_i, \delta(M_j)] = 0 \text{ if and only if } \delta(M_j) \notin L(M_i)$$

Figure 8.1.5.4 describes B, whose entry in row M_i and column $\delta(Mj)$ is 1, so $\delta(M_j) \in L(M_i)$.

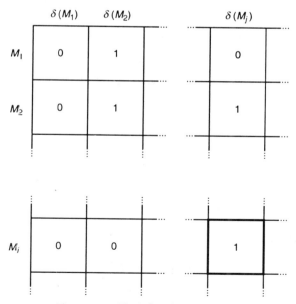

Figure 8.1.5.4 The infinite binary matrix B.

Consider the entries on the diagonal of B. For all $i \geq 1$, the entry in row i and column i equals 1 if and only if $\delta(M_i) \in L(M_i)$; formally,

$$B[M_i, \delta(M_i)] = 1 \text{ if and only if } \delta(M_i) \in L(M_i)$$

Thus, by the definition of $L_{\text{SelfAcceptance}}$,

$$B[M_i, \delta(M_i)] = 1 \text{ if and only if } \delta(M_i) \in L_{\text{SelfAcceptance}}$$

Therefore,

$$B[M_i, \delta(M_i)] = 0 \text{ if and only if } \delta(M_i) \notin L_{\text{SelfAcceptance}}$$

$L_{\text{NonSelfAcceptance}}$ represents the complement of $L_{\text{SelfAcceptance}}$, so

$$B[M_i, \delta(M_i)] = 0 \text{ if and only if } \delta(M_i) \in L_{\text{NonSelfAcceptance}}$$

Figure 8.1.5.5 displays B's diagonal entries, where $\delta(M_n) \in L_{\text{SelfAcceptance}}$ and $\delta(M_m) \in L_{\text{NonSelfAcceptance}}$.

By contradiction, this proof next demonstrates that $L_{\text{NonSelfAcceptance}}$ is not recursively enumerable. Suppose that $L_{\text{NonSelfAcceptance}}$ is recursively enumerable. As

$$L_{\text{NonSelfAcceptance}} \subseteq \{0, 1\}^*$$

Theorem 8.1.3.6 implies that $L_{\text{NonSelfAcceptance}}$ is accepted by a deterministic Turing machine that satisfies the form

$$M = (Q, \{0, 1, B\}, R, q_0, \{q_1\})$$

with $\Sigma_I = \{0, 1\}$ and $Q \subseteq \Theta$. Then, for some $k \geq 1$, M_k in the enumeration $M_1, M_2, \ldots$ satisfies

$$L_{\text{NonSelfAcceptance}} = L(M_k)$$

Consider the kth diagonal entry, $B[M_k, \delta(M_k)]$, and distinguish the two cases $B[M_k, \delta(M_k)] = 1$ and $B[M_k, \delta(M_k)] = 0$.

1. Suppose that $B[M_k, \delta(M_k)] = 1$, so

$$\delta(M_k) \in L(M_k)$$

As $L(M_k) = L_{\text{NonSelfAcceptance}}$,

$$\delta(M_k) \in L_{\text{NonSelfAcceptance}}$$

Generalized models

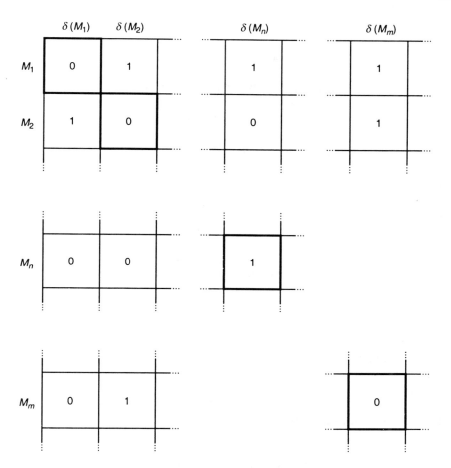

Figure 8.1.5.5 The diagonal of B.

Because $\delta(M_k) \in L_{\text{NonSelfAcceptance}}$ if and only if $B[M_k, \delta(M_k)] = 0$,

$$B[M_k, \delta(M_k)] = 0$$

However, $B[M_k, \delta(M_k)] = 0$ contradicts $B[M_k, \delta(M_k)] = 1$.

2. Suppose that $B[M_k, \delta(M_k)] = 0$, so

$$\delta(M_k) \notin L(M_k)$$

As $L(M_k) = L_{\text{NonSelfAcceptance}}$,

$$\delta(M_k) \notin L_{\text{NonSelfAcceptance}}$$

Thus,

$$\delta(M_k) \in L_{\text{SelfAcceptance}}$$

Because $\delta(M_i) \in L_{\text{SelfAcceptance}}$ if and only if $B[M_i, \delta(M_i)] = 1$,

$$B[M_k, \delta(M_k)] = 1$$

However, $B[M_k, \delta(M_k)] = 1$ contradicts $B[M_k, \delta(M_k)] = 0$.

In both cases, a contradiction arises, so $L_{\text{NonSelfAcceptance}}$ is not recursively enumerable.

Therefore, Lemma 8.1.5.5 holds. ∎

From Lemma 8.1.5.5, $L_{\text{NonSelfAcceptance}}$ represents a language that no Turing machine accepts. Therefore, not all languages are recursively enumerable, as the next theorem states.

Theorem 8.1.5.6
The family of all languages properly contains the family of recursively enumerable languages.

Proof
This theorem follows from Lemma 8.1.5.5. ∎

Lemmas 8.1.5.4 and 8.1.5.5 also imply the following non-closure property concerning the family of recursively enumerable languages.

Theorem 8.1.5.7
The family of recursively enumerable languages is not closed under complement.

Proof
Recall that $L_{\text{NonSelfAcceptance}}$ is the complement of $L_{\text{SelfAcceptance}}$. From Lemma 8.1.5.4, $L_{\text{SelfAcceptance}}$ represents a recursively enumerable language. By contrast, Lemma 8.1.5.5 demonstrates that $L_{\text{NonSelfAcceptance}}$ is not a recursively enumerable language. Hence, Theorem 8.1.5.7 holds. ∎

8.1.6 Turing machines that always halt

From Church's thesis, Turing machines can simulate all procedures. By investigating deterministic Turing machines that always halt, this section restricts its attention to Turing machines that simulate algorithms (see Section 2.3). These machines are less powerful than Turing machines. Indeed, deterministic Turing machines that always halt define the family of recursive languages, that is properly included in the family of recursively enumerable languages.

Definition — recursive language
Let L be a language. If $L = L(M)$, where M is a deterministic Turing machine that always halts, then L is a *recursive language*.

◆

To prove that some recursively enumerable languages are not recursive, first establish a closure property concerning the family of recursive languages.

Theorem 8.1.6.1
The family of recursive languages is closed under complement

Proof
Let L be a recursive language, and let $L = L(M)$, where M is a deterministic Turing machine that always halts. Construct a deterministic Turing machine M' so that with every input word, w, M' acts as M except that M' decides the acceptance of w according to these two equivalences:

1. M' accepts w by entering a final state and halts if and only if M halts without accepting its input;
2. M' halts without accepting its input if and only if M accepts w.

As M always halts, M' always halts as well. Furthermore, observe that M' accepts the complement of $L(M)$, so this complement is recursive.

Thus, Theorem 8.1.6.1, whose detailed proof is left to the Exercises, holds.

■

Theorem 8.1.6.2
The family of recursively enumerable languages properly contains the family of recursive languages.

Proof
As every recursive language is recursively enumerable, the family of recursively enumerable languages surely contains the family of recursive languages. By

Theorem 8.1.5.7, the family of recursively enumerable languages is not closed under complement. By Theorem 8.1.6.1, however, the family of recursive languages is closed under complement. Consequently, some recursively enumerable languages are not recursive, so the family of recursively enumerable languages properly contains the family of recursive languages.

Thus, Theorem 8.1.6.2 holds. ∎

From Theorem 8.1.6.2, deterministic Turing machines that always halt cannot accept all recursively enumerable languages. In other words, some recursively enumerable languages can be accepted only by deterministic Turing machines that run endlessly on some input words. $L_{\text{SelfAcceptance}}$ and $L_{\text{Acceptance}}$, defined in the previous section, represent languages of this kind.

Theorem 8.1.6.3

$L_{\text{SelfAcceptance}}$ is a recursively enumerable language that is not recursive.

Proof
From Lemma 8.1.5.4, $L_{\text{SelfAcceptance}}$ represents a recursively enumerable language. From Lemma 8.1.5.5, $L_{\text{NonSelfAcceptance}}$ is not recursively enumerable. As $L_{\text{NonSelfAcceptance}}$ is the complement of $L_{\text{SelfAcceptance}}$, Theorem 8.1.6.1 implies that $L_{\text{SelfAcceptance}}$ is a nonrecursive language. Thus, Theorem 8.1.6.3 holds. ∎

Theorem 8.1.6.4

$L_{\text{Acceptance}}$ is a recursively enumerable language that is not recursive.

Proof
From Lemma 8.1.5.3, $L_{\text{Acceptance}}$ is recursively enumerable.

The following part of this proof, demonstrating that $L_{\text{Acceptance}}$ is not recursive, is made by contradiction. Suppose that $L_{\text{Acceptance}}$ is recursive. Let $L = L(M_1)$, where M_1 is a deterministic Turing machine that always halts. From M_1, construct another deterministic Turing machine, M_2, as follows. First, M_2 checks whether its input word satisfies the form $\delta(M)$, where $M = (Q, \{0, 1, B\}, R, s, \{f\})$ is a deterministic Turing machine with $\Sigma_I = \{0, 1\}$ and $Q \subseteq \Theta$ (Θ has the same meaning as in the previous section). If the input does not satisfy this form, M_2 rejects the input and halts. However, if the input word satisfies the form $\delta(M)$, M_2 places $\delta(M)\delta(M)$ on its tape and then works as M_1. M_2 accepts $\delta(M)$ and halts if and only if M_1 accepts $\delta(M)\delta(M)$. M_2 rejects $\delta(M)$ and halts if and only if M_1 rejects $\delta(M)\delta(M)$. Observe that M_2 represents a deterministic Turing machine that always halts and, in addition, satisfies $L(M_2) = L_{\text{SelfAcceptance}}$. Hence, $L_{\text{SelfAcceptance}}$ is recursive, and this statement contradicts Theorem 8.1.6.3. Thus, $L_{\text{Acceptance}}$ is not recursive.

Consequently, the present theorem, whose detailed proof is left to the exercises, holds. ∎

It is worth noting that Turing machines that always halt are as powerful as deterministic Turing machines that always halt. Indeed, they both characterize the family of recursive languages, as follows from the next theorem.

Theorem 8.1.6.5
Let L be a language. Then, $L = L(M)$ for a Turing machine M that always halts if and only if L is recursive.

Proof
Let L be a language.

If
If L is recursive, then there exists a deterministic Turing machine M that always halts and, in addition, satisfies $L = L(M)$. Consequently, the 'if' part of this proof holds.

Only if
Let $L = L(M)$, where M is a Turing machine that always halts. The exercises modify the conversion described in Section 8.1.3 so the modified conversion transforms M to an equivalent deterministic Turing machine that always halts. Consequently, the 'only if' part of this proof holds.
Consequently, Theorem 8.1.6.5 holds.
∎

8.1.7 Linear-bounded automata

A linear-bounded automaton M is a Turing machine that never extends its tape. More precisely, with an input word w on its tape, M use no more than the first $|w|$ tape squares. To guarantee this restriction, M's tape initially contains $w\#$, where $\#$ is a special tape symbol called the *endmarker* and, during its computation, M's tape head always remains left of $\#$ (see Figure 8.1.7.1).

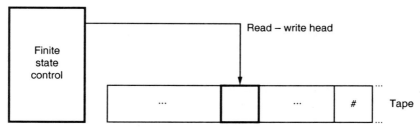

Figure 8.1.7.1 A linear bounded automaton.

Definition — linear-bounded automaton
A *linear-bounded automaton* is a quintuple

$$M = (Q, \Sigma, R, s, F)$$

where $Q, \Sigma, R, s,$ and F have the same meaning as for a Turing machine; # is a symbol in Σ_I, and for every rule, $qX \vdash pYt \in R$, either $\{\#\} \cap \{X, Y\} = \emptyset$ or $X = \#$, $Y = \#, t \in \{\downarrow, \lrcorner\}$.

◆

Both $\vdash$ and $\vdash^*$ are defined as for a Turing machine. If $w\# \vdash^* ufv\#$, where $w \in (\Sigma_I - \{\#\})^*, u, v \in (\Sigma - \{\#\})^*$, and $f \in F$, then M accepts w. The language $L(M)$ accepted by M is the set of all words accepted in this way.

Later on, Section 8.3.4.2 determines the power of linear-bounded automata. Although they are less powerful than Turing machines, they are more powerful than pushdown automata.

Deterministic linear-bounded automata are defined by analogy with deterministic Turing machines. The question as to whether deterministic linear-bounded automata are as powerful as linear-bounded automata represents a famous long-standing problem, known as the *LBA problem*.

8.2 Two-pushdown automata

First, Section 8.2.1 introduces the basic model of a two-pushdown automaton. Then, Section 8.2.2 introduces the deterministic version of a two-pushdown automaton. Finally, Section 8.2.3 establishes the equivalence of Turing machines and two-pushdown automata.

8.2.1 Basic definitions

By attaching an additional pushdown, the pushdown automaton is extended to the two-pushdown automaton (see Figure 8.2.1.1).

A two-pushdown automaton M consists of a finite state control, an input tape with its read head, and two pushdowns with their read-write heads. During a move, M rewrites the top symbols of both pushdowns; otherwise, it works by analogy with a pushdown automaton.

Definition — two-pushdown automaton
A *two-pushdown automaton* is a quintuple

$$M = (Q, \Sigma, R, s, F)$$

Generalized models

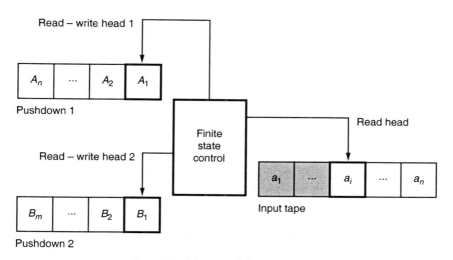

Figure 8.2.1.1 A two-pushdown automaton.

where

Q is a finite set of states;
Σ is an alphabet such that $\Sigma \cap Q = \emptyset$ and $\Sigma = \{|\} \cup \Sigma_I \cup \Sigma_{PD}$, where $|$ is a special symbol such that $| \notin \Sigma_I \cup \Sigma_{PD}$, Σ_I is an input alphabet, and Σ_{PD} is a pushdown alphabet containing S, the start symbol;
$R \subseteq \Sigma_{PD}\{|\}\Sigma_{PD}Q(\Sigma_I \cup \{\varepsilon\}) \times \Sigma_{PD}^* \{|\}\Sigma_{PD}^* Q$ is a finite relation;
$s \in Q$ is the start state;
$F \subseteq Q$ is a set of final states. ◆

Let $M = (Q, \Sigma, R, s, F)$ be a two-pushdown automaton. Consider $(B|Apa, w|vq) \in R$, where $A, B \in \Sigma_{PD}, p, q \in Q, a \in \Sigma_I \cup \{\varepsilon\}$, and $v, w \in \Sigma_{PD}^*$. The special symbol $|$ distinguishes one pushdown of M from the other pushdown. Customarily, the present section calls $(B|Apa, w|vq)$ a *rule* and writes it as

$$B|Apa \vdash w|vq$$

Accordingly, R is referred to as a finite *set of rules*. For brevity, this section sometimes labels the rules of R and, then, uses these labels to refer to the rules. To express that a label r denotes the rule $B|Apa \vdash w|vq$, this is written as

$$r: B|Apa \vdash w|vq,$$

where $B|Apa$ represents the left-hand side of r, lhs(r), and $w|vq$ represents the right-hand side of r, rhs(r). Besides this notation, the conventions introduced for pushdown automata are also used (see Section 5.2).

Example 8.2.1.1 Part 1 Two-pushdown automaton

This part of Example 8.2.1.1 defines the two-pushdown automaton M by its seven rules:

1: $S|Ssa \vdash S|Sas$
2: $S|asa \vdash S|aas$
3: $S|asb \vdash Sb|q$
4: $b|aqb \vdash bb|q$
5: $b|Sqc \vdash |Sp$
6: $b|Spc \vdash |Sp$
7: $S|Sp \vdash |f$

where f is the final state of M. All subsequent parts of Example 8.2.1.1 discuss this two-pushdown automaton.

△

A pushdown automaton M makes moves according to its computational rules. A move depends on the current state, the top symbols of the two pushdowns, and the input symbol. During a move, M changes the state, rewrites the two top pushdown symbols with some words, and shifts the read head zero or one square right.

Definition — configuration

Let $M = (Q, \Sigma, R, s, F)$ be a pushdown automaton. A *configuration* of M is a word χ satisfying

$$\chi \in \Sigma_{PD}^*\{|\}\Sigma_{PD}^* Q \Sigma_I^*$$

◆

Consider a configuration of M,

$$yB|xApaz$$

where $A, B \in \Sigma_{PD}$, $x, y \in \Sigma_{PD}^*$, $a \in \Sigma_I \cup \{\varepsilon\}$, and $z \in \Sigma_I^*$. Notice that $yB|xApaz$ represents an instantaneous description of M. Specifically, yB and xA represent the first pushdown and the second pushdown, respectively. A is the top symbol of the first pushdown, and B is the top symbol of the second pushdown. The current state is p. The current input symbol, scanned by the read head, is the leftmost symbol of az.

Definition — move

Let $M = (Q, \Sigma, R, s, F)$ be a two-pushdown automaton. Let $yB|xApaz$ be a configuration of M, where $A, B \in \Sigma_{PD}$, $x, y \in \Sigma_{PD}^*$, $a \in \Sigma_I \cup \{\varepsilon\}$, and $z \in \Sigma_I^*$. If $r: B|Apa \vdash$

Generalized models

$w|vq \in R$, then M makes a *move* from $yB|xApaz$ to $yw|xvpaz$ according to r, written as

$$yB|xApaz \vdash yw|xvqz \quad [r]$$

♦

Convention
If the specification of the rule r used is immaterial, $yB|xApaz \vdash yw|xvpz$ $[r]$ is simplified to

$$yB|xApaz \vdash yw|xvpz$$

●

Example 8.2.1.1 Part 2 Moves
Return to the two-pushdown automaton M defined in the first part of this example. Consider the configuration

$$S|Ssaabbcc$$

By using thee rule 1: $S|Ssa \vdash S|Sas$, M makes the move

$$S|Ssaabbcc \vdash S|Sasabbcc$$

Furthermore, consider

$$S|Saasbbcc$$

From this configuration, by using the rule 3: $S|asb \vdash Sb|q$, M makes the following move

$$S|Saasbbcc \vdash Sb|Saqbcc$$

△

Generalize $\vdash$ to $\vdash^n$, where $n \geq 0$, for two-pushdown automata by analogy with the corresponding generalization in terms of pushdown automata. Then, based on $\vdash^n$, introduce $\vdash^+$ and $\vdash^*$ for two-pushdown automata. The Exercises define and discuss these notations in detail.

Example 8.2.1.1 Part 3 Sequences of moves
Reconsider the two-pushdown automaton M discussed in the previous two parts of this example. Observe that

$S|Ssaabbcc \vdash S|Sasabbcc$

$\vdash S|Saasbbcc$

$\vdash Sb|Saqbcc$

Therefore,

$S|Ssaabbcc \vdash^3 Sb|Saqbcc$

Thus,

$S|Ssaabbcc \vdash^+ Sb|Saqbcc$ and $S|Ssaabbcc \vdash^* Sb|Saqbcc$

△

A two-pushdown automaton, $M = (Q, \Sigma, R, s, F)$, accepts a word $w \in \Sigma_I^*$ as follows. Initially, M is in its start state s with w on its input tape; both pushdowns contain the start symbol S. If starting from this initial configuration, M can make a sequence of moves so it enters a final state after reading all w, then M accepts w. The collection of all words accepted in this way forms the language that M accepts.

Definition — accepted language

Let $M = (Q, \Sigma, R, s, F)$ be a two-pushdown automaton and $w \in \Sigma_I^*$. If $S|Ssw \vdash^* x|yf$ in M, where $x, y \in \Sigma_{PD}^*$ and $f \in F$, then M accepts w. The *language accepted* by M, $L(M)$, is defined as

$$L(M) = \{w: w \in \Sigma_I^*, \text{ and } M \text{ accepts } w\}$$

◆

Example 8.2.1.1 Part 4 Accepted language

This example determines $L(M)$, where M is the two-pushdown automaton discussed previously.

Consider *aabbcc*, and observe that

$S|Ssaabbcc \vdash S|Sasabbcc$

$\vdash S|Saasbbcc$

$\vdash Sb|Saqbcc$

$\vdash Sbb|Sqcc$

$\vdash Sb|Spc$

$\vdash S|Sp$

$\vdash |f$

in M. Therefore,

$$S|Ssaabbcc \vdash^* |f,$$

where f is a final state. As a result, M accepts $aabbcc$. As this computation illustrates, M initially pushes as onto the first pushdown. When the leftmost b appears, M pops as from the first pushdown and pairs them off with bs; in addition, M pushes bs onto the second pushdown. If the bs exactly exhaust the as, M compares the bs with the following cs in the same way. That is, when the leftmost c appears, M pops bs from the second pushdown and pairs them off with cs. If the number of bs coincides with the number of cs, M accepts the input word. Consequently,

$$L(M) = \{a^n b^n c^n : n \geq 1\}$$

To explain the reason why $L(M) = \{a^n b^n c^n : n \geq 1\}$ in somewhat greater detail, take a closer look at changes in the states and the pushdowns when M works.

State changes
M remains in s while reading as, and when the first b appears, it enters q. M remains in q while scanning bs, and it makes a move to p when the leftmost c appears. Finally, M makes an ε-move to f when S appears on the top of both pushdowns.

Pushdown changes and the applied rules
M begins its computation by copying as from its input tape onto the first pushdown by using the rule 1: $S|Ssa \vdash S|Sas$ followed by zero or more applications of 2: $S|asa \vdash S|aas$. When M scans the first b, it pops one a from the first pushdown while copying the b from the input tape onto the second pushdown according to the rule 3: $S|asb \vdash Sb|q$. By zero or more applications of 4: $b|aqb \vdash bb|q$, M then pops one a from the first pushdown for each b and, in addition, it pushes the b onto the second pushdown. When M has S on the first pushdown's top and, simultaneously, scans the first c, M uses 5: $b|Sqc \vdash |Sp$ to pop one b from the second pushdown while reading c. After this move, by zero or more applications of 6: $b|Spc \vdash |Sp$, M pops b from the second pushdown for each c. When S appears on the second pushdown's top, M makes its last move according to 7: $S|Sp \vdash |f$, by which M enters its final state, f, and empties both pushdowns. Observe that M makes this computation if and only if the input word contains n as followed by n bs followed by n cs, for some $n \geq 1$. Thus, M accepts $\{a^n b^n c^n : n \geq 1\}$ as formally verified in the exercises.

△

Consider a two-pushdown automaton $M = (Q, \Sigma, R, s, F)$. Recall that M accepts an input word $w \in \Sigma_I^*$ if and only if $S|Ssw \vdash^* x|yf$ in M, where $x, y \in \Sigma_{PD}^*$ and $f \in F$. That is, M accepts w if and only if after reading w, M enters a final state f; notice that x and y are irrelevant regarding the acceptance of w. When this section wants to point out this type of acceptance, it refers to $L(M)$ as the *language accepted* by M *by final state*; at this point, it symbolically writes $L(M)_f$ instead of $L(M)$.

Convention

For a two-pushdown automaton M, $L(M)_f$ and $L(M)$ are used synonymously throughout.

●

In addition to this type of acceptance is acceptance by empty pushdowns and, subsequently, the combination of acceptance by final state and acceptance by empty pushdowns.

Definition — language accepted by empty pushdowns

Let $M = (Q, \Sigma, R, s, F)$ be a pushdown automaton and $w \in \Sigma_I^*$. If $S|Ssw \vdash^* |q$, where $q \in Q$, then M *accepts w by empty pushdowns*. The set of all words accepted in this way is denoted by $L(M)_\varepsilon$ and called the *language that M accepts by empty pushdowns*; formally,

$$L(M)_\varepsilon = \{w: w \in \Sigma_I^*, \text{ and } M \text{ accepts } w \text{ by empty pushdowns}\}$$

◆

Example 8.2.1.1 Part 5 Language accepted by empty pushdowns

Reconsider the two-pushdown automaton M discussed in the previous parts of Example 8.2.1.1. Part 4 demonstrates that

$$L(M)_f = \{a^n b^n c^n : n \geq 1\}$$

Modify this demonstration to see that M also accepts $\{a^n b^n c^n : n \geq 1\}$ by empty pushdowns, so

$$L(M)_f = L(M)_\varepsilon = \{a^n b^n c^n : n \geq 1\}$$

A detailed version of this modification is left to the exercises.

△

Return to Algorithm 5.2.1.1 and modify this algorithm so it transforms any two-pushdown automaton accepting by final state to an equivalent two-pushdown automaton accepting by empty pushdowns. Then, return to Algorithm 5.2.1.3 and modify it so that it transforms any two-pushdown automaton accepting by empty pushdowns to an equivalent two-pushdown automaton accepting by final state. These two modifications lead to the next theorem.

Theorem 8.2.1.1

Let L be a language. Then, $L = L(M_f)_f$ for a two-pushdown automaton M_f if and only if $L = L(M_\varepsilon)_\varepsilon$ for a two-pushdown automaton M_ε.

Proof
A detailed proof of this theorem is left to the exercises. ∎

The next definition combines acceptance by final state and acceptance by empty pushdowns.

Definition — language accepted by final state and empty pushdowns
Let $M = (Q, \Sigma, R, s, F)$ be a pushdown automaton and $w \in \Sigma_I^*$. If $S|Ssw \vdash^* |f$, for some $f \in F$, then M accepts w by final state and empty pushdowns. The *language that M accepts by final state and empty pushdowns* is denoted by $L(M)_{f\varepsilon}$ and defined as

$$L(M)_{f\varepsilon} = \{w: w \in \Sigma_I^*, \text{ and } M \text{ accepts } w \text{ by final state and empty pushdowns}\}$$

◆

Example 8.2.1.1 Part 6 Language accepted by final state and empty pushdowns
Return to the pushdown automaton M discussed throughout the previous parts of this example. By analogy with Part 4, demonstrate that

$$L(M)_{f\varepsilon} = \{a^n b^n c^n : n \geq 1\}$$

Thus,

$$L(M)_f = L(M)_\varepsilon = L(M)_{f\varepsilon} = \{a^n b^n c^n : n \geq 1\}$$

A detailed proof that $L(M)_{f\varepsilon} = \{a^n b^n c^n : n \geq 1\}$ is left to the exercises.

△

Theorem 8.2.1.2
Let L be a language. Then, $L = L(M_\varepsilon)_\varepsilon$ for a two-pushdown automaton, M_ε, if and only if $L = L(M_{f\varepsilon})_{f\varepsilon}$ for a two-pushdown automaton, $M_{f\varepsilon}$.

Proof
Prove this theorem by analogy with the proof of Theorem 5.2.1.6. A detailed version of this proof is left to the exercises. ∎

Corollary 8.2.1.3
Let L be a language.

1. $L = L(M_f)_f$ for a two-pushdown automaton M_f if and only if
   $L = L(M_\varepsilon)_\varepsilon$ for a two-pushdown automaton M_ε.

2. $L = L(M_\varepsilon)_\varepsilon$ for a two-pushdown automaton M_ε if and only if
   $L = L(M_{f\varepsilon})_{f\varepsilon}$ for a two-pushdown automaton $M_{f\varepsilon}$.

3. $L = L(M_{f\varepsilon})_{f\varepsilon}$ for a two-pushdown automaton $M_{f\varepsilon}$ if and only if
   $L = L(M_f)_f$ for a two-pushdown automaton M_f.

Proof
Theorems 8.2.1.1 and 8.2.1.2 state the first equivalence and the second equivalence, respectively. The third equivalence follows from these two equivalences. ∎

8.2.2 Determinism

This section defines the notion of a deterministic two-pushdown automaton. However, the next example first presents nondeterministic two-pushdown automata, which make several different move sequences with the same input word.

Example 8.2.2.1 Nondeterministic two-pushdown automaton
Consider

$$L = \{a^n b^n c^n : n \geq 1\}$$

Recall that the two-pushdown automaton M defined in Example 8.2.1.1 accepts L; symbolically,

$$L(M) = \{a^n b^n c^n : n \geq 1\}$$

By adding $S|Sp \vdash S|Ss$ to M's rules (see Part 1 of Example 8.2.1.1), the present example obtains the two-pushdown automaton N satisfying

$$L(N) = L^*$$

a formal proof of this identity is left to the exercises. Thus, N contains these eight rules:

1: $S|Ssa \vdash S|Sas$
2: $S|asa \vdash S|aas$
3: $S|asb \vdash Sb|q$
4: $b|aqb \vdash bb|q$

5: $b|Sqc \vdash |Sp$
6: $b|Spc \vdash |Sp$
7: $S|Sp \vdash |f$
8: $S|Sp \vdash S|Ss$

Assume that N's current state is p and that S appears on the top of both pushdowns. At this point, N can make two different moves, by using

7: $S|Sp \vdash |f$ or 8: $S|Sp \vdash S|Ss$

Therefore, N works nondeterministically.

▲

The notion of a deterministic two-pushdown automaton follows next.

Definition — deterministic two-pushdown automaton
Let $M = (Q, \Sigma, R, s, F)$ be a two-pushdown automaton. M is *deterministic* if each rule $r \in R$, where lhs$(r) = A|Bpa$ with $a \in \Sigma_I \cup \{\varepsilon\}$, satisfies

$$\{r\} = \{r': r' \in R, A|Bpa = \text{lhs}(r') \text{ or } A|Bp = \text{lhs}(r')\}$$

♦

From the definition of a deterministic two-pushdown automaton, $M = (Q, \Sigma, R, s, F)$, for every $A, B \in \Sigma_{PD}$, $q \in Q$, and $a \in \Sigma_I \cup \{\varepsilon\}$, $B|Aqa$ is the left-hand side of no more than one rule in R; in addition, if $a = \varepsilon$, then R contains no rule with $B|Aqb$ on the left-hand side, where $b \in \Sigma_I$. Consequently, with any input word, M makes a unique sequence of moves, and this property makes M easy to implement. Therefore, pragmatically oriented computer science mostly uses deterministic two-pushdown automata, whose power equals the power of nondeterministic Turing machines, as the next section demonstrates.

8.2.3 Equivalence of two-pushdown automata and Turing machines
To prove the equivalence stated in this section's title, the next lemma first demonstrates that for every deterministic Turing machine, there exists an equivalent deterministic two-pushdown automaton.

Lemma 8.2.3.1
Let L be a language. If $L = L(M)$, where M is a deterministic Turing machine, then $L = L(D)$, where D is a deterministic two-pushdown automaton.

Proof
Let L be a language such that $L = L(M)$, where M is a deterministic Turing machine. From M, construct a deterministic two-pushdown automaton D that simulates M by using its two pushdowns as follows. D stores the symbols to the left of M's tape head onto one pushdown so that symbols closer to M's tape head appear closer to this pushdown's top than symbols further from M's tape head. Analogously, D stores the symbols to the right of M's tape head onto the other pushdown. By using these two pushdowns, D then simulates moves made by M so D accepts $L(M)$; that is, $L(D) = L$. Thus, Lemma 8.2.3.1, whose detailed proof is left to the exercises, holds. ■

Observe that every deterministic two-pushdown automaton D constitutes a procedure. Thus, according to Church's thesis, there exists a Turing machine equivalent to D. Furthermore, Theorem 8.1.2.1 implies that there exists a deterministic Turing machine, M, equivalent to D. Consequently, for every deterministic two-pushdown automaton D, there exists a deterministic Turing machine M, so $L(D) = L(M)$. The next lemma states this result; in addition, its proof explains how to construct M from D.

Lemma 8.2.3.2
Let L be a language. If $L = L(D)$, where D is a deterministic two-pushdown automaton, then $L = L(M)$, where M is a deterministic Turing machine.

Proof
Let L be a language such that $L = L(D)$, where D is a deterministic two-pushdown automaton. From D, construct a three-tape Turing machine N that uses its tapes as follows. N's first tape corresponds to the input tape of D. Furthermore, N's second tape simulates one pushdown of D, and N's third tape simulates the other pushdown of D. By using its tapes in this way, N simulates moves made by D so $L(D) = L(N)$. Section 8.1.4 explain how to convert any three-tape Turing machine to an equivalent deterministic Turing machine; use this conversion to transform N to a deterministic Turing machine, M, satisfying $L(N) = L(M)$. Thus, $L(M) = L$. Hence, Lemma 8.2.3.2, whose detailed proof is left to the exercises, holds. ■

Theorem 8.2.3.3
Let L be a language, $L = L(D)$, where D is a deterministic two-pushdown automaton, if and only if $L = L(M)$, where M is a deterministic Turing machine.

Proof
Theorem 8.2.3.3 follows from the previous two lemmas. ■

Theorem 8.2.3.4
The following classes of computational models characterize the family of recursively enumerable languages:

1. Turing machines;
2. deterministic Turing machines;
3. two-pushdown automata;
4. deterministic two-pushdown automata.

Proof
From Theorems 8.1.4.9 and 8.2.3.3, Turing machines, deterministic Turing machines, and deterministic two-pushdown automata characterize the family of recursively enumerable languages. By their definition, deterministic two-pushdown automata are no more powerful than two-pushdown automata and, by Church's thesis, two-pushdown automata are no more powerful than Turing machines. Thus, Theorem 8.2.3.4 holds.
∎

Recall that deterministic pushdown automata, characterizing the family of deterministic context-free languages, are less powerful than pushdown automata, characterizing the family of context-free languages (see Theorem 7.1.7). By contrast, Theorem 8.2.3.4 states that deterministic two-pushdown automata are as powerful as two-pushdown automata.

Finally, notice that the generalization of two-pushdown automata to k-pushdown automata, where $k \geq 3$, does not increase these automata's power. Indeed, by Church's thesis, k-pushdown automata are no more powerful than Turing machines, whose power coincides with the power of two-pushdown automata by Theorem 8.2.3.4.

The exercises continue the investigation of two-pushdown automata and their properties.

8.3 Unrestricted grammars

This section generalizes context-free grammars to unrestricted grammars, in which the right-hand side of each production consists of a non-empty word. Section 8.3.1 formalizes unrestricted grammars. Section 8.3.2 establishes the equivalence between these grammars and Turing machines. Section 8.3.3 normalizes the form of productions in unrestricted grammars. Finally, Section 8.3.4 discusses unrestricted grammars in which each production has its right-hand side at least as long as its left-hand side; grammars restricted in this way are called context-sensitive grammars, and they are less powerful than unrestricted grammars.

8.3.1 Basic definitions

An unrestricted grammar has productions of the form

$$u \to v$$

where u is a non-empty word; otherwise, the definition of an unrestricted grammar coincides with the definition of a context-free grammar.

Definition — unrestricted grammar
A unrestricted grammar is a quadruple

$$G = (N, T, P, S)$$

where

N is an alphabet of nonterminals;
T is an alphabet of terminals such that $N \cap T \neq \emptyset$;
$P \subseteq (N \cup T)^+ \times (N \cup T)^*$ is a finite relationships;
$S \in N$ is the start symbol.

◆

Hereafter, P's members are called *productions*; accordingly, P is referred to as a finite *set of productions*. A production, $(u, v) \in P$, is customarily written as

$$u \to v$$

For brevity, productions in P are labelled; thus, a label p denotes a production $u \to v$ as

$$p: u \to v,$$

where u represents the left-hand side of p, lhs(p), and v represents the right-hand side of p, rhs(p). unrestricted grammars are specified by the same conventions as for context-free grammars (Section 5.1).

Example 8.3.1 Part 1 Unrestricted grammars
Consider the unrestricted grammar G defined by these seven productions:

1: $S \to CAaD$
2: $Aa \to aaA$

3: $AD \to BD$
4: $aB \to Ba$
5: $CB \to CA$
6: $CA \to A$
7: $AD \to \varepsilon$

G contains nonterminals A, B, C, D and S, where S is the start symbol. Furthermore, G has one terminal, a.

△

An unrestricted grammar $G = (N, T, P, S)$ uses its productions to derive words from other words. Consider a word xuy and a production $p: u \to v \in P$. By using p, G directly derives xvy from xuy.

Definition — direct derivation
Let $G = (N, T, P, S)$ be an unrestricted grammar, $p \in P$, and $x, y \in (N \cup T)^*$. Then, $x\text{lhs}(p)y$ *directly derives* $x\text{rhs}(p)y$ according to p in G; symbolically,

$$x\text{lhs}(p)y \Rightarrow x\text{rhs}(p)y \qquad [p]$$

or, briefly,

$$x\text{lhs}(p)y \Rightarrow x\text{rhs}(p)y$$

◆

Example 8.3.1 Part 2 Direct derivations
Return to the unrestricted grammar defined in the previous part of this example. Consider $CAaD$. By the rule 2: $Aa \to aaA$, G performs a derivation step from $CAaD$ to $CaaAD$; symbolically,

$$CAaD \Rightarrow CaaAD \qquad [2]$$

in G.
 Similarly, consider $aaaaAD$. Using 7: $AD \to \varepsilon$, G makes the derivation step

$$aaaaAD \Rightarrow aaaa$$

△

Consider an unrestricted grammar $G = (N, T, P, S)$. By analogy with the corresponding definition for a context-free grammar (see Section 5.1), for all $n \geq 0$, define

$$v \Rightarrow^n w \quad [\pi]$$

in G, where π is the production word denoting the sequence of n productions according to which G makes $v \Rightarrow^n w$. In a similar manner, introduce

$$v \Rightarrow^+ w \ [\pi] \quad \text{and} \quad v \Rightarrow^* w \ [\pi]$$

If π represents an immaterial piece of information, it is omitted in these notations; for example, $v \Rightarrow^n w \ [\pi]$ is frequently simplified to $v \Rightarrow^n w$.

Example 8.3.1 Part 3 Derivations

Reconsider the unrestricted grammar G defined in Part 1 of this example. From $CAaD$, G derives $CAaaD$ by carrying out these five derivation steps:

$$\begin{aligned}
CAaD &\Rightarrow CaaAD & [2] \\
&\Rightarrow CaaBD & [3] \\
&\Rightarrow CaBaD & [4] \\
&\Rightarrow CBaaD & [4] \\
&\Rightarrow CAaaD & [2]
\end{aligned}$$

Symbolically,

$$CAaD \Rightarrow^5 CAaaD \quad [23442]$$

or, briefly,

$$CAaD \Rightarrow^5 CAaaD$$

Therefore,

$$CAaD \Rightarrow^+ CAaaD \text{ and } CAaD \Rightarrow^* CAaaD$$

△

Definition — generated language

Let $G = (N, T, P, S)$ be an unrestricted grammar. If $S \Rightarrow^* w$ in G, then w is a *sentential form* of G. A sentential form w satisfying $w \in T^*$ represents a sentence generated by G. The *language generated* by G, $L(G)$, is the set of all sentences that G generates; formally,

$$L(G) = \{w : w \in T^* \text{ and } S \Rightarrow^* w \text{ in } G\}$$

◆

Example 8.3.1 Part 4 Sentential forms and sentences

Consider the unrestricted grammar, G, discussed in previous parts of this example. Notice that $CAaaaaD$ is a sentential form of G because $S \Rightarrow^* CAaaaaD$. However, as $CAaaaaD$ contains some nonterminals, $CAaaaaD$ is not a sentence. Observe that $aaaaaaaa$ is a sentence of G. Indeed, $aaaaaaaa$ contains only terminals and $S \Rightarrow^* aaaaaaaa$, as follows from this derivation:

$$
\begin{aligned}
S &\Rightarrow CAaD && [1] \\
&\Rightarrow^* CAaaD && [23445] \\
&\Rightarrow^* CAaaaaD && [22344445] \\
&\Rightarrow^* aaaaaaaa && [622227]
\end{aligned}
$$

△

Example 8.3.1 Part 5 Generated language

All previous parts of this example have discussed the unrestricted grammar G that has these productions:

1: $S \rightarrow CAaD$

2: $Aa \rightarrow aaA$

3: $AD \rightarrow BD$

4: $aB \rightarrow Ba$

5: $CB \rightarrow CA$

6: $CA \rightarrow A$

7: $AD \rightarrow \varepsilon$

This part of first studies how G uses its productions to generate w, where $w \in L(G)$; that is, it studies the form of the production word π in a derivation of the form

$$S \Rightarrow^* w \, [\pi]$$

where $w \in \{a\}^*$. Then, based on this study, this part determines $L(G)$.

Use of production 1

In the first derivation step, G rewrites S with $CAaD$ by using 1: $S \rightarrow CAaD$. In the subsequent sentential forms, C and D represent the leftmost symbol and the rightmost symbol, respectively.

Use of productions 2 through 5

By using 2: $Aa \rightarrow aaA$, G moves A to the right in $CAaD$, and during this move G changes a to aa; more formally,

$$CAaD \Rightarrow CaaAD \quad [2]$$

A reaches the rightmost symbol D, and at this point G uses 3: $AD \to BD$ to change A to B. By using 4: $aB \to Ba$, G then moves B left until B reaches the leftmost symbol, C. Finally, by using 5: $CB \to CA$, B becomes A. To summarize the use of these productions,

$$CAaD \Rightarrow^* CAaaD \quad [23445]$$

Use of productions 2 or 6
G rewrites $CAaaD$ by using 2: $Aa \to aaA$ or 6: $CA \to A$.

1 If G uses 2: $Aa \to aaA$, then G subsequently uses productions 3 through 5 so that

$$CAaaD \Rightarrow^* CAaaaaD \quad [22344445]$$

2 If G uses 6: $CA \to A$, then G erases the leftmost symbol C. After this erasure, by using 2: $Aa \to aaA$, G moves A through the sentential form from left to right and, simultaneously, doubles the number of as. When A reaches the right-most symbol D, G makes its last step by 7: $AD \to \varepsilon$. In brief,

$$CAaaD \Rightarrow^* aaaa \quad [6227]$$

Notice that $w = aaaa$ at this point.

Use of productions 2 or 6 — general approach
More generally, consider $CAa^{2^{i-1}}D$, for some $i \geq 1$. G rewrites $CAa^{2^{i-1}}D$ by using 2: $Aa \to aaA$ or 6: $CA \to A$ as described next.

1 If G rewrites $CAa^{2^{i-1}}D$ by using 2: $Aa \to aaA$, it subsequently performs the derivation

$$CAa^{2^{i-1}}D \Rightarrow^* CAa^{2^i}D \quad [2^{2^{i-1}}34^i 5]$$

2 If G rewrites $CAa^{2^{i-1}}D$ by using 6: $CA \to A$, then

$$CAa^{2^{i-1}}D \Rightarrow^* a^{2^i} \quad [62^{2^{i-1}}7]$$

in G, so $w = a^{2^i}$.

All derivations
Consequently, G generates w as follows:

$$S \Rightarrow CAaD \quad [1]$$
$$\Rightarrow^* CAaaD \quad [23445]$$

$$\Rightarrow^* CAaaaaD \quad [22344445]$$
$$\vdots$$
$$\Rightarrow^* CAa^{2^{i-1}}D$$
$$\Rightarrow^* CAa^{2^i}D \quad [2^{2^{i-1}}34^i5]$$
$$\Rightarrow^* a^{2^{i+1}} \quad [62^{2^i}7]$$

That is, if

$$S \Rightarrow^* w\ [\pi]$$

in G, where $w \in \{a\}^*$, then

$$\pi = 1p_1\ldots p_i 62^{i+1} 7$$

for some $i \geq 1$, with

$$p_j = 2^j 34^{j+1} 5$$

for $j = 1, \ldots, i$. Therefore,

$$w = a^{2^{i+1}}$$

Consequently,

$$L(G) = \{a^{2^i} : i \geq 1\}$$

as formally verified in the exercises.

▲

8.3.2 Equivalence of unrestricted grammars and Turing machines

This section demonstrates the equivalence of unrestricted grammars and Turing machines. First, it explains how to transform any unrestricted grammar to an equivalent Turing machine. Then, it transforms any Turing machine to an equivalent unrestricted grammar. Finally, based on these two transformations, the equivalence between unrestricted grammars and Turing machines is established.

From unrestricted grammars to Turing machines

Observe that any unrestricted grammar G represents a procedure; therefore, by Church's thesis, there surely exists a Turing machine M that accepts $L(G)$. This section explains how to convert G to M so $L(M) = L(G)$. Two alternative methods of this conversion are given.

The first method resembles the technique used in Section 8.1.2 because it converts any unrestricted grammar to an equivalent three-tape Turing machine by exploring all possible derivations in the grammar. More precisely, let $G = (N, T, P, S)$ be an unrestricted grammar and let $w \in T^*$. M has w placed on its first tape. On the second tape, M systematically generates production words, consisting of productions from P. According to these production words, M simulates the derivations in G on the third tape.

1. Assume that $w \in L(G)$. Then M eventually generates a production word π according to which M simulates a derivation of the form $S \Rightarrow^* w\ [\pi]$; at this point, M accepts w and halts.
2. Assume that $w \notin L(G)$. Then M never generates a production word that causes this machine to simulate the generation of w in G. Therefore, M runs endlessly and it never accepts w.

Therefore, $w \in L(G)$ if and only if $w \in L(M)$, so

$$L(G) = L(M)$$

The exercises examine this method in greater detail.

The proof of the next theorem describes another method that transforms an unrestricted grammar to an equivalent Turing machine.

Theorem 8.3.2.1

Let G be an unrestricted grammar. Then, there exists a Turing machine M that satisfies $L(G) = L(M)$.

Proof

Let $G = (N, T, P, S)$ be an unrestricted grammar. First, construct a three-tape Turing machine M accepting $L(G)$ as follows. Consider a word $w \in T^*$. With w on its first tape, M begins its computation by writing a list of all productions in P on the second tape. Then, it writes S on the third tape, which always records the current sentential form of G during the computation. From this point on, M iterates the following four-step computational cycle:

1. Nondeterministically select a position, i, in the current sentential form on the third tape.
2. Nondeterministically select a production, p, on the second tape.
3. If $lhs(p)$ appears on the third tape at positions i through $i + |lhs(p)| - 1$, then replace $lhs(p)$ with $rhs(p)$; otherwise, reject.
4. If the first tape and third tape coincide, accept; otherwise, go to 1.

Consider step 1: starting from the leftmost symbol of the current sentential form placed on the third tape, M proceeds right towards the right end of this form. During each move, M can either shift the third tape head a square right or select the present position as i. Analogously, M performs step 2.

Consider step 3: if $|\text{lhs}(p)| = |\text{rhs}(p)|$, then M replaces lhs(p) with rhs(p) without any prearranging of the second tape. If, however, $|\text{lhs}(p)| \neq |\text{rhs}(p)|$, M shifts the non-blank suffix following lhs(p) before M carries out this replacement. More specifically, M distinguishes $|\text{lhs}(p)| < |\text{rhs}(p)|$ and $|\text{lhs}(p)| > |\text{rhs}(p)|$:

1. Let $|\text{rhs}(p)| - |\text{lhs}(p)| = h$, where $h > 0$. At this point, M shifts the non-blank suffix following $|\text{lhs}(p)|$ to the right by h squares, then performs the replacement.
2. Let $|\text{lhs}(p)| - |\text{rhs}(p)| = h$, where $h > 0$. Then, M shifts the non-blank suffix following lhs(p) to the left by h squares before it carries out the replacement.

Observe that x represents a sentential form of G if and only if x appears on the third tape of M. Hence, $L(M) = L(G)$.

Section 8.1.4 explains how to transform any k-tape Turing machine, where $k \geq 1$, to an equivalent Turing machine. Use this transformation to convert M to an equivalent Turing machine. Thus, Theorem 8.3.2.1, whose detailed proof is left to the exercises, holds.

∎

From Turing machines to unrestricted grammars

The next algorithm converts any Turing machine to an equivalent unrestricted grammar.

Algorithm 8.3.2.2: Conversion of a Turing machine to an equivalent unrestricted grammar

Input: A Turing machine $M = (Q, \Sigma, R, s, F)$.

Output: An unrestricted grammar $G = (N, T, P, S)$, such that $L(G) = L(M)$.

Method

begin
  $T := \Sigma_I$ {Σ_I is the input alphabet of M};
  $N := \{\langle aX \rangle: a \in \Sigma_I \cup \{\varepsilon\}, X \in \Sigma\} \cup Q \cup \{S, A\}$ {S and A are new symbols};
  for each $a \in \Sigma_I$ **do**
    $P := P \cup \{S \to S\langle B \rangle, S \to A\langle B \rangle\}$;
  for each $a \in \Sigma_I$ **do**
    $P := P \cup \{A \to A\langle aa \rangle, A \to s\}$;

for each $pY \vdash qX\downarrow \in R$, where $p \in Q - F$, and $a \in \Sigma_I \cup \{\varepsilon\}$ do
$P := P \cup \{p\langle aY\rangle \to q\langle aX\rangle\}$;
for each $pY \vdash qX\hookrightarrow \in R$, where $p \in Q - F$, and $a \in \Sigma_I \cup \{\varepsilon\}$ do
$P := P \cup \{p\langle aY\rangle \to \langle aX\rangle q\}$;
for each $pY \vdash qX\lrcorner \in R$, where $p \in Q - F$, and $a \in \Sigma_I \cup \{\varepsilon\}$, and each $\langle bZ\rangle \in N$, where
$b \in \Sigma_I \cup \{\varepsilon\}$ and $Z \in \Sigma$ do
$P := P \cup \{\langle bZ\rangle p\langle aY\rangle \to q\langle bZ\rangle\langle aX\rangle\}$;
for each $f \in F$ and each $\langle aX\rangle \in N$, where $a \in \Sigma_I \cup \{\varepsilon\}$ and $X \in \Sigma$ do
$P := P \cup \{\langle aX\rangle f \to faf, f\langle aX\rangle \to faf, f \to \varepsilon\}$
end.

Consider the unrestricted grammar $G = (N, \Sigma_I, P, S)$, produced by Algorithm 8.3.2.2. Every nonterminal in N has the form

$$\langle aX\rangle$$

where $a \in \Sigma_I \cup \{\varepsilon\}$ and $X \in \Sigma$. During the simulation of M, G never changes a in $\langle aX\rangle$; however, G changes the second component, X, during this simulation. Initially, G derives

$$s\langle a_1 a_1\rangle\langle a_2 a_2\rangle\ldots\langle a_n a_n\rangle\langle B\rangle\ldots\langle B\rangle$$

where a_1 through a_n belong to Σ_I — the input alphabet of M. After this initial derivation, G simulates M's moves by using the second component of the nonterminals appearing in the derived sentential forms. If G simulates a move during which M enters a final state and, thus, $a_1 a_2 \ldots a_n \in L(M)$, then G generates $a_1 a_2 \ldots a_n$. If, by contrast, $a_1 a_2 \ldots a_n \notin L(M)$, G never generates $a_1 a_2 \ldots a_n$. Therefore, $L(G) = L(M)$.

Lemma 8.3.2.3
Let $M = (Q, \Sigma, R, s, F)$ be a Turing machine. With M as its input, Algorithm 8.3.2.2 halts and correctly constructs an unrestricted grammar, $G = (N, \Sigma_I, P, S)$, such that $L(G) = L(M)$.

Proof
Termination
Because Σ_I, R and F are finite, all **for** loops of Algorithm 8.3.2.2 are repeated a finite number of times; as a result, this algorithm surely terminates.

Correctness
Observe that G begins every derivation by using productions introduced in the first **for** loop; then, it applies productions introduced in the second **for** loop. More precisely, according to productions introduced in the first **for** loop:

for each $a \in \Sigma_I$ **do**
$P := P \cup \{S \rightarrow S\langle B\rangle, S \rightarrow A\langle B\rangle\}$,

G makes an m-step derivation, where $m \geq 1$, of the form

$$S \Rightarrow^m A\langle B\rangle^m$$

so that it uses $S \rightarrow S\langle B\rangle$ $(m-1)$ times and, then, applies $S \rightarrow A\langle B\rangle$ once. After $S \Rightarrow^m A\langle B\rangle^m$, G uses productions introduced in the second **for** loop:

for each $a \in \Sigma_I$ **do**
$P := P \cup \{A \rightarrow A\langle aa\rangle, A \rightarrow s\}$;

using these productions, it produces

$$A\langle B\rangle^m \Rightarrow^n A\langle a_1 a_1\rangle\langle a_2 a_2\rangle\ldots\langle a_n a_n\rangle\langle B\rangle^m$$
$$\Rightarrow s\langle a_1 a_1\rangle\langle a_2 a_2\rangle\ldots\langle a_n a_n\rangle\langle B\rangle^m$$

for some $n \geq 0$ so that G makes the first n steps according to productions of the form $A \rightarrow A\langle aa\rangle$, where $a \in \Sigma_I$, and it performs the last step by $A \rightarrow s$ (s is the start state of M).

To summarize these two partial derivations, G begins every derivation as

$$S \Rightarrow^* s\langle a_1 a_1\rangle\langle a_2 a_2\rangle\ldots\langle a_n a_n\rangle\langle B\rangle^m$$

From this point on, by using productions introduced in the third **for** loop through the fifth **for** loop, G simulates M, which never moves more than m squares to the right of its input — $a_1\ldots a_n$. The next claim demonstrates this simulation rigorously.

Claim
For all $a_1, \ldots, a_n \in \Sigma_I, X_1, \ldots, X_k \in \Sigma, q \in Q$, where $n \geq 0$ and $j, k \geq 1$ such that $j \leq k$, this equivalence holds:

$$sa_1\ldots a_n B \vdash^* X_1\ldots X_{j-1} q X_j \ldots X_k \text{ in } M$$

if and only if

$$s\langle a_1 a_1\rangle\ldots\langle a_n a_n\rangle\langle B\rangle^m \Rightarrow^* \langle a_1 X_1\rangle\ldots\langle a_{j-1} X_{j-1}\rangle q\langle a_j X_j\rangle\ldots\langle a_k X_k\rangle\ldots\langle a_{n+m} X_{n+m}\rangle$$

in G, where m is a natural number such that $n + m \geq k$, $a_{n+1} = \ldots = a_{n+m} = \varepsilon$, and $X_{k+1} = \ldots = X_{n+m} = B$.

Proof
Only if
By induction on i, where $i \geq 0$, this part of the proof demonstrates that

if
$$sa_1...a_nB \vdash^i X_1...X_{j-1}qX_j...X_k \text{ in } M$$

then
$$\langle a_1a_1\rangle...\langle a_na_n\rangle\langle B\rangle^m \Rightarrow^* \langle a_1X_1\rangle...\langle a_{j-1}X_{j-1}\rangle q\langle a_jX_j\rangle...\langle a_{n+m}X_{n+m}\rangle \text{ in } G$$

Basis
This part of the proof is left to the exercises.

Induction hypothesis
Assume that the 'only if' part holds for all $i = 0, ..., t$, where t is an integer such that $i \geq 0$.

Induction step
Consider
$$sa_1...a_nB \vdash^* X_1...X_{j-1}qX_j...X_k \quad [\rho r]$$

in M such that ρ consists of t rules and $r \in R$. By the definition of a Turing machine, r has one of these three forms:

1. $r: pY \vdash qX_j\downarrow$
2. $r: pY \vdash qX_j \hookrightarrow$
3. $r: pY \vdash qX_j\lhookleftarrow$

Next, this proof considers these three forms of r.

1. Suppose r has the first form; that is,
$$r: pY \vdash qX_j\downarrow$$

Express
$$sa_1...a_nB \vdash^* X_1...X_{j-1}qX_j...X_k \quad [\rho r]$$

as
$$sa_1...a_nB \vdash^* X_1...X_{j-1}pY...X_k \quad [\rho]$$
$$\vdash X_1...X_{j-1}qX_j...X_k \quad [r]$$

Recall that ρ consists of t rules, so by the induction hypothesis,
$$s\langle a_1a_1\rangle...\langle a_na_n\rangle\langle B\rangle^m \Rightarrow^* \langle a_1X_1\rangle...\langle a_{j-1}X_{j-1}\rangle p\langle a_jY\rangle...\langle a_{n+m}X_{n+m}\rangle \text{ in } G$$

Consider the third **for** loop of Algorithm 8.3.2.2:

for each $pY \vdash qX{\downarrow} \in R$ and $a \in \Sigma_I \cup \{\varepsilon\}$ **do**
$P := P \cup \{p\langle aY \rangle \to q\langle aX \rangle\}$;

Because $r\colon pY \vdash qX_j{\downarrow} \in R$, this loop introduces

$$p\langle aY \rangle \to q\langle aX_j \rangle \in P$$

Consequently,

$$\langle a_1 X_1 \rangle \ldots \langle a_{j-1} X_{j-1} \rangle p \langle a_j Y \rangle \ldots \langle a_{n+m} X_{n+m} \rangle \Rightarrow \langle a_1 X_1 \rangle \ldots \langle a_{j-1} X_{j-1} \rangle q \langle a_j X_j \rangle \ldots \langle a_{n+m} X_{n+m} \rangle$$

according to $p\langle aY \rangle \to q\langle aX_j \rangle$, so

$$\langle a_1 a_1 \rangle \ldots \langle a_n a_n \rangle \langle B \rangle^m \Rightarrow^* \langle a_1 X_1 \rangle \ldots \langle a_{j-1} X_{j-1} \rangle q \langle a_j X_j \rangle \ldots \langle a_{n+m} X_{n+m} \rangle$$

2. Suppose that

$$r\colon pY \vdash qX_j \hookrightarrow$$

Express

$$s a_1 \ldots a_n B \vdash^* X_1 \ldots X_{j-1} q X_j \ldots X_k \quad [\rho r]$$

as

$$s a_1 \ldots a_n B \vdash^* X_1 \ldots X_{j-1} p Y \ldots X_k \quad [\rho]$$
$$\vdash X_1 \ldots X_{j-1} X_j q \ldots X_k \quad [r]$$

From the induction hypothesis,

$$s\langle a_1 a_1 \rangle \ldots \langle a_n a_n \rangle \langle B \rangle^m \Rightarrow^* \langle a_1 X_1 \rangle \ldots \langle a_{j-1} X_{j-1} \rangle p \langle a_j Y \rangle \ldots \langle a_{n+m} X_{n+m} \rangle$$

in G because ρ consists of t rules. Return to the fourth **for** loop:

for each $pY \vdash qX \hookrightarrow \in R$ and $a \in \Sigma_I \cup \{\varepsilon\}$ **do**
$P := P \cup \{ p\langle aY \rangle \to \langle aX \rangle q \}$;

As $r\colon pY \vdash qX_j \hookrightarrow \in R$, this loop introduces

$$p\langle aY \rangle \to \langle aX_j \rangle q \in P$$

Hence,

$$\langle a_1 X_1 \rangle \ldots \langle a_{j-1} X_{j-1} \rangle p \langle a_j Y \rangle \ldots \langle a_{n+m} X_{n+m} \rangle \Rightarrow \langle a_1 X_1 \rangle \ldots \langle a_{j-1} X_{j-1} \rangle \langle a_j X_j \rangle q \ldots \langle a_{n+m} X_{n+m} \rangle$$

according to $pY \vdash qX_j \hookrightarrow$; consequently,

$$\langle a_1 a_1 \rangle \ldots \langle a_n a_n \rangle \langle B \rangle^m \Rightarrow^* \langle a_1 X_1 \rangle \ldots \langle a_{j-1} X_{j-1} \rangle \langle a_j X_j \rangle q \ldots \langle a_{n+m} X_{n+m} \rangle$$

3. Suppose that

$$r: pY \vdash qX_j \lrcorner$$

Express

$$sa_1 \ldots a_n B \vdash^* X_1 \ldots X_{j-1} qX_j \ldots X_k \quad [\rho r]$$

as

$$sa_1 \ldots a_n B \vdash^* X_1 \ldots X_{j-1} pY \ldots X_k \quad [\rho]$$
$$\vdash X_1 \ldots qX_{j-1} X_j \ldots X_k \quad [r]$$

From the induction hypothesis,

$$s\langle a_1 a_1 \rangle \ldots \langle a_n a_n \rangle \langle B \rangle^m \Rightarrow^* \langle a_1 X_1 \rangle \ldots \langle a_{j-1} X_{j-1} \rangle p\langle a_j Y \rangle \ldots \langle a_{n+m} X_{n+m} \rangle$$

in G. Consider the fifth **for** loop:

for each $pY \vdash qX \lrcorner \in R$, where $p \in Q - F$, and $a \in \Sigma_I \cup \{\varepsilon\}$,
  and each $\langle bZ \rangle \in N$, where $b \in \Sigma_I \cup \{\varepsilon\}$ and $Z \in \Sigma$ **do**
  $P := P \cup \{ \langle bZ \rangle p\langle aY \rangle \to q\langle bZ \rangle\langle aX \rangle \}$;

This loop implies that

$$\langle a_{j-1} X_{j-1} \rangle p\langle a Y \rangle \to q\langle a_{j-1} X_{j-1} \rangle\langle a X_j \rangle \in P$$

because $r: pY \vdash qX_j \lrcorner \in R$. Thus,

$$\langle a_1 X_1 \rangle \ldots \langle a_{j-1} X_{j-1} \rangle p\langle a_j Y \rangle \ldots \langle a_{n+m} X_{n+m} \rangle \Rightarrow \langle a_1 X_1 \rangle \ldots q\langle a_{j-1} X_{j-1} \rangle\langle a_j X_j \rangle \ldots \langle a_{n+m} X_{n+m} \rangle$$

according to $pY \vdash qX_j \lrcorner$. Consequently,

$$\langle a_1 a_1 \rangle \ldots \langle a_n a_n \rangle \langle B \rangle^m \Rightarrow^* \langle a_1 X_1 \rangle \ldots q\langle a_{j-1} X_{j-1} \rangle\langle a_j X_j \rangle \ldots \langle a_{n+m} X_{n+m} \rangle$$

Therefore, the inductive step is completed, so the 'only if' part of the claim holds.

If
This part of the claim states that if

Generalized models

$$\langle a_1 a_1 \rangle \ldots \langle a_n a_n \rangle \langle B \rangle^m \Rightarrow^i \langle a_1 X_1 \rangle \ldots \langle a_{j-1} X_{j-1} \rangle q \langle a_j X_j \rangle \ldots \langle a_{n+m} X_{n+m} \rangle$$

in G, where $i \geq 0$, then

$$sa_1 \ldots a_n B \vdash^* X_1 \ldots X_{j-1} q X_j \ldots X_k$$

in M. Prove this part by analogy with the only-if part; a detailed version of this proof is left to the exercises.

Therefore, the claim holds.

□

Consider this claim only for final states. More precisely, for all $a_1, \ldots, a_n \in \Sigma_I$, $X_1, \ldots, X_k \in \Sigma, f \in F$, where $n \geq 0$ and $j, k \geq 1$ such that $j \leq k$, this equivalence holds:

$$sa_1 \ldots a_n B \vdash^* X_1 \ldots X_{j-1} f X_j \ldots X_k \text{ in } M$$

if and only if

$$s\langle a_1 a_1 \rangle \ldots \langle a_n a_n \rangle \langle B \rangle^m \Rightarrow^* \langle a_1 X_1 \rangle \ldots \langle a_{j-1} X_{j-1} \rangle f \langle a_j X_j \rangle \ldots \langle a_k X_k \rangle \ldots \langle a_{n+m} X_{n+m} \rangle$$

in G, where m is a natural number such that $n + m \geq k$, $a_{n+1} = \ldots = a_{n+m} = \varepsilon$, and $X_{k+1} = \ldots = X_{n+m} = B$. Return to the sixth **for** loop of Algorithm 8.3.2.2:

for each $f \in F$ and each $\langle aX \rangle \in N$, where $a \in \Sigma_I \cup \{\varepsilon\}$ and $X \in \Sigma$ **do**
  $P := P \cup \{\langle aX \rangle f \to faf, f\langle aX \rangle \to faf, f \to \varepsilon\}$

Furthermore, recall that G begins every derivation as

$$S \Rightarrow^* s \langle a_1 a_1 \rangle \langle a_2 a_2 \rangle \ldots \langle a_n a_n \rangle \langle B \rangle^m$$

Consequently,

$$sa_1 \ldots a_n B \vdash^* X_1 \ldots X_{j-1} f X_j \ldots X_k \text{ in } M$$

if and only if

$$\begin{aligned} S &\Rightarrow^* s\langle a_1 a_1 \rangle \ldots \langle a_n a_n \rangle \langle B \rangle^m \\ &\Rightarrow^* \langle a_1 X_1 \rangle \ldots \langle a_{j-1} X_{j-1} \rangle f \langle a_j X_j \rangle \ldots \langle a_{n+m} X_{n+m} \rangle \\ &\Rightarrow^* a_1 \ldots a_n \end{aligned}$$

Therefore, for all $w \in \Sigma_I^*$,

$$w \in L(M) \text{ if and only if } w \in L(G)$$

In other words,

$$L(M) = L(G)$$

In summary, with M as its input, Algorithm 8.3.2.2 halts and correctly constructs an unrestricted grammar $G = (N, T, P, S)$ such that $L(G) = L(M)$. Thus, Lemma 8.3.2.3 holds. ∎

Equivalence of Turing machines and unrestricted grammars

Theorem 8.3.2.4
Let L be a language. Then, $L = L(M)$ for a Turing machine M if and only if $L = L(G)$ for an unrestricted grammar G.

Proof
This theorem follows from Theorem 8.3.2.1, Algorithm 8.3.2.2 and Lemma 8.3.2.3. ∎

8.3.3 Normal forms

Section 5.1.4 explains how to modify context-free grammars so their productions satisfy some normal forms, such as Chomsky normal form. The present section normalizes productions in unrestricted grammars. Specifically, it covers the Kuroda normal form and its special case the Pentonnen normal form. Both forms somewhat resemble the Chomsky normal form. Indeed, every production in a Kuroda normal form grammar G has one of the four forms

$$AB \to DC, A \to BC, A \to a, A \to \varepsilon$$

If, in addition, every production of the form $AB \to DC$ satisfies $A = D$, then G is in Pentonnen normal form.

Definition — Kuroda normal form
Let $G = (N, T, P, S)$ be an unrestricted grammar. G is in *Kuroda normal form* if every production, $p \in P$, has one of these four forms

1. $AB \to DC$ with $A, B, C, D \in N$

2. $A \to BC$ with $A, B, C \in N$
3. $A \to a$ with $A \in N$ and $a \in T$
4. $A \to \varepsilon$ with $A \in N$.

◆

Theorem 8.3.3.1
Let $G = (N, T, P, S)$ be an unrestricted grammar. Then, there exists an unrestricted grammar, $G_{KNF} = (N_{KNF}, T, P_{KNF}, S)$, such that $L(G) = L(G_{KNF})$, and G_{KNF} is in Kuroda normal form.

Proof
This proof resembles Algorithm 5.1.4.1.1 and the proof of Theorem 5.1.4.1.2. Therefore, an outline proof is given here; a rigorous verification is left to the exercises.

Let $G = (N, T, P, S)$ be an unrestricted grammar. Transform G to an equivalent Kuroda normal form grammar, $G_{KNF} = (N_{KNF}, T, P_{KNF}, S)$, as follows. Move all nonterminals from N into N_{KNF}. In P, select all productions that satisfy Kuroda normal form, and move these productions from P into P_{KNF}. Then, carry out the following five steps.

1. In all productions of P, replace each occurrence of a terminal, $a \in T$, with a new nonterminal a' and add a' to N_{KNF}. Include

$$a' \to a$$

into P_{KNF}. Then, select all productions in P that satisfy Kuroda normal form, and move these productions from P to P_{KNF}.

2. In P, replace every production of the form

$$A_1...A_m \to B_1...B_n,$$

where n and m satisfy $0 \le n < m$ ($n = 0$ implies $B_1...B_n = \varepsilon$), with

$$A_1...A_m \to B_1...B_n C_{n+1}...C_m$$

where C_{n+1} through C_m denote $m - n$ occurrences of a new nonterminal C. Then, add C to N_{KNF}, and include

$$C \to \varepsilon$$

in P_{KNF}. Finally, in P, select all productions that satisfy Kuroda normal form, and move them from P to P_{KNF} (after this move, each production of P has its left-hand side no longer than its right-hand side).

3. For every production of the form

$$A \to B$$

in P, add a new nonterminal C to N_{KNF}, and include these two productions

$$A \to BC$$
$$C \to \varepsilon$$

into P_{KNF}. In addition, remove $A \to B$ from P.

4. For every context-free production of P,

$$A \to B_1 \ldots B_n$$

where $3 \leq n$, include the following $n - 1$ productions

$$A \to B_1 \langle B_2 \ldots B_n \rangle$$
$$\langle B_2 \ldots B_n \rangle \to B_2 \langle B_3 \ldots B_n \rangle$$
$$\vdots$$
$$\langle B_{n-2} \ldots B_n \rangle \to B_{n-2} \langle B_{n-1} \ldots B_n \rangle$$
$$\langle B_{n-1} B_n \rangle \to B_{n-1} B_n$$

into P_{KNF}; moreover, add the $n - 2$ new nonterminals

$$\langle B_2 \ldots B_n \rangle \text{ through } \langle B_{n-1} B_n \rangle$$

to N_{KNF}. Then, remove $A \to B_1 \ldots B_n$ from P (after this removal, every production of P, $u \to v$, satisfies $u \in N \cup N^2$, and $v \in N \cup N^2 \cup N^3$.

5. For every production of the form

$$A_1 A_2 \ldots A_m \to B_1 B_2 \ldots B_n$$

in P, where $2 \leq m$ and $3 \leq n$, add a new nonterminal C to N_{KNF}. Then, include

$$A_1 A_2 \to B_1 C$$

into P_{KNF}. Moreover, if $|B_2 \ldots B_n| \leq 2$, add

$$CA_3 \ldots A_m \to B_2 \ldots B_n$$

into P_{KNF}; however, if $|B_2 \ldots B_n| \geq 3$, place $CA_3 \ldots A_m \to B_2 \ldots B_n$ into P. Remove $A_1 \ldots A_m \to B_1 \ldots B_n$ from P. Repeat step 5 until $P = \emptyset$.

The resulting unrestricted grammar $G_{KNF} = (N_{KNF}, T, P_{KNF}, S)$ satisfies the Kuroda normal form. In addition,

$$L(G) = L(G_{KNF})$$

Therefore, Theorem 8.3.3.1 holds. ∎

Example 8.3.3.1 Kuroda normal form

Return to the unrestricted grammar G discussed in Example 8.3.1.1. Formally, this grammar is defined as

$$G = (N, \{a\}, P, S)$$

where

$$N = \{A, B, C, D, S\}$$

and P contains the seven productions

$$S \rightarrow CAaD$$
$$Aa \rightarrow aaA$$
$$AD \rightarrow BD$$
$$aB \rightarrow Ba$$
$$CB \rightarrow CA$$
$$CA \rightarrow A$$
$$AD \rightarrow \varepsilon$$

Using the technique described in the proof of the previous theorem, this example constructs a Kuroda normal form grammar, $G_{KNF} = (N_{KNF}, \{a\}, P_{KNF}, S)$ such that $L(G) = L(G_{KNF})$. Initially, set

$$N_{KNF} = \{A, B, C, D, S\}$$

G has these two Kuroda normal form productions:

$$AD \rightarrow BD \text{ and } CB \rightarrow CA$$

Remove these productions from P, then use them to initialize P_{KNF}:

$$P_{KNF} = \{AD \rightarrow BD, CB \rightarrow CA\}$$

Now perform the five-step procedure described in the proof of the previous theorem, as follows.

1. In productions $S \to CAaD$, $Aa \to aaA$, and $aB \to Ba$, replace each a with a'. Add a' to N_{KNF} and $a' \to a$ to P_{KNF}. Because $a'B \to Ba'$ satisfies the Kuroda normal form, remove this production from P, and add $a'B \to Ba'$ to P_{KNF}. At this point, G contains four productions:

$$S \to CAa'D$$
$$Aa' \to a'a'A$$
$$CA \to A$$
$$AD \to \varepsilon$$

Concerning G_{KNF}, after step A, N_{KNF} and P_{KNF} are defined as follows:

$N_{KNF} = \{A, B, C, D, S, a'\}$

$P_{KNF} = \{AD \to BD, CB \to CA, a' \to a, a'B \to Ba'\}$

2. In G, replace

$$CA \to A$$

with

$$CA \to AX$$

Furthermore, replace

$$AD \to \varepsilon$$

with

$$AD \to XX$$

Moreover, add X to N_{KNF}, and include

$$X \to \varepsilon$$

into P_{KNF}. Because $CA \to AX$ and $AD \to XX$ satisfy the Kuroda normal form, move both from P to P_{KNF}. At this point,

$P = \{S \to CAa'D, Aa' \to a'a'A\}$

$N_{KNF} = \{A, B, C, D, S, a', X\}$

$P_{KNF} = \{AD \to BD, CB \to CA, a' \to a, a'B \to Ba', CA \to AX, AD \to XX, X \to \varepsilon\}$

3. Because G has no unit production (a unit production has one nonterminal on both of its sides), this step does not change G or G_{KNF}.

4. As

$$S \to CAa'D \in P,$$

add $\langle Aa'D \rangle$ and $\langle a'D \rangle$ to N_{KNF}. In addition, include

$$S \to C\langle Aa'D \rangle$$
$$\langle Aa'D \rangle \to A\langle a'D \rangle$$
$$\langle a'D \rangle \to a'D$$

in P_{KNF}, and remove $S \to CAa'D$ from P. As a result,

$P = \{Aa' \to a'a'A\}$

$N_{KNF} = \{A, B, C, D, S, a', X, \langle Aa'D \rangle, \langle a'D \rangle\}$

$P_{KNF} = \{AD \to BD, CB \to CA, a' \to a, a'B \to Ba', CA \to AX, AD \to XX, X \to \varepsilon,$
$\qquad S \to C\langle Aa'D \rangle, \langle Aa'D \rangle \to A\langle a'D \rangle, \langle a'D \rangle \to a'D\}$

5. Because

$$Aa' \to a'a'A \in P,$$

add the new nonterminal Y to N_{KNF}. Include

$$Aa' \to a'Y$$

in P_{KNF}. Moreover, as $|a'A| \le 2$, introduce

$$Y \to a'A$$

and add this production to P_{KNF} as well. Remove $Aa' \to a'a'A$ from P. After this removal $P = \varnothing$, so the construction of G_{KNF} is completed. Thus,

$$G_{KNF} = (N_{KNF}, \{a\}, P_{KNF}, S)$$

where

$N_{KNF} = \{A, B, C, D, S, X, Y, \langle Aa'D \rangle, \langle a'D \rangle, a'\}$
$P_{KNF} = \{S \to C\langle Aa'D \rangle, Aa' \to a'Y, AD \to BD, AD \to XX, CA \to AX, CB \to CA,$
$\qquad X \to \varepsilon, Y \to a'A, \langle Aa'D \rangle \to A\langle a'D \rangle, \langle a'D \rangle \to a'D, a' \to a, a'B \to Ba'\}$

To make G_{KNF} more readable, change $\langle Aa'D \rangle, \langle a'D \rangle$, and a' to U, V and W, respectively. Then, G_{KNF} is defined by these productions:

$S \to CU$
$AW \to WY$
$AD \to BD$
$AD \to XX$
$CA \to AX$
$CB \to CA$
$X \to \varepsilon$
$Y \to WA$
$U \to AV$
$V \to WD$
$W \to a$
$WB \to BW$

Observe that G_{KNF} satisfies the Kuroda normal form. The exercises verify that

$$L(G_{KNF}) = \{a^{2^n} : n \geq 1\}$$

Part 6 of Example 8.3.1 proves

$$L(G) = \{a^{2^n} : n \geq 1\}$$

Thus, G_{KNF} represents a Kuroda normal form grammar equivalent to G.

▲

Recall that Kuroda normal form grammars permit these four forms of production

1. $AB \to DC$
2. $A \to BC$
3. $A \to a$
4. $A \to \varepsilon$

Unless these grammars have productions for all these four forms, their power is decreased:

1. Without productions of the form $AB \to DC$, these grammars actually become context-free grammars, which are less powerful than unrestricted grammars (see Theorem 8.4.1).
2. Without productions of the form $A \to BC$, these grammars cannot expand the start symbol, so they can generate only symbols and ε.

Generalized models

3. Without productions of the form $A \to a$, these grammars can generate only ε.
4. Without productions of the form $A \to \varepsilon$, these grammars also decrease their power because they are as powerful as context-sensitive grammars, which are less powerful than unrestricted grammars (see Theorems 8.3.4.4.1 and 8.4.1).

Pentonnen normal form

Consider a Kuroda normal form grammar G. If in G, every production of the form $AB \to DC$ satisfies $A = D$, G represents a Pentonnen normal form grammar.

Definition — Pentonnen normal form
Let $G = (N, T, P, S)$ be an unrestricted grammar. G is in *Pentonnen normal form* if every production $p \in P$ has one of these four forms

1. $AB \to AC$ with $A, B, C \in N$
2. $A \to BC$ with $A, B, \in N$
3. $A \to a$ with $A \in N$ and $a \in T$
4. $A \to \varepsilon$ with $A \in T$

Theorem 8.3.3.2
Let $G = (N, T, P, S)$ be an unrestricted grammar. Then, there exists an unrestricted grammar, $G_{PNF} = (N_{PNF}, T, P_{PNF}, S)$, such that $L(G) = L(G_{PNF})$, and G_{PNF} is in Pentonnen normal form.

Proof
Let $G = (N, T, P, S)$ be an unrestricted grammar. From Theorem 8.3.3.1, without any loss of generality, assume that G satisfies the Kuroda normal form. Convert G to an equivalent unrestricted grammar, G_{PNF}, in Pentonnen normal form. A detailed description of this conversion is left to the exercises.

∎

8.3.4 Context-sensitive grammars

Context-sensitive grammars represent special cases of unrestricted grammars in which each production has its right-hand side at least as long as its left-hand side. Section 8.3.4.1 defines context-sensitive grammars and demonstrates that they are more powerful than context-free grammars. Section 8.3.4.2 returns to linear-bounded automata, introduced in Section 8.1.7, and demonstrates that these automata are equivalent to context-sensitive grammars. Section 8.3.4.3 proves that the family of recursive languages properly contains the family of languages generated by context-sensitive grammars. Finally, Section 8.3.4.4 normalizes context-sensitive grammars by analogy with the normalization presented in the previous section.

8.3.4.1 Basic definitions

Definition — context-sensitive grammar
Let $G = (N, T, P, S)$ be an unrestricted grammar. G is a *context-sensitive grammar* if $p \in P$ implies $|\text{lhs}(p)| \leq |\text{rhs}(p)|$.
◆

Definition — context-sensitive language
A language L is a *context-sensitive language* if there exists a context-sensitive grammar G such that $L = L(G)$.
◆

Observe that every context-sensitive grammar $G = (N, T, P, S)$ satisfies these three properties.

1. For all $p \in P$, $1 \leq |\text{rhs}(p)|$, so $\varepsilon \notin L(G)$.
2. If every $p \in P$ satisfies $\text{lhs}(p) \in N$, then G, in effect, represents an ε-free context-free grammar (see Section 5.1.3.2).
3. As $p \in P$ implies $|\text{lhs}(p)| \leq |\text{rhs}(p)|$, $x \Rightarrow y$ in G implies $|x| \leq |y|$; therefore, if $w \in L(G)$ and $S \Rightarrow^* v \Rightarrow^* w$, then $|v| \leq |w|$. Hence, G generates w by a derivation in which no sentential form is longer than $|w|$.

Example 8.3.4.1.1 Context-sensitive grammar
Example 8.3.1.1 discusses the following unrestricted grammar:

$S \to CAaD$
$Aa \to aaA$
$AD \to BD$
$aB \to Ba$
$CB \to CA$
$CA \to A$
$AD \to \varepsilon$

Recall that this grammar generates

$$\{a^{2^i} : i \geq 1\}$$

This grammar is not context-sensitive because its productions $CA \to A$ and $AD \to \varepsilon$ have the right-hand side shorter than the left-hand side. However, $\{a^{2^i} : i \geq 1\}$ is a context-free language because there exists a context-sensitive grammar that generates this language. Indeed, the following grammar is context-sensitive and generates $\{a^{2^i} : i \geq 1\}$:

1: $S \to CAD$
2: $Aa \to aaA$
3: $AD \to BaD$
4: $aB \to Ba$
5: $CB \to CA$
6: $CA \to AA$
7: $AD \to aE$
8: $AE \to aa$
9: $S \to aa$

where A, B, C, D, E and S are nonterminals, S is the start symbol, and a is a terminal. Consider a^{16}; G generates this word as follows

$$\begin{aligned}
S &\Rightarrow CAD & [1] \\
&\Rightarrow CBaD & [3] \\
&\Rightarrow CAaD & [5] \\
&\Rightarrow CaaAD & [2] \\
&\Rightarrow^* CBaaaD & [344] \\
&\Rightarrow AAaaaD & [6] \\
&\Rightarrow^* AaaaaaaaE & [2227] \\
&\Rightarrow^* a^{16} & [22222228]
\end{aligned}$$

By analogy with the technique described in Part 5 of Example 8.3.1, the exercises formally verifies that

$$L(G) = \{a^{2^i} : i \geq 1\}$$

▲

Context-free languages and context-sensitive languages

By using the previous example, the next theorem states the relationship between the family of context-free languages and the family of context-sensitive languages.

Theorem 8.3.4.1.1
The family of context-sensitive languages properly contains the family of context-free languages without ε.

Proof
From Corollary 5.1.3.2.5, for every context-free language L there exists an ε-free context-free grammar G satisfying $L(G) = L - \{\varepsilon\}$. As already noted, every ε-free context-free grammar represents a special case of a context-sensitive grammar. Consequently, the family of context-sensitive languages contains the family of context-free languages without ε.

Example 8.3.4.1.1 presents a context-sensitive grammar that generates $\{a^{2^i}: n \geq 1\}$. By using Lemma 6.1.3, the pumping lemma for context-free languages, prove that $\{a^{2^i}: i \geq 1\}$ is not context-free; a detailed version of this proof is left to the exercises. Therefore, the family of context-sensitive languages properly contains the family of context-free languages without ε, so Theorem 8.3.4.1.1 holds. ∎

8.3.4.2 Context-sensitive grammars and linear-bounded automata

This section demonstrates that context-sensitive grammars are equivalent to linear-bounded automata, discussed in Section 8.1.7. First, the proof of Theorem 8.3.4.2.1 explains how to transform any context-sensitive grammar to an equivalent linear-bounded automaton. Then, Algorithm 8.3.4.2.2 converts any linear-bounded automaton to an equivalent context-sensitive grammar. Finally, Theorem 8.3.4.2.4 states the equivalence between context-sensitive grammars and linear-bounded automata.

From context-sensitive grammars to linear-bounded automata

Theorem 8.3.4.2.1
For every context-sensitive grammar G there exists a linear-bounded automaton M that satisfies $L(M) = L(G)$.

Proof
From a context-sensitive grammar, this proof constructs an equivalent linear-bounded automaton with a three-track tape. Observe that this construction resembles the transformation of any unrestricted grammar to an equivalent Turing machine (see Theorem 8.3.2.1 and its proof).

More precisely, let $G = (N, T, P, S)$ be a context-sensitive grammar, and let $w \in T^*$, where $|w| = k$, for some $k \geq 0$. Assume that M's tape is initialized with w (see Figure 8.3.4.2.1); recall that # represents a special tape symbol, called the endmarker, which bounds the input word (see Section 8.1.7). If $k = 0$, M immediately halts and rejects

Generalized models

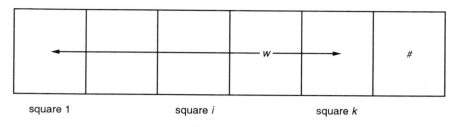

Figure 8.3.4.2.1 Initial containment of M's tape.

w because $w = \varepsilon$ and $\varepsilon \notin L(G)$. If $k \geq 1$, M divides its tape into three tracks. The first track contains w. The second track keeps the productions of P (if P has more than k productions, some of the second track's squares contain more than one production). Finally, during its computation, M uses the third track to keep the current sentential form; therefore, initially, this track contains S (see Figure 8.3.4.2.2).

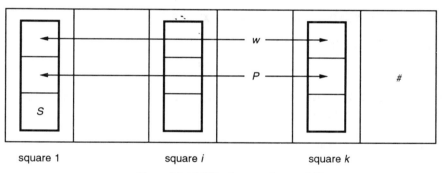

Figure 8.3.4.2.2 The three-track tape of M.

From this point on, M iterates the following four-step computational cycle:

1. Nondeterministically select a position, i, in the current sentential form on the third track.
2. Nondeterministically select a production p on the second track.
3. Let x be the current sentential form on the third track. Consider these two conditions:

    A. $|w| \geq |x| + (|\text{rhs}(p)| - |\text{lhs}(p)|)$
    B. on the third track, positions i through $i + |\text{lhs}(p)| - 1$ contain lhs(p)

    If A and B are true, then replace this occurrence of lhs(p) with rhs(p) on the third track; otherwise, reject w and halt.
4. If the third track contains w, accept w and halt; otherwise, go to step 1.

Steps 1, 2 and 4 are similar to the corresponding steps in the proof of Theorem 8.3.2.1. Concerning step 3, if $|w| < |x| + (|\text{rhs}(p)| - |\text{lhs}(p)|)$, then M rejects w because the sentential form obtained by replacing lhs(p) with rhs(p) is longer than w (recall that a context-sensitive grammar generates every sentence, z, by a derivation that does not contain a sentential form longer than z). On the other hand, if $|w| \geq |x| + (|\text{rhs}(p)| - |\text{lhs}(p)|)$ and, in addition, the third track's positions i through $i + |\text{lhs}(p)| - 1$ contain lhs(p), then M replaces this occurrence of lhs(p) with rhs(p). More exactly, M first shifts the nonblank suffix that follows lhs(p) to the right by $(|\text{rhs}(p)| - |\text{lhs}(p)|)$ squares, then M carries out this replacement.

Notice that $S \Rightarrow^* x$ in G if and only if x appears on the third track of M's tape, so $w \in L(G)$ if and only if $w \in L(M)$. In other words,

$$L(M) = L(G)$$

As a result, Theorem 8.3.4.2.1, whose detailed proof is left to the exercises, holds. ∎

From linear-bounded automata to context-sensitive grammars

By analogy with Algorithm 8.3.2.2 the next algorithm converts any linear-bounded automaton into an equivalent context-sensitive grammar.

Algorithm 8.3.4.2.2: Conversion of a linear-bounded automaton to an equivalent context-sensitive grammar

Input: A linear-bounded automaton $M = (Q, \Sigma, R, s, F)$.

Output: A context-sensitive grammar $G = (N, \Sigma_I, P, S)$, such that $L(G) = L(M)$.

Method

begin
$\quad N := \{\langle aqXZ\rangle : a \in \Sigma_I, q \in Q \cup \{\varepsilon\}, X \in \Sigma - \{\#\}, Z \in \{\#, \varepsilon\}\} \cup \{S, A\}$ {S and A are new symbols};
$\quad$**for** each $a \in \Sigma_I$ **do**
$\quad\quad P := P \cup \{S \to A\langle aa\#\rangle, S \to \langle asa\#\rangle\}$;
$\quad$**for** each $a \in \Sigma_I$ **do**
$\quad\quad P := P \cup \{A \to A\langle aa\rangle, A \to \langle asa\rangle\}$;
$\quad$**for** each $pY \vdash qX\!\downarrow\, \in R$ with $p \in Q - F, a \in \Sigma_I$, and $Z \in \{\#, \varepsilon\}$ **do**
$\quad\quad P := P \cup \{\langle apYZ\rangle \to \langle aqXZ\rangle\}$;
$\quad$**for** each $p\# \vdash q\#\!\downarrow\, \in R$ with $p \in Q - F, a \in \Sigma_I$, and $X \in \Sigma - \{\#\}$ **do**
$\quad\quad P := P \cup \{\langle apX\#\rangle \to \langle aqX\#\rangle\}$;
$\quad$**for** each $pY \vdash qX\!\lrcorner\, \in R$ with $p \in Q - F, a \in \Sigma_I, X \in \Sigma - \{\#\}$, and $\langle bV\rangle \in N$, where $b \in \Sigma_I$ and $V \in \Sigma - \{\#\}$ **do**

$P := P \cup \{\langle bV\rangle\langle apX\#\rangle \to \langle bqV\rangle\langle aX\#\rangle\}$;
 for each $p\# \vdash q\#\lrcorner \in R$ with $p \in Q - F, a \in \Sigma_I, X \in \Sigma - \{\#\}$, and $\langle bV\rangle \in N$, where $b \in \Sigma_I$ and $V \in \Sigma - \{\#\}$ **do**
$P := P \cup \{\langle bV\rangle\langle apX\#\rangle \to \langle bqV\rangle\langle aX\#\rangle\}$;
 for each $pY \vdash qX \hookrightarrow \in R, a \in \Sigma_I$, and $\langle bVZ\rangle \in N$
 where $b \in \Sigma_I, V \in \Sigma - \{\#\}, Z \in \{\#, \varepsilon\}$ **do**
$P := P \cup \{\langle apY\rangle\langle bVZ\rangle \to \langle aX\rangle\langle bqVZ\rangle\}$;
 for each $f \in F, a, b \in \Sigma_I, X \in \Sigma - \{\#\}, Z \in \{\#, \varepsilon\}$ **do**
$P := P \cup \{\langle afXZ\rangle \to a, b\langle aXZ\rangle \to ba, \langle aX\rangle b \to ab\}$
end

Lemma 8.3.4.2.3
Let $M = (Q, \Sigma, R, s, F)$ a linear-bounded automaton. With M as its input, Algorithm 8.3.4.2.2 halts and correctly constructs a context-sensitive grammar G such that $L(G) = L(M) - \{\varepsilon\}$.

Proof
Verify this lemma by analogy with the proof of Lemma 8.3.2.3. A detailed proof of Lemma 8.3.4.2.3 is left to the exercises. ∎

Equivalence of linear-bounded automata and context-sensitive grammars

Theorem 8.3.4.2.4
Let L be a language. Then, $L = L(M)$ for a linear-bounded automaton M if and only if $L - \{\varepsilon\} = L(G)$ for a context-sensitive grammar G.

Proof
This theorem follows from Theorem 8.3.4.2.1, Algorithm 8.3.4.2.2 and Lemma 8.3.4.2.3. ∎

8.3.4.3 Context-sensitive languages and recursive languages

This section proves that every context-sensitive language is recursive; however, some recursive languages are not context-sensitive. In other words, the family of recursive languages properly contains the family of context-sensitive languages. Consequently, from Theorems 8.1.6.2 and Theorem 8.3.4.2.4, context-sensitive grammars are less powerful than unrestricted grammars. In terms of automata, from Theorem 8.3.4.2.4, linear-bounded automata are less powerful than Turing machines.

To demonstrate the recursiveness of context-sensitive languages, recall that a context-sensitive grammar generates every sentence by a derivation that contains no sentential form longer than the sentence. This property implies that every context-sensitive language is recursive. Indeed, consider a context-sensitive grammar $G = (N, T, P, S)$ and a word $w \in T^*$. In addition, consider the set of all sequences of the form

$$x_0, \ldots, x_n$$

where n is a natural number, and these three properties hold:

1. $x_i \in (N \cup T)^*$, for $i = 0, \ldots, n$;
2. $x_0 = S$, and $x_n = w$;
3. $|x_j| \leq |x_k|$ and $x_j \neq x_k$, for all j, k such that $0 \leq j < k \leq n$.

The set of these sequences is finite because $|\text{lhs}(p)| \leq |\text{rhs}(p)|$ for any $p \in P$. Consequently, a deterministic Turing machine M can decide whether $w \in L(G)$ by generating this set on the tape, then checking if for some $m \geq 1$, this set contains a sequence,

$$y_0, \ldots, y_m$$

so

$$y_i \Rightarrow y_{i+1}$$

in G for $i = 0, \ldots, m-1$. If so, M accepts w and halts because

$$S = y_0, y_0 \Rightarrow y_1 \Rightarrow \ldots y_{n-1} \Rightarrow y_m, \text{ and } y_m = w,$$

so $w \in L(G)$; otherwise, M rejects and halts. As M always halts and $L(G) = L(M)$, $L(G)$ is recursive. The exercises reconsider in detail this method of demonstrating that every context-sensitive language is recursive. The proof of the following theorem makes this demonstration in a different way.

Theorem 8.3.4.3.1
Every context-sensitive language is recursive.

Proof
Given a context-sensitive grammar $G = (N, T, P, S)$ this proof construct a three-tape nondeterministic Turing machine M that always halts and accepts $L(G)$. Observe that this construction resembles the construction described in the proof of Theorem

8.3.2.1. However, there exists an important difference between these two constructions: M, constructed next, records all sentential forms of a derivation on the third tape, whereas the machine produced in the proof of Theorem 8.3.2.1 records only the current sentential form.

Let $w \in T^*$. Initially, with w placed on the first tape, M writes a list of all productions in P on the second tape. In addition, M writes $\$S$ on the third tape, where $\$$ is a special tape symbol acting as a separator of the sentential forms written on this tape. Then, M repeats the following four-step computational cycle:

1. On the third tape, nondeterministically select a position i so square i contains a symbol of a word x that appears between $\$$ and B as $\$xB$.
2. On the second tape, nondeterministically select a production p on the second tape.
3. If on the third tape, $\$xB$ equals $\$u\mathrm{lhs}(p)vB$ with $\mathrm{lhs}(p)$ appearing at positions i through $i + |\mathrm{lhs}(p)| - 1$, write $\$u\mathrm{rhs}(p)v$ behind the non-blank portion of the third tape (this portion begins at position $i + |\mathrm{lhs}(p)v|$); otherwise, reject w and halt.
4. Consider the following two conditions

    A. the third tape contains $\$u\mathrm{rhs}(p)v\$$ besides $\$u\mathrm{rhs}(p)vB$
    B. $|u\mathrm{rhs}(p)v| > |w|$

    If A or B is true, M rejects w and halts. If A and B are false, then test whether $u\mathrm{rhs}(p)v$ coincides with w. If so, accept w and halt; otherwise, go to step 1.

In step 1, x in $\$xB$ represents the most recent sentential form written on the third tape. Step 2 is analogous to the corresponding step in the proof of Theorem 8.3.2.1. In step 3, if the production, p, selected in step 2 is not applicable to x at positions i through $i + |\mathrm{lhs}(p)| - 1$, where i is selected in step 1, M rejects w and halts. Return to conditions A and B described in step 4: if A or B is true, M rejects w and halts. Informally, these two conditions are explained next.

Condition A
If $u\mathrm{rhs}(p)v$ appears on the third tape twice, then M has simulated a cyclic computation of the form

$$S \Rightarrow^* u\mathrm{rhs}(p)v \Rightarrow^+ u\mathrm{rhs}(p)v$$

Observe that if $S \Rightarrow^* x_1 \Rightarrow^+ x_2 \Rightarrow^* w$, where $x_1 = u\mathrm{rhs}(p)v = x_2$, then

$$S \Rightarrow^* x_1 \Rightarrow^* w$$

That is, G can generate every sentence by a noncyclic derivation. As a result, without any loss of generality, M simulates only noncyclic derivations.

Condition B
If $|\text{urhs}(p)v| > |w|$, G cannot derive w from $\text{urhs}(p)v$ because for every $p' \in P$, $|\text{lhs}(p')| \le |\text{rhs}(p')|$. Therefore, M rejects w and halts

If A and B are false, M checks if $\text{urhs}(p)v = w$. If so, M has simulated a derivation of the form

$$S \Rightarrow^* w$$

in G, so M accepts w and halts; otherwise, M goes to step 1 in order to simulate another step of the derivation written on the third tape.

Observe that M represents a Turing machine that always halts. In addition, $L(M) = L(G)$. By using *OneTapeDTM* presented in Section 8.1.4, convert M to an equivalent one-tape Turing machine. Thus, by Theorem 8.1.6.5, $L(G)$ is recursive. A detailed proof of this theorem is left to the exercises. ∎

The next lemma presents a non-context-sensitive language that is recursive.

Lemma 8.3.4.3.2
There exists a recursive language that is not context-sensitive.

Proof
Notice that some parts of the present proof resemble the proof of Lemma 8.1.5.5. Let

$$\mathbb{N} = \{A_0, A_1, A_2, \ldots\}$$

be an infinite set. Throughout this proof, assume that every context-sensitive grammar $G = (N, T, P, S)$, satisfies

$$N \subseteq \mathbb{N} \text{ and } S = A_0$$

This assumption represents no loss of generality because nonterminals in N can be always renamed so that $N \subseteq \mathbb{N}$ and $L(G)$ remains unchanged. Consider an enumeration

$$G_1, G_2, \ldots$$

of all context-sensitive grammars that possess only two terminals, 0 and 1. This enumeration can be obtained by analogy with the method producing an enumeration of all deterministic Turing machines with input symbols 0 and 1 (see Section 8.1.5). Moreover, let

Generalized models

$$x_1, x_2, \ldots$$

be an enumeration of all nonempty words over $\{0, 1\}$. Set

$L_{\text{Generation}} = \{ x_i : x_i \in L(G_i)$, where $G = (N, \{0, 1\}, P, S)$ is a context-sensitive grammar and $i \geq 1 \}$

and let $L_{\text{NonGeneration}}$ be the complement of $L_{\text{Generation}}$; that is,

$$L_{\text{NonGeneration}} = \{0, 1\}^* - L_{\text{Generation}}$$

The rest of this proof demonstrates that $L_{\text{NonGeneration}}$ represents a recursive language that is not context-sensitive.

Claim A
$L_{\text{NonGeneration}}$ is recursive.

Proof
Return to the enumeration

$$G_1, G_2, \ldots$$

From Theorem 8.3.4.3.1, for all $i \geq 1$, $L(G_i)$ is recursive. Let M_i be a deterministic Turing machine that always halts and satisfies

$$L(M_i) = L(G_i)$$

Construct a deterministic Turing machine M that takes a given input word, $w \in \{0, 1\}^*$, and in the enumeration $x_1, x_2, \ldots$, finds x_i, where $i \geq 1$, that satisfies

$$w = x_i$$

Then, M works as M_i except that

M rejects and halts if and only if M_i accepts and halts

by this equivalence,

M accepts and halts if and only if M_i rejects and halts

Observe that M represents a deterministic Turing machine that always halts and satisfies

$$L(M) = L_{\text{NonGeneration}}$$

Hence, $L_{\text{NonGeneration}}$ is recursive, so Claim A holds.

Claim B
$L_{\text{NonGeneration}}$ is not context-sensitive.

Proof
This proof is made by contradiction. Assume that $L_{\text{NonGeneration}}$ is context-sensitive. Return to the enumeration $G_1, G_2, \ldots$. As $L_{\text{NonGeneration}} \subseteq \{0, 1\}^*$, this enumeration contains G_k, where $k \geq 1$, satisfying

$$L_{\text{NonGeneration}} = L(G_k)$$

Consider the kth binary word x_k in the enumeration $x_1, x_2, \ldots$. Next, this proof considers two cases, $x_k \in L(G_k)$ and $x_k \notin L(G_k)$.

1. Suppose that $x_k \in L(G_k)$. By the definition of $L_{\text{Generation}}$, $x_k \in L_{\text{Generation}}$, so $x_k \notin L_{\text{NonGeneration}}$. As $L_{\text{NonGeneration}} = L(G_k)$, $x_k \notin L(G_k)$ – a contradiction.
2. Suppose that $x_k \notin L(G_k)$. Thus, $x_k \notin L_{\text{Generation}}$. Therefore, $x_k \in L_{\text{NonGeneration}}$. As $L_{\text{NonGeneration}} = L(G_k)$, $x_k \in L(G_k)$ – a contradiction.

As a result, $L_{\text{NonGeneration}}$ is not context-sensitive.

$L_{\text{NonGeneration}}$ represents a recursive language that is not context-sensitive, so Lemma 8.3.4.3.2 holds. ∎

Theorem 8.3.4.3.3
The family of recursive languages properly contains the family of context-sensitive languages.

Proof
This theorem follows from Theorems 8.3.4.3.1 and 8.3.4.3.2. ∎

8.3.4.4 Normal forms of context-sensitive grammars

Section 8.3.3 introduces Kuroda normal form and Pentonnen normal forms for unrestricted grammars. The present section adapts these forms for context-sensitive grammars.

Definition — Kuroda normal form

Let $G = (N, T, P, S)$ be a context-sensitive grammar. G is in *Kuroda normal form* if every production $p \in P$ has one of these three forms

1. $AB \to DC$ with $A, B, C, D \in N$
2. $A \to BC$ with $A, B, \in N$
3. $A \to a$ with $A \in N$ and $a \in T$

◆

Theorem 8.3.4.4.1

Let $G = (N, T, P, S)$ be a context-sensitive grammar. Then, there exists a context-sensitive grammar G_{KNF} such that $L(G) = L(G_{KNF})$, and G_{KNF} is in Kuroda normal form.

Proof
Demonstrate this theorem by analogy with the proof of Theorem 8.3.3.1; a detailed version of this demonstration is left to the exercises.

■

Definition — Pentonnen normal form

Let $G = (N, T, P, S)$ be a context-sensitive grammar. G is in *Pentonnen normal form* if every production $p \in P$ has one of these three forms

1. $AB \to AC$ with $A, B, C \in N$
2. $A \to BC$ with $A, B, \in N$
3. $A \to a$ with $A \in N$ and $a \in T$

◆

Theorem 8.3.4.4.2

Let $G = (N, T, P, S)$ be a context-sensitive grammar. Then, there exists a context-sensitive grammar G_{PNF} such that $L(G) = L(G_{PNF})$, and G_{PNF} is in Pentonnen normal form.

Proof
This proof is left to the exercises.

■

8.4 Hierarchy of language families

This section summarizes the relationships between several important families of languages.

Theorem 8.4.1
The following seven statements are true.

1. The family of regular languages properly contains the family of finite languages.
2. The family of deterministic context-free languages properly contains the family of regular languages.
3. The family of context-free languages properly contains the family of deterministic context-free languages.
4. The family of context-sensitive languages properly contains the family of context-free languages without ε.
5. The family of recursive languages properly contains the family of context-sensitive languages.
6. The family of recursively enumerable languages properly contains the family of recursive languages.
7. The family of all languages properly contains the family of recursively enumerable languages.

Proof
The first three statements hold by Theorem 7.1.8. Theorem 8.3.4.1.1 has stated the fourth statement. By Theorem 8.3.4.3.3, the fifth statement is true. Theorem 8.1.6.2 has established the sixth statement. Finally, by Theorem 8.1.5.6, the seventh statement holds. Therefore, Theorem 8.4.1 is true. ■

Finite automata and regular expressions represent fundamental computational modes that characterize the family of regular languages (see Chapters 3 and 4). Deterministic pushdown automata define the family of deterministic context-free languages (see Sections 5.2.3 and 7.1). Context-free grammars and pushdown automata characterize the family of context-free languages (see Chapters 5 and 6). Linear-bounded automata and context-sensitive grammars are basic models that characterize the family of context-sensitive languages (see Sections 8.1.7 and 8.3.4). Deterministic Turing machines that always hold define the family of recursive languages (see Section 8.1.6). Finally, Turing machines, two-pushdown automata and unrestricted grammars represent fundamental computational modes that characterize the family of recursively enumerable languages (see Chapter 8).

Generalized models   743

Exercises

1. Turing machines

1.1 Solve (A) through (C):
   (A) Give a Turing machine $M = (Q, \Sigma, R, s, F)$ and an input word $w \in \Sigma_I$ such that for some $f \in F$, $swB \vdash^* fB$ according to infinitely many rule words.
   (B) Give a Turing machine $M = (Q, \Sigma, R, s, F)$, and an input word $w \in \Sigma_I$ such that for some $f \in F$, $swB \vdash^* fB$ according to eight rule words.
   (C) Give a Turing machine $M = (Q, \Sigma, R, s, F)$, and an input word $w \in \Sigma_I$, such that for some $f \in F$, $swB \vdash^* fB$ according to one word.

1.2 Consider the following Turing machines M:

   1: $sB \vdash pB\lefthookdownarrow$
   2: $sa \vdash sa\hookrightarrow$
   3: $sb \vdash sc\hookrightarrow$
   4: $sc \vdash sc\hookrightarrow$
   5: $pa \vdash qB\lefthookdownarrow$
   6: $pc \vdash fB\downarrow$
   7: $qa \vdash qa\lefthookdownarrow$
   8: $qc \vdash qc\lefthookdownarrow$
   9: $qc \vdash sB\hookrightarrow$

   where f is its final state. Solve (A) through (D):

   (A) give M's state diagram;
   (B) give five words that M accepts;
   (C) give five words that M rejects;
   (D) determine the language that M accepts.

1.3 Return to the Turing machine in Example 8.1.1.1. Recall that this machine has nine rules. The language accepted by this machine is $\{a^n b^n : n \geq 0\}$. Construct another Turing machine that has fewer than nine rules and that also accepts $\{a^n b^n : n \geq 0\}$.

1.4 Exercise 1.1 in Chapter 6 discusses the following languages:

   (a) $\{a^i b^j c^k : i, j, k \geq 0 \text{ and } i < j < k\}$
   (b) $\{a^i b^j : i, j \geq 0 \text{ and } j = i^2\}$
   (c) $\{a^i : i \text{ is a prime}\}$
   (d) $\{w : w \in \{a, b, c\}^* \text{ and } \#_a w = \#_b w = \#_b w\}$
   (e) $\{a^i b^i c^j : i, j \geq 0 \text{ and } j \leq i\}$
   (f) $\{a^i b^i c^j : i, j \geq 0 \text{ and } i \leq j \leq 2i\}$
   (g) $\{a^i b^j c^k : i, j, k \geq 0, i \neq j, k \neq i, \text{ and } j \neq k\}$

(h) $\{a^i b^j c^j d^i : i, j \geq 0 \text{ and } j \leq i\}$
(i) $\{a^i b^{2i} c^i : i \geq 0\}$
(j) $\{ww : w \in \{a, b\}^*\}$
(k) $\{wvw : w \in \{a, b\}^* \text{ and } v = reversal(w)\}$

For each of these languages, construct a Turing machine that accepts the language.

1.5 Convert each of the Turing machines obtained in the previous exercise to an equivalent deterministic Turing machine by using the method described in Section 8.1.2.

1.6 Convert each of the deterministic Turing machines obtained in Exercise 1.5 to an equivalent deterministic Turing machine with only one noninput symbol, B. Base this conversion on OneTapeSymbolDTM (see Section 8.1.3).

1.7 Convert each of the deterministic Turing machines obtained in Exercise 1.5 to an equivalent deterministic Turing machine with only one final state. Base this conversion on Algorithm 8.1.3.4.

1.8 Restrict the definition of a Turing machine by disallowing stationary moves. A Turing machines restricted in this way thus shifts its tape head on every move. Formalize this restriction. Prove that for every Turing machine, there exists an equivalent Turing machine restricted in this way.

1.9 In a move, a *simple Turing machine* changes its state and either rewrites the tape symbol or shifts its head; consequently, a simple Turing machine cannot simultaneously change its state, rewrite the tape, and shift its head. Formalize the notion of a simple Turing machine. Prove that for every Turing machine, there exists an equivalent simple Turing machine.

1.10 Restrict the definition of the language accepted by a Turing machine $M = (Q, \Sigma, R, s, F)$ so that a word w is accepted by M if and only if $sw \vdash^* fw$, for some $f \in F$. Formalize this restriction. Prove that for every Turing machine M there exists a Turing machine that accepts $L(M)$ in this restricted way.

1.11 Restrict the definition of the language accepted by a Turing machine M so that a word w is accepted by M if and only if with w on its tape, M can reach a final state f and halt in f (that is, M cannot leave f by making another move). Formalize this restriction. Prove that the family of languages accepted by Turing machines in this restricted way coincides with the family of recursively enumerable languages.

1.12 Consider the languages discussed in Exercise 1.4 of this chapter. For each of these languages, construct a k-tape Turing machine that accepts the language. Make this construction so that the resulting k-tape Turing machine has fewer states, fewer tape symbols, or fewer rules than the corresponding one-tape machine obtained in Exercise 1.4 of this chapter.

1.13 Convert each of the k-tape Turing machines obtained in Exercise 1.12 to an equivalent deterministic Turing machine. Base this conversion on OneTapeDTM (see Section 8.1.4).

1.14 Consider the languages discussed in Exercise 1.4 of this chapter. For each of these languages, construct a k-head Turing machine that accepts the language.

1.15 Make this construction so that the resulting k-head Turing machine has fewer states, fewer tape symbols, or fewer rules than the corresponding one-head machine obtained in Exercise 1.4.

1.15 Section 8.1.4 explains how to transform any k-head deterministic Turing machine to an equivalent deterministic Turing machine. By using this transformation, convert each of the k-head Turing machines obtained in Exercise 1.14 to an equivalent deterministic Turing machine.

1.16 Consider the languages discussed in Exercise 1.4 of this chapter. For each of these languages, construct a Turing machine M with a two-way infinite tape so that M accepts the language. Make this construction so M has fewer states, fewer tape symbols, or fewer rules than the corresponding machine obtained in Exercise 1.4.

1.17 Section 8.1.4 explains how to transform any Turing machine with a two-way infinite tape to an equivalent deterministic Turing machine. By using this transformation, convert each of the machines constructed in Exercise 1.16 to an equivalent deterministic Turing machine.

1.18 Generalize the definition of a Turing machine by allowing a set of start states. Formalize this generalization. Prove that for every Turing machine generalized in this way, there exists an equivalent Turing machine.

1.19 In a move, a *lazy Turing machine* rewrites a word, consisting of several tape symbols. Formalize the notion of a lazy Turing machine. Prove that for every lazy Turing machine, there exists an equivalent Turing machine.

1.20 Section 8.1.5 has introduced the function δ. Consider its purpose, and define an alternative function for this purpose.

1.21 Return to the languages discussed in Exercise 1.4 of this chapter. For each of these languages, construct a deterministic Turing machine that accepts the language and that always halts.

1.22 Return to the languages discussed in Exercise 1.4 of this chapter. For each of these languages, construct a linear-bounded automaton that accepts the language.

1.23 Complete Part 8 of Example 8.1.1.1.

1.24 Complete Part 1 of Example 8.1.2.1.

1.25 For all natural numbers m and n, Section 8.1.2 has introduced the function

$$\text{Next}_{m,n}$$

over the set of sequences

$$\{ i_1, \ldots, i_m : i_k \text{ is an integer such that } 0 \leq i_k < n, \text{ where } k = 1, \ldots, m \}$$

Recall that:

1. For all $i_1, \ldots, i_m$ such that $n^{m-1} i_m + n^{m-2} i_{m-1} + \ldots n i_2 + i_1 < n^m - 1$:

$$\text{Next}_{m,n}(i_1, \ldots, i_m) = j_1, \ldots, j_m$$

if and only if

$$(n^{m-1}i_m + n^{m-2}i_{m-1} + \ldots + ni_2 + i_1) + 1 = n^{m-1}j_m + n^{m-2}j_{m-1} + \ldots + nj_2 + j_1$$

2. For $i_1, \ldots, i_m$ such that $n^{m-1}i_m + n^{m-2}i_{m-1} + \ldots ni_2 + i_1 = n^m - 1$:

$\text{Next}_{m,n}(i_1, \ldots, i_m)$ is undefined

Consider the set

$$\{j_1, \ldots, j_m: \text{Next}_{m,n}(i_1, \ldots, i_m) = j_1, \ldots, j_m, \text{ where } 0 \le i_k < n,$$
$$k = 1, \ldots, m, \text{ and } n^{m-1}i_m + n^{m-2}i_{m-1} + \ldots + i_1 < n^m - 1\}$$

and design an algorithm enumerating all members of this set.

1.26 Complete the proof of Theorem 8.1.2.2.
1.27 Complete the proof of Theorem 8.1.3.1
1.28 Prove Lemma 8.1.3.5.
1.29 Prove Theorem 8.1.3.7.
1.30 Prove Theorem 8.1.4.1 in detail.
1.31 Complete the proof of Theorem 8.1.4.2.
1.32 Formalize the notion of a k-head Turing machine.
1.33 Complete the proof of Theorem 8.1.4.3.
1.34 Complete the proof of Theorem 8.1.4.4.
1.35 Prove Theorem 8.1.4.5 in detail.
1.36 Prove Lemma 8.1.4.6 in detail.
1.37 Consider the functions Transformation and Replace (see Section 8.1.5). Describe both in detail.
1.38 Prove Theorem 8.1.5.1.
1.39 Complete the proof of Lemma 8.1.5.4.
1.40 Complete the proof of Theorem 8.1.6.5.
1.41 Formalize all Pascal-like descriptions of Turing machines given in this chapter in terms of the precise definition of a Turing machine (see Section 8.1.1).
1.42* Consider the families of recursively enumerable, recursive, and context-sensitive languages. Establish closure properties of these families under union, intersection, complement, substitution, and concatenation.
1.43 Consider the transformation of any Turing machine M to an equivalent deterministic Turing machine D (see Section 8.1.2). Recall that D works so that it explores all nonempty sequences of moves that M can make. Consequently, this exploration excludes the empty sequence. Explain why this exclusion represents no loss of generality.
1.44 Section 8.1.3 explains how to convert any deterministic Turing machine M to an equivalent deterministic Turing machine T that contains only one non input tape symbol, B. This conversion has assumed that M's input alphabet contains 0 and 1. Explain why this assumption represents no loss of generality.

Generalized models

1.45 Let n and m be two natural numbers. Consider deterministic Turing machines with no more than n tape symbols and no more than m states. Explain why Turing machines restricted in this way are less powerful than Turing machines without this restriction.

1.46 Consider the function δ in section 8.1.5. Design an algorithm that finds out whether a binary word w satisfies $w = \delta(M)$, where M is a deterministic Turing machine and, if $w = \delta(M)$, this algorithm converts $\delta(M)$ to M.

1.47 Section 8.1.5 has sketched how to enumerate all deterministic Turing machines that have the form $M = (Q, \{0, 1, B\}, R, q_0, \{q_1\})$, where $\Sigma_I = \{0, 1\}$ and $Q \subseteq \Theta$. Explain how to obtain this enumeration in detail.

1.48 Formalize the three-head Turing machine in Example 8.1.4.1.

2. Two-pushdown automata

2.1 Generalize $\vdash$ to $\vdash^n$, where $n \geq 0$, for two-pushdown automata by analogy with the corresponding generalization in terms of pushdown automata. Then, based on $\vdash^n$, introduce $\vdash^+$ and $\vdash^*$ for two-pushdown automata.

2.2 Solve (A) through (C):

(A) Give a two-pushdown automaton $M = (Q, \Sigma, R, s, F)$ and an input word $w \in \Sigma_I$, such that for some $f \in F$, $S|Ssw \vdash^* |f$ according to infinitely many rule words.

(B) Give a two-pushdown automaton $M = (Q, \Sigma, R, s, F)$ and an input word $w \in \Sigma_I^*$, such that for some $f \in F$, $S|Ssw \vdash^* |f$ according to five rule words.

(C) Give a two-pushdown automaton $M = (Q, \Sigma, R, s, F)$ and an input word $w \in \Sigma_I$, such that for some $f \in F$, $S|Ssw \vdash^* |f$ according to one rule word.

2.3 Consider the following two-pushdown automaton M,

$r_1: S|Ssa \vdash Sa|Saas$
$r_2: a|asa \vdash aa|aaas$
$r_3: a|asb \vdash a|p$
$r_4: a|apb \vdash a|p$
$r_5: a|Spc \vdash |Sq$
$r_6: a|Sqc \vdash |Sq$
$r_7: S|Sq \vdash |f$

where f is the final state of M. Solve (A) through (D):

(A) give five words that M accepts;
(B) give five words that M rejects;
(C) determine $L(M)$.

2.4 Consider these three two-pushdown automata:

M:

1: $S|Ssa \vdash Sa|Sas$

2: $a|asa \vdash aa|aas$
3: $a|as \vdash a|aq$
4: $a|aqb \vdash a|q$
5: $a|aqc \vdash |aq$
6: $S|Sq \vdash S|Ss$
7: $S|Sq \vdash |q$

M':

1: $S|Ssa \vdash S|Saas$
2: $S|Ssa \vdash Saa|Ss$
3: $a|asa \vdash a|aaas$
4: $a|asa \vdash aaa|as$
5: $a|asb \vdash a|q$
6: $a|aqb \vdash a|q$
7: $a|Sqc \vdash |Sp$
8: $a|Spc \vdash |Sp$
9: $S|Sp \vdash |s$

M'':

1: $S|Ssa \vdash Saa|Sas$
2: $a|asa \vdash aaa|aas$
3: $a|as \vdash a|aq$
4: $a|aqc \vdash |aq$
5: $a|aqb \vdash |q$
6: $S|Sq \vdash |s$

Determine $L(M)_\varepsilon$, $L(M')_\varepsilon$, and $L(M'')_\varepsilon$.

2.5 Consider these three two-pushdown automata:

M:

1: $S|Ssa \vdash Sa|Sas$
2: $a|asa \vdash aa|aas$
3: $a|as \vdash a|aq$
4: $a|aqb \vdash |q$
5: $a|aqc \vdash |q$
6: $S|Sq \vdash |f$

M':

1: $S|Ssa \vdash S|Sas$
2: $S|Ssa \vdash Sa|Ss$

3: $a|asa \vdash a|aas$
4: $a|asa \vdash aa|as$
5: $a|asc \vdash a|q$
6: $a|aqc \vdash a|q$
7: $a|Sqb \vdash |Sp$
8: $a|Spb \vdash |Sp$
9: $S|Sp \vdash |f$

M'':

1: $S|Ssa \vdash Saa|Sas$
2: $a|asa \vdash aaa|aas$
3: $a|as \vdash a|aq$
4: $a|aqc \vdash |aq$
5: $a|aq \vdash a|af$
6: $a|afb \vdash |f$

Determine $L(M)_f$, $L(M')_f$, $L(M'')_f$, $L(M)_{fe}$, $L(M')_{fe}$, and $L(M'')_{fe}$.

2.6 Consider these languages:

$$L_1 = \{a^{2^i} b^i c^{2^i} : i \geq 0\}$$

$$L_2 = \{a^{2^{2^i}} : i \geq 0\}$$

$$L_3 = \{w : w \in \{a, b, c\}^*, \#_a w = \#_b w = \#_c w\}$$

Construct three two-pushdown automata, M_1, M_2 and M_3, such that $L_1 = L(M_1)_f$, $L_2 = L(M_2)_e$, and $L_3 = L(M_3)_{fe}$.

2.7 For each language L discussed in Exercise 1.4, construct three two-pushdown automata, M, M', and M'', such that $L = L(M)_f$, $L = L(M')_e$, and $L = L(M'')_{fe}$.

2.8 A *lazy two-pushdown automaton* can read a word during a move. Formalize this generalization. Design an algorithm that converts any lazy two-pushdown automaton to an equivalent two-pushdown automaton.

2.9 A *two-way pushdown automaton* moves in both directions on its input. Formalize this generalization. Design an algorithm that converts any two-way two-pushdown automaton to an equivalent two-pushdown automaton.

2.10 Introduce two-pushdown state diagrams by analogy with pushdown state diagrams.

2.11 By analogy with extended pushdown automata, introduce extended two-pushdown automata. Define the language accepted by an extended two-pushdown automata by final state, by empty pushdowns, and by final state and empty pushdowns.

2.12 By analogy with deterministic extended pushdown automata, define deterministic extended two-pushdown automata.

2.13 Adapt Algorithm 5.2.2.1 so it converts any extended two-pushdown automaton to an equivalent two-pushdown automaton.

2.14* Let L be a recursively enumerable language. Then, these six statements hold

(1) $L = L(M_f)_f$ for a two-pushdown automaton M_f;
(2) $L = L(M_\varepsilon)_\varepsilon$ for a two-pushdown automaton M_ε;
(3) $L = L(M_{f\varepsilon})_{f\varepsilon}$ for a two-pushdown automaton $M_{f\varepsilon}$;
(4) $L = L(M_f)_f$ for a deterministic two-pushdown automaton M_f;
(5) $L = L(M_\varepsilon)_\varepsilon$ for a deterministic two-pushdown automaton M_ε;
(6) $L = L(M_{f\varepsilon})_{f\varepsilon}$ for a deterministic two-pushdown automaton $M_{f\varepsilon}$.

Prove these statements.

2.15 Complete Part 4 of Example 8.2.1.1.
2.16 Complete Part 5 of Example 8.2.1.1.
2.17 Prove Theorem 8.2.1.1.
2.18 Prove Part 6 of Example 8.2.1.1.
2.19 Prove Theorem 8.2.1.2.
2.20 Complete Example 8.2.2.1.
2.21 Complete the proof of Lemma 8.2.3.1.
2.22 Complete the proof of Lemma 8.2.3.2.

3 Unrestricted grammars

3.1 Consider the following four unrestricted grammars:
(a) 1: $S \to aAbc$
    2: $S \to \varepsilon$
    3: $A \to aAbC$
    4: $A \to \varepsilon$
    5: $Cb \to bC$
    6: $Cc \to cc$
(b) 1: $S \to CAaDS$
    2: $Aa \to aA$
    3: $AD \to BD$
    4: $aB \to Baaa$
    5: $CB \to CA$
    6: $CA \to A$
    7: $AD \to \varepsilon$
(c) 1: $S \to CAaSD$
    2: $S \to \varepsilon$
    3: $Aa \to aaA$
    4: $AD \to BD$
    5: $aB \to Ba$
    6: $CB \to CA$

7: $CA \to A$
8: $AD \to \varepsilon$

(d) 1: $S \to AaB$
2: $A \to AC$
3: $Ca \to aaC$
4: $CB \to B$
5: $A \to \varepsilon$
6: $B \to \varepsilon$

For each of these grammars, solve (A) through (C):

(A) give five sentences generated by the grammar;
(B) give five words that the grammar does not generate;
(C) determine the language that the grammar generates.

3.2 Consider these languages:
(a) $\{a^i b^j c^k : i, j, k \geq 0 \text{ and } i = j = k\}$
(b) $\{a^i b^j c^k : i, j, k \geq 0 \text{ and } j \leq i \leq k\}$
(c) $\{a^i b^j c^k : i, j, k \geq 0 \text{ and } i \neq j \neq k\}$
(d) $\{a^i b^j c^k : i, j, k \geq 0 \text{ and } i = j = 2k\}$
(e) $\{a^i b^j c^k : i, j, k \geq 0 \text{ and } j > k > i\}$
(f) $\{a^i b^j c^k : i, j, k \geq 0 \text{ and } j = i + k\}$
(g) $\{a^i b^j c^k : i, j, k \geq 0 \text{ and } i = 2j = 3k\}$
(h) $\{a^i b^j c^k : i, j, k \geq 0 \text{ and } i = j = k^i\}$
(i) $\{a^i b^j c^k : i, j, k \geq 0 \text{ and } i < 2j < 2^k\}$
(j) $\{a^i b^j : i, j \geq 0 \text{ and } i \leq 2^j\}$
(k) $\{a^i b^j : i, j \geq 0 \text{ and } i^2 = j\}$
(l) $\{a^i b^i c^j : i, j \geq 0 \text{ and } i^4 = j\}$
(m) $\{a^i b^j c^j a^i : i, j \geq 0\}$
(n) $\{a^i b^j c^k d^l : i, j, k, l \geq 0, i < l < j \text{ and } j \neq k\}$
(o) $\{a^i b^j b^i a^j : i, j \geq 0 \text{ and } j^2 = i^4\}$
(p) $\{a^i b^j c^k d^i : i, j \geq 0 \text{ and } j^2 = i^4 = k\}$
(q) $\{a^i b^i c^i d^{2i} : i \geq 0\}$

For each of these languages, construct an unrestricted grammar that generates the language.

3.3 Consider the unrestricted grammars produced in the previous exercise. Convert each of them to an equivalent unrestricted grammar in Kuroda normal form.

3.4 Consider the Kuroda normal form grammars produced in the previous exercise. Convert each of them to an equivalent unrestricted grammar in Pentonnen normal form.

3.5 Let G be an unrestricted grammar in Pentonnen normal form, and $w \in L(G)$. What is the minimum number of derivation steps that G needs to make in order to generate w?

3.6   For each language L given in Exercise 3.2 of this chapter, construct a context-sensitive grammar G so $L(G) = L - \{\varepsilon\}$.
3.7   Consider the context-sensitive grammars produced in the previous exercise. Convert each of them to an equivalent context-sensitive grammar in Kuroda normal form.
3.7   Generalize $\Rightarrow$ to $\Rightarrow^n$, where $n \geq 0$, for unrestricted grammars by analogy with the corresponding generalization in terms of context-free grammars. Then, based on $\Rightarrow^n$, introduce $\Rightarrow^+$ and $\Rightarrow^*$ for unrestricted grammars.
3.8   A pure unrestricted grammar has only terminals. More precisely, a *pure unrestricted grammar* G is a triple,

$$G = (T, P, S)$$

where

T is an alphabet;
$P \subseteq T^+ \times T^*$ is a finite relationship;
$S \in T^+$ is the start word.

The language, $L(G)$, generated by G is defined as

$$L(G) = \{x: S \Rightarrow^* x\}$$

where $\Rightarrow^*$ has an analogous meaning to $\Rightarrow^*$ in terms of context-free grammars. Consider these languages

(a) $\{bbb, aa\}$
(b) $\{aa, aaaa\}$
(c) $\{a^n c^n b^n : n \geq 1\}$
(d) $\{a^n b^n : n \geq 1\}$

For each of these languages, prove or disprove that there exists a pure unrestricted grammar that generates the language.
3.9   Complete Part 5 of Example 8.3.1.
3.10 Section 8.3.2.1 has sketched a method that converts any unrestricted grammar to an equivalent three-tape Turing machine M by exploring all possible derivations in G. Describe this conversion in detail.
3.11 Complete the proof of Theorem 8.3.2.1.
3.12 Complete the proof of Lemma 8.3.2.3.
3.13 Complete Example 8.3.3.1.
3.14 Complete the proof of Theorem 8.3.3.1.
3.15 Prove Theorem 8.3.3.2.
3.16 Complete Example 8.3.4.1.1.
3.17 Complete the proof of Theorem 8.3.4.1.1.
3.18 Complete the proof of Theorem 8.3.4.2.1.

3.19 Prove Lemma 8.3.4.2.3.
3.20 Recall that every context-sensitive grammar generates each sentence w by a derivation that contains no sentential form longer than w. By using this property, Section 8.3.4.3 has sketched how to prove the recursiveness of context-sensitive languages. Give this proof in detail.
3.21 Complete the proof of Theorem 8.3.4.3.1.
3.22 Prove Theorem 8.3.4.4.1.
3.23 Prove Theorem 8.3.4.4.2.

Programming Projects

1. Turing machines

1.1 Write a program that decides whether a given Turing machine is deterministic.
1.2 Write a program that simulates a deterministic Turing machine. Base this program on Algorithm 8.1.2.1.
1.3 Write a program that simulates a deterministic two-tape Turing machine.
1.4 Write a program that simulates a deterministic ten-head Turing machine.
1.5 Write a program that simulates a deterministic Turing machine with a two-way infinite tape.
1.6 Section 8.1 describes several methods that modify Turing machines. Implement each of these methods.
1.7 Write a program that simulates a universal Turing machine (see Section 8.1.5).

2. Two-pushdown automata

2.1 Write a program that decides whether a given two-pushdown automaton is deterministic.
2.2 Write a program that simulates a deterministic two-pushdown automaton.
2.3 Consider Programming Project 2.3 in Chapter 5. This project transforms any deterministic pushdown automaton M to a program that simulates M. Recall that M is specified by its rules, and the output program, simulating M, has the form of Algorithm 5.2.3.10. Reformulate and solve this project in terms of deterministic two-pushdown automata.
2.4 Write a program that converts any deterministic Turing machine to an equivalent two-pushdown automaton. Base this program on the conversion given in the proof of Lemma 8.2.3.1.
2.5 Write a program that converts any deterministic two-pushdown automaton to an equivalent deterministic Turing machine. Base this program on the conversion given in the proof of Lemma 8.2.3.2.

3. Unrestricted grammars

3.1 Design a data structure for representing unrestricted grammars.

3.2 Given an unrestricted grammar G write a program that reads a natural number n and generates all n-step derivations in G.

3.3 Write a program that converts any unrestricted grammar to an equivalent Turing machine. Base this program on the conversion given in the proof of Theorem 8.3.2.1.

3.4 Write a program that converts any Turing machine to an equivalent unrestricted grammar. Base this program on Algorithm 8.3.2.2.

3.5 Write a program that converts any unrestricted grammar to an equivalent unrestricted grammar in Kuroda normal form. Base this program on the conversion given in the proof of Theorem 8.3.3.1.

3.6 Write a program that decides whether a given unrestricted grammar is context-sensitive.

3.7 Write a program that converts any context-sensitive grammar to an equivalent linear-bounded automaton. Base this program on the conversion given in the proof of Theorem 8.3.4.2.1.

3.8 Write a program that converts any linear-bounded automaton to an equivalent context-sensitive grammar, using Algorithm 8.3.4.2.2.

Bibliographical Notes

Turing Machines

Turing machines were introduced by Turing, (1936); Kleene, (1936), Church, (1936), and Post, (1936) gave alternative formulations of these machines. Turing, (1936) also described a universal Turing machine. Church (1936) presented his famous thesis that the notion of a procedure is equivalent to the notion of a Turing machine. Shannon, (1956) proved that the three-state deterministic Turing machines are as powerful as Turing machines. Hartmanis et al., (1965) discussed some important variants of Turing machines. Hartmanis sand Stearns, (1965) demonstrated how to simulate multihead Turing machines by one-head Turing machines. Hartmanis sand Stearns, (1965), Hartmanis et al., (1965) and Lewis et al., (1965) represent a series of crucial papers about resource-bounded Turing machines. Myhill, (1957) defined and studied linear-bounded automata.

Buchi, (1962), Hartmanis, (1967), Hennie and Stearns, (1966), Kleine and Ottmann, (1977), Minsky, (1960), Minsky, (1962), Priese, (1979), Watanabe, (1960, 1961) are important early studies of Turing machines. Beigel and Floyd, (1994), Berstel, (1979), Book, (1980), Brookshear, (1989), Bucher and Maurer, (1984), Carroll and Long, (1989), Eilenberg, (1974), Eilenberg, (1976), Harrison, (1965), Harrison, (1978), Hopcroft and Ullman, (1979), Kelley, (1995), Kuich and Salomaa, (1985), Lewis and Papadimitriou, (1981), Linz, (1990), Martin, (1991), Minsky, (1967), McNaughton, (1982), Revesz, (1983), Salomaa, (1969), Sudkamp, (1988), Salomaa, (1985) and Wood, (1987) discuss Turing machines in depth. Wood (1987) also covers two-pushdown automata.

Unrestricted grammars

Chomsky (1956, 1957) introduced unrestricted grammars. Chomsky, (1959) studied their properties and, most importantly, proved that these grammars characterize the family of recursively enumerable languages. Landweber, (1963) proved that the family of context-sensitive languages contains the family of languages accepted by deterministic linear-bounded automata. Kuroda, (1964) demonstrated that linear-bounded automata are equivalent to context-sensitive grammars.

Banerji (1963), Bar-Hillel, Perles and Shamir (1961), Floyd (1962) and Greibach (1965) are important early studies of unrestricted grammars. Beigel and Floyd (1994), Brookshear (1989), Bucher and Maurer (1984), Carroll and Long (1989), Denning et al. (1978), Harrison (1978), Hopcroft and Ullman (1979), Kelley (1995), Kuich and Salomaa (1985), Linz (1990), Martin (1991), McNaughton (1982), Pagan (1981), Prather (1976), Revesz (1983), Rozenberg and Salomaa (1997), Salomaa (1973), Sudkamp (1988), Salomaa (1985), and Savitch (1982) cover unrestricted grammars in detail.

Part V
Translations

The previous parts of this book have introduced and examined several models for languages. The present part adapts these models for translations. Chapter 9 modifies finite automata, pushdown automata and context-free grammars to finite transducers, pushdown transducers and translation grammars, respectively. To demonstrate the use of these models in practice, Chapter 9 also constructs a compiler based on these translation models. Chapter 10 derives Turing transducers from Turing machines. Based upon Turing transducers, Chapter 10 discusses the fundamental topics of computational theory, such as computability, decidability and computational complexity.

9 Finite and Pushdown Transducers

This chapter adapts the models introduced in Parts II and III for translations. Specifically, Section 9.1 modifies finite automata to finite transducers. Then, Section 9.2 generalizes context-free grammars and pushdown automata to translation grammars and pushdown transducers, respectively. Finally, based on the models introduced in Sections 9.1 and 9.2, Section 9.3 builds up a compiler.

9.1 Finite transducers

To obtain a finite transducer, extend a finite automaton so that it can read and also write (see Figure 9.1.1).

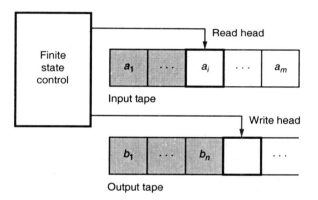

Figure 9.1.1 Finite transducer.

More precisely, a finite transducer, M, possesses two tapes — a read-only input tape and a write-only output tape. Both tapes are divided into squares. Each square of the input tape contains one symbol of a given input word, $a_1...a_i...a_m$. The symbol a_i, scanned by the read head, represents the current input symbol. The output tape is semi-infinite: its squares may extend infinitely to the right. If the output tape contains a word $b_1...b_n$, then the write head occurs over the square following the square filled with b_n. The finite control is represented by a finite set of states together with a finite relation, which is customarily specified as a set of computational rules. M works by making moves according to its computational rules. During a move, M

changes the current state, reads zero or one input symbol, and writes an output word. If M reads the input symbol a_i, then it shifts its read head one square to the right; however, if M reads no symbol, then it keeps this head stationary. Concerning the write head, M shifts this head a square behind the output word. One of M's states is defined as the start state, and some states are designated as final states. With its input tape containing a word x and with its output tape completely blank, M begins the translation of x from the start state. If M can make a sequence of moves so it reads all x, writes a word y on the output tape, and enters a final state, then M translates x to y (see Figure 9.1.2). The set that contains all pairs of words translated in this way forms the translation defined by M.

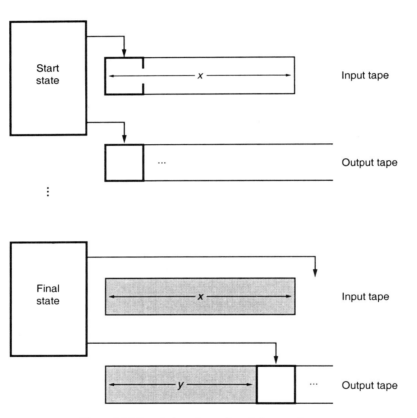

Figure 9.1.2 Translation of x to y by a finite transducer.

Example 9.1.1 Part 1 Intuitive design of a finite transducer

Consider the language

$$L = \{!\}^*\{a\}$$

Finite and pushdown transducers

Let $x \in L$. Notice that x has this form

$$!^i a$$

for some $i \geq 0$. In terms of the programming language C, ! denotes *not*. This initial part of Example 9.1.1 informally design a finite transducer M that reads x and removes all redundant !s from x. For instance, M translates !!a to a; however, it translates !!!!!a to !a.

M works so it counts the number of !s appearing in front of a. If this number is odd, M writes !a; if this number is even, it writes a. More precisely, M has the three states

$$s, q \text{ and } f$$

where s is the start state, and f is the final state. State s indicates an even number of !s and q indicates an odd number of !s. The input symbols of M are

$$! \text{ and } a$$

The output symbols coincide with the input symbols. M begins its computation in s, which corresponds to an even number of !s. Depending on the input symbol from s, M makes one of these two moves

with a, M enters f and writes a
with !, M enters q

From q, which which corresponds to an odd number of !s, M makes one of these two moves

with !, M enters s
with a, M enters f and writes a

Consequently, M works according to these four rules:

Rule 1: go from s to q on !
Rule 2: go from s to f on a and write a
Rule 3: go from q to s on !
Rule 4: go from q to f on a and write !a

$\triangle$

Definition — finite transducer

A *finite transducer* is a quintuple

$$M = (Q, \Sigma, R, s, F)$$

where

Q is a finite set of states;
Σ is an alphabet such that $\Sigma \cap Q = \Delta$ and $\Sigma = \Sigma_I \cup \Sigma_O$, where Σ_I is an input alphabet, and Σ_O is an output alphabet;
$R \subseteq Q(\Sigma_I \cup \{\varepsilon\}) \times Q\Sigma_O^*$ is a finite relationship;
$s \in Q$ is the start state;
$F \subseteq Q$ is a set of final states.

◆

Consider a finite transducer $M = (Q, \Sigma, R, s, F)$. Members of R are called rules, and R is thus referred to as a finite set of rules. Consider a rule $(pa, qz) \in R$ with $p, q \in Q$, $a \in \Sigma_I \cup \{\varepsilon\}$, and $z \in \Sigma_O^*$; instead of (pa, qw), this is written hereafter as

$$pa \vdash qz$$

To reference rules in a shorthand manner, they are labelled. To express that a label r denotes the rule, $pa \vdash qz$, write

$$r: pa \vdash qz,$$

where pa is the left-hand side of r, lhs(r), and qz is the right-hand side, rhs(r). Otherwise, this section specifies M by using the conventions introduced in Section 3.2 for finite automata.

Example 9.1.1 Part 2 Formal specification

Consider the finite transducer M defined in Part 1 of this example. Formally, M is defined by the rules

1: $s! \vdash q$
2: $sa \vdash fa$
3: $q! \vdash s$
4: $qa \vdash f!a$

△

Graphically, a finite transducer $M = (Q, \Sigma, R, s, F)$ is represented by its finite state diagram, whose nodes are labelled with states of Q. The start state is indicated by an arrow, and the final states are doubly circled. If $pa \vdash qx \in R$, then there exists an edge going from p to q labelled with a/x (see Figure 9.1.3)

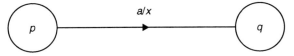

Figure 9.1.3 The representation of $pa \vdash qx$.

Example 9.1.1 Part 3 Finite state diagram

Figure 9.1.4 depicts the finite state diagram corresponding to M, discussed in the previous two parts of this example.

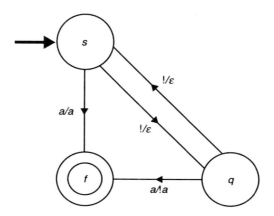

Figure 9.1.4 The finite state diagram of M.

△

As already noted, a finite transducer M works by making moves according to its rules. In a move, M changes the current state, reads zero or one input symbol, and emits an output word. The following definitions formalize the notion of a move made by M.

Definition — input finite automaton

Let $M = (Q, \Sigma, R, s, F)$ be a finite transducer. The *input finite automaton* M_I underlying M, is defined as

$$M_I = (Q, \Sigma_I, R_I, s, F)$$

where Σ_I is the input alphabet of M, and

$$R_I = \{qa \vdash p : qa \vdash px \in R \text{ for some } x \in \Sigma_O^*\}.$$

◆

Definition — configuration

Let $M = (Q, \Sigma, R, s, F)$ be a finite transducer. A *configuration* of M is a word χ that has the form

$$\chi = \chi_1 | y$$

where χ_I is a configuration of the input finite automaton M_I, underlying M, | is a special symbol (| $\notin \Sigma$), and $y \in \Sigma_O^*$.

◆

Convention
Given a finite transducer M, χ_M denotes a configuration of M. This section drops the subscript M in χ_M whenever no confusion exists; in other words, it simplifies χ_M to χ.

●

Definition — move
Let $M = (Q, \Sigma, R, s, F)$ be a finite transducer. Furthermore, let

$$\chi = \chi_I | y \text{ and } \chi' = \chi'_I | yz$$

be two configurations of M, and let $r: qa \vdash pz \in R$. If

$$\chi_I \vdash \chi'_I \ [qa \vdash p]$$

in the input finite automaton M_I underlying M, then M makes a *move* from χ to χ' according to r, symbolically written as

$$\chi \Vdash \chi' \quad [r]$$

◆

Convention
When the specification of the used rule r in $\chi \Vdash \chi'$ $[r]$ represents an immaterial piece of information, then $\chi \Vdash \chi'$ $[r]$ is simplified to $\chi \Vdash \chi'$.

●

Consider a finite transducer $M = (Q, \Sigma, R, s, F)$ and a configuration of M

$$\chi = \chi_I | y$$

where $y \in \Sigma_O^*$, and χ_I is a configuration of M_I such that

$$\chi_I = qax$$

where $q \in Q, a \in \Sigma_I$, and $x \in \Sigma_I^*$; that is,

$$\chi = qax | y$$

As Figure 9.1.5 indicates, $qax|y$ represents an instantaneous description of M:

1. q is the current state of M;
2. ax is the unread suffix of the input word, whose leftmost symbol a occurs under the input head
3. y is the output word emitted up to this point — the output head is over the square following this written portion of the output tape.

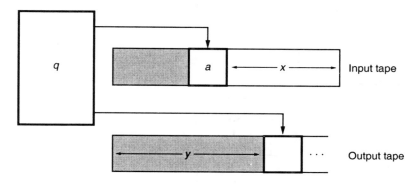

Figure 9.1.5 Configuration.

Consider a move according to $r: qa \vdash pz \in R$. As both a and z may equal ε, distinguish these four cases:

A. $a \in \Sigma_I$ and $z \in \Sigma_O^+$
B. $a = \varepsilon$ and $z \in \Sigma_O^+$
C. $a \in \Sigma_I$ and $z = \varepsilon$
D. $a = \varepsilon$ and $z = \varepsilon$.

A. Assume that $a \in \Sigma_I$ and $z \in \Sigma_O^+$. At this point, M leaves q for p, reads a on the input tape, shifts the input head one square to the right, writes z on the output tape, and positions the output head at the square following z (see Figure 9.1.6).
B. If $a = \varepsilon$ and $z \in \Sigma_O^+$, r has the form $r: q \vdash pz$. According to this rule, M goes from q to p and, in addition, writes z on the output tape; however, M does not shift the input head, so M scans the same input symbol in the next move.
C. If $a \in \Sigma_I$ and $z = \varepsilon$, r has the form $r: qa \vdash p$. At this point, M goes from q to p, shifts the input head one square to the right, but writes no symbol on the output tape.
D. If $a = \varepsilon$ and $z = \varepsilon$, r is of the form $r: q \vdash p$. According to this rule, M goes from q to p without reading or writing any symbols.

By analogy with Figure 9.1.6, the exercises pictorially describes cases B through D.

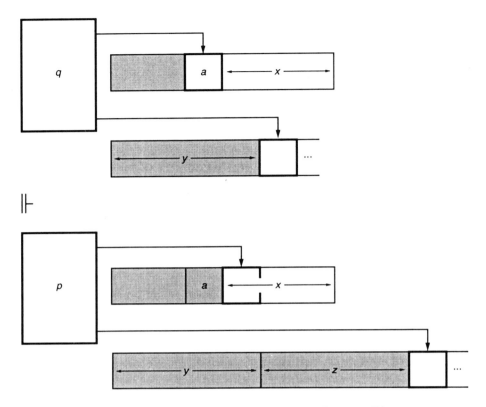

Figure 9.1.6 Move according to $qa \vdash pz$ with $a \in \Sigma_I$ and $z \in \Sigma_O^+$.

Example 9.1.1 Part 4 Moves

Consider the finite transducer M discussed in the previous parts of this example. Consider the configuration

$$qa|$$

and the rule

$$4: qa \vdash q!a.$$

By using this rule, M makes the move

$$qa| \vdash f|!a \ [10]$$

Furthermore, consider

$$s!a| $$

and

$$1: s! \vdash q$$

According to this rule, M computes

$$s!a| \vdash qa|$$

△

The following definition extends $\vdash$ to $\vdash^n$, where $n \geq 0$.

Definition — sequence of moves, part 1
Let $M = (Q, \Sigma, R, s, F)$ be a finite transducer.

1. Let χ be any configuration of M. M makes *zero moves* from χ to χ according to ε, written as

$$\chi \vdash^0 \chi \, [\varepsilon]$$

2. Let there exist a sequence of configurations

$$\chi_0, \ldots, \chi_n$$

for some $n \geq 1$ such that

$$\chi_{i-1} \vdash \chi_i \, [r_i]$$

where $r_i \in R$, $i = 1, \ldots, n$. Then, M makes n *moves* from χ_0 to χ_n according to $r_1 \ldots r_n$, written as

$$\chi_0 \vdash^n \chi_n \, [r_1 \ldots r_n]$$

◆

Let $M = (Q, \Sigma, R, s, F)$ be a finite transducer. Consider $\chi \vdash^n \chi' \, [\rho]$ in M, where ρ denotes a sequence of n rules from R ($\rho = \varepsilon$ if $n = 0$). Observe that ρ, called the *rule word* corresponding to $\chi \vdash^n \chi'$, specifies the sequence of rules according to which M makes $\chi_0 \vdash^n \chi_n$. Whenever this specification is immaterial, $\chi \vdash^n \chi' \, [\rho]$ is simplified to $\chi \vdash^n \chi'$.

Definition — sequence of moves, part 2
Let $M = (Q, \Sigma, R, s, F)$ be a finite transducer, and let χ and χ' be two configurations of M.

1. If there exists $n \geq 1$ so $\chi \models^n \chi'\ [\rho]$ in M, then $\chi \models^+ \chi'\ [\rho]$.
2. If there exists $n \geq 0$ so $\chi \models^n \chi'\ [\rho]$ in M, then $\chi \models^* \chi'\ [\rho]$.

◆

For brevity, the present section frequently writes $\chi \models^+ \chi'$ and $\chi \models^* \chi'$ instead of $\chi \models^+ \chi'\ [\rho]$ and $\chi \models^* \chi'$, respectively.

Example 9.1.1 Part 5 Move sequences
Reconsider M investigated in the previous parts of this example. Observe that

$$s!!!a| \models^4 f|!a \qquad [2324]$$

or, simply,

$$s!!!a| \models^4 f|!a$$

Therefore,

$$s!!!a| \models^+ f|!a \text{ and } s!!!a| \models^* f|!a$$

△

A finite transducer, $M = (Q, \Sigma, R, s, F)$, translates words over its input alphabet Σ_I, into words over its output alphabet Σ_O. Initially, an input word x is written on the input tape, the output tape is completely blank, and M is in the start state with both heads over the leftmost squares. If, starting from this initial configuration M can make a sequence of moves so it reads all x, writes a word y on the output tape, and enters a final state, then M translates x to y. The set that contains all pairs of words translated in this way forms the translation defined by M.

Definition — translation defined by finite transducer
Let $M = (Q, \Sigma, R, s, F)$ be a finite transducer, $x \in \Sigma_I^*$, and $y \in \Sigma_O^*$. M translates x into y if and only if

$$sx| \models^* f|y$$

in M, for some $f \in F$. The *translation defined by M*, $T(M)$, is

$$T(M) = \{(x, y): x \in \Sigma_I^*, y \in \Sigma_O^*, \text{ and } M \text{ translates } x \text{ into } y\}$$

The input language corresponding to $T(M)$ is defined as

$$L_I(M) = \{x: (x, y) \in T(M) \text{ for some } y \in \Sigma_O^*\}$$

The output language corresponding to $T(M)$ is defined as

$$L_O(M) = \{ y: (x, y) \in T(M) \text{ for some } x \in \Sigma_I^* \}$$

◆

Let $M = (Q, \Sigma, R, s, F)$ be any finite transducer. Then, as demonstrated in the exercises, both $L_I(M)$ and $L_O(M)$ are regular.

Example 9.1.1 Part 6 Translation
Return to M investigated throughout this example. Recall that

$$s!!!a| \vdash^* f|!a$$

in M. Therefore,

$$(!!!a, !a) \in T(M)$$

The exercises proves that

$$T(M) = \{ (!^i a, a): i \geq 0, \text{ and } i \text{ is even}\} \cup \{ (!^j a, !a): j \geq 1, \text{ and } j \text{ is odd}\}$$

▲

Determinism

According to the definition presented in the beginning of this section, finite transducers work nondeterministically because they can make several different moves from the same configuration. As a rule, however, practically oriented computer science uses their deterministic versions, defined next.

Definition — deterministic finite transducer
Let $M = (Q, \Sigma, R, s, F)$ be a finite transducer. M is *deterministic* if each rule, $r \in R$, where $\text{lhs}(r) = pa$ with $a \in \Sigma_I \cup \{\varepsilon\}$, satisfies

$$\{r\} = \{r': r' \in R, pa = \text{lhs}(r') \text{ or } p = \text{lhs}(r')\}$$

◆

Let $M = (Q, \Sigma, R, s, F)$ be a deterministic finite transducer. Notice that for every $q \in Q$ and $a \in \Sigma_I \cup \{\varepsilon\}$, if qa forms the left-hand side of a rule r, then no rule in $R - \{r\}$ has its left-hand side equal to qa or q. This property guarantees that M cannot make different moves from the same configuration. Observe, however, that although M is deterministic, it can translate the same input word into several different output words as the following example illustrates.

Example 9.1.2 Empty word translated to infinitely many words

Consider the one-rule deterministic finite transducer M defined by its rule

$$f \vdash f0,$$

where f is the start state and the final state. Observe that M translates ε into these infinitely many words

$$\varepsilon, 0, 00, \dots$$

That is,

$$T(M) = \{ (\varepsilon, 0^i): i \geq 0\}$$

▲

The exercises discusses how to guarantee that a given deterministic finite transducer translates every input word to no more than one output word.

9.2 Translation grammars and pushdown transducers

This section adapts context-free grammars and pushdown automata so they define translations rather than languages. Section 9.2.1 modifies context-free grammars to translation grammars, and Section 9.2.2 introduces pushdown transducers based on pushdown automata.

9.2.1 Translation grammars

A translation grammar G resembles a context-free grammar except that each productions in G has two words on its right-hand side. By using productions of this form, G generates pairs of words that belong to the translation defined by G.

Definition — translation grammar
A *translation grammar* is a quadruple

$$G = (N, T, P, S)$$

where

N is an alphabet of nonterminals;
T is an alphabet such that $T \cap N = \emptyset$ and $T = T_I \cup T_O$, where T_I is an input alphabet, and T_O is an output alphabet;

P is a finite set of productions of the form

$$A \twoheadrightarrow u_0 B_1 u_1 \ldots B_n u_n | v_0 B_1 v_1 \ldots B_n v_n$$

where $|$ is a special symbol such that $| \notin T \cap N$, for $j = 1, \ldots, n$, $B_j \in N$, for $i = 0, \ldots, n$, $u_i \in T_I^*$ and $v_i \in T_O^*$ ($n = 0$ implies $x = u_0$ and $y = v_0$); $S \in N$ is the start symbol.

◆

Consider a translation grammar $G = (N, T, P, S)$. This section frequently labels productions in P and uses these labels to refer to the productions that they denote in a shorthand manner. Thus, a label p denotes a production

$$A \twoheadrightarrow u_0 B_1 u_1 \ldots B_n u_n | v_0 B_1 v_1 \ldots B_n v_n \in P$$

as

$$p: A \twoheadrightarrow u_0 B_1 u_1 \ldots B_n u_n | v_0 B_1 v_1 \ldots B_n v_n$$

In $p: A \twoheadrightarrow u_0 B_1 u_1 \ldots B_n u_n | v_0 B_1 v_1 \ldots B_n v_n \in P$, A represents the left-hand side of p, lhs(p). Furthermore, $u_0 B_1 u_1 \ldots B_n u_n$ is the input right-hand side of p, irhs(p), and $v_0 B_1 v_1 \ldots B_n v_n$ is the output right-hand side of p, orhs(p). Otherwise, this section uses the conventions that Section 5.1 has introduced for context-free grammars.

Example 9.2.1.1 Part 1 Translation grammar
Consider the translation grammar G defined by the following six productions

1: ⟨expression⟩ ↠ ⟨expression⟩+⟨term⟩|⟨expression⟩⟨term⟩+

2: ⟨expression⟩ ↠ ⟨term⟩|⟨term⟩

3: ⟨term⟩ ↠ ⟨term⟩*⟨factor⟩|⟨term⟩⟨factor⟩*

4: ⟨term⟩ ↠ ⟨factor⟩|⟨factor⟩

5: ⟨factor⟩ ↠ (⟨expression⟩)|⟨expression⟩

6: ⟨factor⟩ ↠ a|a

G has three nonterminals — ⟨expression⟩, ⟨term⟩, and ⟨factor⟩, where ⟨expression⟩ is the start symbol of G. The input alphabet of G possesses five symbols — +, *, (,) and a. The output alphabet of G has three symbols — +, * and a.

△

Let $G = (N, T, P, S)$ be a translation grammar. By using productions in P, derive pairs of words from other pairs of words. More precisely, consider two words, $u_1 A u_2$ and $v_1 A v_2$, such that the same number of of nonterminals appears in u_1 and v_1.

Furthermore, let $p \in P$ with $\text{lhs}(p) = A$. By using p, G rewrites $u_1Au_2|v_1Av_2$ as $u_1\text{irhs}(p)u_2|v_1\text{orhs}(p)v_2$.

Definition — direct derivation

Let $G = (N, T, P, S)$ be a translation grammar, $p \in P$, and $x, y, u, v \in (N \cup T)^*$ so that the same number of nonterminals appears in x and u. Then, $x\text{lhs}(p)y|u\text{lhs}(p)v$ *directly derives* $x\text{irhs}(p)y|u\text{orhs}(p)v$ according to p in G; symbolically,

$$x\text{lhs}(p)y|u\text{lhs}(p)v \Longrightarrow x\text{irhs}(p)y|u\text{orhs}(p)v \quad [p]$$

or, briefly,

$$x\text{lhs}(p)y|u\text{lhs}(p)v \Longrightarrow x\text{irhs}(p)y|u\text{orhs}(p)v$$

◆

Example 9.2.1.1 Part 2 Direct derivations

Return to the translation grammar G defined in Part 1 of this example. Observe that G makes the direct derivation step

$$\langle\text{factor}\rangle*\langle\text{term}\rangle|\langle\text{factor}\rangle\langle\text{term}\rangle* \Longrightarrow (\langle\text{expression}\rangle)*\langle\text{term}\rangle|\langle\text{expression}\rangle\langle\text{term}\rangle* \quad [5]$$

where

$$5: \langle\text{factor}\rangle \twoheadrightarrow (\langle\text{expression}\rangle)|\langle\text{expression}\rangle$$

Furthermore,

$$(\langle\text{expression}\rangle)*\langle\text{term}\rangle|\langle\text{expression}\rangle\langle\text{term}\rangle* \Longrightarrow (\langle\text{term}\rangle)*\langle\text{term}\rangle|\langle\text{term}\rangle\langle\text{term}\rangle*$$

in G according to

$$2: \langle\text{expression}\rangle \twoheadrightarrow \langle\text{term}\rangle|\langle\text{term}\rangle$$

△

By analogy with the extension of $\Rightarrow$ to $\Rightarrow^n$ (see Section 5.1), the next definition extends $\Longrightarrow$ to $\Longrightarrow^n$, for $n \geq 0$.

Definition — derivation, part 1

Let $G = (N, T, P, S)$ be a translation grammar.

1. For any $u \in (N \cup T_I)^*$ and any $v \in (N \cup T_O)^*$, G makes *zero derivation steps* from $u|v$ to $u|v$ according to ε, written as

$$u|v \Longrightarrow^0 u|v \qquad [\varepsilon]$$

2. Let $u_0, ..., u_n \in (N \cup T_I)^*$ and $v_0, ..., u_n \in (N \cup T_O)^*$, for some $n \geq 1$, and let for $i = 1, ..., n$,

$$u_{i-1}|v_{i-1} \Longrightarrow u_i|v_i \qquad [p_i]$$

where $p_i \in P$. Then, G makes an *n-step derivation* from $u_0|v_0$ to $u_n|v_n$ according to $p_1...p_n$, written as

$$u_0|v_0 \Longrightarrow^n u_n|v_n \qquad [p_1...p_n]$$

◆

Consider a translation grammar G. Let $u_0|v_0 \Longrightarrow^n u_n|v_n\ [\pi]$ in G, where π denotes a sequence of n productions of P ($\pi = \varepsilon$ if $n = 0$). Note that π, called the *production word* corresponding to $u_0|v_0 \Longrightarrow^n u_n|v_n$, represents the sequence of productions according to which G makes $u_0|v_0 \Longrightarrow^n u_n|v_n$. When the representation is immaterial, this is simplified by writing $u_0|v_0 \Longrightarrow^n u_n|v_n$ instead of $u_0|v_0 \Longrightarrow^n u_n|v_n\ [\pi]$.

Definition — derivation, part 2
Let $G = (N, T, P, S)$ be a translation grammar, and let $u, x \in (N \cup T_I)^*$ and $v, y \in (N \cup T_O)^*$.

1. If there exists $n \geq 1$ so $u|v \Longrightarrow^n x|y\ [\pi]$ in G, then $u|v$ *properly derives* $x|y$ according to π in G, written as

$$u|v \Longrightarrow^+ x|y \qquad [\pi]$$

2. If there exists $n \geq 0$ so $u|v \Longrightarrow^n x|y\ [\pi]$ in G, then $u|v$ *properly derives* $x|y$ according to π in G, written as

$$u|v \Longrightarrow^* x|y \qquad [\pi]$$

◆

This chapter frequently simplifies $u|v \Longrightarrow^+ x|y\ [\pi]$ and $u|v \Longrightarrow^* x|y\ [\pi]$ to $u|v \Longrightarrow^+ x|y$ and $u|v \Longrightarrow^* x|y$, respectively.

Example 9.2.1.1 Part 4 Derivations
Consider the translation grammar G discussed in the previous parts of this example. Observe that

$(\langle\text{expression}\rangle)*\langle\text{term}\rangle|\langle\text{expression}\rangle\langle\text{term}\rangle*$
$\Rightarrow (\langle\text{expression}\rangle+\langle\text{term}\rangle)*\langle\text{term}\rangle|\langle\text{expression}\rangle\langle\text{term}\rangle+\langle\text{term}\rangle*$
$\Rightarrow (\langle\text{term}\rangle+\langle\text{term}\rangle)*\langle\text{term}\rangle|\langle\text{term}\rangle\langle\text{term}\rangle+\langle\text{term}\rangle*$
$\Rightarrow (\langle\text{factor}\rangle+\langle\text{term}\rangle)*\langle\text{term}\rangle|\langle\text{factor}\rangle\langle\text{term}\rangle+\langle\text{term}\rangle*$
$\Rightarrow (a+\langle\text{term}\rangle)*\langle\text{term}\rangle|a\langle\text{term}\rangle+\langle\text{term}\rangle*$

Thus,

$(\langle\text{expression}\rangle)*\langle\text{term}\rangle|\langle\text{expression}\rangle\langle\text{term}\rangle* \Rightarrow^4 (a+\langle\text{term}\rangle)*\langle\text{term}\rangle|a\langle\text{term}\rangle+\langle\text{term}\rangle*$

Therefore,

$(\langle\text{expression}\rangle)*\langle\text{term}\rangle|\langle\text{expression}\rangle\langle\text{term}\rangle* \Rightarrow^+ (a+\langle\text{term}\rangle)*\langle\text{term}\rangle|a\langle\text{term}\rangle+\langle\text{term}\rangle*$

and

$(\langle\text{expression}\rangle)*\langle\text{term}\rangle|\langle\text{expression}\rangle\langle\text{term}\rangle* \Rightarrow^* (a+\langle\text{term}\rangle)*\langle\text{term}\rangle|a\langle\text{term}\rangle+\langle\text{term}\rangle*$

△

Definition — translation defined by translation grammar

Let $G = (N, T, P, S)$ be a translation grammar. If $S|S \Rightarrow^* u|v$ in G, where $u \in T_I^*$ and $v \in T_O^*$, G translates u to v. The *translation defined by* G, $T(G)$, is

$$T(G) = \{ u|v : S|S \Rightarrow^* u|v, \text{ where } u \in T_I^* \text{ and } v \in T_O^*\}$$

◆

Example 9.2.1.1 Part 5 Translation

Observe that G, defined in Part 1 of this example, makes the following derivation:

$\langle\text{expression}\rangle|\langle\text{expression}\rangle$
$\Rightarrow \langle\text{term}\rangle|\langle\text{term}\rangle$
$\Rightarrow \langle\text{term}\rangle*\langle\text{factor}\rangle|\langle\text{term}\rangle\langle\text{factor}\rangle*$
$\Rightarrow \langle\text{factor}\rangle*\langle\text{factor}\rangle|\langle\text{factor}\rangle\langle\text{factor}\rangle*$
$\Rightarrow (\langle\text{expression}\rangle)*\langle\text{term}\rangle|\langle\text{expression}\rangle\langle\text{term}\rangle*$
$\Rightarrow (\langle\text{expression}\rangle+\langle\text{term}\rangle)*\langle\text{term}\rangle|\langle\text{expression}\rangle\langle\text{term}\rangle+\langle\text{term}\rangle*$
$\Rightarrow (\langle\text{term}\rangle+\langle\text{term}\rangle)*\langle\text{term}\rangle|\langle\text{term}\rangle\langle\text{term}\rangle+\langle\text{term}\rangle*$
$\Rightarrow (\langle\text{factor}\rangle+\langle\text{term}\rangle)*\langle\text{term}\rangle|\langle\text{factor}\rangle\langle\text{term}\rangle+\langle\text{term}\rangle*$
$\Rightarrow (a+\langle\text{term}\rangle)*\langle\text{term}\rangle|a\langle\text{term}\rangle+\langle\text{term}\rangle*$

$\Rightarrow$ $(a+\langle\text{factor}\rangle)*\langle\text{term}\rangle|a\langle\text{factor}\rangle+\langle\text{term}\rangle*$
$\Rightarrow$ $(a+a)*\langle\text{term}\rangle|aa+\langle\text{term}\rangle*$
$\Rightarrow$ $(a+a)*a|aa+a*$

Thus,

$$\langle\text{expression}\rangle|\langle\text{expression}\rangle \Rightarrow^* (a+a)*a|aa+a*$$

Therefore, G translates $(a+a)*a$ to $aa+a*$. As rigorously verified in the exercises, G translates infix arithmetic expressions to equivalent postfix Polish expressions.

△

There exist two context-free grammars (the input grammar G_I and the output grammar G_O) that underlie every translation grammar G. To obtain G_I, remove the second word occurring on the right-hand side of each production in G. Analogously, to obtain G_O, remove the first word occurring on the right-hand side of each production in G. The following definition formalizes G_I and G_O.

Definition — input and output grammars
Let $G = (N, T, P, S)$ be a translation grammar. The *input grammar* G_I, underlying G, is defined as

$$G_I = (N, T_I, P_I, S)$$

where

$$P_I = \{ A \to x: A \twoheadrightarrow x|y \in P\}.$$

The *output grammar* G_O, underlying G, is defined as

$$G_O = (N, T_O, P_O, S)$$

where

$$P_O = \{ A \to y: A \twoheadrightarrow x|y \in P\}.$$

◆

Example 9.2.1.1 Part 6 Input and Output Grammars
Return to the translation grammar G that the first part of this example defined by these six productions:

1: ⟨expression⟩ ↠ ⟨expression⟩+⟨term⟩|⟨expression⟩⟨term⟩+
2: ⟨expression⟩ ↠ ⟨term⟩|⟨term⟩
3: ⟨term⟩ ↠ ⟨term⟩*⟨factor⟩|⟨term⟩⟨factor⟩*
4: ⟨term⟩ ↠ ⟨factor⟩|⟨factor⟩
5: ⟨factor⟩ ↠ (⟨expression⟩)|⟨expression⟩
6: ⟨factor⟩ ↠ a|a

The input grammar G_I underlying G has the productions

⟨expression⟩ → ⟨expression⟩+⟨term⟩
⟨expression⟩ → ⟨term⟩
⟨term⟩ → ⟨term⟩*⟨factor⟩
⟨term⟩ → ⟨factor⟩
⟨factor⟩ → (⟨expression⟩)
⟨factor⟩ → a

The output grammar G_O, underlying G consists of the productions

⟨expression⟩ → ⟨expression⟩⟨term⟩+
⟨expression⟩ → ⟨term⟩
⟨term⟩ → ⟨term⟩⟨factor⟩*
⟨term⟩ → ⟨factor⟩
⟨factor⟩ → ⟨expression⟩
⟨factor⟩ → a

▲

The exercises generalize translation grammars by permitting productions of the form

$$A \twoheadrightarrow u_0 B_1 u_1 \ldots B_n u_n | v_0 C_1 v_1 \ldots C_n v_n$$

where n is a nonnegative integer, B_j and C_j are nonterminals for $j = 1, \ldots, n$ and, in addition, there exists a bijection β on $\{1, \ldots, n\}$ such that $B_j = C_{\beta(j)}$. Note that translation grammars generalized in this way are more powerful than the translation grammars discussed in this section.

9.2.2 Pushdown transducers

A pushdown transducer is based on a pushdown automaton. In addition to a pushdown and an input tape, a pushdown transducer has an output tape, on which it writes words (see Figure 9.2.2.1).

Finite and pushdown transducers

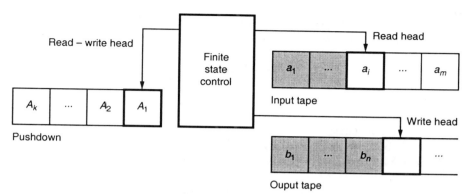

Figure 9.2.2.1 Pushdown transducer.

A pushdown transducer M has both tapes divided into squares. Each square of the input tape contains one symbol of an input word, $a_1 \ldots a_i \ldots a_m$. The symbol under the read head, a_i, is the current input symbol. The output tape is semi-infinite — that is, it's squares may extend infinitely to the right. If the output tape contains a word $b_1 \ldots b_n$, then the write head occurs over the square following the square filled with the rightmost symbol, b_n. The pushdown has the same meaning as in a pushdown automaton. The finite control of M is represented by a finite set of states together with a finite relationship, customarily specified as a finite set of rules. One of M's states is defined as the start state; some states are designated as final states. By using its rules, M computes moves. A move consists of changing the current state, replacing the top pushdown symbol with a word, reading zero or one input symbol, and writing an output word. Initially, the input tape contains a word x, the pushdown contains the start symbol S, the output tape is completely blank, and M occurs in the start state. If, from this initial configuration, M can read all input word x, write a word y, on the output tape, and reach a final state, then M translates x to y (see Figure 9.2.2.2) The set containing all pairs of words translated in this way forms the translation defined by M.

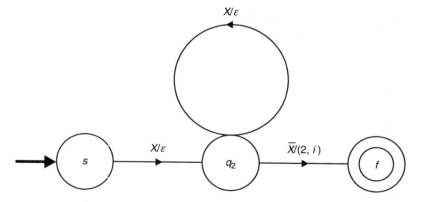

Figure 9.2.2.2 Translation of x to y by a pushdown transducer.

Definition — pushdown transducer
A *pushdown transducer* is a quintuple

$$M = (Q, \Sigma, R, s, F)$$

where

Q is a finite set of states;
Σ is an alphabet such that $\Sigma \cap Q = \emptyset$ and $\Sigma = \Sigma_I \cup \Sigma_O \cup \Sigma_{PD}$, where Σ_I is an input alphabet, Σ_O is an output alphabet and Σ_{PD} is a pushdown alphabet containing S, the start symbol;
$R \subseteq \Sigma_{PD} Q (\Sigma_I \cup \{\varepsilon\}) \times \Sigma_{PD}^* Q \Sigma_O^*$ is a finite relationship;
$s \in Q$ is the start state;
$F \subseteq Q$ is a set of final states.

◆

Consider a pushdown transducer $M = (Q, \Sigma, R, s, F)$. Members of R are called rules, and, R is thus referred to as a finite set of rules. Let $(Apa, wqv) \in R$, where $A \in \Sigma_{PD}$, $p, q \in Q$, $a \in \Sigma_I \cup \{\varepsilon\}$, $w \in \Sigma_{PD}^*$, and $v \in \Sigma_O^*$; instead of (Apa, wqv), it is convenient to write

$$Apa \vdash uqv$$

To express that a label r denotes a rule $Apa \vdash uqv$, write

$$r: Apa \vdash uqv$$

where the left-hand side of r, Apa, is denoted by lhs(r), and the right-hand side, uqv, is denoted by rhs(r). In addition, M is specified using the conventions introduced in Section 5.2 for pushdown automata.

Example 9.2.2.1 Part 1 Pushdown transducer
Consider the following pushdown transducer M:

1: $Ss \vdash SAq$
2: $Aqa \vdash qa$
3: $Aq+ \vdash +AAq$
4: $Aq* \vdash *AAq$
5: $+q \vdash q+$
6: $*q \vdash q*$
7: $Sq \vdash f$

M has three states — s, q and f — where s is the start state, and f is the final state. Its pushdown alphabet consists of $A, S, +$ and $*$, where S is the start pushdown symbol.

The input alphabet and the output alphabet of M contain the three symbols a, $+$ and $*$.

△

Section 5.2 represents pushdown automata by their pushdown state diagrams. The present section analogously represents pushdown transducers except that a rule, $Apa \vdash uqv$, is depicted as described in Figure 9.2.2.3.

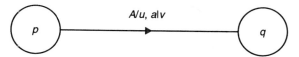

Figure 9.2.2.3 Graphical specification of $Apa \vdash uqv$.

Example 9.2.2.1 Part 2 Pushdown state diagram

Figure 9.2.2.4 depicts the pushdown state diagram corresponding to the pushdown transducer M defined in the previous part of this example.

△

A pushdown transducer M makes moves according to its rules. In a move, M changes the state of the finite control, replaces the top pushdown symbol with a word, reads zero or one input symbol, and writes a word on the output tape. The following definitions formalize the notion of a move.

Definition — input pushdown automaton

Let $M = (Q, \Sigma, R, s, F)$ be a pushdown transducer. The *input pushdown automaton* M_I, underlying M, is defined as

$$M_I = (Q, \Sigma_I \cup \Sigma_{PD}, R_I, s, F)$$

where Σ_I is the input alphabet of M, Σ_{PD} is the pushdown alphabet of M, and

$$R_I = \{Aqa \vdash up \colon Aqa \vdash upv \in R \text{ for some } v \in \Sigma_O^*\}.$$

◆

Definition — configuration

Let $M = (Q, \Sigma, R, s, F)$ be a pushdown transducer. A *configuration* of M is a word χ that has the form

$$\chi = \chi_1 | y$$

where χ_1 is a configuration of the input pushdown automaton, M_I, underlying M, $|$ is a special symbol ($| \notin \Sigma$), and $y \in \Sigma_O^*$.

◆

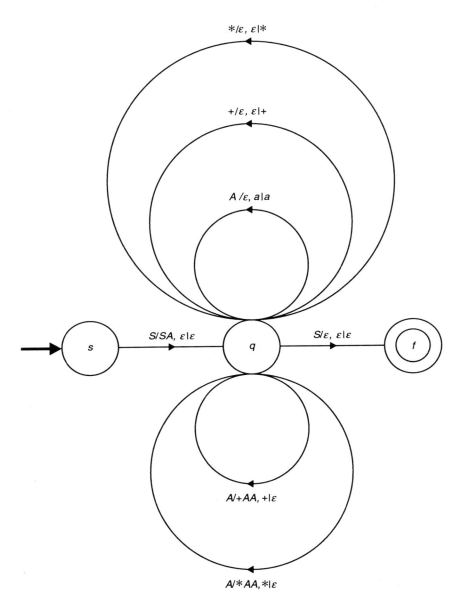

Figure 9.2.2.4 The pushdown state diagram of M.

Convention
Given a pushdown transducer M, χ_M denotes a configuration of M. Whenever no confusion exists, this is simplified χ_M to χ.

Definition — move

Let $M = (Q, \Sigma, R, s, F)$ be a pushdown transducer. Furthermore, let

$$\chi = \chi_I|y \text{ and } \chi' = \chi'_I|yv$$

be two configurations of M, and let $r\colon Aqa \vdash upv \in R$. If

$$\chi_I \vdash \chi'_I \quad [Aqa \vdash up]$$

in M_I, where M_I is the input pushdown automaton underlying M, then M makes a *move* from χ to χ' according to r, written as

$$\chi \Vdash \chi' \quad [r]$$

♦

Convention

Whenever the specification of the used rule, r, in $\chi \Vdash \chi'\ [r]$ is immaterial, $\chi \Vdash \chi'\ [r]$ is simplified to $\chi \Vdash \chi'$.

●

Consider a pushdown transducer $M = (Q, \Sigma, R, s, F)$ and a configuration of M,

$$\chi = \chi_I|y$$

where $y \in \Sigma_O^*$, and χ_I is a configuration of M_I such that

$$\chi_I = zAqax$$

for some $z \in \Sigma_{PD}^*$, $A \in \Sigma_{PD}$, $q \in Q$, $a \in \Sigma_I \cup \{\varepsilon\}$, and $x \in \Sigma_I^*$; consequently,

$$\chi = zAqax|y$$

As Figure 9.2.2.5 demonstrates, $zAqax|y$ represents an instantaneous description of M:

1. zA represents the current contents of the pushdown, whose rightmost symbol A occurs on the pushdown top.
2. q is the current state of M.
3. ax is the unread suffix of the input word, whose leftmost symbol occurs under the input head.
4. y is the output word emitted up to this point; the output head is over the square following this written portion of the output tape.

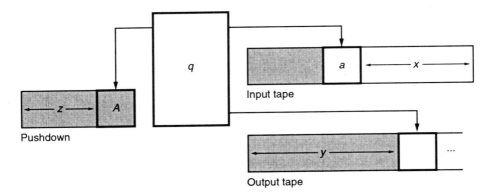

Figure 9.2.2.5 Configuration.

Next, is described a move according to $r: Aqa \vdash upv \in R$, where $a \in \Sigma_I$, $u \in \Sigma_{PD}^+$, and $v \in \Sigma_O^+$. During a move according to $r: Aqa \vdash upv$, M leaves q for p, replaces A with u on the pushdown top, reads a on the input tape, shifts the input head one square to the right, writes v on the output tape, and positions the output head at the square following v (see Figure 9.2.2.6).

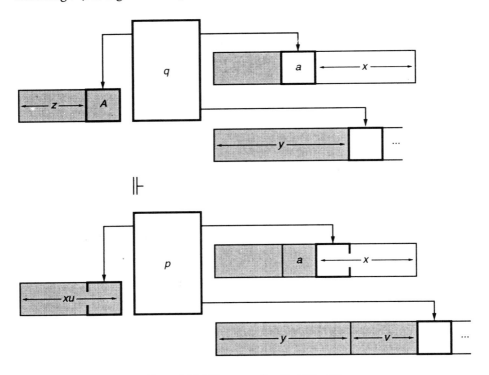

Figure 9.2.2.6 Move according to $Aqa \vdash upv$.

Finite and pushdown transducers

Consider a move according to r: $Aqa \vdash upv \in R$ with $\{a, u, v\} \cap \{\varepsilon\} \neq \emptyset$. If $a = \varepsilon$, M does not shift the read head. If $u = \varepsilon$, M actually removes A from the pushdown. If $v = \varepsilon$, M does not shift the write head. The exercises discusses a move according to r: $Aqa \vdash upv \in R$ with $\{a, u, v\} \cap \{\varepsilon\} \neq \emptyset$ in greater detail.

Example 9.2.2.1 Part 3 Moves

Consider the pushdown transducer M discussed in the previous parts of this example. Consider the configuration

$$S*A+qa|aa$$

and the rule

$$5: +q \vdash q+$$

(Part 2 of this example contains all rules of M). By using this rule, M makes the move

$$S*A+qa|aa \vDash S*Aqa|aa+$$

To describe another move, M computes

$$Sq|aa*a+ \vdash f|aa*a+ \qquad [7]$$

where 7: $Sq \vdash f$.

△

The next definition extends $\vdash$ to $\vdash^n$, where $n \geq 0$.

Definition — sequence of moves, part 1

Let $M = (Q, \Sigma, R, s, F)$ be a pushdown transducer.

1. Let χ be any configuration of M. M makes *zero moves* from χ to χ according to ε, written as

$$\chi \vdash^0 \chi \qquad [\varepsilon]$$

2. Let there exist a sequence of configurations

$$\chi_0, ..., \chi_n$$

for some $n \geq 1$ such that

$$\chi_{i-1} \vdash \chi_i \qquad [r_i]$$

where $r_i \in R, i = 1, \ldots, n$. Then, M makes n moves from χ_0 to χ_n according to $r_1\ldots r_n$, written as

$$\chi_0 \vdash^n \chi_n \qquad [r_1\ldots r_n]$$

♦

Let $M = (Q, \Sigma, R, s, F)$ be a pushdown transducer. Let $\chi \vdash^n \chi'$ $[\rho]$ in M, where ρ denotes the sequence of n rules according to which M makes $\chi \vdash^n \chi'$ ($\rho = \varepsilon$ if $n = 0$); ρ is called the *rule word corresponding to* $\chi \vdash^n \chi'$. Whenever ρ represents an immaterial piece of information, $\chi \vdash^n \chi'$ $[\rho]$ is simplified to $\chi \vdash^n \chi'$.

Definition — sequence of moves, part 2
Let $M = (Q, \Sigma, R, s, F)$ be a pushdown transducer, and let χ and χ' be two configurations of M.

1. If there exists $n \geq 1$ so $\chi \vdash^n \chi'$ $[\rho]$ in M, then $\chi \vdash^+ \chi'$ $[\rho]$.
2. If there exists $n \geq 0$ so $\chi \vdash^n \chi'$ $[\rho]$ in M, then $\chi \vdash^* \chi'$ $[\rho]$.

♦

For brevity, the present section frequently writes $\chi \vdash^+ \chi'$ and $\chi \vdash^*$ instead of $\chi \vdash^+ \chi'$ $[\rho]$ and $\chi \vdash^* \chi'$ $[\rho]$, respectively.

Example 9.2.2.1 Part 4 Sequences of moves
Reconsider the pushdown transducer M investigated in the previous parts of this example. Observe that

$$\begin{aligned}
Ss+*aaa| &\vdash SAq+*aaa| & [1] \\
&\vdash S+AAq*aaa| & [3] \\
&\vdash S+A*AAqaaa| & [4] \\
&\vdash S+A*Aqaa|a & [2] \\
&\vdash S+A*qa|aa & [2] \\
&\vdash S+Aq|aa* & [6] \\
&\vdash S+q|aa*a & [2] \\
&\vdash Sq|aa*a+ & [5] \\
&\vdash f|aa*a+ & [7]
\end{aligned}$$

Consequently,

$$Ss+*aaa| \vdash^9 f|aa*a+ \qquad [134226257]$$

or, more simply,

$$Ss+{*}aaa| \vdash^9 f|aa{*}a+$$

Consequently,

$$Ss+{*}aaa| \vdash^+ f|aa{*}a+ \text{ and } Ss+{*}aaa| \vdash^* f|aa{*}a+$$

△

A pushdown transducer M translates words over its input alphabet into words over the output alphabet. Initially, the pushdown contains the start symbol, the input tape contains an input word x the output tape is blank, and M occurs in the start state with both heads over the leftmost squares. If, from this initial configuration, M can make a sequence of moves so that M reads x, writes a word y on the output tape, and enters a final state, then M translates x to y. The set that contains all pairs of words translated in this way forms the translation that M defines.

Definition — translation defined by pushdown transducer

Let $M = (Q, \Sigma, R, s, F)$ be a pushdown transducer, $x \in \Sigma_I^*$, and $y \in \Sigma_O^*$. M translates x into y if and only if

$$Ssx| \vdash^* zf|y$$

in M, where $z \in \Sigma_{PD}^*$ and $f \in F$. The *translation defined by* M, $T(M)$, is

$$T(M) = \{ (x, y) : x \in \Sigma_I^*, y \in \Sigma_O^*, \text{ and } M \text{ translates } x \text{ into } y\}$$

The *input language* $L_I(M)$ corresponding to $T(M)$ is defined as

$$L_I(M) = \{x : (x, y) \in T(M) \text{ for some } y \in \Sigma_O^*\}$$

The *output language* $L_O(M)$ corresponding to $T(M)$ is defined as

$$L_O(M) = \{y : (x, y) \in T(M) \text{ for some } x \in \Sigma_I^*\}$$

◆

Example 9.2.2.1 Part 5 Translation

Return to the pushdown transducer M studied throughout this example. The previous part of Example 9.2.2.1 has demonstrated that

$$Ss+{*}aaa| \vdash^* f|aa{*}a+$$

in M, so

$$(+{*}aaa, aa{*}a+) \in T(M)$$

$L_I(M)$ consists of prefix Polish arithmetic expressions over $\{+, *, a\}$, and $L_O(M)$ consists of postfix Polish arithmetic expressions over $\{+, *, a\}$. As formally verified in the exercises, M translates prefix Polish arithmetic expressions over $\{+, *, a\}$ to the equivalent postfix Polish arithmetic expressions over $\{+, *, a\}$.

▲

Equivalence of translation grammars and pushdown transducers

Theorem 9.2.2.1
Let τ be a translation. Then, $\tau = T(G)$ for a translation grammar if and only if $\tau = T(M)$ for a pushdown transducer.

Proof
Prove this theorem by analogy with the proof of Theorem 5.3.3.1, stating the equivalence between pushdown automata and context-free grammars. A detailed version of this proof is left to the exercises.

■

Determinism

According to the definition presented in the beginning of this section, pushdown transducers work nondeterministically because they can make several different moves from the same configuration. Practically oriented computer science, however, usually deals with their deterministic versions, defined next.

Definition — deterministic pushdown transducer
Let $M = (Q, \Sigma, R, s, F)$ be a pushdown transducer. M is *deterministic* if each rule, $r \in R$, where $\text{lhs}(r) = Apa$ with $a \in \Sigma_I \cup \{\varepsilon\}$, satisfies this identity

$$\{r\} = \{r': r' \in R, Apa = \text{lhs}(r')) \text{ or } Ap = \text{lhs}(r'))\}$$

♦

By this definition, for each $q \in Q, A \in \Sigma_{PD}, a \in \Sigma_I \cup \{\varepsilon\}$, if Aqa forms the left-hand side of a rule r then no other rule has its left-hand side equal to Aqa or Aq. Therefore, with any input word, a deterministic pushdown transducer M makes a unique sequence of moves, and this property simplifies the implementation of M very much.

Extension

The next definition introduces an extended pushdown transducer, which is based upon an extended pushdown automaton (see Figure 9.2.2.7).

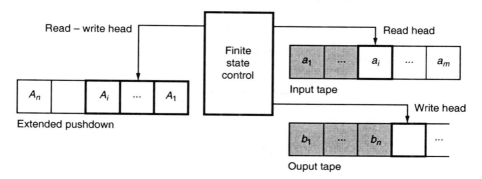

Figure 9.2.2.7 Extended pushdown transducer.

Definition — extended pushdown transducer
An *extended pushdown transducer* is a quintuple

$$M = (Q, \Sigma, R, s, F)$$

where $R \subseteq \Sigma_{PD}^* Q(\Sigma_I \cup \{\varepsilon\}) \times \Sigma_{PD}^* Q \Sigma_O^*$ is a finite relation, and the other components — Q, Σ, s and F — have the same meaning as in a pushdown transducer.

♦

The exercises discuss extended pushdown transducers in detail.

9.3 Compilers

This section demonstrates an application of the translation models introduced in Sections 9.1 and 9.2. Based upon these models, it designs a complete compiler for the programming language COLA (see Section 1.3). Section 9.3.1 outlines the structure of a compiler. Section 9.3.2 constructs a COLA scanner. Section 9.3.3 designs a parser, a semantic analyzer, and a code generator for COLA. Together, these parts form a COLA compiler. Section 9.3.4 optimizes the translation made by this compiler. Finally, Section 9.3.5 traces the computation of a program produced by the COLA compiler.

9.3.1 Compiler structure

A compiler reads a program written in a source language and converts this program to an equivalent program written in a target language (see Figure 9.3.1.1). Typically, a high-level language, such as Pascal or C, represents the source language. The target language is usually an assembly language, which is easily transformable to the machine language of a particular computer.

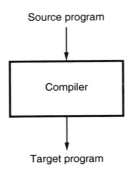

Figure 9.3.1.1 Compiler.

A compiler consists of these two fundamental parts

- source program analyzer
- target program synthesizer

(see Figure 9.3.1.2). The former decomposes the source program into its elementary parts so the latter can produce the equivalent target program.

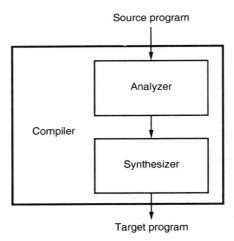

Figure 9.3.1.2 Analyzer and synthesizer.

The analyzer has the following three components:

- scanner
- parser
- semantic analyzer

The scanner reads the source program characters and produce tokens, representing lexemes, i.e. logically cohesive lexical entities, such as identifiers. The scanner sends the produced tokens to the parser. The parser determines the syntactical structure of the whole source program by constructing a derivation tree for the word consisting of tokens, which represent the program. The semantic analyzer verifies various semantic aspects of the source program; for instance, it makes sure that each label denotes precisely one statement in the source program.

The synthesizer is composed of two parts:

- code generator
- optimizer

The code generator produces the target program, and then, the optimizer makes this program as efficient as possible. Figure 9.3.1.3 depicts a compiler as described above.

The five components of a compiler cooperate closely. The parser is at the heart of the compiler heart, and controls the actions of the other components. Upon receiving a command from the parser, the scanner reads the source program characters, produces the next token, and passes this token to the parser. The parser also controls the semantic analyzer's actions. In addition, the parser commands the code generator to produce the target program.

Based on the compiler concepts given in this section, Sections 9.3.2 through 9.3.4 construct a compiler for the programming language COLA (see Section 1.3).

9.3.2 Scanner

The main task of a scanner is the recognition of the next lexeme that occurs in the source program. In practice, however, a scanner also accomplishes another task: the production of a token representing the recognized lexeme. In effect, a scanner acts as a finite transducer that recognizes the next source program lexeme and produces a token that represents the recognized lexeme.

Tokens

A token has the format

$$(\text{type}, \text{index})$$

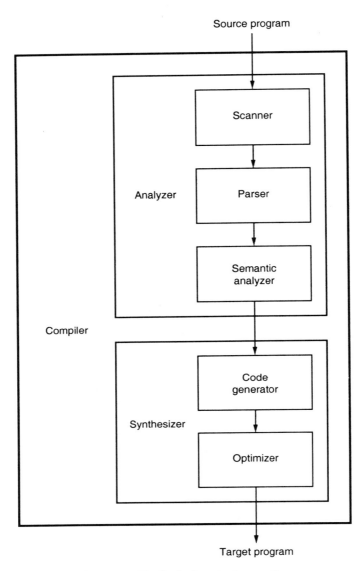

Figure 9.3.1.3 The five basic parts of a compiler.

The type of a token is a natural number, and the index of a token is a nonnegative integer. The token type coincides with the lexeme type (see Section 3.3.1.2). For instance, 1, 2 and 3 represent identifiers, integers and labels, respectively. With some token types, the scanner associates tables, which record all necessary information about the scanned lexemes of these types. For instance, the table of identifiers contains the scanned identifiers appearing in the source program. With other types, however, the scanner associates no tables because these types uniquely determine the lexemes that they represent. For instance, if 6 is the type of +, 6 uniquely specifies +, so there exists no table associated with type 6.

More precisely, a token has the form

$$(t, i)$$

where $t \geq 1$ and $i \geq 0$. If $i \geq 1$, there exists table t, which contains information about type-t lexemes; if $i = 0$, no table associated with type t exists. Assume that $i \geq 1$. At this point, the ith entry in table t describes the scanned lexeme represented by token (t, i). To illustrate, assume that the scanner reads ID1, classifies this lexeme as an identifier, and represents it by token (1, 2), where 1 is the type of identifiers. At this point, entry 2 in table 1 records ID1 — that is, the scanned lexeme represented by (1, 2). As another example, suppose that the scanner reads + and represents it by token (6, 0), where 6 is the type of +. Because 6 uniquely specifies +, there is no table corresponding to type 6.

Scanner

The rest of this section designs a scanner for COLA (see Section 1.2). As a matter of fact, Section 3.3.1.2 has already constructed a substantial part of this scanner — GetLexeme. However, GetLexeme acts as a finite automaton that recognizes the next lexeme appearing in a COLA program. Therefore, the present section extends GetLexeme to a new procedure, called GetToken, which acts as a finite transducer that not only recognizes the next lexeme but also produces a token that represents this lexeme.

Recall the definition of COLA lexemes (see Section 3.3.1.2):

Identifiers

$$XY^*$$

where X is the set of all letters, and Y is the set of all letters and digits.

Integers

$$X^+$$

where X is the set of all digits.

Labels

$$\{@\}X^+$$

where X is the set of all letters and digits.

Text literals

$$\{'\}X^*\{'\}$$

where X is the set of all symbols except ' or ".

New-line text literals

$$\{"\}X^*\{"\}$$

where X is the set of all symbols except ' or ".

Arithmetic operators

$$\{+, -, *, /\}$$

Relational operators

$$\{=, >, <\}$$

Parentheses

$$\{(,)\}$$

Separators

$$\{,\} \text{ and } \{;\}$$

Assignment operator

$$\{:=\}$$

Reserved words

$$\{\textbf{begin, end, goto, if, read, write}\}$$

Section 3.3.1.2 has classified all COLA lexemes into 24 types, denoted by integers 1 through 24. The following table recalls these integers. In addition, this table associates tables T1 through T5 with types 1 through 5, respectively (the contents of these tables are described in detail later on in this section).

Type	Lexeme	Tables
1	Identifier	T1
2	Integer	T2
3	Label	T3
4	Text literal	T4
5	New-line text literal	T5
6	+	
7	−	
8	*	
9	/	
10	=	
11	>	
12	<	
13	(	
14	)	
15	,	
16	;	
17	:=	
18	**begin**	
19	**end**	
20	**goto**	
21	**if**	
22	**read**	
23	**write**	
24	error	

Type 24 indicates an error occurrence. To specify this error occurrence in greater detail, GetToken uses the second component of a type-24 token to classify the given error as follows:

(24, 1) invalid label — @ is followed by no letter or digit
(24, 2) invalid text literal — the literal begins with ' but ends with "
(24, 3) invalid new-line text literal — the literal begins with " but ends with '
(24, 4) invalid assignment operator — the second symbol differs from =
(24, 5) illegal character occurrence.

By analogy with the scanner depicted in Figure 3.3.1.2.1, this section next designs the COLA scanner, which recognizes the next lexeme in the source program and, in addition, produces the token representing this lexeme. This scanner contains 18 finite transducers — M_1, ..., M_{17}, and M_{24}. M_1 produces tokens representing lexemes of type 1 and lexemes of types 18 through 23. For $j = 2$ through 17, M_j produces tokens corresponding to type-j lexemes. Finally, M_{24}, which corresponds to type-24 lexemes, specifies errors.

The following procedure, GetToken, implements the COLA scanner. GetToken uses several components, including Concatenate, Digits, Empty, GetSymbol, Lexeme, LexemeType, Letters, and UnGetSymbol, that have the same meaning as in GetLexeme (see Section 3.3.1.2). Besides these components, the procedures in GetToken use a global variable, Token, that represents a token and, therefore, has the format described in the beginning of this section. More exactly, Token's first component, Token[1], specifies one of the 24 token types. If Token[1] = i with $i \in \{1, \ldots, 5\}$, then Token's second component, Token[2], equals the index of an entry in table T_i, and this entry contains all necessary information about the scanned lexeme represented by Token. If Token[1] $\in \{6, \ldots, 23\}$, then Token[2] = 0. Finally, If Token[1] = 24, then Token[2], where Token[2] $\in \{1, \ldots, 5\}$, represents an error classification. When GetToken exits, Token represents the recognized lexeme.

procedure GetToken;

begin
   Empty; {Lexeme is empty}
   repeat GetSymbol
   until Symbol ≠ ' ' {read the next nonblank symbol};
   case Symbol **of**
      'a'..'z':P1;
      '0'..'9': P2;
      '@': P3;
      '''': P4;
      '"': P5;
      '+': P6;
      ⋮
      ':': P17;
      otherwise: P24
   end
end

where P1, ..., P17, and P24 are procedures such that Pj implements transducer M_j. These procedures follow next.

Procedure P1

Figure 9.3.2.1 depicts the finite transducer, M_1, which translates identifiers into their tokens. In this figure, X and Y are the set of letters and the set of letters and digits, respectively, and $\overline{Y}$ denotes the complement of Y. The token produced by M_1 is $(1, i)$, where $i \geq 1$; accordingly, T1's entry i contains the scanned identifier represented by $(1, i)$.

Procedure P1, which implements M_1, contains the two procedures SetType and StoreInT1:

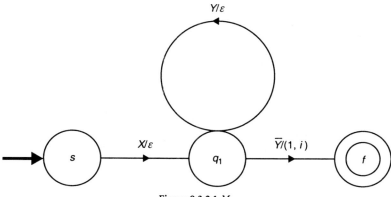

Figure 9.3.2.1 M_1.

1. SetType resembles procedure ReservedWord, used in GetLexeme. SetType finds out whether Lexeme, which contains the scanned lexeme, equals a reserved word of type j, for some $j = 18, \ldots, 23$. If so, SetType sets Token[1] to j; otherwise, SetType sets Token[1] to 1 because Lexeme contains an identifier.
2. As its title indicates, StoreInT1 stores the scanned identifier, contained in Lexeme, in the identifier table T1. More precisely, StoreInT1 first searches the identifier table to determine whether the identifier in Lexeme occurs in T1. If this identifier appears as item j in T1, the same identifier has previously occurred in the source program; at this point, StoreInT1 sets Token[2] to j and returns. If, however, T1 has not recorded the identifier in Lexeme, StoreInT1 creates a new item, k, at the end of T1, stores this identifier in entry k, sets Token[2] to k, and returns. In either case, when StoreInT1 exits, Token[2] addresses the T1 entry that contains the identifier in Lexeme.

When P1 begins, Symbol contains a member of Letters.

procedure P1;

begin
   repeat
      Concatenate{concatenation of Lexeme and Symbol};
      GetSymbol
   until not(Symbol **in** (Letters **or** Digits)) {this loop exits when it reads a nonalphanumeric symbol};

   UnGetSymbol{the nonalphanumeric symbol in Symbol is pushed back onto the standard input};

   SetType{Token[1] is set};

  if Token[1] = 1
  then StoreInT1{the identifier in Lexeme is stored in an entry of T1, and Token[2] is set to the index of this entry}
end

Procedure P2
M_2 which translates integers into their tokens, is displayed in Figure 9.3.2.2, where X is the set of digits, $\overline{X}$ denotes the complement of X, and i is an index in the integer table T2. M_1 produces $(2, i)$, i.e. the token that represents the scanned integer, whose value is contained in T2's entry i.

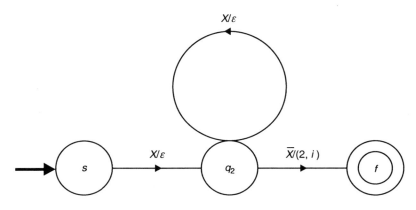

Figure 9.3.2.2 M_2.

  M_2 is implemented by procedure P2, which contains procedure StoreInT2. StoreInT2 stores the value of the nonnegative integer represented by the scanned lexeme, contained in Lexeme, in the integer table T2. More precisely, StoreInT2 first searches the integer table to determine whether the value of the integer in Lexeme occurs in T2. If this value appears as an item j of T2, StoreInT2 sets Token[2] to j and returns. If this value does not appear in T2, StoreInT2 creates a new item k at the end of the table, stores the integer value in this newly created item, sets Token[2] to k, and returns. In either case, StoreInT2 exits with Token[2] addressing the T2 item that contains the value of the integer in Lexeme.
  Recall that when GetToken calls P2, Symbol contains a digit.

procedure P2;

begin
 repeat
  Concatenate;
  GetSymbol

until not(Symbol **in** Digits) {this loop exits when it reads a nonnumeric symbol};

UnGetSymbol{the nonnumeric symbol in Symbol is pushed back onto the standard input};

Token[1] := 2 {the token type is set to 2, which represents integers };

StoreInT2 {the value of the integer in Lexeme is stored in an item of T2, and Token[2] is set to this item's index}
end

Procedure P3
Figure 9.3.2.3 shows the finite transducer M_3 that translates labels into their corresponding tokens. In this figure, X denotes the set of letters and digits, $\overline{X}$ is the complement of X, and i is an index in T3. If M_3 recognizes a well-formed label @x, where x is a non-empty alphanumeric word, then M_3 produces a token of the form $(3, i)$, where i indicates that entry i in T3 contains x. However, if M_3 reads a symbol from $\overline{X}$ in state q_3, then it produces $(24, 1)$ and, thereby, makes an error specification, stating that no letter or digit follows @.

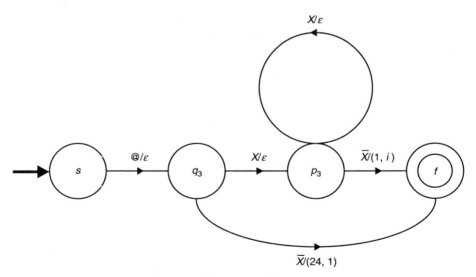

Figure 9.3.2.3 M_3.

Procedure P3, which implements M_3, contains another procedure, StoreInT3. If the scanned label has the form @x, where x is a non-empty alphanumeric word, then

StoreInT3 stores x in T3. More precisely, when P3 calls StoreInT3, Lexeme contains x. StoreInT3 searches T3 to determine whether x has been previously stored in T3. If an item j in T3 stores x, StoreInT3 sets Token[2] to j and returns. However, if x does not occur in T3, StoreInT3 creates a new item, k, at the end of T3, places x in this new item, sets Token[2] to k, and returns. In either case, when StoreInT3 exits, Token[2] points to the T3 item that contains x.

Recall that GetToken calls procedure P3 when Symbol contains @.

procedure P3;

begin
  GetSymbol;

  while Symbol **in** Letters **or** Digits **do**
  begin
    Concatenate;
    GetSymbol
  end;

  UnGetSymbol {the nonalphanumeric symbol in Symbol is pushed back onto the standard input};

  if Lexeme is empty {Concatenate has placed the alphanumeric word following @ into Lexeme}
  then {invalid label — no letter or digit follows @}
  begin
    Token[1] := 24;
    Token[2] := 1
  end
  else {valid label — Lexeme contains the nonempty alphanumeric word following @}
  begin
    Token[1] := 3 {the token type is set to 3, which represents labels};
    StoreInT3 {the word in Lexeme is stored in an item of T3, and Token[2] is set to the index of this item}
  end
end

Procedure P4

Figure 9.3.2.4 displays M_4, which translates text literals into their corresponding tokens. M_4 enters state q_4 on '; then, M_4 remains in q_4 until the input symbol is " or '. If M_4 reads " in q_4, it enters f and writes (24, 2), to make an error specification, stating the literal begins with ' but ends with ". If M_4 reads ' in q_4, it enters f and generates (4, i), where i is an index in T4. This index addresses the T4 item that contains the word occurring between the two apostrophes; that is, if 'x' forms the scanned text literal, then item i contains x.

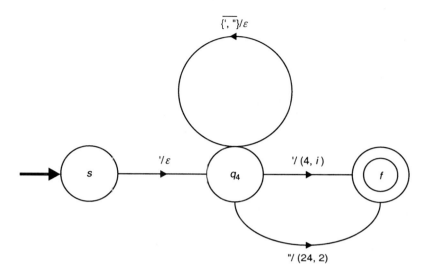

Figure 9.3.2.4 M_4.

Procedure P4, implementing M_4, contains the procedure StoreInT4. If 'x' is the scanned text literal, where x is a word not containing ' or ", then StoreInT4 stores x in T4. More precisely, P4 calls StoreInT4 with Lexeme containing x (x is the word occurring between the two apostrophes). StoreInT4 first searches T4 to determine whether x appears in T4. If an item j in T4 contains x, StoreInT4 sets Token[2] to j and returns. If, however, x does not occur in T4, StoreInT4 creates a new item k at the end of T4, places x in this new item, sets Token[2] to k, and returns. As a result, when StoreInT4 exits, Token[2] addresses the T5 item containing x.

When GetToken calls P4, Symbol contains '.

procedure P4;

begin
  GetSymbol;

  while not(Symbol in [', "]) **do**
  begin
    Concatenate;
    GetSymbol
  end;
  if Symbol = ""
  then {invalid text literal — the literal begins with ' but ends with "}

```
begin
    Token[1] := 24;
    Token[2] := 2
end
else {valid text literal}
begin
    Token[1] := 4 {the token type is set to 4, which represents text literals};
•   StoreInT4 {the word in Lexeme is stored in an item of T4, and Token[2] is set
    to this item's index}
end
end
```

Procedure P5

Figure 9.3.2.5 depicts M_5, which translates new-line text literals into tokens representing them. M_5 enters q_5 with "; then, M_5 remains in q_5 until the input symbol equals " or '. If M_5 reads ' in q_5, then it enters f and writes (24, 3), which makes an error specification, stating that the new-line text literal begins with " but ends with '. If M_5 reads " in q_5, it enters f and generates (5, i), where i is an index in the text literal table, T5. This index indicates that item i in T5 records the word occurring between the two quotation marks; that is, if "x" forms the scanned new-line text literal, then item i in T5 contains x.

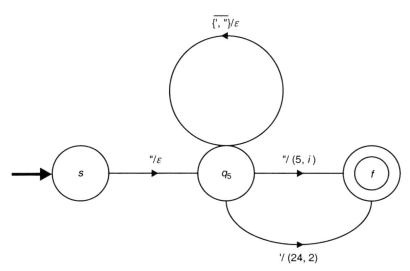

Figure 9.3.2.5 M_5.

Procedure P5 contains the procedure StoreInT5, that works in the following way. Suppose that the scanned new-line text literal is of the form "x", where x is a word containing neither ' nor "; then, StoreInT5 stores x in T5. More formally, P5 calls StoreInT5 with Lexeme containing x. StoreInT5 first searches T5 to find out whether x appears in T5. If an item j in T5 contains x, StoreInT5 sets Token[2] to j and returns. However, if x does not occur in T5, StoreInT5 creates a new item k at the end of T5, places x in this new item, sets Token[2] to k, and returns. Consequently, in either case, Token[2] addresses the T5 item recording x when StoreInT4 exits.

Recall that when GetToken calls P5, Symbol contains ".

procedure P5;

begin
  GetSymbol;

  while not(Symbol **in** [', "]) **do**
  begin
    Concatenate;
    GetSymbol
  end;

  if Symbol = '''
  then {invalid new-line text literal — the literal begins with " but ends with '}
  begin
    Token[1] := 24;
    Token[2] := 3
  end
  else {valid new-line text literal}
  begin
    Token[1] := 5 {the token type is set to 5, which
                   represents new-line text literals};
    StoreInT5 {the word in Lexeme is stored in an item of T4, and Token[2] is set
            so it addresses this item}
  end
end

Procedure P6

Figure 9.3.2.6 depicts M_6, translating + to the corresponding token, i.e. (6, 0).

When GetToken calls P6, which implements M_6, Symbol contains +. P6 follows next.

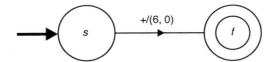

Figure 9.3.2.6 M_6.

procedure P6;

begin
  Token[1] := 6;
  Token[2] := 0
end

By analogy with P6, the exercises design P7 through P16.

Procedure P17

M_{17}, which translates := to (17, 0), is displayed in Figure 9.3.2.7. Note that if : is followed by a symbol that is different from =, M_{17} specifies this error by writing (24, 4).

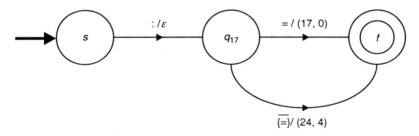

Figure 9.3.2.7 M_{17}.

GetToken calls P17 with Symbol containing :

procedure P17;

begin
  GetSymbol;

  if Symbol ≠ '='
  then {invalid assignment operator — the second symbol differs from =}
  begin

```
        Token[1] := 24;
        Token[2] := 4
    end
    else {valid assignment operator}
    begin
        Token[1] := 17;
        Token[2] := 0
    end
end
```

Recall that lexemes of types 18 through 23 are translated to their tokens by P1.

Procedure P24

Figure 9.3.2.8 depicts M_{24}, which produces (24, 5) and, thereby, specifies an illegal symbol occurrence.

Figure 9.3.2.8 M_{24}.

procedure P24;

```
begin
    Token[1] := 24;
    Token[2] := 5
end
```

Note that as well as an illegal symbol occurrence, GetToken indicate four other kinds of errors (see P3, P4, P5 and P17).

The descriptions of P1, ..., P17, and P24 complete the construction of the COLA scanner, GetToken, which produces the token that represents the next lexeme appearing in the source program.

Tokens produced by the scanner

Section 3.3.1.2 discusses the program

```
begin
  read(n);
  write(" resulting factorial ", n, '! = ');
  factorial := 1;
  @iteration;
    if n = 0 goto @stop;
    factorial := factorial*n;
    n := n - 1;
  goto @iteration;
  @stop;
  write(factorial)
end
```

By repeatedly calling GetToken, this program is decomposed into its lexemes and the tokens that these lexemes represent. The next table describes this decomposition.

Lexeme	Token
begin	(18, 0)
read	(22, 0)
(	(13, 0)
n	(1, 1)
)	(14, 0)
;	(16, 0)
write	(23, 0)
(	(13, 0)
" resulting factorial "	(5, 1)
,	(15, 0)
n	(1, 1)
,	(15, 0)
'! = '	(4, 1)
)	(14, 0)
;	(16, 0)
factorial	(1, 2)
:=	(17, 0)
1	(2, 1)
;	(16, 0)
@iteration	(3, 1)
;	(16, 0)
if	(21, 0)
n	(1, 1)
=	(10, 0)
0	(2, 2)
goto	(20, 0)
@stop	(3, 2)

Finite and pushdown transducers

;	(16, 0)
factorial	(1, 2)
:=	(17, 0)
factorial	(1, 2)
*	(8, 0)
n	(1, 1)
;	(16, 0)
n	(1, 1)
:=	(17, 0)
n	(1, 1)
−	(7, 0)
1	(2, 1)
;	(16, 0)
goto	(20, 0)
@iteration	(3, 1)
;	(16, 0)
@stop	(3, 2)
;	(16, 0)
write	(23, 0)
(	(13, 0)
factorial	(1, 2)
)	(14, 0)
end	(19, 0)

After this decomposition, tables T1, T2, T3, T4 and T5 contain the following items.

T1:
1. n
2. factorial

T2:
1. 1
2. 0

T3
1. iteration
2. stop

T4
1. ! =

T5
1. resulting factorial

9.3.3 Parser, semantic analyzer and code generator

By using context-free grammars and pushdown automata, Section 5.3.1.2 designs a parser that accepts well-formed programs written in COLA. Based upon translation grammars and pushdown transducers, this present section extends this parser so that the extended parser not only accepts COLA programs but also controls the actions of the code generator. In addition, the end of this section sketches the semantic analyzer for COLA.

Parser for expression

First, the parser is constructed that translates COLA expressions to the equivalent postfix Polish expressions. The COLA expressions are defined by the following context-free grammar $G_{expression}$:

r_1: <expression> → <expression>+<term>
r_2: <expression> → <expression>−<term>
r_3: <expression> → <term>
r_4: <term> → <term>*<factor>
r_5: <term> → <term>/<factor>
r_6: <term> → <factor>
r_7: <factor> → (<expression>)
r_8: <factor> → i

$G_{expression}$ contains three nonterminals — <expression>, <factor> and <term> — where <expression> is the start symbol of this grammar. Furthermore, $G_{expression}$ possesses the seven terminals $i, +, -, *, /, ($ and $)$. $G_{expression}$ underlies the translation grammar G_{infix} and the context-free grammar $G_{postfix}$, as follows:

G_{infix}:

q_1: <expression> ⇢ <expression>+<term>|p_1
q_2: <expression> ⇢ <expression>−<term>|p_2
q_3: <expression> ⇢ <term>|p_3
q_4: <term> ⇢ <term>*<factor>|p_4
q_5: <term> ⇢ <term>/<factor>|p_5
q_6: <term> ⇢ <factor>|p_6
q_7: <factor> ⇢ (<expression>)|p_7
q_8: <factor> ⇢ i|p_8

Finite and pushdown transducers

$G_{postfix}$:

p_1: <expression> → <expression><term>+
p_2: <expression> → <expression><term>−
p_3: <expression> → <term>
p_4: <term> → <term><factor>*
p_5: <term> → <term><factor>/
p_6: <term> → <factor>
p_7: <factor> → <expression>
p_8: <factor> → i

PostfixExpression uses G_{infix} and $G_{postfix}$ to translate a given COLA expression x to the equivalent postfix Polish expressions y. This translation consists of two phases:

1. In the rightmost way, G_{infix} translates x to a sequence π consisting of labels that denote productions in $G_{postfix}$.
2. By the rightmost derivation according to π, $G_{postfix}$ generates y.

To illustrate this translation, consider $i*i+i$. $G_{expression}$ derives $i*i+i$ in the following rightmost way.

<expression>	$\Rightarrow_{rm}$ <expression>+<term>	$[r_1]$
	$\Rightarrow_{rm}$ <expression>+<factor>	$[r_6]$
	$\Rightarrow_{rm}$ <expression>+i	$[r_8]$
	$\Rightarrow_{rm}$ <term>+i	$[r_3]$
	$\Rightarrow_{rm}$ <term>*<factor>+i	$[r_4]$
	$\Rightarrow_{rm}$ <term>*i+i	$[r_8]$
	$\Rightarrow_{rm}$ <factor>*i+i	$[r_6]$
	$\Rightarrow_{rm}$ $i*i+i$	$[r_8]$

That is,

$$<\text{expression}> \Rightarrow_{rm}^* i*i+i \qquad [r_1 r_6 r_8 r_3 r_4 r_8 r_6 r_8]$$

PostfixExpression translates $i*i+i$ as follows. First, G_{infix} translates $i*i+i$ to $p_1 p_6 p_8 p_3 p_4 p_8 p_6 p_8$. Then, according to $p_1 p_6 p_8 p_3 p_4 p_8 p_6 p_8$, $G_{postfix}$ makes this rightmost derivation

<expression>	$\Rightarrow_{rm}$ <expression><term>+	$[p_1]$
	$\Rightarrow_{rm}$ <expression><factor>+	$[p_6]$
	$\Rightarrow_{rm}$ <expression>i+	$[p_8]$

$\Rightarrow_{rm}$ <term>i+   [p_3]
$\Rightarrow_{rm}$ <term><factor>*i+   [p_4]
$\Rightarrow_{rm}$ <term>i*i+   [p_8]
$\Rightarrow_{rm}$ <factor>i*i+   [p_6]
$\Rightarrow_{rm}$ ii*i+   [p_8]

As a result, PostfixExpression produces *ii*i+*, which represents the postfix Polish equivalent to *i*i+i*.

PostfixExpression is implemented as an integer function consisting of four computational steps:

A. Read the input expression *x* appearing between the current input symbol and the first occurrence of ;, >, <, =, **goto**, or **end** in the source COLA program
B. Translate *x* to the equivalent postfix Polish expression *y* by applying the two-phase method based on G_{infix} and $G_{postfix}$.
C. Place *y* as the last item *i* in TE, where TE denotes the expression table maintained by the COLA compiler.
D. Exit with PostfixExpression = *i* to specify that TE[*i*] contains *y*.

The complete COLA parser, described next, assumes that PostfixExpression is implemented in this way. A detailed description of this implementation is left as a programming project.

Parser with code generator

Section 5.3.1.2 describes a parser that accepts well-formed programs written in COLA. The present section extends this parser so that the resulting parser not only accepts COLA programs but also produces the equivalent target program. The following 16-production grammar defines well-formed COLA programs. Notice that this definition excludes COLA expressions because this section has already described PostfixExpression, which parse these expressions.

1: <program> → **begin**<statement list>**end**
2: <statement list> → <statement>;<statement list>
3: <statement list> → <statement>
4: <statement> → label
5: <statement> → **goto** label
6: <statement> → identifier := <expression>
7: <statement> → **read**(<read list>)
8: <statement> → **write**(<write list>)
9: <statement> → **if**<expression>relational operator<expression> **goto** label
10: <read list> → identifier, <read list>
11: <read list> → identifier

12: <write list> → <write member>,<write list>
13: <write list> → <write member>
14: <write member> → identifier
15: <write member> → text literal
16: <write member> → new-line text literal

This grammar contains the following nonterminals:

<expression>
<program>
<read list>
<statement>
<statement list>
<write list>
<write member>

where <program> is the start symbol. Furthermore, it possesses the following terminals

identifier
label
text literal
new-line text literal
relational operators
=
>
<
(
)
:=
begin
end
goto
if
read
write
,
;

The COLA parser translates COLA programs into the target language, called Target. A program in Target is a sequence consisting of the following instructions.

Input

$$I\ T1[j]$$

where $j \geq 1$. This instruction inputs the next integer from the standard input and places the value of this integer into $T1[j]$, the jth item of the identifier table T1 (Section 9.3.4 describes the form of this placement in greater detail).

Output

$$O\ Ti[j]$$

where $i = 1, 2, 4, 5$ and $j \geq 1$. This instruction writes the containment of the jth item in table Ti onto the standard output. If $i = 5$, the output begins on the next line; otherwise, it continues on the same line.

Evaluate

$$E\ T1[i], TE[j]$$

where $i, j \geq 1$. This instruction evaluates the postfix expression in the jth item of the expression table, TE, and places the resulting value into the ith item of the identifier table, T1.

Label

$$L\ T3[i]$$

where $i \geq 1$. This instruction acts as a label used by the following two branch instructions, Branch and Conditional Branch.

Branch

$$B\ T3[i]$$

where $i \geq 1$. This instruction causes the computation to continue at instruction $L\ T3[i]$.

Conditional Branch

$$C\ TE[i], r, TE[j], T3[k]$$

where $r \in \{=, <, >\}$, and $i, j, k \geq 1$. This instruction first determines the values of the postfix expressions in $TE[i]$ and $TE[j]$. Let v_i and v_j be the resulting values corresponding to $TE[i]$ and $TE[j]$, respectively. If $v_i\ r\ v_j$ is true, the computation continues at instruction L

Finite and pushdown transducers

T3[k]; otherwise, the next instruction is performed. The following translation grammar $G_{\text{COLA-Target}}$ defines the translation of well-formed COLA programs to the equivalent programs in Target.

1: \<program\> →» **begin**\<statement list\>**end**|ε
2: \<statement list\> →» \<statement\>;\<statement list\>|ε
3: \<statement list\> →» \<statement\>|ε
4: \<statement\> →» label| L T3[i]
5: \<statement\> →» **goto** label| B T3[i]
6: \<statement\> →» identifier := \<expression\>| E T1[i],TE[j]
7: \<statement\> →» **read**(\<read list\>)|ε
8: \<statement\> →» **write**(\<write list\>)|ε
9: \<statement\> →» **if**\<expression\>r\<expression\> **goto** label| C TE[i],r,TE[j],T3[k]
10: \<read list\> →» identifier, \<read list\>| I T1[j]
11: \<read list\> →» identifier| I T1[j]
12: \<write list\> →» \<write member\>,\<write list\>|ε
13: \<write list\> →» \<write member\>|ε
14: \<write member\> →» identifier|O T1[j]
15: \<write member\> →» text literal|O T4[j]
16: \<write member\> →» new-line text literal|O T5[j]

$G_{\text{COLA-Target}}$ contains the same nonterminals as G_{COLA}; \<program\> is the start symbol. The input alphabet of $G_{\text{COLA-Target}}$ coincides with the alphabet of terminals in G_{COLA}. The output alphabet of $G_{\text{COLA-Target}}$ is the alphabet of Target. Some productions contain variables i, j and r, whose values are set in the following procedures Statement, ReadList and WriteMember.

By analogy with the procedures described in Section 5.3.1.2, this section next constructs the procedures corresponding to the nonterminals of $G_{\text{COLA-Target}}$. First, it presents the procedure ColaProgram, which corresponds to \<program\>. There exists one production with \<program\> on its left-hand side:

1: \<program\> →» **begin**\<statement list\>**end**|ε

As | is followed by no Target instruction, this production does not generate any output instruction, so the following description of ColaProgram parallels the corresponding description in Section 5.3.1.2.

function ColaProgram:**boolean**;

begin
 ColaProgram := **false**;
 GetToken;

```
        if Token[1] = 18 {18 is the token type of begin}
        then if StatementList
             then if Token[1] = 19 {19 is the token type of end}
                  then ColaProgram := true
end
```

StatementList corresponds to <statement list>, which forms the left-hand side of these two productions:

2: <statement list> →» <statement>;<statement list>|ε
3: <statement list> →» <statement>|ε

As neither production produces a Target instruction, StatementList is specified by analogy with the corresponding function in Section 5.3.1.2.

function StatementList:**boolean**;

```
begin
  StatementList := false;
  if Statement
  then
  begin
    GetToken;
    if Token[1] = 16 {16 is the token type of ;}
    then StatementList := StatementList
    else StatementList := true
  end
end
```

Statement is the function corresponding to <statement>, which occurs on the left-hand side of the six productions

4: <statement> →» label| L T3[i]
5: <statement> →» **goto** label| B T3[i]
6: <statement> →» identifier := <expression>| E T1[i],TE[j]
7: <statement> →» **read**(<read list>)|ε
8: <statement> →» **write**(<write list>)|ε
9: <statement> →» **if**<expression>r<expression> **goto** label| C TE[i],r,TE[j],T3[k]

Productions 7 and 8 produce no output, whereas productions 4, 5, 6, and 9 generate some Target instructions. Observe that Statement, described next, produces these Target instructions.

function Statement:**boolean**;

procedure Success {this procedure is used in the following
case statement to exit for StatementList with Statement := **true** and the next token in Token};
begin
  Statement := **true**;
  GetToken
end;

begin
  Statement := **false**;
  GetToken;

  case Token[1] **of**

    3:{3 is the token type of labels, so production 4 is simulated}
      begin
        writeln(' L T3[',Token[2],']') {the output Targetinstruction is L T3[i] with i = Token[2]};
        Success
      end;

    20: {20 is the token type of **goto**, so production 5 is simulated}
      begin
        GetToken;
        if Token[1] = 3
        then
        begin
          writeln('B T3[',Token[2],']') {the output Target instruction is L T3[i] with i = Token[2]};
          Success
        end
      end;

  1: {1 is the token type of identifiers, so production 6 is simulated}
    begin
      writeln('E T1[', Token[2],'],') {the first part of the output Target instruction is
          E T1[i], where i = Token[2]};
      GetToken;
      if Token[1] = 17
      then

begin
      write('TE[''PostfixExpression,'']') {the other part of the output Target instruction is TE[j] with j = PostfixExpression, so E T1[i],TE[j] represents the complete output Target instruction};
      Statement := **true**
   end
end;

22: {22 is the token type of **read**, so production 7 is simulated}
   begin
      GetToken;
      if Token[1] = 13 {13 is the token type of (}
      then if ReadList
         then if Token[1] = 14 {14 is the token type of)}
            then Success
   end;

23: {23 is the token type of **write**, so production 8 is simulated}
   begin
   GetToken;
   if Token[1] = 13 {13 is the token type of (}
   then if WriteList
      then if Token[1] = 14 {14 is the token type of)}
         then Success
   end;

21: {21 is the token type of **if**, so production 9 is simulated}
   begin
      writeln('C TE['',PostfixExpression,''],') {the first part of the output Target instruction is C TE[i], where i = PostfixExpression};

      case Token[1] **of**
      10: **write**('=,');
      11: **write**('>,');
      12: **write**('<,')
      {the second part of the output Target instruction is r with r ∈ {=, >, <,}}
   end;

   write('TE['', PostfixExpression,''],') {the third part of the output Target instruction is TE[j] with j = PostfixExpression};

   if Token[1] = 20 {20 is the lexeme type of **goto**}
   then
   begin
      GetToken;
      if Token[1] = 3 {3 is the type of labels}

```
        then
        begin
        write('T3[',Token[2],']') {the remaining part of the output Target instruction
        is T3[k] with j = Token[2], so C TE[i],r,TE[j],T3[k] represents the complete
        output Target instruction};
        Success
        end
    end
  end
end
```

ReadList is the function corresponding to <read list>, which form the left-hand side of these two productions:

10: <read list> $\rightarrow\!\!\!\rightarrow$ identifier, <read list>| I T1[j]
11: <read list> $\rightarrow\!\!\!\rightarrow$ identifier| I T1[j]

Both of these productions produce I T1[j], so ReadList is described as follows.

function ReadList:**boolean**;

```
begin
  ReadList := false;
  GetToken;
  if Token[1] = 1
  then
  begin
    writeln('I T1[',Token[2],']') {the output Target instruction is I T1[j] with
    j = Token[2]};
    GetToken;
    if Token[1] = 15
    then ReadList := ReadList
    else ReadList := true
  end
end
```

WriteList corresponds to <write list>, which occurs on the left-hand side of the following two productions:

12: <write list> $\rightarrow\!\!\!\rightarrow$ <write member>,<write list>|ε
13: <write list> $\rightarrow\!\!\!\rightarrow$ <write member>|ε

Neither of these productions produces any output, so the following description of WriteList parallels the corresponding description in Section 5.3.1.2.

```
function WriteList: boolean;

begin
  WriteList := false;
  if WriteMember
  then
  begin
    GetToken;
    if Token[1] = 15
    then WriteList := WriteList
    else WriteList := true
  end
end
```

WriteMember corresponds to <write member>. This nonterminal occurs on the left-hand side of these three productions

14: <write member> —» identifier|O   T1[j]
15: <write member> —» text literal|O   T4[j]
16: <write member> —» new-line text literal|O   T5[j]

As each of these productions produces a Target instruction, WriteMember is defined as follows.

```
function WriteMember: boolean;

begin
  WriteMember := true;
  GetToken;
  case Token[1] of
  1: writeln('O T1[',Token[2],']');
  4: writeln('O T4[',Token[2],']');
  5: writeln('O T5[',Token[2],']');
  otherwise: WriteMember := false
  end
end
```

Having defined boolean functions corresponding to the nonterminals in $G_{\text{COLA-Target}}$, this section next completes the COLA parser with the code generator by adding the following main program body. Given a COLA program, the main program calls ColaProgram. If ColaProgram returns **true** and, in addition, the next lexeme is the end-of-file symbol, then the parser has verified the syntactical correctness of the input program, and the code generator has produced the equivalent Target program.

```
begin
   if ColaProgram
   then if eof {eof is the end-of-file symbol}
         then writeln(' successful parsing and code generation')
end
```

Semantic analyzer

Besides scanning and parsing, the source program analysis necessaties some semantic actions, which verify the semantic correctness of the source program. For example, the COLA sematic analyzer needs to verify that labels are correctly defined in the source program; most importantly, it makes sure that each label denotes precisely one **label** statement in the source program. As a rule, a compiler easily performs semantic actions of this kind by using various tables and results obtained by the parser, which usually invokes these actions. The exercises discuss the semantic analysis of a source program in more detail.

Compiler translation

Assembled together, the procedures described in Sections 9.3.2 and 9.3.3 represent a COLA compiler. The rest of this section explains how this compiler translates the COLA program presented in the end of Section 9.3.2. Recall that this program as

```
begin
   read(n);
   write(" resulting factorial ", n, '! = ');
   factorial := 1;
   @iteration;
      if n = 0 goto @stop;
      factorial := factorial*n;
      n := n - 1;
      goto @iteration;
   @stop;
   write(factorial)
end
```

The COLA compiler translates this program to the following equivalent Target program

I T1[1]
O T5[1]
O T1[1]

O T4[1]
E T1[2],TE[1]
L T3[1]
C TE[1],=,TE[2],T3[2]
E T1[2],TE[4]
E T1[1],TE[5]
B T3[1]
L T3[2]
O T1[2]

where tables T1, T2, T3, T4, T5, and TE have these contents:

T1:
1. n
2. factorial

T2:
1. 1
2. 0

T3
1. iteration
2. stop

T4
1. ! =

T5
1. resulting factorial

TE
1. T2[1]
2. T1[1]
3. T2[2]
4. T1[2]T1[1]*
5. T1[1]T2[1]−

9.3.4 Optimizer

A compiler usually contains an optimizer, to make the resulting target program as efficient as possible. Most importantly, the optimizer reduces the program's size and time requirements. By using the Target program obtained in the end of the previous section, the present section sketches some of these reductions.

Reduction of tables

The table of labels, T3, plays an important role during the source program analysis; however, after the COLA compiler completes this analysis and generates the Target program, T3 becomes completely useless. As a result, the COLA optimizer removes T3.

The table of identifiers, T1, no longer needs to store the lexemes, which form the identifiers occurring in the COLA program. On the other hand, T1 can record the values of these identifiers during the execution of the Target program. Therefore, the code optimizer replaces these lexemes with integer items, whose values are defined during the execution of the Target program (see Section 9.3.5).

Reduction of program size

Consider the Target instruction

$$L \quad T3[i]$$

which serves as a label used by the two branch instructions—B and C. This instruction itself invokes no computational action. Consequently, if the branch instructions address the instruction following L $T3[i]$, this instruction can be removed. To carry out this removal, number the Target program instructions and modify the two branch instructions as follows.

Branch

$$B\ i$$

where $i \geq 1$. This instruction causes the computation to continue at the instruction numbered by i.

Conditional Branch

$$C\ TE[i], r, TE[j], k$$

where $r \in \{=, <, >\}$, and $i, j, k \geq 1$. This instruction determines the values of the postfix expressions in TE[i] and TE[j]. Let v_i and v_j be the resulting values corresponding to TE[i] and TE[j], respectively. If $v_i\ r\ v_j$ is **true**, the computation continues at the instruction numbered by k; otherwise, the next instruction is performed.

The use of these modified branch instructions allows the optimizer to remove the two label instructions from the Target program and, thereby, reduce the twelve-instruction program

```
I  T1[1]
O  T5[1]
O  T1[1]
O  T4[1]
E  T1[2],TE[1]
L  T3[1]
C  TE[2],=,TE[3],T3[2]
E  T1[2],TE[4]
E  T1[1],TE[5]
B  T3[1]
L  T3[2]
O  T1[2]
```

to the ten-instruction program:

1. I T1[1]
2. O T5[1]
3. O T1[1]
4. O T4[1]
5. E T1[2],TE[1]
6. C TE[2],=,TE[3],10
7. E T1[2],TE[4]
8. E T1[1],TE[5]
9. B 6
10. O T1[2]

Other approaches to optimization

This section has sketched optimization techniques that make the given target program more efficient by reducing its space and time requirements. There are several other optimization methods. To illustrate one of these, assume that the source program has an awkward expression containing several integers but no identifier. At this point, the optimizer evaluates this expression during the translation of this program and substitute the obtained value for the expression. For example, if the expression is 1 + 2 * 2, the optimizer substitutes 5 for it. The Exercises discusses other optimization strategies of this kind.

9.3.5 Execution

This section describes the execution of the Target program obtained in the previous section. Recall that the COLA compiler translates

```
begin
  read(n);
  write(" resulting factorial ", n, '! = ');
  factorial := 1;
  @iteration;
    if n = 0 goto @stop;
    factorial := factorial*n;
    n := n - 1;
    goto @iteration;
  @stop;
  write(factorial)
end
```

to the Target program

1. *I* T1[1]
2. *O* T5[1]
3. *O* T1[1]
4. *O* T4[1]
5. *E* T1[2],TE[1]
6. *C* TE[2],=,TE[3],10
7. *E* T1[2],TE[4]
8. *E* T1[1],TE[5]
9. *B* 6
10. *O* T1[2]

whose instructions use the following tables.

T1:
1. undefined integer item
2. undefined integer item

T2:
1. 1
2. 0

T4
1. ! =

T5
1. resulting factorial

TE
1. T2[1]
2. T1[1]

3. T2[2]
4. T1[2]T1[1]*
5. T1[1]T2[1]–

The next table traces the output Target program with 3 as its input in order to determine the factorial of 3.

Instruction	Effect	Notes
1	T1[1] = 3	
2	output T5[1]	T5[1] = resulting factorial
3	output T1[1]	T1[1] = 3
4	output T4[1]	T4[1] = ! =
5	T1[2] = 1	TE[1] = T2[1] and T2[1] = 1
6	continue at 7	TE[2] = T1[1] = 3 ≠ TE[3] = T2[2] = 0
7	T1[2] = 3	T1[2]T1[1]* with T1[2]=1 and T1[1] = 3
8	T1[1] = 2	TE[4] = T1[1]T2[1] – with T1[1] = 3 and T2[1] =1
9	continue at 6	
6	continue at 7	TE[2] = T1[1] = 2 ≠ TE[3] = T2[2] = 0
7	T1[2] = 6	T1[2]T1[1]* with T1[2]= 3 and T1[1] = 2
8	T1[1] = 1	TE[4] = T1[1]T2[1]– with T1[1] = 2 and T2[1] = 1
9	continue at 6	
6	continue at 7	TE[2] = T1[1] = 1 ≠ TE[3] = T2[2] = 0
7	T1[2] = 6	T1[2]T1[1]* with T1[2]= 6 and T1[1] = 1
8	T1[1] = 0	TE[4] = T1[1]T2[1]– with T1[1] = 1 and T2[1] = 1
9	continue at 6	
6	continue at 10	TE[2] = T1[1] = 0 = TE[3] = T2[2] = 0
10	output T1[2]	T1[2] = 6

Consequently, this program writes

$$\text{resulting factorial } 3! = 6$$

That is, it correctly determines the factorial of 3.

Exercises

1 Finite transducers

1.1   Consider a finite transducer $M = (Q, \Sigma, R, s, \{s\})$. Does $R = \varnothing$ imply $T(M) = \{(\varepsilon, \varepsilon)\}$?

Finite and pushdown transducers

1.2 Give

    (a) a finite transducer $M = (Q, \Sigma, R, s, F)$
    (b) a word $w \in \Sigma_I$
    (c) an infinite language $L \in \Sigma_O^*$
    (d) a final state $f \in F$

so that for each $v \in L$,

$$sw \vdash^* fv$$

1.3 Consider these finite transducers:

    (a) 1: $sa \vdash sb$
        2: $sb \vdash sa$
        3: $sb \vdash qa$
        4: $qb \vdash qa$
        5: $qa \vdash qb$
        6: $qa \vdash sb$
        7: $s \vdash f$
    (b) 1: $sa \vdash qaa$
        2: $sb \vdash pbb$
        3: $qa \vdash qaa$
        4: $pb \vdash pbb$
        5: $qa \vdash saa$
        6: $pb \vdash sbb$
        7: $s \vdash f$
    (c) 1: $sa \vdash qc$
        2: $qa \vdash pc$
        3: $pb \vdash qc$
        4: $qb \vdash sc$
        5: $sc \vdash fa$
    (d) 1: $sa \vdash qabc$
        2: $sb \vdash pbac$
        3: $qc \vdash scab$
        4: $pc \vdash scab$
        5: $sc \vdash fcab$

For each of these transducers,
(A) give its finite state diagram;
(B) give five pairs of words that belong to the translation defined by the transducer;
(C) give five pairs of words that do not belong to the translation defined by the transducer;
(D) determine the translation that the transducer defines.

1.3 Consider the following translations, defined by regular languages and regular expressions.

(a) $\{(abxba, baxab): x \in \{c\}^*\}$
(b) $\{(aaxbbbb, bbbbxxaa): x \in \{c\}^*\}$
(c) $\{(xbc, xxbcc): x \in \{c\}^*\}$
(d) $\{(xc, cx): x \in L(r) \text{ where } r = ((abba)^* + (baab)^*)^*\}$
(e) $\{(ax, aax): x \in L(r) \text{ where } r = ((ab + ba)^* + (aabb)^*)^*\}$
(f) $\{(x, xy): x \in L(r) \text{ where } r = ((ab + ba)^* + (aabb)^*)^*, \text{ and } y \in L(r') \text{ where } r' = a(a + b)^*b\}$
(g) $\{(yx, y): x \in L(r) \text{ where } r = ((ab + ba)^* + (aabb)^*)^*, \text{ and } y \in L(r') \text{ where } r' = a(a + b)^*b\}$
(h) $\{(a^i b, a^i b^j): i, j \geq 0\}$
(i) $\{(a^i b, a^j b^i): i, j \geq 0\}$
(j) $\{(c_1...c_n, d_1...d_n) : c_i, d_i \in \{a, b\}, c_i = a \text{ if and only if } d_i = b, 1 \leq i \leq n, \text{ for } n \geq 1\} \cup \{(\varepsilon, \varepsilon)\}$

For each of these translations, construct a finite transducer that defines the translation.

1.4 By analogy with ε-free finite automata, define ε-free finite transducers. Does the power of finite transducers coincide with the power of ε-free finite transducers?

1.5 By analogy with well-specified finite automata, define well-specified finite transducers. Does the power of finite transducers coincide with the power of well-specified finite transducers?

1.6 Generalize the definition of a finite transducer by permitting a set of start states. Prove that this generalization does not increase the power of finite transducers.

1.7 A *lazy finite transducer* reads a word, consisting of several symbols, during a move. Formalize the notion of a lazy finite transducer. Prove that this generalization does not increase the power of finite transducers.

1.8 A *two-head finite transducer*, $M = (Q, \Sigma, R, s, F)$, possesses two tape heads, H_0 and H_1, that move independently from left to right on the input tape. Its state set, Q, is divided into two disjoint sets, Q_0 and Q_1. If the current state is in Q_i, for some $i \in \{0, 1\}$, the input symbol is read by H_i. M translates a word x to a word y if M can make a sequence of moves so that it reads the entire input word, x, by H_0 and H_1, writes y on the output tape, and reaches a final state. Formalize the notion of a two-head finite transducer. Prove that the power of finite transducers is less than the power of two-head finite transducers.

1.9 A *two-way finite transducer* can move either way on its input. Formalize the notion of a two-way finite transducer. Does the power of finite transducers coincide with the power of two-way finite transducers?

1.10 Let $M = (Q, \Sigma, R, s, F)$ be a finite transducer, $qax|y$ be a configuration of M, and $r: qa \vdash pz \in R$. Consider these three cases:

(a) $a = \varepsilon$ and $z \in \Sigma_O^+$
(b) $a \in \Sigma_I$ and $z = \varepsilon$
(c) $a = \varepsilon$ and $z = \varepsilon$

For each of these three cases, depict a move that M computes from $qax|y$ by using r. Make this depiction by analogy with Figure 9.1.1.8.

1.11 Let $M = (Q, \Sigma, R, s, F)$ be a finite transducer. Recall that the input language corresponding to $T(M)$ is defined as

$$L_I(M) = \{x: (x, y) \in T(M) \text{ for some } y \in \Sigma_O^*\}$$

and the output language corresponding to $T(M)$ is defined as

$$L_O(M) = \{y: (x, y) \in T(M) \text{ for some } x \in \Sigma_I^*\}$$

Prove that $L_I(M)$ and $L_O(M)$ are regular.

1.12 Prove that a deterministic finite transducer M translates every input word to no more than one output word if M can make no ε-move in any of its final states.

1.13 Complete Example 9.1.1 Part 6.

2 Translation grammars and pushdown transducers

Translation grammars

2.1 Consider these translation grammars:

(a) 1: $S \twoheadrightarrow abSba|baSab$
   2: $S \twoheadrightarrow A|A$
   3: $S \twoheadrightarrow aAa|bAb$
   4: $A \twoheadrightarrow bb|aa$
(b) 1: $S \twoheadrightarrow ASB|ASB$
   2: $S \twoheadrightarrow \varepsilon|\varepsilon$
   3: $A \twoheadrightarrow aSb|bSa$
   4: $A \twoheadrightarrow \varepsilon|\varepsilon$
   5: $B \twoheadrightarrow aBb|bBa$
   6: $B \twoheadrightarrow ba|ab$
(c) 1: $S \twoheadrightarrow a_1 S a_2 | a_2 a_1 S a_2$
   2: $S \twoheadrightarrow a_1 a_2 | a_2 a_1 a_2$

3: $S \twoheadrightarrow a_3 S a_4 | a_4 a_3 S a_4$
4: $S \twoheadrightarrow a_3 a_4 | a_4 a_3 a_4$
5: $S \twoheadrightarrow a_5 S a_6 | a_6 a_5 S a_6$
6: $S \twoheadrightarrow a_5 a_6 | a_6 a_5 a_6$

For each of these grammars,

(A) give five pairs of words that belong to the translation generated by the grammar;
(B) give five pairs of words that do not belong to the translation generated by the grammar.

2.2 Determine the translations defined by the following translation grammars:

(a) 1: $S \twoheadrightarrow aSa|bSb$
    2: $S \twoheadrightarrow bSb|aSa$
    3: $S \twoheadrightarrow \varepsilon|\varepsilon$
(b) 1: $S \twoheadrightarrow aSa|aaSaa$
    2: $S \twoheadrightarrow bSb|bbSbb$
    3: $S \twoheadrightarrow a|aa$
    4: $S \twoheadrightarrow b|bb$
(c) 1: $S \twoheadrightarrow aS|Sb$
    2: $S \twoheadrightarrow Sb|aS$
    3: $S \twoheadrightarrow a|a$
(d) 1: $S \twoheadrightarrow aSa|abSba$
    2: $S \twoheadrightarrow bb|aa$

2.3 Construct translation grammars that define the following translations.

(a) $\{(a^i b^j c^k, a^{2i} b^{2j} c^{2k}): i, j, k \geq 0 \text{ and } i = j + k\}$
(b) $\{(a^i b^j c^k, a^i b^{4j} c^k): i, j, k \geq 0 \text{ and } j = i + k\}$
(c) $\{(a^i b^j c^k, a^i b^j c^8): i, j, k \geq 0 \text{ and } i \neq j + k\}$
(d) $\{(a^i b^j c^k, d^{2(i+j+k)}): i, j, k \geq 0 \text{ and } j \neq i\}$

2.4 Consider the homomorphism γ representing all digits in binary in the following way:

$$\gamma(i) = 01^i \text{ for } i = 1, \ldots, 9$$

By using γ, represent all natural numbers as

$\gamma(1) = 01, \gamma(2) = 011, \ldots, \gamma(12) = 01011, \ldots$

Construct a translation grammar that defines this translation

$$\{ (j, \gamma(j)) : j \geq 1 \}$$

2.5 Define a binary representation of parenthesized logical expressions consisting of the logical variable p and the logical operators **and**, **or** and **not** such that **not** has a higher priority than **and**, and **and** has a higher priority than **or**. By analogy with the previous exercise, design a binary representation of these expressions. Construct a translation grammar that translates these expressions to the corresponding binary representations. Trace the translations of the following three expressions

(a) **not** p **or** p
(b) **not** (p **and** p) **or** p
(c) (p **or** p) **or** (p **and** **not** p)

2.6 Recall that an E0S system is a context-free grammar that can rewrite terminals; more precisely, an *E0S system* is a quadruple $G = (N, T, P, S)$, where N is an alphabet of nonterminals, T is an alphabet of terminals, $P \subseteq (N \cup T) \times (N \cup T)^*$ is a finite relationship, and S in N is the start symbol. Define translation grammars based on E0S systems. Does the power of translation grammars defined in this way coincide with the power of translation grammars defined in Section 9.2.1?

2.7 Generalize translation grammars by permitting productions of the form

$$A \twoheadrightarrow u_0 B_1 u_1 \ldots B_n u_n | v_0 C_1 v_1 \ldots C_n v_n$$

where n is a nonnegative integer, B_j and C_j are nonterminals, for $j = 1, \ldots, n$, and there exists a bijection, β, on $\{1, \ldots, n\}$ such that $B_j = C_{\beta(j)}$. Prove that translation grammars generalized in this way are more powerful than translation grammars as defined in Section 9.2.1.

2.8 Recall that a pure context-free grammar has only terminals; more precisely, a *pure context-free grammar* G is a triple $G = (T, P, S)$, where T is an alphabet, $P \subseteq T \times T^*$ is a finite binary relationship, and $S \in T^+$ is the start word. Define pure translation grammars based on pure context-free grammars. Consider the following four translations.

(a) $\{(b, a), (aa, bb)\}$
(b) $\{(a, a), (aa, a)\}$
(c) $\{(a^n cb^n, \varepsilon): n \geq 1\}$
(d) $\{(a^n b^n, \varepsilon): n \geq 1\}$

For each of these translations, decide whether there exists a pure translation grammar that defines the translation.

2.9 By analogy with ambiguous context-free grammars, define ambiguous translation grammars.

2.10 Consider the following translation grammar G:

1: $S \twoheadrightarrow S + S | SS+$
2: $S \twoheadrightarrow S * S | SS*$
3: $S \twoheadrightarrow (S) | S$
4: $S \twoheadrightarrow i | i$

Observe that G translates arithmetic expressions, whose alphabet has $+, *, (,)$ and i, to the corresponding postfix expressions. Is G ambiguous?

2.11 By analogy with inherently ambiguous context-free languages, define inherently ambiguous translations.

2.12 Consider the language L defined as

$$L = \{x \text{reversal}(x): x \in \{a, b\}^*\}$$

Does there exist a translation grammar G that defines the translation

$$\{(v, \text{reversal}(v)): v = w\text{reversal}(w) \text{ and } w \in L\}$$

If so, is this translation inherently ambiguous?

Pushdown transducers

2.14 Give

(a) a pushdown transducer $M = (Q, \Sigma, R, s, F)$
(b) a word $w \in \Sigma_I$
(c) an infinite language $L \in \Sigma_O^*$
(d) a final state $f \in F$

so that for each $v \in L$,

$$Ssw \vDash^* fv$$

Finite and pushdown transducers

2.15 Consider the following pushdown transducer M:

r_1: $Ssa \vdash aqb$
r_2: $Ssa \vdash aaqbb$
r_3: $Ssb \vdash bqa$
r_4: $Ssb \vdash bbqaa$
r_5: $aqa \vdash aaqbb$
r_6: $aqa \vdash aaaqbbb$
r_7: $bqb \vdash bbqaa$
r_8: $bqb \vdash bbbqaaa$
r_9: $aqb \vdash f$
r_{10}: $bqa \vdash f$
r_{11}: $afb \vdash f$
r_{12}: $bfa \vdash f$

For this transducer,

(A) give its pushdown state diagram;
(B) give five pairs of words that belong to $T(M)$;
(C) give five pairs of words that do not belong to $T(M)$.

2.16 Section 9.2.2 describes extended pushdown transducers informally. Formalize this description. Specifically, define $\vdash$ and $\vdash^*$ for extended pushdown transducers. Then, based on $\vdash^*$, describe the translations defined by extended pushdown transducers.

2.17 By analogy with the languages that pushdown automata accept by empty pushdown, introduce the translations that pushdown transducers define by empty pushdown.

2.18 Consider these pushdown transducers:

(a) 1: $Ssa \vdash Sasbb$
    2: $asa \vdash aasbbbb$
    3: $asb \vdash q$
    4: $aqb \vdash q$
    5: $Sq \vdash Ss$
    6: $Sq \vdash s$
(b) 1: $Ss \vdash SSs$
    2: $Ssa \vdash Sasa$
    3: $asa \vdash aasaa$
    4: $asb \vdash qab$
    5: $aqb \vdash qab$
    6: $Sq \vdash s$

(c) 1: $Ssa \vdash Asc$
2: $Asa \vdash AAsc$
3: $Asc \vdash qa$
4: $Ssb \vdash Asb$
5: $Asb \vdash AAsb$
6: $Aqc \vdash qa$

Determine the translations that these transducers define by empty pushdown.

2.19 Prove or disprove that the family of translations that pushdown transducers define by final state coincides with the family of translations that pushdown transducers define by empty pushdown.

2.20 By analogy with the languages that pushdown automata accept by empty pushdown and final state, introduce the translations that pushdown transducers define by empty pushdown and final state.

2.21 Consider these two pushdown transducers:

(a) 1: $Ssa \vdash Sqc$
2: $aqa \vdash aascc$
3: $aqb \vdash qcc$
4: $Sq \vdash f$
(b) 1: $Ssa \vdash Saaqc$
3: $bqb \vdash qc$
4: $bqa \vdash qc$
5: $bqa \vdash bqc$
6: $Sq \vdash f$

Determine the translations that these transducers define by final state and empty pushdown.

2.21 Prove or disprove that the family of translations that pushdown transducers define by final state and empty pushdown coincides with the family of translations that pushdown transducers define by empty pushdown.

2.22 A lazy pushdown transducer can read a word, consisting of several symbols, during a move.

Formalize the notion of a lazy pushdown transducer. Does this generalization add to the power of pushdown transducers?

2.23 Let $M = (Q, \Sigma, R, s, F)$ be a pushdown transducer. M is a counter pushdown transducer if Σ_{PD} has only one element, the start symbol. Formalize this transducer. Is the power of pushdown transducers greater than the power of counter pushdown transducers?

2.24 Consider a pushdown transducer $M = (Q, \Sigma, R, s, F)$, and a configuration of M,

$$zAqax|y$$

for some $z \in \Sigma_{PD}^*, A \in \Sigma_{PD}^*, q \in Q, a \in \Sigma_I \cup \{\varepsilon\}, x \in \Sigma_I^*,$ and $y \in \Sigma_O^*.$ Let

$$r: Aqa \vdash upv \in R$$

where $p \in Q, u \in \Sigma_{PD}^*,$ and $v \in \Sigma_O^*.$

(a) If $a = \varepsilon, M$ does not shift the read head.
(b) If $u = \varepsilon, M$ removes A from the pushdown.
(c) If $v = \varepsilon, M$ does not shift the write head.

Describe these three cases in detail.

2.25 Complete Example 9.2.2.1 Part 5
2.26 Prove Theorem 9.2.2.1

3. Compiler

3.1 Section 9.3.2 has sketched procedures P7 through P16. Describe these procedures in detail.

3.2 Many programming languages require that an object is defined exactly once; for instance, in Pascal, an identifier must be declared uniquely. Consider a programming language that has a requirement of this kind. Design a semantic analyzer procedure that verifies this requirement.

3.3 A typical semantic analyzer checks that each operator is used with compatible operands and reports an error whenever this compatibility is violated.

Consider a common programming language, and design a semantic analyzer procedure that verifies the operand compatibility of this language.

3.4 In some programming languages, a statement that causes flow of control to leave a construct require the specification of another statement to which to transfer the flow of control. For example, in the programming language C, a break statement leaves for the smallest enclosing **while**, **for** or **switch** statement; consequently, an error occurs if no such enclosing statement exists. Consider a common programming language that places a requirement of this kind on the flow of control. Design a semantic analyzer procedure that verifies this requirement.

3.5 There exist programming languages requiring some names to appear several times; for instance, in Ada, loops and blocks begin and end with the same name. Consider a common programming language that has a requirement of this kind, and design a semantic analyzer procedure that verifies this requirement.

3.6 Design some optimization techniques that simplify expressions by using algebraic laws and identities, such as $x + 0 = x$ or $x/1 = x$.

3.7 A variable occurring in a program is useless if its removal does not effect the program. For instance, a variable that is declared but unused in a given program represents a useless variable. Design an optimization technique that eliminates all useless variables.

Programming projects

1. Finite transducers

1.1 Design a data structure for representing finite transducers.
1.2 Write a program that decides whether a given finite transducer is deterministic.
1.3 Write a program that simulates a deterministic finite transducer.
1.4 Write a deterministic finite transducer compiler — that is, a program that reads a deterministic finite transducer and produces a program that simulates this transducer.
1.5 Write a program that simulates a nondeterministic finite transducer.

2. Translation grammars and pushdown transducers

2.1 Design a data structure for representing translation grammars.
2.2 Given a translation grammar G and a natural number n write a program that produces $\{(x, y): |xy| \leq n, \text{and } (x, y) \in T(G)\}$.
2.3 Write a program that decides whether a given pushdown transducer is deterministic.
2.4 Write a program that simulates a deterministic pushdown transducer.
2.5 Write a deterministic pushdown transducer compiler — that is, a program that reads a deterministic pushdown transducer and produces a program that simulates this transducer.
2.6 Write a program that simulates a nondeterministic pushdown transducer.

3. Compilers

3.1 Write a program that implements the COLA scanner GetToken, described in Section 9.3.2.
3.2 Section 9.3.3 has sketched the **integer** function PostfixExpression. Write a program that implements this function.
3.3 Write a program that implements the COLA parser described in Section 9.3.3.
3.4 Based on the previous two projects, write the complete COLA compiler.

10 Turing Transducers

Is the power of computers limitless? Can computers execute any function? Can they decide any problem? The present chapter discusses fundamental problems of this kind in terms of Turing transducers, which are based on Turing machines (see Section 8.1).

Section 10.1 introduces Turing transducers. Based upon these transducers, Section 10.2 formalizes computers and investigates which functions computers can compute. Finally, Section 10.3 studies Turing transducers acting as decision-making algorithms, examines the time and space complexity of these algorithms, and presents several problems that computers cannot decide.

10.1 Basic definitions

As Figure 10.1.1 depicts, a Turing transducer resembles a Turing machine with two tapes, the input tape and the output tape. However, whereas a two-tape Turing machine accepts a language, a Turing transducers translates a language into another language.

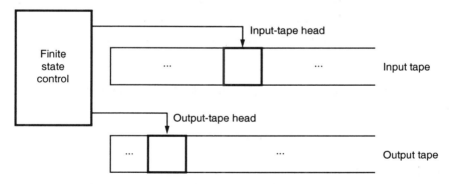

Figure 10.1.1 Turing transducer.

A Turing transducer M works by making moves. Initially, M's input tape contains a word x and its output tape is completely blank. If M can make a computation so it erases x on the input tape, writes a word y on the output tape, and enters a final state with both heads over the leftmost squares, then M translates x into y (see Figure 10.1.2). The set that contains all pairs of words translated in this way forms the translation defined by M.

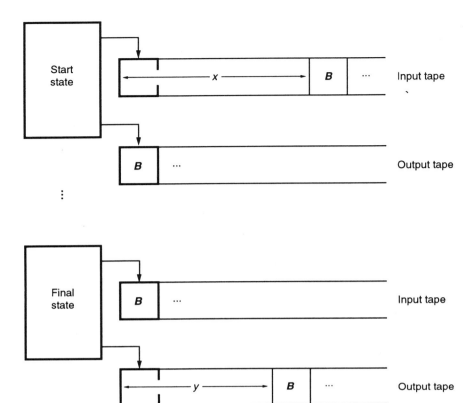

Figure 10.1.2 Translation of x to y by a Turing machine.

Example 10.1.1 Part 1 Intuitive design of a Turing machine

Consider the translation

$$\tau = \{ (x, x0): x \in \{1\}\{0, 1\}^* \}$$

That is, τ contains

$$(1, 10), (10, 100), (11, 110), \ldots$$

This example describes a Turing transducer M that defines τ. In the beginning, M's input tape contains x, where $x \in \{0, 1\}^*$, and the output tape is blank. M copies x onto the output tape provided that x begins with 1. When performing this copy, M marks the leftmost square of the input tape by placing 0 in this square and fills all other input tape's squares with blanks, i.e. Bs. Having finished this copy, M writes 0 behind x on the output tape to produce $x0$. Then, M keeps shifting both heads left until 0 appears on the input tape; at this point, both heads are over the leftmost squares. To complete the translation, M writes B into the leftmost square of the input tape and halts in a final state. Figure 10.1.3 shows this computation for $x = 11$.

Definition — Turing transducer
A *Turing transducer* is a quintuple

$$M = (Q, \Sigma, R, s, F)$$

where

Q is a finite set of states;
Σ is a tape alphabet such that $\Sigma \cap Q = \emptyset$ and $\Sigma = \Sigma_I \cup \Sigma_O \cup \{B\}$, where Σ_I is an input alphabet, Σ_O is an output alphabet, and $B \in \Sigma - (\Sigma_I \cup \Sigma_O)$ is the blank;
R is a finite set of rules of the form

$$qX_IX_O \vdash pY_It_IY_Ot_O$$

where $q, p \in Q$; $X_I, Y_I \in \Sigma_I \cup (\Sigma - \Sigma_O)$; $X_O, Y_O \in \Sigma_O \cup (\Sigma - \Sigma_I)$; $t_I, t_O \in \{\downarrow, \hookrightarrow, \dashv\}$;
$s \in Q$ is the start state;
$F \subseteq Q$ is a set of final states.

♦

Consider a Turing transducer, $M = (Q, \Sigma, R, s, F)$. To refer to the rules in R succinctly, they are labelled. If a rule $qX_IX_O \vdash pY_It_IY_Ot_O$ is denoted with a label r this is written as

$$r: qX_IX_O \vdash pY_It_IY_Ot_O$$

Consider $r: qX_IX_O \vdash pY_It_IY_Ot_O \in R$. The left-hand side of r, qX_IX_O, is denoted by lhs(r), and its right-hand side, $pY_It_IY_Ot_O$, is denoted by rhs(r). The present section also makes use of the conventions introduced in Section 8.1 for Turing machines.

Example 10.1.1 Part 2 Formal specification of a Turing transducer
This part of Example 10.1.1 formalizes the Turing transducer M informally described in Part 1. M has the states

$$s, q \text{ and } f$$

where s is the start state and f is the final state of M. M's tape alphabet is

$$\{0, 1, B\}$$

△

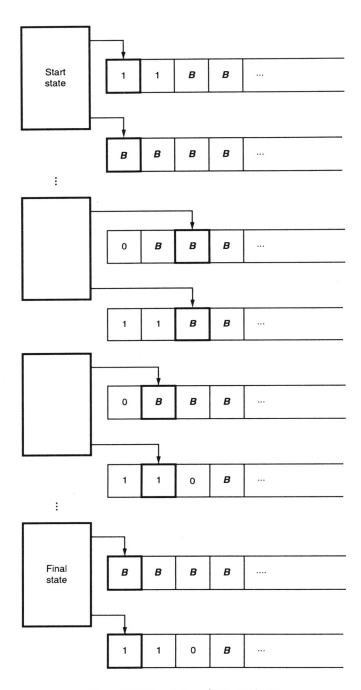

Figure 10.1.3 Translation of 11 to 110 by M.

Both the input alphabet and the output alphabet are

$$\{0, 1\}$$

M's rules complete the formalization of M:

1: $s1B \vdash q0 \hookrightarrow 1 \hookrightarrow$
2: $q0B \vdash qB \hookrightarrow 0 \hookrightarrow$
3: $q1B \vdash qB \hookrightarrow 1 \hookrightarrow$
4: $qBB \vdash qB\lrcorner 0\lrcorner$
5: $qB0 \vdash qB\lrcorner 0\lrcorner$
6: $qB1 \vdash qB\lrcorner 1\lrcorner$
7: $q01 \vdash fB\downarrow 1\downarrow$

△

A Turing transducer M works by making moves according to its rules. During a move, M changes the current state and rewrites the scanned symbols; in addition, M shifts its tape heads zero or one square to the right or left.

Definition — configuration
Let $M = (Q, \Sigma, R, s, F)$ be a Turing transducer, $q \in Q$, $I = \Sigma_I \cup (\Sigma - \Sigma_O)$, and $O = \Sigma_O \cup (\Sigma - \Sigma_I)$. Then, χ is a *configuration* of M if

$$\chi = \chi_I | \chi_O$$

where

$\chi_I \in I^*\{q\}(I^*(I - \{B\}) \cup \{B\})$,
$\chi_O \in O^*\{q\}(O^*(O - \{B\}) \cup \{B\})$,
$| \notin \Sigma^*$.

◆

Conventions
Given a Turing transducer M, χ_M denotes a configuration of M; when no confusion exists, χ_M is simplified to χ.

●

Consider a Turing transducer $M = (Q, \Sigma, R, s, F)$ and a configuration of M

$$\chi = \chi_I | \chi_O$$

where | separates the input tape from the output tapes. Let

$$\chi_I = xqy \text{ and } \chi_O = uqv$$

where $q \in Q, x \in I^*, y \in I^*(I - \{B\}) \cup \{B\}, u \in O^*,$ and $v \in O^*((O - \{B\}) \cup \{B\})$. As Figure 10.1.4 displays, χ represents an instantaneous description of M. Indeed, q specifies the current state of M. The word xy is the currently written portion of the input tape with the input-tape head over the leftmost symbol of y. Analogously, uv represents the currently written portion of the output tape with the output-tape head over the leftmost symbol of v.

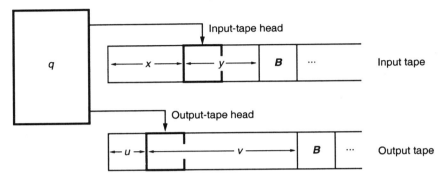

Figure 10.1.4 Configuration of M.

Definition — input Turing machine

Let $M = (Q, \Sigma, R, s, F)$ be a Turing transducer. The *input Turing machine* M_I underlying M is defined as

$$M_I = (Q, \Sigma, R_I, s, F)$$

where

$$R_I = \{qU_I \vdash pV_I t_I : qU_I U_O \vdash pV_I t_I V_O t_O \in R\}.$$

◆

Definition — output Turing machine

Let $M = (Q, \Sigma, R, s, F)$ be a Turing transducer. The *output Turing machine* M_O underlying M is defined as

$$M_O = (Q, \Sigma, R_O, s, F)$$

where

$$R_O = \{qU_O \vdash pV_O t_O : qU_I U_O \vdash pV_I t_I V_O t_O \in R\}.$$

◆

Theorem 10.1.1
Consider the following two classes of Turing machines:

1. input Turing machines underlying Turing transducers;
2. output Turing machines underlying Turing transducers.

Both of them characterize the family of recursively enumerable languages.

Proof
This theorem follows from Theorem 8.1.4.9 and the previous two definitions. A detailed version of this proof is left to the exercises. ∎

Definition — move
Let $M = (Q, \Sigma, R, s, F)$ be a Turing transducer, and let

$$\chi = \chi_I | \chi_O \text{ and } \chi' = \chi'_I | \chi'_O$$

be two configurations of M. Furthermore, let

$$r: qX_IX_O \vdash pY_It_IY_Ot_O \in R$$

If

$$\chi_I \vdash \chi'_I \qquad [qX_I \vdash pY_It_I]$$

in the input Turing machine M_I underlying M, and

$$\chi_O \vdash \chi'_O \qquad [qX_O \vdash pY_Ot_O]$$

in the output Turing machine M_O underlying M, then M makes a move from χ to χ' according to r, symbolically written as

$$\chi \vdash \chi' \quad [r]$$

◆

Conventions
Whenever in $\chi \vdash \chi'$ $[r]$, r represents an immaterial piece of information, then write $\chi \vdash \chi'$.

●

Example 10.1.1 Part 3 Moves
Consider the Turing transducer M discussed throughout the previous two parts of this example. Let

$$0BqB|11qB$$

be the current configuration of M. According to

$$4: qBB \vdash qB \lrcorner 0 \lrcorner$$

M makes the move

$$0BqB|11qB \vdash 0qB|1q10 \quad [4]$$

To describe another move, suppose that

$$q0BB\ |q110B$$

be the current configuration of M. According to

$$7: q01 \vdash fB \downarrow 1 \downarrow,$$

M makes the move

$$q0BB|q110B \vdash fB|f110B \quad [4]$$

△

The next definition extends a move to a sequence of moves.

Definition — sequence of moves, part 1
Let $M = (Q, \Sigma, R, s, F)$ be a Turing transducer.

1. Let χ be any configuration of M. M makes *zero moves* from χ to χ according to ε, written as

$$\chi \vdash^0 \chi \qquad [\varepsilon]$$

2. Let

$$\chi_0, ..., \chi_n$$

be a sequence of n configurations, for some $n \geq 1$, such that

$$\chi_{i-1} \vdash \chi_i \qquad [r_i]$$

where $r_i \in R, i = 1, \ldots, n$. Then, M makes n *moves* from χ_0 to χ_n according to $r_1 \ldots r_n$, written as

$$\chi_0 \vdash^n \chi_n \qquad [r_1 \ldots r_n]$$

Consider a Turing transducer $M = (Q, \Sigma, R, s, F)$. Let $\chi \vdash^n \chi'\ [\rho]$ in M, where ρ denotes a sequence of n rules ($\rho = \varepsilon$ if $n = 0$). Notice that ρ, called the rule word corresponding to $\chi \vdash^n \chi'$, represents the sequence of n rules according to which M makes the n moves from χ to χ'. For brevity, omits ρ in $\chi \vdash^n \chi'\ [\rho]$ and write $\chi \vdash^n \chi'$.

Definition — sequence of moves, part 2

Let $M = (Q, \Sigma, R, s, F)$ be a Turing transducer, and let χ and χ' be two configurations of M.

1. If there exists $n \geq 1$ so $\chi \vdash^n \chi'\ [\rho]$ in M, then $\chi \vdash^+ \chi'\ [\rho]$.
2. If there exists $n \geq 0$ so $\chi \vdash^n \chi'\ [\rho]$ in M, then $\chi \vdash^* \chi'\ [\rho]$.

◆

This chapter frequently simplifies $\chi \vdash^+ \chi'\ [\rho]$ and $\chi \vdash^* \chi'\ [\rho]$ to $\chi \vdash^+ \chi'$ and $\chi \vdash^* \chi'$, respectively.

Example 10.1.1 Part 4 Sequences of moves

Return to the Turing transducer M discussed throughout the previous parts of this example. Observe that

$$s11|sB \vdash^* fB|f110 \qquad [13467]$$

in M because

$$\begin{aligned}
s11|sB &\vdash 0q1|1qB & [1]\\
&\vdash 0BqB|11qB & [3]\\
&\vdash 0qB|1q10B & [4]\\
&\vdash q0B|q110B & [6]\\
&\vdash fB|f110B & [7]
\end{aligned}$$

where

1: $s1B \vdash q0 \hookrightarrow 1 \hookrightarrow$
3: $q1B \vdash qB \hookrightarrow 1 \hookrightarrow$

4: $qBB \vdash qB\lrcorner 0\lrcorner$
6: $qB1 \vdash qB\lrcorner 1\lrcorner$
7: $q01 \vdash fB\downarrow 1\downarrow$

Because $s11|sB \vdash^5 fB|f110$,

$$s11|sB \vdash^+ fB|f110 \text{ and } s11|sB \vdash^* fB|f110$$

in M.

△

A Turing transducer M translates words over its input alphabet Σ_I into words over its output alphabet Σ_O. Initially, an input word x is written on the input tape while the output tape is completely blank. M begins its computation from the start state with both heads over the leftmost squares of the tapes. If M can make a move sequence so that it erases x on the input tape, writes a word y on the output tape, and enters a final state with both heads over the leftmost squares, then M translates x into y. The set containing all pairs of words translated in this way forms the translation defined by M.

Definition — translation of word by Turing transducer
Let $M = (Q, \Sigma, R, s, F)$ be a Turing transducer, $x \in \Sigma_I^*$, and $y \in \Sigma_O^*$. M *translates x into y* if

$$sx'|sB \vdash^* fB|fy'$$

in M, where

1. $f \in F$;
2. if $x = \varepsilon$, then $x' = B$; otherwise $x' = x$;
3. if $y = \varepsilon$, then $y' = B$; otherwise $y' = y$.

◆

Definition — translation defined by Turing transducer
Let $M = (Q, \Sigma, R, s, F)$ be a Turing transducer. The *translation defined by M*, $T(M)$, is

$$T(M) = \{ (x, y): x \in \Sigma_I^*, y \in \Sigma_O^*, \text{ and } M \text{ translates } x \text{ into } y\}$$

◆

Example 10.1.1 Part 5 Translation
Return to the Turing transducer M discussed throughout Example 10.1.1. The previous part demonstrates that

$$s11|sB \vdash^* fB|f110$$

Thus,

$$(11, 110) \in T(M)$$

The exercises proves that

$$T(M) = \{\, (x, x0) : x \in \{1\}\{0, 1\}^* \,\}$$

△

Determinism

According to the basic definition given in the beginning of the present section, a Turing transducer works nondeterministically. Indeed, a Turing transducer may possess a number of rules with the same left-hand side and, therefore, make different moves from the same configuration. As a result, with the same word, it can make different move sequences. The next definition introduces the notion of a deterministic Turing transducer, which rules out this multiplicity of move sequences with the same word.

Definition — deterministic Turing transducer
Let $M = (Q, \Sigma, R, s, F)$ be a Turing transducer. M is a *deterministic Turing transducer* if every rule $r \in R$ satisfies

$$\text{lhs}(r) \notin \{\text{lhs}(r') : r' \in (R - r)\}$$

◆

Notice that the Turing transducer M studied in Example 10.1.1 is deterministic because M does not have two different rules with the same left-hand side.

Theorem 10.1.2
Let τ be a translation. Then, $\tau = T(M)$ for a Turing transducer M if and only if $\tau = T(D)$ for a deterministic Turing transducer D.

Proof
Prove this theorem by analogy with the conversion of a Turing machine to an equivalent deterministic Turing machine (see Section 8.1.2). A detailed version of this proof is left to the exercises.

■

Simplification

The following sections investigate deterministic Turing transducers that define translations representing functions, not relationships. To simplify this investigation, the conclusion of this section introduces some conventions concerning the form of these transducers.

Theorem 10.1.3

Let $M = (Q, \Sigma, R, s, F)$ be a deterministic Turing transducer such that $T(M)$ represents a function; that is, $(x, y) \in T(M)$ and $(x, y') \in T(M)$ imply $y = y'$. Then, there exists a deterministic Turing transducer M' satisfying these three properties:

1. $T(M) = T(M')$;
2. M' has one final state f;
3. for every $x \in \Sigma_I^*$, the following equivalences holds:

$$(x, y) \in T(M') \text{ for a word } y \in \Sigma_O^*,$$

if and only if

M' translates x into y and halts in f.

Proof
Let $M = (Q, \Sigma, R, s, F)$ be a deterministic Turing transducer such that $(x, y) \in T(M)$ and $(x, y') \in T(M)$ imply $y = y'$. Construct a deterministic Turing transducer M' that has one final state, f. M' works so it simulates M move by move. When M translates a word x into a word y, M' translates x into y so it enters f and halts. As formally verified in the exercises, M' constructed in this way satisfies the requirements of Theorem 10.1.3. ∎

Conventions

Let M be a Turing transducer. Whenever $T(M)$ represents a function, the rest of this chapter assumes that M has the form

$$M = (Q, \Sigma, R, s, \{f\})$$

where f is the final state of M and, in addition, M satisfies the following two conditions:

1. M is deterministic;
2. $(x, y) \in T(M)$ for some $y \in \Sigma_O^*$ if and only if M translates x into y and halts in f. ●

From Theorems 10.1.2 and 10.1.3, these conventions significantly simplify the study of Turing transducers, and represent no loss of generality.

10.2 Computability

By using the Turing transducers defined above, Section 10.2.1 formalizes computers. Then, Section 10.2.2 establishes some fundamental results about functions computable by computers. By contrast, Section 10.2.3 discusses uncomputable functions. Most importantly, this section introduces some simple functions over natural numbers and demonstrates that no computer can compute them. This demonstration leads to some crucial results concerning the limit of computer power.

10.2.1 Computers

Based upon deterministic Turing transducers, the present section formalizes computers. It restricts its attention to functions over nonnegative integers represented in binary. This representation is defined by the function BiInt, mapping nonnegative integers into $\{0, 1\}^*$, as follows:

1. BiInt(0) = 0;
2. for any natural number i

$$\text{BiInt}(i) = x$$

where x is defined by these two properties

A. $x \in \{1\}\{0, 1\}^*$
B. $\text{Binary}_{|x|}(i) = x$

(See Section 3.2.3 for the definition of Binary). Less formally, if $i = 0$, then BiInt(i) equals 0. If $i \geq 1$, BiInt(i) equals the shortest representation of i defined by Binary because, by property A, BiInt forbids any leading zeros; for example, 11 validly represents 3, but 011 is not valid.

Definition — computer
Let $M = (Q, \Sigma, R, s, \{f\})$ be a deterministic Turing transducer, such that $\Sigma = \{0, 1, B\}$ with $\Sigma_I = \{0, 1\}$ and $\Sigma_O = \{0, 1\}$. Furthermore, let ϕ be a function over nonnegative integers. M is a *computer* of ϕ if, for all $x, y \in \{0, 1\}^*$, this equivalence holds

$$(x, y) \in T(M)$$

if and only if

$$x = \text{BiInt}(i) \text{ and } y = \text{BiInt}(\phi(i)), \text{ for some } i \geq 0$$

◆

Let M be a computer of a function ϕ. Then, by the previous definition, M translates a binary word x to a binary word y if and only if there exists $i \geq 0$ such that $x = \text{BiInt}(i)$ and $y = \text{BiInt}(\phi(i))$ (see Figure 10.2.1.1). In other words,

$$T(M) = \{(x, y): x = \text{BiInt}(i) \text{ and } y = \text{BiInt}(\phi(i)) \text{ for some } i \geq 0\}$$

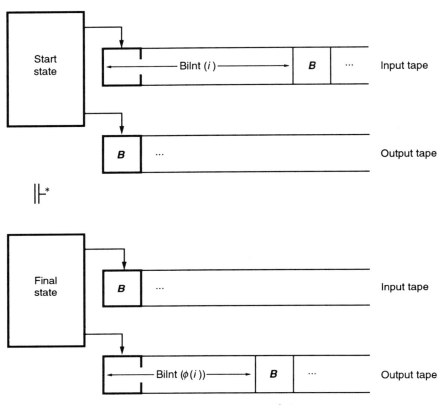

Figure 10.2.1.1 Computation of $\phi(i)$.

Convention
The rest of Section 10.2 narrows its attention to functions over natural numbers. ●

Example 10.2.1.1 Computer for multiplication
Let ϕ be the total function multiplying natural numbers by two:

$$\phi(i) = 2i$$

for $i = 1, \ldots$. Consider the Turing transducer M defined in Part 1 of Example 10.1.1. This example demonstrates that M represents a computer of ϕ. Indeed, from Part 6 of this example,

$$T(M) = \{ (x, x0) : x \in \{1\}\{0, 1\}^* \}$$

Equivalently, in terms of BiInt,

$$T(M) = \{ (\text{BiInt}(i), \text{BiInt}(2i)) : i \geq 1 \}$$

That is,

$$T(M) = \{ (\text{BiInt}(i), \text{BiInt}(\phi(i))) : i \geq 1 \}$$

Thus, for all $x, y \in \{0, 1\}^*$, $(x, y) \in T(M)$ if and only if there exists $i \geq 1$ so $x = \text{BiInt}(i)$ and $y = \text{BiInt}(\phi(i)))$. As a result, M is a computer of ϕ.

▲

Example 10.2.1.2 Computer of the successor function

Let ϕ be the successor function, defined as

$$\phi(i) = i + 1$$

for $i = 1, \ldots$. This example constructs a deterministic Turing transducer M that represents a computer of ϕ.

In the beginning, M's input tape contains a binary word x while the output tape is blank. M copies x onto the output tape provided that x begins with 1 and, thus, validly represents a natural number, $i \geq 1$; that is,

$$\text{BiInt}(i) = x$$

When making this copy, M marks the leftmost square of the input tape by placing 0 into this square and fills all other input tape's squares with Bs. Moreover, by using a special state, M remembers whether x contains 0. This information, specifying whether x contains 0, determines the rest of the computation. Indeed, if x contains 0, M performs the following computation A; otherwise, M carries out computation B. Both kinds of computation are described from the configuration in which M has finished the copy of x from the input tape to the output tape; in this configuration, the input tape and the output tape contain $0B^{|x|}$ and xB, respectively, and both heads occur over the $(|x| + 1)$th square.

Computation A

If x contains 0, M keeps shifting the input head and the output head left until the rightmost appearance of 0 appears on the output tape; at this point, M replaces this appearance of 0 with 1. Then, M shifts both heads left until 0 appears on the input tape and, consequently, both heads occur over the leftmost squares. To complete this translation, M places B into the leftmost square of the input tape and enters a final state. Figure 10.2.1.2 describes how M translates 10 into 11, where $10 = \text{BiInt}(2)$ and $11 = \text{BiInt}(3)$; in this way, M computes $\phi(i) = i + 1$ for $i = 2$.

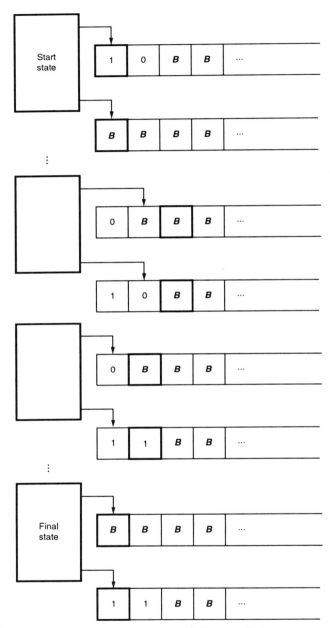

Figure 10.2.1.2 Computation of $\phi(i) = i + 1$ for $i = 2$.

Computation B
If x contains no 0, M writes 0 behind x on the output tape, then shifts both heads left until 0 appears on the input tape. When making this shift, M replaces each symbol

Turing transducers

of x, except for the leftmost 1, with 0 on the output tape. By analogy with Computation A, M completes the translation by placing B into the leftmost square of the input tape and halting in a final state. Figure 10.2.1.3 indicates the way M determines $\phi(i) = i + 1$ for $i = 3$ by translating 11 into 100, where 11 = BiInt(3) and 100 = BiInt(4).

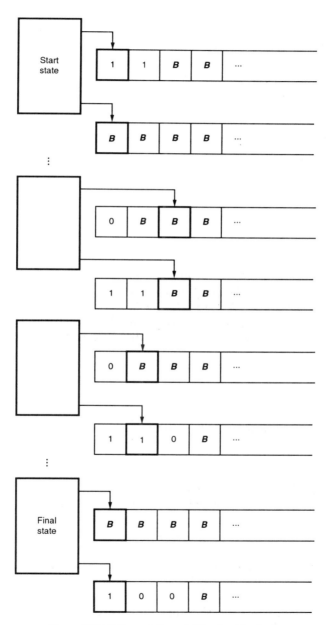

Figure 10.2.1.3 Computation of $\phi(i) = i + 1$ for $i = 3$.

Formally, M has states s, q, p, t and f, where f is the final state. M possesses these 15 rules:

$r_1: s1B \;\; \vdash q0 \hookrightarrow 1 \hookrightarrow$
$r_2: q0B \;\; \vdash pB \hookrightarrow 0 \hookrightarrow$
$r_3: q1B \;\; \vdash qB \hookrightarrow 1 \hookrightarrow$
$r_4: p0B \;\; \vdash pB \hookrightarrow 0 \hookrightarrow$
$r_5: p1B \;\; \vdash pB \hookrightarrow 1 \hookrightarrow$
$r_6: pBB \;\; \vdash pB \hookleftarrow B \hookleftarrow$
$r_7: pB0 \;\; \vdash tB \hookleftarrow 1 \hookleftarrow$
$r_8: pB1 \;\; \vdash pB \hookleftarrow 1 \hookleftarrow$
$r_9: tB1 \;\; \vdash tB \hookleftarrow 1 \hookleftarrow$
$r_{10}: tB0 \;\; \vdash tB \hookleftarrow 0 \hookleftarrow$
$r_{11}: t01 \;\; \vdash fB \downarrow 1 \downarrow$
$r_{12}: qBB \vdash qB \hookleftarrow 0 \hookleftarrow$
$r_{13}: qB1 \vdash qB \hookleftarrow 0 \hookleftarrow$
$r_{14}: qB0 \vdash qB \hookleftarrow 0 \hookleftarrow$
$r_{15}: q01 \vdash fB \downarrow 1 \downarrow$

M copies a given input x onto the output tape by using rules r_1 through r_5. When this copy is completed, M is in state p or q. State p means that x contains 0, whereas q indicates that x does not contain any 0. If x contains 0, M uses rules r_6 through r_{11} to perform Computation A. If x does not contain any 0, M applies rules r_{12} through r_{15} to carry out Computation B. A detailed proof that M computes $\phi(i) = i + 1$, where $i \geq 1$, is left to the exercises.

▲

Convention
For a computer M, ϕ_M denotes the function computed by M throughout.

●

Definition — computable function
A function γ is a *computable function* if there exists a computer M such that

$$\phi_M = \gamma$$

A function that is not computable is called an *uncomputable function*.

◆

Section 10.2.2 discusses computable functions. Then, Section 10.2.3 investigates uncomputable functions.

10.2.2 Computable functions

The recursion theorem, established in this section, represents a crucial result concerning computable functions. This theorem states that for every total computable function γ there exists a natural number n, referred to as the *fixed point* of γ, satisfying $\phi_n = \phi_{\gamma(n)}$. Less formally, if all computers are modified in a uniform manner, then there always exists a computer M that computes the same function as the modified version of M.

Indices

Before giving the proof of the recursion theorem, this section introduces some notation, used not only in this proof but also in later sections of this chapter. Let

$$M_1, M_2, \ldots$$

be an enumeration of all computers; this enumeration can be obtained by analogy with the method that enumerates all deterministic Turing machines (see Section 8.1.5). Corresponding to $M_1, M_2, \ldots$, there exists the enumeration of all computable functions,

$$\phi_{M_1}, \phi_{M_2}, \ldots$$

Convention

Instead of ϕ_{M_i}, write ϕ_i whenever no confusion exists. Therefore, instead of $\phi_{M_1}, \phi_{M_2}, \ldots$, write

$$\phi_1, \phi_2, \ldots$$

●

Let $i \geq 1$, and let M be the ith computer in $M_1, M_2, \ldots$; then, i is called the *index* of M, denoted by I_M. Observe that I_M uniquely determines the ith computer in

$$M_1, M_2, \ldots$$

In addition, I_M also determines the ith function ϕ in

$$\phi_1, \phi_2, \ldots$$

at this point, I_M is referred to as the *index* of ϕ.

Recursion Theorem

Theorem 10.2.2.1 Recursion theorem
For every total computable function γ there exists a natural number n satisfying

$$\phi_n = \phi_{\gamma(n)}$$

Proof
For every natural number j introduce the computer denoted by $j\text{-}M$, that works as follows. Let $\text{BiInt}(i)$ be an input of $j\text{-}M$. First, $j\text{-}M$ simulates M_j with the input $\text{BiInt}(j)$ (M_j is the jth computer in $M_1, M_2, \ldots$). If $\phi_j(j)$ is defined, $j\text{-}M$ simulates $M_{\phi_j(j)}$ with the input $\text{BiInt}(i)$.

By using $j\text{-}M$, for all $j \geq 1$, define the total computable function η as

$$\eta(j) = I_{j\text{-}M}$$

where $I_{j\text{-}M}$ is the index of $j\text{-}M$. Notice that

$$\phi_{\eta(j)} = \phi_{\phi_j(j)}$$

for every $j \geq 1$.

Let γ be any total computable function. Because both γ and η are computable, their composition, $\gamma\eta$, is surely computable, too. Let p be the index of a computer that computes $\gamma\eta$; that is,

$$\phi_p = \gamma\eta$$

Set

$$n = \eta(p)$$

As a result,

$$\phi_n = \phi_{\eta(p)}$$

Consider $\phi_{\eta(j)} = \phi_{\phi_j(j)}$ with $j = p$. Under this consideration,

$$\phi_{\eta(p)} = \phi_{\phi_p(p)}$$

As $\phi_p = \gamma\eta$,

$$\phi_{\phi_p(p)} = \phi_{\gamma(\eta(p))}$$

Since $n = \eta(p)$,

$$\phi_{\gamma(\eta(p))} = \phi_{\gamma(n)}$$

To summarize the previous parts of this proof,

$$\phi_n = \phi_{\eta(p)} = \phi_{\phi_p(p)} = \phi_{\gamma(\eta(p))} = \phi_{\gamma(n)}$$

Thus,

$$\phi_n = \phi_{\gamma(n)},$$

and the present theorem holds.

■

The recursion theorem represents a powerful tool that is often used in proofs involving a fixed-point requirement. Indeed, Section 10.3.2 uses this theorem to establish another important result, Rice's theorem. The exercises demonstrate other uses of the recursion theorem.

10.2.3 Uncomputable functions

The present section discusses uncomputable functions. Specifically, it introduces a function over natural numbers and proves that this function is uncomputable. Before this proof, however, reconsider Church's thesis.

Church's thesis

Section 8.1.1 presents Church's thesis, which states that the notion of a procedure is equivalent to the notion of a Turing machine. In terms of computable functions, the present section next reformulates this thesis, as follows:

Church's thesis for computable functions

A function ϕ can be computed by a procedure if and only if ϕ is computable.

Uncomputable function

From Church's thesis, if a function is uncomputable, then no procedure can compute this function. The next definition introduces the function γ, which is uncomputable, as proved subsequently.

Definition — function γ

Let k be a natural number. Consider the collection of deterministic Turing transducers

$$C(k) = \{M: M \text{ is a deterministic Turing transducer with } k + 1 \text{ states}\}$$

Define the function γ as

$\gamma(k)$ is the greatest number in $\{ i: (1, 1^i) \in T(M) \text{ for some } M \in C(k)\}$

for $k = 1, 2, \ldots$. ◆

Informally, $\gamma(k)$ equals the greatest number of 1s that any transducer in $C(k)$ can produce as the translation of a single 1. Observe the following three properties that γ satisfies for every natural number k:

1. $C(k)$ contains a finite number of transducers, so γ is well-defined.
2. $C(k)$ has a Turing transducer translating 1 into a word of 1s; consequently, γ is total.
3. The value of $\gamma(k)$ can be exactly determined, so γ is precisely defined.

In view of these properties, it might seem that γ is computable. Surprisingly, however, the next theorem demonstrates that this function is uncomputable.

Theorem 10.2.3.1
The function γ is uncomputable.

Proof
This lemma is proved by contradiction. Assume that γ is computable. Let M be a computer computing γ; that is,

$$\phi_M = \gamma$$

Consider the translation

$$\tau_1 = \{ (1^k, 1^{\gamma(k)}): k \geq 1\}$$

Because γ is computable, there surely exists a deterministic Turing transducer M_1 such that

$$\tau_1 = T(M_1)$$

To construct M_1 from M, proved as follows. First, M_1 converts 1^k into $\text{BiInt}(k)$ on the input tape. Then, M_1 works as M until $\gamma(k)$ is produced on the output tape. Finally, M_1 converts $\gamma(k)$ into $1^{\gamma(k)}$, i.e. the translation of 1^k.

Based upon τ_1, define τ_2 as

$$\tau_2 = \{ (1^k, y1): k \geq 1 \text{ and } (1^{2k}, y) \in \tau_1\}$$

From M_1, construct a deterministic Turing transducer M_2 such that

$$\tau_2 = T(M_2)$$

Let t be the natural number satisfying $M_2 \in C(t)$. Without any loss of generality, assume that the states of M_2 are named as

$$q_t, q_{t+1}, \ldots, q_{2t}$$

where q_t is the initial state, and q_{2t} is the only final state; symbolically,

$$M_2 = (\{q_t, \ldots, q_{2t}\}, \Sigma_2, R_2, q_t, \{q_{2t}\})$$

Observe that for every $j \geq 1$, M_2 computes

$$q_t 1^j | q_t B \vdash^* q_{2t} B | q_{2t} y1$$

where y is defined by $(1^{2j}, y) \in \tau_1$. Consider the Turing transducer M_3 defined as

$$M_3 = (\{q_0, \ldots, q_{t-1}, q_t, \ldots, q_{2t}\}, \Sigma, R_2 \cup R_3, q_0, \{q_{2t}\})$$

where

$R_3 = \{q_0 1 B \vdash q_1 B \hookrightarrow 1\downarrow\}$
  $\cup \{q_i B 1 \vdash q_{i+1} 1 \hookrightarrow 1\downarrow : i = 1, \ldots, t-1\}$
  $\cup \{q_{t-1} B 1 \vdash q_{t-1} 1 \lrcorner B\downarrow, q_{t-1} 1 B \vdash q_{t-1} 1 \lrcorner B\downarrow, q_{t-1} B B \vdash q_t 1 \downarrow B\downarrow\}$

Consider the input 1 on the input tape of M_3. By using the rules of R_3, M_3 first changes 1 into 1^t on the input tape, then works exactly as M_2 by using the rules of R_2. More precisely,

$q_0 1 | B \vdash B q_1 B | q_1 1$ $[q_0 1 B \vdash q_1 B \hookrightarrow 1\downarrow]$
$\vdash B 1 q_2 B | q_2 1$ $[q_1 B 1 \vdash q_2 1 \hookrightarrow 1\downarrow]$
$\vdots$

$\vdash B 1^{t-2} q_{t-1} B | q_{t-1} 1$ $[q_{t-2} B 1 \vdash q_{t-1} 1 \hookrightarrow 1\downarrow]$
$\vdash B 1^{t-3} q_{t-1} 1 1 | q_{t-1} B$ $[q_{t-1} B 1 \vdash q_{t-1} 1 \lrcorner B\downarrow]$
$\vdots$

$\vdash q_{t-1} B 1^{t-1} | q_{t-1} B$ $[q_{t-1} 1 B \vdash q_{t-1} 1 \lrcorner B\downarrow]$
$\vdash q_t 1^t | q_t B$ $[q_{t-1} B B \vdash q_t 1 \downarrow B \downarrow]$
$\vdash^* q_{2t} B | q_{2t} y 1$ $[\rho]$

where ρ is a rule word consisting of rules from R_2, and y is defined by $(1^{2t}, y) \in \tau_1$. From the definition of τ_1, $|y| = |\gamma(2t)|$. As a result, M_3 translates a single 1 into $|\gamma(2t)|$ + 1 occurrences of 1. However, because M_3 has $2t + 1$ states, $M_3 \in C(2t)$; hence, by the definition of γ, M_3 cannot translate 1 into more than $|\gamma(2t)|$ occurrences of 1. This contradiction implies that γ is an uncomputable function. ∎

From a mathematical point of view, γ represents a simple function. The previous theorem and Church's thesis therefore imply the surprising conclusion that even some mathematically trivial functions, such as γ, can never be computed by any computer.

10.3 Decidability

Based upon the computers defined in Section 10.2, the present section introduces decision makers, which represent computational models for deciding problems. Section 10.3.1 formalizes decision makers. Section 10.3.2 investigates problems decidable by decision makers, whose computational complexity is subsequently studied in Section 10.3.3. Section 10.3.4 presents several problems that are undecidable by any decision maker, and Section 10.3.5 discusses undecidability in general.

10.3.1 Decision makers

This section modifies computers, as defined in Section 10.2, so they can decide problems. Before this modification, this section explains how to specify problems in a formal way.

Problems

As already stated in Section 2.3, a problem specification consists of a *question* and an *instance*. The question formulates the problem. The set of problem instances is the collection of all allowable values for the problem's unknowns. This section restricts its attention to questions with yes–no answers. Given a problem p, the present section encodes all instances of p by nonnegative integers, denotes the set consisting of these integers by E_p, and says that E_p *encodes* p. At this point, p requires the decision as to whether $i \in E_p$ for any nonnegative integer i: if $i \in E_p$, the answer to p is yes, and if $i \notin E_p$, the answer is no. A computer M decides p if and only if M computes the total *characteristic function* of E_p, X_{E_p}. This function, mapping nonnegative integers to $\{1, 0\}$, is defined by

$$X_{E_p}(i) = 1 \text{ if and only if } i \in E_p$$

for $i = 0, 1, \ldots$. Notice that

$$X_{E_p}(i) = 0 \text{ if and only if } i \notin E_p$$

because X_{E_p} is total. To illustrate these notions, this section formulates Halting, which represents an important problem concerning Turing machines. The following lemma and conventions simplify this formulation.

Lemma 10.3.1.1
For every deterministic Turing machine M there exists a deterministic Turing transducer M' satisfying these three properties:

1. M' has one final state f;
2. $x \in L(M')$ if and only if M' accepts x and halts in f;
3. $L(M) = L(M')$.

Proof
Let M be a deterministic Turing machine. Use Algorithm 8.1.3.4 to convert M to a deterministic Turing machine M' satisfying the three properties of this lemma. ∎

Convention
Without any loss of generality, the following formulation of Halting assumes that a deterministic Turing machine M satisfies these two conditions:

1. M has one final state f;
2. $x \in L(M)$ if and only if M accepts x and halts in f. ●

Given a deterministic Turing machine M and an input word w, the Halting problem asks whether, with w as its input tape, M halts in its final state f.

Halting

Instance: A deterministic Turing machine $M = (Q, \Sigma, R, s, \{f\})$ and a word $w \in \Sigma_I^*$.
Question: Does M halt in f with w as its input?

Encode **Halting** is encoded as follows:

$$E_{\text{Halting}} = \{\, i\colon \text{BiInt}(i) = \delta(M)\delta(w),\, M = (Q, \Sigma, R, s, \{f\}) \text{ is a deterministic Turing machine},\, w \in \Sigma_I^*, \text{ and } w \in L(M) \,\}$$

The characteristic function of $E_{Halting}$, $X_{E_{Halting}}$, is defined as

$$X_{E_{Halting}}(i) = 1 \text{ if and only if } i \in E_{Halting}$$

for $i = 0, 1, \ldots$. Note that

$$X_{E_{Halting}}(i) = 0 \text{ if and only if } i \notin E_{Halting}$$

The discussion concerning Halting continues in Section 10.3.4.

The next definition formalizes the notion of a decision maker.

Definition — decision maker
Let $M = (Q, \{0, 1, B\}, R, s, \{f\})$ be a computer, and let E be a set of nonnegative integers. M is a *decision maker* for E if and only if M computes the characteristic function of E, X_E; that is,

$$\phi_M = X_E$$

The *1-language* of M, denoted by $L_1(M)$, is defined as

$$L_1(M) = \{ \text{BiInt}(i): \phi_M(i) = 1 \}$$

The *0-language* of M, denoted by $L_0(M)$, is defined as

$$L_0(M) = \{ \text{BiInt}(i): \phi_M(i) = 0 \}$$

◆

Definition — decidable set
A set of nonnegative integers E is *decidable* if and only if there exists a decision maker for E; otherwise, E is *undecidable*.

◆

Definition — decidable language
A binary language L is *decidable* if and only if there exists a decidable set of nonnegative integers E such that $L = \{\text{BiInt}(i): i \in E\}$; otherwise, E is *undecidable*.

◆

Definition — decidable problem
A problem is *decidable* if and only if there exists a decidable set of nonnegative integers that encodes this problem; otherwise, the problem is *undecidable*.

◆

Example 10.3.1.1 Decision maker
Consider the following function γ:

$$\gamma(n) = \sum_{i=0}^{2n} 2^i - 2^n$$

for $n = 1, \ldots$. Given $m \geq 1$, the present example studies the problem of whether there exists a natural number, n, satisfying

$$\gamma(n) = m$$

For instance, for $m = 4$, the answer is no because $\gamma(n) \neq m$ for all $n \geq 1$; however, for $m = 5$, the answer is yes because $\gamma(1) = 5$.

Next, this example constructs a decision maker M that decides this problem by computing the characteristic function X_E with E defined as

$$E = \{\gamma(n): n \geq 1\}$$

Observe that

$$\{\text{BiInt}(j) : j \in E\} = \{1^n 01^n: n \geq 1\}$$

Indeed,

$$\text{BiInt}(\gamma(1)) = \text{BiInt}(5) = 101$$
$$\text{BiInt}(\gamma(2)) = \text{BiInt}(29) = 11011$$
$$\vdots$$

Therefore, design M so

$$L_1(M) = \{1^n 01^n: n \geq 1\}$$

and

$$L_0(M) = \{0, 1\}^* - \{1^n 01^n: n \geq 1\}$$

Consider a binary word, $x \in \{0, 1\}^*$. Without any loss of generality, express x as $x = 1^i 0y$ where $i \geq 0$ and $y \in \{0, 1\}^*$. M begins its computation by writing 0 on the output tape and copying the prefix 1^i behind this 0. Then, M shifts the input head right until it reaches the B following y. At this point, M's input tape contains $1^i 0yB$, the output tape contains $01^i B$, and both heads read the Bs following the nonblank portions of these tapes. Synchronously shifting both heads left, M compares y on the input tape with 1^i on the output tape; while making this comparison, M replaces all scanned symbols with Bs. If M finds out that $y = 1^i$, then $x \in L$, and M performs the following Computation 1; otherwise, $x \notin L$, and M carries out Computation 2.

Computation 1
If $x \in L$, M's input tape contains $1^n 0B$, the output tape contains $0B$, and both heads are over the 0s. At this point, M replaces $1^n 0$ with B^{n+1} on the input tape, rewrites 0 with 1 on the output tape, and halts with both heads over the leftmost squares.

Computation 2
If $x \notin L$, M replaces all nonblank symbols following the leftmost 0 with Bs on the output tape, then halts with both heads over the leftmost squares.

A detailed construction of M is left to the exercises.

▲

10.3.2 Decidable problems

The present section establishes some basic results concerning decision makers, decidable problems and decidable languages.

Church's thesis

Observe that any decision maker M always halts because

$$\{0, 1\}^* = L_0(M) \cup L_1(M)$$

A decision maker thus represents a computational model that formalizes an algorithm; that is, a procedure that halts on all inputs. This observation gives rise to the following version of Church's thesis.

Church's thesis for decision problems

A problem can be decided by an algorithm if and only if the problem is decidable by a decision maker.

Decidable problems

From Church's thesis for decision problems, if there exists an algorithm that decides a problem, then there surely exists a decision maker for a language encoding this problem. To demonstrate some decidable problems, return to Sections 4.3 and 6.3.

These sections have described several algorithms that decide problems, concerning models for regular and context-free languages. As there algorithms exist that decide these problems, by Church's thesis, all these problems are decidable.

Decidable languages

The definition of a decidable language is based on decision makers, which halt on all inputs. It thus comes as no surprise that every decidable language belongs to the family of recursive languages, which are characterized by deterministic Turing machines that always halt (see Section 8.1.6).

Theorem 10.3.2.1
Let L be a decidable language. Then, L is recursive.

Proof
Let L be a decidable language, and let M be a decision maker for E, where

$$E = \{\, i : \mathrm{BiInt}(i) \in L \,\}$$

Observe that M satisfies the following three properties:

1. $\phi_M = X_E$
2. $L = L_1(M) = \{\, \mathrm{BiInt}(i) : \phi_M(i) = 1 \,\}$
3. $L_0(M) = \{\, \mathrm{BiInt}(i) : \phi_M(i) = 0 \,\}$

Convert M to a deterministic Turing machine M' that always halts and accepts the inputs that M translates to 1; as a result,

$$L(M') = L_1(M) = L$$

Therefore, L is recursive. A detailed version of this proof is left to the exercises. ∎

10.3.3 Computational complexity

According to Church's thesis for decision problems, decision makers formalize algorithms that decide problems. The present section studies the computational complexity of these algorithms. This complexity is measured according to these two criteria:

1. the time required by these algorithms;
2. the space required by these algorithms.

To express these criteria in terms of decision makers, the time complexity equals the number of moves made by a given decision maker, and the space complexity is defined as the number of squares visited by this decision maker. Based upon these criteria, pragmatically oriented computer science distinguishes decidable problems whose solutions require reasonable amount of time and space from those decidable problems whose solutions can hardly be implemented in practice for their unreasonably high requirements.

Section 10.3.4.1 studies the time complexity, then Section 10.3.4.2 briefly discusses the space complexity. The exercises also investigate computational complexity.

10.3.3.1 Time complexity

Consider a decision maker M and a function τ over nonnegative integers. If for every input word w, M makes no more than $\tau(|w|)$ moves before halting, then τ represents the time complexity of M.

Definition — time complexity
Let $M = (Q, \{0, 1, B\}, R, s, \{f\})$ be a decision maker, and let τ be a function over nonnegative integers. Then, τ represents the *time complexity* of M provided that for all $w \in \{0, 1\}^*$, $b \in \{0, 1\}$, and $n \geq 0$, this implication holds:

$$sw|sB \models^n fB|fb \text{ in } M \text{ implies } \tau(|w|) \geq n$$

◆

Let $M = (Q, \{0, 1, B\}, R, s, \{f\})$ be a decision maker, and let τ be its time complexity. Observe that for all $n \geq 0$, $\tau(n)$ is at least as great as the maximum number of moves that M can make on any input word of length n; in other words, the previous definition considers the worst-case measure of time complexity. To illustrate this definition, return to the decision maker M in Example 10.3.1.1. Notice that for any word of length n, where $n \geq 0$, M makes at most $2n + 2$ moves before halting, so the time complexity of M is

$$\tau(n) = 2n + 2$$

for $n = 1, \ldots$.

Consider a decision maker M whose time complexity is τ. Instead of τ, we frequently represent the time complexity of M by the *growth rate* of τ, customarily expressed in terms of the O notation, defined next.

Definition — O notation
Let ϕ and γ be two functions over nonnegative integers. If there exist natural numbers c and d such that for every $n \geq d$, $\phi(n)$ and $\gamma(n)$ are defined and

$$\phi(n) \leq c\gamma(n),$$

then ϕ is of the order of γ, i.e.

$$\phi(n) = O(\gamma(n))$$

or, simply,

$$\phi = O(\gamma)$$

◆

Observe the following three properties, that follow from this definition.

1. $\phi = O(\gamma)$ implies $k\phi = O(\gamma)$ for any constant k; informally, the multiplication constants are ignored.
2. As $\phi(n) \leq c\gamma(n)$ holds for $n = d, d + 1, \ldots$, where d is a natural number, the values of n less than d are ignored.
3. $\phi \neq O(\gamma)$ implies that for any natural number c there exists $m \geq c$ so $\phi(m) > c\gamma(m)$; in other words, if $\phi \neq O(\gamma)$, then for any natural number c there exist infinitely many values of n satisfying $\phi(n) > c\gamma(n)$.

The next topic of interest is the polynomial growth rate of functions.

Definition — polynomial growth rate
Let γ be a *polynomial function*; that is, either γ is identically 0 or has the form

$$\gamma(n) = a_k n^k + a_{k-1} n^{k-1} + \ldots + a_1 n + a_0$$

where a_i is an integer, $i = 1, \ldots, k$, and $a_k \geq 1$, for some nonnegative integer k. If ϕ is a total function satisfying $\phi = O(\gamma)$ and $\gamma = O(\phi)$, then ϕ has a *polynomial growth rate*.

◆

Based on the polynomial growth rate of functions, this section distinguishes between tractable and intractable decision problems.

Definition — tractable decision problem
Let p be a decidable problem. If p can be decided by a decision maker M whose time complexity has a polynomial growth rate, then p is *tractable*; otherwise, p is *intractable*.

◆

Informally, this definition states that although intractable problems are decidable in principle, they can hardly be solved in reality as no decision maker can solve them in polynomial time. However, tractable problems can be solved in polynomial time, so they are central to practically oriented computer science. Besides their practical significance, tractable problems lead to some crucial topics of theoretical computer science as demonstrated next.

According to the definition given in Section 10.3.1, decision makers work deterministically. However, the concept of time complexity also applies to decision makers underlain by nondeterministic Turing machines. Leaving the rigorous definition of nondeterministic decision makers to the exercises, the present section next defines a polynomial-time-bounded language and a nondeterministic-polynomial-time-bounded language.

Definition — polynomial-time-bounded language
Let L be a language.

1. If there exists a decision maker M whose time complexity has polynomial growth rate and $L = L_1(M)$, then L is a *polynomial-time-bounded language*.
2. If there exists a nondeterministic decision maker M' whose time complexity has polynomial growth rate and $L = L_1(M')$, then L is a *nondeterministic polynomial-time-bounded language*.

◆

Convention
The term P denotes the family of all polynomial-time-bounded languages; NP denotes the family of all nondeterministic polynomial-time-bounded languages.

●

Notice that any decision maker represents a special case of a nondeterministic decision maker, so $P \subseteq NP$. However, it is a longstanding open problem, known as the *$P = NP$ problem*, as to whether P and NP coincide.

By using various methods, theoretical computer science has intensively attempted to solve the $P = NP$ problem. One of the most important approaches to this problem is based upon ordering all NP languages. The equivalence classes defined by this ordering consist of languages coding equally difficult problems. Consider the class corresponding to the most difficult problems. Any problem coded by a language from this class is as difficult as any other problem coded by a language from NP. Consequently, if it is proved that this class contains a language that also belongs to P, then $P = NP$; however, if it is demonstrated that this class contains a language that does not belong to P, then $P \subset NP$. The following definition formalizes this approach to the $P = NP$ problem.

Definition — polynomially transformable language

Let L and L' be two languages over $\{0, 1\}$. Then, L_1 is *polynomially transformable* into L_2, written as

$$L \propto L'$$

if there exist a decision maker M and a total function γ from $\{0, 1\}^*$ to $\{0, 1\}^*$, satisfying these three properties:

1. the time complexity of M has a polynomial growth rate;
2. $L_1(M) = L'$;
3. for every $x \in \{0, 1\}^*$, $x \in L$ if and only if $\gamma(x) \in L'$.

◆

Intuitively, $L \propto L'$ indicates that the difficulty of deciding L is no greater than the difficulty of deciding L', so the problem coded by L is no more difficult than the problem coded by L'.

Definition — NP-complete language

Let $L \in NP$. If $L' \propto L$ for every $L' \in NP$, then L is *NP-complete*.

◆

A decision problem coded by an NP-complete language is an *NP-complete problem*. There exist a number of NP-complete problems, including time-bounded acceptance.

Time-bounded acceptance

Instance: A nondeterministic Turing machine, $M = (Q, \{0, 1, B\}, R, s, \{f\})$, $w \in \{0, 1\}^*$, and a natural number, i.
Question: Does M accept w by making no more than i moves?

Theorem 10.3.3.1

Time-bounded acceptance is an *NP*-complete problem.

Proof
This proof is left to the exercises.

∎

As already noted, to solve the $P = NP$ problem, it is sufficient to find an *NP*-complete language L and prove that $L \in P$ or $L \notin P$. Indeed, $L \in P$ implies $P = NP$, whereas $L \notin P$ implies $P \subset NP$. So far, however, the theory of computation has not achieved a proof of this kind, so the $P = NP$ problem remains open.

10.3.3.2 Space complexity

A decision maker M has the space complexity σ, where σ is a function over non-negative integers, provided that for every input word w, M visits no more than $\sigma(|w|)$ squares on either of its tapes.

Definition — space complexity
Let $M = (Q, \{0, 1, B\}, R, s, \{f\})$ be a decision maker, and let σ be a function over non-negative integers. Then, σ represents the *space complexity* of M provided that for all $w \in \{0, 1\}^*, b \in \{0, 1\}$, and $i = 1, 2$, this implication holds:

$$sw|sB \vdash^* x_1qy|x_2qz \vdash^* fB|fb \text{ in } M \text{ implies } \sigma(|w|) \geq |x_i|$$

◆

By analogy with the time complexity, this section considers the worst-case measure of space complexity: $\sigma(n)$ is greater or equal to the maximum number of squares M can visit on any input word of length n. To give an example illustrating this definition, reconsider the decision maker M in Example 10.3.1.1. With any word of length n, where $n \geq 0$, M visits at most $n + 1$ squares on either tape before halting, so the space complexity of M is

$$\sigma(n) = n + 1$$

Definition — polynomial-space-bounded language
Let L be a language.

1. If there exists a decision maker M whose space complexity has polynomial growth rate and $L = L_1(M)$, then L is a *polynomial-space-bounded language*.
2. If there exists a nondeterministic decision maker M' whose space complexity has polynomial growth rate and $L = L_1(M')$, then L is a *nondeterministic polynomial-space-bounded language*.

◆

Section 10.3.4.1 points out that some crucial questions about the family of polynomial-time-bounded languages remain open. Regarding the family of polynomial-space-bounded languages, however, the fundamental results have been established. Most importantly, computational theory has achieved the following three results concerning the family of polynomial-space-bounded languages and its relationship to other language families

1. The family of polynomial-space-bounded languages contains NP (where NP denotes the family of nondeterministic polynomial-time-bounded languages).
2. The family of recursive languages properly contains the family of polynomial-space-bounded languages.
3. The family of polynomial-space-bounded languages coincides with the family of nondeterministic polynomial-space-bounded languages.

The proofs of these results are left to the exercises, which continues the study of computational complexity.

10.3.4 Undecidable problems

This section discusses several undecidable problems. To prove that a problem p is undecidable, it is frequently easier to consider a restricted version of this problem, p', and demonstrate that p' is undecidability; at this point, the undecidability of p' implies the undecidability of p. To illustrate, consider the following restricted version of Halting (see Section 10.3.1).

Restricted Halting

Instance: A deterministic Turing machine $M = (Q, \{0, 1, B\}, R, s, \{f\})$ with $\Sigma_I = \{0, 1\}$ and $w \in \{0, 1\}^*$.
Question: Does M halt in f with w on its input?

Theorem 10.3.4.1
Restricted Halting is undecidable.

Proof
This theorem is proved by contradiction. Assume that Restricted Halting is decidable. Recall that Section 8.1.5 introduced the function δ and, by using δ, defined this language:

$L_{\text{Acceptance}} = \{\delta(M)\delta(w): M = (Q, \{0, 1, B\}, R, s, \{f\})$ is a deterministic Turing machine with $\Sigma_I = \{0, 1\}, w \in \{0, 1\}^*,$ and $w \in L(M)\}$

Observe that the decidability of Restricted Halting implies that $L_{\text{Acceptance}}$ is a decidable language. Then, by Theorem 10.3.2.1, $L_{\text{Acceptance}}$ is recursive; however, by Theorem 8.1.6.4, $L_{\text{Acceptance}}$ is not recursive — a contradiction. Thus, Restricted Halting is undecidable. ∎

Corollary 10.3.4.2
Halting is undecidable

Proof
Restricted Halting uses two non-blank tape symbols, 0 and 1. More generally, Halting permits any tape alphabet. Consequently, Halting is undecidable because its restricted version, Restricted Halting, is undecidable by Theorem 10.3.4.1.
∎

Observe that Theorem 8.1.6.4 underlies the proof of Theorem 10.3.4.1. The proof demonstrating the undecidability of the following problem, called Restricted Empty Word Membership, also makes use of Theorem 8.1.6.4.

Restricted empty word membership

Instance: A deterministic Turing machine of the form $M = (Q, \{0, 1, B\}, R, s, \{f\})$.
Question: Is ε a member of $L(M)$?

Theorem 10.3.4.3
Restricted Empty Word Membership is undecidable.

Proof
Prove this theorem by contradiction. Assume that Restricted Empty Word Membership is decidable, and consider the following language:

$L_{\varepsilon\text{-Acceptance}} = \{\delta(M): M = (Q, \{0, 1, B\}, R, s, \{f\})$ is a deterministic Turing machine with $\Sigma_I = \{0, 1\}$, and $\varepsilon \in L(M)\}$

Notice that the decidability of Restricted Empty Word Membership implies that $L_{\varepsilon\text{-Acceptance}}$ is a decidable language. Then, by Theorem 10.3.2.1, $L_{\varepsilon\text{-Acceptance}}$ is recursive. Let N be a deterministic Turing machine that always halts and accepts $L_{\varepsilon\text{-Acceptance}}$. Transform N into another deterministic Turing machine, N', that performs the following Computation 1 and, then, Computation 2.

Computation 1
N' checks whether its input has the form $\delta(M)\delta(w)$, where $w \in \{0, 1\}^*$. If not, N' rejects and halts. If the input is of the form $\delta(M)\delta(w)$, N' replaces $\delta(M)\delta(w)$ with $\delta(w\text{-}M)$ on the input tape, where $w\text{-}M$ is a deterministic Turing machine that works as follows. First, $w\text{-}M$ checks whether its input equals ε; if so, it replaces the input ε with w. Then, $w\text{-}M$ works as M.

Computation 2
N' works as N on $\delta(w\text{-}M)$.

Observe these three properties.

1. N' is a deterministic Turing machine that always halts.
2. M accepts w if and only if w–M accepts ε.
3. N' accepts $\delta(M)\delta(w)$ if and only if N accepts $\delta(w$–$M)$.

As N is a deterministic Turing machine that always halts and accepts $L_{\varepsilon\text{-Acceptance}}$, N' is a deterministic Turing machine that always halts and accepts $L_{\text{Acceptance}}$ (the proof of Theorem 10.3.4.1 contains the definition of $L_{\text{Acceptance}}$). Consequently, $L_{\text{Acceptance}}$ is recursive, and this conclusion contradicts Theorem 8.1.6.4. Thus, Restricted Empty Word Membership is undecidable. ■

The following problem, called Empty Word Membership, generalizes Restricted Empty Word Membership.

Empty word membership

Instance: A deterministic Turing machine $M = (Q, \Sigma, R, s, \{f\})$.
Question: Is ε a member of $L(M)$?

Corollary 10.3.4.4
Empty Word Membership is undecidable.

Proof
From Theorem 10.3.4.3, Restricted Empty Word Membership is undecidable. This undecidability implies the undecidability of Empty Word Membership. ■

Frequently, the undecidability of a problem follows from the undecidability of another problem. Proofs of this kind are made by contradiction according to the following format. Consider two problems p and p'. Assume that the undecidability of p has been established. To prove that p' is undecidable, suppose that p' is decidable and demonstrate that the decidability of p' implies the decidability of p; in other words, if an algorithm solves p', then a modified version of this algorithm decides p. However, p is undecidable. By this contradiction, p' is undecidable. A proof of this format is called a *reduction* of p' to p. Theorem 10.3.4.5 is established by using this method of proof.

Restricted emptiness

Instance: A deterministic Turing machine of the form $M = (Q, \{0, 1, B\}, R, s, \{f\})$.
Question: Is $L(M)$ empty?

Theorem 10.3.4.5
Restricted Emptiness is undecidable.

Proof
This proof reduces Restricted Emptiness to Restricted Empty Word Membership. Assume that Restricted Emptiness is decidable. Consider

$$L_{\text{Empty}} = \{\delta(M): M = (Q, \{0, 1, B\}, R, s, \{f\}) \text{ is a deterministic Turing machine with } \Sigma_I = \{0, 1\}, \text{ and } L(M) = \varnothing\}$$

The decidability of Restricted Emptiness implies that L_{Empty} is decidable, so L_{Empty} is recursive by Theorem 10.3.2.1. Let N be a deterministic Turing machine that always halts and accepts L_{Empty}. Transform N into a deterministic Turing machine N' that performs the following Computation 1 and, then, Computation 2.

Computation 1
1. N' checks whether its input has the form $\delta(M)$ where $M = (Q, \{0, 1, B\}, R, s, \{f\})$ is a deterministic Turing machine with $\Sigma_I = \{0, 1\}$. If not, N' rejects and halts. If the input is of the form $\delta(M)$, N' replaces $\delta(M)$ with $\delta(M_\varepsilon)$ on the input tape, where M_ε is a deterministic Turing machine that rewrites its input word with ε and, then, works exactly as M.
2. With $\delta(M_\varepsilon)$ on its input, N' works as N; however, N' rejects if and only if N accepts, and N' accepts if and only if N rejects.

Observe that

$$\varepsilon \in L(M) \text{ if and only if } L(M_\varepsilon) = \{0, 1\}^*$$

Therefore,

$$\varepsilon \notin L(M) \text{ if and only if } L(M_\varepsilon) = \varnothing$$

Thus, as N is a deterministic Turing machine that always halts and accepts L_{Empty}, N' is a deterministic Turing machine that always halts and accepts $L_{\varepsilon\text{-Acceptance}}$ (the proof of Theorem 10.3.4.3 gives the definition of $L_{\varepsilon\text{-Acceptance}}$). Consequently, Restricted Empty Word Membership is decidable. However, this conclusion contradicts Theorem 10.3.4.3. As a result, Restricted Emptiness is undecidable. ∎

Emptiness

Instance: A deterministic Turing machine $M = (Q, \Sigma, R, s, \{f\})$.
Question: Is $L(M)$ empty?

Corollary 10.3.4.6
Emptiness is undecidable.

Proof
This corollary follows from Theorem 10.3.4.5. ∎

Restricted finiteness

Instance: A deterministic Turing machine of the form $M = (Q, \{0, 1, B\}, R, s, \{f\})$.
Question: Is $L(M)$ finite?

Theorem 10.3.4.7
Restricted Finiteness is undecidable.

Proof
Prove Theorem 10.3.4.7 by analogy with the proof of Theorem 10.3.4.5. ∎

Finiteness

Instance: A deterministic Turing machine $M = (Q, \Sigma, R, s, \{f\})$.
Question: Is $L(M)$ finite?

Corollary 10.3.4.8
Finiteness is undecidable.

Proof
This corollary follows from Theorem 10.3.4.7. ∎

This section has concentrated on undecidable results concerning Turing machines. However, there are also many undecidable problems about other computational models. To illustrate this, an undecidable problem concerning context-free grammars is briefly discussed.

Context-free universalness

Instance: A context-free grammar, $G = (N, T, P, S)$.
Question: Is $L(G)$ equal to T^*?

Theorem 10.3.4.9
Context-free Universalness is undecidable.

Proof
This proof is made by contradiction. Assume that Context-Free Universalness is decidable. As demonstrated in the exercises, for any deterministic Turing machine M there exists an algorithm that produces a context-free grammar, $G = (N, T, P, S)$, satisfying

$$L(G) = T^* \text{ if and only if } L(M) = \varnothing$$

Thus, the decidability of Context-free universalness implies the decidability of Emptiness. From Corollary 10.3.4.6, Emptiness is undecidable — a contradiction. Therefore, Context-free Universalness is undecidable. ∎

The exercises introduce several other undecidable problems.

10.3.5 Undecidability: a general approach

The previous section formulates several specific problems and proves that they are undecidable. The present section studies undecidability from a more general point of view. Most importantly, it establishes Rice's theorem, which is frequently used in proofs that demonstrate the undecidability of problems concerning computable functions. To give an insight into this theorem, consider whether a given computable function has a property; by Rice's theorem, this problem is undecidable whenever there exist two computable functions, ϕ and ϕ', such that ϕ satisfies the property and ϕ' does not. Before the proof of this theorem, recall the following two notions, introduced in Sections 10.2.2 and 10.3.1.

1. ϕ_i denotes the ith function in the enumeration of all computable functions

$$\phi_1, \phi_2, \ldots$$

2. For a set of nonnegative integers E, the characteristic function of E, X_E, is the total function that maps all nonnegative integers into $\{0, 1\}$ so that

   A. $X_E(i) = 1$ if and only if $i \in E$
   B. $X_E(i) = 0$ if and only if $i \notin E$

   for $i = 0, 1, \ldots$.

Theorem 10.3.5.1 Rice's theorem
Let Y be a nonempty proper subset of the set of computable functions, and let X_{CY} be the characteristic function of the set

$$C_Y = \{ i: \phi_i \in Y \}$$

Then, X_{C_Y} is uncomputable.

Proof
Prove this theorem by contradiction. Assume that Y is a nonempty proper subset of the set of all computable functions and that X_{C_Y} is computable. Then, there necessarily exist two integers, j and k, such that

$$X_{C_Y}(j) = 1 \text{ and } X_{C_Y}(k) = 0$$

Compute $X_{C_Y}(1), X_{C_Y}(2), \ldots$ until j and k satisfying these identities are found. At this point,

$$\phi_j \in Y \text{ and } \phi_k \notin Y.$$

For all $m \geq 1$, define the total function γ by these two equivalences

1. $\gamma(m) = k$ if and only if $\phi_m \in Y$
2. $\gamma(m) = j$ if and only if $\phi_m \notin Y$

As ϕ is computable, γ is surely computable, too. By the recursion theorem (see Theorem 10.2.2.1) for γ, there exists a fixed point n satisfying

$$\phi_n = \phi_{\gamma(n)}$$

This proof now distinguishes two cases, $\phi_n \in Y$ and $\phi_n \notin Y$.

A. If $\phi_n \in Y$, $\gamma(n) = k$, so $\phi_{\gamma(n)} \notin Y$. From $\phi_n = \phi_{\gamma(n)}$, $\phi_n \notin Y$ — a contradiction.
B. If $\phi_n \notin Y$, $\gamma(n) = j$; therefore, $\phi_{\gamma(n)} \in Y$. At this point, the equation $\phi_n = \phi_{\gamma(n)}$ implies $\phi_n \in Y$ — a contradiction.

Because a contradiction arises in both cases, X_{C_Y} is uncomputable, and the theorem holds. ∎

Rice's theorem fulfils an important role in many proofs that demonstrate the undecidability of problems about computable functions. Indeed, whenever one computable function satisfies a property and another computable function does not satisfy this property, then this property is undecidable. In this way, this section uses Rice's theorem in the proof of the next theorem.

Computable function totalness

Instance: A computable function ϕ.
Question: Is ϕ total?

Theorem 10.3.5.2
Computable function totalness is undecidable.

Proof
Naturally, some computable functions are total while other computable functions are not; in other words, the set of all total computable functions forms a nonempty proper subset of the set of all computable functions. Consequently, Computable Function Totalness is undecidable by Theorem 10.3.5.1.

∎

Rice's theorem implies the undecidability of many other problems concerning computable functions as demonstrated in the Exercises.

Exercises

1. Basic definitions

1.1 Solve (A) through (C):
 (A) Give an example of a Turing transducer $M = (Q, \Sigma, R, s, F)$ and an input word $x \in \Sigma_I$, such that for a final state $f \in F$, and an output word $y \in \Sigma_O$,

$$sx|sB \vdash^* fB|fy$$

according to infinitely many rule words.
 (B) Give an example of a Turing transducer $M = (Q, \Sigma, R, s, F)$ and an input word $x \in \Sigma_I$, such that for a final state $f \in F$, and an output word $y \in \Sigma_O$,

$$sx|sB \vdash^* fB|fy$$

according to precisely eight rule words.
 (C) Give an example of a Turing transducer $M = (Q, \Sigma, R, s, F)$ and an input word $x \in \Sigma_I$, such that for a final state $f \in F$, and an output word $y \in \Sigma_O$,

$$sx|sB \vdash^* fB|fy$$

according to one rule word.

1.2 Consider the following Turing transducer M:

1: $s1B \vdash q0 \hookleftarrow 1 \hookleftarrow$
2: $q0B \vdash qB \hookleftarrow 0 \hookleftarrow$
3: $qBB \vdash pB\lrcorner B\lrcorner$
4: $pB0 \vdash qB\lrcorner 1\lrcorner$

5: $qB0 \vdash qB\llcorner 0\lrcorner$
6: $q01 \vdash fB\downarrow 1\downarrow$

where f is the final state. Solve the following tasks (A) through (C):

(A) Give five pairs of words that belong to $T(M)$.
(B) Give five pairs of words that do not belong to $T(M)$.
(C) Describe the translation that M defines.

1.3 Consider the Turing transducer in Example 10.1.1. Recall that this transducer has seven rules and defines this translation:

$$\{(x, x0): x \in \{1\}\{0, 1\}^*\}$$

Does there exist a Turing transducer that defines this translation by using fewer than seven rules?

1.4 Consider the following translations.

(a) $\{(a^i b^j c^k, a^{i+1} b^{j+1} c^{k+1}): i, j, k \geq 0 \text{ and } i < j < k\}$
(b) $\{(a^i b^j, a^j b^i): i, j \geq 0 \text{ and } j = i^2\}$
(c) $\{(a^j, a^i): j \geq 1, i \text{ is a prime, and } j < i\}$
(d) $\{(w, v): v, w \in \{a, b, c\}^*, \#_a w > \#_b w > \#_c w, \text{ and } \#_a w < \#_b w < \#_c w\}$
(e) $\{(a^i b^i c^j, a^i b^j c^j): i, j \geq 0 \text{ and } j \leq i\}$
(f) $\{(a^j b^i, c^j): i, j \geq 0 \text{ and } i \leq j \leq 2^i\}$
(g) $\{(a^i b^j c^k, c^{i+j} b^{j+k} c^{k+i}): i, j, k \geq 0, i \neq j, k \neq i, \text{ and } j \neq k\}$
(h) $\{(a^i b^j c^j d^i, a^j b^i c^i d^j): i, j \geq 0 \text{ and } j \leq i\}$
(i) $\{(a^i, b^{2i} c^i b^{2i}): i \geq 0\}$
(j) $\{(ww, \text{reversal}(w)): w \in \{a, b\}^*\}$
(k) $\{(wvw, ww): w \in \{a, b\}^* \text{ and } v = \text{reversal}(w)\}$

For each of these translation, construct a Turing transducer that defines the translation. Provide a proof that the construction is correct.

1.5 Convert each of the Turing transducers obtained in the previous exercise to an equivalent deterministic Turing transducer.

1.6 Consider each deterministic Turing transducer M obtained in Exercise 1.5. Prove or disprove that M satisfies

if $(x, y) \in T(M)$ and $(x, y') \in T(M)$ then $y = y'$

If M satisfies this implication, convert M to a deterministic Turing transducer M' satisfying these three properties:

(1) $T(M) = T(M')$;
(2) M' has one final state f;
(3) for any input word, $x \in \Sigma_I^*$, this equivalences holds:

$(x, y) \in T(M')$ for an output word y

if and only if

M' translates x into y and halts in f

1.7 Consider each translation τ presented in Exercise 1.4. Prove or disprove that τ satisfies

if $(x, y) \in \tau$ and $(x, y') \in \tau$ then $y = y'$

If τ satisfies this implication, construct a deterministic Turing transducer M such that M has the form described in Exercise 1.6, and M defines τ.

1.8 Base the definition of a Turing transducer upon a one-tape Turing machine. A Turing transducer defined in this way reads and writes words on the same tape. Describe this modified definition in detail. Show that this modification does not affect the power of Turing transducers.

1.9 Consider each of translations (a) through (k) in Exercise 1.4. Construct a one-tape Turing transducer, obtained from Exercise 1.8, that defines the translation.

1.10 Base the definition of a Turing transducer upon a Turing machine with a two-way infinite tape. Describe this modified definition in detail. Show that this modification does not affect the power of Turing transducers.

1.11 Consider each of translations (a) through (k) in Exercise 1.4. Construct a two-way-infinite-tape Turing transducer, obtained in Exercise 1.10, that defines the translation.

1.12 By analogy with a simple Turing machine, a *simple Turing transducer* changes its state and either rewrites the tape symbols or shifts the heads. Therefore, in a move, a simple Turing transducer cannot simultaneously change its state, rewrite the tape symbols, and shift the heads. Formalize the notion of a simple Turing transducer. Show that simple Turing transducers are as powerful as Turing transducers.

1.13 Construct a simple Turing transducer for each of the translations (a) through (k) in Exercise 1.4.

1.14 Modify the translation defined by a Turing transducer $M = (Q, \Sigma, R, s, F)$, so

M translates an input word x into an output word y

if and only if

$sx|sB \vdash^* fx|fy$ in M, where $f \in F$

Formalize this modification. Show that this modification does not affect the family of translations defined by Turing transducers.

1.15 For each of languages (a) through (k) in Exercise 1.4, construct a Turing transducer M that defines $T(M)$ by the modified way described in Exercise 1.14.

1.16 Generalize the definition of a Turing transducer by allowing a set of start states rather than a single start state. Formalize this generalization. Show that this generalization does not add to the power of Turing transducers.

1.17 In a move, a *lazy Turing transducer* rewrites a word, consisting of several symbols, on its tapes. Formalize the notion of a lazy Turing transducer. Show that lazy Turing transducers are as powerful as Turing transducers.

1.18 Section 8.1.5 defines the function δ and demonstrates how to describe any deterministic Turing machine M by δ. Adapt δ so this function can describe any Turing transducer.

1.19 Introduce a Turing transducer description that differs from the description based upon the function δ discussed in Exercise 1.18.

1.20 Formalize the notion of a Turing transducer $M = (Q, \Sigma, R, s, F)$, so R is defined as a finite relationship rather than a finite set of rules.

1.21 Prove that input Turing machines underlying Turing transducers characterize the family of recursively enumerable languages.

1.22 Prove that output Turing machines underlying Turing transducers characterize the family of recursively enumerable languages.

1.23 Complete Example 10.1.1 Part 5.

1.24 Prove Theorem 10.1.1.

1.25 Complete the proof of Theorem 10.1.2.

2. Computability

2.1 The *constant function* Zero is defined as

$$\text{Zero}(n) = 0$$

for all $n \geq 0$. Return to the definition of a computer given in Section 10.2.1. In terms of this definition, design a computer that computes Zero.

2.2 For each of the following functions over nonnegative integers, design a computer that computes the function.

(a) $\gamma(n) = n!$
(b) $\gamma(n) = n^2$
(c) $\gamma(n) = 2^n$
(d) $\gamma(n) = n^n$

2.3* Let $M_1, M_2, \ldots$ be any enumeration of all computers. By using Theorem 10.2.2.1, prove that there exists a natural number n such that M_n and M_{n+1} compute the same function.

2.4 Section 10.2.1 has represented nonnegative integers by function BiInt. Consider the following binary specification of nonnegative integers

0^i1 represents i

for $i = 0, \ldots$. Modify all Section 10.2.1 in terms of this new representation.

2.5 Extend computers of one-variable functions to computers of n-variable functions, where $n \geq 1$.

Note: Most of the following exercises deal with functions of many variables and, consequently, necessitate the use of the computers extended in this exercise.

2.6 Design a computer of the following two-variable functions over nonnegative integers.

(a) $\gamma(n, m) = n + m$
(b) $\gamma(n, m) = nm$
(c) $\gamma(n, m) = n^m$

2.7 For all i and m satisfying $1 \leq i \leq m$, the *projection function i-m-proj* is defined by

$$i\text{-}m\text{-}proj(n_1, \ldots, n_i, \ldots, n_m) = n_i$$

where $n_1, \ldots, n_m$ are nonnegative integers. Design a computer that computes this function.

2.8* Let γ be a function of i variables, and let η_1 through η_i be i functions of j variables. Then, the following function θ defined by

$$\theta = \gamma(\eta_1(n_1, \ldots, n_j), \ldots, \eta_i(n_1, \ldots, n_j))$$

where $n_1, \ldots, n_j$ are nonnegative integers, represents the *composition of functions* γ and $\eta_1, \ldots, \eta_i$. Design a computer that computes θ.

Note: Notice that the case when $i = j = 1$ in $\gamma(\eta_1(n_1, \ldots, n_j), \ldots, \eta_i(n_1, \ldots, n_j))$ corresponds to the basic definition of composition, discussed in the exercises to chapter 0.

2.9* Let γ, η and θ be three functions satisfying the following conditions:

1. γ is a function of m variables;
2. η is a function of $m + 2$ variables;
3. θ is the function of $m + 1$ variables, defined by

$$\theta(n_1, \ldots, n_{m+1}) = \gamma(n_1, \ldots, n_m) \text{ if } n_{m+1} = 0;$$

otherwise, $\theta(n_1, \ldots, n_{m+1}) = \eta(\, n_{m+1} - 1, \theta(n_1, \ldots, n_{m+1} - 1), n_1, \ldots, n_m)$

Then, θ is the *recursion of functions* γ and η. Design a computer that computes θ.

Turing transducers

2.10 Let η be one of the following three functions

(a) the constant function Zero (see Exercise 2.1);
(b) a projection function (see Exercise 2.7);
(c) the successor function (see Example 10.2.1.2).

Then, η is called an *initial function*. A function γ is a *primitive recursive function* provided that γ is one of these three functions:

(A) an initial function;
(B) the composition of some primitive recursive functions (see Exercise 2.8);
(C) the recursion of some primitive recursive functions (see Exercise 2.9).

Formalize the notion of a primitive recursive function.

2.11 Consider the following primitive recursive function Test:

(a) for $n = 0$, $\text{Test}(n) = 1$
(b) for $n > 0$, $\text{Test}(n) = \text{Zero}(12\text{proj}(n - 1, \text{Test}(n - 1)))$.

Design a computer that computes Test. Demonstrate that the definition of test actually means that:

(A) $\text{test}(n) = 1$ if and only if $n = 0$
(B) $\text{test}(n) = 0$, for any $n > 0$.

That is, this function tests whether its argument is zero.

2.12 Prove that all primitive recursive functions are computable.
2.13* Prove that some computable functions are not primitive recursive functions.
2.14* *Ackermann's function*, A, is a function of two variables defined by:

(1) for $m \geq 0$, $A(0, m) = m + 1$
(2) for $n \geq 1$, $A(n, 0) = A(n - 1, 1)$
(3) for $n, m \geq 1$, $A(n, m) = A(n - 1, A(n, m - 1))$

Is A a primitive recursive function?

2.15* Let γ be a total function of $j + 1$ variables, and let η be a j-variable partial function satisfying these two properties;

(1) $\eta(n_1, \ldots, n_j)$ equals the smallest k satisfying $\gamma(n_1, \ldots, n_j, k) = 0$, if there exists such a k
(2) $\eta(n_1, \ldots, n_j)$ is undefined if there does not exist any nonnegative integer, k, such that $\gamma(n_1, \ldots, n_j, k) = 0$

Then, η is the *minimization* of γ. Formalize this notion in more detail. Design a computer that computes η.

2.16 A function γ is a *recursive function* provided γ is one of the four functions

   (1) an initial function;
   (2) the composition of some primitive recursive functions (see Exercise 2.8)
   (3) the recursion of some recursive functions (see Exercise 2.9).
   (4) the minimization of a recursive function (see Exercise 2.15).

   Formalize the notion of a recursive function.
2.17 Prove that every primitive recursive function is recursive.
2.18* Prove that some recursive functions are not primitive recursive functions.
2.19* Prove that Ackermann's function, defined in Exercise 2.14, represents a recursive function.
2.20** Prove that a function γ is recursive if and only if γ is computable.
2.21 Complete Example 10.2.1.2.
2.22 Complete the proof of Lemma 10.2.3.1.

3 Decidability

3.1 Let γ, η and θ be three functions over natural numbers such that

$$\gamma = O(\theta) \text{ and } \eta = O(\theta)$$

Prove that

$$\gamma + \eta = O(\theta)$$

3.2 Let γ and θ be two functions such that θ is polynomial, and $\gamma = O(\theta)$. Prove that there exists a polynomial function η such that $\gamma(n) \leq \eta(n)$ for all $n \geq 1$.
3.3 Let γ be an *exponential function*; that is, γ has the form

$$\gamma(n) = a^n$$

where a is a natural number. If ϕ is a total function satisfying $\phi = O(\gamma)$ and $\gamma = O(\phi)$, then ϕ has an *exponential growth rate*. Prove that every exponential function has a growth rate greater than the growth rate of any polynomial function.
3.4 Consider the following three functions:

   (a) $n!$
   (b) n^n
   (c) 2^{2^n}

   Solve these three tasks.

(A) Prove that each of these functions has a growth rate greater than a growth rate of any exponential function.
(B) Decide which of these functions has the largest growth rate.
(C) Decide which of these functions has the smallest growth rate.

3.5* Consider $n^{\log n}$. Prove that this function has a growth rate less than the growth rate of any exponential function. Then, prove that this function has a growth rate greater than the growth rate of any polynomial function.

3.6 Formalize the notion of a nondeterministic decision maker.

3.7* Prove that the family of polynomial-space-bounded languages contains NP, where NP denotes the family of nondeterministic polynomial-time-bounded languages (see Section 10.3.3.1).

3.8* Prove that the family of recursive languages properly contains the family of nondeterministic polynomial-space-bounded languages.

3.9* Prove that the family of polynomial-space-bounded languages coincides with the family of nondeterministic polynomial-space-bounded languages.

3.10* Recall that Section 10.3.3 formulates the time-bounded acceptance problem:

Instance: A nondeterministic Turing machine, $M = (Q, \{0, 1, B\}, R, s, \{f\})$, $w \in \{0, 1\}^*$, and a natural number, i.
Question: Does M accept x by making no more than i moves?

Prove that time-bounded acceptance is an NP-complete problem.

3.11* Consider the regular-language difference problem:

Instance: Two finite automata M and M'.
Question: Is $L(M)$ different from $L(M')$?

Prove that this problem is an NP-complete problem.

3.12* Consider the question of whether each automaton in a finite set of deterministic finite automata accepts a word w. Formulate this problem rigorously. Prove that this is an NP-complete problem.

3.13* Consider the linear regularness problem:

Instance: A linear grammar $G = (N, T, P, S)$.
Question: Is $L(G)$ regular?

Prove that this problem is undecidable.

3.14 Consider the linear-complement linearness problem:

Instance: A linear grammar $G = (N, T, P, S)$.
Question: Is the complement of $L(G)$ linear?

Prove that this problem is undecidable.

3.15* Consider the linear-complement context-freeness problem:

Instance: A linear grammar $G = (N, T, P, S)$.
Question: Is the complement of $L(G)$ context-free?

Prove that this problem is undecidable.

3.16* Consider the context-free linearness problem:

Instance: A context-free grammar $G = (N, T, P, S)$.
Question: Is $L(G)$ linear?

Prove that this problem is undecidable.

3.17* Consider the context-free-complement context-freeness problem:

Instance: A context-free grammar $G = (N, T, P, S)$.
Question: Is the complement of $L(G)$ context-free?

Prove that this problem is undecidable.

3.18* Consider the context-sensitive emptiness problem.

Instance: A context-sensitive grammar $G = (N, T, P, S)$.
Question: Is $L(G)$ empty?

Prove that this problem is undecidable.

3.19* Consider the containment problem:

Instance: Two Turing machines M and M'.
Question: Is $L(M)$ contained in $L(M')$?

Prove that this problem is undecidable.

3.20* Consider the equivalence problem:

Instance: Two Turing machines M and M'.
Question: Is M equivalent to M'?

Prove that this problem is undecidable.

3.21* Consider the intersection problem:

Instance: Two Turing machines M and M'.
Question: Is the intersection of $L(M)$ and $L(M')$ empty?

Prove that this problem is undecidable.

3.22 A *Post tag system* G is a triple,

$$G = (T, P, S)$$

where

T is an alphabet;
P is a finite set of productions of the form

$$u \to v$$

where $u, v \in T^*$;
S in T^+ is the start word.

If $x \in T^*$ and $u \to v \in P$, then $ux \Rightarrow xv$ in G; $\Rightarrow$ is extended to $\Rightarrow^*$ in the standard manner. The language generated by G, $L(G)$, is defined by

$$L(G) = \{w : S \Rightarrow^* w\}$$

Formalize the notion of a Post tag system in greater detail.

3.23* Consider the Post-tag-system membership problem:

Instance: A Post tag system $G = (T, P, S)$, and a word $w \in T^*$.
Question: Is w a member of $L(G)$?

Prove that this problem is undecidable.

3.24* Consider the Post's correspondence problem:

Instance: A finite, binary relation, $\rho \subseteq T^+ \times T^+$, where T is an alphabet.
Question: Does there exist a sequence

$$(x_1, y_1), \ldots, (x_n, y_n)$$

for some $n \geq 1$ such that $x_1 \ldots x_n = y_1 \ldots y_n$, and $(x_i, y_i) \in \rho$, for $i = 1, \ldots, n$?

Prove that this problem is undecidable.

3.25 Consider the one-symbol Post's correspondence problem:

Instance: A finite, binary relation, $\rho \subseteq T^+ \times T^+$, where T is an alphabet that contains one symbol.
Question: Does there exist a sequence

$$(x_1, y_1), \ldots, (x_n, y_n)$$

for some $n \geq 1$ such that $x_1 \ldots x_n = y_1 \ldots y_n$, and $(x_i, y_i) \in \rho$, for $i = 1, \ldots, n$? Prove that the one-symbol Post's correspondence problem is decidable.

3.26* Consider the problem of whether a computer program, written in a real programming language, can loop forever. Prove that this problem is undecidable.

3.27* Consider the problem of whether a computer program, written in a real programming language, can ever produce any output. Prove that this problem is undecidable.

3.28* Consider the problem of whether two computer programs, written in a real programming language, produce the same output with all inputs. Prove that this problem is undecidable.

3.29 Complete Example 10.3.1.1.

3.30 Complete the proof of Theorem 10.3.2.1.

Programming projects

1 Basic definitions

1.1 Write a program that decides whether a Turing transducer is deterministic.

1.2 Write a program that simulates a deterministic Turing transducer.

1.3 Write a program that simulates a deterministic one-tape Turing transducer (see Exercise 1.9).

1.4 Write a program that simulates a deterministic Turing transducer with a two-way infinite tape (see Exercise 1.11).

1.5 Write a program that simulates a universal Turing transducer — that is, a Turing transducer that can simulate any Turing transducer.

2 Computability

2.1 Write a program that decides whether a given Turing transducer represents a computer.

2.2 Write a program that simulates a computer.

2.3 Write a program that reads a set of rules specifying a computer M and produces a program simulating M.

2.4 In Section 10.2, computers have represented nonnegative integers by using BiInt. Exercise 2.4 produces another representation of nonnegative integers. Write a program that converts any computer M that represents nonnegative integers by BiInt to a computer, M', that uses the representation produced in Exercise 2.4 so that $\phi_M = \phi_{M'}$.

2.5 Observe that primitive recursive functions, defined in Exercise 2.10, actually represent a simple programming language for functions over nonnegative integers. Design and implement a compiler for this language.

3 Decidability

3.1 Write a program that decides whether a given Turing transducer represents a decision maker.
3.2 Write a program that simulates a decision maker.
3.3 Write a program that reads a set of rules specifying a decision maker M and produces a program simulating M.

Bibliographical notes

Finite and Pushdown Transducers

Finite transducers were introduced by Elgot and Mezei (1965). Irons (1961) and Barnett and Futrelle (1962) presented pragmatically oriented versions of translation grammars, which were formalized by Lewis and Stearns (1968). Evey (1963) introduced pushdown transducers, and Choffrut and Culik II (1983) examined their properties in detail.

Aho and Ullman (1969a,b), Conway (1963), Floyd (1964), Foster (1968), Johnson (1974), Kasami (1965), Knuth (1967), Knuth (1971), Lewis et al. (1965), Lewis and Stearns (1968), McCarthy and Painter (1967), Valiant (1975) and Younger (1976) are important early studies of translation models. Aho and Ullman (1972, 1973, 1977), Beigel and Floyd (1994), Berstel (1979), Book (1980), Brainerd and Landweber (1974), Brookshear (1989), Bucher and Maurer (1984), Carroll and Long (1989), Denning et al. (1978), Gries (1971), Hopcroft and Ullman (1979), Kelley (1995), Kuich and Salomaa (1985), Lewis et al. (1976), Linz (1990), Martin (1991), McNaughton (1982), Pagan (1981), Prather (1976), Revesz (1983), Rozenberg and Salomaa (1997), Salomaa (1973), Sudkamp (1988), Salomaa (1985), Savitch (1982) and Wood (1987) contain useful material dealing with various theoretical and practical aspects of compiler construction. Sippu and Soisalon-Soininen (1987) provide a thorough treatment of modern parsing techniques.

Turing transducer

Turing transducers are based on Turing machines, which were introduced by Turing (1936). Kleene (1936), Church (1936) and Post (1936) defined these machines in an alternative way. Church's thesis is given in Church (1936). Godel (1931) introduced the basic ideas about decidability. Rice (1953) established Rice's theorem. Hartmanis and Stearns (1965) represents a fundamental study of computational complexity. Cook (1971a) introduced NP-completeness, further discussed by Karp (1972).

Buchi (1962), Cobham (1964), Davis (1965), Dekke (1962), Greibach (1963), Hartmanis et al. (1965), Hartmanis (1967), Hennie and Stearns (1966), Hartmanis and Hopcroft (1971), Kleene (1943), Kleine and Ottmann (1977), McCarthy (1960), McCarthy (1963), Minsky (1960, 1962), Priese (1979), Post (1947), Shepherdson and Sturgis (1963), Watanabe (1960) and Watanabe (1961) are important early studies of various aspects of the material that this chapter covers. Rogers (1967) is an excellent reference concerning all the topics discussed in this chapter even though it was published more than 30 years ago. Davis (1958), Davis and Weyuker (1983) and Salomaa (1985) study computability and decidability in depth. Papadimitriou (1995) comprehensively covers computational complexity. Beigel and Floyd (1994), Berstel (1979), Book (1980), Brookshear (1989), Bucher and Maurer (1984), Carroll and Long (1989), Eilenberg (1974, 1976), Harrison (1965, 1978), Hopcroft and Ullman (1979), Kelley

(1995), Kuich and Salomaa (1985), Lewis and Papadimitriou (1981), Linz (1990), Martin (1991), Minsky (1967), McNaughton (1982), Revesz (1983), Salomaa (1969), Sudkamp (1988) and Wood (1987) are good sources for further study.

Bibliography

Aho, A. V.: (1968) Indexed Grammars–An Extension of Context-free Grammars. *Journal of the ACM* 15, 647–671.
Aho, A. V.(ed.): (1973) *Currents in the Theory of Computing*, Prentice-Hall, Englewood Cliffs, New Jersey.
Aho, A. V.: (1980) Pattern Matching in Strings, in Book, R.V.(ed.), *Formal Language Theory: Perspectives and Open Problems*, Academic Press, New York, 325–247.
Aho, A. V., and Ullman, J. D.: (1969a) Syntax Directed Translations and the Pushdown Assembler, *Journal of Computer and System Sciences* 3, 37–56.
Aho, A. V., and Ullman, J. D.: (1969b) Properties of Syntax Directed Relations, *Journal of Computer and System Sciences* 3, 319–334.
Aho, A. V., and Ullman, J. D.: (1972) *The Theory of Parsing, Translation and Compiling*, Volume I: Parsing. Prentice Hall, Englewood Cliffs, New Jersey.
Aho, A. V., and Ullman, J. D.: (1973) *The Theory of Parsing, Translation and Compiling*, Volume II: Compiling. Prentice Hall, Englewood Cliffs, New Jersey.
Aho, A. V., and Ullman, J. D.: (1977) *Principles of Compiler Design*, Addison-Wesley, Reading, Massachusetts.
Alagic, S., and Arbib, M. A.: (1978) *The Design of Well-Structured and Correct Programs*, Springer-Verlag, Heidelberg.
Altman, E. B.: (1964) *The Concept of Finite Representability*, Systems Research Center Report SRC 56-A-64-20, Case Institute of Technology.
Anderson, R. B.: (1979) *Proving Programs Correct*, John Wiley & Sons, New York.
Arbib, M. A., Kfoury, A. J., and Moll, R. N.: (1981) *A Basis for Theoretical Computer Science*, Springer-Verlag, New York.
Ashcroft, E. A., and Wadge, W. W.: (1976) LUCID, a Formal System for Writing and Proving Programs, *SIAM Journal on Computing* 5, 336–354.
Backus, J. W.: (1959) The Syntax and Semantics of the Proposed International Algebraic Language of the Zurich ACM-GAMM Conference. *Proceedings of the International Conference on Information Processing*, UNESCO, 125–132.
Banerji, R. B.: (1963) Phrase Structure Languages, Finite Machines, and Channel Capacity, *Information and Control* 6, 153–162.
Bar-Hillel, Y., Perles, M., and Shamir, E.: (1961) On Formal Properties of Simple Phrase Structure Grammars. *Zeitschrift für Phonetik Sprachwissenschaft und Kommunikations-Forschung* 14, 143–172.
Bar-Hillel, Y.: (1964) *Language and Information*. Addison-Wesley, Reading, Massachusetts.
Barnes, B. H.: (1970) A Programmer's View of Automata, *Computing Surveys* 4, 221–239.
Barnett, M. P., and Futrelle, R. P.: (1962) Syntactic Analysis by Digital Computer, *Communications of the ACM* 5, 515–526.
Becker, C. B.: (1983) *Software Testing Techniques*, Van Nastrand Reinhold, New York.
Beckmann, F. S.: (1980) *Mathematical Foundations of Programming*, Addison-Wesley, Reading, Massachusetts.
Beigel, R., and Floyd, R. W.: (1994) *The Language of Machines*; Freeman, New York.
Bellmann, R. E., and Dreyfus, S. E.: (1962) *Applied Dynamic Programming*, Princeton University Press, Princeton, New Jersey.
Bentley, J. L., and Ottmann, Th.: (1981) The Complexity of Manipulating Hierarchically Defined Sets of Rectangles, Mathematical Foundations of Computer Science 1981, *Springer-Verlag Lecture Notes in Computer Science* 118, 1–15.
Bentley, J. L., Ottmann, Th., and Widmayer, P.: (1983) The Complexity of Manipulating Hierarchically Defined Sets of Rectangles, in Preparata, F.P.(ed.), *Advances in Computing Research 1*, JAI Press, Greenwich, Connecticut, 127–158.

Berger, R.: *The Undecidability of the Domino Problem*, (1966) Memoirs of the American Mathematical Society 66.
Berlekamp, E. R., Conway, J. H., and Guy, R. K.: (1982) *Winning Ways*, Volume 2: Games in Particular, Academic Press, New York.
Berstel, J.: (1979) *Transductions and Context-Free Languages*, Teubner, Stuttgart, West Germany.
Berstel, J., and Boasson, L.: (1974) Une Suite Décroissante de Cônes Rationnels, *Springer-Verlag Lecture Notes in Computer Science* 14, 383-397.
Bobrow, L. S., and Arbib, M. A.: (1974) *Discrete Mathematics: Applied Algebra for Computer and Information Science*, W. B. Saunders, Philadelphia, Pensylvania.
Bobrow, L. S., and Arbib, M. A.: (1974) *Discrete Mathematics: Applied Algebra for Computer and Information Science*, W. B. Saunders, Philadelphia, Pensylvania.
Book, R. V. (ed.): (1980) *Formal Language Theory: Perspectives and Open Problems*, Academic Press, New York.
Borodihn, H., and Fernau, H.: (1995) Remarks on Accepting Parallel Systems, *International Journal of Computer Mathematics* 14, 51-67.
Bourne, S. R.: (1983) *The UNIX System*, Addison-Wesley, Reading, Massacussetts.
Braffort, P., and Hirschberg, D. (eds): (1963) *Computer Programming and Formal Systems*, North-Holland, Amsterdam.
Brainerd, W. S., and Landweber, L. H.: (1974) *Theory of Computation*, John Wiley & Sons, New York.
Brookshear, J. G.: (1989) *Theory of Computation*, Benjamin/Cummings, Redwood City, California.
Brzozowski, J. A.: (1962) A Survey of Regular Expressions and Their Applications, *IEFE Transactions on Electronic Computers* 11, 324-335.
Brzozowski, J. A.: (1964) Derivates of Regular Expressions, *Journal of the ACM* 11, 481-494.
Brzozowski, J. A.: (1980) Open Problems about Regular Languages, in Book, R. V. (ed.). *Formal Language Theory: Perspectives and Open Problems*, Academic Press, New York, 23-47.
Brzozowski, J. A.., and McCluskey, Jr., E. J.: (1963) Signal Flow Graph Techniques for Sequential Circuit State Diagrams, IEEE *Transactions on Electronic Computers* EC-12, 67-76.
Brzozowski, J. A., and Yoeli, M.: (1976) *Digital Networks*, Prentice-Hall, Englewood Cliffs, New Jersey.
Bucher, W., and Maurer, H. A.: (1984) *Teoretische Grundlagen der Programmiersprachen: Automatem und Sprachen*, Bibliographisches Institut, Zurich.
Büchi, J. R.: (1962) Turing-Machines and the Entscheidungsproblem, *Mathematische Annalen* 148, 201-213.
Burge, W. H.: (1975) *Recursive Programming Techniques*, Addison-Wesley, Reading, Massachusetts.
Burks, A. W. (ed.): (1970) *Essays in Cellular Automata*, University of Illinois Press.
Burks, A. W., Warren, D. W., and Wright, J. B.: (1954) An Analysis of a Logical Machine Using Parenthesis-Free Notation, *Mathematical Tables and Other Aids to Computation* 8, 55-57.
Cantor, D. C.: (1962) On the Ambiguity Problem of Backus Systems, *Journal of the ACM* 9, 477-479.
Carroll, J., and Long, D.: (1989) *Theory of Finite Automata*, Prentice Hall, New Jersey.
Choffrut, C., and Culik II, K.: (1983) Properties of Finite and Pushdown Transducers, *SIAM Journal on Computing* 12, 300-315.
Chomsky, N.: (1956) Three Models for the Description of Language. *IRE Transactions on Information Theory* 2, 113-124.
Chomsky, N.: (1957) *Syntactic Structures*,The Hague, Netherlands.
Chomsky, N.: (1959) On Certain Formal Properties of Grammars. *Information and Control* 2, 137-167.
Chomsky, N.: (1962) Context-Free Grammars and Pushdown Storage. Quarterly Progress Report No. 65, MIT Research Laboratory of Electronics, Cambridge, Massachusetts, 187-194.
Chomsky, N.: (1963) *Formal Properties of Grammars, Handbook of Mathematical Psychology*, Vol. 2, John Wiley & Sons, New York, 323-418.
Chomsky, N. and Miller, G. A.: (1958) Finite-State Languages. *Information and Control* 1, 91-112.
Chomsky, N., and Schutzenberger, M. P.: (1963) The Algebraic Theory of Context Free Languages, in Braffort, P., and Hirschberg, D. (eds.), *Computer Programming and Formal Systems*, North-Holland, Amsterdam, 118-161.
Christofides, N.: (1976) *Worst-Case Analysis of a New Heuristic for the Traveling Salesman Problem*, Technical Report, Graduate School of Industrial Administration, Carnegie-Mellon University, Pittsburg, Pensylvania.

References and bibliography

Church, A.: (1936) An Unsolvable Problem of Elementary Number Theory, *American Journal of Mathematics* 58, 345–363.

Church, A.: (1941) *The Calculi of Lambda-Conversion, Annals of Mathematics Studies* 6, Princeton University Press, Princeton New Jersey.

Cleaveland, J. C., and Uzgalis, R.: (1977) *Grammars for Programming Languages*, Elsevier North-Holland, New York.

Clocksin, W. F., and Mullish, C. S.: (1981) *Programming in PROLOG*, Springer-Verlag, Heideeberg.

Cobham, A.: (1964) The Intrinsic Computational Difficulty of Functions, *Proceedings 1964 Congress for Logic, Mathematics, and Philosophy of Science, North Holland*, Amsterdam, 24–30.

Cohen, J.: (1979) Nondeterministic Algorithms, *Computing Surveys* 11, 79–94.

Cohen, D. J., and Gotlieb, C. C.: (1970) A List Structure Form of Grammars for Syntactic Analysis, *Computing Surveys* 2.

Comer, D.: (1979) Heuristic for Trie Index Minimization, *ACM Transactions on Data Base Systems* 4, 383–395.

Conway, M. E.: (July 1963) Design of a Separable Transition-Diagram Compiler, *Communications of the ACM* 6, 396–408.

Cook, S. A.: (1971a) The Complexity of Theorem-Proving Procedures, *Proceedings Third Annual ACM Symposium on the Theory of Computing*, 151–158.

Cook, S. A.: (1971b) Linear-Time Simulation of Deterministic Two-Way Pushdown Automata, *Proceeding of the 1971 IFIP Congress, North-Holland*, Amsterdam, 75–80.

Csuhaj-Varju, E., Dassow, J., Kelemen, J., Paun, Gh.: (1994) *Grammar Systems: A Grammatical Approach to Distribution and Cooperation*, Gordon and Breach, London.

Csuhaj-Varju, E., Kelemen, J., Kelemenova, J., Paun, Gh.:(1996) Eco-Grammar Systems: A grammatical framework for life-like interactions, *Artificial Life* 3 27–38.

Dantzig, G. B.: (1960) On the Significance of Solving Linear Programming Problems with Integer Variables, *Econometrica* 28, 30–44.

Dassow, J. and Paun, Gh.: (1989) *Regulated Rewriting in Formal Language Theory*, Springer, Berlin.

Davis, M.: (1958) Computability and Unsolvability, McGraw-Hill, New York.

Davis, M. (ed.): (1965) *The Undecidable: Basic Papers on Undecidable Propositions, Unsolvable Problems, and Computable Functions*, Raven Press, Hewlett, New York.

Davis, M.: (1973) Hilbert's Tenth Problem is Unsolvable, *American Mathematical Monthly* 80, 233–269.

Davis, M. D., and Weyuker, E. J.: (1983) *Computability, Complexity, and Languages*, Academic Press, New York.

de Bakker, J. W.: (1969) Semantics of Programming Languages, in Tou, J.(ed.), *Advances in Information Systems and Sciences*, Vol. 2, Plenum Press, New York, 173–227.

Dekker, J. C. E. (ed.): (1962) *Recursive Function Theory, Proceedings of Symposia in Pure Mathematics* 5, American Mathematical Society, Providence, Rhode Island.

DeMillo, R. A., Dobkin, D. P., Jones, A. K., and Lipton, R. J.(eds.): (1978) *Foundations of Secure Computation*, Academic Press, New York.

DeMillo, R. A., Lipton, R. J., and Perlis, A. J.: (1979) Social Processes and Proofs of Theorems and Programs, *Communications of the ACM* 22, 271–280.

Denning, P. J., Dennis, J. B., and Qualitz, J. E.: (1978) *Machines, Languages, and Computation*, Prentice-Hall, Englewood Cliffs, New Jersey.

Dewdney, A., K.: (August 1984) Computer Recreations: A Computer Trap for the Busy Beaver, the Hardest-Working Turing Machine, *Scientific American* 251, 19–23.

Dewdney, A., K.: (March 1985) Computer Recreations, *Scientific American* 252, 23.

Dijkstra, E. W.: (1976) *A Discipline of Programming*, Prentice-Hall, Englewood Cliffs, New Jersey.

Edmonds, J.: (1962) Covers and Packings in a Family of Sets, Bulletin of the *American Mathematical Society* 68, 494–499.

Edmonds, J.: (1965) Paths, Trees and Flowers, *Canadian Journal of Mathematics* 17, 499–467.

Ehrenfeucht, A., Karhumaki, J., and Rozenberg, G.: (1982) The (Generalized) Post Correspondence Problem with Lists Consisting of two Words is Decidable, *Theoretical Computer Science* 21, 119–144.

Ehrenfeucht, A., Parikh, R., and Rozenberg, G.: (1981) Pumping Lemmas for Regular Sets, *SIAM Journal on Computing* 10, 536–541.

Eilenberg, S.: (1974) *Automata, Languages, and Machines*, Volume A Academic Press, New York.
Eilenberg, S.: (1976) *Automata, Languages, and Machines*, Volume B, Academic Press, New York.
Elgot, C. C. and Mezei, J. E.: (1965) On Relations Defined by Generalized Finite Automata, *IBM Journal of Research and Development* 9, 47–68.
Elspas, B., Levitt, K., Waldinger, R., and Waksman, A.: (1972) An Assessment of Techniques for Proving Program Correctness, *Computing Surveys* 4, 97–147.
Engelfriet, J.: (1980) Some Open Questions and Recent Results on Tree Transducers and Tree Languages, in Book, R.V. (ed.), *Formal Language Theory: Perspectives and Open Problems*, Academic Press, New York 241–286.
Engelfriet, J., Schmidt, E. M., and van Leeuwen, J.: (1980) Stack Machines and Classes of Nonnested Macro Languages, *Journal of the ACM* 27, 6–17.
Evey, J.: (1963) Application of Pushdown Store Machines, *Proceedings 1963 Fall Joint Computer Conference*, AFIPS Press, Montvale, New Jersey, 215–227.
Fernau, H.: (1996) On Grammar and Language Families, *Fundamenta Informaticae* 25, 17–34
Fischer, M. J.: (1968) Grammars with Macro-like Productions, *Proceedings of the Ninth Annual IEEE Symposium on Switching and Automata Theory*, 131–142.
Floyd, R. W.: (1962) On Ambiguity in Phrase Structure Languages. *Communications of the ACM* 5, 526–534.
Floyd, R. W.: (1964a) *New Proofs and Old Theorems in Logic and Formal Linguistics*, Computer Associates, Wakefield, Massachusetts.
Floyd, R. W.: (August 1964b) The Syntax of Programming Languages-A Survey, *IEEE Transactions on Electronic Computers*, Vol. EC-13, 346–353. (Reprinted in Rosen, S. (ed.), *Programming Systems and Languages*, McGraw-Hill, New York, 1967; and Pollack, B.W., *Compiler Techniques*, Auerbach Press, Philadelphia, Pensylvania, 1972.)
Floyd, R. W.: (1967a) Assigning Meaning to Programs, in Schwartz, J. T.(ed.), *Mathematical Aspects of Computer Science*, American Mathematical Society, Providence, Rhode Island 19–32.
Floyd, R. W.: (1967b) Nondeterministic Algorithms, *Journal of the ACM* 14, 636–644.
Floyd, R. W., and Ullman, J. D.: (1984) The Compilation of Regular Expressions into Integrated Circuits, *Journal of the ACM* 29, 603–622.
Fosdick, L. D., and Osterweil, L. J.: (1976) Data Flow Analysis in Software Reliability, *Computing Surveys* 8, 305–330.
Foster, J. M.: (1968) A Syntax-Improving Program, *Computer Journal* 11, 31–34.
Foster, J. M.: (1970) *Automatic Syntactic Analysis*, American Elsevier, New York.
Galler, B. A., and Perlis, A. J.: (1970) *A View of Programming Languages*, Addison-Wesley, Reading, Massachusetts.
Gardner, M.: (1983) *Wheels, Life and Other Mathematical Amusements*, W.H. Freeman, San Francisco.
Gardner, M.: (April 1985) The Traveling Saleman's Travail, *Discover* 6, 87–90.
Garey, M. R., and Johnson, D. S.: (1979) *Computers and Intractability: A Guide to the Theory of NP-Completeness*, W.H. Freeman, San Francisco.
Gesceg, F. and Steinby, M.: (1984) *Tree Automata*, Akademia Kiado, Budapest.
Ginsburg, S.: (1966) *The Mathematical Theory of Context-Free Languages*, McGraw Hill, New York.
Ginsburg, S., Greibach, S. A., and Hopcroft, J. E.: (1969) Studies in Abstract Families of Languages, *Memoirs of the American Mathematical Society* 87, Providence, Rhode Island.
Ginsburg, S. and Greibach, S. A.: (1966) Deterministic Context-Free Languages. *Information and Control* 9, 563–582.
Ginsburg, S. and Rice, H. G.: (1962) Two Families of Languages Related to ALGOL. *Journal of the ACM* 9, 350–371.
Ginsburg, S., and Rose, G. F.: (1963b) Operations Which Preserve Definability in Languages, *Journal of the ACM* 10, 175–195.
Ginsburg, S., and Spanier, E. H.: (1963) Quotients of Context-Free Languages, *Journal of the ACM* 10, 487–492.
Gödel, K.: (1931) Über formal unentscheidbare Sätze der Principia Mathematica und verwandter Systeme I. *Monathefte für Mathematik und Physik* 38, 173–198.
Gonnet, G. H.: (1984) *Handbook of Algorithms and Data Structures*, Addison-Wesley, Reading, Massachusetts.

Gonnet, G. H., and Tompa, F. W.: (1983) A Constructive Approach to the Design of Algorithms and Data Structures, *Communications of the ACM* 26, 912-920.

Gouda, M. G., and Rosier, L. E.: (1985) Priority Networks of Communicating Finite State Machines, *SIAM Journal on Computing* 14, 569-584.

Graham, R. L.: (1978) The Combinatorial Mathematics of Scheduling, *Scientific American* 238, 3, 124-132.

Gray, J. N., and Harison, M. A.: (1966) The Theory of Sequential Relations, *Information and Control* 9, 435-468.

Greibach, S. A.: (1963) The Undecidability of the Ambiguity Problem for Minimal Linear Grammars, *Information and Control* 6, 117-125.

Greibach, S. A.: (1965) A New Normal Form Theorem for Context-Free Phrase Structure Grammars, *Journal of the ACM* 12, 42-52.

Greibach, S. A.: (1970) Chains of Full AFLs, *Mathematical Systems Theory* 4, 231-242.

Greibach, S. A.: (1972) A Generalization of Parikh's Theorem, *Discrete Mathematics* 2, 347-355.

Greibach, S. A.: (1973) The Hardest Context-Free Language, *SIAM Journal on Computing* 2, 304-310.

Greibach, S. and Hopcroft, J.: (1969) Scattered Context Grammars, *Journal of Computer and Systems Sciences* 3, 233-247.

Gries, D.: (1971) *Compiler Construction for Digital Computers*, John Wiley & Sons, New York.

Gries, D.: (1981) *The Science of Programming*, Springer-Verlag, New York.

Gruska, J.: (1971) A Characterization of Context-Free Languages, *Journal of Computer and System Sciences* 5, 353-364.

Habel, A.: (1992) *Hyperedge Replacement: Grammars and Languages*, LNCS 643, Springer, Berlin.

Habel, A., Heckel, R., and Taentzer, G.: (1996) Graph Grammars with Negative Application Conditions, *Fundamenta Informaticae* 26, 287-313

Hantler, S. L., and King, J. C.: (1976) An Introduction to Proving the Correctness of Programs, *Computing Surveys* 8, 331-353.

Harrison, M. A.: (1965) *Introduction to Switching and Automata Theory*, McGraw-Hill, New York.

Harrison, M. A.: (1978) *Introduction to Formal Language Theory*, Addison-Wesley, Reading, Massachusetts.

Harrison, M. A., Ruzzo, W. L., and Ullman, J. D.: (1976) Protection in Operating Systems, *Communications of the ACM* 19, 461-471.

Hartmanis, J.: (1967) Context-Free Languages and Turing Machine Computations, in Schwartz, J.T. (ed.), *Mathematical Aspects of Computer Science*, American Mathematical Society, Providence, Rhode Island, pp. 42-51.

Hartmanis, J. and Hopcroft, J. E.: (1971) An Overview of the Theory of Computational Complexity, *Journal of the ACM* 18 444-475.

Hartmanis, J., Lewis, P. M., II, and Stearns, R. E.: (1965) Hierarchies of Memory Limited Computations, *Proceedings of the Sixth Annual Symposium on Switching Circuit Theory and Logical Design*, pp. 179-190.

Hartmanis, J., and Stearns, R. E.: (1965) On the Computational Complexity of Algorithms, *Transactions of the AMS* 117, 285-306.

Hayes, B.: (December 1983) Computer Recreations, *Scientific American* 249, 19-28.

Hayes, B.: (March 1984) Computer Recreations, *Scientific American* 250, 10-16.

Hays, D. G.: (1967) *Introduction to Computational Linguistics*, Elsevier, New York.

Hein, J. L.: (1995) *Discrete Structures, Logic, and Computability*. Jones and Bartlett, London.

Heman, G. T.: (1973) A Biologically Motivated Extension of ALGOL-like Languages, *Information and Control* 22, 487-502.

Henderson, P.: (1980) *Functional Programming: Application and Implementation*, Prentice-Hall, Englewood Cliffs, New Jersey.

Hennie, F. C.: (1977) *Introduction to Computability*, Addison-Wesley, Reading, Massachusetts.

Hennie, F. C., and Stearns, R. E.: (1966) Two-Tape Simulation of Multitape Turing Machines, *Journal of the ACM* 13, 533-546.

Herman, G. T., and Rozenberger, G.: (1975) *Developmental Systems and Languages*, American Elsevier, New York.

Hermes, H.: (1969) *Enumerability, Decidability, Computability*, Springer-Verlag, New York.

Hoare, C. A. R., and Allison, D. C. S.: (1972) Incomputability, *Computing Surveys* 4, 169-178.

Hoare, C. A. R., and Lauer, P.: (1974) Consistent and Complementary Formal Theories of the Semantics of Programming Languages, *Acta Informatica* 3, 135–153.
Hoare, C. A. R., and Wirth, N.: (1973) An Axiomatic Definition of the Programming Language PASCAL, *Acta Informatica* 2, 335–355.
Hodges, A.: (1983) *Alan Turing: The Enigma*, Burnett Books Ltd., London.
Hopcroft, J. E.: (1971) An n log n Algorithm for Minimizing the States in a Finite Automaton, in Kohavi, Z., and Paz, A. (eds.), *Theory of Machines and Computations*, Academic Press, New York, pp 189–196.
Hopcroft, J. E.: (May 1984) Turing Machines, *Scientific American* 250, 86–98.
Hopcroft, J. E., and Ullman, J. D.: (1979) *Introduction to Automata Theory, Languages, and Computation*; Second Edition, Addison-Wesley, Reading, Massachusetts.
Horowitz, E., and Sahni, S.: (1978) *Fundamentals of Computer Algorithms*, Computer Science Press, Potomac, Maryland.
Hotz, G. and Pitsch, G.: (1996) On Parsing Coupled Context-Free Languages, *Theoretical Computer Science* 161, 205–233.
Irons, E. T: (1961) A Syntax Directed Compiler for ALGOL 60, *Communications of the ACM* 4, 51–55.
M. Ito (ed.): (1992) *Words, Languages, and Combinatorics*, World Scientific, Singapore.
Kelley, D.: (1995) *Automata and Formal Languages*; Prentice Hall, Englewood Cliffs.
Johnson, J. H.: (1983) *Formal Models for String Similarity*, Ph.D. Dissertation, Department of Computer Science, University of Waterloo.
Johnson, S. C.: (1974) YACC-Yet Another Compiler Compiler, *Computer Science Technical Report* 32, Bell Laboratories, Murray Hill, New Jersey.
Johnson, W. L., Porter, J. H., Ackley, S. I., and Ross, D. T.: (1968) Automatic Generation of Efficient Lexical Analyzers Using Finite-State Techniques, *Communications of the ACM* 11, 805–813.
Karp, R. M.: (1972) Reducibility Among Combinatorial Problems, in Miller, R. E., and Thatcher, J. W. (eds.), *Complexity of Computer Computations*, Plenum Press, New York, pp 85–103.
Karp, R. M.: (1986) Combinatorics, Complexity, and Randomness, *Communications of the ACM* 29, 98–109.
Kasami, T.: (1965) *An Efficient Recognition and Syntax Algorithm for Context-Free Languages*, Scientific Report AFCRL-65-758, Air Force Cambridge Research Laboratory, Bedford, Massachusetts.
Kernighan, B. W., and Plauger, P. J.: (1976) *Software Tools*, Addison-Wesley, Reading, Massachusetts.
Kfoury, A. J., Moll, R. N., and Arbib, M. A.: (1982) *A Programming Approach to Computability*, Springer-Verlag, New York.
Kleene, S. C.: (1936) General Recursive Functions of Natural Numbers, *Mathematische Annalen* 112, 727–742.
Kleene, S. C.: (1943) Recursive Predicates and Quantifiers, *Transactions of the American Mathematical Society* 53, 41–73.
Kleene, S. C.: (1952) *Introduction to Metamathematics*, D. Van Nostrand, Princeton, New Jersey.
Kleene, S. C.: (1956) Representation of Events in Nerve Nets and Finite Automata, in Shannon, C. E., and McCarthy, J. (eds.), *Automata Studies*. Princeton University Press, Princeton, New Jersey, pp. 3–42.
Kleine Buning, H., and Ottmann, Th.: (1977) Kleine Universelle Mehrdimensionale Turingmaschinen, *Elektronische Informationsverarbeitung und Kybernetik* 13, 179–201.
Knuth, D. E.: (1967) On the Translation of Languages from Left to Right, *Information and Control* 8, 611–618.
Knuth, D. E.: (1967) The Remaining Trouble Spots in ALGOL 60, *Communications of the ACM* 10, 611–618.
Knuth, D. E.: (1971) Top-Down Syntax Analysis, *Acta Informatica* 1, 79–110.
Knuth, D. E.: (1973) *The Art of Computer Programming*, Vol. 3: Sorting and Searching, Addison-Wesley Publishing Co., Reading, Massachusetts.
Knuth, D. E.: (1976) Big Omicron and Big Omega and Big Theta, *SIGACT News* 8, 18–23.
Knuth, D. E., Morris, J. H., Jr., and Pratt, V. R.: (1977) Fast Pattern Matching in Strings, *SIAM Journal on Computing* 6, 323–350.
Korenjak, A. J., and Hopcroft. J. E.: (1966) Simple Deterministic Languages, *Proceedings of the Seventh Annual IEEE Symposium on Switching and Automata Theory*, pp 36–46.
Kuich, W., and Salomaa, A.: (1985) *Semirings, Automata, Languages*, Springer-Verlag, New York.
Kurki-Suonio, R.: (1964) Note on Top-Down Languages, *Information and Control* 7, 207–223.
Kuroda, S. Y.: (1969) Classes of Languages and Linear Bounded Automata, *BIT* 9, 225–238.

Landin, P. J.: (1965) A Correspondence between Algol 60 and Church's Lambda-Notation, *Communications of the ACM* 8, pp 89-101 and 158-165.
Landweber, L. H.: (1963) Three Theorems on Phrase Structure Grammars of Type 1, *Information and Control* 6, 131-136.
Larson, L. C.: (1983) *Problem-Solving through Problems*, Springer-Verlag, New York.
Lauer, P. E., Torrigiani, P.R., and Shields, M. W.: COSY: (1979) A System Specification Language Based on Paths and Processes, *Acta Inform.* 12, 109-158.
Lewis, H. R., and Papadimitriou, C.: (1981) *Elements of the Theory of Computation*, Prentice-Hall, Englewood Cliffs, New Jersey.
Lewis, P. M., II, Rosenkrantz, D. J., and Stearns, R. E.: (1976) *Compiler Design Theory*, Addison-Wesley, Reading, Massachusetts.
Lewis, P. M., II, and Stearns, R. E.: (1968) Syntax-Directed Transduction, *Journal of the ACM* 15, 465-488.
Lewis, P. M., II, Stearns, R. E., and Hartmanis, J.: (1965) Memory Bounds for Recognition of Context-Free and Context-Sensitive Languages, *Proceedings of the Sixth Annual IEEE Symposium on Switching Circuit Theory and Logical Design*, 191-202.
Lindenmayer, A.: (1971) Mathematical Models for Cellular Interactions in Development, Parts I and II, *Journal of Theoretical Biology* 30, 455-484.
Linger, R. C., Mills, H. D., and Witt, B. I.: (1979) *Structured Programming:Theory and Practice*, Addison-Wesley, Reading, Massachusetts.
Linz, P.: (1990) *An Introduction to Formal Languages and Automata*, D.C. Heath and Co., Lexigton, Mass.
Loeckxx, J., and Sieber, K.: (1978) *The Foundations of Program Verification*, John Wiley & Sons, New York.
Mallozi, J. S., and De Lillo, N. J.: (1984) *Computability with PASCAL*, Prentice-Hall, Englewood Cliffs, New Jersey.
Marcotty, M., Ledgard, H.F., and Bochmann, G. V.: (1976) A Sampler of Formal Definitions, *Computing Surveys* 8, 191-276.
Markov, A. A.: (1960) *The Theory of Algorithms* (translated from the Russian by J.J. Schorr-kon), U.S. Dept. of Commerce, Office of Technical Services, No. OTS 60-5108.
Martin, J. C.: (1991) *Introduction to Languages and the Theory of Computation*. McGraw-Hill, New York.
McCarthy, J.: (1960) Recursive Functions of Symbolic Expressions and Their Computation by Machine, Part I, *Communications of the ACM* 3, 184-195.
McCarthy, J.: (1963) A Basis for a Mathematical Theory of Computation, in Braffort, P., and Hirschberg, D. (eds.), *Programming and Formal Systems*, North-Holland, Amsterdam 33-70.
McCarthy, J., and Painter, J.: (1967) Correctness of a Compiler for Arithmetic Expressions, in Schwartz, J. T. (ed.), *Mathematical Aspects of Computer Science*, American Mathematical Society, Providence, Rhode Island, pp 33-41.
McCulloch, W. S., and Pitts, W.: (1943) A Logical Calculus of the Ideas Immanent in Nervous Activity. *Bulletin of Mathematical Biophysics* 5, 115-133.
McNaughton, R.: (1982) *Elementary Computability, Formal Languages, and Automata*, Prentice-Hall, Englewod Cliffs, New Jersey.
McNaughton, R., and Papert, S.: (1971) *Counter-Free Automata*, The M.I.T. Press, Cambridge, Massachusetts.
McNaughton, R., and Yamada, H.: (1960) Regular Expressions and State Graphs for Automata, *IEEE Transactions on Electronic Computers* 9, 39-47.
McWhirter, I. P.: (1971) Substitution Expressions, *Journal of Computer and System Sciences* 5, 629-637.
Mead, C. A., and Conway, L. A.: (1980) *Introduction to VLSI Systems*, Addison-Wesley, Reading, Massachusetts,.
Mealy, G. H.: (1955) A Method for Synthesizing Sequentail Circuits, *Bell System Technical J.* 34, 1045-1107.
Meduna, A.: (1986) A Note on Exponential Density of ETOL Languages, *Kybernetika* 22, 514-518.
Meduna, A.: (1987a) Evaluated Grammars, *Acta Cybernetika* 8, 169-176.
Meduna, A.: (1987b) Characterization of the Chomsky Hierarchy through Sequential-Parallel Grammars, *Rostock. Math. Kolloq.* 32, 4-14
Meduna, A. and Horvath, G.: (1988) On State Grammars, *Acta Cybernetica* 8, 237-245.
Meduna, A.: (1990a) Context Free Derivations on Word Monoids, *Acta Informatica* 27, 781-786.
Meduna, A.: (1990b) Generalized Forbidding Grammars, *International Journal of Computer Mathematics* 36, 31-38.

Meduna, A.: (1991) Global Context Conditional Grammars, *J. Inform. Process. Cybern.* 27 159–165.

Meduna, A.: (1992) Symbiotic E0L Systems, *Acta Cybernetika* 12, 164–172.

Meduna, A.: (1993a) A Formalization of Sequential, Parallel, and Continuous Rewriting, *International Journal of Computer Mathematics* 39, 24 –32.

Meduna, A.: (1993b), Canonical Scattered Rewriting, *International Journal of Computer Mathematics* 51, 122–129.

Meduna, A. and Csuhaj-Varju, E.: (1993) Grammars with Context Conditions, *EATCS Bulletin* 32, 112–124.

Meduna, A.: (1994) Matrix Grammars under Leftmost and Rightmost Restrictions, in *Mathematical Linguistics and Related Topics* (Gh. Paun, ed.), The Publ. House of the Romanian Academy, Bucharest, 243–257.

Meduna, A., Crooks, C., and Sarek, M.: (1994) Syntactic Complexity of Regulated Rewriting, *Kybernetika* 30, 177–186.

Meduna, A., and Gopalaratnam, M.: (1994) On Semi-Conditional Grammars with Productions Having either Forbidding or Permitting Conditions, *Acta Cybernetica* 11, 309–323.

Meduna, A.: (1995a) Syntactic Complexity of Scattered Context Grammars, *Acta Informatica* 32, 285–298.

Meduna, A.: (1995b) A Trivial Method of Characterizing the Family of Recursively Enumerable Languages by Scattered Context Grammars, *EATCS Bulletin* 56, 104–106.

Meduna, A.: (1996) Syntactic Complexity of Context-Free Grammars over Word Monoids, *Acta Informatica* 33, 457–462.

Meduna, A.: (1997a) Four-Nonterminal Scattered Context Grammars Characterize the Family of Recursively Enumerable Languages, *International Journal of Computer Mathematics* 63, 67–83.

Meduna, A.: (1997b) On the Number of Nonterminals in Matrix Grammars with Leftmost Derivations, *LNCS* 1217, 27–38.

Meduna, A.: (1997c) Six-Nonterminal Multi-Sequential Grammars Characterize the Family of Recursively Enumerable Languages, *International Journal of Computer Mathematics* 65, 179–189.

Meduna, A.: (1998b) Economical Transformation of Phrase-Structure Grammars to Scattered Context Grammars, *Acta Cybernetica* 13, 225–242.

Meduna, A.: (1998c) Uniform Rewriting Based on Permutations, *International Journal of Computer Mathematics* 69, 57–74.

Meduna, A.: (1998d) Descriptional Complexity of Multi-Continues Grammars, *Acta Cybernetica* 13, 375–384.

Meyer, A. R., and Stockmeyer, L. J.: (1972) The Equivalence Problem for Regular Expressions with Squaring Requires Exponential Time, *Proceedings of the Thirteenth Annual IEEE Symposium on Switching and Automata Theory*, pp. 125–129.

Minsky, M. L.: (August 1960) *A 6-Symbol, 7-State Universal Turing Machine*, MIT Laboratory Group Report 54G-OO27.

Minsky, M. L.: (1962) *Size and Structure of Universal Turing Machines Using Tag Systems*, Marcel Dekker, pp. 229–238.

Minsky, M. L.: (1967) *Computation: Finite and Infinite Machines.* Prentice Hall, Englewood Cliffs, New Jersey.

Moore, E. F.: (1956) Gedanken Experiments on Sequential Machines, in Shannon, C. E. and McCarthy, J. (eds.), *Automata Studies*. Princeton University Press, Princeton, New Jersey 129–153.

Moore, G. B., Kuhns, J. L., Trefftzs, J. L., and Montgomery, C.A.: (1977) *Accessing Individual Records from Personal Data Files Using Non-Unique Identifiers.* NBS Special Publication 500-2, U.S. Department of Commerce, National Bureau of Standards.

Myhill, J.: (1957) *Finite Automata and the Representation of Events*, WADD TR-57-624, Wright Patterson AFB, Ohio, 112–137.

Naur, P. (ed.): (1960) Report on the Algorithmic Language ALGOL 60. *Communications of the ACM* 3, 299–314; revised in *Communications of the ACM* 6, 1963, 1–17.

Newell, A., and Shaw, J. C.: (1957) Programming the Logic Theory Machine, *Proceedings of the Western Joint Computer Conference*, 230–240.

Newman, W., and Sproul, R.: (1979) *Principles of Interactive Computer Graphics*, Second Edition, McGraw-Hill, New York.

Oettinger, A. G.: (1961) Automatic Syntactic Analysis and Pushdown Store. *Proceedings of the Symposia in Applied Mathematics* 12, American Mathematical Society, Providence, Rhode Island, pp 104–109.

Ogden, W.: (1968) A Helpful Result for Proving Inherent Ambiguity, *Mathematical Systems Theory* 2, 191-194.
Pagan, F. G.: (1981) *Formal Specification of Programming Languages L: A Panoramic Primer*, Prentice-Hall, Englewood Cliffs, New Jersey.
Pansiot, J. J.: (1981) A Note on Post's Correspondence Problem, *Information Processing Letters* 12, 233.
Papadimitriou, C. H., and Steiglitz, K.: (1982) *Combinatorial Optimization: Algorithms and Complexity*, Prentice-Hall, Englewood Cliffs, New Jersey.
Parikh, R. J.: (1966) On Context-Free Languages, *Journal of the ACM* 13, 570-581.
Gh. Paun (ed.) (1995a) *Artificial Life: Grammatical Models*, Black Sea University Press, Bucharest, Romania.
Gh. Paun (ed.) (1995b) *Mathematical Linguistics and Related Topics*, The Publ. House of the Romanian Academy, Bucharest, Romania.
Pavlenko, V. A.: (1981) Post Combinatorial Problem with Two Pairs of Words, *Dokladi AN Ukr. SSR* 33, 9-11.
Peter, R.: (1967) *Recursive Functions*, Academic Press, New York.
Pilling, D. L.: (1973) Commutative Regular Equations and Parikh's Theorem, *Journal of the London Mathematical Society II*, 6, 663-666.
Pippenger, N.: (1978) Complexity Theory, *Scientific American* 238, 6, 114-124.
Post, E. L.: (1936) Finite Combinatory Processes-Formulation I, *Journal of Symbolic Logic* 1, 103-105.
Post, E. L.: (1947) Recursive Unsolvability of a Problem of Thue, *Journal of Symbolic Logic* 12, 1-11.
Prather, R. E.: (1976) *Discrete Mathematical Structures for Computer Science*, Houghton Mifflin, Boston.
Pratt, T. W.: (1982) The Formal Analysis of Computer Programs, in Pollack, S.V. (ed.) *Studies in Mathematics*, The Mathematical Association of America, 169-195.
Priese, L.: (1979) Towards a Precise Characterization of the Complexity of Universal and Nonuniversal Turing Machines, *SIAM Journal on Computing* 8, 508-523.
Rabin, M. O. and Scott, D.: (1959) Finite Automata and Their Decision Problems. *IBM Journal of Research and Development* 3, 115-125.
Rado, T.: (1962) On Noncomputable Functions, *Bell System Technical Journal* 41, 877-884.
Revesz, G. E.: (1983) *Introduction to Formal Language Theory*, McGraw-Hill, New York.
Reynolds, J. C.: (1981) *The Craft of Programming*, Prentice-Hall, Englewood Cliffs, New Jersey.
Rice, H, G,: (1953) Classes of Recursively Enumerable Sets and their Decision Problems. *Transactions of AMS* 74, 358-366.
Rogers, Jr., H.: (1967) *The Theory of Recursive Functions and Effective Computability*, McGraw-Hill, New York.
Rosenkrantz, D. J.: (1967) Matrix Equations and Normal Forms for Contex-Free Grammars, *Journal of the ACM* 14, 501-507.
Rosenkrantz, D. J.: (1969) Programmed Grammars and Classes of Formal Languages, *Journal of the ACM* 16, 107-131.
Rosenkrantz, D. J., and Stearns, R. E.: (1970) Properties of Deterministic Top-Down Grammars, *Information and Control* 17, 226-256.
Rosenkrantz, D. J., Stearns, R. E., and Lewis, P. M.: (1977) An Analysis of Several Heuristic for the Travelling Salesman Problem, *SIAM Journal on Computing* 6, 563-581.
Rozenberg, G.: (1973) Extension of Tabled 0L Systems and Languages, *International Journal of Computer and Information Sciences* 2, 311-334.
Rozenberg, G.: (1977) Selective Substitution Grammars (Towards a Framework for Rewriting Systems), Part I: Definitions and Examples, *J. Inform. Process. Cybern.* 13, 455-463.
Rozenberg, G., and Salomaa, A.: (1980) *The Mathematical Theory of L Systems*, Academic Press, New York.
Rozenberg, G. and Salomaa, A. (eds.): (1994) *Developments in Language Theory*, World Scientific, Singapore.
Rozenberg, G. and Salomaa, A. (eds.): (1997) *Handbook of Formal Languages*, Volume 1 through 3, Springer.
Rustin, R. (ed.): (1972) *Formal Semantics of Programming Languages*, Prentice-Hall, Englewood Cliffs, New Jersey.
Salomaa, A.: (1969) *Theory of Automata*, Pergamon Press, London.
Salomaa, A.: (1973) *Formal Languages*, Academic Press, New York.
Salomaa, A.: (1985) *Computation and Automata*, Cambridge University Press, Cambridge, England.
Savitch, W. J.: (1982) *Abstract Machines and Grammars*, Little, Brown, Boston.

Savitch, W. J.: (1970) Relationships between Nondeterministic and Deterministic Tape Complexities, *Journal of Computer and System Sciences* 4, 177-192.
Scheinberg, S.: (1963) Note on the Boolean Properties of Context-Free Languages, ???*Information and Control* 6, 246-264???.
Schutzenberger, M. P.: (1963) On Context-Free Languages and Pushdown Automata. ???*Information and Control* 6, 246-264???.
Scott, D.: (1967) Some Definitional Suggestions for Automata Theory, *Journal of Computer and System Sciences* 1, 187-212.
Scowen, R. S.: (1983) *An Introduction and Handbook for the Standard Syntactic Metalanguage*, National Physical Laboratory Report DITC 19/83.
Shannon, C. E.: (1956) A Universal Turing Machine with Two Internal States, in *Automata Studies*, Princeton University Press, Princeton, New Jersey, pp 129-153.
Shannon, C. E., and McCarthy, J. (eds.): (1956) *Automata Studies*, Princeton University Press, Princeton, New Jersey.
Shyr, H. J.: (1991) *Free Monoids and Languages*, Hon Min Book Comp., Taichung.
Shepherdson, J. C.: (1959) The Reduction of Two-Way Automata to One-Way Automata, *IBM Journal of Research and Development* 3, 198-200.
Shepherdson, J. C., and Sturgis, H. E.: (1963) Computability of Recursive Functions, *Journal of the ACM* 10, 217-255.
Sippu, S., and Soisalon-Soininen, E.: (1987) *Parsing Theory*. Springer-Verlag, New York.
Sippu, S., and Soisalon-Soininen, E., and Ukkonen, E.: (1983) The Complexity of LALR(k) Testing, *Journal of the ACM* 30, 259-270.
Smith, A. R.: (1984) Plants, Fractals, and Formal Languages, *Computer Graphics* 18, 1-10.
Solow, D.: (1982) *How to Read and Do Proofs*, John Wiley & Sons, New York.
Stanat, D. F., and McAllister, D. F.: (1977) *Discrete Mathematics in Computer Science*, Prentice-Hall, Englewood Cliffs, New Jersey.
Stockmeyer, L. J., and Chandra, A. K.: (1979) Intrinsically Difficult Problems, *Scientific American* 240, 5, 140-159.
Stone, H.S.: (1973) *Discrete Mathematical Structures and Their Applications*, SRA, Chicago, Illinois.
Sudkamp, T. A.: (1988) *Languages and Machines*, Addison Wesley, Reading, Massachusetts.
Tarjan, R. E.: (1981) A Unified Approach to Path Problems, *Journal of the ACM* 28, 577-593.
Tennet, R. D.: (1981) *The Denotational Semantics of Programming Languages*, Prentice-Hall, Englewood Cliffs, New Jersey.
Thatcher, J. W.: (1967) Characterizing Derivation Trees of a Context-Free Grammar through a Generalization of Finite-Automata Theory, *Journal of Computer and System Sciences* 1, 317-322.
Thatcher, J. W.: (1973) Tree Automata: An Informal Survey, in Aho, A. V. (ed.), *Currents in the Theory of Computing*, Prentice-Hall, Englewood Cliffs, New Jersey, 143-172.
Thompson, K.: (1968) Regular Expression Search Algorithm, *Communications of the ACM* 11, 419-422.
Thue, A.: (1906) Über unedlische Zeichenreihen, *Skrifter utgit av Videnskapsselskapet i Kristiania* 1, 1-22.
Thue, A.: (1914) Probleme über Veränderungen von Zeichenreihen nach gegebenen Regeln, *Skrifter utgit av Videnskapsselskapet i Kristiania* 10.
Tremblay, R. E., and Manohar, R. P.: (1975) *Discete Mathematical Structures with Applications to Computer Science*, McGraw-Hill, New York.
Turing, A. M.: (1936) On Computable Numbers with an Application to the Entscheidungs-Problem. *Proceedings of the London Mathematical Society* 2, 230-265.
Ullman, J. D.: (1984) *Computational Aspects of VLSI*, Computer Science Press, Rockville, Maryland.
Valiant, L. G.: (1975) General Context-Free Recognition in Less than Cubic Time, *Journal of Computer and Systems Sciences* 10, 308-315.
van Dalen, D.: (1971) A Note on some Systems of Lindenmayer, *Mathematical Systems Theory* 5, 128-140.
van Leewen, J.: (1974a) A Generalization of Parikh's Theorem in Formal Language Theory, Proceedings of ICALP '74, *Springer-Verlag Lecture Notes in Computer Science* 14, 17-26.
van Leewen, J.: (1974b) Notes on Pre-Set Pushdown Automata, *Springer-Verlag Lecture Notes in Computer Science* 15, 177-188.

van Wijngaarden, A. (ed.): (1969) Report on the Algorithmic Language ALGOL 68, *Numerische Mathematik* 14, 79–218.
van Wijngaarden, A., Mailloux, B. J., Peck, J. E. L., Koster, C. H. A., Sintzoff, M., Lindsey, C. H., Meertens, L. G. L. T., Fisker, R. G. (eds.): (1974) Revised Report on the Algorithmic Language ALGOL 68, *Acta Informatica* 5, 1–236.
Vere, S.: (1970) Translation Equations, *Communications of the ACM* 13, 83–89.
Watanabe, S.: (1960) *On a Minimal Universal Turing Machine*, MCB Report, Tokyo.
Watanabe, S.: (1961) 5-Symbol 8-State and 5-Symbol 6-State Universal Turing Machines, *Journal of the ACM* 8, 476–483.
Wegner, P.: (1972a) Programming Language, *Computing Syrveyes* 4, 5–63.
Wegner, P.: (1972b) Programming Language Semantics, in Rustin, R. (ed.), *Formal Semantics of Programming Languages*, Prentice-Hall, Englewood Cliffs, New Jersey, pp 149–248.
Winston, P. H.: (1977) *Artificial Intelligence*, Addison-Wesley Publishing Co., Reading, Massachusetts.
Wirth, N.: (1973) *Systematic Programming: An Introduction*, Prentice-Hall, Englewood Cliffs, New Jersey.
Wirth, N.: (September 1984) Data Structures and Algorithms, *Scientific American* 251, 60–69.
Wise, D. S.: (1976) A Strong Pumping Lemma for Context-Free Languages, *Theoretical Computer Science* 3, 359–370.
Wolfram, S., Farmer, J. D., and Toffoli, T. (eds.): (1984) Cellular Automata: Proceedings of an Inter-Disciplinary Workshop, *Physica* 10D, Nos. 1 and 2.
Wood, D.: (1969a) The Normal Form Theorem–Another Proof, *Computer Journal* 12, 139–147.
Wood, D.: (1969b), The Theory of Left-Factored Languages, *Computer Journal* 12, 349–356; and 13 (1970), 55–62.
Wood, D.: (1987) *Theory of Computation*, Harper and Row, New York.
Wood, D.: (1984) *Paradigms and Programming with PASCAL*, Computer Science Press, Rockville, Maryland.
Yentema, M. K.: (1971) Cap Expressions for Context-Free Languages, *Information and Control* 8, 311–318.
Younger, D. H.: (1976) Recognition and Parsing of Context-Free Languages in Time n 3, *Information and Control* 10, 189–208.

Indices

Index to Special Symbols

	Page
◆	ix
●	ix
□	ix
■	ix
△	ix
▲	ix
∅	3
∪	6
∩	6
×	7
∈	3
∉	3
⊆	4
⊂	5
∨	16
∧	16
ε	25
⊢	101
⊢	103
⊢$^+$	107
⊢*	107
⊩	762
⊩	764
⊩$^+$	768
⊩*	768
→	270
⇒	271
⇒$^+$	273
⇒*	273
⇒$_{lm}$	284
⇒$_{rm}$	286
↓	613
⌐	614
↪	613
⊨	123
⊨$^+$	125
⊨*	125

$\twoheadrightarrow$	771
$\Rrightarrow$	772
$\Rrightarrow^{+}$	773
$\Rrightarrow^{*}$	773
$\lceil$	36
$\rfloor$	36
$\nearrow$	671
$\searrow$	671
Σ^{∞}	865
$\overline{\Sigma}$	7
$\#_{a}x$	26
$\mathrm{card}(\Sigma)$	3
$O(\gamma)$	863

Index to Decision Problems

Chapter 4

Membership problem for finite automata	251
Emptiness problem for finite automata	252
Infiniteness problem for finite automata	254
Finiteness problem for finite automata	257
Equivalence problem for finite automata	257
Equivalence problem for finite automata and regular expressions	263
Computational multiplicity problem for finite automata	263
Rejection problem for two finite automata	263
Suffix membership problem for finite automata	264
Prefix membership problem for finite automata	264
Subword membership problem for finite automata	264

Chapter 6

Membership problem for context-free grammars	551
Emptiness problem for context-free grammars	555
Finiteness problem for context-free grammars	556
Infiniteness problem for context-free grammars	558
Recursive nonterminal problem for context-free grammars	562
Emptiness problem for pushdown automata	563
Derivation problem for context-free grammars	563
Leftmost derivation problem for context-free grammars	563
Rightmost derivation problem for context-free grammars	563

Chapter 7

Equivalence problem for deterministic finite automata and deterministic pushdown automata	571
Containment problem for deterministic finite automata and deterministic pushdown automata	572
Emptiness problem for the complement of deterministic context-free languages	573
Context-freeness problem for the complement of deterministic context-free languages	573
Regularness problem for deterministic context-free languages	573

Chapter 10

Halting	857
Time-bounded acceptance	865
Restricted halting	867
Restricted empty word membership	868
Empty word membership	869
Restricted emptiness	869
Emptiness	870
Restricted finiteness	871
Finiteness	871
Context-free universalness	871
Computable-function totalness	873
Regular-language difference	881
Linear regularness	881
Linear-complement linearness	881
Linear-complement context-freeness	882
Context-free linearness	882
Context-free-complement context-freeness	882
Context-sensitive emptiness	882
Containment	882
Equivalence	882
Intersection	882
Post-tag-system membership	883
Post's correspondence problem	883
One-symbol Post's correspondence	883

Index to Algorithms

Chapter 3

Algorithm 3.2.2.1: Determination of computation without reading.	126
Algorithm 3.2.2.3: Conversion of a finite automaton to an equivalent ε-free finite automaton.	130
Algorithm 3.2.2.7: ε-Free finite automaton implementation	141
Algorithm 3.2.2.8: ε-Free finite automaton implementation based on set operations	144
Algorithm 3.2.3.1: Conversion of an ε-free finite automaton to an equivalent deterministic finite automaton — the subset method	146
Algorithm 3.2.3.4: Conversion of an ε-free finite automaton to an equivalent deterministic finite automaton — the binary method	150
Algorithm 3.2.4.1: Conversion of an ε-free finite automaton to an equivalent deterministic finite automaton without inaccessible states — the binary method	156
Algorithm 3.2.4.3: Removal of non-terminating states from a deterministic finite automaton	161
Algorithm 3.2.4.5: Conversion of an incomplete finite automaton to an equivalent complete deterministic finite automaton	164
Algorithm 3.2.4.7: Conversion of a deterministic finite automaton to an equivalent well-specified finite automaton	165
Algorithm 3.2.4.10: Well-specified finite automaton implementation — the tabular method	167
Algorithm 3.2.4.11: Well-specified finite automaton implementation — the case method	170
Algorithm 3.2.5.1: Well-specified finite automaton minimization	172
Algorithm 3.3.1.4: Construction of a finite automaton for the union of two languages accepted by finite automata	177
Algorithm 3.3.1.7: Construction of a finite automaton for the concatenation of two languages accepted by finite automata	181
Algorithm 3.3.1.9: Construction of a finite automaton for the closure of the language accepted by a finite automaton	183
Algorithm 3.3.1.11: Conversion of any regular expression to an equivalent finite automaton	187
Algorithm 3.3.2.1: Conversion of a deterministic finite automaton to an equivalent regular expression	210

Chapter 4

Algorithm 4.2.2: Construction of a finite automaton for the complement of the language accepted by a well-specified finite automaton — 219
Algorithm 4.2.7: Construction of a finite automaton for a regular substitution — 242
Algorithm 4.3.1: Membership problem decision for finite automata — 251
Algorithm 4.3.4: Emptiness problem decision for finite automata — 252
Algorithm 4.3.7: Infiniteness problem decision for finite automata — 255
Algorithm 4.3.11: Equivalence problem decision for finite automata — 258

Chapter 5

Algorithm 5.1.3.1.1: Determination of terminating symbols — 306
Algorithm 5.1.3.1.3: Conversion of a context-free grammar to an equivalent context-free grammar without nonterminating symbols — 311
Algorithm 5.1.3.1.5: Determination of accessible symbols — 313
Algorithm 5.1.3.1.7: Conversion of a context-free grammar to an equivalent context-free grammar without inaccessible symbols — 317
Algorithm 5.1.3.1.9: Conversion of a context-free grammar to an equivalent context-free grammar without useless symbols — 119
Algorithm 5.1.3.2.1: Determination of ε-nonterminals — 322
Algorithm 5.1.3.2.3: Conversion of a context-free grammar to an equivalent ε-free context-free grammar — 327
Algorithm 5.1.3.3.1: Determination of nonterminals derived by unit derivations — 335
Algorithm 5.1.3.3.3: Conversion of an ε-free context-free grammar to an equivalent unit-free ε-free context-free grammar — 340
Algorithm 5.1.4.1.1: Conversion of a context-free grammar to an equivalent context-free grammar in Chomsky normal form — 348
Algorithm 5.1.4.2.1: Elimination of a directly left-recursive nonterminal — 359
Algorithm 5.1.4.2.3: Nonterminal substitution — 368
Algorithm 5.1.4.2.5: Elimination of left recursion — 370
Algorithm 5.1.4.2.8: Conversion of a context-free grammar to an equivalent context-free grammar in Greibach normal form — 376
Algorithm 5.2.1.1: Conversion of a pushdown automaton accepting by final state to an equivalent pushdown automaton accepting by empty pushdown — 401
Algorithm 5.2.1.3: Conversion of a pushdown automaton accepting by empty pushdown to an equivalent pushdown automaton accepting by final state — 406
Algorithm 5.2.2.1: Conversion of an extended pushdown automaton to an equivalent pushdown automaton — 419
Algorithm 5.2.3.1: Conversion of a deterministic finite automaton to an equivalent deterministic extended pushdown automaton accepting by final state and empty pushdown — 434
Algorithm 5.2.3.10: Deterministic pushdown automaton implementation — 440

Algorithm 5.3.1.1.1: Conversion of a context-free grammar in Greibach normal form to an equivalent pushdown automaton accepting by empty pushdown — 444

Algorithm 5.3.1.1.4: Conversion of a context-free grammar in Greibach normal form to an equivalent pushdown automaton accepting by final state — 454

Algorithm 5.3.1.1.9: Conversion of a context-free grammar to an equivalent pushdown automaton accepting by empty pushdown — 456

Algorithm 5.3.1.1.11: Conversion of a context-free grammar to an equivalent extended pushdown automaton — 462

Algorithm 5.3.2.1: Conversion of a pushdown automaton to an equivalent context-free grammar — 486

Chapter 6

Algorithm 6.2.1: Construction of a context-free grammar for the union of two context-free languages — 528

Algorithm 6.2.5: Construction of a pushdown automaton for the intersection of a context-free language and a regular language — 533

Algorithm 6.2.9: Construction of an extended pushdown automaton for a context-free substitution — 539

Algorithm 6.3.1: Membership problem decision for context-free grammars in Chomsky normal form — 551

Algorithm 6.3.3: Membership problem decision of the for context-free grammars — 553

Algorithm 6.3.6: Emptiness problem decision of the for context-free grammars — 555

Algorithm 6.3.9: Finiteness problem decision of the for context-free grammars — 556

Chapter 7

Algorithm 7.1.1: Construction of a deterministic pushdown automaton for the complement of a deterministic context-free language — 566

Algorithm 7.2.1: Conversion of a right-linear grammar to an equivalent finite automaton — 575

Algorithm 7.2.3: Conversion of a deterministic finite automaton to an equivalent regular grammar — 583

Algorithm 7.2.5: Conversion of a deterministic finite automaton to an equivalent right-linear grammar — 587

Algorithm 7.2.9: Construction of a left-linear grammar that generates the reversal of the language generated by a right-linear grammar — 591

Algorithm 7.2.11: Construction of a right-linear grammar that generates the reversal of the language generated by a left-linear grammar — 594

Chapter 8

Algorithm 8.1.2.1: Deterministic Turing machine implementation 633
Algorithm 8.1.3.4: Conversion of a deterministic Turing machine to an equivalent deterministic Turing machine with one final state 651
Algorithm 8.3.2.2: Conversion of a Turing machine to an equivalent unrestricted grammar 715
Algorithm 8.3.4.2.2: Conversion of a linear-bounded automaton to an equivalent context-sensitive grammar 743

Subject Index

acceptance 61
  by a finite automaton 64, 107
  by a pushdown automaton 388
    by empty pushdown 400
    by empty pushdown and final state 411
    by final state 399
  by a Turing machine 621
accessible state 156
Ackermann's function 879
algorithm 78
alphabet 25
  input 48, 382, 613, 762, 835,
  output 48, 762, 835
  pushdown 382
  tape 835, 613
ambiguity 299
  in a context-free grammar 299
  in a programming language 300
and 16, 139
ancestor 12
arithmetic expression 35
assembly language 788
assignment statement 43
associative law 23
associativity 23
automaton 59
  cellular 265
  finite 59, 101
    complete 162
    deterministic 145
    minimum-state 172
    nondeterministic 145
    well-specified 165
    linear bounded 695
  pushdown 65, 382
    deterministic 437
    extended 415
    nondeterministic 413
  systolic 265
  tree 266
  two-pushdown 696
    deterministic 705
    nondeterministic 704
axiom 15

Backus-Naur form 34
  extended 36
balanced words of parentheses 457
basis of an inductive proof 17
big-O notation 862
bijection 10
binary relation 7

blank 613
Boolean
  algebra 23, 240
  operation 23
bottom-up parsing 443, 462

cardinality 3
cartesian product 7
characteristic function 22, 856
child 13
Chomsky normal form 348
Church's thesis 80, 81, 630, 853, 860
closed under an operation 32, 237
closure
  of a language 31
  reflexive and transitive 9
  transitive 9
closure properties 32
  of context-free languages 528, 546
  of regular languages 237
COLA 39
commutative law 23
compiler 788
complement
  of a context-free language 537
  of a deterministic context-free language 567
  of a language 30
  of a recursive language 693
  of a recursively enumerable language 692
  of a regular language 240
  of a set 7
complete finite automaton 162
composition 10
computability 845
computable function 850
computational complexity 861
computer 845
concatenation
  of context-free languages 545
  of deterministic context-free languages 600
  of languages 30
  of regular languages 181, 238
  of words 26
configuration
  of a finite automaton 103
  of a pushdown automaton 384
  of a Turing machine 616
  of a Turing transducer 837
  of a finite transducer 763
  of a pushdown transducer 779
containment 3

constant function 877
context-free
　grammar 269
　language 278
　substitution 538
　closure properties 528
　inherent ambiguity 303
context-sensitive
　grammar 730
　language 730
　recursiveness 736
contradiction 16
contrapositive law 16
correctness 80
correspondence
　one-to-one 10
　problem 87, 883
countable set 10
cycle 11, 335

dead configuration 439
decidability 81, 856
decidable
　language 858
　set 858
decision
　algorithm 81
　maker 858
　problem 858
　　decidable 858, 860
　　involving context-free languages 551
　　involving regular languages 250
　　involving Turing machines 860, 867
　　undecidable 867
decision-making Turing machine 858
de-Morgan law 54
derivation 271
　leftmost 284
　rightmost 286
derivation tree 289
deterministic 289
　context-free language 565
　finite automaton 145
　finite transducer 769
　parsing 477
　pushdown automaton 437
　pushdown transducer 786
　Turing machine 632
　Turing transducer 843
diagonalization 691
difference 6
　of languages 30
　of sets 6
direct left recursion 358
directed graph 11
　acyclic 12
distinguishable states 171
domain 7
Dyck language 603

ε-free context-free grammar 326
ε-move 103
ε-production 270, 321
emptiness problem 252, 555
empty
　pushdown 400
　set 3
　word 25
endmarker 695
English 4, 550
enumerability
E0L system 605
equivalence 16
　class 20
　problem 257
　relation 20
exponential
　function 880
　growth rate 880
extended
　pushdown automaton 415
　pushdown transducer 787

factorial 79
family relationships 742
final state 101, 382, 613
finite
　automaton 59, 101
　　as a language acceptor 61
　　as a computational model 59
　　complete 162
　　deterministic 145
　　ε-free 130
　　lazy 226
　　minimum-state 172
　　nondeterministic 63
　　two-head 225
　　two-tape 225
　　two-way 225
　　well-specified 165
　substitution 248
　control 61
　language 29
　set 3
　transducer 761
　　deterministic 769
　　nondeterministic 761
finiteness problem 257, 556
formal language 29
fully parenthesized regular expression 94
function 9
　computable 850
　one-to-one 10
　partial 9
　polynomial 863
　primitive recursive 879
　total 9
　uncomputable 81

Subject index

grammar 33, 34
    context-free 39, 269
    context-sensitive 730
    left-linear 591
    linear 597
    meta-linear 603
    over word monoids 605
    pure 752, 499
    regular 582
    regulated 605
    right-linear 574
    selective substitution 605
    translation 770
    unrestricted 708
    graph 11
Greibach normal form 357, 381
growth rate 862

halting problem 82, 857
hierarchy of language families 742
homomorphism 50

if and only if 15
inaccessibility 313
inaccessible state 156
in-degree 11
index
    of equivalence relation 20
    of function 851
    of Turing machine 851
indistinguishable states 171
induction 17
    basis 17
    hypothesis 17
    step 17
infinite set 3
infinitness problem 254, 558
inherent ambiguity 303
injection 10
input
    alphabet 48, 382, 613, 762, 835
    head 61, 101, 382, 613, 833
    language 48
    symbol 100, 382, 613
    tape 61, 100, 382, 613
    word 100, 382, 613
instance of a problem 82
intersection 6
    of context-free languages 532
    of deterministic context-free
        languages 568
    of languages 30
    of regular languages 240
    of sets 6
intractable problem 863
inverse 7
    homomorphism 50
    substitution 49
    relation 7

language 29
    accepted by
        finite automaton 107
        pushdown automaton 388
        Turing machine 621
    context-free 278
    context-sensitive 730
    deterministic context-free 565
    E0L 605
    finite 29
    infinite 29
    inherently ambiguous 303
    linear 597
    generated by
        context-free grammar 274
        linear grammar 597
        unrestricted grammar 710
    recursive 693
    recursively enumerable 69, 631
    regular 94
LBA problem 696
left-linear grammar 591
left recursion 367
leftmost derivation 284
length of a word 26
lexical analysis 789
lexicographical order 688
linear-bounded automaton 696
linear grammar 597
logic 15
logical
    connective 15, 139
    statement 15
looping configuration 439

mathematical induction 17
membership problem 251
metalanguage 33
metalinear language 603
minimalization 171
minimum-state finite automaton 172
model of computation 32
move 105
multihead Turing machine 663
multitape Turing machine 653
multitrack tape of a Turing machine 658
natural
    language 4, 550
    number 3
node 11
non-context-free language 526, 527
nondeterministic
    finite automaton 145
    pushdown automaton 413
    Turing machine 613
nondeterministic polynomial time 864
nondeterministic space complexity 866
nondeterministic time complexity 864
nonrecursively-enumerable languages 689

nonregular languages 234, 235
nonterminal 269
   recursive 367
normal form
   for context-free grammars 347
      Chomsky 348
      Greibach 357, 375, 381
   for context-sensitive grammars 740
      Kuroda 741
      Pentonnen 741
   for unrestricted grammars 722
      Kuroda 722
      Pentonnen 729
not 15
NP-complete problem 865

Ogden's lemma 559
one-to-one correspondence 10
ordered pair 7
output
   alphabet 48, 835
   language 48
   tape 833

$P=NP$ problem 864
parsing 442, 477
   bottom-up 443, 462
   top-down 443, 447
partial
   function 9
   order 21
partition 20
Pascal 549
path 11
polish notation 38
   postfix 38
   prefix 38
polynomial
   function 863
   growth rate 863
polynomial-space-bounded
   language 866
polynomial-time-bounded language 864
Post correspondence problem 87
power set 5
prefix 27
problem 856
procedure 78
production
   in a context-free grammar 270
   in a left-linear grammar 591
   in a linear grammar 597
   in a regular grammar 582
   in a right-linear grammar 574
   in an unrestricted grammar 708
programming language 39
proof 15
   based on the contrapositive law 16
   by contradiction 16
   by induction 17

proper
   containment 5
   context-free grammar 346
   prefix 27
   subset 5
   subword 27
   suffix 27
properties
   associativity 23
   commutativity 23
   distributivity 23
pumping lemma 598
   for context-free languages 514
   for regular languages 230
pushdown
   automaton 382
      acceptance 388
      atomic 506
      configuration 384
      determinism 437
      diagram 390
      lazy 505
      two-way 505
      one-turn 601
      extension 415
   transducer 74, 778

question 82, 856

range 7
recursive
   definition 8
   function 879, 880
   language 693
recursion theorem 852
recursively enumerable language 69, 631
   nonrecursiveness 694
reflexivity 19
reflexive and transitive closure 9
regular
   expression 93
   grammar 582
   language 94
      acceptance by a finite automaton 187
      closure properties 237
      decidability 250
      generation by regular grammar 582
      nonregularity 230, 234
relation 7
   domain 7
   from one set to another set 7
   on a set 7
   range 7
reversal
   of a language 30
   of a word 27
Rice's theorem 872
right move 616
right-linear grammar 574
rightmost derivation 286

Subject index

rule 101
Russell's paradox 19

sentence 274
sentential form 274
set
   cardinality 3
   complement 7
   countable 10
   difference
   empty 3
   definition 3
   finite 3
   infinite 3
   of natural numbers 3
   operations 6
   uncountable 10
shuffle 561
simplification
   of context-free grammars 305
   of finite automata 122
   of Turing machines 631
source program 788
space complexity 866
state diagram 110, 623
start state
   in a finite automaton 101
   in a pushdown automaton 382
   in a Turing machine 613
start symbol 269
state
   diagram 110
      of a finite automaton 110
      of a Turing machine 623
   table 109, 139
      of a deterministic finite automaton 154, 155
      of a nondeterministic finite automaton 109
string 26
subrelation 7
subset 4
substitution 49
   context-free 538
   regular 241
subtree 14
subword 27
successor function 71
suffix 27
symbol 25
   terminating 306
   accessible 313
   useful 319
   useless 319
symmetric relation 19
syntactic analysis 788
syntax graph 37

tape 68
   alphabet 613, 835
   head 68
   square 68

symbol 69, 643
   two-way infiniteness 667
terminal 269
termination 80
theorem 15
time complexity 862
token 789
top-down parsing 443, 477
total function 9
track 658
tractable problem 863
transducer 71
   finite 71
   pushdown 74, 778
   Turing 77, 835
translation 48
   defined by
      finite transducer 72
      pushdown transducer 74, 785
      translation grammar 774
      Turing transducer 77, 842
transitive closure 9
tree 12
   depth 13
   elementary 13
   frontier 13
   root 12
Turing computable function 850
Turing machine 68, 613
   acceptance 621
   as a language acceptor 609
   as a computational model 845
   configuration 616
   description 675
   lazy 745
   multihead 663
   multitape 653
   multitrack 658
   nondeterministic 613, 631
   simple 744
   state diagram 623
   time complexity 862
   two-way 667
   universal 678, 686
   variations 652
two-pushdown automaton 696
two-way
   finite automaton 226
   infinite tape 667
   pushdown automaton 749
   deterministic 705
   lazy 749

unambiguousness 299
uncomputable function 853
undecidability 81
undirected graph 22
union 6
   of context-free languages 528
   of languages 30

of regular languages 177, 238
of sets 6
uniqueness of minimum-state finite automaton 175
unit production 334
unit-free context-free grammar 340
universal
   language 29
   Turing machine 678, 686
universe 7

unrestricted grammar 708
useful symbol 319
useless symbol 319

value
   falsehood 15
   true 15
word 25
   empty 25